CONTENTS

8.	THE ATLANTIC SOUTH - ROUTE 1
74.	THE NEW ENGLAND TRAIL - ROUTE 2
110.	THE JAZZ/WHISKY RUN - ROUTE 3
168.	THE DETROIT HUB - ROUTE 4
186.	THE SOUTHBOUND TRAIL - ROUTE 5
226.	THE SOUTHERN TRAIL - ROUTE 6
248.	THE NORTHERN TRAIL - ROUTE 7
280.	THE CANADIAN BORDERLANDS - ROUTE 8
300.	THE PACIFIC TRAIL - ROUTE 9
348.	THE INNER NEVADA TRAIL - ROUTE 10
376.	SAN FRAN TO THE MIDWEST - ROUTE 11
412.	SAN DIEGO TO TENNESSEE - ROUTE 12

INTRODUCTION

Whether you are looking to embark on the journey of a lifetime, to bring back tall tales of weird and wonderful locations or are simply and inexplicably drawn to sit in the World's Largest Frying Pan, this book is for you.

Nowhere in the world has quite the fascination with and number of eclectic roadside oddities as can be found in the United States of America, the scale of the country matched only by the giant versions of mundane things that have been built along its interstates.

The USA, however, offers much more than the daft and pointless by way of obscure landmarks; its long and illustrious history of extreme entrepreneurship, eccentric oddballs, American Dreaming, pioneering, cowboys, con-men and showbiz, all underlined by a hefty dose of Patriotism, has left the territory marked by countless examples of history and anthropology at its colourful best.

Upon encountering each of these often bizarre and outlandish destinations, it is easy to view them as distinct from one another; each tells its own story, however where these stories become truly fascinating is when they are viewed from the perspective of the historic American backdrop. When one reads of an abandoned theater for example, the building itself will have likely have a wonderfully vivid history of its own, however when one views it through the lens of America's then-new obsession with film, with recorded soundtracks and with automobiles, one can understand why the next location, a drive-in movie theater, was such a roaring success, combining as it did these three new fads in one, leaving the theatre, its black tie cocktails and its Wurlitzer decaying and forgotten. By now the drive-in too is long lost, replaced by 4k TVs and surround sound in the home; yet both the original theater and the drive-in, due to the large scale of land in the USA, remain rooted in place, crumbling slowly in on themselves whilst elsewhere in the world such places are immediately torn down to make way for concrete jungle.

While they exist, one can catch a glimpse of real bygone Americana - some are even now being lovingly restored. The vast majority however will eventually be lost and I hope that this book encourages you to see these sometimes silly, sometimes marvellous wonders before they are obliterated. If you can't make the trip, I hope you enjoy the entries from the comfort of your sofa and encourage others to have an appreciation for those places that open a window on the past. I hope too that this book will kindle in readers of other nations the frivolity and whimsy that Americans seem to foster. I secretly hope you will launch into a backyard project involving reclaimed bowling balls or a giant rooster of your own in celebration of them.

Sadly, given the nature of the subject matter, I have to caveat that some of these places may no longer be around by the time you reach them, and we suggest you research them before your departure to save yourself the trip should this be the case. The entry in the book will remain as a reminder of what went before and we

hope you enjoy reading about these places whether or not they are currently visible; perhaps if you pass a place that once was, your imagination may be kick-started to view that location a little differently than you otherwise would have. These locations are not helpfully located. They are not in straight lines. Some of the most obscure are...well quite inconvenient. We think this adds to the joy of reaching them but again suggest you check their locations carefully to ensure you are willing to trek that distance to a Mustard Museum.

Enjoy!

Top: Galleta Meadows
Bottom : Ringling Circus Museum

INTRODUCTION

5

NAVIGATING

This book allows you to plan a delightfully outlandish road trip by simply following one of the routes provided. All entries are in (approximate!) geographic order, just set your navigation to the provided address or coordinates (useful for the more obscure locations) and follow along the route. Don't fancy a particular location? Just miss it out, or add your own 'normal' locations to your route!

Sometimes the book will give you direction choices along the way - just look through the entries and decide which you fancy and head in that direction! There are clear markers throughout telling you which pages to jump to to continue your journey, as well as suggested entries which you could include from elsewhere in the book should they be nearby. Consider it a 'make your own adventure' book!

Of course you can simply armchair travel - why leave your home at all when you can enjoy the weird and wonderful side of the USA with your feet up and a gin in hand?

Alternatively just pick your favourite entries that are near your holiday destination and include a couple to add a bit of quirk to your vacation.

The boring stuff:

Many of these locations are private buildings - please be respectful, enjoy from a distance and needless to say we do not condone trespass.

Many of these locations are in hostile environments - plan your journey carefully and be safe! Death Valley is so called for good reason!

Many of these locations are abandoned, historic, in decline, please leave them as you found them so that many more people can enjoy them.

By the very nature of the subject matter, again many of these locations are capturing a moment in time - a brilliant store, a work of art, an individual's contribution to Unusual America - it is therefore possible that a location will have closed or even disappeared by the time you visit. Please check before you travel and please enjoy these sites' preservation in these pages.

> Right: The Big Duck

The Big Duck
1012 NY-24, Flanders, NY 11901
40.90750, -72.62243

We will be kicking off in New York, however if you find yourself in nearby Long Island near the Riverhead entrance to the Hamptons, why not check out The Big Duck, a 'ferrocement' building in the shape of, you guessed it, a sizeable duck, built by a duck farmer in 1931 as a shop to sell his ducks and duck eggs. The duck's eyes are made from Ford Model T tail lights and oddly, Christie Brinkley has voiced the duck as a welcome message. In architecture, the term 'duck architecture' is used to describe buildings in the shape of an everyday object to which they relate, coined from The Big Duck itself.

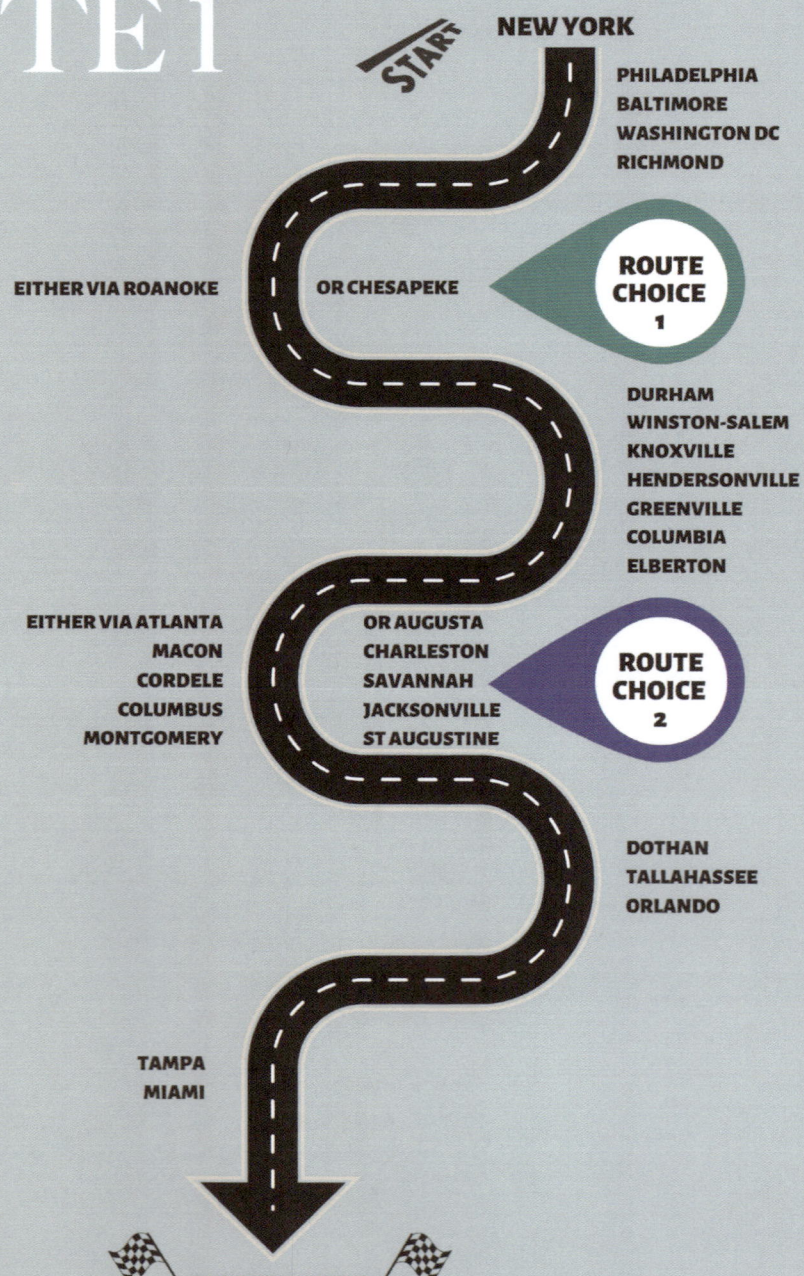

THE ATLANTIC SOUTH ROUTE 1

START — NEW YORK
PHILADELPHIA
BALTIMORE
WASHINGTON DC
RICHMOND

ROUTE CHOICE 1

EITHER VIA ROANOKE   OR CHESAPEKE

DURHAM
WINSTON-SALEM
KNOXVILLE
HENDERSONVILLE
GREENVILLE
COLUMBIA
ELBERTON

ROUTE CHOICE 2

EITHER VIA ATLANTA   OR AUGUSTA
MACON   CHARLESTON
CORDELE   SAVANNAH
COLUMBUS   JACKSONVILLE
MONTGOMERY   ST AUGUSTINE

DOTHAN
TALLAHASSEE
ORLANDO

TAMPA
MIAMI

FLORIDA KEYS

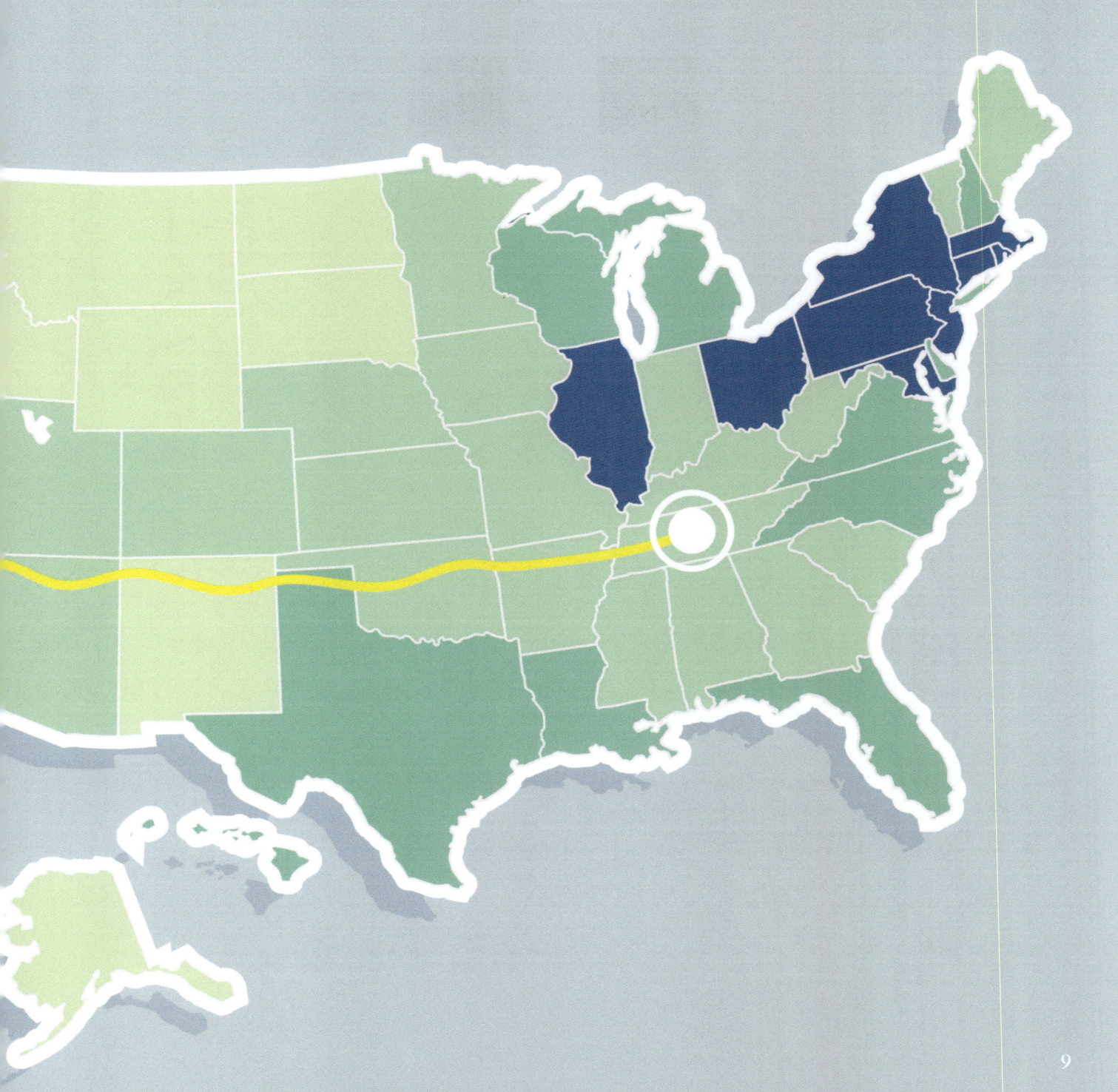

THE ATLANTIC SOUTH ROUTE 1

OFFBEAT AMERICA

The Atlantic South Route will take you from the bright lights of Manhattan, to the Deep South, to the far reaches of the Florida Keys, via one of the ugliest buildings in the world, humans with naturally bright blue skin, abandoned amusement parks and the creepiest cabin in the woods imaginable. Think Weird America was the remit of the West Coast? Think again.

STARTING CITY - NEW YORK

Top: 112 Ocean Avenue

1. 112 OCEAN AVE
40.66656, -73.41477
112 Ocean Ave, Amityville, NY 11701
The real Amityville Horror house (notwithstanding house number and name changes aimed at shaking off the notoriety) and the site of Ronald Butch DeFeo's all too real horrific murderous rampage which left 6 of his family members slain. The house went on to gain further infamy when a family, George and Kath Lutz and their children moved into the house having acquired it for a bargain price due to its dark past, only to be plagued by so say poltergeists and hauntings; from George waking up every morning at

3:15, the hour of the murders, to plagues of flies, vivid nightmares of the murders, cold spots, images of demons, the sounds of doors slamming, the sound of a clock radio playing off frequency, locks on doors and windows malfunctioning, slime oozing from walls and keyholes and rotating crucifixes. Were that not enough, George began to realise that he bore an uncanny likeness to Butch DeFeo and also one day discovered a tiny hidden room behind shelving in the basement which did not appear on the house's blueprints and which was painted deep red. Known as 'The Red Room', the family dog would not approach it, cowering in terror. When their 5 year old daughter Missy gained an imaginary friend called Jodie who transpired to be a demonic pig-like apparition with glowing eyes which George would see standing behind Missy when he would look up at the window of her bedroom, the Lutz Family had enough and were so scared that they left the house containing all their belongings behind without retrieving them, such was their rush. Whilst the Amityville episode is widely thought to be a hoax, details such as this have garnered a huge following of believers too and the events have spawned a multitude of movies including The Amityville Horror.

2. HARRY HOUDINI GRAVE

40.69381, -73.88636
Glendale, NY 11385

Houdini's grave can be found in Machpelah Cemetery along with that of his brother Theodore Hardeen, (also a world famous magician) and the rest of his family, except his wife Bess. Houdini's grave stone, during her lifetime, was engraved with her name and her year of death, the final two numbers of which were left blank ready to be carved at a later time, but as she was Catholic and this cemetery is Jewish, her family in fact buried her at Gates of Heaven Catholic cemetery when she died on a train heading to NY in 1943. At Halloween, this monument becomes a site of Pilgrimage where hordes pay homage to the greatest escape artist that ever lived.

3. BROOKLYN SUPERHERO SUPPLY STORE

40.67137, -73.98466
372 5th Ave, Brooklyn, NY 11215
www.superherosupplies.com
+1 718-499-9884

This awesome store which asks that you ring prior to visiting on a weekday because 'we are staffed by volunteers and sometimes their schedules are as volatile as a can of Anti-Matter' has a double identity: by day, a store selling everything a superhero might need, whilst by...well also in the day actually, a non-profit dedicated to supporting young people with their writing skills.

4. STEVES AUTHENTIC KEY LIME PIES

40.67777, -74.01816

185 Van Dyke St, Brooklyn, NY 11231

The most authentic you can get outside of the Keys, at least according to Steve. Stop by for a slice and let the taste whisk you away to sunny Southern Florida.

5. NEW YORK FEDERAL GOLD VAULT

40.7085, -74.0086
33 Liberty St, New York, NY 10045

This building contains the world's largest stockpile of gold. A mere $200 billion mind you, all just 30 ft. below the city's subway system in a jolly big vault. Surprisingly few of the 540,000 gold bars belong to the US government - only about 5% of them in fact, the rest belonging to the likes of foreign central banks and international organizations such as The International Monetary Fund. Gold is stored for free but $1.75 must be paid for each bar moved (presumably this fee isn't too much of an issue for the gold-bar--owning amongst us). About 25% of the world's gold reserves are stored in this one vault, more than the entire annual economy of the UAE.

6. HARRY JENNINGS RAT PIT

40.7122, -73.99829
James St, New York, NY 10038

Harry Jennings was quite a man. An English 'sports hall' promoter in the 1850s operating in the infamous Five Points area known for its villainous activities, Harry

< Top: Harry Houdini Grave
< Bottom left & centre: Brooklyn Superhero Supply Store
< Bottom right: New York Federal Gold Vault

could offer prostitution, dog fights and even the horrendous underground sport of the time 'rat baiting' where dogs were released into a pen of rats, which had to be pre-caught by young lads down by the river, and had to catch as many as possible before the time ran out. 47-49 Madison St was one of the most notorious rat pits in Manhattan, advertised proudly as having 'a good supply of rats constantly on hand' (what self-respecting establishment doesn't?), where fights were held twice a month leading New York papers to refer to Jennings as of 'rat-killing notoriety' (today's dubious fame equivalent might be reality TV, perhaps things haven't gone downhill quite as far as we thought). Jennings continued his trade until he was jailed in 1869 for a robbery of $13,000, then a very large sum. Upon his release, in 1886 he attended 'The Fanciers' Show' at Madison Square Garden where in an effort to regain some respectability he represented himself as a rat-catcher and appears to have won over New Yorkers in a somewhat unorthodox manner: 'A feature of the day that pleased visitors was the performance of Harry Jennings, the rat-catcher. Every few minutes he went into the big rat cage and made free with the brown-coated inmates, picking them up and flinging them about as though he thought he was giving them pleasure. Occasionally he enticed a lad to enter the cage with him to get a lesson in the way to handle and tame rats'. The location is now a church, belying its inhumane past.

7. CITY HALL STATION
40.7134, -74.0046
258 Broadway, New York, NY 10007
A subway station lies abandoned from its time of closure in the early 1900s, intact with original ornate decorations which led it to be called one of the most beautiful subway stations in the world, beneath the public area in front of City Hall. At the time it was built, it represented the showpiece of the subway network, featuring skylights, colored glass tiling and grand chandeliers in solid brass. It is the only station in the system which uses Romanesque Revival architecture and was designed by Rafael Guastavino, the man behind the Whispering Gallery in Grand Central Station who revolutionised the concept of vaulted tiled ceilings. Its opening event was so popular that every policeman in the city was on duty all day and late into that night, whilst all New Yorkers were asked to join the celebration by blowing whistles and ringing bells. From above, a concrete slab inset with glass tiles, the skylights, can still be found today in the middle of a grouping of dogwoods in front of City Hall near Broadway. One street entrance has also been restored and high demand tours are sometimes conducted, although glimpses can be had from certain subway routes...

8. NINJA
40.71673, -74.00934
25 Hudson St, New York, NY 10013
www.ninjanewyork.com
A restaurant that takes its theme seriously; pick one of two paths to your table, (simple or dangerous), watch out for your waiter, marvel at your dishes and flee on exit.

9. GHOSTBUSTERS' FIRESTATION
40.7197, -74.00659
14 N Moore St, New York, NY 10013
The iconic building - Who you gonna call?

10. AMERICAN NUMISMATIC SOCIETY
40.7235, -74.00644
75 Varick St, New York, NY 10013
www.numismatics.org
Coin flipping reaches whole new levels at this New York society specialised in coin collecting and research – Its collection of around 1 million objects is one of the largest in the world whilst its library is the most comprehensive collection of numismatic literature in existence at over 100,000 volumes. A small public museum can be visited.

11. THE MANHATTAN WELL MURDER
40.72399, -74.0004
129 Spring St, New York, NY 10012
As your wander past this unassuming address, pause to remember that a murder remaining unsolved to this day in which a

> Top: City Hall Station
> Bottom: Ninja
Overleaf: The Ghostbusters' Firehouse

OFFBEAT AMERICA

14

woman was killed and her body hidden in a well in the basement of this site (which was until recently restaurant 'The Manhattan Bistro'….mmmm… why on earth didn't it prove a hit!?), involved her family displaying the victim's body outside their boarding house to encourage public speculation as to who her murderer might be. It didn't work but one assumes that public speculation certainly went through the roof.

12. SHOPSINS
40.71919, -73.98758
120 Essex St, New York, NY 10002
www.shopsins.com
This restaurant, owned by notorious head cook Kenny Shopsin and run by himself and his family, featured in a 2004 documentary entitled 'I Like Killing Flies: Kenny Shopsin's Legendary Eatery' and has been profiled by The New Yorker. Shopsin is renowned for his profanity, as well as for his eclectic menu featuring some 900 dishes and eatery rules: All customers must eat, parties of four or more are very much NOT welcome, anyone who in any way irritates the owner are quickly thrown out. Try it at your peril.

13. THE SAD TINY DINER
40.7302, -74.01069
357 West St, New York 10014
For fans of urban exploration, this diner ran for 50 years before closing in 2006, was known variously in that time as the Lunchbox Diner, the Lost Diner, Rib, Reel Diner and the Terminal Diner and served travellers of the West Side Highway, before presumably the rise of the McDonald's generation took its toll leaving it falling slowly into decrepitude. Now looking sad sandwiched between an Auto Repair and a Car Wash, this miniscule diner looks unlikely to reopen any time soon.

14. HESS' TRIANGLE
40.73348, -74.0031
110 7th Ave S, New York, NY 10014
The kind of quirk that is not liable to be around forever, this tiny triangle represents the smallest plot of real estate in New York City. An apartment building owned by a Mr. David Hess was, in a bid to widen Seventh Avenue and expand the subway, claimed by the City of New York in 1910, expropriated and demolished along with many other buildings. Heirs to Hess later discovered that a survey conducted at the time omitted a tiny corner of the plot and thus established a claim of possession to it. To rectify this error, an official request was made for them to donate the square to the public but they refused and moreover installed this tiny mosaic of ownership in defiance in 1922. It was sold for the modern day equivalent of $17,000 to the Village Cigars shop nearby and thus far remains intact.

15. BELLEVUE HOSPITAL
40.7392, -73.9753
462 1st Avenue, New York, NY 10016

Above: Hess' Triangle
> Right: Bellevue Hospital

Built in 1736, Bellevue is the oldest public hospital in the USA and housed New York's first ever morgue (as well as a pest house, an execution ground, a pathological museum and some rather ghastly conditions along the way). Situated on the waterfront which gave the hospital its name, its location ensured its success at a time in which transport by road could be less that ideal. The hospital is still operating today, now seeing nearly 670,000 outpatient visits a year. It was originally the city's first permanent Almshouse, occupying a building which is now New York City Hall, before being relocated in 1798 to Belle Vue farm near the East River which had been used to house yellow fever patients in quarantine. The area was unsettled at the time, which is why when the grid system came in, First Avenue was situated outside Bellevue. Its revolutionary 'Pavilion for the Insane' built in 1879 has made Bellevue's name a less than complimentary byword for psychiatric hospitals of the time with poor conditions that today seem barbaric, although compared to other practices on offer such as the Barber Surgeons who provided a rather unappealing alternative, letting blood and advertising their barbershop-based services via a large congealed bowl of blood in their windows (later replaced, due to gathering flies, with poles outside the shop flying blood soaked bandages, later happily replaced by the modern day rotating red and white signage we see today recalling the bandages wrapping around the pole in the wind), they were relatively advanced and did much to take in the sick and needy. Many medical firsts have occurred at the hospital (and with the 2014 admittance of an Ebola patient, continue to occur), including the origins of the first ambulance which at the time was horse-drawn and featured a gong to break through busy streets and a large bottle of brandy as a pain reliever for use en route. The Barnum and Bailey circus also visited the old hospital every year, entertaining the patients who watched from grand iron balconies.

16. EXCHANGE BAR & GRILL
40.7375, -73.9844
256 3rd Ave, New York, NY 10010

exchangebarandgrill.com
New York's first and only fully automated 'drink market' – watch the ticker tape as the prices for your drinks fluctuate in real time depending on the laws of supply and demand at any given moment! Try to catch the market crash when all drinks hit rock bottom, or hold out until your favourite drink is at an all time low.

17. THE NEW YORK NEW CHURCH
40.74724, -73.98012
114 E 35th St, New York, NY 10016
http://spiritualistchurchnyc.com/
Ever fancied joining a séance? This is your chance at this new age gathering of The Spiritualist Church of New York City at the New York New Churh. Seances occur after service and are known as Message Services which the church promises 'prove the existence of life after death' and are conducted by what is referred to as a certified Psychic Medium.

18. TANNEN'S MAGIC STORE
40.74973, -73.98692
45 W 34th St #608, New York, NY 10001
www.tannens.com
Tannen's takes magic seriously. The best magic shop you are likely to find anywhere and the oldest one operating in New York City, founded as it was by Louis Tannen in 1925. The shop also holds a Magic Camp for young magicians which has been unning since the early 70s.

< Left: Houdini Museum

19. HOUDINI MUSEUM
40.75034, -73.99067
3rd floor, 421 7th Ave, New York, NY 10001
houdinimuseumny.com
A tribute to a phenomenal character with several hundred wonderful Houdiniana exhibits of the most rare and vital pieces that were used by or belonged to the great escapologist himself, among them some of his most rare publicity challenge posters, handcuffs, large escape restraints, secret escape tools, magic propos, spiritualistic expose items, photographs and other items never before on public display. The collection, houses in the headquarters of leading manufacturer of magic tricks Fantasma Magic, even contains the renowned original Metamorphosis trunk. Some Houdini items are even for sale and admission is free, 7 days a week. Be sure to read William Kalush and Larry Sloman's excellent biography The Secret Life of Houdini before you go.

20. WEST SIDE COW TUNNELS
40.7536, -73.9949
West 35th St, New York 10001
New York is well known for its trendy Meatpacking District but less known for the releated subterranean meat packing infrastructure created to ease the cattle jams in the aforementioned area. It is said that in the 1870s, with traffic at a standstill, a 'Cow Tunnel' was built under Twelfth Avenue and is still there to this day. Why did the Cow Tunnel fall from grace? Allegedly because refrigerated train cars made the city's livestock slaughtering and handling areas redundant, and with the demise of the area so too went the Cow Tunnel. Is it beneath Twelfth Avenue at either 34th or 38th? Is it on Harrison Street? Renwick? Greenwich? Near the entrance to the Holland Tunnel or Gansevoort Street in the West Village? Is it oak vaulted as the rumour goes? A labourer did apparently smash a hole in a wall of wood about 10 ft. below Greenwich St, finding a void which transpired to be an oak vaulted tunnel 10ft by 8ft , leading a local old timer to exclaim 'Why I see you found the cattle tunnel'. The MTA and Department of City Planning also reported the following: 'The Manhattan Abattoir had a dock at the foot of West 34th Street in the 1870s, and cattle were brought to their slaughterhouse between Eleventh and Twelfth Avenues beneath the streets via a cow tunnel. Sometime between 1928 and 1930 a two-story concrete cattle pen was built at the south-eastern intersection of West 39th Street and Twelfth Avenue. Another underground cattle pass was built from the shoreline to this pen to allow cows to be driven under, instead of across, Twelfth Avenue.' Is it a myth? The report concludes that 'if intact, the cattle tunnels may meet the criteria for inclusion on the National Register of Historic Places'. For now, at least, this

> Right : Van Sandt Crybaby Bridge
Below: Laurel Hill Cemetery
Overleaf: Mount Moriah Cemetery

remains a moo..t.. point.

21. VAN SANDT CRYBABY BRIDGE
40.32634, -74.95768
New Hope, PA 18938
Legend has it that a man killed a woman and her child on the bridge hence the name, or variously that a woman drowned her child there herself after giving birth outside of marriage. A commonly replicated urban legend in America, this has led to such bridges being commonly termed 'cry-baby bridges' across the country and ghoul hunters are quick to throng here to attempt to catch proof of a guilt ridden soul on camera

22. LAUREL HILL CEMETERY
40.00419, -75.18755
3822 Ridge Ave, Philadelphia, PA 19132
Founded in 1836, this garden cemetery is listed on the National Historic Register and near the front gates features the headstone of Adrian Balboa, the fictional Rocky's wife, a leftover from when the graveyard scene of the eponymous movie was filmed at Laurel Hill.

23. LICK FORK
38.0537, -82.1568
Lick Fork, Western, WV
A small town/area, the reasoning behind its name unknown. Other lick towns in the US include Lick, Licking, Big Lick, Lick Mountain, Lickskillet, Lick Skillet, Otter Lick, Lizard Lick, Beaver Lick, Big Beaver Lick, Huge Beaver Lick (not really), French Lick, Lickinghole, Knob Lick, Big Bone Lick, Mud Lick, Salt Lick, Paint Lick, Bullitt Lick, Elk Lick and Sand Lick.

24. MOUNT MORIAH CEMETERY
39.93567, -75.23842
Yeadon, PA 19142
A beautiful cemetery set in Deadwood's Black Hills, with burials including notables such as Calamity Jane and Wild Bill Hickock.

< Left: Mount Moriah Cemetery
Below: Lawyers Winterbrook Farm
Overleaf: Lucy The Elephant

25. LAZARETTO QUARANTINE STATION
39.8606, -75.3006
Wanamaker Ave, Essington, PA 19029
This is the oldest surviving quarantine facility in the Western Hemisphere and the sixth oldest in the world, used primarily to quarantine sick individuals arriving on ships - the name Lazaretto came from its European use to mean 'maritime quarantine centre' in the late 14th century.

26. GOOD INTENT
39.80416, -75.07777
Good Intent, Deptford Township, NJ 08096
For those who like to hunt for a quirky sign to photograph – Sadly, the reason behind its name is unknown.

27. LOVELADIES
39.72373, -74.13374
Loveladies, Long Beach Township, NJ 08008
Innocuously named for a Thomas Lovelady who owned an adjacent island.

28. LUCY THE ELEPHANT
39.3209, -74.5117
9200 Atlantic Ave, Margate City, NJ 08402
www.lucytheelephant.org
Said by locals to be the greatest elephant in the world, surely the only one that is six stories high and fully climbable.

29. LITTLE HEAVEN
39.04167, -75.45694
Little Heaven, DE 19946
While on the hunt for another quirky US location sign to photograph, look out also for the house of town founder Jehu Reed, a dilapidated pile built in 1771 next to 7615 Bay Road, Frederica, DE 19946. The house, once 2 and a half stories but expanded to keep pace with Reed's extravagant lifestyle, at one time included a rooftop observatory and was a highly profitable farm with barns, stables and milk houses. Perhaps most unbelievably to look at it today, the house was occupied as recently as 2000.

30. ASSAWOMAN
37.87403, -75.52357
Assawoman, VA 23302
Weirdly named US location - The name is a corruption of Assawaman, the Native American name for the area.

31. LAWYERS WINTERBROOK FARM

> Top: Forest Haven Asylum

39.59043, -77.3813
13001 Creagerstown Rd, Thurmont, MD 21788
www.thurmontfarm.com
Stop by to check out Jan Lawyer's fantastic junk robots at the farm now run by his children and whilst there enjoy a serious corn maze and whatever a pumpkin cannon might be as it sounds awesome. Seasonal.

32. HELL HOUSE ALTAR
39.2402, -76.74739
Nearest Rd: 1501 Hilton Ave, Catonsville, MD 21228
St Mary's College and Chapel was a school for young men entering the Catholic priesthood, which due to declining numbers was closed in 1972. For years the abandoned buildings including a large cruciform altar were left to decay and be explored, but as is so often the way, someone helpfully set light to it in '97, leading the owners to raze the remains to the ground in 2006 to prevent forest fires. The Altar was used in the intervening years, legend has it, by Satanists for their rituals, hence the name Hell House. Now you would have to look hard to find any remnants, but several large stone staircases lead to nowhere and the site makes for good ruin hunting.

33. FOREST HAVEN ASYLUM
39.09863, -76.78644
Fort Meade, MD 20755
Deemed one of the most deadly institutions in the USA, this asylum was built in 1925 with promising ideals of operating a farm-like facility to educate its 1000 plus patients who suffered from intellectual disabilities. Despite its beautiful surroundings, the hospital soon became known for under staffing, patient abuse and neglect due to city budget restrictions which also forced the facility to accept patients with a wider range of issues including severe epilepsy. A large number of lawsuits, (many of which focussed on deaths from aspiration pneumonia caused by feeding patients while they are lying down and unable to process food correctly) as well as a lack of funding caused the centre to be shut down in 1991. During its 80 year operation, hundreds of inpatients died and the remainder suffered an undignified deterioration dogged by mental, physical and sexual abuse at this facility. Many were buried in a mass unmarked grave and several graves have since been uncovered by erosion. Guarded by the Park Police, many of the original items still remain in place within the building.

34. NATIONAL PARK SEMINARY
39.01197, -77.05649
9615 Dewitt Dr, Silver Spring, MD 20910
This boarding school stands in dilapidated state, gaining attention from urban explorers. Notable for its whimsical architecture featuring multiple sorority buildings in a range of somewhat outlandish architectural styles including a Dutch style windmill. The area is at the time of writing slated for residential redevelopment.

35. WASHINGTON DC MORMON TEMPLE
39.01404, -77.06567
9900 Stoneybrook Dr, Kensington, MD 20895
If a big Mormon temple isn't enough for you, this is the tallest in the entire world.

36. THE ADAMS MEMORIAL
38.9474, -77.0103
201 Allison St NW, Washington, DC 20011
This captivating memorial sculpture of a shrouded figure was commissioned by a husband as a memorial to his wife who had killed herself whilst suffering from depression by ingesting potassium cyanide, a substance she used regularly to develop her photos. The architect was directed to consider Buddhist art when devising the sculpture, one such figure being Kannon, frequently visualised as a shrouded seated figure linked to the ideal of compassion.

37. DARTH VADER GARGOYLE AT THE WASHINGTON NATIONAL CATHEDRAL
38.9304, -77.07159
3101 Wisconsin Ave NW, Washington, DC 20016
One gargoyle is strangely out of place on this otherwise normal Cathedral

> Bottom left: Hell House Altar
> Bottom right: Darth Vader Grotesque
> Overleaf: The Adams Memorial

Right: Hollywood Cemetery
Below: Grand Kugel

38. GLEN ECHO AMUSEMENT PARK
38.9664, -77.1381
MacArthur Blvd, Glen Echo, MD 20812
Abandoned amusement park closed in 1968, built on the welcoming site of a suspected malaria outbreak.

39. WARP DRIVE STREET SIGN
39.01385, -77.43085
Warp Drive, Sterling, VA 20166
After presumably tempting US road management workers for years, this name clearly proved too seductive to bear for one Sterling planner.

40. NATIONAL FIREARMS MUSEUM
38.86303, -77.33567
11250 Waples Mill Rd, Fairfax, VA 22030
www.nramuseums.com
If you were in any doubt as to where the gun control debate was heading, this museum will shoot down any residual hope you might still be clinging to. Who says hunters don't need semi automatic military grade weaponry!?

41. AMERICAN CELEBRATION ON PARADE
38.71407, -78.66673
397 Caverns Rd, Quicksburg, VA 22847
shenandoahcaverns.com
50 years' worth of parade floats under one warehouse roof and enough patriotism for another 50.

42. BARBOURSVILLE RUINS
38.16239, -78.2807
Mansion Rd, Barboursville, VA 22923
The ruins of U.S. Senator, Secretary of War and Virginia Govenor James Barbour's mansion, preserved after its destruction by fire and now run as a vineyard

43. THE MARKEL BUILDING
37.5846, -77.4993
5310 Markel Rd # 203, Richmond, VA 23230
This bizarre building officially ranks as one of the Top Ten Most Horrendously Ugly Buildings In The World. Its eccentric architect was not only inspired by a foil-wrapped baked potato (aren't we all), he also hand--sledge hammered almost all of the dents into the giant single sheet of aluminium that wraps the structure. Perhaps pure bottled rage incarnate was what drew him to architecture and that process entirely released it, as no other work of his exists today.

44. GRAND KUGEL
37.56164, -77.46597
2500 W Broad St, Richmond, VA 23220
Unparalleled elsewhere in the world this marvel of physics is at once a 29 ton ball of granite and yet also able to be moved by anyone with the slightest touch. Try it for yourself.

45. HOLLYWOOD CEMETERY
37.53636, -77.45527
412 S Cherry St, Richmond, VA 23220

< Top left: Warp Drive
< Top right: National Firearms Museum
< Bottom left: Barboursville Ruins
< Bottom right: The Markel Building

THE ATLANTIC SOUTH ROUTE 1

hollywoodcemetery.org

This notable cemetery has one legendary guest and it's not one of its two resident Presidents - W.W. Pool's tomb is said to house a vampire who was seen dripping rotting flesh with pointed fangs and head to toe in blood leaving the scene of a railroad tunnel collapse towards a river in a legend known as the Richmond or Hollywood Vampire. William Pool, a bookkeeper who spent most of his life doing accounts in a tobacco company, was buried in the cemetery with his wife although the bodies later had to be moved to escape the onslaught of Vampire legend-seeking vandals. It is thought that the legend, which was rife in the 1960s, first started due to the tomb's architecture which is both Masonic and Egyptian in nature as well as from the fact that the double Ws look somewhat like fangs. The legend was then thought to have proliferated due to the cemetery's proximity to a University, as the students fell in the love with the tale and it spread like wildfire. The additional detail of the vampire being linked to the collapse of the Chesapeake and Ohio railroad's Church Hill Tunnel under neighbouring Church Hill which buried several workers alive in 1925 was only added in 2001 and gained traction since that time. It is said that when fleeing from the scene with a group of onlookers in pursuit, it took refuge in the Pool mausoleum. More recent research suggests that the creature that escaped was actually a 28 year old 'railroad fireman', poor Benjamin F. Mosby, who had been shovelling coal into the firebox of a steam chain with no shirt on when the cave in happened and the entire firebox and boiler exploded, leaving Mosby horribly burnt and with severely broken teeth. He may have indeed fled to the river to cool his wounds. He was reportedly in shock and layers of his skin were hanging from his body; he died shortly after at Grace Hospital and was indeed buried at Hollywood Cemetery. It appears perhaps that a more exciting looking grave was chosen to live up to the legend spawned by the tragic Mosby, a story in itself no less horrifying.

46. JAMES RIVER PARK PIPELINE WALKWAY
37.5232, -77.471
Hillcrest Rd, Richmond, VA 23225
Walk this concrete industrial-style pathway through beautiful terrain and fauna.

ROUTE A VIA CHESAPEAKE

Or skip to p.37 to follow Route B via Roanoke

47. WORLD'S LARGEST HAMMOCK
36.0944, -75.8048
Gallop Road, Point Harbor, NC 27964
Relaxation takes on a whole new scale here.

48. LIZARD LICK
35.81639, -78.37527
Lizard Lick, NC 27591
The name was allegedly from a 'passing observer who saw many lizards sunning and licking themselves on a rail fence'. In 1998 the town was thrust into the spotlight when Nintendo launched Nintendo 64 game Yoshi's Story there, due to Yoshi's ability to extend his tongue over a long distance. Yoshi was technically a dinosaur but this was deemed a minor detail by PR

Right: James River Park Pipeline Walkway

consultant Dereck Andrade of Pasadena who came up with the stunt, which was covered by ABC World News Tonight, CBS Evening News and NBC's The Today Show. Today the town has retained the spotlight thanks to Lizard Lick Towing and Recovery, a TruTV show starring Lizard Lick's honorary Mayor and evangelist Ronnie Shirley and his wife Amy. Talent scouts signed the series on the spot upon meeting Amy Shirley, finding her to be not only a power lifter but also a mortician and co-owner of a recovery business. When they discovered that her husband was quote unquote a walking reality show, they knew they'd struck big.

49. BARBECUE
35.33599, -79.03863
Barbecue, NC 27332
This location was named by early settler 'Red' McNeill who saw steam rising from a nearby creek which reminded him of the meat-roasting pits he had encountered in the Caribbean; he named the creek Barbecue Creek, the name becoming official in the early 1750s as other settlers moved into the area and documented the township.

50. ERECT
35.5588, -79.65945
Erect, NC 27341
Good place to spot a weird US signpost or two, etymology sadly unknown.

JUMP TO THE CUP HOUSE P.40 TO CONTINUE YOUR JOURNEY

ROUTE B - VIA ROANOKE

51. THE MONROE INSTITUTE
37.86002, -78.83038
365 Roberts Mountain Rd, Faber, VA 22938
www.monroeinstitute.org
A research centre for out of body experiences, in more recent times this facility appears more inclined to provide paying visitors with a range of esoteric courses on achieving what some might call pseudosciency states of being such as Remote Viewing.

52. LOVE
37.88541, -79.01002
Love, AZ 85357
Original named Lockhart, the town was renamed for soldier Ernest Love who died in France during World War and whose father was a long standing railroad engineer in the area.

53. THE PEST HOUSE MEDICAL MUSEUM
37.4095, -79.1513
401 Taylor St, Lynchburg, VA 24501
www.gravegarden.org
Few that entered this building to be locked away from the healthy population left it alive, and many remain in the grounds to this day

54. FOAMHENGE
37.64041, -79.54018
Natural Bridge, VA 24578
www.thefoamhenge.com
Because it's easier to transport than stone, and...let's be honest... Basically exactly the same.

ROUTES A & B CONVERGE HERE AT WINSTON-SALEM

55. THE CUP HOUSE
35.9469, -81.04599
2085-2199 Old Johns River Rd, Collettsville,

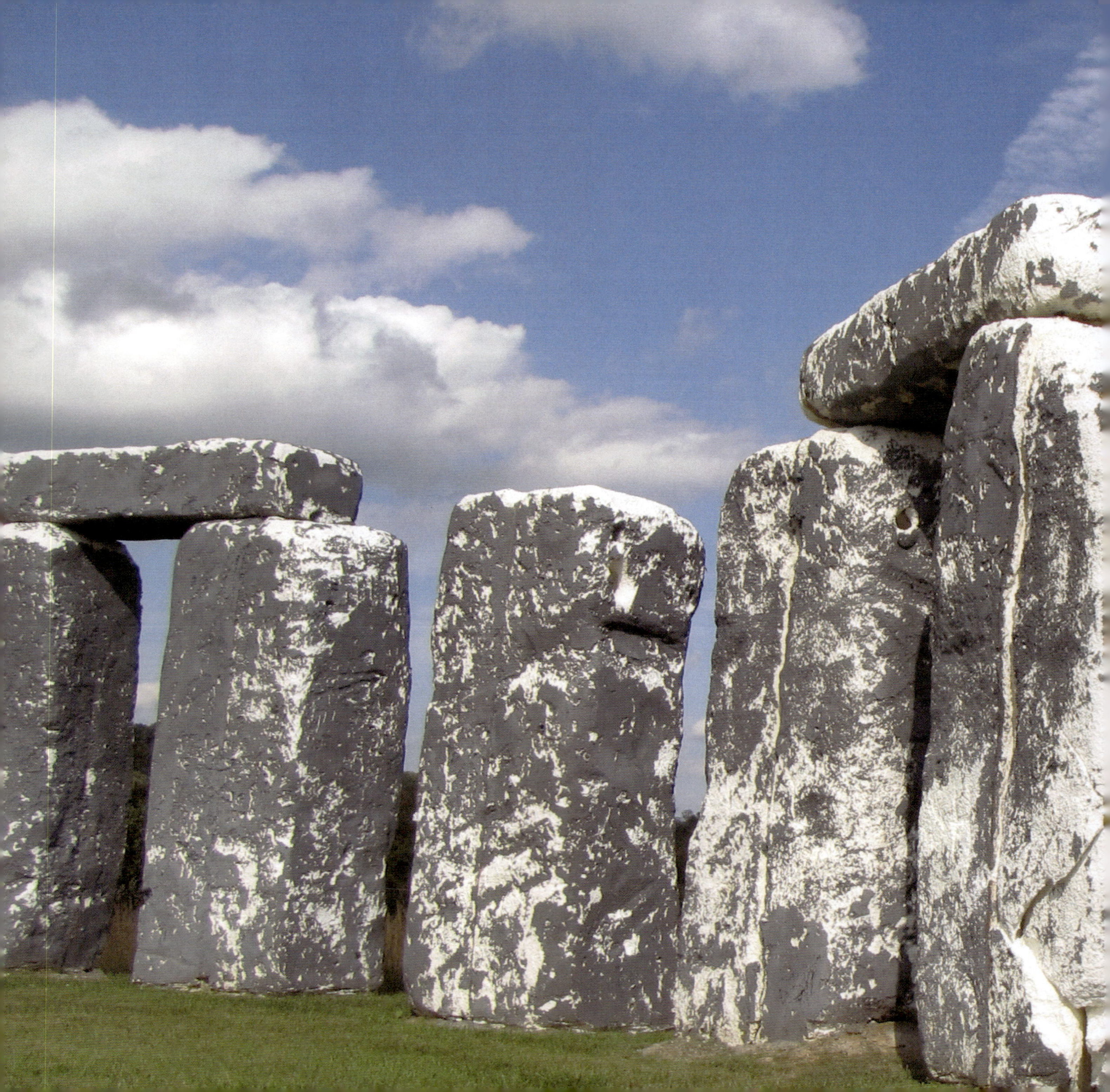

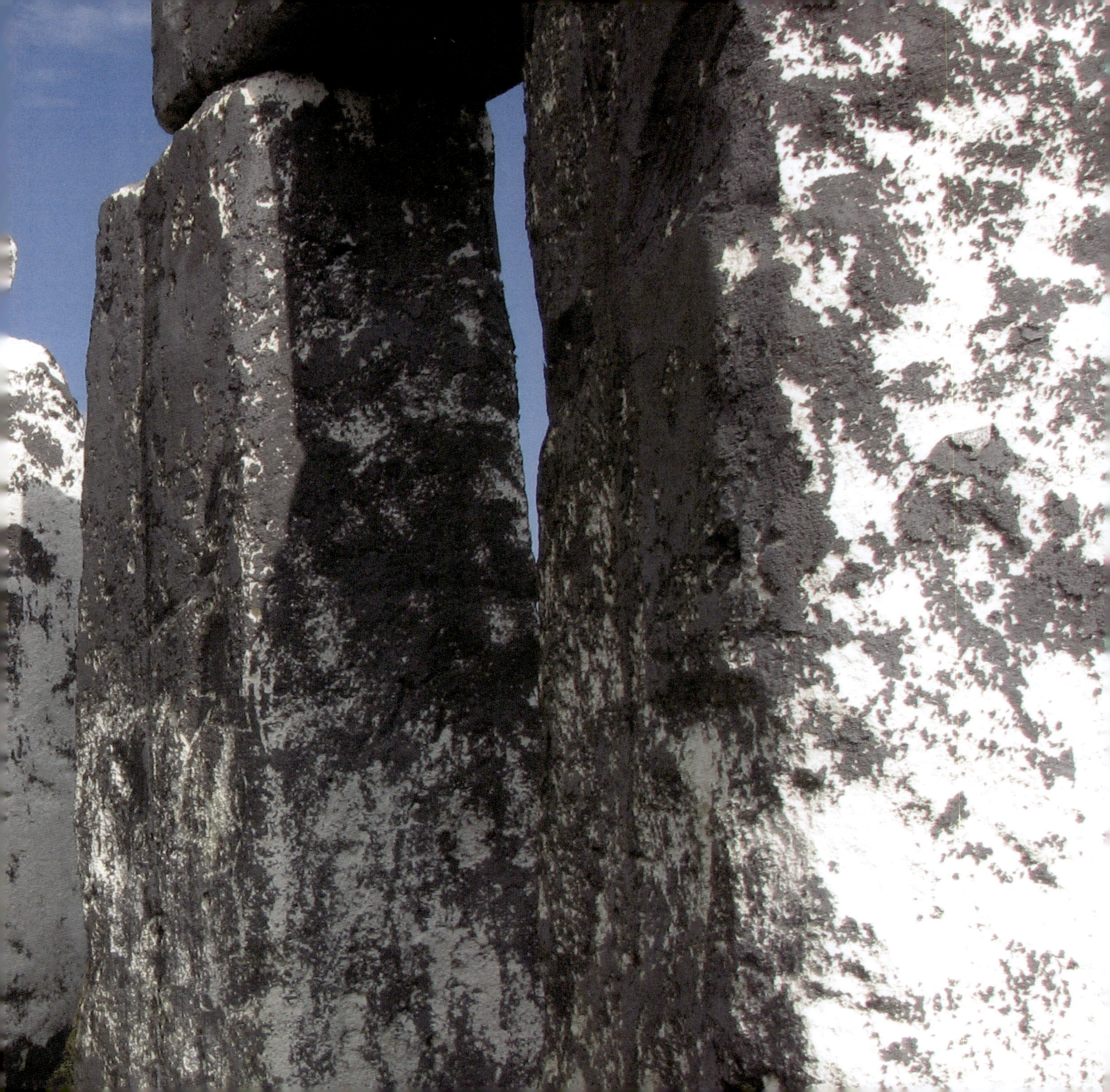

Bottom left: The Evil Dead Cabin
Bottom right: Gaffney Peachoid

NC 28611
A cabin entirely covered in cups, yet still requesting visitors to leave more.

56. ABANDONED HENRY RIVER VILLAGE & MILL
35.69624, -81.42919
Henry River Rd, Hildebran, NC 28637
This early industrial planned community was a self-sustaining village with its own store and mill and remains largely untouched since that time - despite being private property one can drive through the area on the Henry River Road. The village was used as a Hunger Games filming location.

57. BITTER END
36.21166, -82.04
Old Buck Mountain Rd, Roan Mountain, TN 37687
Good 'weird town sign' fodder, etymology unknown.

58. LOST COVE
36.0708, -82.4025
Nearest Road: Ephiram Place Rd, Erwin, TN 37650
Once a hotbed of illegal alcohol trafficking, this settlement was once home to around 100 people before its timber trading ran out leading all the inhabitants to leave the town by the late fifties. Several structures remain relatively intact and a keen eye may be able to find the local cemetery buried within the woodland.

59. THE PEACHOID
35.09533, -81.68587
Peachoid Rd, Gaffney, SC 29341
www.gbpw.com
When the name 'World's Largest Peach' just doesn't cut it. As featured in House of Cards.

60. BLUE GHOST FIREFLIES
35.197, -82.59429
Nearest Road: Buck Forest Rd, Hendersonville, NC 28739
See these ethereal beauties glow in the night sky.

61. BIG BUTT MOUNTAIN SIGN
35.5976, -82.79902
Big Butt Mountain, Beaverdam, NC 28716
Rather sadly, the name Butt is simply a corruption of Butte, now meaning an isolated hill with steep or vertical sides and a small, flattish top; originally French meaning simply 'small hill'. Those viewing your photos will never know this.

62. THE EVIL DEAD CABIN
36.2226, -83.3766
Inman Bend Rd, Morristown, TN 37814
Visit the archetypal creepy woodland cabin and stay away from the trees.

63. THE BLUE FUGATES OF TROUBLESOME CREEK
37.4038, -83.17412
Troublesome Creek Kentucky
'Blue all over', 'the bluest woman I ever saw' and 'as blue as Lake Louise'; these were just a few of the descriptions given at the time to the Fugate family of Troublesome Creek, Kentucky. The Fugates were a family suffering from an extremely rare genetic condition called 'Methemoglobinemia', which is passed down via recessive genes. Martin Fugate who suffered from the disease came to Troublesome Creek from France in 1820 and exhibited blue skin. He married Elizabeth Smith, also a carrier of the recessive gene. Of their seven subsequent progeny, 4 were blue. Due to a total lack of transportation (few roads or railroads), the Fugates intermarried cousins and families living nearby. One of their blue boys married his aunt by way of example. This continued through the generations resulting in a proliferation of blue individuals in the area. This persists to this day; an American Heart Association clinic nurse in Hazard, Cawein called Ruth Pendergrass cited seeing a dark blue woman for a blood test whose 'face and fingernails were almost indigo blue - it scared me to death. I thought she would die right there in the health department but she wasn't at all alarmed. She told me that her family were the blue Combses who lived up on Ball Creek, a sister to one of the Fugate women.' Others have been located, such as Luke Combs and Patrick and Rachel Richie

Top: The Blue Fugates of Troublesome Creek
Bottom: Blue Ghost Fireflies

THE ATLANTIC SOUTH ROUTE 1

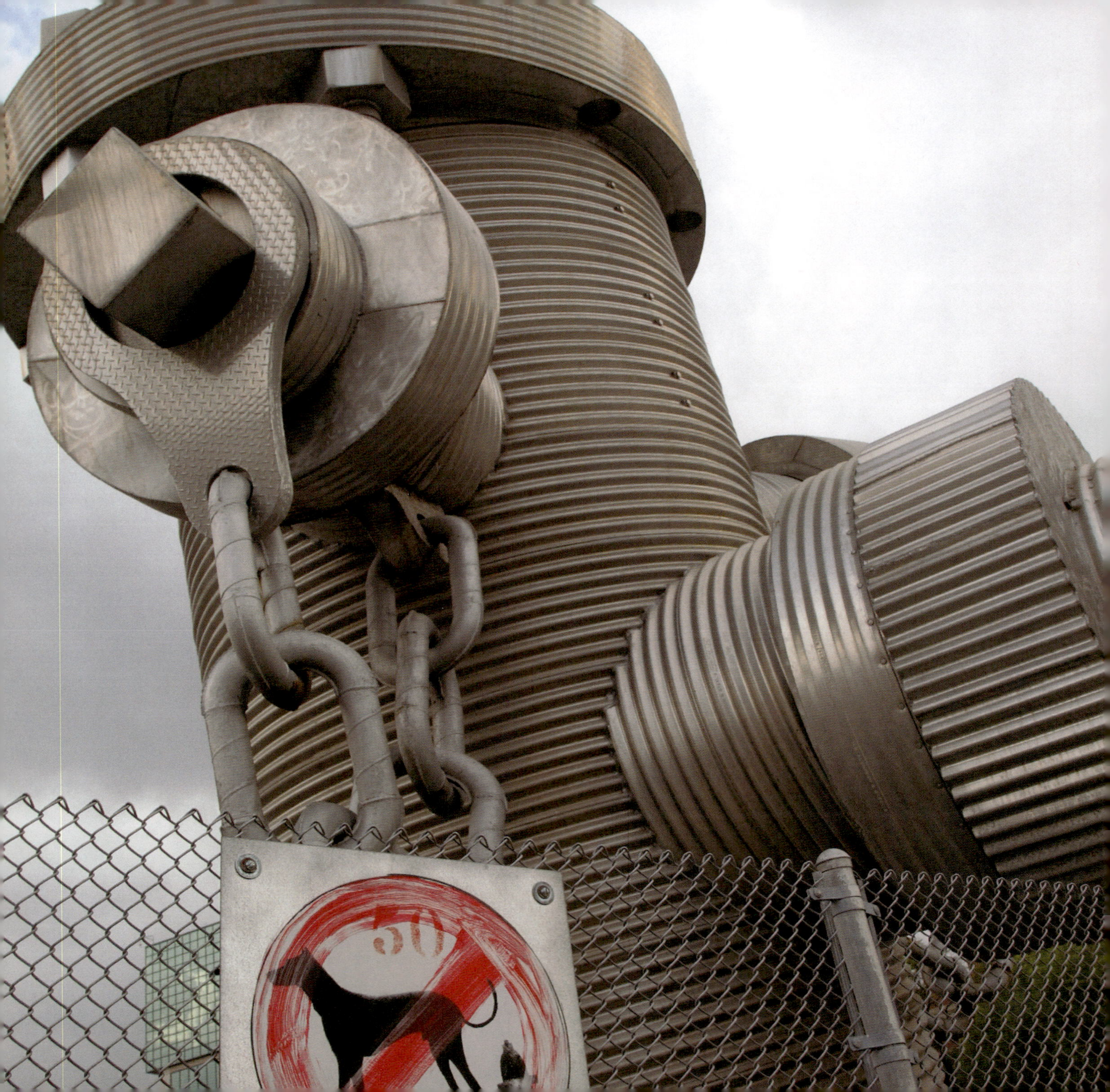
50

(these are common surnames in the lineage) who were quoted as being 'bluer'n hell' and embarrassed by the condition. It has been determined that when both parents have the trait, their child has a 25% of getting the condition and exhibiting a blood disorder in which an abnormal amount of methemoglobin is produced, responsible for distributing oxygen to the body. With this condition, they are unable to carry oxygen and cannot release it effectively into body issues, the lips and skin looking purple or blue due to the lack of oxygenisation of their blood. Today it is much rarer to find than it was back in the original time of the Fugates as people are more freely able to relocate and disperse the gene pool.

64. THE BODY FARM
35.94098, -83.93954
2102 Cherokee Blvd, Knoxville, TN 37919
This 10,000m2 plot places bodies in different settings across the area, exposing them in a number of ways to natural erosion (sun, rain, wind, tree mulch etc) in order to provide insight into decomposition processes. Over 100 human bodies are donated to the facility each year. 60% of donations are given by family members of individuals who were not pre-registered to self-donate prior to their death. The facility is also used to train forensics and law enforcement.

65. THE FUGITIVE TRAIN WRECK
35.37039, -83.2633

< Left: Busted Plug Plaza
Top right: The Body Farm
Overleaf: Tunnelvision

973 Haywood Rd, Sylva, NC 28779
Visit the famed scene from Harrison Ford movie The Fugitive, left in the Great Smokeys since 1993.

66. FAIR PLAY
34.51132, -82.98555
Fair Play, SC 29643
Amusing location name - Allegedly the name originates from an incident in which a bystander had to implore two brawling pioneers to play fair.

67. CHEDDAR
34.57816, -82.49623
Cheddar, South Carolina 29627
Etymology unknown, pronounced SHEDur (because when it comes to cheese, Americans are never top of their game).

68. WELCOME
34.8265, -82.43901
Welcome, SC 29611
Strange place name, etymology unknown.

69. BUSTED PLUG PLAZA
34.00762, -81.032
Busted Plug, Taylor St, Columbia, SC 29201
This giant hydrant's big claim to fame is that it is made to survive through natural disasters (which is somewhat ironic given that it's already broken).

70. TUNNELVISION
34.00719, -81.0325
Marion Street, Columbia, SC 29220
This stunning piece of trompe l'oeil looks brand new but was actually painted in 1976 and is real enough to be a traffic liability.

71. ELBERTON GRANITE MUSEUM
34.11586, -82.87218
1 Granite Plaza, Elberton, GA 30635
egaonline.com
A museum dedicated to all things granite in

THE ATLANTIC SOUTH ROUTE 1

CLEAR

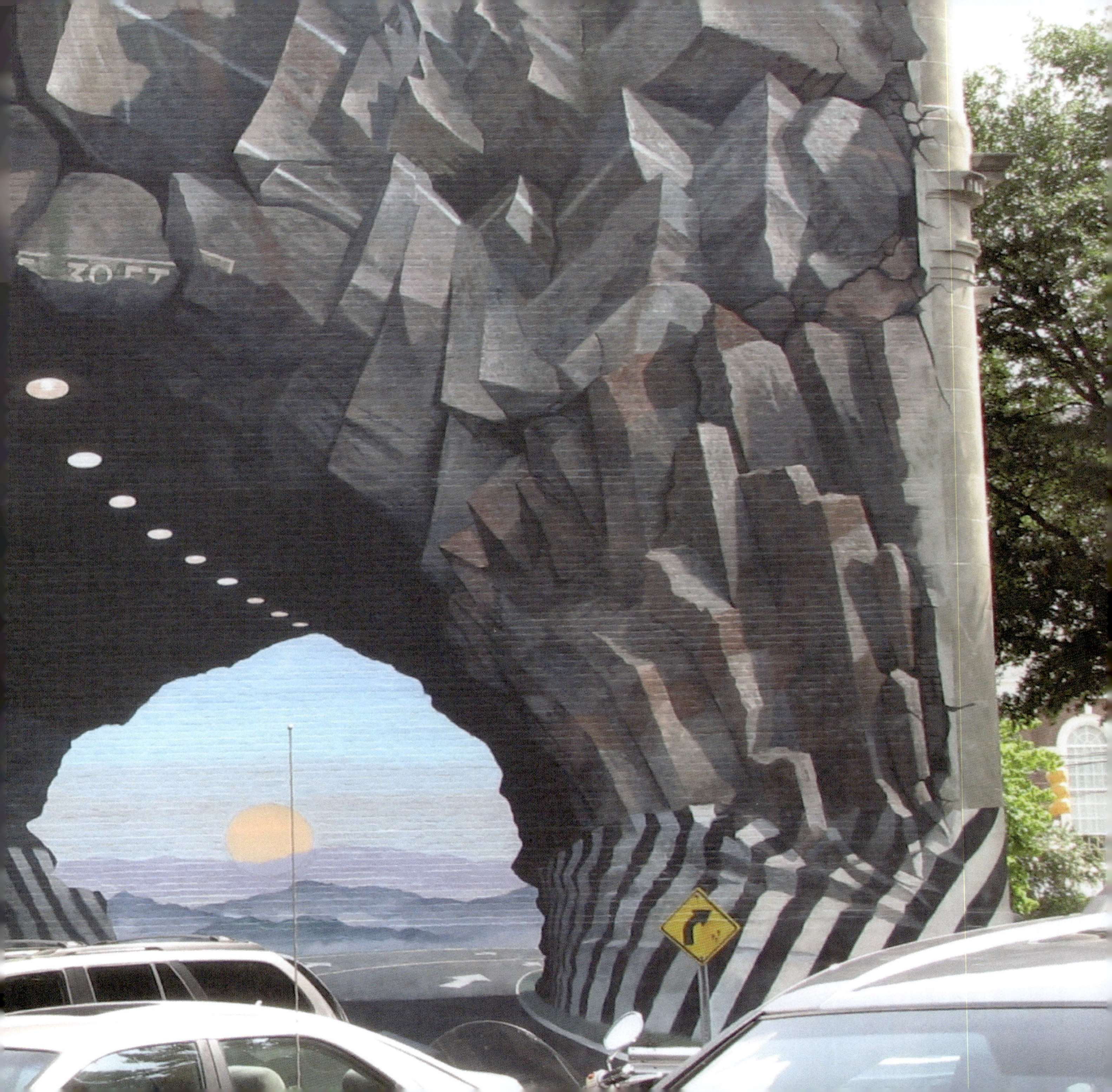

a town which features more granite than most.

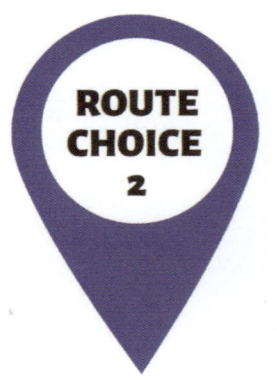

ROUTE CHOICE 2

NOW CHOOSE ROUTE A - via ATLANTA

or jump to p. 57 to follow Route B via Augusta

72. THE TREE THAT OWNS ITSELF
33.9551, -83.3823
S Finley St & Dearing St, Athens, GA 30605
One man loved this tree so much that he relinquished ownership of it and the land it stands on..to the tree itself. For those yet to get on the property ladder, this tree is ahead of you.

73. CAGLE CASTLE
34.0888, -84.3607
Arnold Mill Rd, Alpharetta, GA 30004
A tasteful family home that just happens to look like a castle replete with gnomes. Does it have much of its living space below ground, or is it really just an incredibly small but incredibly ostentatious residence? We may never know. What we do know is that a truck driver called Rudy promised to build his wife (who he referred to as his princess) a castle and that he is a man who stays true to his word.

74. BIG CHICKEN
33.95137, -84.52032
Big Chicken, 12 Cobb Pkwy S, Marietta, GA 30062
An eggcelent roadside attraction to visit.

75. ATLANTA WHITE HOUSE
33.8437, -84.2894
3691 Briarcliff Rd NE, Atlanta, Georgia
Almost, but not quite as big as the actual White House (itself known for being disappointingly small) but otherwise pretty much identical. The house foreclosed in 2011.

> Top left: Big Chicken
> Top right: CDC Museum Atlanta
> Bottom right: Atlanta White House

OFFBEAT AMERICA

47

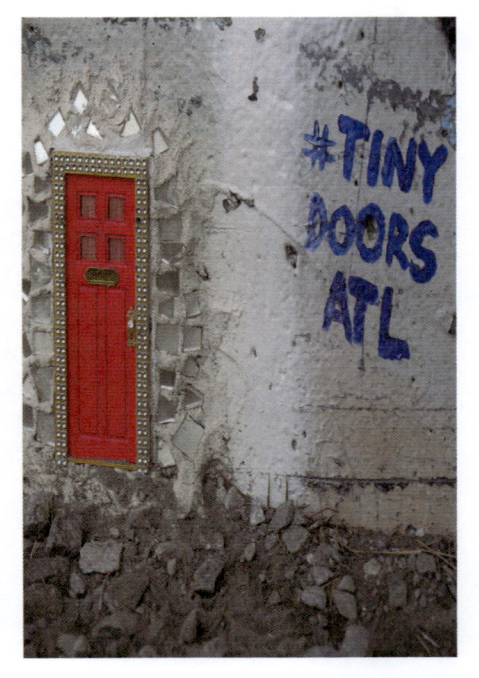

76. CDC MUSEUM ATLANTA
33.79911, -84.32971
1600 Clifton Road Northeast, Atlanta, GA 30333
Relive every zombie apocalypse movie ever by visiting a real life disease control centre.

77. GRAVITY RESEARCH FOUNDATION MONUMENT
33.7904, -84.3265
400 Dowman Dr, Atlanta, GA 30307
After suffering the loss of his sister in a drowning accident, the eccentric Roger Babson decided enough was enough and that someone had to take the blame for the tragedy. The logical culprit was gravity, and further thought on that matter revealed to Babson that gravity was in fact responsible for all kinds of ills in the world not least the deaths of people due to innumerous accidents. This led him to found the Gravity Research Foundation with the sole aim of developing an anti-gravity shield, which provided grants to a number of universities for related projects. Upon receipt of such a fund, the recipient received a dedicated monolith and this is one such stone. Happily the foundation is alive and kicking today.

78. JUNKMAN'S DAUGHTER
33.76681, -84.34945
464 Moreland Ave NE, Atlanta, GA 30307
thejunkmansdaughter.com
A real life junkman's daughter opened her own store to sell excess wares from the junkyard and this beauty is the result - 10,000 plus square feet of joy which has been frequented by the likes of Lenny Kravitz, Courtney Love, Usher, Pink, Alice Cooper, Bono and Steven Tyler.

79. TINY DOORS ATL
33.77358, -84.3644
692 Ponce De Leon Ave NE, Atlanta, GA 30306
www.tinydoorsatl.com
Atlanta may be a big city but it contains some very small doors if you know where to look.

Top left: Gravity Research Monument
Bottom left: Tiny Doors ATL
Top: Junkmans Daughter
Overleaf: Spectre Ruins

OFFBEAT AMERICA

80. THE VARSITY
61 North Avenue NW, Atlanta, GA 30308
www.thevarsity.com
This wonderful institution is the World's Largest Drive-in and has been running since 1928 when it was opened by a man named Frank Gordy with $2000 in savings. Once named 'The Yellow Jacket', the main location (for there are 6 others in the area) is responsible for more retail sales of Coke on an annual basis than any other single location in the world. US Presidents Jimmy Carter, George H. W. Bush, Bill Clinton and Obama have all been patrons of The Varsity during their tenures.

81. ATLANTA PRISON FARM
33.69699, -84.338
Key Rd SE, Atlanta, GA 30316
Within 400 acres of deserted land, the Atlanta Prison Farm (APF) was a functional correctional institute from 1945 to as recently as 1995 and could house 700 individuals who were deemed redeemable via training. As many as 1000 inmates were known to have stayed at any one time, working on the dairy, with livestock and canning vegetables - a barbershop and commissary store were also present. Every inmate in good health was expected to work. It still stands abandoned due to the land being owned by City of Atlanta but falling within the bounds of DeKalb County with neither party wishing to take ownership. Rumour has it than when a fire broke out on the premises, DeKalb county fire dept. refused to visit, letting it burn itself out.

82. THE RUINS OF SWEETWATER CREEK
33.7524, -84.62934
1750 Mt Vernon Rd, Lithia Springs, GA 30122
Evocative ruins of the Sweetwater Factory, a cotton mill on the banks of Sweetwater Creek built on Cherokee land which was operated almost independently by a tightknit community of workers from local farming families as the mill owners themselves lived in Marietta some distance from the mill itself, leading to a particularly strong sense of comradeship amongst the staff.

83. WORLD'S LARGEST PEANUT MONUMENT
31.70638, -83.63536
Ashburn, GA 31714
Not just a giant peanut, but a monument too.

Top: World's Largest Peanut Monument
Bottom: Atlanta Prison Farm

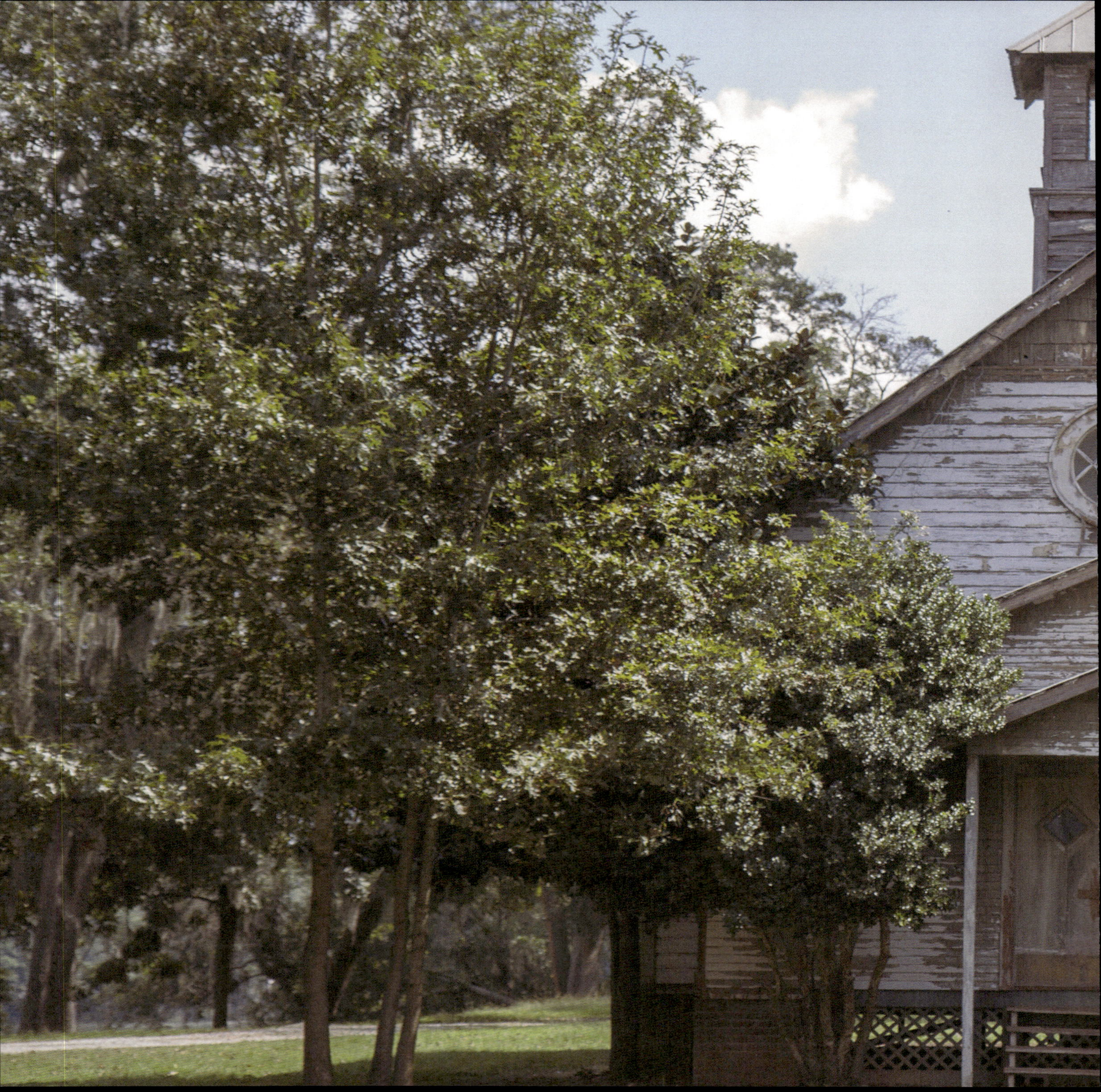

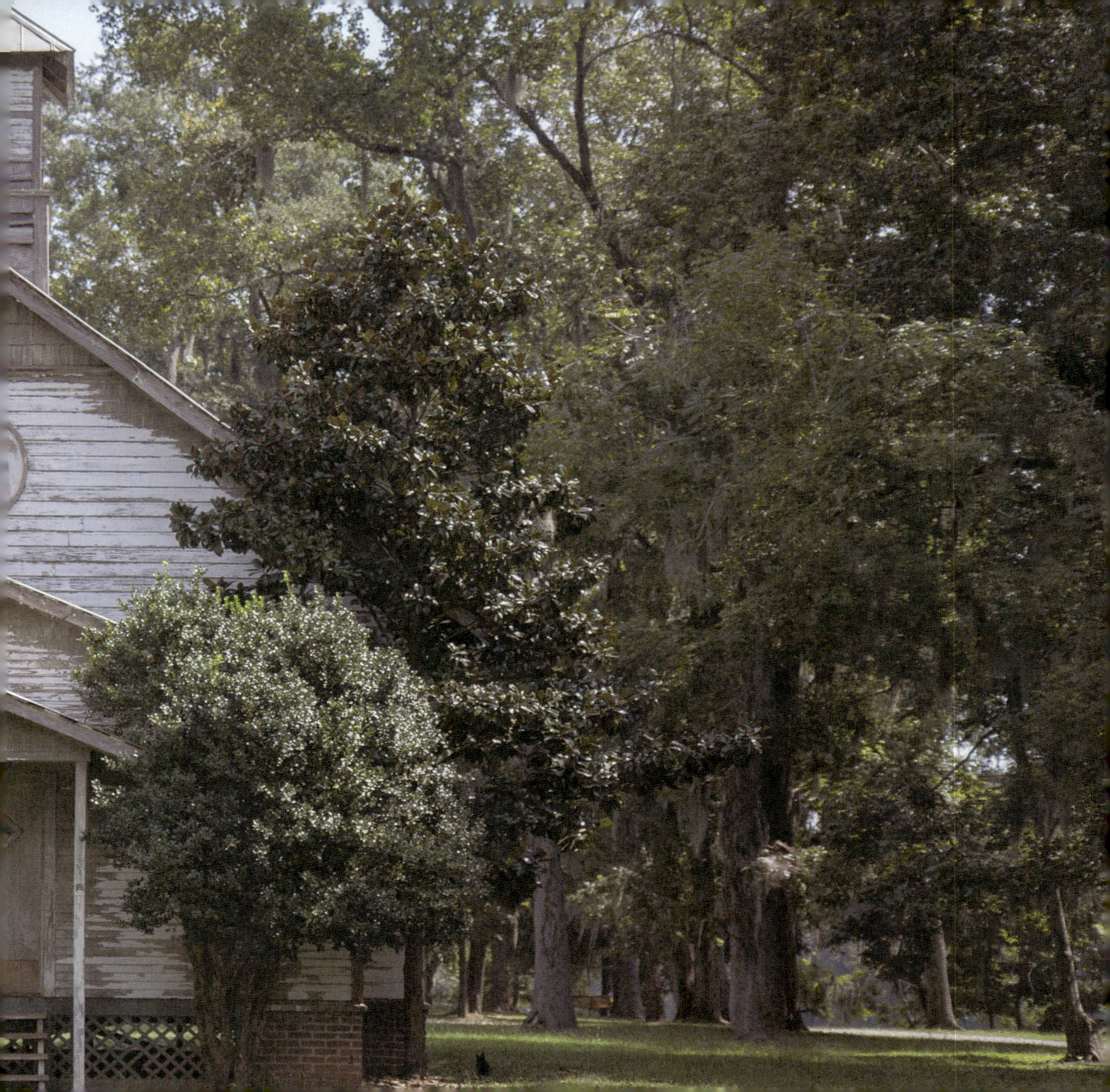

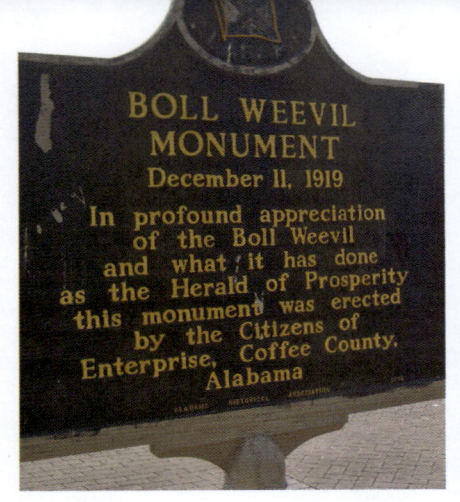

Go nuts for it.

84. PASAQUAN
32.34628, -84.58143
238 Eddie Martin Rd, Buena Vista, GA 31803
www.pasaquan.com
Georgia born Eddie Owens Martin, residing in New York, had a fever-fuelled vision that men from the future instructed him to build a perfect land of unity called Pasaquan in Georgia. Off he obediently trotted and began work on this colourful, rather hippyish series of structures (but not before renaming himself St. EOM). Things took a turn for the tragic in 1986 when he took his own life leaving Pasaquan abandoned to the elements, but a preservation society has taken up the mantle and it now stands bright and proud.

85. CIRCUS TRAIN WRECK VICTIMS MEMORIAL
32.4468, -84.97899
1000 Victory Dr, Columbus, GA 31901
A circus train wreck in which a circus train ran headlong into a passenger train that was on the wrong route in 1915. The passenger train, being made of metal, survived well, but the circus train was made of wood and incinerated most of the animals as well as one or two dozen performers and rousties. The monument to this tragic event is fittingly shaped like a large tent.

86. SPECTRE SET RUINS
32.44853, -86.33051
Dirt road near, Cypress Ln, Millbrook, AL 36054
This 'Big Fish' set remains abandoned in a woodland clearing and is an evocative and magical place to visit.

87. THE ALABAMA BOLL WEEVIL MONUMENT
31.31445, -85.85401
Main St, Enterprise, AL 36330
Enterprise, Alabama considers itself indebted to the Boll Weevil and knows how to show its appreciation in style. This otherwise classic monument of a beautiful female figure holds aloft a pedestal, on which is balanced… a large boll weevil. The Mexican beetle was responsible, in 1915, for the destruction of crop after crop of cotton until the enterprising Mr H. M. Sessions stepped in, heralding the horror as a golden opportunity to convert the area to peanut farming. Peanuts proved a hit and although cotton farming did return to the area, the event exemplified diversification. A local businessman named Bon Fleming decided to give the humble boll weevil its due (not H.M. Sessions who one imagines might have been a tad put out at the oversight), financing this monumental tribute which was built in 1919 and fashioned in Italy prior to being shipped over to the States. Disappointingly, the original boll weevil monument was sans boll weevil (I know right?!!?) but thankfully Mr Luther Baker saw the idiocy of this half-baked worship and thinking a Boll Weevil Monument without a boll weevil no Boll Weevil Monument at all, fashioned one himself and set it atop the statue. Sadly, probably due to publications such as this one, both the boll weevil itself as well as the entire statue has been stolen countless times.

Above: The Alabama Boll Weevil Monument
> Right: Original Boll Weevil Monument
Overleaf: Circus Train Wreck

53

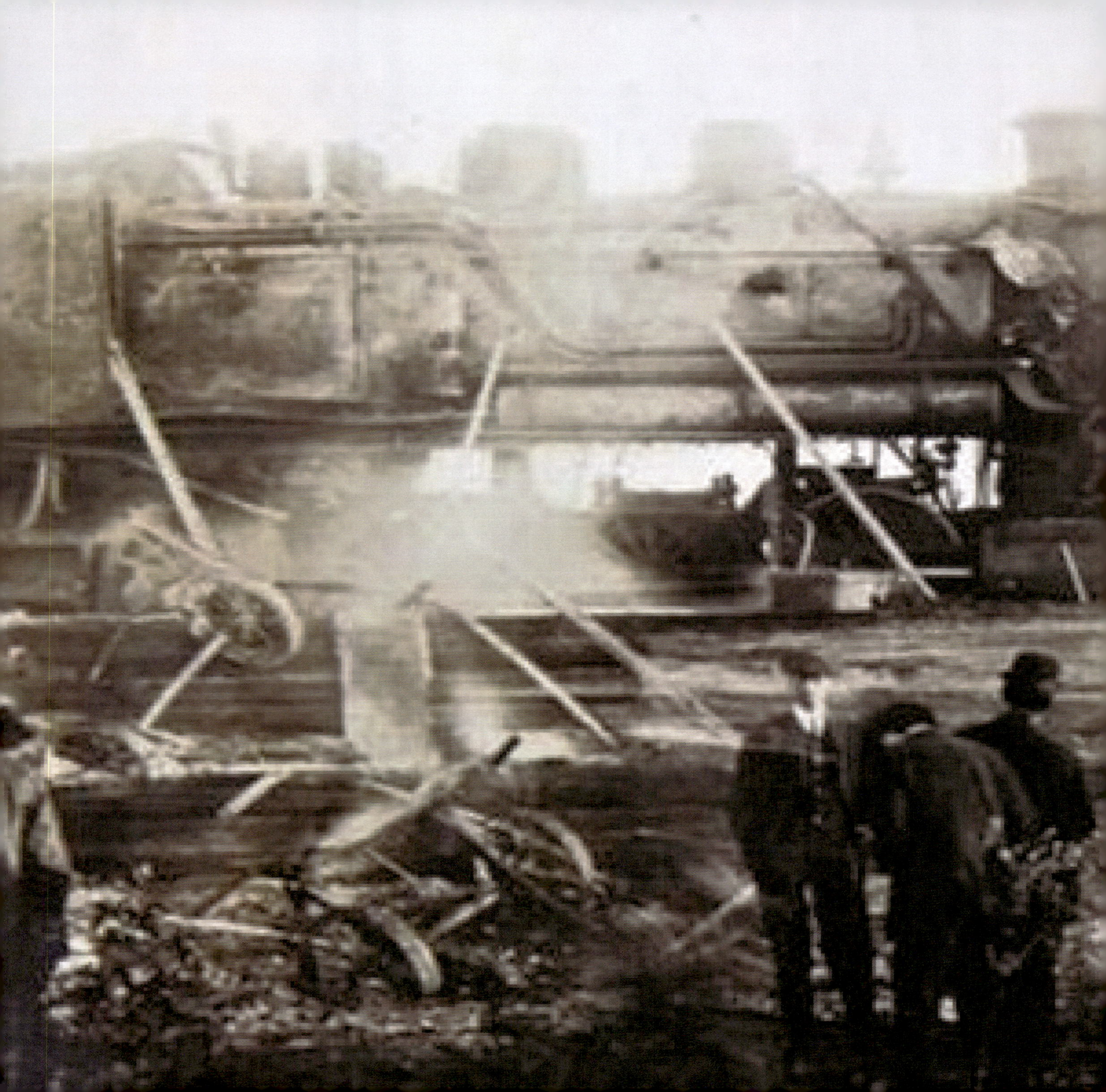

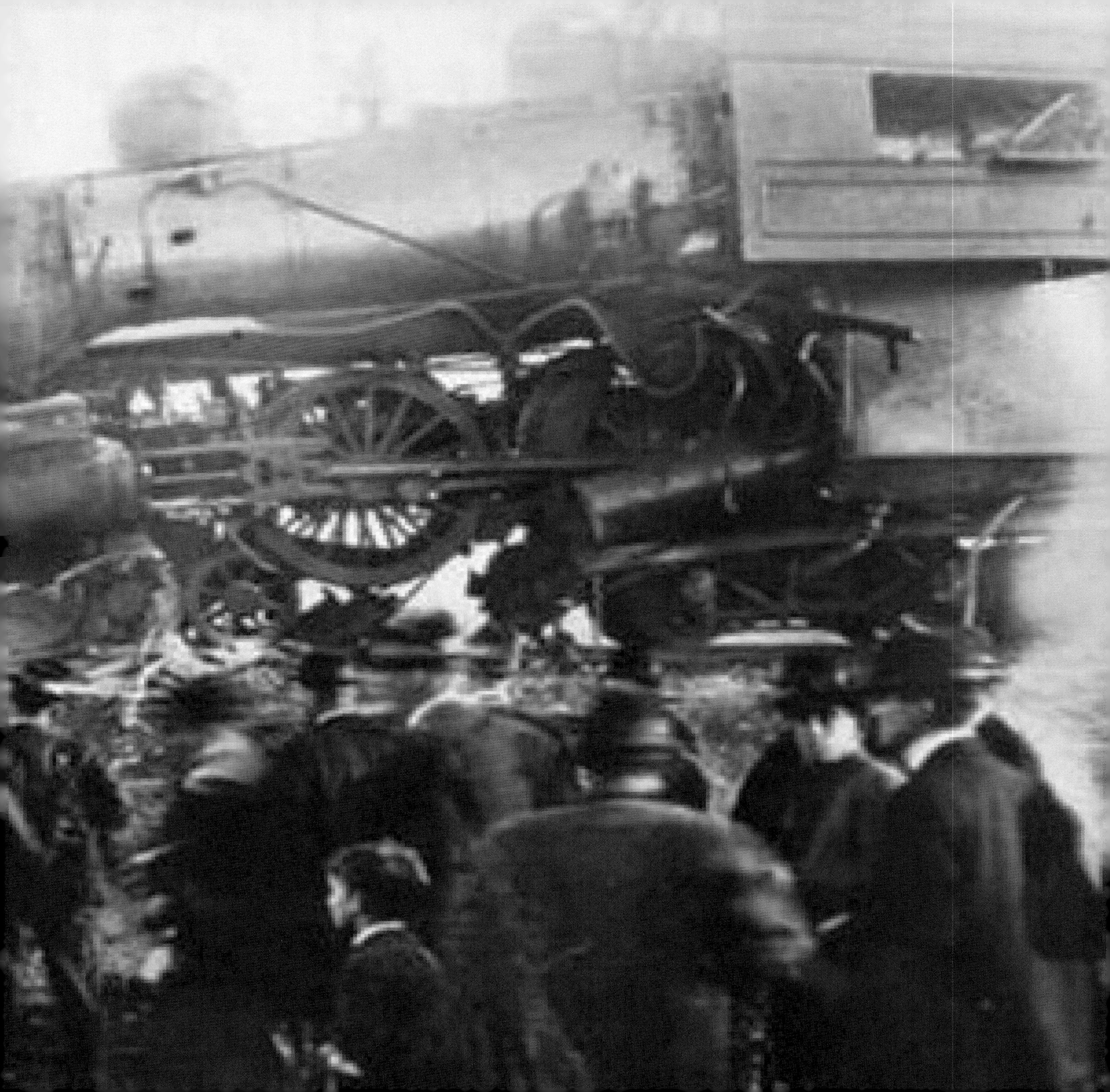

Each time it has been tracked down but on the latest iteration the boll weevil was callously ripped from the statue's hands, irreparably damaging it – now you will see a polymer-resin replica whilst the original can be viewed at Enterprise's Depot Museum at 106 Railroad Street. Be warned, the prized weevil is now monitored around the clock on cctv.

88. PEANUT-TASTIC DOTHAN
31.14522, -85.40425
201-209 N College St, Dothan, AL 36303, USA

Dothan, Alabama is literally peanut obsessed and various humanoid peanuts (Peanut Elvis, Peanut Policeman, Peanut Film Director) are to be spotted around the town. Stop in at the November National Peanut Festival and whilst in town visit the World's Smallest City Block in the World at the address provided.

89. THE WORLD'S SMALLEST POLICE STATION
29.85143, -84.66509
Ave A N, Carrabelle, FL 32322

Built in the sixties, the original version of this police call booth-come-station had its phone ripped out, bullets shot through its glass, was knocked over by a truck and got caught up in Hurricane Kate before a local gas station attendant was asked to help a tourist load it into the back of his truck in order to take it back with him to Tennessee. This is now a slightly more recent replacement and is firmly fixed to the ground.

90. FORD TRUCK GRAVEYARD
30.0933, -84.3856
Coastal Hwy south on Highway 319 between Crawfordville and Medart, just before the intersection of 319 and 98. FL 32327 (near Sarablake Lane)

This collection of classic and somewhat rust-orientated Fords, left here by Pat Harvey after their use on the Harvey family farm by both his father and grandfather before him, hasn't hit the road for a while. They are arranged in chronological order from the 1900s to the mid 1970s.

91. NEW SALEM AIRPORT CEMETERY
30.3909, -84.2765
3815 Woodville Hwy, Tallahassee, FL 32305

Despite appearing to be situated amongst a considerable number of no entry signs, fear not -this cemetery is public. Thought to be a pauper's graveyard dating back to 1922, it is still used for burials despite the airport's runways having been built around the site.

92. GEORGE FIRESTONE PRISON
30.4352, -84.27761
George Firestone Building, Tallahassee, FL 32301
This art-deco prison was the site of a tragedy in which two black prisoners were taken from the jail and lynched and has been abandoned since 2007.

93. UTOPIAN FALLSCHASE
30.4619, -84.2096
Fallschase Pkwy, Tallahassee, FL 32317
Ruins of a utopian development.

94. THE VERDURA PLANTATION
30.4906, -84.1857
Miccosukee Road, Tallahassee, FL 32308
The ruins of an early example of an antebellum plantation home are now being overtaken by the Florida fauna.

95. ELLAVILLE GHOST TOWN
30.4586, -83.507
Unnamed Road, Madison, FL 32340
Named after the first governor of Florida's favourite servant Ella, the town became one of Florida's largest mills employing over 500 people. Today, very little remains, other than an old bridge and the remnants of the once great mill.

< Bottom Left: Hampton Springs Hotel
< Bottom right: World's Smallest Police Station
Right: The Old Slave Mart Museum

96. HAMPTON SPRINGS HOTEL
30.042, -83.7155
Hampton Springs Rd, Perry, FL 32348
Once a top end resort, today the abandoned ruins of this 1908 spa hotel built on a spring with so-called healing properties lie vacant and open, belying the once extravagant fountains, tennis courts, golf course, stabling, ballrooms, casino and indoor pool that previously lay there. Bottled water from the spring was once shipped nationwide prior to the facility and hotel burning to the ground in the mid-fifties.

**- END ROUTE A–
JUMP TO THE HOLY LAND EXPERIENCE, p.60 TO CONTINUE YOUR JOURNEY**

ROUTE B - via AUGUSTA

97. KILLER PILLAR
33.47261, -81.95886
200 5th St, Augusta, GA 30901
More of a point of ridicule than of interest, this column is almost the column that was left standing after a priest, who was banned from speaking in front of the town's marketplace, threatened that the market would be smote down leaving only one pillar standing, and that anyone who so touched it would die a slow painful death. Almost because - well... despite tales that the attempted removal of the pillar (which was indeed left standing alone after a hurricane) resulted in the death of those who tried, the pillar was indeed torn down. And this one...well this is another one built by local residents. In a different location from the original. An underwhelming testament to the folly of mankind perhaps.

98. UFO WELCOME CENTER
33.35179, -80.68459
4004 Homestead Rd, Bowman, SC 29018
Not 'if' they come, but 'when'... An eccentric gentleman by the name of Jody has built not one but two UFOs ready to be taken by our otherworldly guests to distant lands and is ready to welcome them at their convenience. Should you find him at home, he may well show you around.

99. THE OLD SLAVE MART MUSEUM

THE ATLANTIC SOUTH ROUTE 1

32.77783, -79.9284
6 Chalmers St, Charleston, SC 29401
www.oldslavemartmuseum.com
Slaves were once sold in public but the practice was banned in 1856, leading to the markets merely reopening as private auction houses. This is one such auction house and is very rare in that the vast majority of these buildings were torn down once the slavery practice ended. Here, slaves were sold alongside animals to willing buyers with well over a third of all slaves in the American South passing through this 'mart' in Charleston.

100. EDISTO ISLAND TREE
32.5509, -80.2803
Where Botany Bay Road meets the 174, Edisto Island, SC 29438
Visitors leave their own mementos on this tree for no apparent reason.

101. THE KAZOOBIE KAZOO FACTORY & MUSEUM
32.43467, -80.72017
12 John Galt Rd, Beaufort, SC 29906
www.thekazoofactory.com
Learn about all things irritating and sub--musical and even buy your own at this kazoo-tastic venue

102. US NATIONAL TICK COLLECTION

32.4261, -81.7805
Herty Drive, Statesboro, GA 30458
The tick collection has been moved around rather a lot - one might even (although probably unfairly) surmise that owners for the prestigious collection have been rather unforthcoming. As with all such things, despite being gifted to the Smithsonian, it was swiftly passed along to its current home in good Ol' Georgia which can always be relied upon to appreciate the unusual. Want to see over a million ticks in one place? This is for you. Given that ticks are responsible for many of the world's most virulent diseases, the collection in fact has very significant research value.

103. DOTSON RUNWAY GRAVES
32.13559, -81.2088
400 Airways Avenue, Savannah, Georgia, 31408
Only in quirky Savannah could graves be set into a runway. Laying flowers proves tricky if not downright deadly here.

104. ALEX RASKIN ANTIQUES
32.07088, -81.09518
441 Bull St, Savannah, GA 31401
alexraskinantiques.com
At 441 Bull St stands not only a beautiful Savannah mansion but the entrance to an unusual antique shop - in true Savannah style, wander the floors of this somewhat dilapidated yet gorgeous building, strewn with antiques for sale from floor to ceiling.

< Left: Alex Raskin Antiques
Right: Jekyll Island Club

105. CORINNE ELLIOT LAWTON'S GRAVE
32.0564, -81.0479
330 Bonaventure Rd, Thunderbolt, GA 31404
Legend has it that the beautiful, intelligent young Corinne threw herself into the river near her home at 15 West Perry St, depressed that she could not marry the man that she loved and was being pushed into marrying another. It is also said that due to her death by suicide, her beautiful likeness in the cemetery, sculpted by a renowned Italian sculpture, has its back turned to a neighbouring statue of Jesus, beckoning others through the gates of salvation.

106. JEKYLL ISLAND CLUB
31.01726, -81.42945
371 Riverview Dr, Jekyll Island, GA 31527
www.jekyllclub.com
Historically one of the world's most prestigious private members clubs which has played host to Rockefellers and Vanderbilts for years, now open to visit.

107. THE CARNEGIE RUINS
30.8511, -81.44839
Cumberland Island National Seashore, St Marys, GA 31558
This 1884 Carnegie family mansion which had the space to house 200 servants

THE ATLANTIC SOUTH ROUTE 1

alongside the family was left vacant during the Depression of the 20s, until fire eventually razed much of it to the ground in 1959, leaving behind only the outline of what once was.

108. DINE WITH AN ASTRONAUT
28.5232, -80.6816
Kennedy Space Center, SR 405, Titusville, FL 32899
www.kennedyspacecenter.com

The Kennedy Space Center Visitor Complex offers patrons the unique ability to dine with a real life astronaut and quiz them about their out of this world experiences.

ROUTES A & B CONVERGE HERE IN ORLANDO

109. THE HOLY LAND EXPERIENCE
28.49545, -81.43355
4655 Vineland Rd, Orlando, FL 32811
www.holylandexperience.com

A theme park of biblical proportions.

110. FLORIDA CITRUS TOWER
28.5639, -81.74299
141 US-27, Clermont, FL 34711
www.citrustower.com

One of the top tourist attractions in Florida prior to the Disney era, this gigantic observation deck lets you see for miles and experience a bygone era when visitors'

breath would be taken away by this tower alone.

111. ABANDONED RIVER COUNTRY PARK
28.3987, -81.571
Walt Disney World Resort, Lake Buena Vista, FL 32830

Disney World's first waterpark has seen better days. Open for 25 years and charging around just $3 entry in 1976, River Country was revolutionary in its time as the first thematic water park, one that was entirely imagined in a rustic, ol' swimmin' hole, Huckleberry Finn style. Furthermore, Disney invented innovative methods by which guests could swim in the actual Bay Lake water safely and hygienically, by pumping and filtering lake water, throwing it down the flumes and then returning it to the lake at 8,500 gallons per minute without reducing the lake levels. Real pebbles were rounded up from Georgia and the Carolinas and scattered on the faux rocks to add realism. The park was extremely successful, with some 5000 guests per day enjoying the flumes. So what went wrong? Safety was a major concern; in 1982 a 14 year old drowned after completing the Whoop 'n Holler flume drop into the Bay Cove lagoon - it later emerged that on some days up to 75 people would need lifeguard assistance after taking the plunge. His parents were awarded $375,000 in damages. Just seven years later, a 13 year old also drowned at the park, yet the park remained open. Beyond accidents, it was then discovered that a rare and deadly amoeba lived in those Florida waters and therefore law was passed preventing paid swimming areas from using freshwater or lakes areas, despite Disney's clever filtration system. An 11 year died after spending his holiday at the park which was attributed to the amoebic meningoencephalitis disease which carries a fatality rate in excess of 95%, but although Disney did ban swimming in its lakes in the mid-1990s, a further 21 years passed prior to the park's closure. Competition then struck the beleaguered park in the form of the Wet 'n Wild park in Orlando built by the founder of Seaworld, as well as two new water parks built by Disney themselves both of which were far larger and more successful than River Country. The location became hard to get to and far from the best resort hotels and with the advent of September 11 which drove Disney to take drastic cost cutting action as tourism plummeted, the park closed in 2001. Parts of the park are still clearly visible from boats passing by on Bay Lake, while if you take the boat from Fort Wilderness to the Magic Kingdom, you can see the Cypress Point Nature Trail boardwalk, now collapsing into the lagoon. Visitors to the Hoop-Dee-Doo Musical Revue can also see through the green fence that separates Fort Wilderness from River Country (turn left out of Crockett's Tavern and walk up the street running next to Bay Lake to reach the fence).

112. SINGING RUNWAY
28.3987, -81.571
Off Vista Blvd near World Drive (next to Bay Lake, close to the Magic Kingdom), Orlando, FL 32830
This runway built in 1971 to service Disney World Airport closed soon after it opened but is still accessible - it has a secret feature, that when planes drive over it at exactly 45mph, the surface plays the tune of ' When you wish upon a star' from Pinocchio.

113. MICKEY PYLON
28.3038, -81.5742
Celebration, FL 34747
Literally nothing in this area can escape the Disney touch.

114. BOK TOWER GARDENS & SINGING TOWER
27.9157, -81.5660
1151 Tower Blvd, Lake Wales, FL 33853
www.boktowergardens.org +1 863-676-1408
The 205 foot tall Singing Tower set in beautiful gardens holds an unusual musical instrument that is the heaviest in the world, a beautiful carillon featuring 60 bells, some of which weigh as much as 12 tons. It was designed and built in 1928 by John Taylor Bellfoundry of England who are still making bells to this day.

115. SPOOK HILL ANTI-GRAVITY ZONE
27.9086, -81.5812
Lake Wales, FL 33853
spookhill.info
Said to be haunted by a Native American and/or crocodile after the two had a terrific and momentus standoff leading to their mutual deaths (it is not clear which is responsible for the haunting itself), this is an area in which cars appear to roll up hill in an illusion to be found at various Anti-Gravity Areas around the USA.

116. WHIMZEYLAND
27.99215, -82.70093

< Left: Citrus Tower
< Centre: Bok Tower Gardens & Singing Tower
< Right: Mickey Pylon

Left: Gibsonton
Right: Big Bend Power Plant Manatee Viewing Area

1206 3rd St N, Safety Harbor, FL 34695
An eccentric private residence where bowling balls are turned into a work of art.

117. AIRSTREAMS OF SEFFNER
28.02092, -82.25196
I-4, Seffner, FL 33584
An arresting sight as you drive through Florida, these airstream trailers appear to have been shot into the ground from above to ensure drivers continue to rear end other drivers whilst gawping.

118. GIBSONTON
27.85363, -82.38259
Gibsonton, FL
An entire town whose purpose is to provide circus entertainers and sideshow exhibitors with a place to relax when they are not touring the Nation. The town sprung up due to unusually lax laws in the area regarding the keeping of animals such as elephants on properties. The town is still used by such people over the winter months but they generally take a dim view of gawking tourists so be respectful should you visit. Previous residents have historically included Lobster Boy (as featured in American Horror Story), Colonel Casper Balsam, a circus midget who played a Munchkin in The Wizard of Oz, Al Tomaini who stood at 8ft 5.5 inches, the Anatomical Wonder and Siamese twin sisters who ran a fruit stand in the town. It was once the only town with a post office counter at dwarf height.

119. BIG BEND POWER PLANT MANATEE VIEWING AREA
27.79251, -82.40123
6990 Dickman Rd, Apollo Beach, FL 33572
www.tampaelectric.com
Because all wildlife viewing centres should be power plant linked.

120. THE JOHN & MABLE RINGLING MUSEUM OF ART
27.38139, -82.56043
5401 Bay Shore Rd, Sarasota, FL 34243
www.ringling.org
This wonderful museum in Sarasota is the private home of circus mogul John Ringling and his wife Mabel, who during their lives filled their lavish mansion with beautiful art; both the collection and their home are now open to the public and offer an intimate

insight into their lives and loves.

121. PINECRAFT
27.32504, -82.4912
Pinecraft, Sarasota Springs, FL 34232
Originally conceived as a tourist resort in 1920, Pinecraft took a twist in becoming a destination for the Amish looking to holiday at the beach, complete with a 'Tourist Church' to permit them to continue to pray whilst on their travels. The accommodations are kept simple and the entertainment is mostly confined to sitting on the beach, but by Amish standards which would expect devotees to work in daylight hours and partake in nothing that could be deemed remotely close to relaxation or frivolity, the mere idea of this place as a destination is somewhat bizarre, whilst its popularity perhaps says something about the struggles of those striving to stick to the strict expectations of the Amish way of life.

122. SOLOMON'S CASTLE
27.3720, -81.9777
4533 Solomon Rd, Ona, FL 33865
www.solomonscastle.org
This extraordinary 1974 castle is entirely made out of aluminium printing plates discarded by a local paper. It has recently been listed for sale for $2.5M.

123. WARM MINERAL SPRINGS
27.05889, -82.26098

Above: Ringling Museum of Art
Right: Solomon's Castle
Overleaf: Airstreams of Seffner

THE ATLANTIC SOUTH ROUTE 1

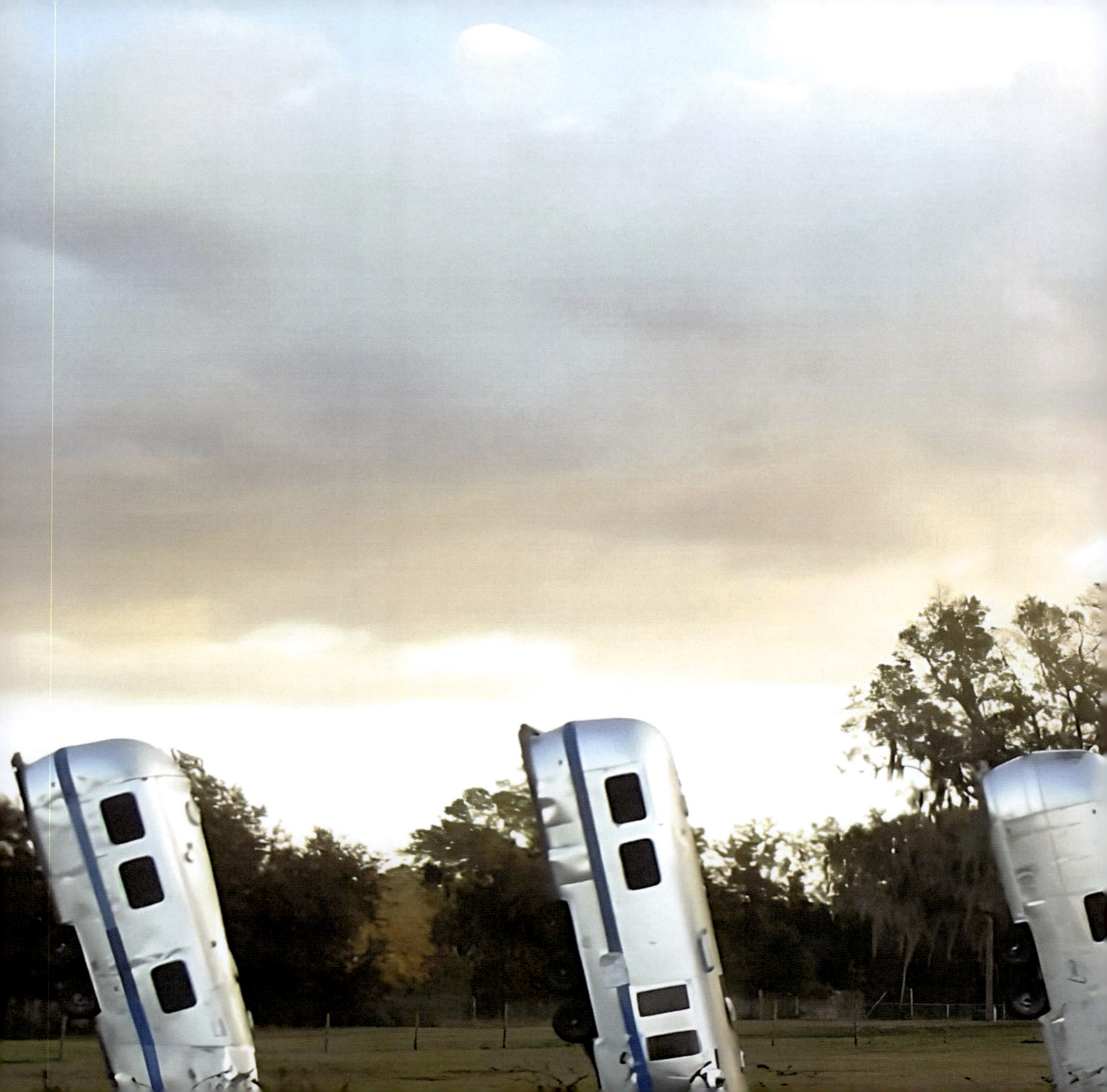

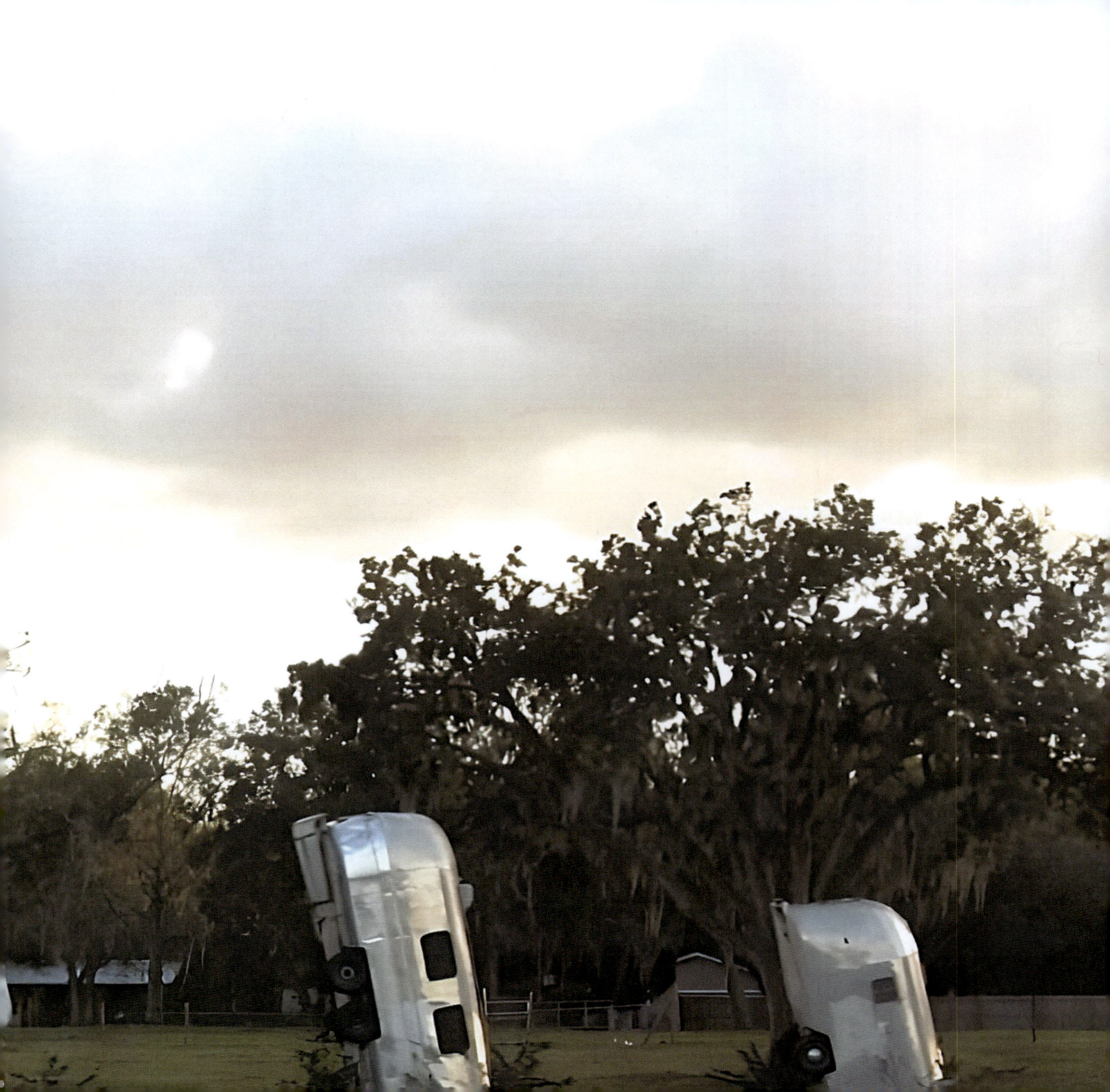

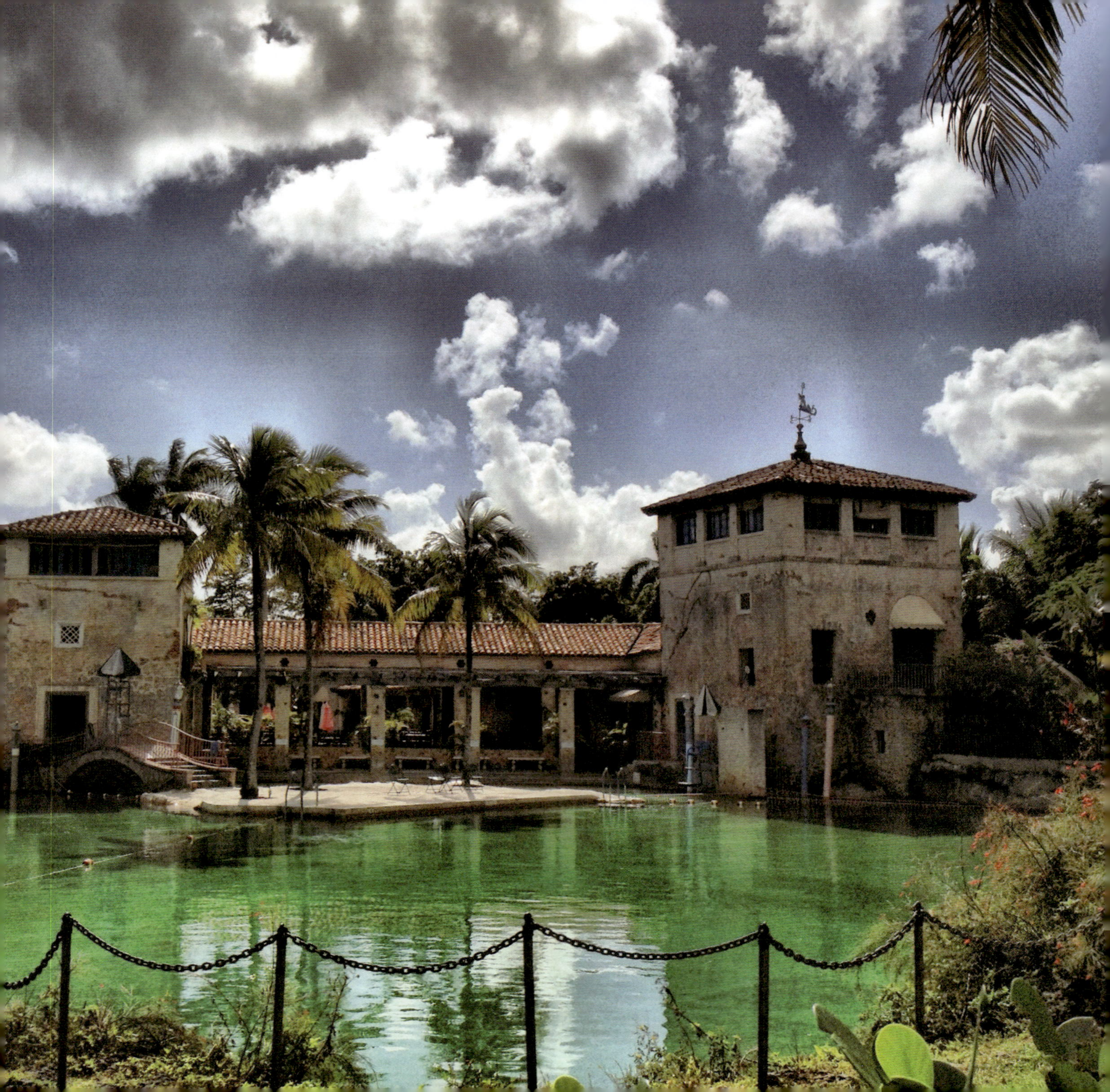

12200 San Servando Ave, North Port, FL 34287
www.warmmineral.com
A collapsed cavern containing pre-historic specimens is now a sink hole full of balmy spring water, all open for you to swim in. It is said that Ponce de Leon died in Florida whilst hunting for the Fountain of Youth which could theoretically be the Springs, although it has equally been renowned for the discovery in the 1950s of the skeletons of at least 7 people which date back to around 10,000 years ago.

124. CAPE ROMANO DOME HOUSES
25.84525, -81.6811
Marco Island, FL 34145
Now only accessible by sea, these once futuristic buildings were a private home built by an inventor but hurricane after hurricane has taken its toll on the coast line and his dream home is now a shell.

125. VENETIAN POOL
25.74553, -80.27335
2701 De Soto Blvd, Coral Gables, FL 33134
coralgables.com
If Venice didn't exist, this would stand up well to it. But it does. So… it doesn't. Pricey but makes for a good swimming spot to escape the Miami heat.

126. VIZCAYA MUSEUM AND GARDENS
25.74438, -80.21047
3251 S Miami Ave, Miami, FL 33129
www.vizcaya.org
An eccentrically grandiose mansion surrounded by luscious gardens and containing what at first glance appears to be a petrified galley ship shipwrecked near the house.

127. VIRGINIA KEY MARINE STADIUM
25.74236, -80.17051
3501 Rickenbacker Causeway, Key Biscayne, FL 33149
This dilapidated water stadium built for speedboat shows and races in the early Sixties was the site of the death of a racer on its opening day and despite successfully continuing to operate until '92, it was then declared unsafe and has been left vacant ever since.

128. NEPTUNE MEMORIAL REEF
25.6902, -80.0908
Key Biscayne, FL 33149
This location, only accessible via scuba

< Left: Venetian Pool
Bottom: Vizcaya Museum and Gardens
Overleaf: Cape Romano Dome Houses

THE ATLANTIC SOUTH ROUTE 1

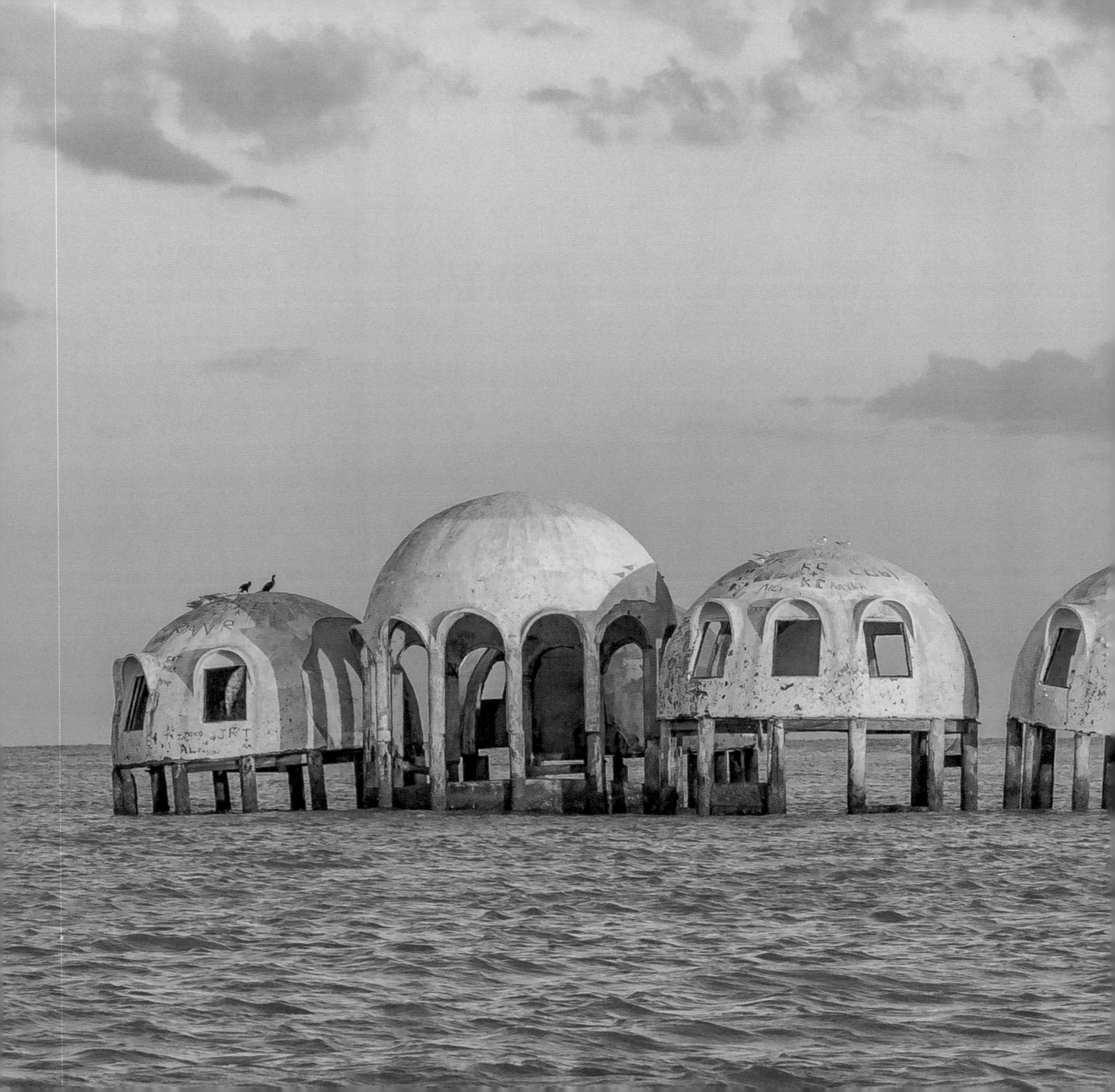

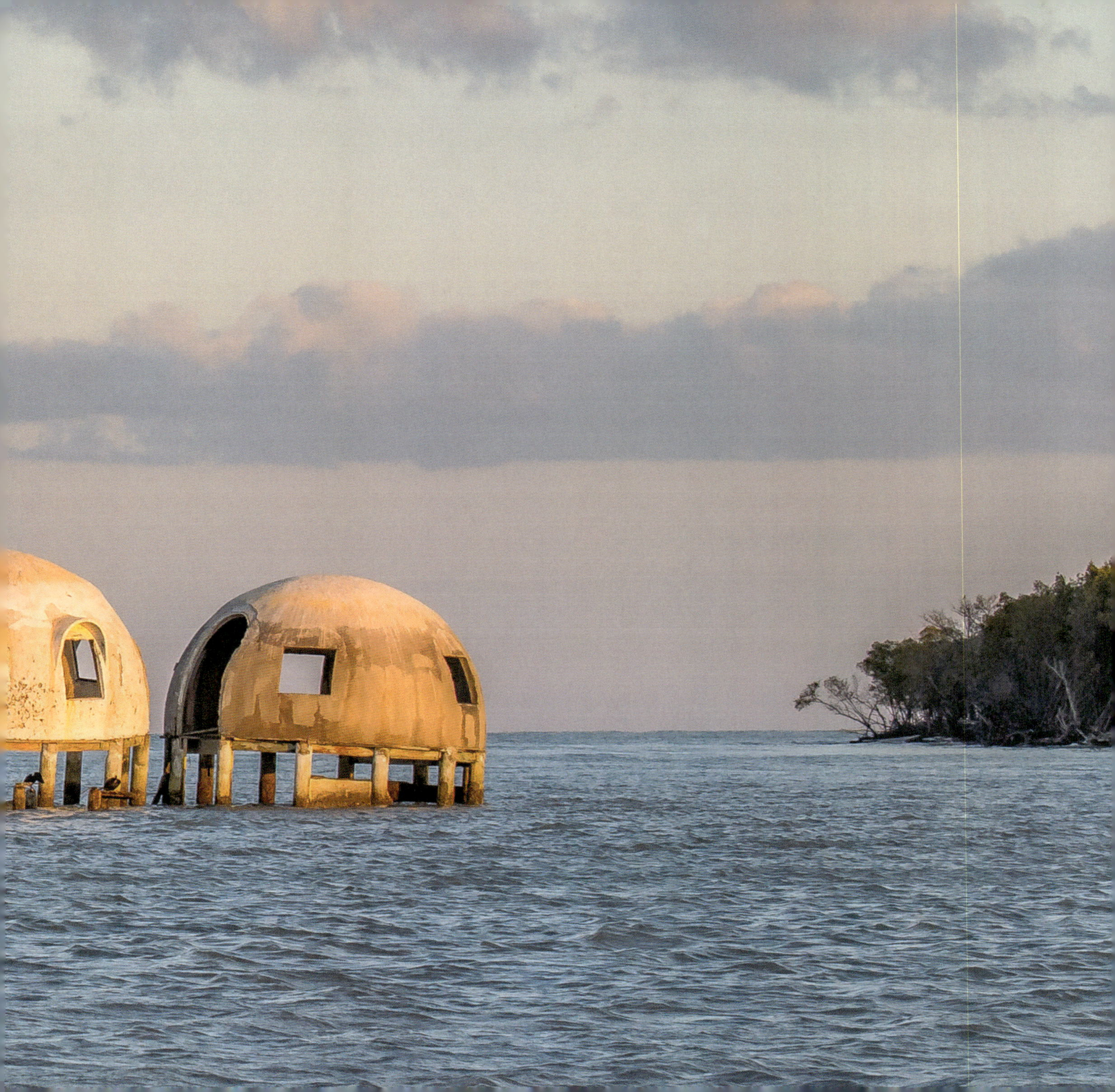

diving, is both a functional underwater cemetery for cremated remains of loved ones who wished to be buried…well in an underwater cemetery, as well as an entire lost city in the style of Atlantis, all created by a Florida artist.

129. STILTSVILLE
25.65457, -80.17444
Key Biscayne, FL 33149
These structures in Biscayne Bay are not simply land residences marooned by rising waters but were part of an entire town built at sea composed of almost 30 such structures, all over a mile into the ocean, developed by Eddie Walker in the twenties during Prohibition Era. It doesn't take a lot of imagination to understand the rationale behind their construction - as gambling and drinking dens, they functioned marvellously far from prying eyes and handcuffs. Unfortunately hurricanes and fires took their toll and only 7 remain.

130. ED LEEDSKALNIN'S CORAL CASTLE
25.5005, -80.4446
28655 S Dixie Hwy, Homestead, FL 33033
coralcastle.com
One man's love lost is another man's bizarre self-built homage-castle.

131. JULES' UNDERSEA LODGE
25.13301, -80.39867
51 Shoreland Dr, Key Largo, FL 33037
www.jul.com
The only hotel imaginable where a scuba suit needs to be donned in order to reach your room.

132. BETSY THE LOBSTER
24.9594, -80.5713
86700 Overseas Hwy, Islamorada, FL 33036
You'll pinch yourself when you see the size of this roadside lobby. Grab a bite at the nearby Lobster Shack in celebration of Betsy.

OFFBEAT AMERICA

Top Left: Stiltsville
Centre left: Ed Leedskalnin's Coral Castle
Bottom left: Jules Undersea Lodge
> Right: Betsy the Lobster
Overleaf: Virginia Key Marine Stadium

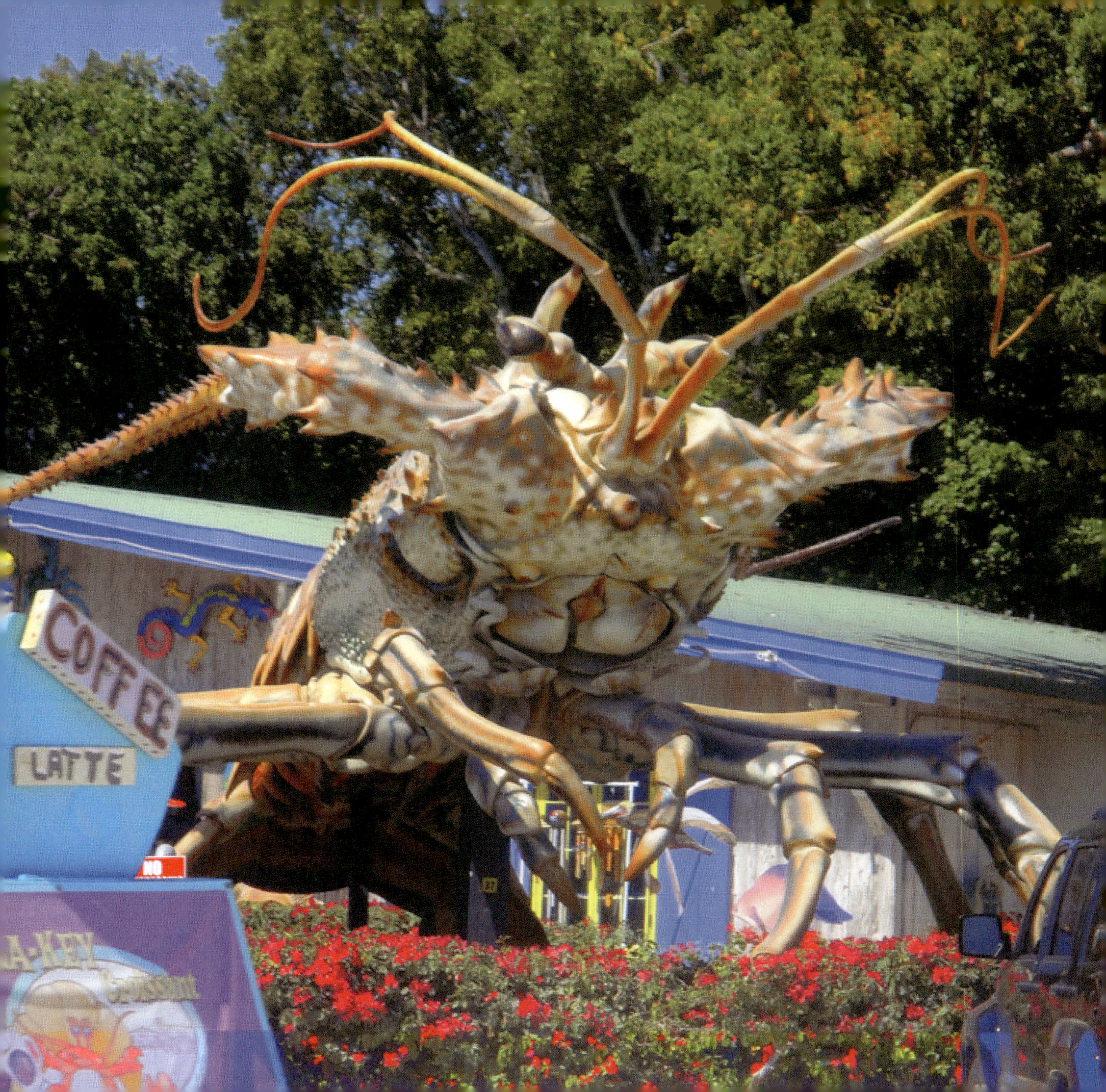
COFFEE
LATTE
NO

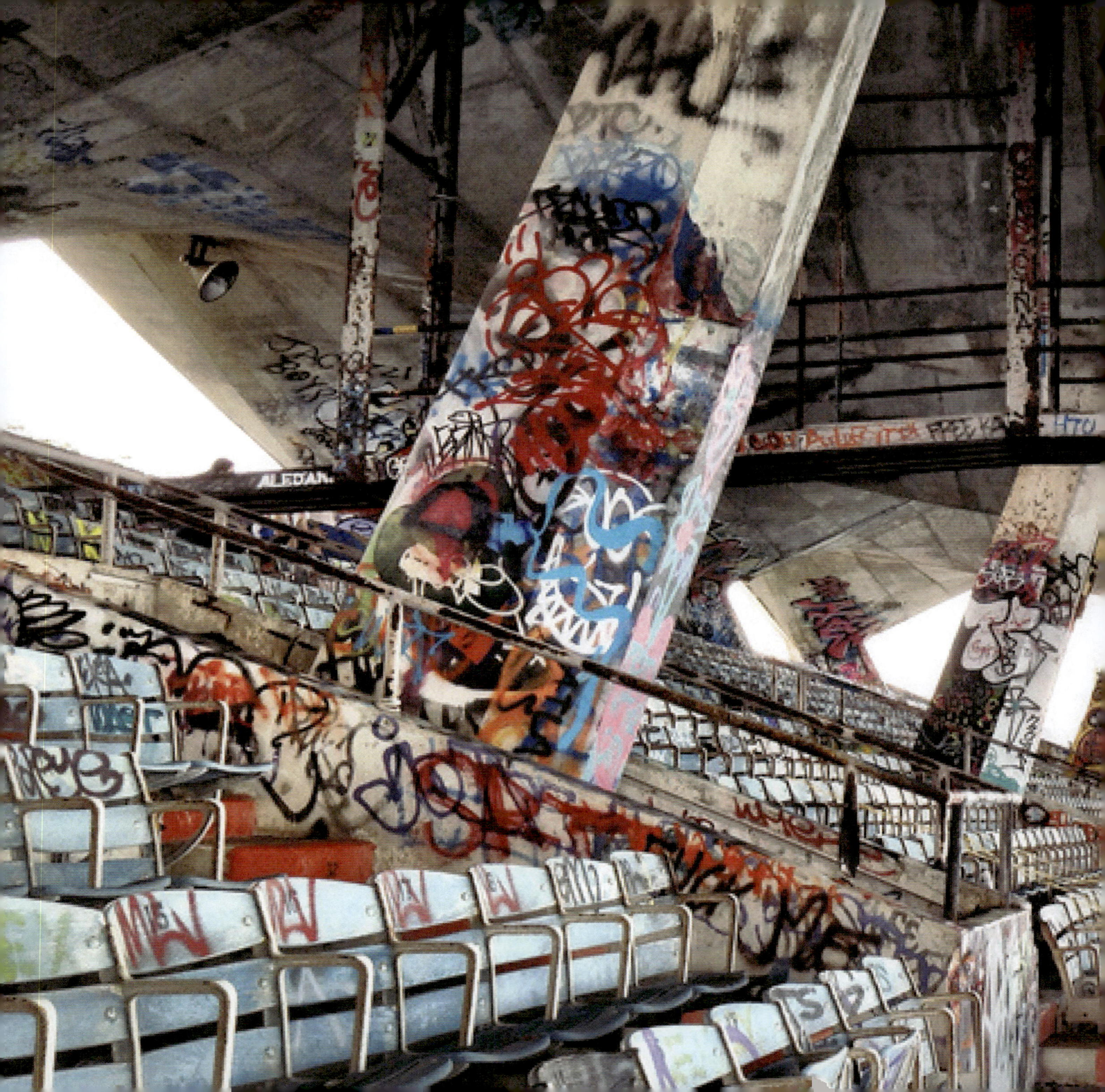

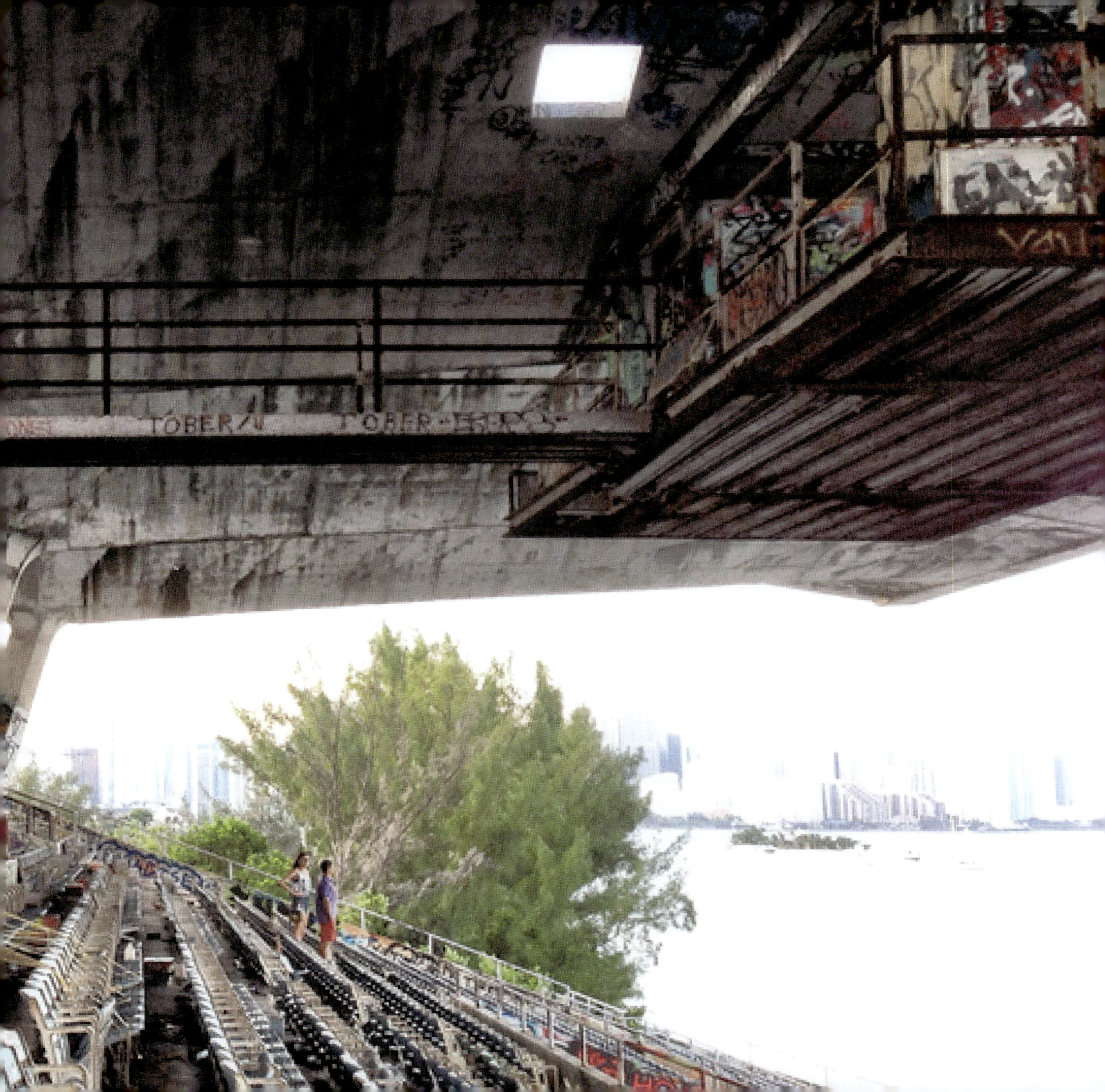
TOBER

THE NEW ENGLAND TRAIL ROUTE 2

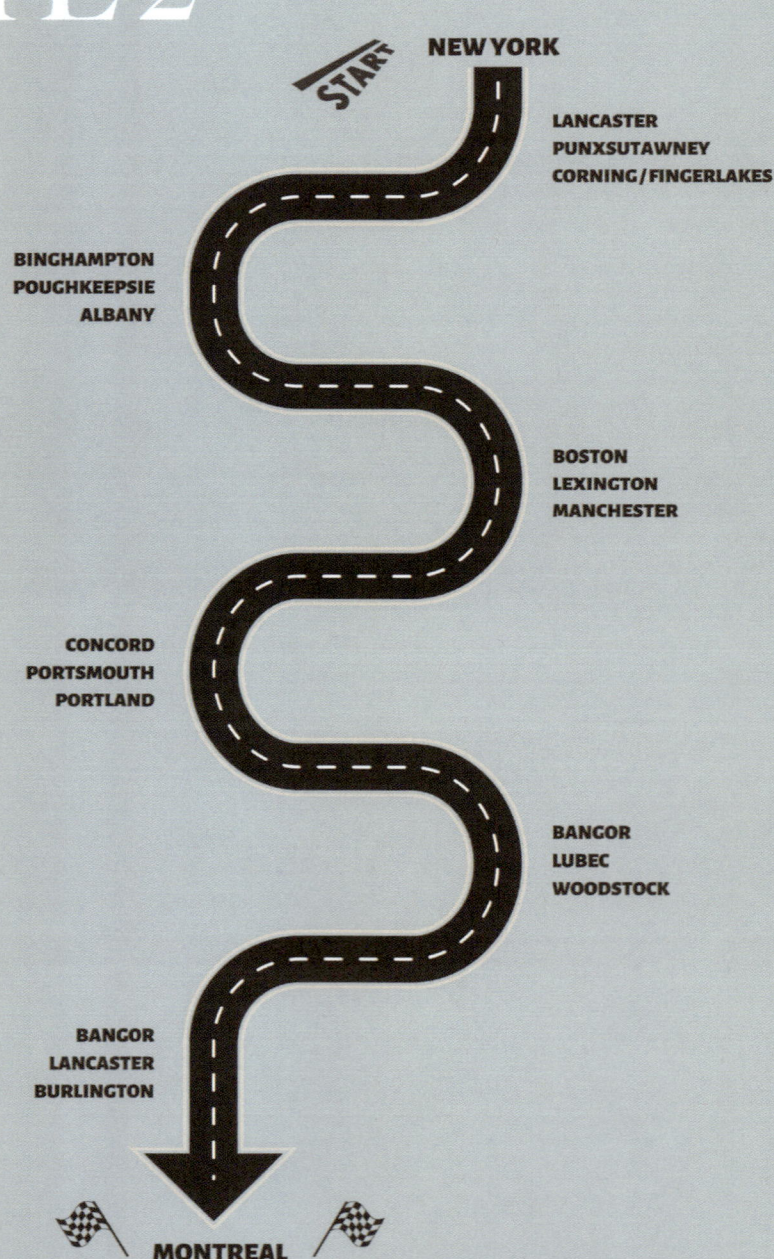

START — **NEW YORK**

LANCASTER
PUNXSUTAWNEY
CORNING/FINGERLAKES

BINGHAMPTON
POUGHKEEPSIE
ALBANY

BOSTON
LEXINGTON
MANCHESTER

CONCORD
PORTSMOUTH
PORTLAND

BANGOR
LUBEC
WOODSTOCK

BANGOR
LANCASTER
BURLINGTON

MONTREAL

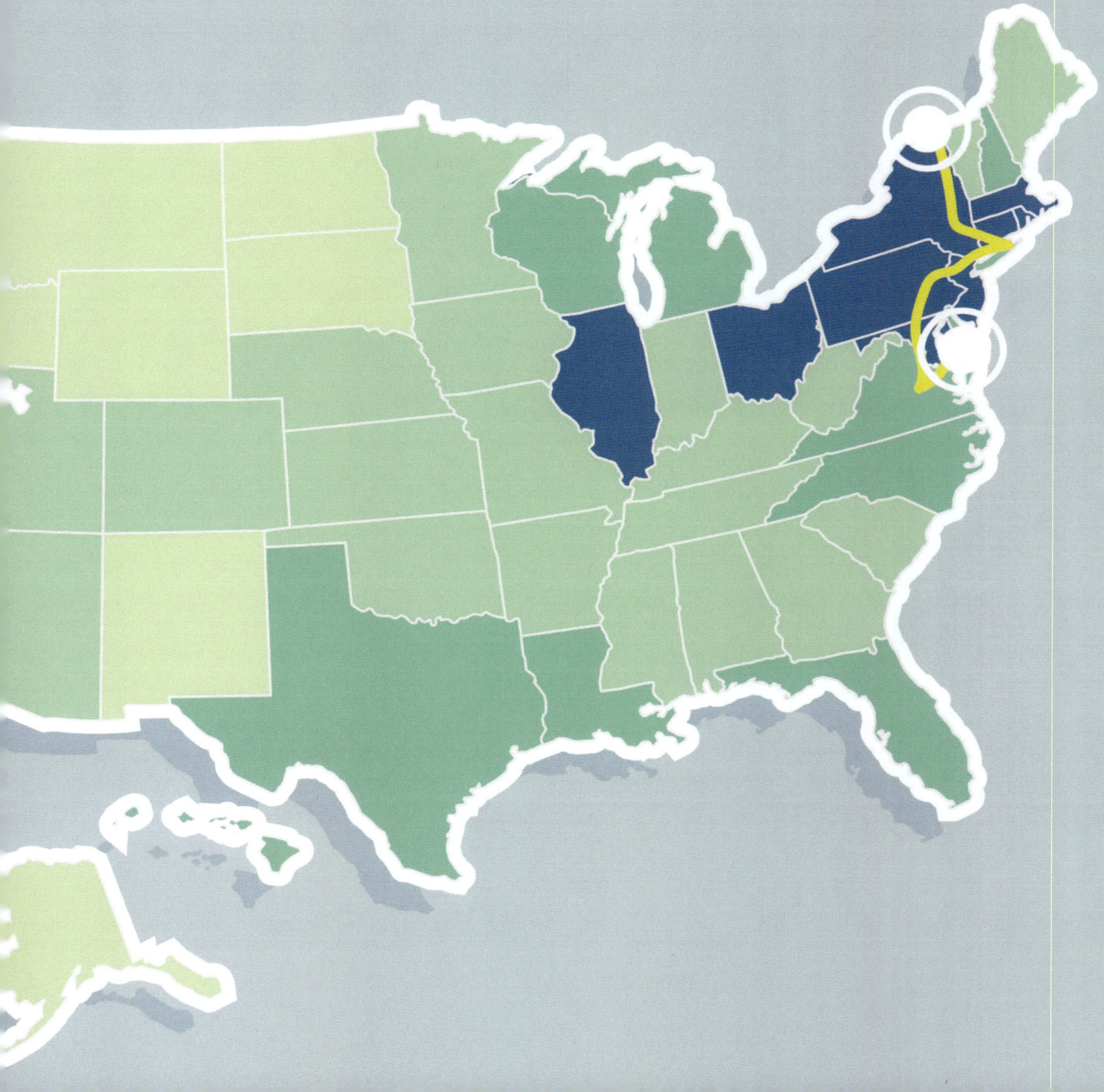

THE NEW ENGLAND TRAIL ROUTE 2

The New England Trail invites you on a weird and wonderful tour of strange places and unusual beliefs, taking you from the bright lights of modernist Manhattan to the gas lamps of Amish country, Lancaster PA before whisking you North to the witch hunts of Salem where every day feels like Halloween. Pay your respects at everything from the graves of gruesome murders, a chapel just for dogs and even a Ben & Jerry's Flavour Graveyard - then go buy a tub or two to recuperate; it's what they would have wanted.

WHILE IN NEW YORK WHY NOT CHECK OUT:

All entries from 112 OCEAN AVENUE to VAN SANT CRYBABY BRIDGE - pages 11-22

1. ROSICRUCIAN PYRAMIDS
40.4386, -75.2715
Just before 5801 Clymer Rd, Quakertown, PA 18951, approaching

from Richlandtown Rd
Strange pyramids stand in a memorial garden which although it no longer provides public access, remains visible from the roadside and is owned to this day by the secretive Fraternitas Rosae Crucis or Rosicrucians, literally 'the Brotherhood of the Rose Cross' (the rose symbolising secrecy in Roman times). Along with various symbols of the Rosicrucian secret sect such as the pyramid itself, skulls and crossbones, a winged globe and several others, this pyramid also features many familiar clandestine symbols matching those featured on the dollar bill (the all seeing eye over an unfinished pyramid, the eagle holding an olive branch and 13 arrows) leading to queries as to the links between the upper echelons of American society and secret societies. These queries are quickly answered at this location as the name of Founding Father Benjamin Franklin is proudly etched in bronze on the side of the pyramid in question as a Council of Nine member.

2. INTERCOURSE
40.03837, -76.1075
Intercourse Pennsylvania 17534
This town was named back in the days when the word conjured

Above: Intercourse, PA

HOME OF
PUNXSY PHIL
WEATHE
WORLD
PHIL

AFGHAN TAKEOUT
CONFLICT KITCHEN

images of 'conversation', perhaps due to the fact that out in Pennsylvanian Amish country you would have to head to the bright lights of this town to talk to a living soul! Another story links the name to a racetrack that once existed just east of the town featuring a sign reading 'Enter Course' at its entrance, leading the locals to refer to the town as 'Entercourse' which eventually evolved into 'Intercourse'!

3. THE HEX HOUSE
39.80034, -76.64429
Rehmeyers Hollow Rd, Stewartstown, PA 17363

This house was home to 'Pow-Wow doctor' Nelson Rehmeyer (Pow-Wow medicine being a Pennsylvanian Dutch settler form of occult practice) until he was beaten to death by another local witch John Blymire who believed Rehmeyer had hexed him. The house failed to burn down when Blymire set fire to it following the beating, further proving Rehmeyer's guilt in the eyes of locals. Now a museum, the street it is on, 'Rehmeyers Hollow', is named for the man himself.

4. ACCIDENT
39.62869, -79.31975
Accident, MD 21520

With residents called Accidentals, the town was thus named due to two speculators, Brooke Beall and William Deakins, Jr, who took each of their surveyors to the area at the same time in order to secure choice areas of land. They realised at a certain juncture that of all the pleasant areas of land up for grabs, they were both laying claim to the same one, leading Beall to point out that he had made numerous axe marks on the trees to prove his stake. Deakins replied that it appeared that they had selected the same land 'by accident'. Beall took the land, naming it Accident after the eventful dispute which lead to his victory.

5. CONFLICT KITCHEN
40.4425, -79.9527
221 Schenley Drive, Pittsburgh, PA 15213
conflictkitchen.org

The restaurant that serves cuisine solely from countries with which the USA in is conflict. This of course provides the kitchen with numerous opportunities to explore varied cultural cuisines, whilst engaging clientele with performances and events around the themes of culture and geopolitical debate. The identity of the restaurant is in a constant state of flux, depending on the current political climate at any given time and strangely has recently presented the only Haudenosaunne, Iranian, Afghan, Venezuelan, North Korean and Palestinian dining experiences that post--industrial Pittsburgh has ever seen.

6. PUNXSUTAWNEY
40.94367, -78.97086
Punxsutawney, PA 15767

Visit Gobbler's Knob, witness the weather predicted by a small furry rodent if you time it well and revel in your very own Groundhog Day here in Punx PA, immortalised by Bill Murray and Tim Minchin in their respective film and musical.

7. THE TOWN OF DESIRE
41.02534, -78.89031
Desire, Henderson Township, PA 15851

Etymology sadly unknown – try asking locals!

8. THE WILLARD ASYLUM SUITCASES
42.9621, -78.8079
3826 Main St, Buffalo, NY 14226

Willard Asylum for the Chronic Insane in Ovid, New York is a stately Victorian asylum now crumbling into disrepair. Willard was opened as a better alternative to existing systems taking so called care of the mentally ill at the time, and was the recipient of patients in all manner of degredation, from those shackled to some arriving in chicken crates. Encouraging patients to turn their hand to agricultural therapy and roam more freely in an environment that incorporated a bowling alley, movie theatre and gymnasium, the asylum however of course still included a morgue, operating theaters, electro-shock and ice bath practices as well as burials in unmarked graves as was typical of the time. After the

< Top: Punxsutawney
< Bottom left: Conflict Kitchen
< Bottom right: The Willard Asylum Suitcases

THE NEW ENGLAND TRAIL ROUTE 2

asylum eventually closed, a cleaner entered the property's attic and found hundreds of dust covered suitcases belonging to ex-residents now deceased, meticulously packed with belongings many of which suggested that patients believed that they would only be passing through. The staff stored these items when family failed to reclaim them, apparently not having the heart to throw them away, and they stand today as a testament to the humanity of those who were forgotten by their society at the time. The Museum of disABILITY History in Buffalo now displays the Willard Suitcases, dating from 1910 to 1960, in a permanent exhibit.

9. WORLD'S LARGEST PANCAKE GRIDDLE
42.663, -77.0541
Near 159 Main St, Penn Yan, NY 14527
Impressively not only is this a giant pancake (or flapjack as those crazy Americans would have it) griddle but furthermore it is a USED pancake griddle, as it cooked the World's Largest Buckwheat Pancake in 1987, requiring a cement mixer to mix the batter, a crane to flip it, 15 gallons of oil, 2000 gallons of water and 2000 pounds of buckwheat, all topped off with 15 gallons of maple syrup and a hunk of butter measuring 2ft by 3ft. It was sliced into 7,200 pieces which fed the 5000 in ways Jesus could only have dreamt of.

10. WILKES-BARRE ABANDONED TRAIN STATION
41.2459, -75.8813
Wilkes-Barre, PA 18701
Two abandoned past lives in one – This location is not only an abandoned station which once served the local mines, it was then converted into a rococo-style cocktail bar and hotel which has also now closed and fallen into disrepair.

11. ECKLEY MINERS VILLAGE MUSEUM
40.99352, -75.86261
2 Eckley Main Street, Weatherly, PA 18255
www.eckleyminersvillagemuseum.com
Incredibly well preserved and restored mining community of the 1850s

12. THE GHOST TOWN OF LAUSANNE
40.8723, -75.7604
Between the 209 E Catawissa St and Lehigh River/ Gorge. Park on highway, lightly worn trail in parking area. Directions on this website: http://www.onlyinyourstate.com/pennsylvania/lausanne-ghost-town-2/ Near E Catawissa St, Nesquehoning, PA 18240
Little known ghost town in rural Pennsylvania with some 5 ruined buildings to be found amongst the woodland.

13. THE PENN HILLS RESORT
41.0578, -75.2141
PA-447, East Stroudsburg, PA 18301(Where Michael Creek joins Brodhead Creek)
This large kitsch honeymoon resort in the Pocono mountains used to be a hub of romance with two outdoor pools in the shape of wedding bells and heart-shaped Jacuzzis in the bedrooms but now lies abandoned, the wedding bells dry. Founded in 1944, the resort had its hey-day in the 60's when it grew to over 100 rooms across 500 acres and offered guests a ski resort and a golf course not to mention attractive floor-to-ceiling carpeting, lamp fixtures from the 1964 World's Fair in New York, round beds, an ice rink (the Pocono Ice-A-Rama), archery, tennis and renowned New Year's Parties where the motto was said to have been 'No balloon goes unpopped'. Sadly, by 2009 the owner had died at the age of 102, leaving the resort owing over a million dollars in unpaid taxes. The location was even once used as a hideout for a police-killing fugitive called Eric Frein who wrote his warped manifesto all over the ice rink walls and those of the hotel itself in 2014. Easily visible from the road.

14. 'GNOME CHOMSKY'
41.7899, -74.2587
5755 US-209, Kerhonkson, NY 12446
Not the largest roadside Gnome in America, just the one with the best name.

15. KAATSKILL KALEIDOSCOPE
42.0441, -74.2836
5340 State Route 28, Mt Tremper, NY 12457

> Top left Eckley Miners Village Museum:
> Top right: The Penn Hills Resort
> Bottom left, right, overleaf: The Penn Hills Resort

81

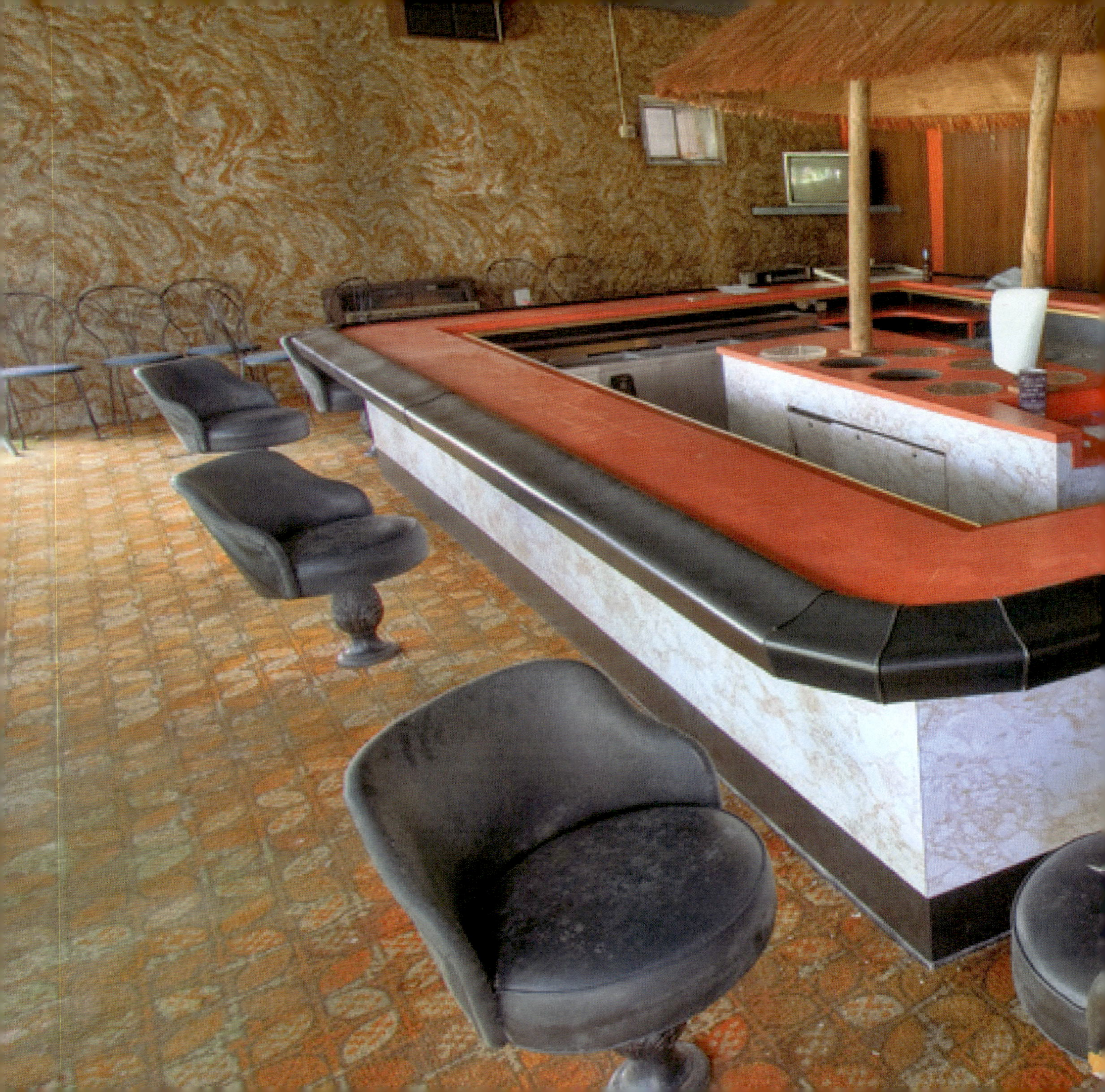

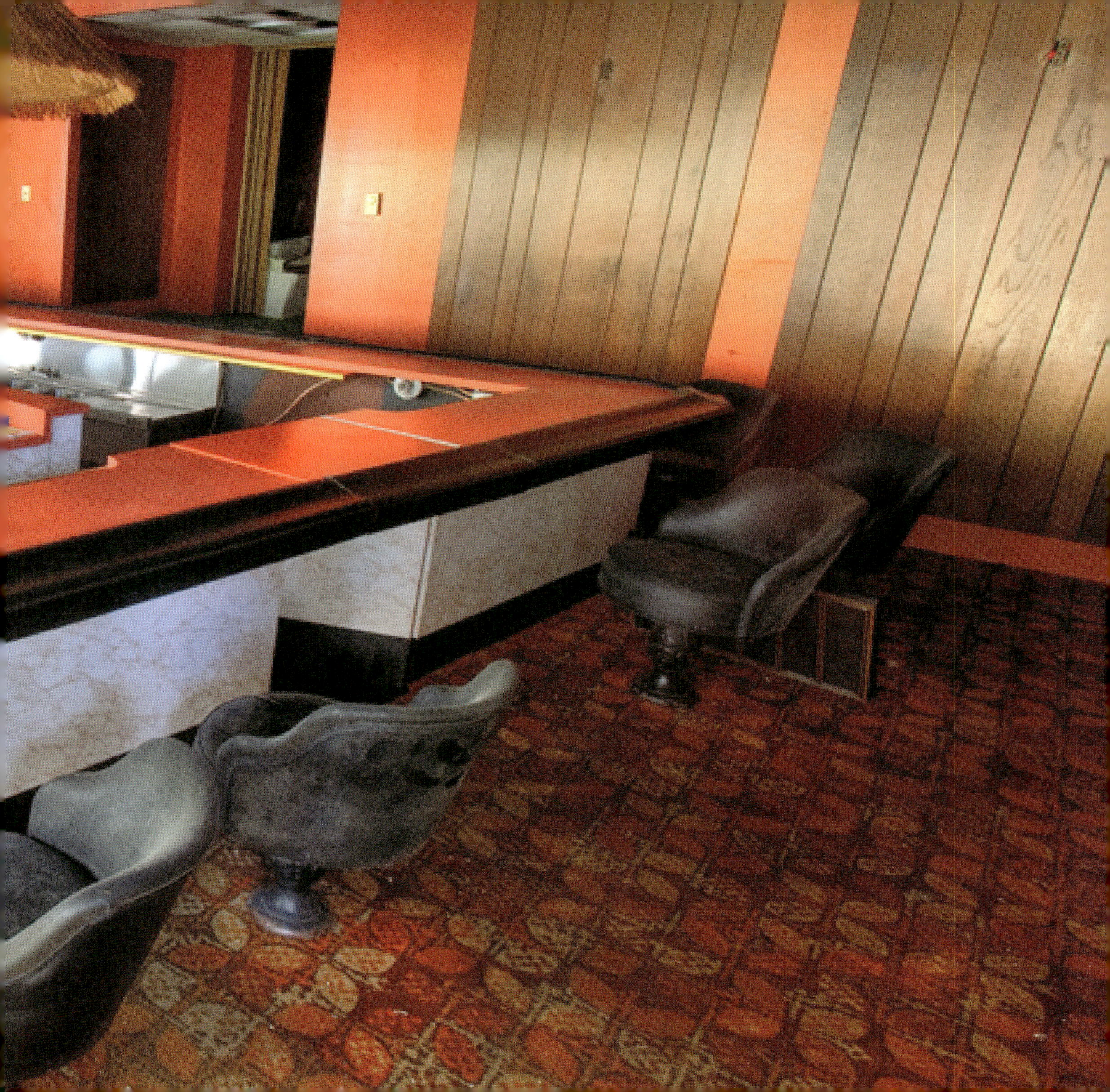

emersonresort.com
A boutique mall like any other, except that this one is complete with the world's largest walk-in kaleidoscope and a hefty dose of hucksterism designed by a psychedelic hippie (or the First Cathedral Of The Third Millennium as he succinctly named it.)

16. HOWE CAVERNS
42.6962, -74.3986
255 Discovery Dr, Howes Cave, NY 12092
howecaverns.com
The second most visited US natural location after Niagara Falls, this cave was discovered in 1842 by a farmer named Lester Howe, a known eccentric, who noticed that his cows tended to gather at the bottom of a hill on hot days where there appeared to be a cool breeze. He discovered the cavern and opened it to the public in 1843, building a hotel over the entrance when it became a popular attraction. Two versions of this hotel burned down, the second in 1872. Lester Howe sold the property owing to personal financial struggles and despite its success, the cavern closed a decade later due to a declining public interest in caves. After its sale, Lester continued to live on his farm within view of the cave and since the 1880s rumour has spread that he came across another cave, this one much larger and more beautiful than the first, which he named the Garden of Eden and the location of which he kept an absolute secret, mentioning its very existence only upon his death bed in 1888. Since his death, many have searched for the cave, but it is yet to be found, laying question to whether it ever existed at all. Lester was an unusual character before his spelunking days began - he once advertised a grand auction on his property to sell everything in his possession. People came from near and far and gathered en masse outside his farmhouse, whereupon he threw open his parlour door and his daughter played the piano relentlessly while he himself stood on his stoop and spoke to the crowd on his life philosophies. No mention of an auction was made and everyone left in fury. Today he is buried with his wife in the Cobleskill Rural Cemetery in Cobleskill, New York.

17. THE TOWN OF HAPPYLAND
41.47438, -72.06607
Happyland, Preston, CT 06365
No municipal taxes makes these townsfolk very happy indeed. Etymology otherwise unknown.

18. TRAVELLER'S RESTAURANT
42.0258, -72.1397
1257 Buckley Hwy #84, Union, CT 06076
The sign outside says 'food and books' and this is what you get from the restaurant that gives away 100,000 free books every year. All of the many books on show in the restaurant are free with the purchase of a meal in this location which is great for the whole family. With framed autographs of literary figures such as Dr. Seuss on the walls, the restaurant was conceptualised by a Mr Marty Doyle, a book collector looking to reduce his own collection and today gifts an estimated 50

tons of books annually, as well as allowing patrons to browse the Book Cellar, whose 20,000 vintage books may not be free but are reasonably priced and could prove to be a treasure.

19. BELCHERTOWN
42.27703, -72.40088
Belchertown, MA 01007
Another day, another silly place name, in this case named for Jonathan Belcher, a large landowner and Royal Governor of Massachusetts from 1730 to 1740. The first town meeting held in 1761 included Jonathan himself, a deer reeve (someone whose job it was to control the illegal killing of deer) and a hog reeve (who had to round up stray hogs and care for them in the town pound.) It was common at the time for domestic hogs to wander the towns, and owners were expected to place rings in their noses so that the hog reeve could do his job. Fines of 10 shillings per hog found without a ring in its nose were issued to owners. In Saxon England, hog reeves were stationed at the doors of cathedrals during services to prevent pigs from entering the church. In Massachusetts specifically, towns were able to vote to stop enforcement of the law against letting hogs run loose and many did so to avoid fines, leaving the hog reeve with nothing to do. Belchertown is also notable for its now abandoned 'State School for the Feeble-Minded', established in 1922 and notorious for its ill--treatment of patients such as healthy teeth being forcibly removed to render their feeding easier.

20. SATANS KINGDOM
42.7125, -72.48055
Satans Kingdom, MA 01360
Another strange US location name, which derived from the area's rough terrain and dangerous wildlife. Originally such names were commonly given to serve as a warning to prevent travellers from entering inhospitable lands.

21. THE TINY MUSEUM
42.37979, -71.09505
71 Union Square, Somerville, MA 02143
tinymuseum.org
The World's most minute museum at only sixteen inches wide. Blink and you might miss it. Despite its size, it took its owner

< Left: Howe Caverns
Above: Belchertown

86

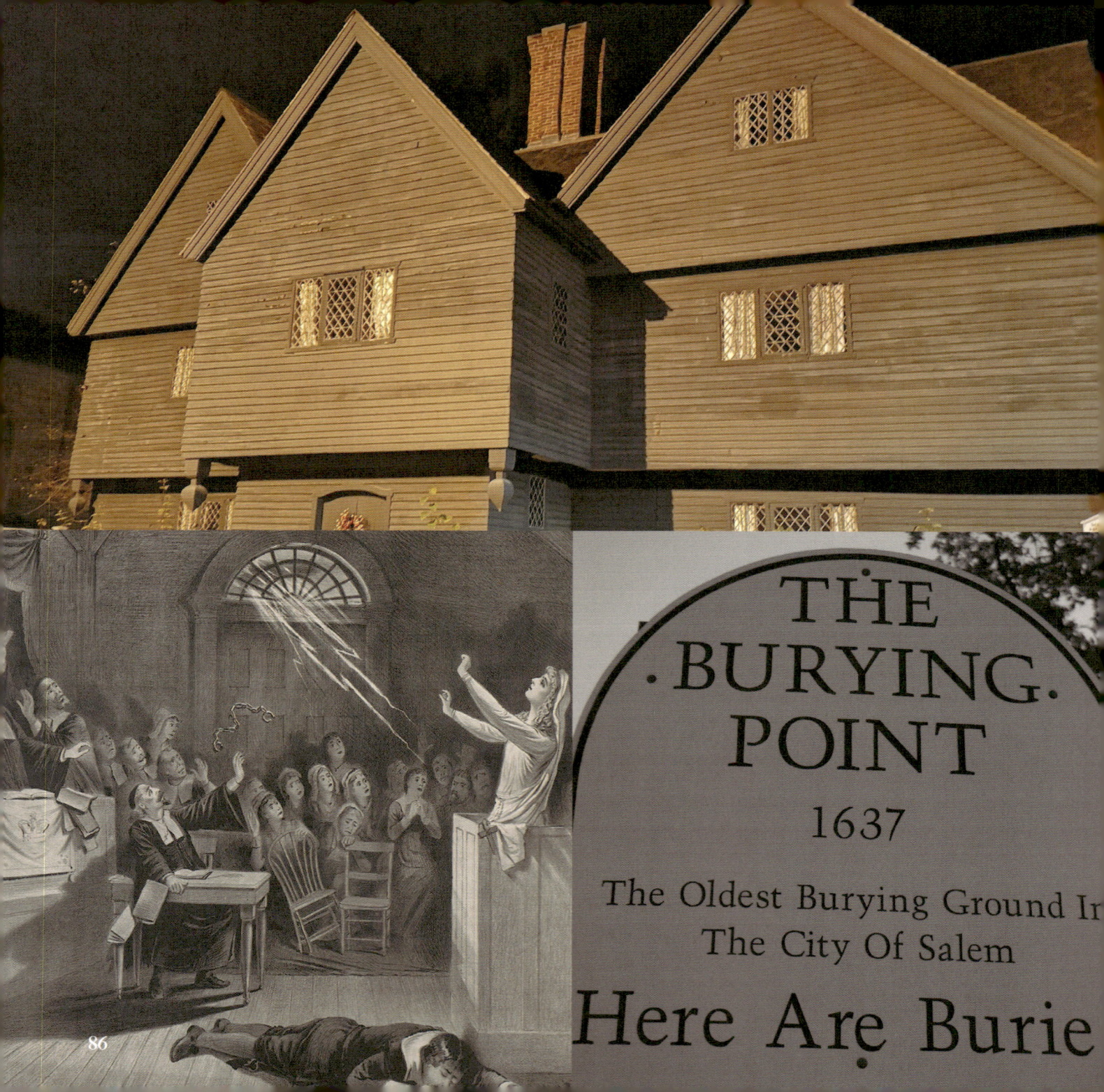

3 years of work to curate. The jury is still out as to whether this is a reflection on the museum, or the curator.

22. BLACK DAHLIA MEMORIAL
42.4219, -71.1027
Fountain St, Medford, MA 02155
Memorial to Elizabeth Short, the victim of an infamous, brutal and entirely unsolved murder in 1947, who was cut in half and whose mouth was mutilated into a macabre grimace in a horrific case that rocked the nation. The Black Dahlia moniker was most probably given due to a popular film noir murder mystery of the time entitled The Blue Dahlia. The case is the oldest unsolved murder in Los Angeles' history.

23. PRISONERS' RESTAURANT
42.47219, -71.39809
Northeast Correctional Center
Route 2 Rotary
Concord, MA 01742
Dine in the Fife & Drum, the only restaurant in the USA where the food is made by prisoners. File through security prior to entering the establishment which is located inside the Northeast Correctional Center, Concord. The meal will cost in the region of $4 and is part of the prison's culinary program which allows prisoners to build the skills needed to work in a restaurant post-release.

24. SKULL CLIFF
42.50879, -71.00314
325 Broadway, Saugus, MA 01906
Quirky giant graffiti of thousands of skulls sprayed across a cliff face, complete with a life affirming if somewhat grim message: 'Take the knowledge that you will someday be these bones and enjoy now all that is precious'.

25. THE WITCH HOUSE OF SALEM
42.5215, -70.8989
310 Essex St, Salem, MA 01970
witchhouse.info
One of the few remaining structures in the town from the time of the infamous witch trials.

26. THE GRAVE OF THE BOSTON STRANGLER
42.5258, -71.00323
185 Lake St, Peabody, MA 01960
www.puritanlawn.com
Grave of Albert DeSalvo, the Boston Strangler, who killed 13 women between 1962 and 1964 in the Boston area. He confessed, although then recanted his confession before dying in prison; in 2013 his remains were exhumed from this plot in order to confirm DNA links to one of his victims, despite his recanted confession, and proved a 100% match.

27. THE DOGTOWN GHOST TOWN & BOULDERS
42.6364, -70.6611
Dogtown Rd, Gloucester, MA 01930
This fascinating ghost town was founded for the families of men at sea, the majority of whom owned dogs to protect them in their husbands' absence, hence the town's name. Upon the deaths of this generation of wives and widows, many of whom also left the town during the War in 1812, only the dogs were left behind to breed and turn wild. Just to make the ghost town a little weirder, Roger Babson (see the Gravity Monument in Atlanta), an eccentric millionaire who famously foretold the stock market crash of 1929, selflessly decided to gift the town his own life platitudes in the form of a 'book made with stones instead of pages', or rather phrases etched into boulders, placed strategically around the town. This fervent inspiration and knowledge-sharing provided the local stone cutters with copious work during the Depression and did therefore actually prove very beneficial to the town, although perhaps not in the intellectual manner he had intended. The road leading to the site is still named Dogtown Road, whilst the nearby reservoir and several roads in the area are named for Babson himself. The boulders, which are now to be found scattered throughout the woodland that is now covering the area, can be spotted from Google Earth with a keen eye in the vicinity of 'Dogtown Square' should you struggle to find them.

< Left: The Witch House of Salem
Overleaf: The Dogtown Ghost Town & Boulders

THE NEW ENGLAND TRAIL ROUTE 2

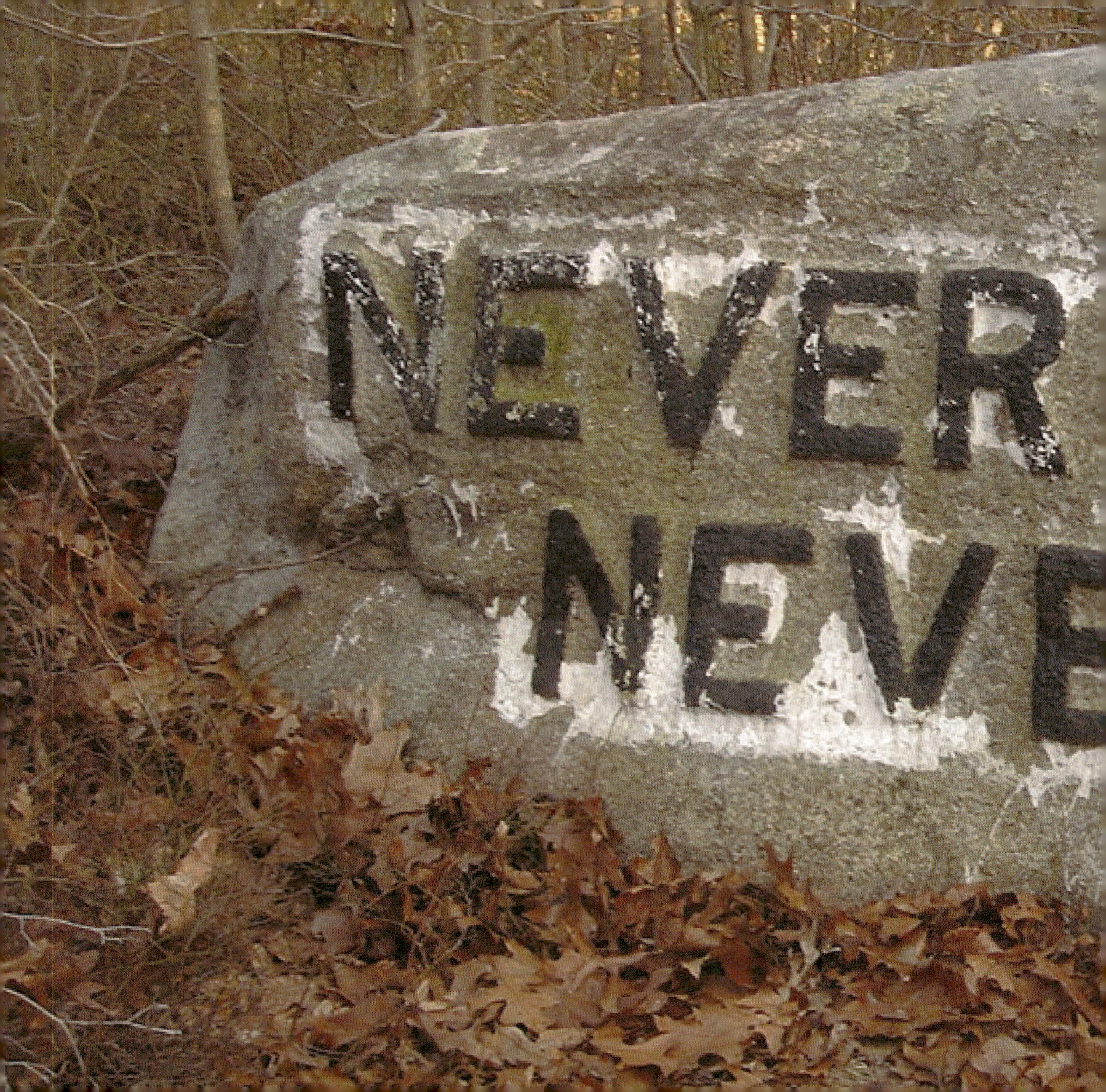
NEVER
NEVE

TRY
RWIN

Below: The Rebecca Nurse Homestead
> Top: Salem Village Witchcraft Victims Memorial
> Bottom: Danvers Hospital for the Criminally Insane

28. PAPER HOUSE
42.6745, -706299
52 Pigeon Hill St, Rockport, MA 01966
paperhouserockport.com
Why dispose of newspapers when you can build out of them. Fingers crossed it doesn't rain.

29. THE REBECCA NURSE HOMESTEAD
42.56553, -70.95767
149 Pine St, Danvers, MA 01923
www.rebeccanurse.org
Rebecca was executed during the Salem witch trials of 1692 at the age of 71. Visit her original house and memorial.

30. SALEM' WITCHCRAFT VICTIMS MEMORIAL
42.56553, -70.95767
172-, 180 Hobart St, Danvers, MA 01923
This monument was erected in 1992 to honour all of the 1692 victims of the witch hunts and has been constructed directly across the road from the site of the Salem Village Meeting House in which many of the trials took place. In terms of symbology, on the memorial one can identify a carved Bible Box, which at the time were used for home based devotional practices rather than linked to mass formal worship, emphasising the legitimacy of personal beliefs and moral standing. There is a quote regarding The Book of Life, pertaining to who should and should not gain eternal life, suggesting that this decision should not rest with Man, but also relating to the time in which victims refused to confess to witch hood because of their desire to be added to the Book of Life. The broken shackles refer to breaking false claims in history. The victim's statements during their trials are also inscribed on the monument.

31. DANVERS HOSPITAL FOR THE CRIMINALLY INSANE
42.5824, -70.9775
450 Maple St, Danvers, MA 01923
The original Asylum building, now apartments, remains externally similar to its previous incarnation and provided the backdrop for Batman's Arkham Asylum . Its

THE NEW ENGLAND TRAIL ROUTE 2

92

< Benson's Park
Below: The Baptist Murder Headstone

cemetery is still intact.

32. ROB ZOMBIE SIGN
42.8074, -71.04489
Amesbury Rd, Haverhill, MA 01830
An unusual 'most famous resident' for an otherwise orthodox town.

33. BENSONS PARK
42.76943, -71.40326
21 Kimball Hill Rd, Hudson, NH 03051
www.hudsonnh.gov
Benson's Park was named for animal trainer John Benson in 1924 who established the park as a training ground before opening it to the public as a circus spectacle two years later. It continued to operate from 1927 to 1987 and was home to a wide range of rides, a miniature train which travelled around the entire 165-acre property as well as a wide number of exotic animals including lions, elephants, tigers, chimps and a gorilla that ran for President. Spectacularly, in what immediately seems like perhaps the best idea of all time but which swiftly upon any further thought whatsoever throws up all manner of obvious problems, the park also featured what was quite possibly the world's only 'Live Carousel', a carousel which featured children riding on the backs of entirely real spotted reindeer. Today the park which lay abandoned for many years after its closure has been reopened as a public space with access granted to the old animal cages. In case the gorilla soundbite is too tantalising to ignore, Colossus the 500-pound silverback entered as a 1980 candidate for the Presidency in both primaries, running against Ronald Reagan and Jimmy Carter in what must have been a first rate publicity stunt for the park.

34. THE BAPTIST MURDER HEADSTONE
42.8353, -71.65409
55 Union Street, Milford, NH 03055
A grave headstone that pushes page margins to the limit. This grave stone manages to squeeze in 150 words of text pertaining to a Baptist church dispute that was apparently so heated that the deceased died of stress, leading her husband to allege that the Baptists were therefore responsible for

his wife's death.

35. THE GRAVE OF WILLIAM G BRUCE
42.8945, -71.67419

17 Route 13, Mont Vernon, NH 03057, entrance via Cemetery Road. Follow path to sharp right turn. Over half way past the avenue of trees, you will see the tomb on the left.

William Bruce was out shooting with his dog at the age of 64 in 1883. He placed his gun back into his wagon but is then thought to have heard his dog pick up a trail, and in his haste to grab his gun, discharged it into his shoulder, almost severing his arm. He was taken to Young's Hotel and his wife summoned in time for him to see her, but he died soon after, his grave stone thereafter adorned by his loving gun dog (who arguably caused this mess in the first place).

36. JOSIE LANGMAID MONUMENT
43.1473, -71.4461

243 Academy Rd, Pembroke, NH 03275 (opposite school)

A funereal monument apparently wasn't enough to memorialise the tragic death of the 17 year old Josie Langmaid whose body was found severed in two in 1875 – it was bizarrely deemed appropriate to moreover erect a marker to the exact location where the torso and head were discovered. Josie's killer, lumberjack Joseph Lapage, hanged for her death in 1878.

37. BIRTHPLACE OF H.H. HOLMES
43.3373, -71.31889

500 Province Road, Gilmanton, NH 03218

America's first serial killer grew up at this spot

38. BETTY AND BARNEY HILL ARCHIVE
43.1364, -70.93439

18 Library Way, Durham, NH, 03824

The University of New Hampshire, where Betty Hill studied, now holds all the papers and artefacts remaining from this renowned alien abduction case of a local couple

39. GRAVES OF THE SMUTTYNOSE MURDER VICTIMS
43.066, -70.7579

Harmony Grove Cemetery, South St, Portsmouth, NH 03801

Graves of two women murdered on Smuttynose Island who were killed by axe wielding Louis Wagner while their friend Maren fled and hid from the killer all night in the bitter cold and eventually was able to provide sufficient eyewitness testimony to bring him to justice. Doubts over Wagner, who hanged for the crime, still continue unabated despite a significant weight of evidence pointing to him.

40. YORK WITCH GRAVE
43.1402, -70.6558

Old Parish Cemetery, opposite 186 York St, York, ME 03909

Legend has it that this is the grave of a witch called Mary Nasson and that the heavyweight tombstone lying horizontally is to prevent her rising from the dead

41. INTERNATIONAL CRYPTOZOOLOGY MUSEUM
43.65166, -70.29052

4 Thompsons Point #106, Portland, ME 04101

cryptozoologymuseum.com

The World's only cryptozoology museum, this quirky marvel has bizarre specimens, information on sightings and features the reassuring quote on its website 'If you don't understand why something is in our exhibits, please ask'. One can but imagine how many queries over dubious inclusions might have prompted this, but surely this makes viewing exhibits relating to all things Big Foot and friends that much more enticing.

42. UMBRELLA COVER MUSEUM
43.656, -70.1983

62-B Island Avenue, Portland, ME, 04108

Possibly the best museum concept to date, this museum cares not for the functional umbrella, but just for its frankly often redundant cover.

43. EARTHA
43.8079, -70.1640

2 DeLorme Dr, Yarmouth, ME 04096

The official world's largest spinning globe, located within Garmin's headquarters

> Top: Umbrella Cover Museum
> Bottom: Eartha

Just let a Smile be Your Umbrella - On a rainy, rainy day!
And if your sweetie cries, just tell her/him   That a smile will always pay.
Whenever skies are gray,   don't worry or fret
A smile will bring the sunshine   and YOU'LL NEVER GET WET!!
So let a Smile be Your Umbrella   On a rainy, rainy day!!!

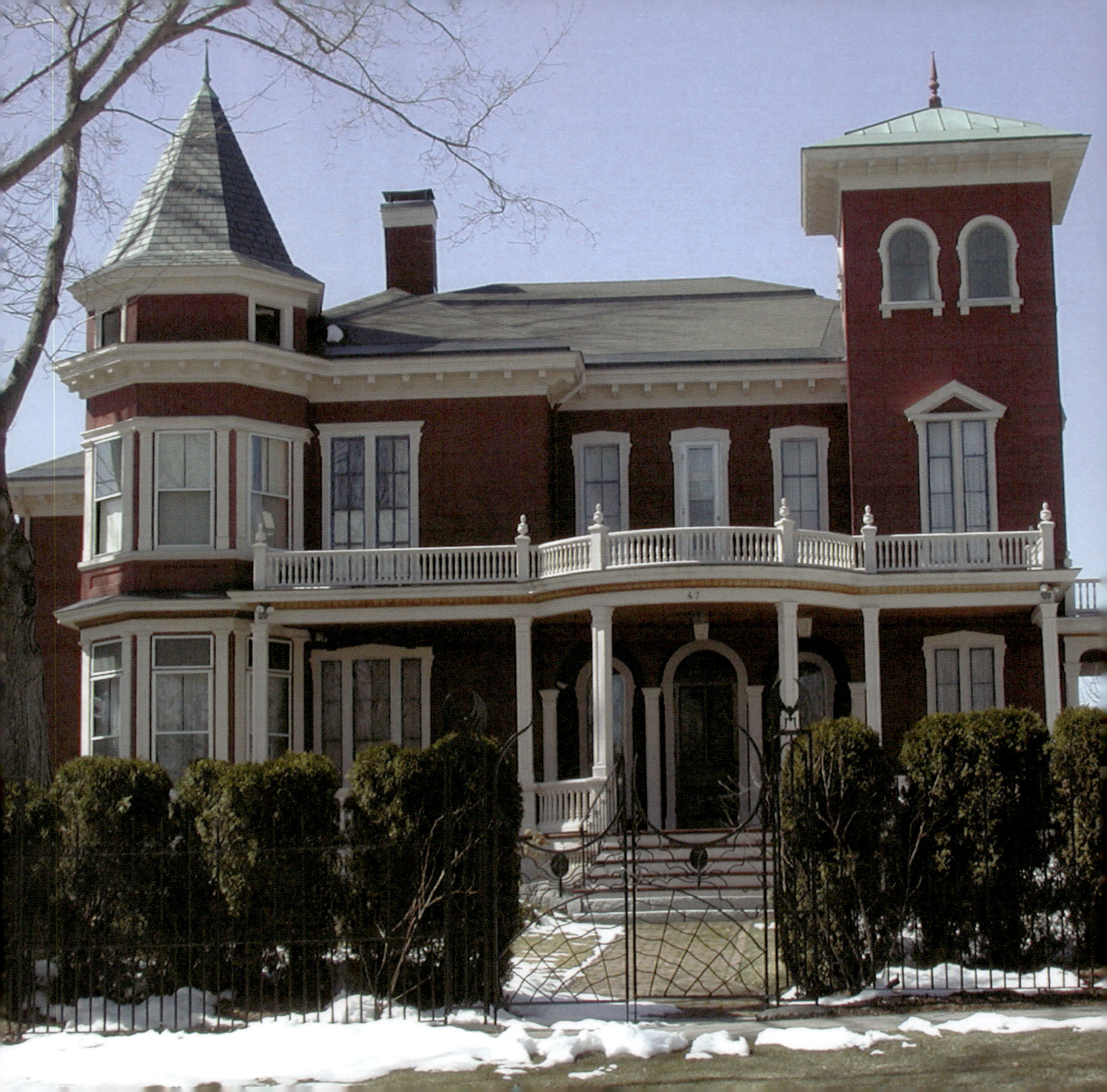

44. GRAVE OF SARAH WARE
44.5743, -68.79669
109-119 Franklin St, Bucksport, ME 04416
Poor Sarah Ware was murdered, found dumped in a field. When she was lifted to be placed in a coffin, her head fell off. Police quickly pointed the finger at a William Treworgy but after 4 years when the case went to trial much evidence had been lost, witnesses recanted and others had died, with the result that he was eventually let off. No one else has ever been charged and she was buried in a poor man's grave, although in a spectacular case of poor organisation skills, her head was found in an evidence lock up 80 years later. It was said that her skull was then reburied with her body, although suspicion has also been raised that her body was moved to a family plot some time later. Now it is unclear where she rests and whether her head is with her.

45. COLONEL BUCK AND THE WITCH'S CURSE
44.5743, -68.79669
109-119 Franklin St, Bucksport, ME 04416
This town founder's monument bears the unmistakeable (maybe) pointed stockinged mark of the witch he killed right beneath his name. Did he burn her as a witch, hang her or kill her for carrying his unborn child? No one knows but the legend lives on.

46. FORT KNOX
44.5661, -68.80247
740 Ft Knox Rd, Prospect, ME 04981
fortknox.maineguide.com
This fortress is one of the best preserved and most accessories forts in the USA complete with plenty of original weaponry still in place, including 24-pounder flank howitzers and Rodman guns weighing as much as 50,000 pounds. The fort also had two shot furnaces, designed to heat cannonballs to such a temperature that when fired into a wooden ship, the ship would immediately ignite. These rapidly became obsolete with the invention of ironclad warships.

47. PAUL BUNYAN STATUE
44.7879, -68.7783
Main St, Bangor, ME 04401
Paul Bunyan the lumberjack is an American folk lore legend and giant statues of him cover the USA. This particularly large one came to life in Stephen King's It.

48. STEPHEN KING'S HOUSE
Bangor
Ever wondered where the King of horror would choose to reside? Wonder no more. Watch the street grates, there be clowns down there.

49. PET SEMETARY FILMING SITES
44.5084, -68.2545
House at 303 Point Road, Hancock, ME 0464. Human cemetery at Mount Hope Cemetery, 1048 State Street, Bangor. The pile of rocks that are climbed in the movie are at Hall Quarry, Acadia National Park, Mt. Desert, ME.
Visit the house and cemetery but don't bring any dead loved ones with you.

50. WILD BLUEBERRY LAND
44.64844, -67.70694
US-1, Columbia Falls, ME 04623
www.wildblueberryland.com
The 'Official Fruit of Maine' is honoured in the only sensible way – with its own dedicated theme park.

51. MURDER IN SMALL TOWN X STATUE
44.9045, -66.9841
51 Water St, Eastport, ME 04631

< Stephen King's House
Top right: Paul Bunyan Statue
Overleaf: Wild Blueberry Land

THE NEW ENGLAND TRAIL ROUTE 2

WILD
BLUEBE
LAN

WILD BLUEBERRY L

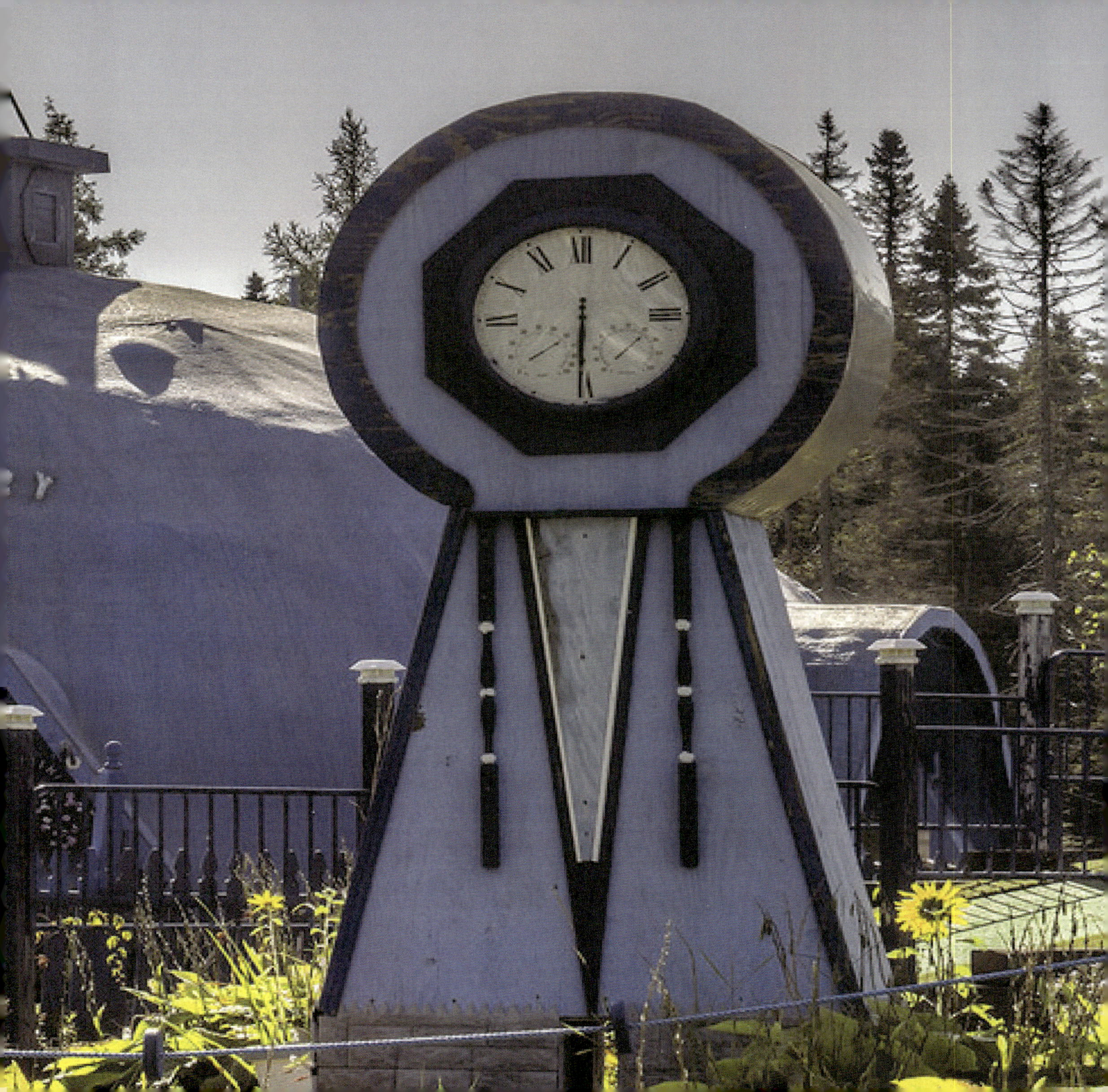

There is a lot going on in this one statue of a man holding a fish. Firstly it was used as a prop on a game show called Murder in Small Town X in which contestants had to solve a murder mystery – it was subsequently gifted to the town of Eastport by way of decoration. Secondly, it was only the second design concept for the statue - it was nearly a lobster in a Macintosh (it is unfair to speculate but some might say this could have been a stronger look). Thirdly, the statue has drawn furore over the flagrant misrepresentation of local fish species, depicting Pacific rather than Atlantic salmon. Finally, the winner on the game show was a fireman called Angel Juarbe Jr who tragically died a hero in the World Trade Center collapse and this multifaceted statue now stands as memorial to him.

52. WORLDS LARGEST AXE
45.99434, -67.23297
Landegger Dr, Nackawic, NB E6G 1H2, Canada
A cut above the rest.

53. BARTLETT YARNS MILL
44.9712, -69.54669
20 Water St, Harmony, ME 04942
www.bartlettyarns.com
This working mill is a spectacularly creepy looking building, which led it to feature as the mill in the adaptation of Stephen King's Graveyard Shift.

54. THE WORLDS LARGEST TELEPHONE
44.37839, -70.64642
1 N Main St, Bryant Pond, ME 04219
The folks of Bryant Pond were the last to use hand-cranked telephones and don't want to let anyone forget their reticence in the face of change, memorialising the fact with…a giant hand-cranked telephone.

55. THE WEARY CLUB OF NORWAY
44.21373, -70.54208
385 Main St, Norway, ME 04268
This evocative 90 year old club's main activity used to be whittling cedar, but most members (or Wearies as they are known) now just pass the time in conversation.

56. WORLD TRAVELER SIGNPOST
44.2443, -70.7853
1435 Valley Road (where Route 5 intersects Route 35), Bethel, ME 04217
This signpost directs you all over the world without leaving Maine.

57. COLEBROOK MURDER VICTIMS MEMORIAL
44.8961, -71.5000
Bridge Street, Colebrook, NH, 03576
Stopped for driving an un-roadworthy vehicle, Carl Drega shot both traffic offices then embarked upon a spree which killed several others including a judge and ended in his death via a shootout with cops. The victims of this tragic event are memorialised with this marker.

58. THE MUSEUM OF EVERYDAY LIFE
44.64127, -72.20563
3482 Dry Pond Rd, Glover, VT 05839
museumofeverydaylife.org
Most museums collect unusual items. This one has cunningly decided to do the (much easier) opposite.

59. DOG MOUNTAIN
44.4445, -71.9766
143 Parks Rd, St Johnsbury, VT 05819
www.dogmt.com
A truly tragic yet wonderful location worth a pilgrimage, ideally with a furry friend for company. An artist called Stephen Huneck who had a severe illness was clinically dead for a period of time prior to being resuscitated and after the experience felt so grateful for the little things in his life, especially the bond he felt with his three cherished dogs, that he decided to build a chapel upon what he named 'Dog Mountain' dedicated to that special relationship between man and his best friend. Built on his home farm in Vermont, the chapel is a shrine to all things canine and all are welcome from any faith or lack of it, especially doggy companions who are welcomed with dog biscuits. The 2010 economic crash took its toll on the chapel and Huneck was forced to sack his staff - feeling extreme

> Top Left: World's Largest Axe
> Top Right: World Traveler Signpost
> Bottom and Overleaf: Dog Mountain

OFFBEAT AMERICA

	NORWAY 14 MI. PARIS 15 MI. DENMARK 23 MI. NAPLES 23 MI. SWEDEN 25 MI. POLAND 27 MI. MEXICO 37 MI. PERU 46 MI. CHINA 94 MI.

WELCOME
ALL CREEDS
ALL BREEDS
NO DOGMAS
ALLOWED

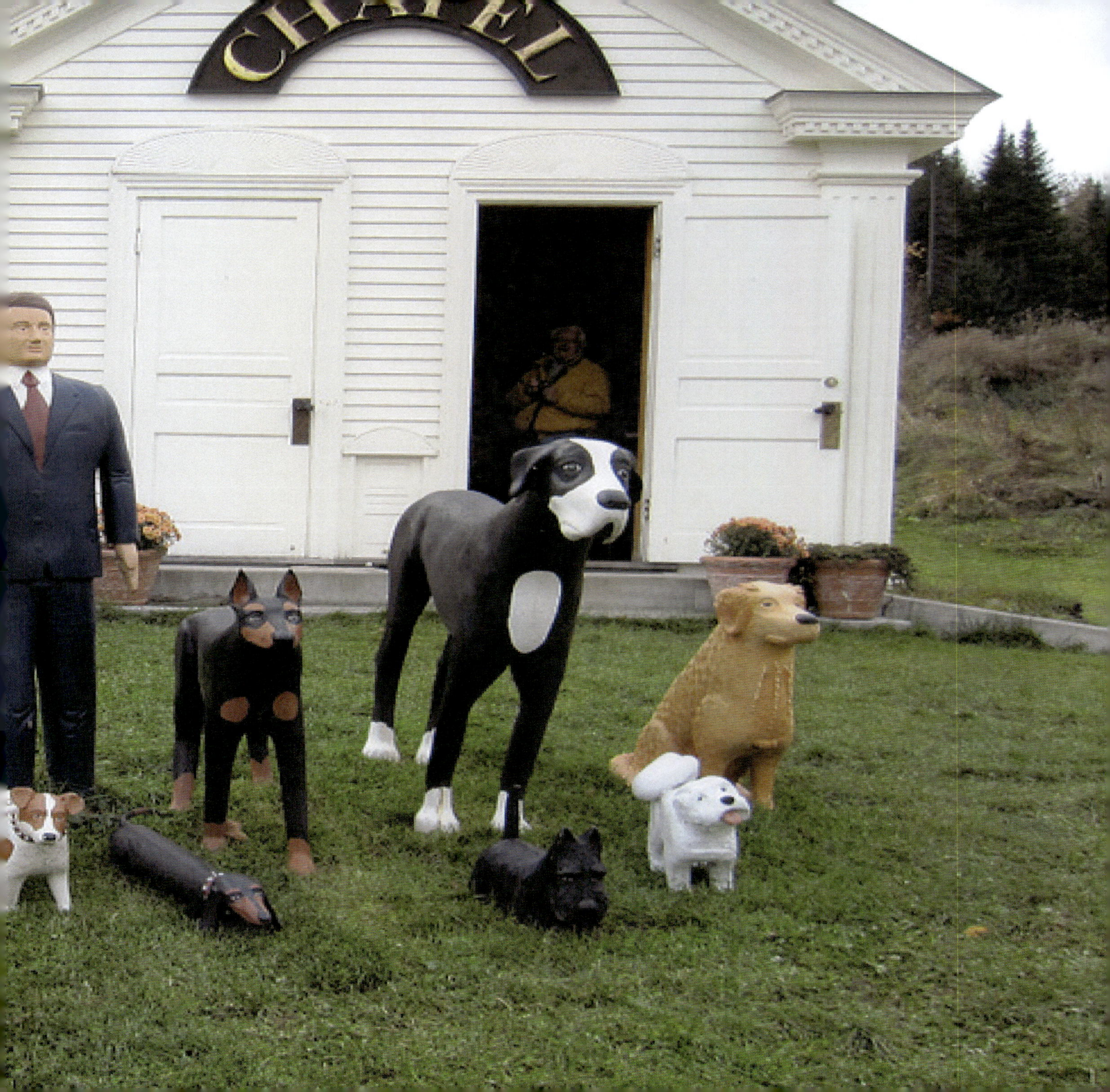
CHAPEL

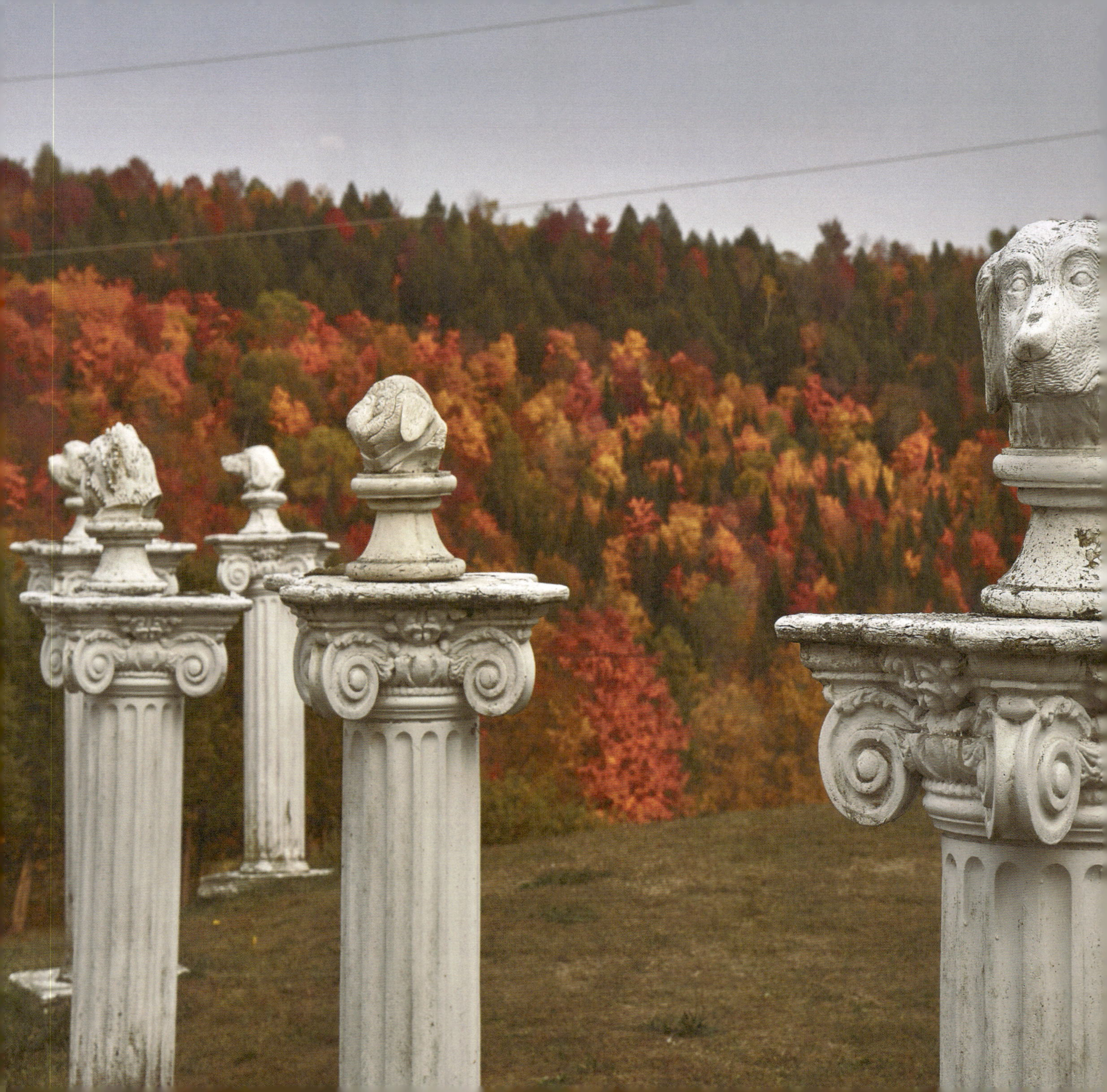

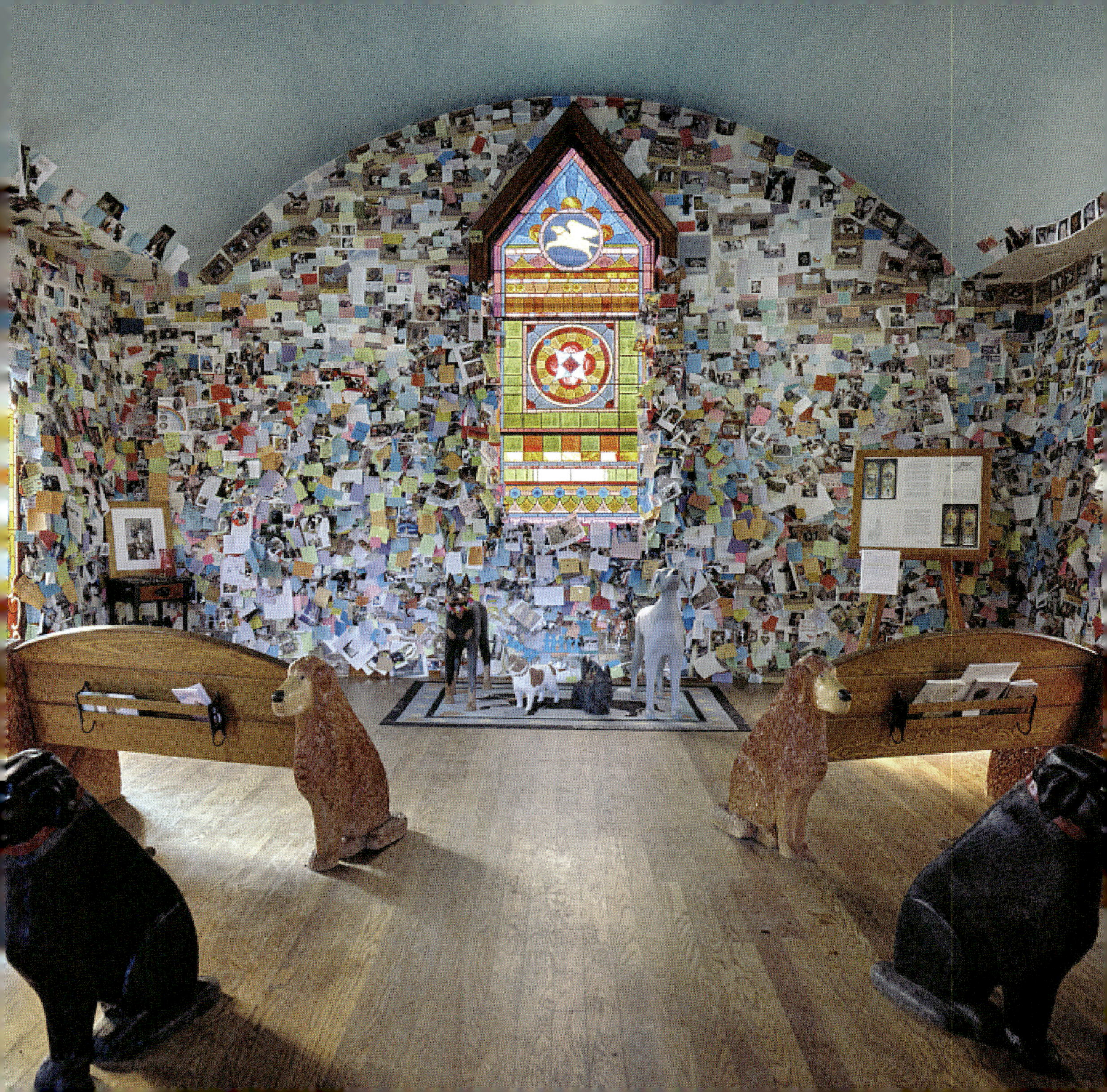

Left: Floating Bridge of Brookfield
Right: Chutters Candy Store

guilt for the effect he had had on the economic stability of the workers, he tragically committed suicide a week later. For three years his wife ran the chapel alone, until yet more tragically, she too killed herself in 2013. The staff have continued to curate the chapel in their absence and happily it remains open to be enjoyed by visitors, their legacy of affection continuing.

60. CHUTTERS CANDY STORE
44.30624, -71.77215
43 Main St, Littleton, NH 03561
www.chutters.com
A Guinness world record holder for the longest counter at a candy store in the world.

61. BETTY AND BARNEY HILL MEMORIALS
44.06414, -71.68674
467 US Route 3, Lincoln, NH 03251
The Franconia Notch Irving Express gas station off exit 33 on I-93/Route 3 (the route the Hills took on THAT night), is a relatively normal gas station - in fact whilst it sells some ubiquitous alien-related wares, it is relatively self-controlled in its selection. Enter the bathroom however and you will find it to be lined with a museum's worth of information about the incident and other such incidents on every available space of wall like a scene from Memento.

62. FUNSPOT
43.61346, -71.47653
579 Endicott St N, Laconia, NH 03246
www.funspotnh.com
Bring your quarters and leave your RSI at home - PlayStation 4 has never looked so dull at this arcade.

63. ALEISTER CROWLEY'S MAGICKAL RETIREMENT
43.6943, -71.80549
Church Ln, Hebron, NH 03241
Owned by a medium who co-authored books with Crowley, this 200 year old house was used by the infamous occultist, magician, poet, painter and novelist in 1916 for four months for what he referred to as his Magick Retirement, during which time he appears to have taken copious amounts of drugs and performed a variety

of questionable rituals

64. VERMONTASAURUS
43.88636, -72.25078
104 Robinson Hill Rd, Post Mills, VT 05058
What do you do if you are a balloon pilot with time on your hands and your hot-air balloon manufacturing facility has just caved in on itself? Why, build a giant dinosaur out of the residual lumber of course.

65. EAST CORINTH
44.06397, -72.22223
East Corinth, Corinth, VT 05040
The filming location for Tim Burton's Beetlejuice movie.

66. BROOKFIELD'S FLOATING BRIDGE
44.0426, -72.6048
VT-65, Brookfield, VT 05036
Is it a bridge? By definition probably not. If you like your roadways damp with a likelihood of sinking, this one is for you. This floating bridge was first built in 1820 and is 321 foot long with just a single lane that carried Route 65 over Sunset Lake in central Vermont. It is one of only three floating bridges in the USA. The bridge has been rebuilt 8 times since its inception, and first came about when a local resident was crossing the frozen lake on foot and fell through the ice to their death. Originally it was built with floating logs, then wooden barrels and later with plastic barrel-pontoons.

Top: Vermontasaurus
Right: Aleister Crowley

THE NEW ENGLAND TRAIL ROUTE 2

107

Makin' Whoopie Pie

Though we sure loved
Makin' Whoopie Pie,
And you loved eatin' the stuff,
After a while we all had to admit
It just wasn't Whoopie enough.

2002-2003

Economic Crunch

1987

Tuskegee Chunk

1989-1990

Bovinity Divinity

1996-2001

67. GREENBANK'S HOLLOW
44.3777, -72.122

525 Greenbanks Hollow Rd, Danville, VT 05828

A village entirely destroyed by fire in 1885 was wiped off the map - but a few foundations can still be found by those who look closely enough. The covered bridge that brought visitors into the town has been restored, giving a fleeting glimpse of what entering the settlement might have been like.

68. EMILY'S BRIDGE
44.44039, -72.67987

Covered Bridge Rd, Stowe, VT 05672

www.emilysbridge.com

This otherwise adorable looking covered wooden bridge in Vermont is rumoured to have a dark past - Emily is said to have awaited her lover in the early 1800s as they were due to elope but when he failed to materialise, she hung herself in a fit of pique. Stories abound as to her ghostly escapades which target anyone that dares to approach the bridge.

69. BEN AND JERRYS FLAVOUR GRAVEYARD
44.3529, -72.7402

1281 Waterbury-Stowe Road, Route 100, Waterbury, VT 05676

www.benjerry.com

Gone but not forgotten.

70. WORLDS TALLEST FILING CABINET
44.4556, -73.21677

220-, 270 Flynn Ave, Burlington, VT 05401

Now this is organisation.

< Left: Ben & Jerry's Flavour Graveyard
Top: Greenbank's Hollow
Bottom: Emily's Bridge

THE NEW ENGLAND TRAIL ROUTE 2

THE JAZZ / WHISKY RUN ROUTE 3

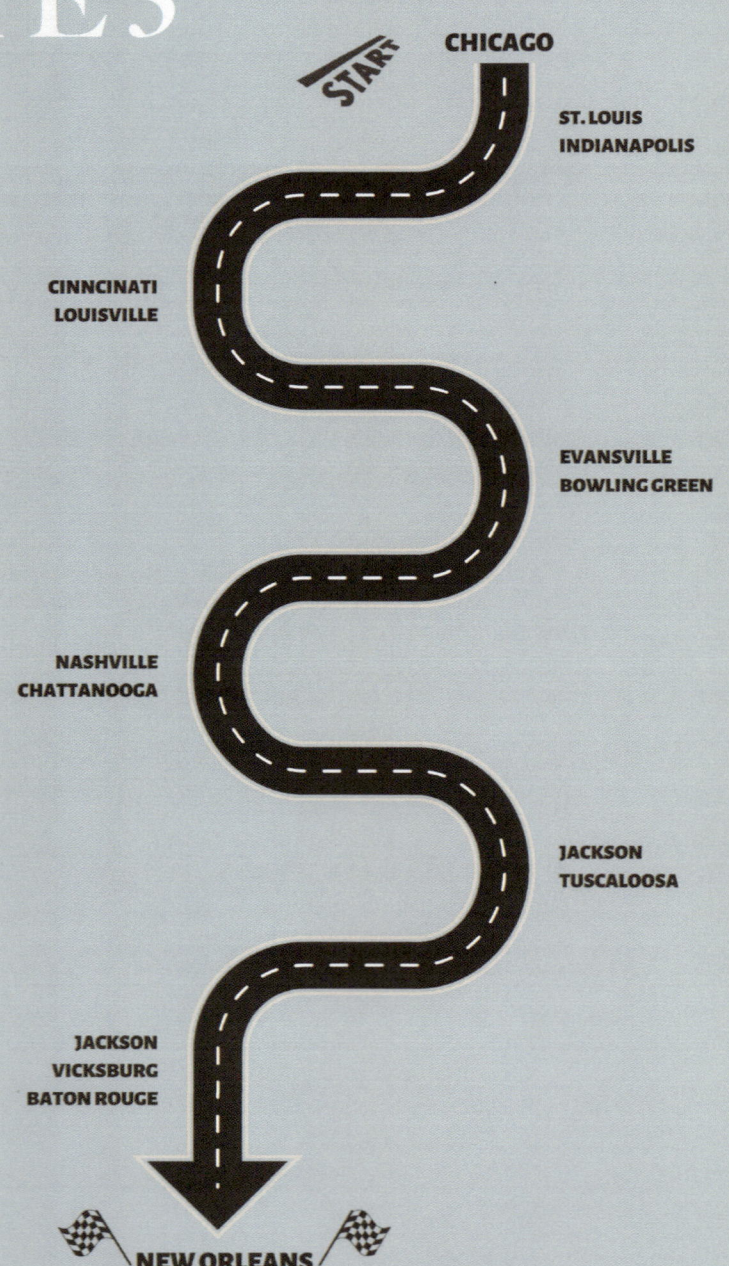

START — CHICAGO
ST. LOUIS
INDIANAPOLIS

CINNCINATI
LOUISVILLE

EVANSVILLE
BOWLING GREEN

NASHVILLE
CHATTANOOGA

JACKSON
TUSCALOOSA

JACKSON
VICKSBURG
BATON ROUGE

NEW ORLEANS

THE JAZZ / WHISKY RUN

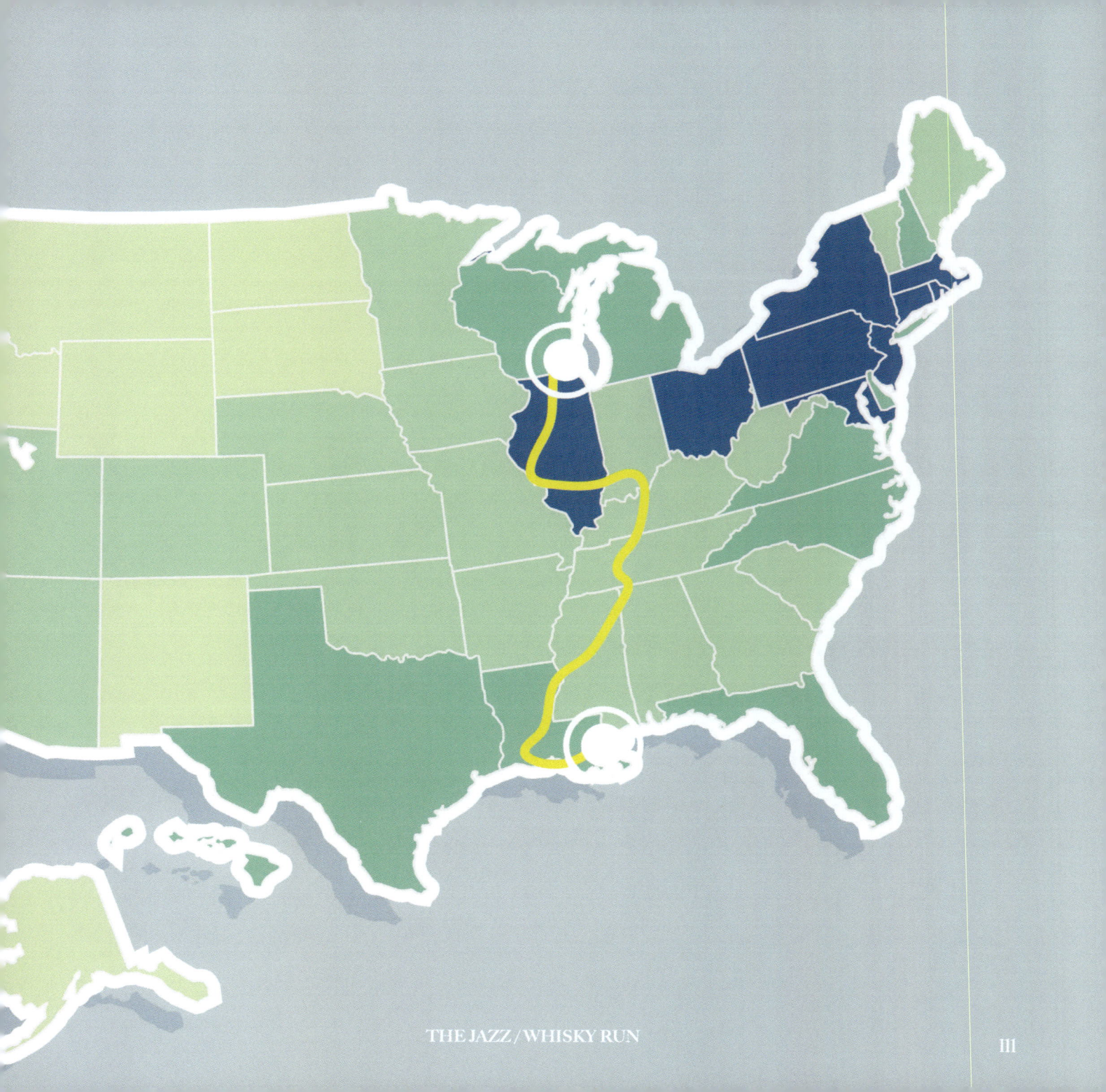

THE JAZZ/WHISKY RUN ROUTE 3

The road to Bourbon Street is paved with terrible fountains, genetically challenged squirrels and over-sized condiments. Journey through the lesser travelled states of Illinois, Missouri, Alabama, Kentucky, Ohio, Indiana and Louisana to name a few as you blitz through the Bible Belt; discover more about the era when Humans rode on Dinosaurs, visit Santa in his natural environment, stay in a wigwam and see what happens when a supercar falls into a giant sinkhole.

1. THE MURDER CASTLE SITE
41.77947, -87.6404
611 W 63rd St, Chicago, IL 60621
A perfectly standard post office sitting on the original site of H. H. Holmes's 'Murder Castle', the residence of America's first serial killer constructed purely with a view to killing all who stayed within it using shoots, trap doors, dead-end passages and secret tunnels to trap and hide victims.

2. MAN-EATING RUGS
41.8662, -87.6186

Above: Man-Eating Rugs

1400 S Lake Shore Dr, Chicago, IL 60605
www.fieldmuseum.org

In 1898 the British were building a bridge over the Tsavo River, Kenya when during 9 months of labour, two male maneless Tsavo lions attacked the camp, dragging 35 Indian workmen from their beds (claimed to be 135 at the time in what is thought to be an exaggeration) and eating them. After much hunting, Colonel Patterson who was leading the project killed both lions. They spent the next 25 years as his floor rugs before being sold to the Chicago Field Museum in 1924 for $5,000 (the exaggerated death toll likely drove the price) and arrived as skins in very poor condition as might be expected for well--worn mats. They were reconstructed, stuffed and are now on display.

3. WORLD'S FIRST CHOCOLATE BROWNIE

41.88066, -87.62706
17 E Monroe St, Chicago, IL 60603
www3.hilton.com

The Palmer House Hilton Hotel is the home of the world's first chocolate brownie - grab one in honour

4. CROWN FOUNTAIN

41.88149, -87.62372
201 E Randolph St, Chicago, IL 60602

This digital artwork is interactive and changes according to the seasons. In the warmer months faces can be seen spitting water at passers-by.

5. LARGEST TIFFANY GLASS DOME

41.88379, -87.62744
78 E Washington St, Chicago, IL 60602

The extraordinary Tiffany Glass dome in the Chicago Cultural Center, the largest of its kind in the world, is 38 foot across and features stunning fish scale glass and the signs of the zodiac. Today it is lit electrically but originally it was meant to be simply lit by sunlight. The quotation running inside the dome is from British author Addison.

6. ROCK 'N' ROLL MCDONALDS AND MUSEUM

41.8925, -87.6313
600 N Clark St, Chicago, IL 60610

One of the most famed McDonalds locations in the World and once the busiest in the States, this museum restaurant has

Above: Crown Fountain
> Right: Rock 'n' Roll Mcdonalds
Overleaf: Largest Tiffany Glass Dome

OFFBEAT AMERICA

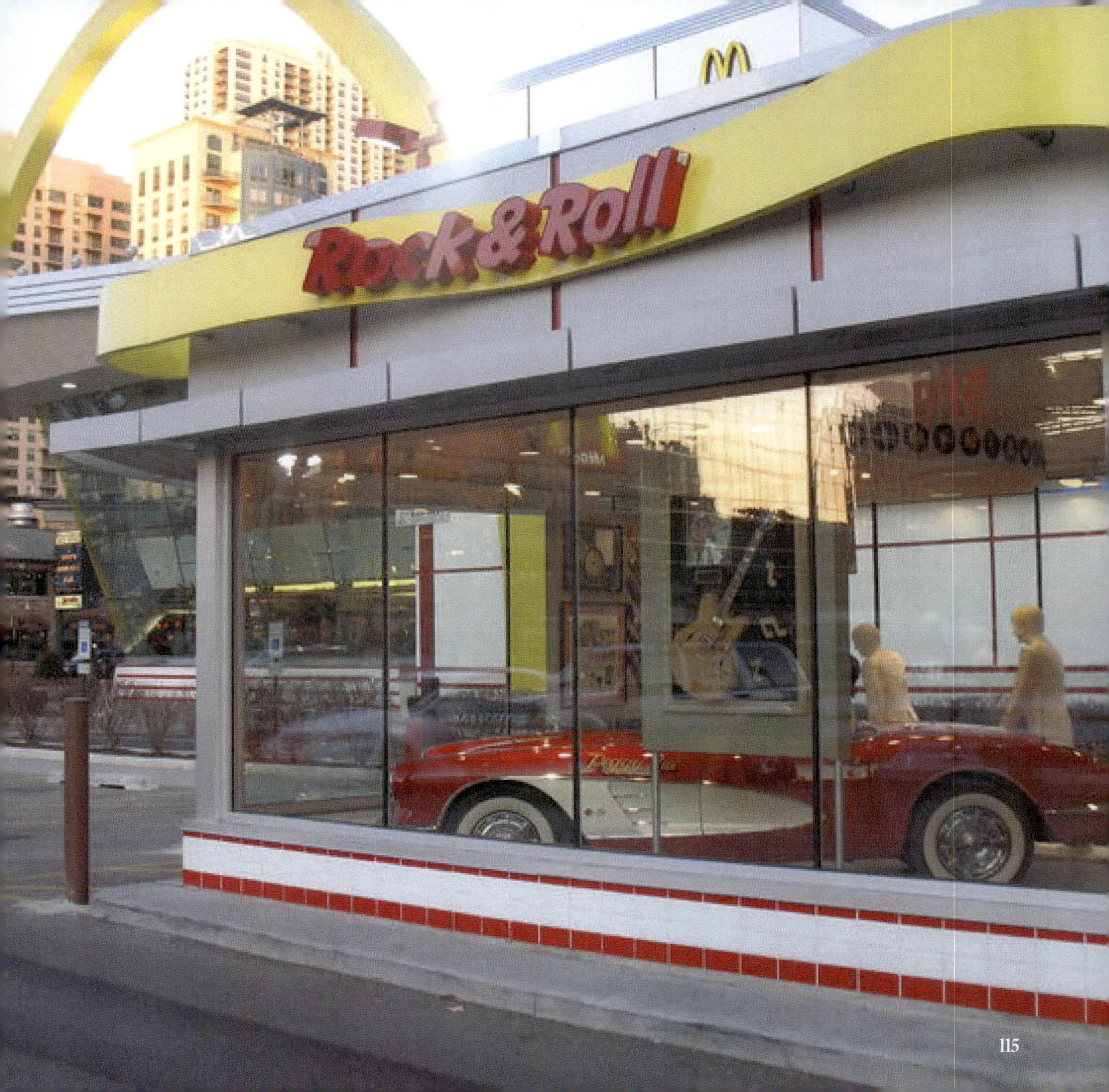
Rock & Roll

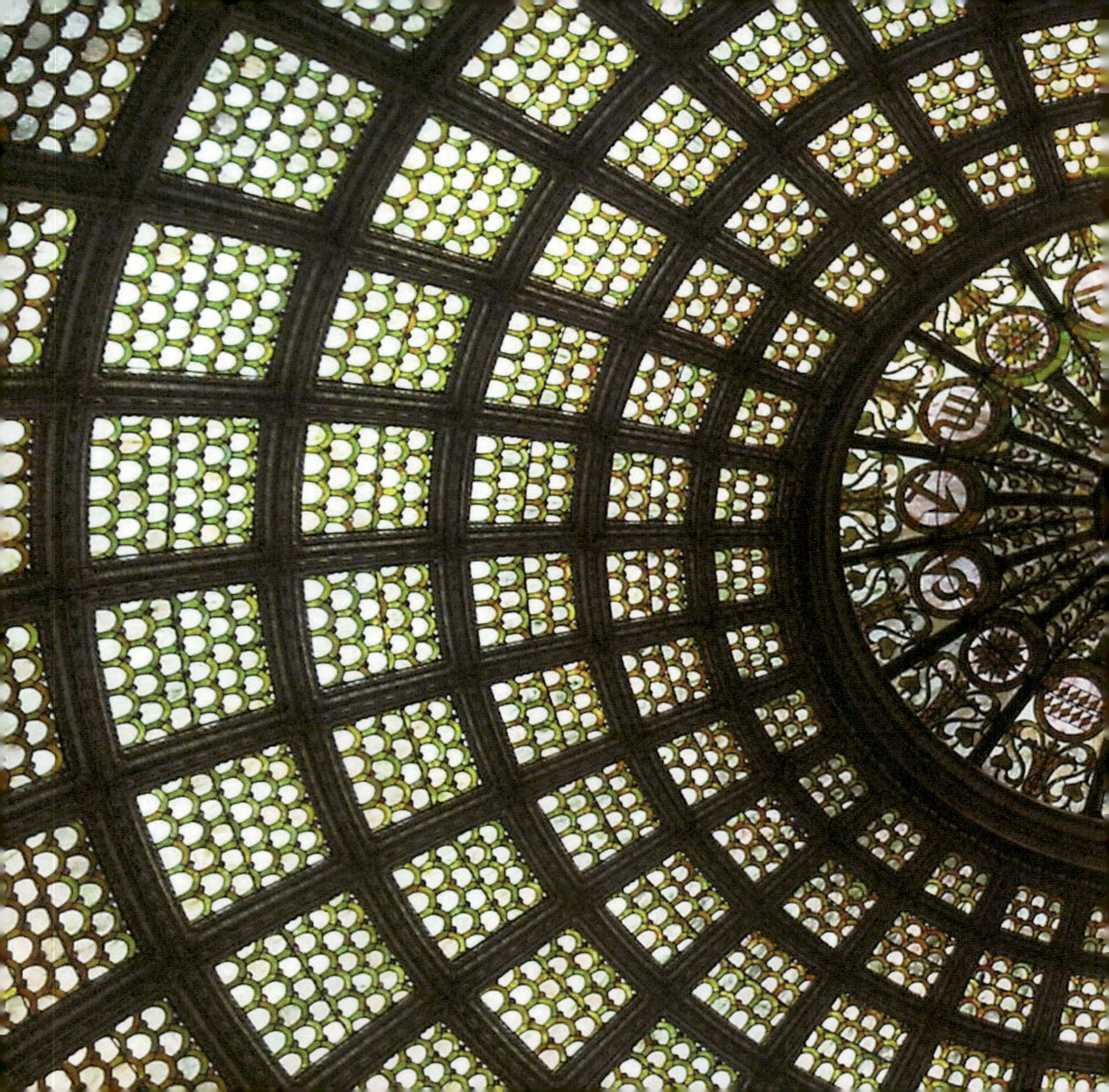

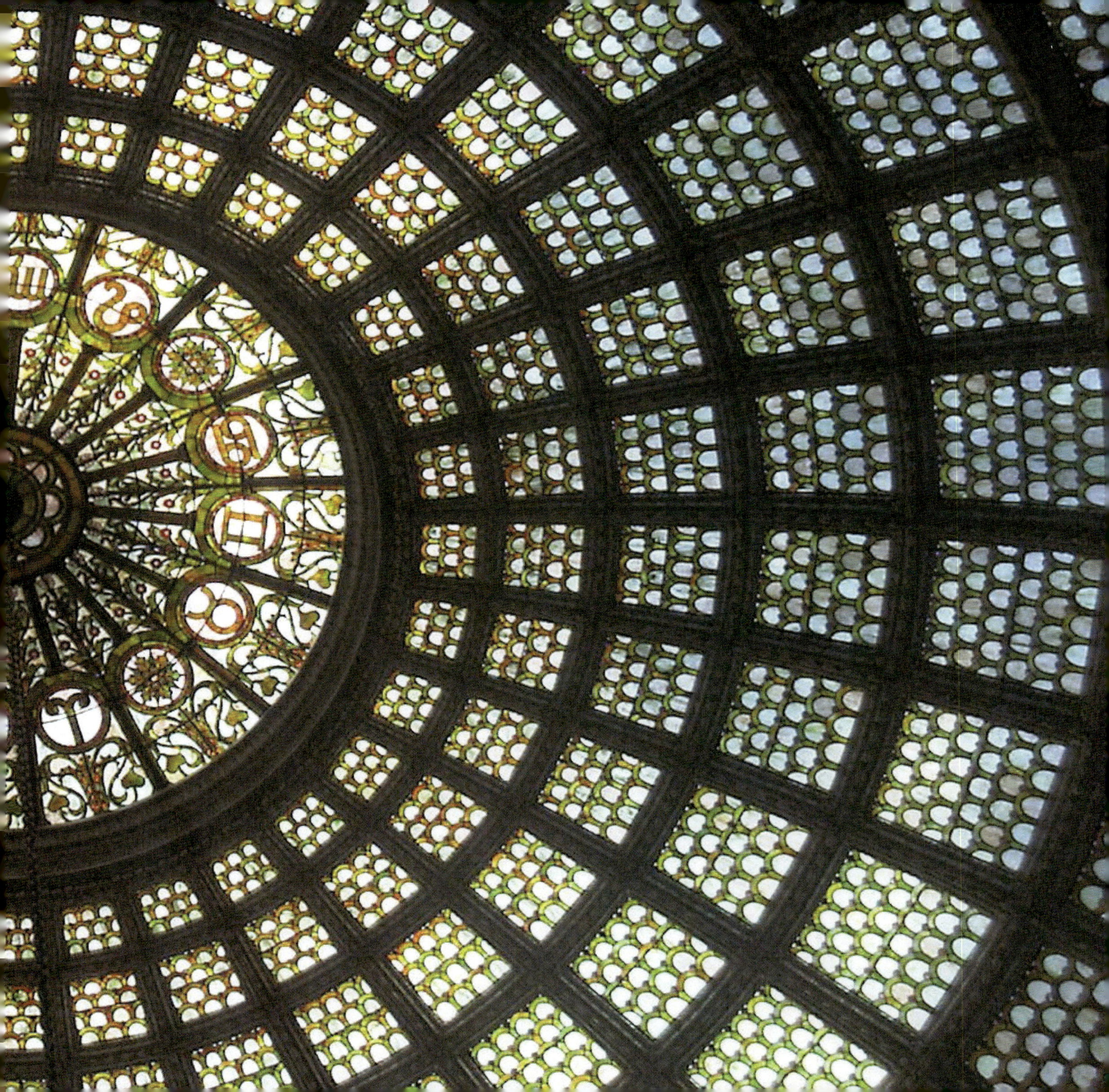

been a tourist attraction since its founding in 1983, and its new incarnation built in 2005 is equally popular. It was built to celebrate the franchise's 50th anniversary and invitees included Colin Powell and Sir Elton John. The prices are higher here than other Chicago McDonalds to offset the costs of the decor.

7. CHICAGO'S WOODEN ALLEYS
41.9103, -87.62763
Wooden Alley, Chicago, IL 60610
Chicago once boasted streets paved with wood, all but two of which are long gone. Visit one before a cigarette butt gets it.

8. SHIT FOUNTAIN
41.8997, -87.6744
1001 North Wolcott Avenue
Chicago, Illinois, 60622
A giant artwork to some, a giant pile of crap to others. Either way, it reminds errant dog walkers to do the business.

9. WICKER PARK SECRET AGENT SUPPLY CO
41.90482, -87.66908
1276 N Milwaukee Ave, Chicago, IL 60622
www.secretagentsupply.com
Every purchase you make at this kooky spy--orientated outlet supports a brilliant free writing program for Chicago students. And all the items on sale aim to unlock creativity in the purchaser.

10. THE OLD BATHHOUSE
41.9104, -87.67899
2039 W. North Avenue
Chicago, Illinois, 60622
This gorgeous Twenties bathhouse was renovated from ruin in the '90s and today houses a great gastro pub.

11. BUSY BEAVER BUTTON CO
41.91707, -87.71001
3407 W Armitage Ave, Chicago, IL 60647
www.busybeaver.net
Buttons in the American sense, aka badges, fill this dedicated museum in Illinois. The humble badge was patented in 1896 and Busy Beaver aim to collect all specimens and document how people have used this humble symbol to commemorate important life events and moments. Open Monday to Friday 10-4pm.

12. CHICAGO SWEATLODGE
41.94444, -87.74729
3500 N Cicero Ave, Chicago, IL 60641
chicagosweatlodge.com
If you're a man and you are au fait with both sweating and eating... in short, if you're a man – this restaurant come Russian bania is for you. Be beaten with bundles of leaves before plunging into a cold water bath, followed by a hearty meal of borsht.

13. THE LEGEND OF ETERNAL SILENCE
41.95483, -87.66188
4001 N Clark St, Chicago, IL 60613
www.gracelandcemetery.org
Beautifully creepy sculpture in Graceland Cemetery in memory of Dexter Graves who died in 1844, financed by his son Henry's will (which also provided $40,000 for a memorial to Ike Cook, Henry's favourite race horse, which would stand by a horse drinking fountain in Washington Park. Sadly, this never came about). Legend has it that visitors looking into the eyes of the Eternal Silence monument would have a vision of their own death. Its design depicts the Grim Reaper, death and silence..

14. WOOLLY MAMMOTH ANTIQUES AND ODDITIES
41.97606, -87.669
1513 W Foster Ave, Chicago, IL 60640
www.woollymammothchicago.com
Love taxidermy, all things vintage, medical oddities, funerary items, military ephemera and more? This is the store for you.

15. CHICAGO MUNICIPAL TUBERCULOSIS SANITARIUM
41.9858, -87.7227
5801 N Pulaski Rd, Chicago, IL 60646
This imposing building built in 1915 was the largest municipal Sanatorium in the country with a capacity of 950 beds. Today repurposed as a gymnasium as part of the North Park Village redevelopment, the

> Top left: Chicago Municipal Tuberculosis Sanitariam
> Bottom left: The Legend of Eternal Silence
Overleaf: Shit Fountain, Baha'i House of Worship

Sanitorium once offered patients occupations such as chess and drawing whilst helping them overcome this often fatal disease.

16. THE AMERICAN TOBY JUG MUSEUM
42.03471, -87.67978
910 Chicago Ave, Evanston, IL 60202
www.tobyjugmuseum.com
Because if you have one mug with a face on it you need several, and once you have several the next logical step is to open a museum.

17. BAHA I HOUSE OF WORSHIP
42.07443, -87.68426
100 Linden Ave, Wilmette, IL 60091
www.bahaitemple.org
The Baha'I faith, a monotheistic Persian religion of the 19th century emphasising commendably the spiritual unity of humankind, states that churches must be open to people of all denominations so that they may worship without denominational restriction and that any holy scripture of any religion may be read inside. Unusually however, no musical instruments may be played in the building, no

THE JAZZ / WHISKY RUN ROUTE 3

SHIT FOUNTAIN

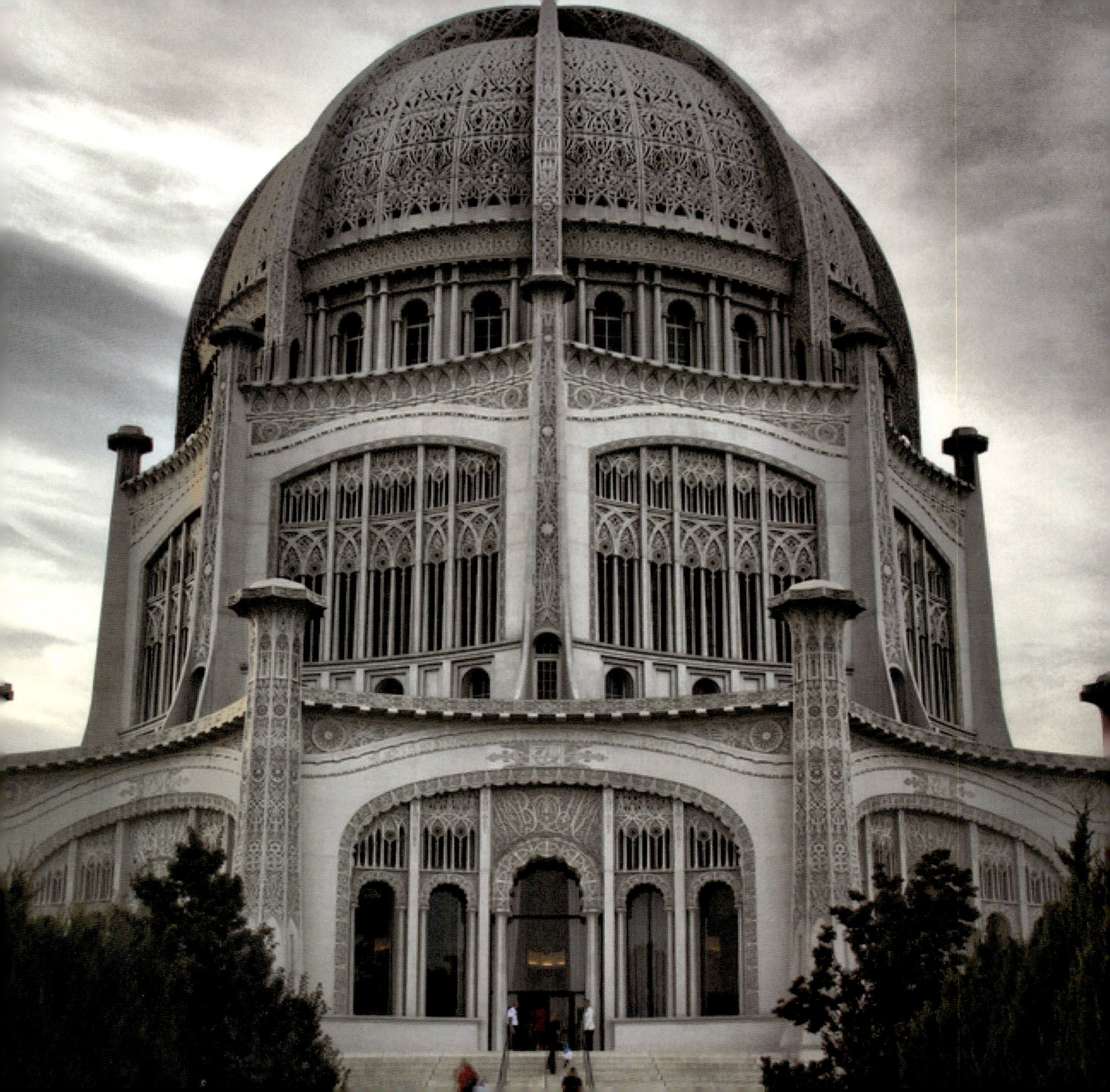

sermons may be delivered and no ritualistic ceremonies practiced which would seem to rule out almost any activity within the building. Furthermore no pictures, statues or images may be displayed and no pulpits or altars incorporated as architectural features. All seats face the Shrine of Baha'u'lIah' in Israel. There are only 8 such Houses of Worship in the World.

18. THE HOME ALONE HOUSE
42.0125, -87.78409
671 Lincoln Ave, Winnetka, IL 60093
Leave the kids behind for this one.

19. THE LEANING TOWER OF NILES
42.0125, -87.7841
6300 Touhy Ave, Niles, IL 60714
Just like Pisa. But smaller. And the lean is deliberate.

20. AHLGRIM FAMILY FUNERAL SERVICES
42.11415, -88.03342
201 N Northwest Hwy, Palatine, IL 60067
This otherwise normal funeral home has a 9 hole miniature golf course and arcade machines in its basement which have macabre themes involving guillotines and mausoleums - they welcome visitors, so drop in for a spot of genuinely crazy golf.

21. THE AWAKING MUSE
42.0253, -88.0629
620 Sherwood Ln, Schaumburg, IL 60193
Curious sculpture of a woman rising from, or sinking into, the earth. It is rumoured that she whispers inspiration to anyone who sits in her outstretched hand. The sculpture forms part of the Chicago Athenaeum International Sculpture Park.

22. EBENEZER FLOPPEN SLOPPERS
41.8633, -87.9619
600 E Riordan Rd
Villa Park, Illinois, 60181
An abandoned waterpark with possibly the best proprietor name of all time.

23. GALLOPING GHOST ARCADE
41.81694, -87.8557
9415 Ogden Ave, Brookfield, IL 60513
www.gallopingghostarcade.com
The largest video arcade in the USA

24. SHOWMEN'S REST, FOREST PARK
41.85069, -87.82187
7750 W Cermak Rd, Forest Park, IL 60130
104 died and 127 were injured in the Hammond Circus Train Wreck during which a troupe train of 20 empty cars collided with the rear of a circus train at about 35 mph. 86 performers and rousties from the Hagenbeck-Wallace circus died in the first 35 seconds of the collision, before the wreck caught fire. Notables among the deceased were the Great Dierckx Brothers and Jennie Ward Todd of The Flying Wards. Most of the dead were buried in Woodlawn Cemetery in Forest Park in a Showmen's Rest section, purchased by the Showmen's League of America. Most were so badly burned they were unable to be identified hence the 'Unknown' name markings. Statues of mourning elephants surround the monument.

25. GEMINI GIANT MUFFLER MAN
41.31044, -88.13856
S East St, Wilmington, IL 60481
A giant 'Muffler Man' advertising prop, many of which were built across the USA in the 1960s. This version is named for the Gemini space program and holds a rock ship.

26. THE TOWN OF NORMAL
40.5142, -88.99063
Normal, IL 61790
A quirky US place name with a scholarly explanation. Originally known as North Bloomington, the town was renamed in 1865 after Illinois State Normal University, a normal school (meaning a teacher training institution). This name originated from the 16th century French école normale, the name normal used to signify 'model', as it was a model school with model classrooms teaching model teaching practices to student teachers.

27. PEORIA STATE HOSPITAL
40.63354, -89.65751

> Right:: Peoria State Hospital
Overleaf: Gemini Giant, The Leaning Tower of Niles, Showmen's Rest

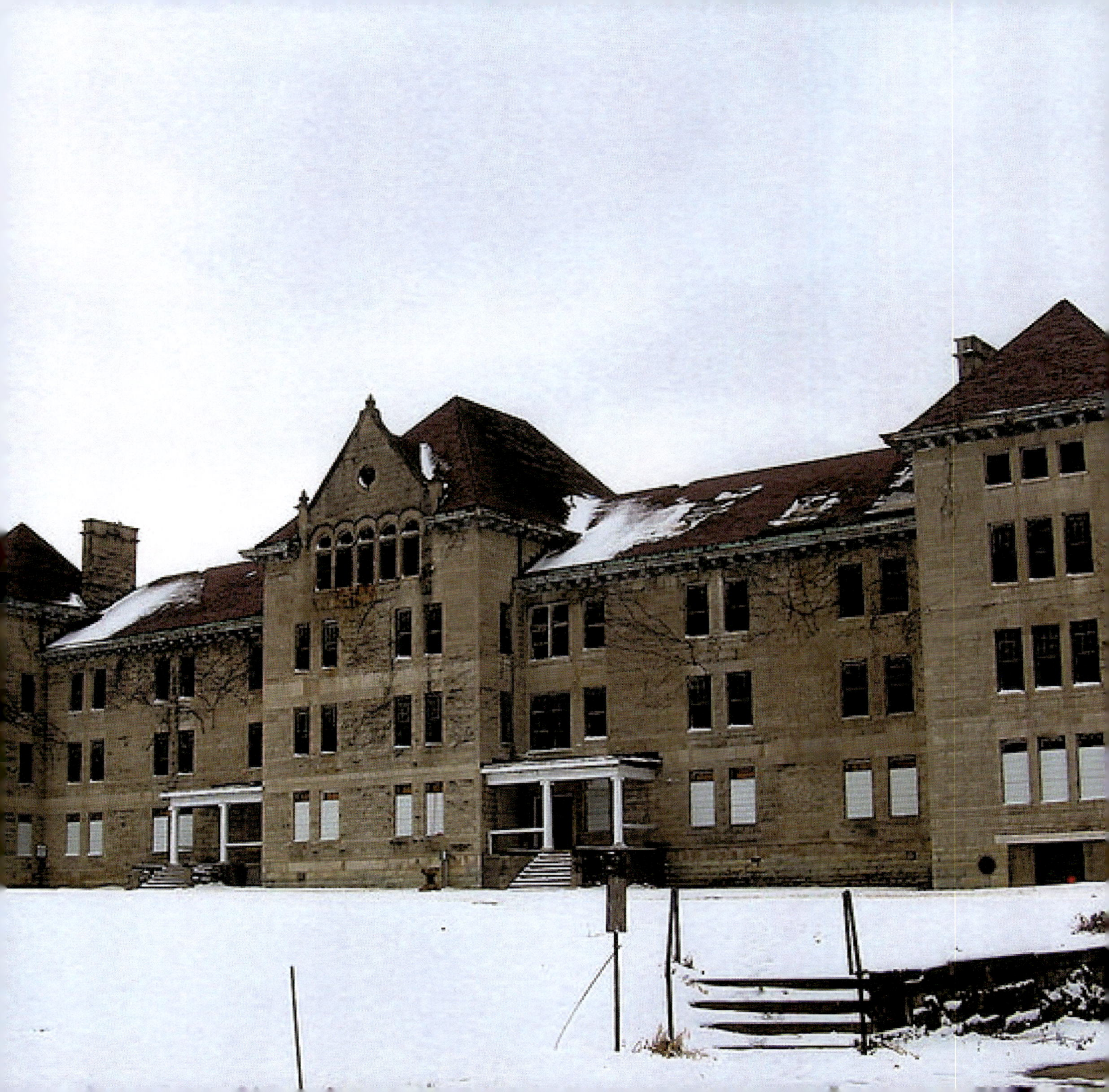

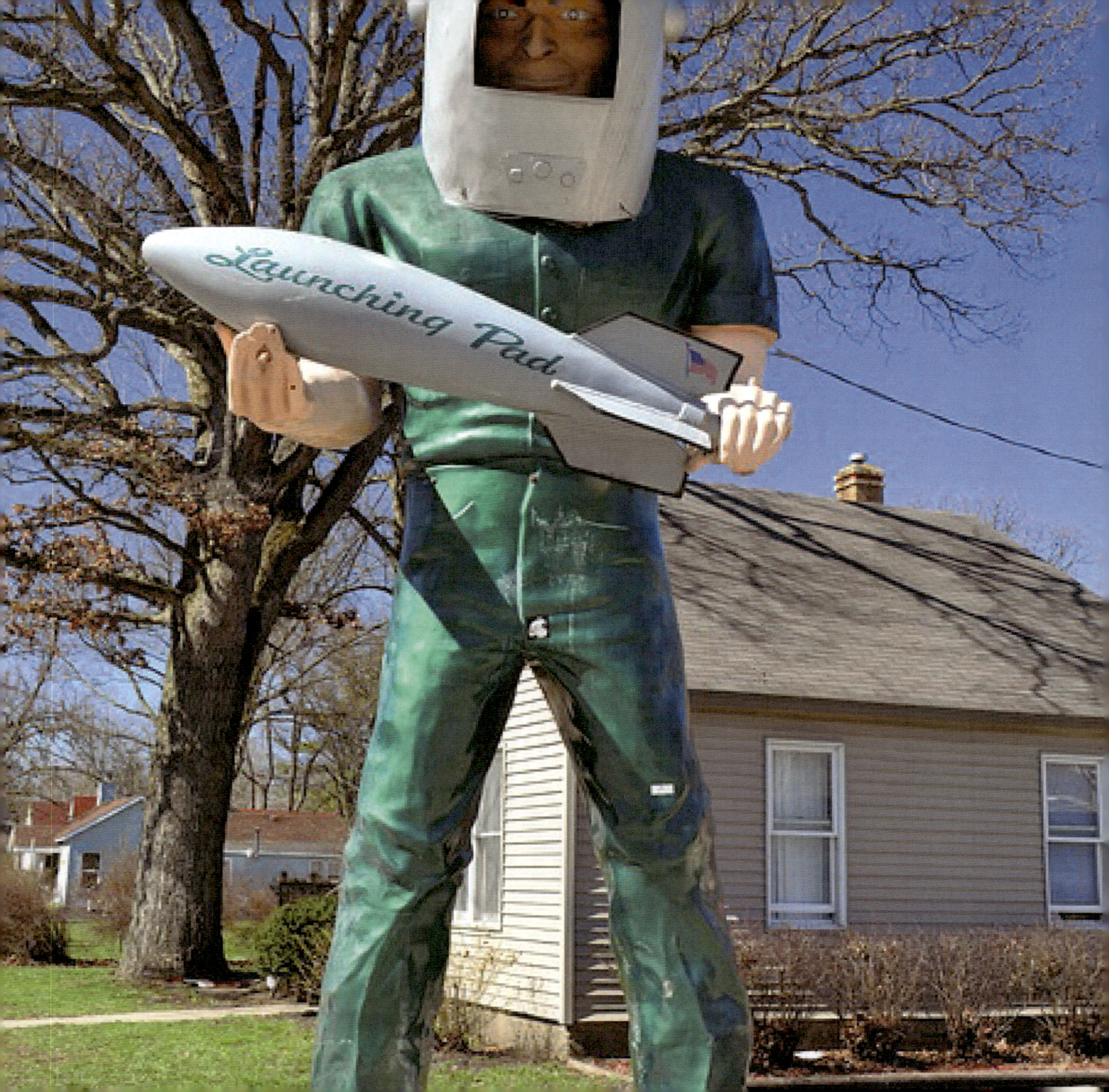
Launching Pad

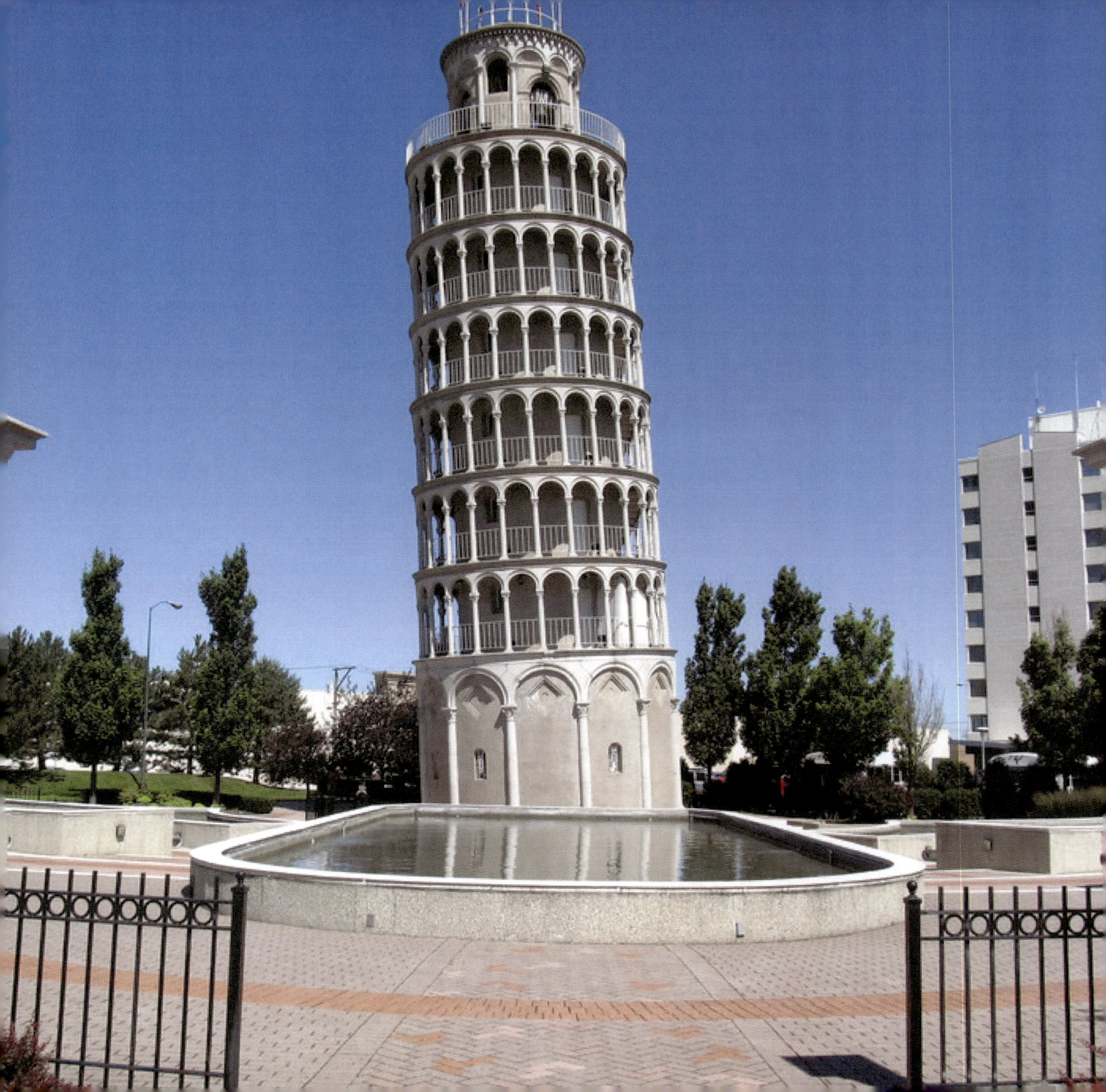

KREBS

FATHER
ALBERT

SHOWM
OF

NS LEAGUE
MERICA

4501 W Pfeiffer Rd, Bartonville, IL 61607
Also known as Bartonville State Hospital or the Illinois Asylum for the Incurable Insane, this hospital ran from 1902 to 1973 and contains 47 buildings in extensive grounds. The first building constructed on the site in the style of a feudal castle was never used, being razed to the ground due to a combination of disused mine shafts compromising the integrity of the building, combined with concerns that the fortress-like style of the building was out of keeping with modern ideas regarding the care of the mentally ill. General patient population was around 2,650 patients at any time, with 13,510 passing through the hospital during its operation. It was well regarded, allowing journalists into the buildings to assess the conditions and focussing on therapeutic treatment of the ill. The property remains largely empty although the town is trying to lease the buildings out to commercial enterprises after developers failed to show interest. The administrative building was purchased by an individual pledging to raise funds to restore and retain it, but in what has to be one of the least successful restoration projects imaginable, his bankruptcy has meant the demolition in 2016 of the building for scrap to pay off his debts. The others he did not attempt to 'save' remaining standing.

28. PHONE BOOTH ON A ROOF
40.14609, -89.36149
700 Broadway St, Lincoln, IL 62656

City Hall has a phone booth improbably balanced on its roof and has done for the past 50 years, bamboozling passers-by. Back in the day, lookouts were posted on the roof for approaching tornadoes who then used the phone to call down to their colleagues on the ground to forewarn them.

29. WORLD'S LARGEST COVERED WAGON
40.14859, -89.38731
1750 5th St, Lincoln, IL 62656
(and Abe Lincoln)

30. HENRYS RABBIT RANCH
39.00437, -89.78188
1107 Historic Old Rte 66, Staunton, IL 62088
www.henrysroute66.com
'Hare it is', as the website says. Follow the rabbity signs off Route 66 whether you like rabbits of the VW or the luffy kind – Henry's caters to both. A classic filling station with a twist and plenty of Route 66 souvenirs.

31. MONUMENT TO THE WORLD'S TALLEST MAN
38.90418, -90.14359
2810 College Ave, Alton, IL 62002
The statue depicts Robert Wadlow, who stood at 8ft 11 in or 2.72 metres tall. He is the tallest human being in history, despite his father measuring a mere 5ft 11 or 1.82 metres in height – Robert exceeded his father and hit 6ft at age 8. He lived from 1918 to 1940, dying at the age of just 24. His height was due to hyperplasia of the pituitary, which results in excessive growth hormone. At the time of his death, he was still growing and had to walk with leg braces with little feeling in his hands and feet. He toured with the Ringling Brothers Circus in 1936 which made him something of a celebrity and thereafter featured in a living advertisement around 1938 for the International Shoe Company which made shoes for him for free and for whom he toured around the nation visiting over 800 towns and 41 states, travelling over 300,000 miles. Sadly, he felt somewhat compelled to take this advertising job in order to secure the supply of free shoes as his own left his feet in so much pain, one of the only health issues he experienced having avoided other common ailments linked to excessive growth. However tragically, whilst soldiering on around the States on his tour the shoes made for him caused him blisters which became infected and ultimately despite surgeries and blood transfusions, he died of the infection. His shoes can be found in several locations across the USA including in Snyder's Shoe Store in Ludlington Michigan, and in the Alton Museum of History and Arts. He was a member of both the Freemasons and the Masonic Order of the DeMolay and was a Master Mason, his Freemason ring the largest that was ever made. He is buried in Oakwood Cemetery, Upper Alton with his parents and siblings in Section 4 of the cemetery.

32. THE MISTAKE HOUSE
38.9488, -90.3484
1 Front Gate Road
Elsah, Illinois, 62028
Also known as the sample house, a noted architect designed this building as an example of what he planned his larger house to look like so that his tradesmen had a point of reference during his absence when he travelled abroad.

33. CEMENTLAND
38.73562, -90.21673
520 Scranton Ave, St. Louis, MO 63137
This tragic location was dreamt up by sculptor Bob Cassilly who was also behind the St Louis City Museum; he decided to create a public art exhibit of huge concrete creations and machinery, funded by companies who use the area as a dump, as they did prior to his purchase of the land. As the project was previously being self-funded, this income has permitted the project to continue. Sadly Cassilly was killed at Cementland in 2011 when the bulldozer he was driving flipped down a hill. It remains closed to the public but reports suggest that his widow is attempting to continue what he began. She would like to fulfil his dream as closely as possible to the latest plans he had created, but as he built much of the park on a whim,

<Left: Monument to the World's Largest Man

this is proving challenging. Hopefully this will come to fruition in the near future.

34. LUNA CAFÉ
38.76191, -90.08881
201 E Chain of Rocks Rd, Granite City, IL 62040
This famed diner was a favourite of the notorious Al Capone.

35. CAHOKIA MOUNDS
38.65506, -90.06182
Collinsville, IL 62234
www.cahokiamounds.org
The site of a pre-Columbian Native American City c. 600-1400 CE, this park contains 80 mounds, (variously used for the raising up of temples and other important buildings, for burials or for political or religious ceremonies as well as to designate important locations,) set in 2,200 acres although the ancient city which was the most influential urban dwelling of Mississippian culture, was much larger with a population of some 40,000, covering some 6 square miles with about 120 human made mounds. Cahokia is one of only 23 UNESCO World Heritage sites in the USA. A notable burial known as the 'birdman' was found, thought to be a ruler, who was buried on 20,000 shell beads arranged in the shape of a falcon. A further 250 plus skeletons have been

OFFBEAT AMERICA

found in Mound 72, over half of which were sacrificial victims, some of which were decapitated, had their hands removed, were buried in layers separated by matting, or buried alive en masse shown by vertical fingers digging in the sand.

36. THE MEATPACKING PLANT
38.64536, -90.15209
Fairmont City Boulevard, Natl Stock Yards, IL 62071

This 1903 abandoned meat packing plant is frozen in time, complete with the latest in late 19th century machinery still in place. Advances in technology rendered the plant too expensive to run and was shut in 1959, remaining in place untouched to this day. Whilst the meat packing business was a grisly process of slaughter and processing, visitors in its heyday would flock to see the revolutionary facility in action; the plant had a slaughterhouse on the top floor of the main building and each subsequent lower floor and room was dedicated to a particular cut of meat / packaging process.

37. PRUITT-IGOE URBAN ABYSS
38.6434, -90.21076
2300 Cass Ave, St. Louis, MO 63106
www.pruittigoenow.org

A classic tale of utopian planning gone wrong akin to Thamesmead of London, Pruitt-Igoe was a giant urban housing project by the architect of the World Trade Center towers in 1954 in St. Louis. As soon as it was fully complete in 1956, things started going drastically downhill and by the mid 1960s it was utterly infamous for its crime, poverty and racial segregation. In the Seventies it was torn down but still represents a failure of both society and town planning. All that now remains are several paths, with sections of streets and parking areas.

38. USS INAUGURAL MINESWEEPER WRECKAGE
38.61147, -90.1881
Rutger St, St. Louis, MO 63104

A minesweeper from WWII, it was launched in 1944 and saw combat in the Pacific Theater, becoming decommissioned in 1946 thereafter. In 1968 the ship became a museum although in 1993 a flood tore the Inaugural from her mooring and left her a mile downstream where she remains to this day. Occasionally the river drops so low that one can walk to the ship - plans continue to scrap her but the river levels continue to rise making this unfeasibly challenging.

39. LEMP MANSION
38.5932, -90.216
3322 Demenil Pl, St. Louis, MO 63118
www.lempmansion.com

This beautiful house is home to tragedy; four Lemp family members committed suicide here after the death of the son of the family Frederick Lemp. Frederick was William Lemp Sr.'s fourth son, born in 1873, and

< Top: USS Inaugural Sunker Minesweeper
< Bottom: Pruitt-Igoe Urban Abyss
Right: Lemp Mansion

THE JAZZ / WHISKY RUN ROUTE 3

Bottom left: World's Largest Catsup Bottle
Bottom centre and right: Demoulin Museum

had significant health problems, dying of heart failure in 1901. This tragedy prompted William Lemp Sr. who had been planning for his much loved son to be the heir to his empire, the William J. Lemp Brewing Company, to commit suicide by gunshot in 1904 at 10.15am. Elsa Lemp, the youngest child of William Sr. shot herself in bed in her own house at 13 Hortense Place in 1920 due to a tumultuous relationship. William Lemp Sr.'s son William Lemp Jr. subsequently shot himself in his office (now the front left dining room) in 1922 when his business was struggling. In 1949 Charles Lemp, William Sr.'s third son who lived alone in the mansion with his dog and never married, shot his dog then himself in the head. In 1970, Edmin Lemp, the last surviving and youngest son of William Sr., died at 90, telling his caretaker to destroy his art collection and all his family heirlooms rather than sell them off, perhaps thinking them cursed or wishing to draw a line under the tragic family history.

40. ROACHTOWN
38.4631, -90.04094
Roachtown, Millstadt Township, IL 62260
Another photogenic town sign to be hunted down. Etymology unknown.

41. WORLD'S LARGEST CATSUP BOTTLE
38.6629, -89.9823
305 Railroad Ave, Collinsville, IL 62234
Is there another World's Largest Ketchup Bottle? Does anyone care?

42. DEMOULIN MUSEUM
38.89191, -89.41197
110 W Main St, Greenville, IL 62246
www.demoulinmuseum.org
'The Ancient Mysteries Of The Goat Are Revealed!' DeMoulin Bros. & Co were founded in 1892 as the foremost manufacturer of fraternal lodge paraphernalia and today are one of the USA's finest specialists in marching band uniforms. Amongst their illustrious history is the creation of 'lodge initiation devices' and this 2010 museum pays tribute to all things created by this heritage company. Initiation rituals and devices have long been a tantalising enigma but this museum lifts the lid on the bizarre practices that go on behind closed doors, with displays which include the Bucking Goat, Invisible Paddle Machine and the

Bottom left: Two Story Outhouse
Bottom centre: Albino Squirrels of Olney
Bottom right: World's Largest Rocking Chair

Lifting and Spraying Machine (?!)

43. WORLDS LARGEST CROSS
39.10656, -88.57193
1900 Pike Ave, Effingham, IL 62401
www.crossusa.org
As symbols of torturous execution in the name of love go, this one is massive. Get your cruci-fix here.

44. TWO STORY OUTHOUSE
39.45888, -88.49558
1022 S Pine St, Gays, IL 61928
'In England they have urinals, in Paris bidets, but nowhere on earth has an outhouse like Gays'.

45. ALBINO SQUIRRELS OF OLNEY
38.73088, -88.08531
502 White Squirrel Cir, Olney, IL 62450
Olney is terribly proud of its albino squirrel population and is fiercely protective of them, restricting the free movement of dogs and cats in their vicinity to ensure their protection. A nearby street is even called White Squirrel Drive in their honour.

46. THE TOWN OF MOONSHINE
39.19074, -87.89546
6017 E 300th Rd, Martinsville, IL 62442
This town has but one building (apart from its toilet…so technically two), which happens to be a grocers built in 1912 run by Helen and Roy Tuttles. But boy does that one building count…home of the infamous Moonburger, the couple who created this renowned delicacy together form the entire population of Moonshine; Population 2. During the Lunchrun Event of 2011 (one assumes a run during which one simultaneously eats lunch?! This is America after all), 2068 burgers were sold, which has to be some kind of record. Technically Moonshine falls short of quite being a town, designated as a quote unquote 'wide spot in the road'.

47. WORLD'S LARGEST ROCKING CHAIR
39.30002, -87.99124
110 E Main St, Casey, IL 62420
bigthingssmalltown.com
One of seemingly several contenders for World's Largest Rocking Chair, this one

designed by Mr Jim Bolin, a prolific 'World's Largest designer', weighs a staggering 46,200 pounds and took two full years to construct. To qualify for the record, this chair had to actually rock and took ten men to move it. It comes complete with its own bible quotation: 'I have told you these things, so that in me you may have peace. In this world you will have trouble. But take heart! I have overcome the world. John 16:33 NIV'. Check out Casey's other 7, (yes 7) contenders for the 'World's Largest' collection, both in this book and by wandering around the town itself.

48. WORLD'S LARGEST WIND CHIME
39.29965, -87.99104

109 E Main St., Casey, IL 62420
Created by the designer of the Rocking Chair in the same town, this monster also took a further two years of this man's life to build. Assembly was complete in 2011 and the chime stands 56 foot high. It too comes complete with its own Romans biblical quotation, however one suspects that the only praying happening in the vicinity is by neighbours begging for a gust-free day.

49. WORLD'S LARGEST GOLF TEE
39.30615, -87.97901
203 NE 13th St., Casey, IL 62420
Presumably hooked on the success of his chair and wind chime, Jim Bolin used 60 gallons of glue and 120lbs. of screws to build this 6659 lb monster in 2013. Why? Presumably to drive tourism and golf balls as high as this tee. The quotation featuring on its plaque, because what giant golf tee would be complete without one: 'For as the heaven is high above the earth, so great is His mercy toward them that fear Him' Psalm 103:11 KJV.

50. WORLD'S LARGEST PITCHFORK
39.31507, -87.9786
607 NE 13th Street, Casey, IL 62420
High off the success of his even higher golf tee, Bolin just couldn't stop himself making a giant pitchfork, this time to represent the farm community (one senses that anyone who was anyone in Casey by this point in the proceedings was demanding their own Giant

Something, in order to feel adequately represented around town.) Accompanied of course by a well chosen quotation, in this case 'His winnowing fork is in his hand, and he will clear his threshing floor, gathering his wheat into the barn and burning up the chaff with unquenchable fire' (Matthew 3:12 NIV), this pronged spectacle weighs in at 1940 lbs and is 60ft. in length, permitting for much burning of chaff with unquenchable fire should the need arise.

51. WORLD'S LARGEST WOODEN SHOES
SE 2nd St/E Albany Ave, Casey, IL 62420
Did Jim restrict himself to the construction of giant objects? Of course not. Well versed too in the art of chainsaw carving (obviously), when he was out and about 'antiquing' (shopping for antiques for the non-American amongst us), he came across a pair of old clogs and couldn't help but attempt to carve them, in giant form, with a chainsaw. Having completed one, a whopping 4ft 11in. in height, he presumably felt that the magic had died as he then handed over the completion of the second shoe to his colleagues at the aptly named 'Big Things in a Small Town Workshop'. Fortunately the pair appear to match. These currently reside in the Workshop whilst a location is found for them (perhaps Casey is now rebelling and trying to find excuses to avoid more Giant Items taking over their town). In a manner which perhaps reflects the somewhat more apathetic feelings of the designer at this point in the proceedings, the giant clogs are accompanied by a quote, but we are only provided with the Chapter and Verse: Ephesians 6:15.

52. WORLD'S LARGEST MAILBOX
39.29733, -87.99916
W Main St, Casey IL 62420
Little detail is provided as to the designer of this Giant Thing however given its location and accompaniment by a verse from Corinthians, one assumes that Jim Bolin might be involved. This brilliant sculpture on Main Street is entirely functional and allows you to post anything anywhere. Even the flag on the side works. 'You yourselves are our letter, written on our hearts, known & read by everyone. You show that you are a letter from Christ, the result of our ministry, written not with ink, but with the Spirit of the living God, not on tablets of stone but on tablets of human hearts' 2 Corinthians 3:2-3. The mailbox is a mere 32ft 6.5in high (to be precise).

53. WORLD'S LARGEST CROCHET HOOK & KNITTING NEEDLES
39.29932, -87.99283
2 E. Main St, Casey IL 62420
These giant needles and hook are to be found in The Yarn Studio and bear the impressive record due to having been successfully used by the store's owned Jeanette to knit and crochet a 10x10 square. Who designed them? We have absolutely no idea. The needles are over 13ft tall whilst the hook is over 6ft tall. Each of these has its OWN quote – 'For you created my inmost being; you knit me together in my mother's womb' (Psalm 139:13 NIV) and 'Whatever you do, work heartily as for the Lord, and not for me.' Colossians 3:23 ESV.

54. THE BIG COIN
39.31612, -87.98389
940 Illinois 49, Casey IL 62420
AND THAT IS NOT ALL. Casey ALSO boasts a further FOUR 'big' things, presumably disappointments which didn't make the record breaking grade and let the town down, now acting as symbols of regret and shame to the world at large. The first is, you guessed it, down to Jim Bolin, and is …well a giant coin. The only quote this item deserved was 'Sadly, the Big Coin did not meet the standards required to earn the title of 'World's Largest', but it is still interesting sight to see'. (sic). One imagines that the lapse in grammar was due to bigthingssmalltown.com sobbing into their keyboard at the time of writing.

55. THE BIG PENCIL
39.29733, -87.99916
W Main St, Casey, Illinois 62420
The pencil got a quote from Proverbs 3:3 NIV, 'Let love and faithfulness never leave you; bind them around you neck, write them on the tablet of your heart (sic) however beyond its majestic length at 32ft 6 inches, no further information is given presumably due to disappointment, and the typos persist.

< Left: World's Largest Wind Chime
< Right: World's Largest Golf Tee

THE JAZZ / WHISKY RUN ROUTE 3

56. THE BIG YARDSTICK
39.30028, -87.9929
101N Central Casey, IL 62420

Again just a quote and a length, this time from Matthew 7:2 'For in the same way you judge others, you will be judged and with the measure you use it will be measured to you'. 36ft. No typos suggest the grief period is waning and recovery, or perhaps the latest giant construction record attempt, may have begun.

57. THE BIG BIRDCAGE
38.25648, -85.75166
101 W Main, Casey, IL 62420

Bigthingssmalltown.com list the height of this item as 'Height: ???'. Perhaps the pain of another record attempt lost was still fresh at this point. 'Look at the birds of the air; they do not sow or reap or store away in barns, and yet your heavenly Father feeds them. Are you not much more valuable than they?' One assumes that the quote is either meant to reassure those who had identified with the tale of the Lazy Mouse as a child, planning to turn their backs on the concept of toiling in the field to ensure that one has provided for one's family, or perhaps it is just to restore a sense of value to those who had just lost another record attempt and spent an inordinate amount of money on a big, but not sufficiently big, birdcage.

58. AIRTIGHT BRIDGE
39.5549, -88.08949
Airtight Rd, Ashmore, IL 61912

Named for a sense of total stillness experienced whilst crossing it, this bridge was the site of the discovery of a dismembered body in 1980 which failed to be identified until 1992 thanks to DNA advances. None the less, the case remains unsolved and is a cold case file. The name stuck to the extent that the road on which it is situated is called Airtight Road.

59. MOORESVILLE'S GRAVITY HILL
39.6043, -86.4107
East Keller Hill Road, Mooresville, Indiana, 46158

A classic American Gravity Hill, any one of which is liable to offer you sightings of people doing strange things to test the phenomenon for themselves, such as leaving their cars in neutral around unsuspecting pedestrians, sprinkling talcum powder on empty roads or closely observing balls rolling around the street in front of them. Leave a ball at the bottom of the hill, and it appears to roll up it. Legend at Mooresville has it that a school bus stalled on the railroad tracks, killing the children when a train collided with it and that today, these children drag items and vehicles backwards out of harm's way. Many sprinkle talc or flour on their cars bumpers as it is said that the kids' finger prints will appear on them from pushing you.

60. ROTARY JAIL MUSEUM
40.04383, -86.90174
225 N Washington St, Crawfordsville, IN 47933
www.rotaryjailmuseum.org

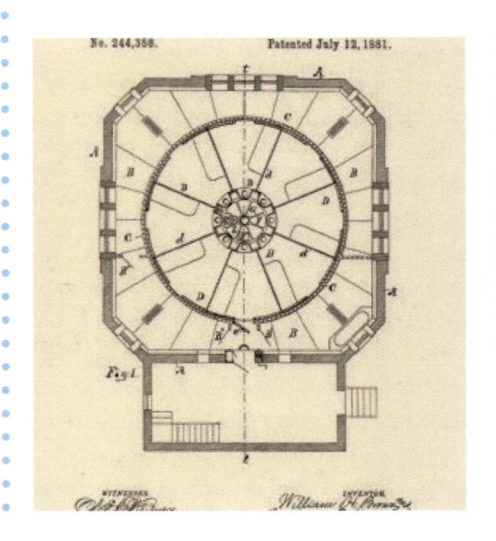

Only three such rotary jails of an original 18 exist today in the USA - this was the first and the last operational one in existence. The concept was a jail which operated as a carousel, with only one of the several cells accessible from a single opening per floor level. The pie shaped cells spun around a central core which had full plumbing, and the entire system could be rotated by one man hand-turning a crank which in turn was connected to gears beneath. Ball bearings facilitated the movement. The concept, whilst rather ingenious, ran into some fairly obvious problems, namely that prisoner's limbs were frequently crushed or prevented the rotation. Eventually, most of the rotary jails had to be welded into a fixed position before being modified to allow for individual access to each pie-shaped cell. The other three such jails can be found at Council Bluffs, Pottawatomie County Iowa, Gallatin, Daviess County Missouri and Sherman, Grayson County Texas. A further five at least in Missouri, Kentucky, Utah and Colorado were demolished.

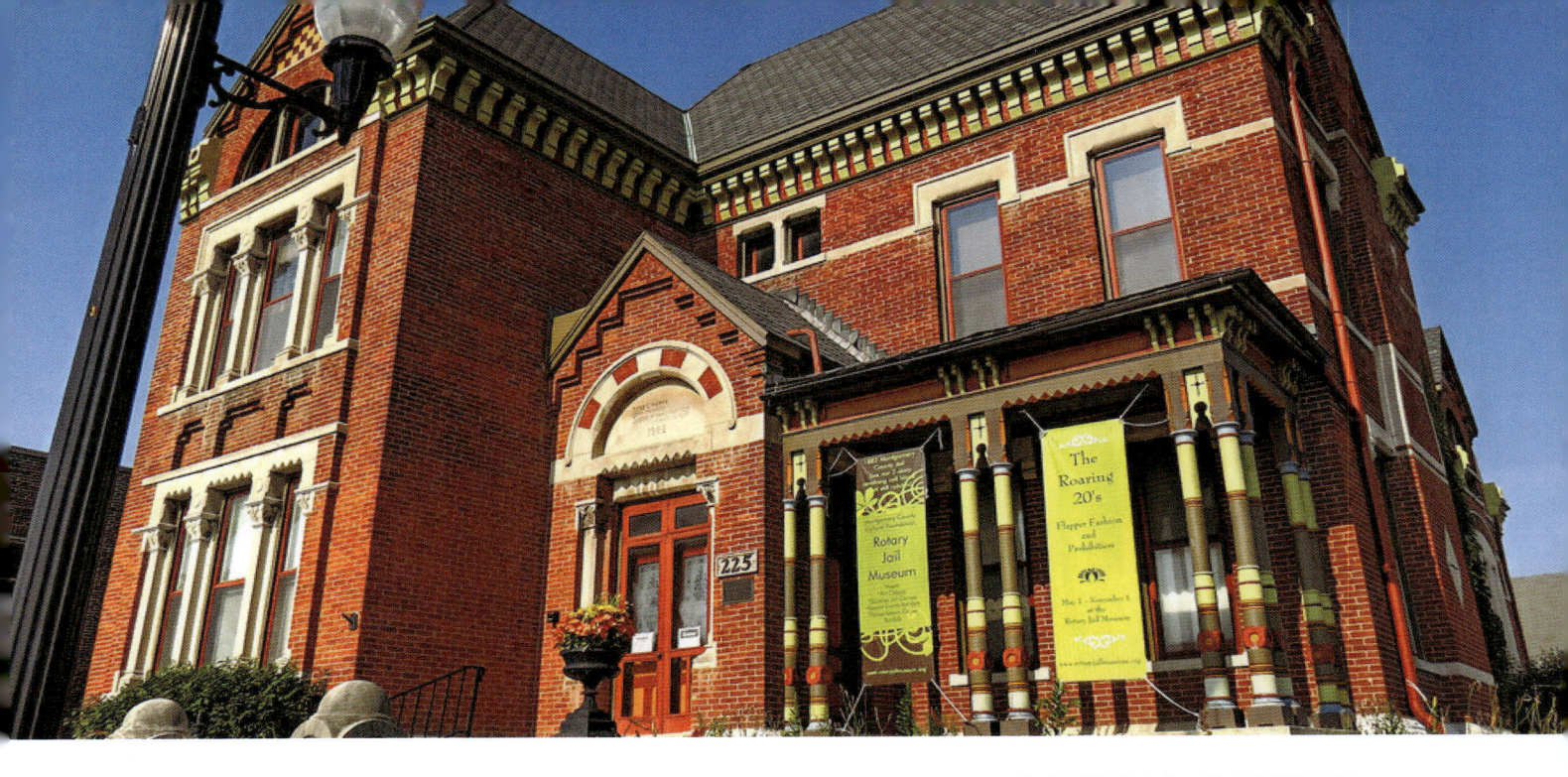

61. THE MARKET STREET CATACOMBS

39.7688, -86.15344
222 E Market St, Indianapolis, IN 46204
www.indianalandmarks.org

< Left and above: Rotary Jail Museum
Bottom right: John Dillinger's Grave

THE JAZZ / WHISKY RUN ROUTE 3

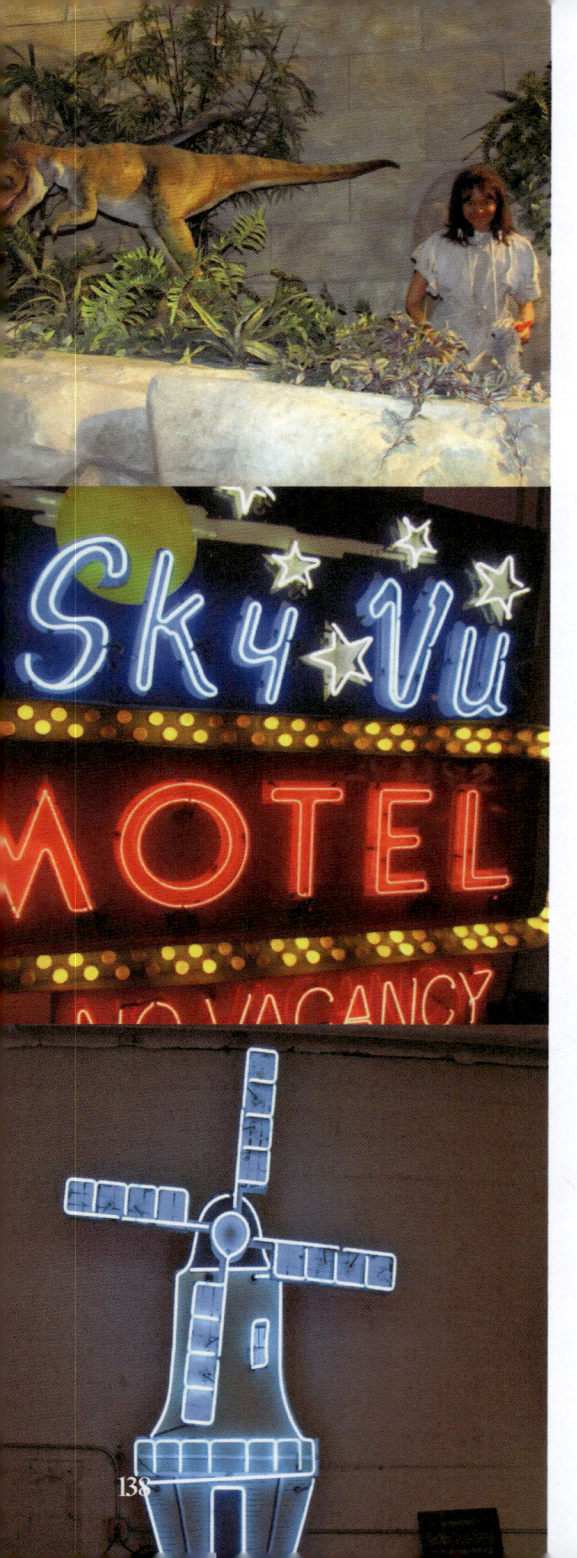

Top left and > bottom right: The Creation Museum
Centre left and bottom left: American Sign Museum
> Top : The Ruins, Holliday Park

These catacombs running beneath the city were built in the 1880s to transport and store meat in the market prior to the advent of refrigeration, as it stayed at such a cool constant temperature. Tours are few and far between - try your luck Googling for them, or ask around the City Market - some caretakers have even been known to let visitors down for a peek.

62. JOHN DILLINGER'S GRAVE
39.82553, -86.17212
700 38th St, Indianapolis, IN 46208
www.crownhill.org
Famed depression-era outlaw Dillinger made this his final resting place after his shootout with police.

63. THE RUINS, HOLLIDAY PARK
39.8711, -86.1612
6363 Spring Mill Rd, Indianapolis, IN 46260
These grandiose stone figures of the 1890s once adorned the now razed St. Paul Building Manhattan and were sculpted to appear as if they were supporting the weight of the high rise towering above them.

64. USS SACHEM RUINS
39.08104, -84.84863
Lawrenceburg Ferry Rd, Petersburg, KY 41080
The Ohio River harbours a ghost ship which first launched in 1902 as the Celt, a luxury yacht for a rich railroad exec, before fighting in two World Wars, firstly as the Sachem after being rented by the Navy who recognised it could potentially out-manoeuvre enemy vessel. Edison was given the boat by the Navy as a base from which to invent new ways of destroying submarines - he sailed it mostly around New York. It then changed hands several times again - one captain used it for fishing and charged the public $2 to board it to drink cocktails on board, fish or otherwise enjoy the feeling of owning a luxury yacht. The Navy called the boat up again after the advent of Pearl Harbour, renaming it the USS Phenakite where it acted as a patrol vessel in Key West Harbour. After briefly returning to its fishing owner, the boat was sold into Circle Line Sightseeing as a passenger tour boat in New York City, taking on the name Circle Line V. Left at an abandoned pier in New Jersey after several years, it was restored by a new owner Mr Miller, during which time he was approached by a man who got out of a limousine, introduced himself as Madonna's representative, and asked whether it could feature in the video for Papa Don't Preach - a keen eye can spot it. Today it is anchored on Miller's property where it is sadly rusting into obscurity.

65. THE CREATION MUSEUM
39.08619, -84.78338
2800 Bullittsburg Church Rd, Petersburg, KY 41080
creationmuseum.org

139

The ideal spot for anyone who is certain that the world is less than 6000 years old despite the existence of…well… natural history and science, and is pretty confident that humans and dinosaurs hung out together.

66. AMERICAN SIGN MUSEUM
39.1435, -84.5399
1330 Monmouth Ave, Cincinnati, OH 45225
www.americansignmuseum.org
This collection does justice to what is a phenomenal history of US signwriting.

67. LUCKY CAT MUSEUM
39.12713, -84.4991
2511 Essex Pl, Cincinnati, OH 45206
www.manekinekomuseum.com
This must be the luckiest museum this side of China.

68. THE CINCINNATI MUSHROOM HOUSE
39.14117, -84.42372
3518 Tarpis Ave, Cincinnati, OH 45208
Burning dream to live in a mushroom? The answer for Mr. Terry Brown was yes.

69. VENT HAVEN MUSEUM
39.0529, -84.5519
33 W Maple Ave, Fort Mitchell, KY 41011
www.venthavenmuseum.com
Over 800 ventriloquial dolls in one place. Ventriloquism originated as a religious practice, coming from the Latin for 'to speak from the stomach', venter (belly) and loqui (speak). In Greek this was known as gastromancy. The religious aspect was due to the notion that the noises produced by the stomach were the noises of the dead taking up residence in the stomach of the ventriloquist - as such figures were thought to be able to not only speak with the dead but foretell the future, they would then interpret the sounds. Prophets in ancient Greece used the technique commonly and this continued into more modern times; when acts of Spiritualism such as mediums took to the stage, leading to acts such as stage magic and escapology, so ventriloquism transitioned into a performance in the early 19th century, losing its religious undertones in the way that a modern Derren Brown has shed the concept that he can 'really' read minds that would have prevailed in earlier times. The first known performance of ventriloquism as an act was in England in 1753 when a Hogarth engraving depicted Sir John Parnell speaking via his hand, whilst in 1757, an Austrian Baron used a small doll in his performance,

Above: Lucky Cat Museum
Right: The Cincinnati Mushroom House
Overleaf: Vent Haven Museum

141

PLEASE DO NOT HANDLE

Kenny Talk

USED BY: Lt. Lee Allen Estes, Lexington, KY

RECEIVED FROM: Ted Estes, son, summer 1967.

FIGURE MAKER: George & Glenn McElroy, Harrison, OH, May 6, 1940.

HISTORY: Figure was made to W.S. specifications in 1940 and later sold to Estes.

launching the ventriloquist's dummy phenomenon. None the less, even by the late 18th century it was rare for dolls to be used; most merely made their voices appear as if from far away. The dolls really caught on in the late 1800s based largely on an influential performer called Fred Russell from Nottingham who used a doll in his acts and who others followed. This museum, apart from being frankly a sight out of a horror movie and founded by a man named William Shakespeare Berger (known as W.S.Berger presumably to avoid derision), is open by appointment only and gathers much memorabilia related to the art. Vent Haven is also come to the conVENTion, a gathering of 'vents' as they are known which has been meeting for 40 some years.

70. FLORENCE Y'ALL WATER TOWER
38.9977, -84.6479
500 Mall Circle Rd, Florence, KY 41042
1970s developers of the (then soon to open) Florence Mall painted a giant advertisement on a Florence water tower.

71. BEAVERLICK
38.87895, -84.69439
Beaverlick, KY 41094
Strange US place name - This fur trading site of the 1780's has a name inspired by the local creek.

72. ARK ENCOUNTER
38.62225, -84.5923
1 Ark Encounter Dr, Williamstown, KY 41097
arkencounter.com
Ever wondered what an EXACT replica of the Ark with EXACT dimensions would look like? No nor did we, but to see what happens when someone figures out what those exact dimensions were and asks supporters to donate a princely sum of $100 million to visualise this calculation in wood form (rather than to say… fighting malaria epidemics) head to Kentucky. The park's opening was due to be protested using a nearby billboard depicting people drowning around the Ark with the caption 'Genocide and Incest Park: Celebrating 2,000 years of myths' but the billboard companies turned down the design. Bill Nye toured the Ark with proponent Ken Ham, stating "It's all very troubling. You have hundreds of school kids there who have already been indoctrinated and who have been brainwashed, this is about the absolutely wrong idea that the Earth is 6,000 years old - that's alarming to me" to which Ken Ham replied "My biggest concern is you're teaching generations of young people that they're just animals". The debate ended when Ham asked "so we're related to a banana?" to which Nye replied "Yes". In December 2016 for Christmas, the Ark was lit with rainbow colours to 'reclaim the symbol from the gay rights movement'. As of February 2017, Ken Ham announced that this rainbow lighting would be made permanent.

73. ROSE ISLAND AMUSEMENT PARK
38.4498, -85.6456
Rose Island, Charlestown Township, IN 47111
Once a rec area belonging to a church camp, Fern Grove (as it was then called) was developed in the early Twenties by the eponymous David Rose to include a classic wooden rollercoaster like that found in Coney Island, (this one named the Devil's Backbone after the nearby rock formation), a Ferris wheel and a small zoo containing wolves, monkeys and a black bear named Teddy Roosevelt. Dances were also held and in winter, ice skating. Access was via a steamboat or footbridge. The Great Depression had its effect on takings but the park's eventual closure was actually due to the great flood of 1937. The concrete pilings of the original footbridge can still be found from a hiking trail and although for a long time there was no land access to the area, in 2011 a bridge was established to cross the creek and connect the island for the first time, although little to nothing remains today but memories, the odd brick footing and for the keen of eye, the swimming pool.

> Top left: Rose Island Amusement Park
> Top right: Pope Lick Trestle Bridge

> Bottom left: Florence Y'all Water Tower
Overleaf: Ark Encounter

74. POPE LICK TRESTLE BRIDGE
38.19761, -85.49267
Pope Lick, Kentucky

The Pope Lick Monster, another of America's die hard urban legends of a man come goat come sheep come demonic farmer come circus freak depending on which version you listen to who either lures or hypnotises his victims to their deaths from or on the bridge, leaps onto cars or pushes pedestrians in front of trains has been going on time immemorial. Which would make it just another urban tale...were it not for the 'legend trippers' and their often deadly tenacity in tracking down an old story. In the case of Pope Lick, a high trestle bridge, the danger is not only in the height of the bridge, but the misconception that it is abandoned whilst it is in fact a major train route. The rail companies have made pleas to young people threatening prosecution and imploring visitors that any movie footage showing train avoiders hanging beneath bridges is unrealistic due to the strength required and force of the train vibrations overhead, but this has not deterred numerous people from getting into

THE JAZZ / WHISKY RUN ROUTE 3

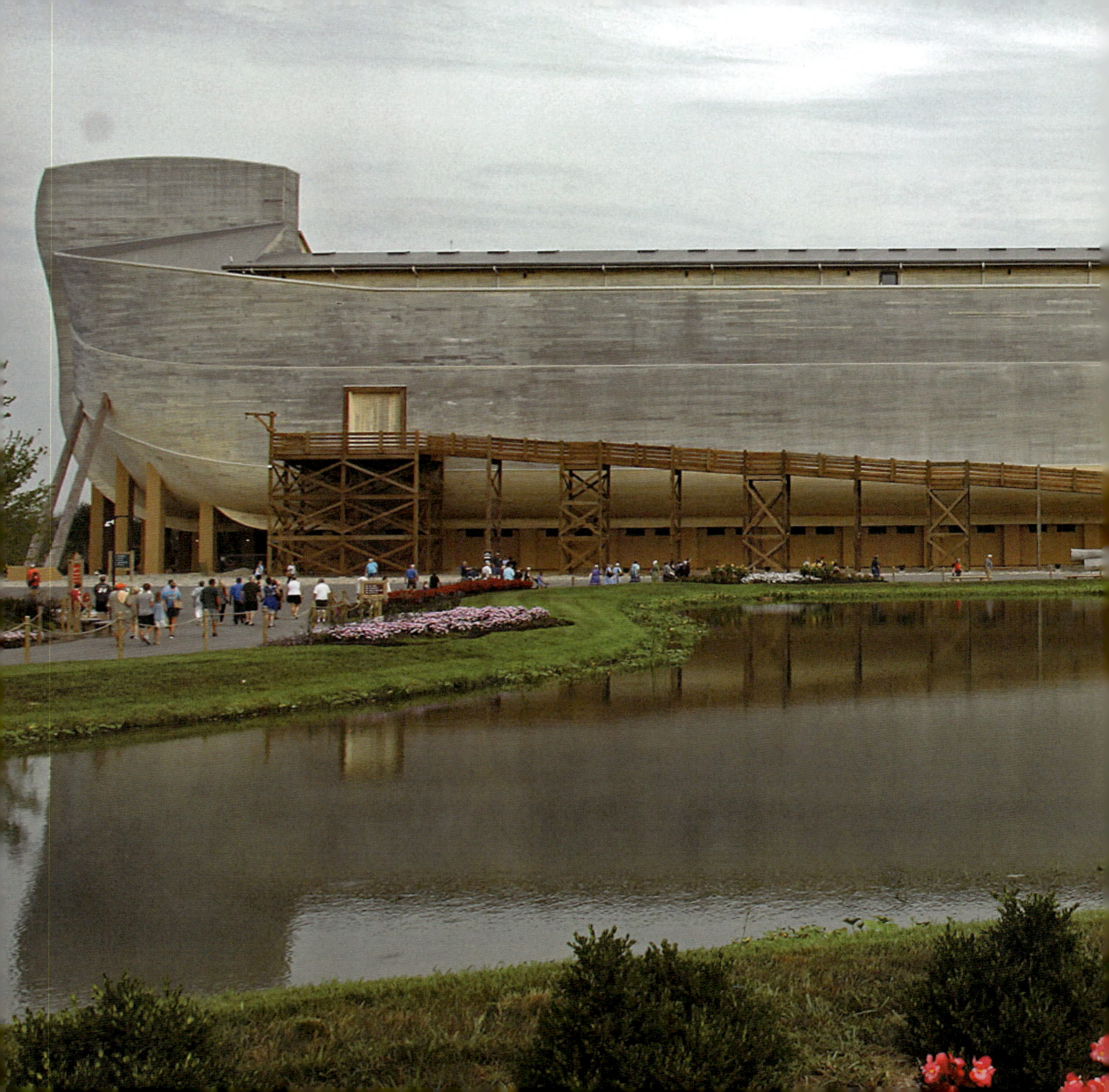

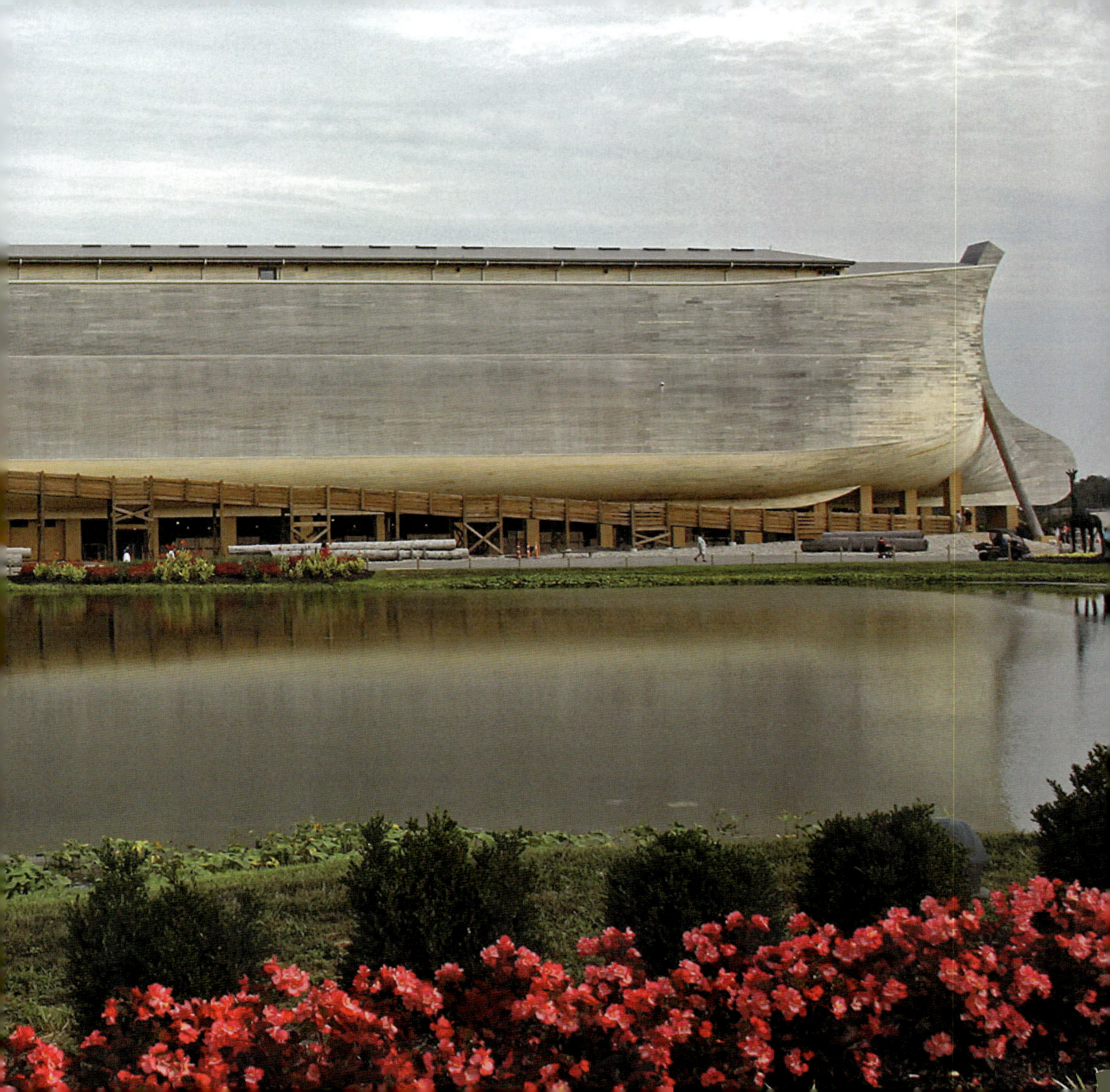

difficulty. One young couple, 26 year old surgical assistant Roquel Bain and her boyfriend, were trailing the monster when they were caught unawares by an oncoming train. Outrunning the train to the other side is almost impossible. The unfortunate girl was hit by the train, falling to the river below, although her boyfriend did in fact manage to grip onto the side of the bridge, climbing back up before being rescued. He later confirmed that he had thought the bridge abandoned. They are not alone - Jack Bahm II, 17, from Spalding University was struck and killed whilst crossing the bridge in 1987; a memorial dedicated to him in graffiti can be found on the bridge's base out of harm's way. In May of the same year, 19 year old David Bryant died of injuries received from jumping from the bridge a year previously to dodge a train. In 2000, 19 year old Nicholas Jewell fell whilst trying to hang off the trestle until a train had passed. The fact that an official Visit Louisville instagram account posted an image of the bridge with 'If you haven't climbed the Pope Lick Train Trestle, you haven't lived!' probably hasn't aided the situation. Many others have committed suicide from the bridge, had close calls or been rescued, but this doesn't stop others from trying. Stay well away and appreciate the legend from a distance if you plan to visit.

75. CAVE HILL CEMETERY
38.24369, -85.72625
701 Baxter Ave, Louisville, KY 40204
Beautiful Victorian garden cemetery containing the graves of Colonel Sanders and most recently Muhammad Ali (Grave -1) .

76. EASTERN CEMETERY
38.24618, -85.72499
641 Baxter Ave, Louisville, KY 40204
One of 3 Louisville Cemeteries (along with Greenwood and Schardein) owned by The Louisville Crematories and Cemetery Company who were discovered, in 1989, to have been burying bodies in occupied graves since the 1920s. The remains of 48,000 people were buried in this stacked manner, enabling the company to keep selling lots when they had long ago run out of them. Maps from 1880, 1907, 162 and 1984 are therefore completely inconsistent with one another and the cemetery now lies largely abandoned, the company dissolved.

77. COLONEL SANDERS' GRAVE
38.2449, -85.72789
641 Baxter Ave, Louisville, KY 40204
The man behind the chicken, immortalized forever in a way that a Twister wrap can't.

78. THE GRAVE OF HARRY L COLLINS
38.2449, -85.72789
641 Baxter Ave, Louisville, KY 40204
Known as the Frito-Lay Magician, this much loved illusionist arranged for a life size monument of a magician to call passing visitors to his graveside. Many leave a red carnation in his outstretched hand.

79. WAVERLY HILLS SANITORIUM
38.13021, -85.84129
4400 Paralee Dr, Louisville, KY 40272
www.therealwaverlyhills.com
This tuberculosis sanatorium opened in 1910 to house 50 patients suffering from the White Plague, but closed in 1961 due to the advent of the Streptomycin antibiotic which outmoded the need for such facilities. The building was initially constructed in wood and patients were housed in tents on the grounds before construction was completed. It was then upgraded to its current style in 1926. Various buyers have tried to convert the buildings; a prison was voiced in 1983 which then lost funding, followed by a proposal by Christ the Redeemer Foundation who planned to build the world's tallest statue of Jesus Christ on the roof of the buildings, along with a worship, arts centre and gift shop. The statue had a proposed cost of $4M, whilst the rest of the buildings were due to cost $8M and relied upon donations; sadly these only came in at $3,000, leading to the project's cancellation in 1997. Featuring on every ghost hunting TV show imaginable, see it now in its original state before currently mooted plans to convert it into a hotel take flight.

> Top left and bottom: Cave Hill Cemetery
> Top right: Waverly Hills Sanitorium

HEFFNER HERMAN

COL. HARLAND SANDERS

COL. HARLAND SANDERS
AND HIS WIFE
CLAUDIA

149

80. WEST BADEN SPRINGS HOTEL
38.5671, -86.61843
8670 W State St, French Lick Township, IN 47432
www.frenchlick.com

Now better known as part of the French Lick Resort, this historic building's dome was, from shortly after it was built from 1902 to 1913, the largest in the world. When it opened it was nicknamed the Eighth Wonder of the World but then several claims were somewhat overstated in the advertising, including the fact that it had 200 rooms more than it actually possessed. That said, what it did have on offer was pretty spectacular, including its stunning natatorium swimming pool. In its day it represented the Disney World of its time and visitors to America would almost always factor in a stay here. Al Capone and his bodyguards were frequent guests as was Diamond Jim Brady and the governor of New York Al Smith. The hotel was substantially renovated in 1918 by a financier called Ballard who started his career in the hotel's bowling alley but hit the big time running a major illegal gambling business in the area. He went on to own several major touring circuses and during this period the hotel was used to treat injured war veterans. The Great Depression hit West Baden as badly as elsewhere and within hours of the crash, the guests began to take their leave. The hotel closed in 1932. Either due to concern over competition or a change of morality, Ballard refused to sell out to anyone who planned to turn the venue into a speakeasy offering gambling or vices - perhaps morality won out, as he later donated all $7 million of the resort to the Society of Jesus. The Jesuits used it as a seminary removing all luxury decor, dumping stone into the mineral pool springs which were capped with concrete and turned into shrines to saints. Low enrolment closed the seminary (a cemetery featuring where priests were buried remains), and a school was founded in its place. It struggled to be successfully redeveloped until someone realised that Ballard's return to grace was what had essentially started the rot and that gambling was the way to go, turning it into a successful casino. Who was awarded the gambling licence? Why The Trump Organisation of course, although his subsequent bankruptcy rendered new plans a necessity. Today a company called Blue Sky run the casino and renovated it back in 2005 to its present condition. Michael Koryta's thriller So Cold the River (2010) is set in the hotel.

81. BLUE FLASH BACKYARD ROLLER COASTER
38.78112, -87.46688
6997 N Ivers Rd, Bruceville, IN 47516
Which self-respecting grandfather hasn't thought of building a rollercoaster in their back yard.

82. THE COMMUNITY OF RAPTURE
38.15222, -87.84194
Rapture, Harmony Township, IN 47633
Once called both Winfield and Bugtown (the airport is called Bugtown Airport), it is thought that this unincorporated community was named after a local horse called Rapture owned by a Dr. James Cooper.

83. THE TOWN OF BACON
38.41061, -86.43331
Bacon, IN 47118
Amusing US place name, etymology unknown.

84. SANTA CLAUS
38.12005, -86.91416
Santa Claus, IN 47579
With a population of 2481, Santa Claus is the largest community in Spencer County. Established in 1854 when it was named Santa Fe (pronounced 'fee' just to be difficult), it was forced to change its name when it was banned from having a post office in the name Santa Fe due to the existence of another Sante Fe, Indiana. Many town meetings were held, and duly the name Santa Claus was chosen. Why? We may never know. This town has the claim of being the world's only post office bearing the name Santa Claus officially. Thousands of letters arrive to Santa each year from all over the world, necessitating that a group of volunteers called Santa's Elves (obviously) reply to every single letter to avoid disappointment - so it has been since 1914 if not earlier. Most residents live within the gated Christmas Lake Village, built on three lakes, Lake Holly, Lake Noel and Christmas Lake. All street names of course are Xmas themed. The remaining residents largely reside in Holiday Village. Visit Santa's Candy Castle, Santa Claus Museum, the somewhat confusingly named Holiday World and Splashin' Safari (home of what is voted the number one wooden rollercoaster in the world), Frosty's Fun Center, Christmas Lake Golf Course and Santa's Stables all built by wily entrepreneurs who don't miss a trick. The locations have been voted by Forbes as one of the World's Top Christmas Destinations.

85. MAMMOTH CAVE
37.18699, -86.10052
1 Mammoth Cave Pkwy, Mammoth Cave, KY 42259
www.nps.gov
Visit the longest stretch of cave in the known world, on Mammoth Cave Parkway, near Old Mammoth Cave Road, in Cave City.

86. FLOYD COLLINS MUSEUM
37.1502, -86.0441
The Wayfarer Bed & Breakfast, 1240 Old Mammoth Cave Rd, Cave City, KY 42127
A bed and breakfast with an exhibit dedicated to poor Floyd Collins, an explorer with a penchant for caves. Having discovered Crystal Cave but being disappointed with the attention the much larger local Mammoth Cave was receiving, Collins was working on a way to enter Sand Cave, a giant cavern, in 1925. In what must be the worst imaginable outcome for a cave explorer, his light went out 100 foot underground and whilst feeling his way around, he knocked a rock onto his leg which held him firmly in place. After some time he was discovered, still hanging onto life, and whilst rescue proved challenging, it was possible to bring him food and water. Whilst this was on-going the media went into full frenzy and souvenir stalls began to gather around the cave to cater to the many onlookers and journalists who hoarded around the cave. On Feb 4th, 5 days after he became

< Left: Santa Claus
Overleaf: Wedt Baden Springs Hotel

THE JAZZ / WHISKY RUN ROUTE 3

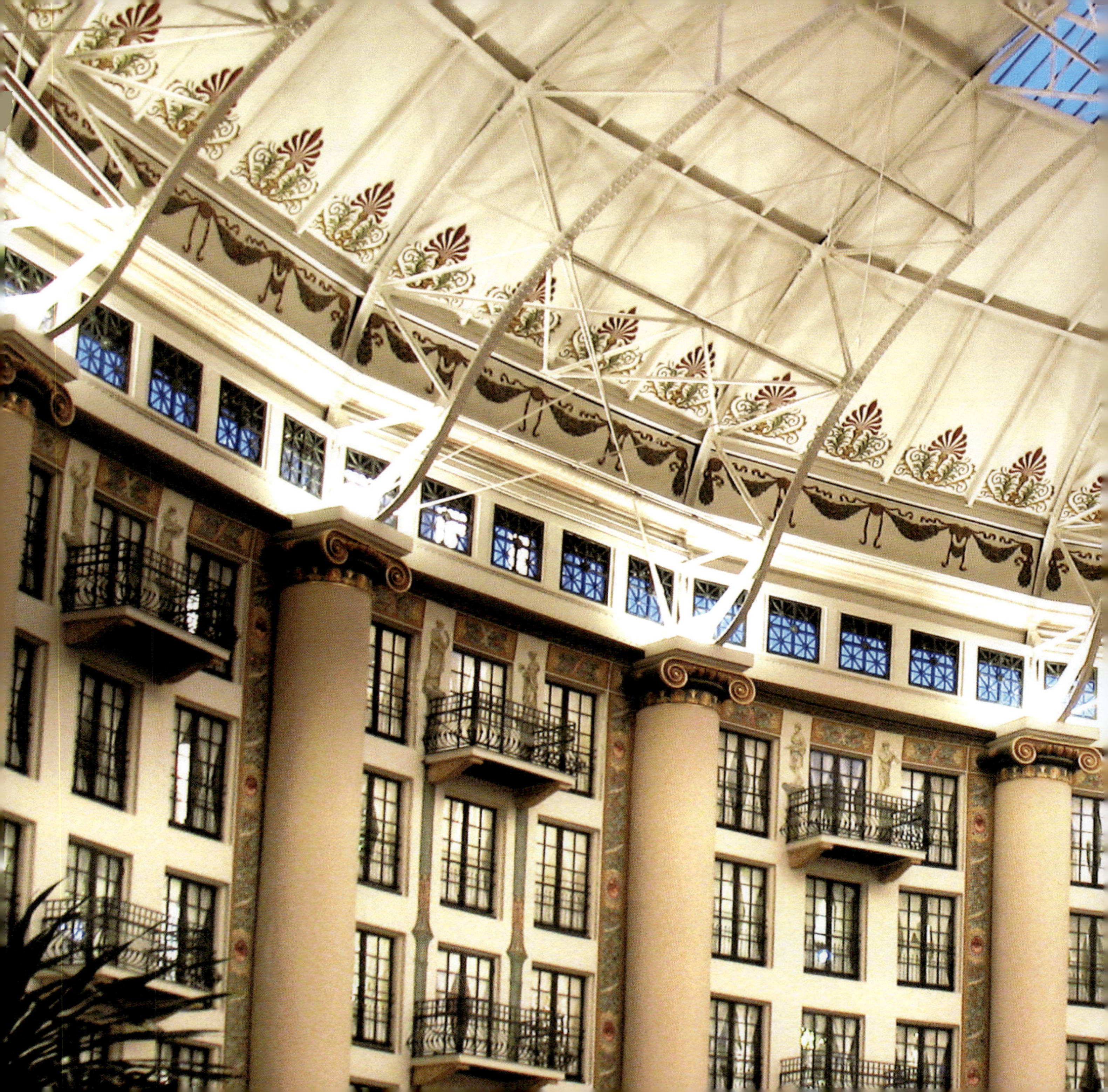

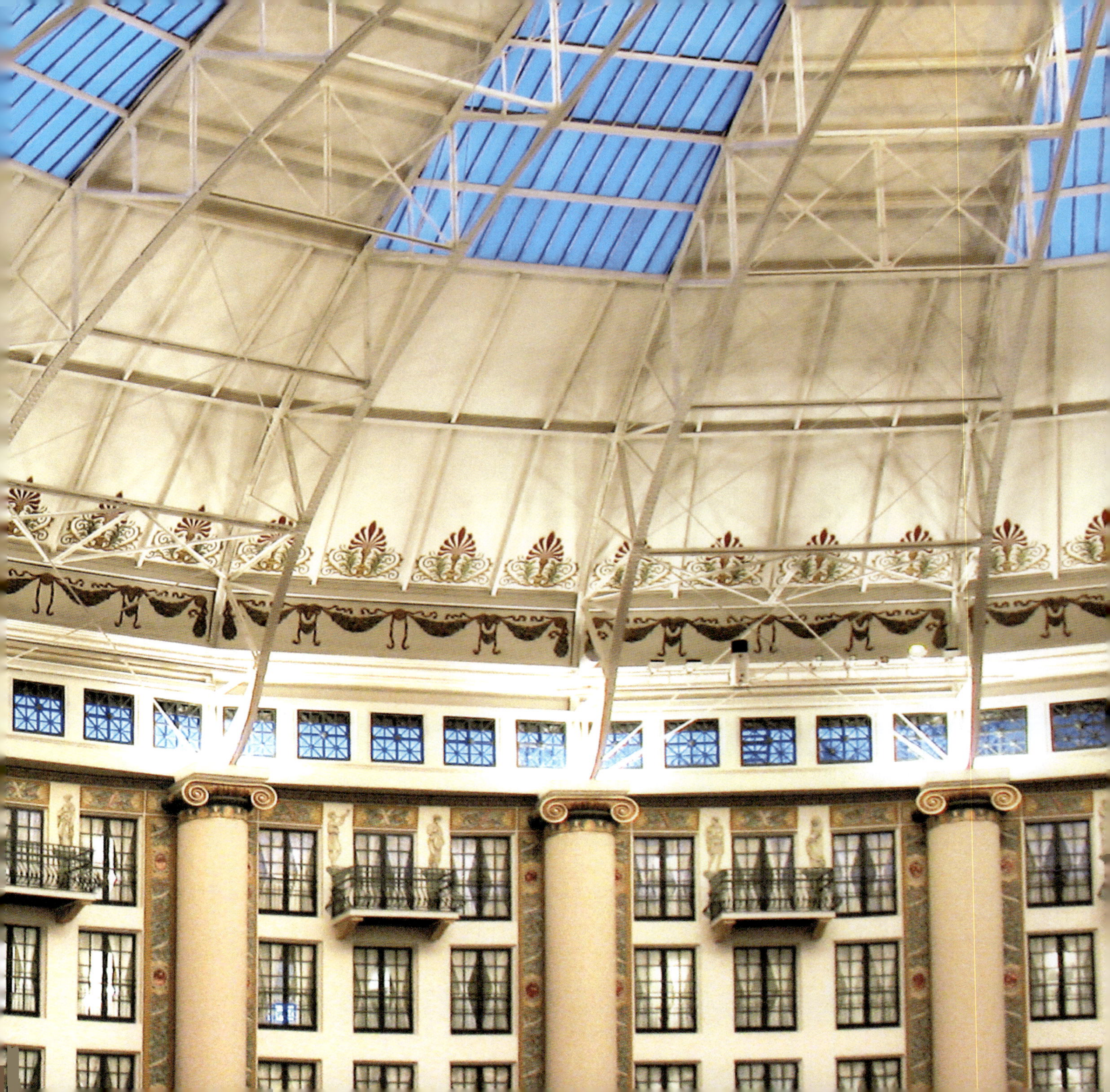

trapped, the unthinkable happened and the tunnel used to reach him collapsed. When it was dug out once again, he was found dead. It took two months to reach his body which was them embalmed and buried on his family's Crystal Cave property. When the Collins family left the house for greener pastures, the new owners had a great idea to attract custom to the afterthought that was Crystal Cave, digging up Collins' body and putting it in a glass lidded coffin for all to see in the middle of the cave, the last place he would undoubtedly have wanted to be trapped. The plan worked a treat and poor Collins didn't make it back into a grave until 1989, where he is now buried in Mammoth Cave Baptist Church Cemetery. The museum at the bed and breakfast documents these occurrences.

87. WIGWAM VILLAGE 2
37.1449, -85.9452
601 N Dixie Hwy, Cave City, KY 42127
www.wigwamvillage.com

Sleep in a throwback to the heyday of themed motels back in the 1900s. Known by its full title of Wigwam Village #2 (as there were originally seven such villages), only two others now remain as the others were razed after falling into decline; #6 in Holbrook Arizon and #7 in Riallton, California. It still stands as one man's incarnation of the American dream come true,

Top left: National Corvette Museum Sinkhole
Bottom left: Dinosaur World

inspired by both an ice-cream shop its creator Frank A. Redford had seen which was shaped like an inverted ice-cream cone as well as a real wigwam on a Dakota reservation. The Village was built to surround Redford's existing museum and gift shop which housed his collection of Native American artefacts. Frank patented his design; when motel operator Chester E. Lewis built Village #6 in Arizona, he had to get permission from Redford to use both the name and the design and in a feat of early royalty-based brand licensing, in 1950 coin-operated radios were installed in the village which would play 30 minutes of broadcast for every dime inserted, with all profits going to Frank Redford. Redford's original designs all incorporated swastikas on the front of the wigwams, which symbolised peace and was associated at the time with the Navajo and Plains Nations such as the Dakota. The name Wigwam is also something of a misnomer - a wigwam is domed which a tipi or tepee is a cone shaped tent, something whilst presumably the somewhat smug Tee Pee Motel of Wharton Texas not only knew but perhaps used to cunningly avoid any royalty issues.

88. DINOSAUR WORLD

37.1358, -85.9830

711 Mammoth Cave Rd, Cave City, KY 42127

www.dinosaurworld.com

If taking snapshots of giant life-like dinos in a natural setting to give your friends the impression you holidayed at Jurassic Park is your thing, get down to Dinosaur World Kentucky, the creation of a Swedish entrepreneur with an eye for opportunity. To add to the realism, kids can dig for real fossils at this location.

89. NATIONAL CORVETTE MUSEUM SINKHOLE

37.00403, -86.37452

National Corvette Museum, 350 Corvette Dr, Bowling Green, KY 42101

This Corvette Museum was struck by an enormous sinkhole which opened up right beneath the valuable corvettes causing untold damage and huge media coverage. See photography of the event and learn about the restoration efforts in the Sinkhole Experience at the self-same site

90. SOUTH UNION SHAKER VILLAGE

36.88418, -86.64411

850 Shaker Museum Rd, Auburn, KY 42206

www.southunionshakervillage.com

Shakers were called such due to their exuberant worship style involving dancing, jumping and twitching. This colony struggled through the Civil War which they objected to and was sold off in 1922, however many of the original buildings remain along with informative exhibits where you can learn more about this religion and its way of life.

Right: The Bell Witch Cave
Overleaf: Wigwam Village

THE JAZZ / WHISKY RUN ROUTE 3

155

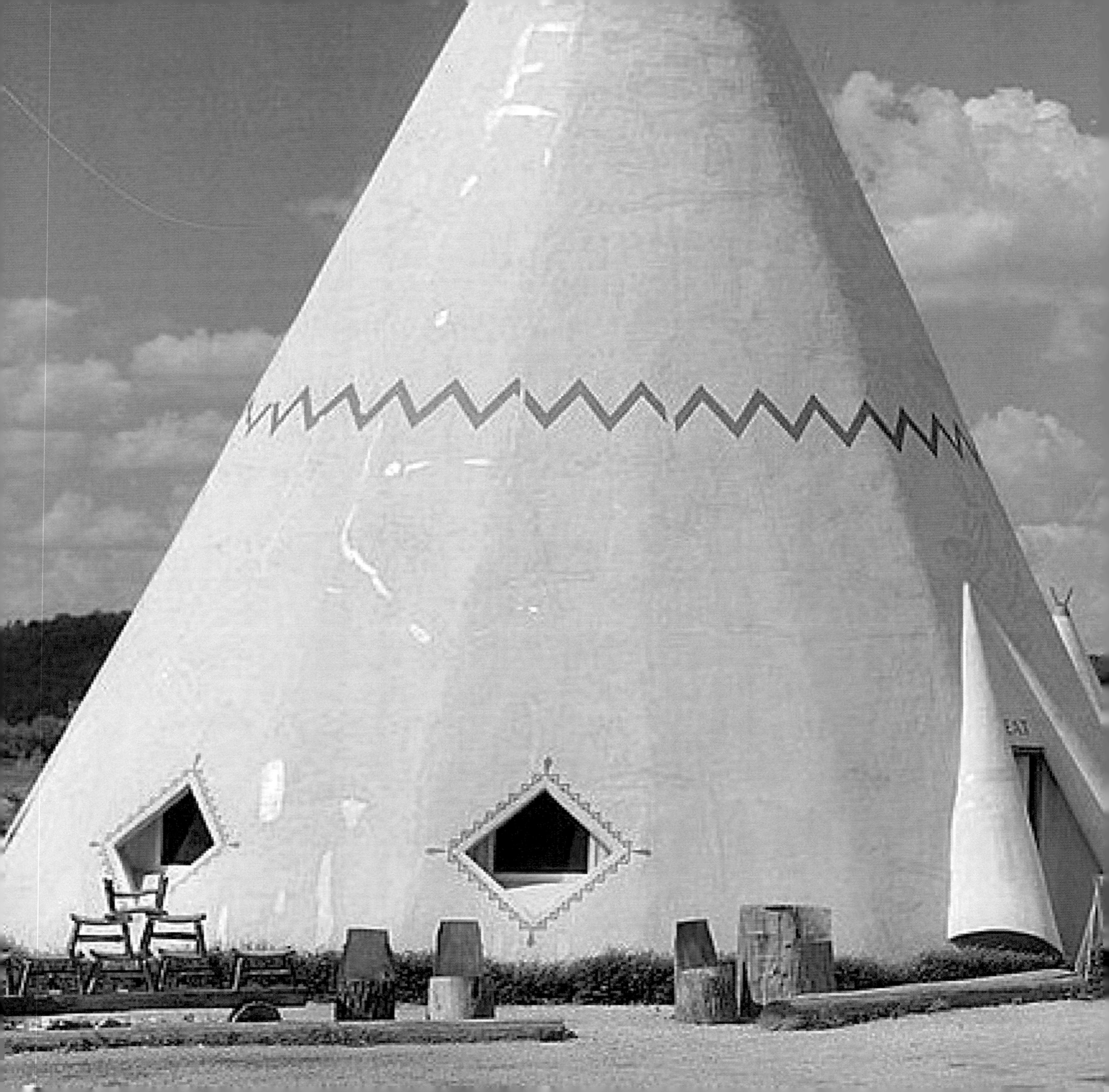

EAT AND SLEEP
IN A
WIGWAM
AAA
STANDARD
OIL
PRODUCTS
ICE CREAM

91. THE BELL WITCH CAVE
36.59074, -87.06072
430 Keysburg Rd, Adams, TN 37010
www.bellwitchcave.com
1817: an evil witch terrorises a family before poisoning the patriarch to death. The cave she was said to reside in when not busy terrorising is said to be hugely haunted and can be explored by the brave today.

92. E T WICKHAM SCULPTURE TRAIL
36.41579, -87.46449
Oak Ridge Road, Palmyra, TN 37142
A tobacco farmer born in 1883 began creating sculptures in his later years and continued until he died. His family are now trying to prevent the works from falling into disrepair as vandals have compromised them in the intervening years.

93. AQUARIUM RESTAURANT
36.20533, -86.69354
516 Opry Mills Dr, Nashville, TN 37214
www.aquariumrestaurants.com
Dine in a 200,000 gallon, subtly underwater-themed restaurant.

94. HERMITAGE HOTEL
36.1637, -86.78245
231 6th Ave N, Nashville, TN 37219
www.thehermitagehotel.com
A grand historic hotel from 1910 with a men's toilet so beautiful and with so many accolades, they now allow women in to view it.

95. CONCRETE PARTHENON
36.1524, -86.7894
2500 West End Ave, Nashville, TN 37203
Authentically sized but less authentically built of..well..concrete, this is 'America telling you to not travel elsewhere' at its best.

96. SPACESHIP HOUSE
35.10629, -85.34839
Palisades Road, Signal Mountain, TN 37377
Flying saucer house, now available as a vacation rental.

97. RACCOON MOUNTAIN CAVERNS
35.0235, -85.4084
319 W Hills Rd, Chattanooga, TN 37419
raccoonmountain.com
Pan for gemstones including amethyst, aventurine, quartz, peridot, ruby, raspberry quartz, topaz, rose quartz, quartz crystal points, sapphire, obsidian, citrine and emerald as well as ancient arrowheads and fossils in this large cave complex and keep what you find.

98. CORPSEWOOD MANOR
34.545, -85.2458
Black Springs Creek Road, Trion, GA 30753
This brick mansion belonged to a doctor and his wife who were murdered by two men with ties to the occult in a botched robbery

99. LICK FORK
34.84638, -86.23787
Lick Fork, Western, WV
Weird location name with etymology unknown although likely to refer simply to a local creek/'lick'.

100. DEAD CHILDREN'S PLAYGROUND
34.73152, -86.56515
1351 McClung Ave SE, Huntsville, AL 35801
The only children's playground liable to be located in the midst of...a graveyard?

Above: Aquarium Restaurant (prior page)
> Top right: Hermitage Hotel (prior page)
> Bottom right: Spaceship House
Overleaf: Concrete Parthenon

Only Cemetery of Its Kind In The World

ONLY COON HOUNDS ARE ALLOWED TO BE BURIED.

TROOP First Dog Laid To Rest Here Sept. 4, 1937

Please Be Careful With Fire

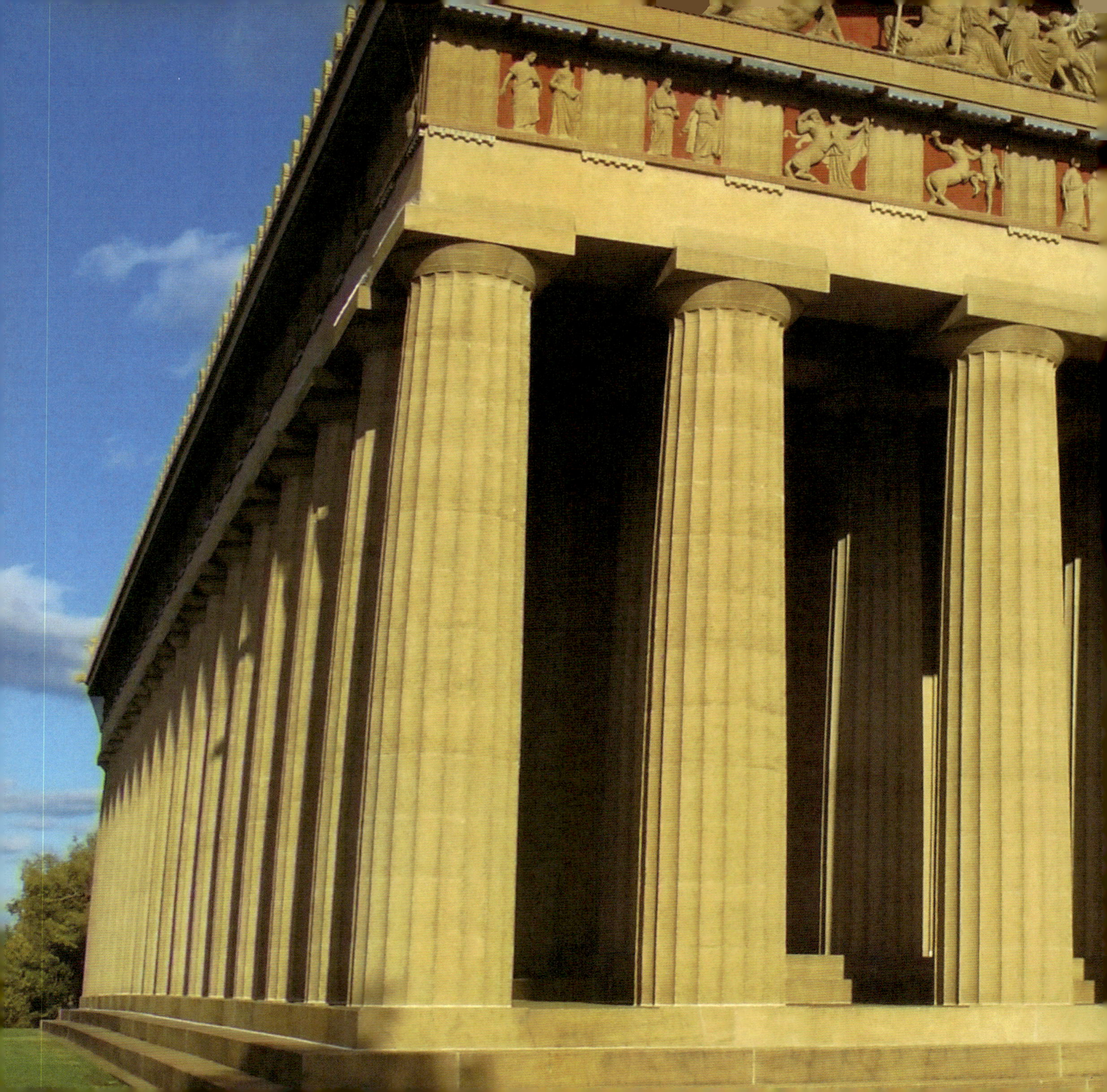

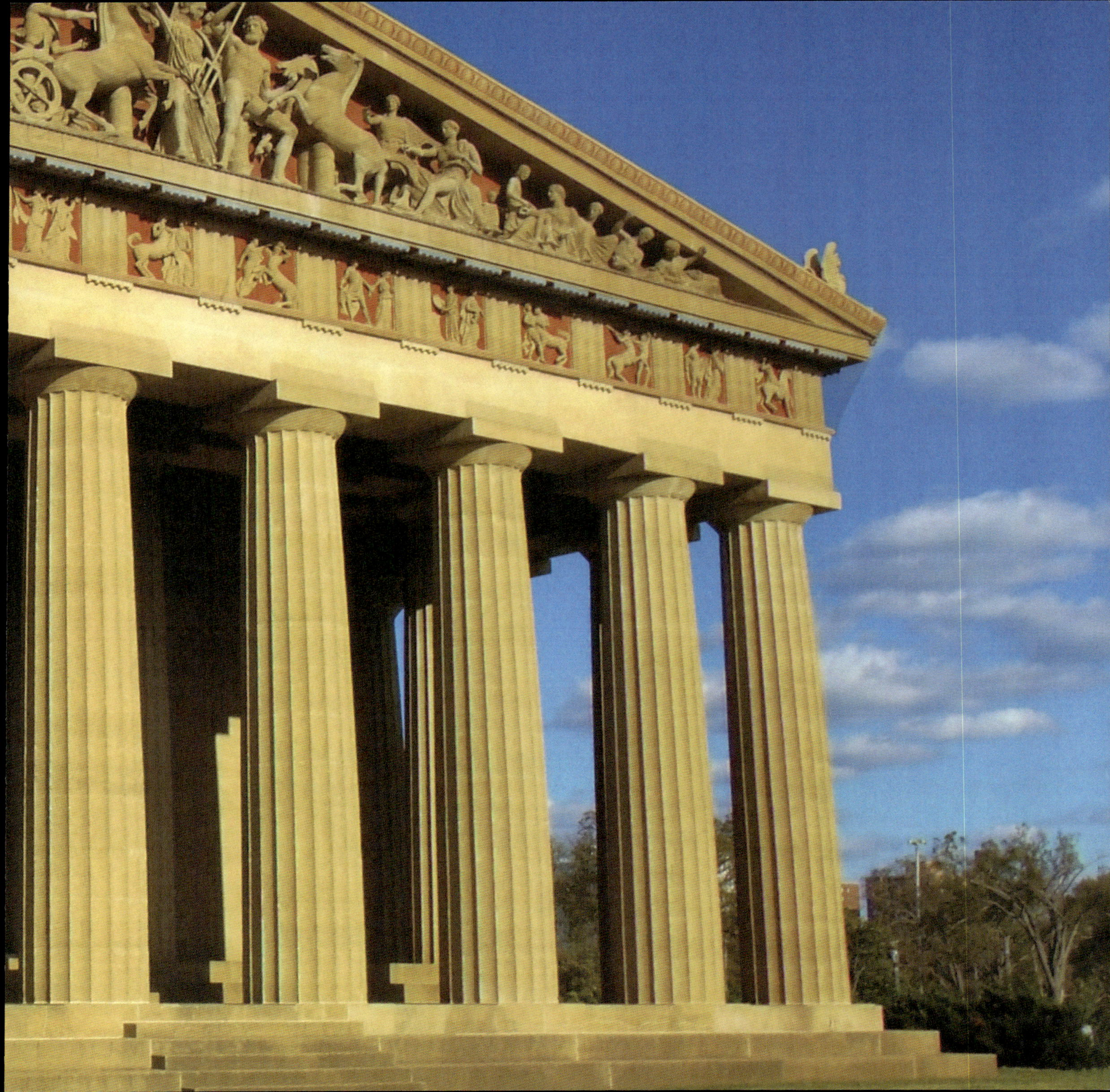

101. RATTLESNAKE SALOON
34.64819, -87.90778
1292 Mt Mills Rd, Tuscumbia, AL 35674
www.sevenspringslodge.net
Dine under a cliff overhang in this Old West style outdoor restaurant built into the rock.

102. KEY UNDERWOOD COON DOG CEMETERY
34.63005, -87.96682
4945 Coondog Cemetery Rd, Cherokee, AL 35616
www.coondogcemetery.com
The wonderfully named Mr Key Underwood of Alabama started this cemetery by burying his faithful hunting coondog (a dog for hunting racoons) named Troop in the camp in which the pair spent many happy years together - since that day, 185 others have travelled from all over the USA to lay their best friends to rest there too.

103. ROWAN OAK
34.35979, -89.52471
916 Old Taylor Rd, Oxford, MS 38655
William Faulkner's early Greek Revival house, which he largely restored himself and which notably contains an outline of his Pulitzer Prize-winning novel A Fable pencilled in graphite on the wall of his study. The house is named after the mythical tree and inspired much of Faulkner's concept that time exists in layers, due to the property's atmosphere of combining past and present in one.

104. THE MISSISSIPPI RIVER BASIN MODEL
32.2992, -90.3086
6180 McRaven Road, Jackson, Mississippi, 39209
This hydraulic large scale model of the Mississippi River basin was built by German and Italian POWs over a period of 23 years from 1943 onwards and operated from 1949 until the early seventies. Such models of which there are several in the USA serve to permit engineers to simulate weather systems and flooding, allowing them to test control measures and how they would affect the whole system. Unfortunately computer modelling came along and although the model was due to be curated as a tourist attraction, the cost proved too high, leading it to become dilapidated. It remains accessible to the public in its run down state today.

105. MARGARET'S GROCERY AND MARKET
32.4107, -90.8421
4535 N. Washington St., Vicksburg, Mississippi, 39183
Proprietors Reverend H. D. Dennis and his fifth wife Margaret Rogers Dennis invite you to The Home of the Double Headed Eagle, a market church complete with church bus which in turn is complete with a pulpit and pews. The sign 'The Church of Christ is the Only One All is Welcome Jews and Gentiles Here at Margaret's Gro. & Mkt. And Bible Class' perhaps gives you further flavour whilst in a twist, the double headed eagle is the symbol of the 32nd degree of the Scottish Rite and the golden letters B and J adorn the pillars outside the store, well known Masonic symbology. Another window carries the symbol for the Order of the Eastern Star.

106. ANGOLA PRISON RODEO
30.9407, -91.5693
17544 Tunica Trace, St Francisville, LA 70775
www.angolarodeo.com
This is either an example of prisoners being afforded too many rights, or a chance for them to get kicked in the teeth for their crimes. Either way, an unusual spectacle worth ticking off your list.

107. COTTAGE PLANTATION
30.85563, -91.37153
10528 Cottage Ln, St Francisville, LA 70775
www.cottageplantation.com
This incredibly intact plantation home is like stepping back in time.

108. THE MYRTLES PLANTATION
30.8034, -91.38804
St Francisville, LA 70775
www.myrtlesplantation.com
Touted as one of the USA's most haunted residences, this pretty plantation home in the Creole Cottage style has 22 rooms and is said to be built on an ancient Tunica Indian burial ground. 10 murders are said to have occurred on the property although only one has been

Overleaf left: Odd Fellows Rest
Overleaf right and following page: Orleans Six Flags Amusement Park

officially validated, that of an attorney who was shot by a stranger, then staggered inside and died attempting to crawl up the stairs on the 17th step in 1871. Stay the night if you dare.

109. CUT OFF
29.54271, -90.33813
W Main St., Cut Off, LA 70345
A strange location name with a logical etymology - A canal cutoff was built here to shorten its route, hence the name.

110. ODD FELLOWS REST
29.98134, -90.11029
5055 Canal St, New Orleans, LA 70119
A cemetery dedicated to the Odd Fellows order, a fraternity first documented in the UK in 1730 in London. One theory behind the unusual name is that most major trades in the UK were organised into Guilds; anyone with an unusual trade might have been labelled an 'odd trade' and may have joined other such individuals to become a larger group of 'odd fellows'. A second theory goes that at the time in which the fraternity came together at the beginning of the 18th century, it was said to be 'odd' to still value benevolence and charity. A third is that it was a lodge that opened its doors to anyone regardless of their position in society, thereby 'odd'.

111. THE SINGING OAK
29.9933, -90.0983
1 Palm Dr, New Orleans, LA 70124
A musical marvel hidden within a beautiful oak tree, the entire tree is effectively tuned to the pentatonic scale so as to be tuneful when caught by gusts of wind in a homage to rebirth in the wake of Katrina.

112. ORLEANS SIX FLAGS AMUSEMENT PARK
30.05515, -89.93169
3011 Michoud Blvd, New Orleans, LA 70129
Previously known as Jazzland, Six Flags has been closed since it was hit by Katrina in 2005 and entirely flooded, as the cost of repair was deemed too extortionate to be commercially viable. Trespassers are prosecuted. There are plans underway to return the park to its origins as Jazzland which is due to open in 2018. Portions of both Dawn of the Planet of the Apes and Jurassic World were filmed in the park.

Above: The Myrtles Plantation

ODD FELLOW'S REST

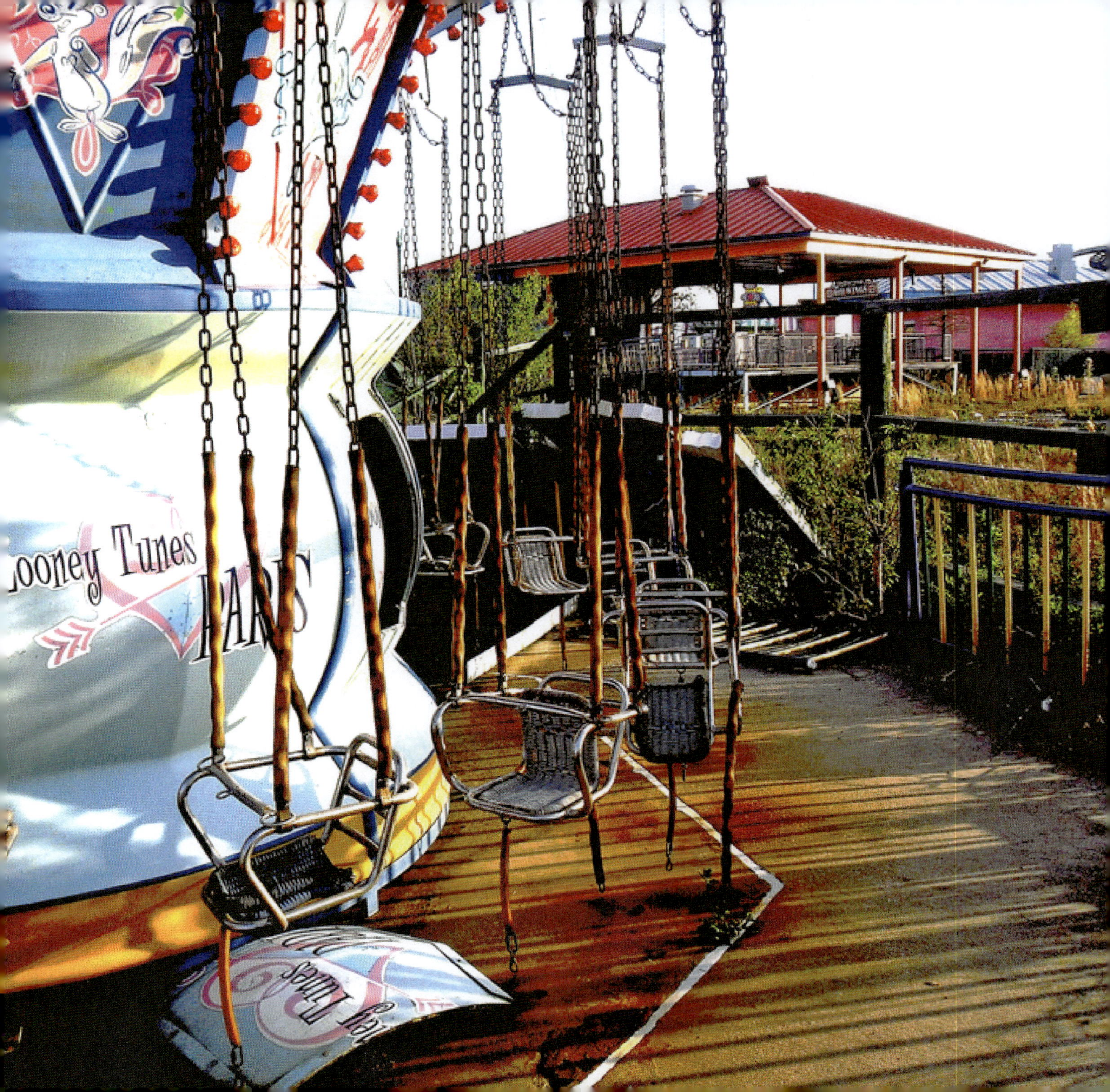
Looney Tunes
PARIS

2012
coming soon

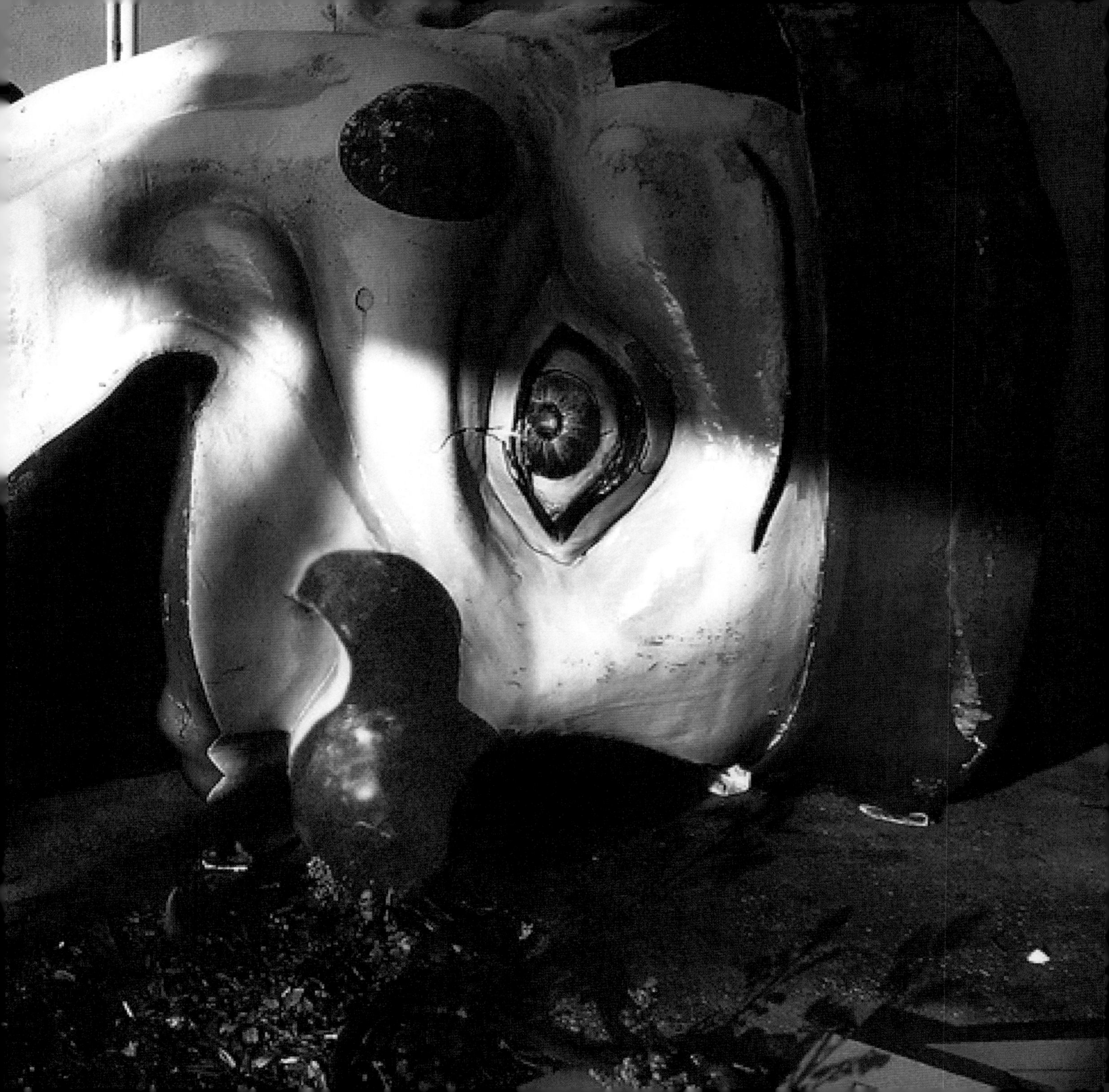

THE DETROIT HUB ROUTE 4

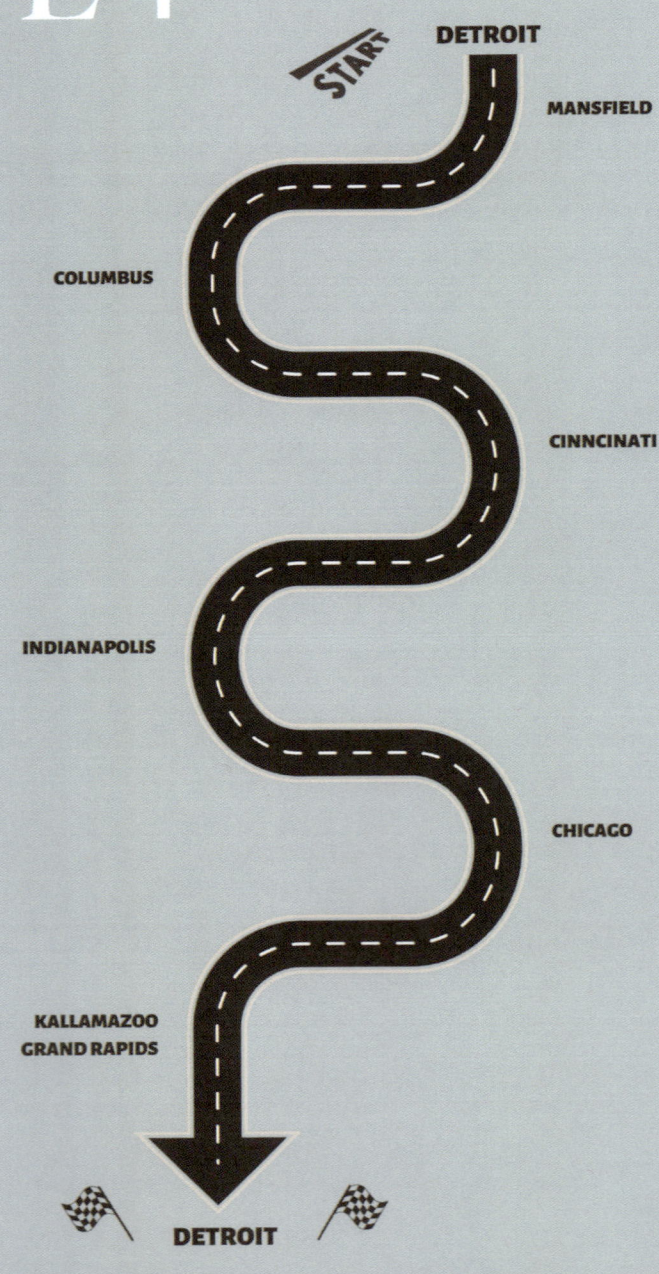

START

DETROIT

MANSFIELD

COLUMBUS

CINNCINATI

INDIANAPOLIS

CHICAGO

KALLAMAZOO
GRAND RAPIDS

DETROIT

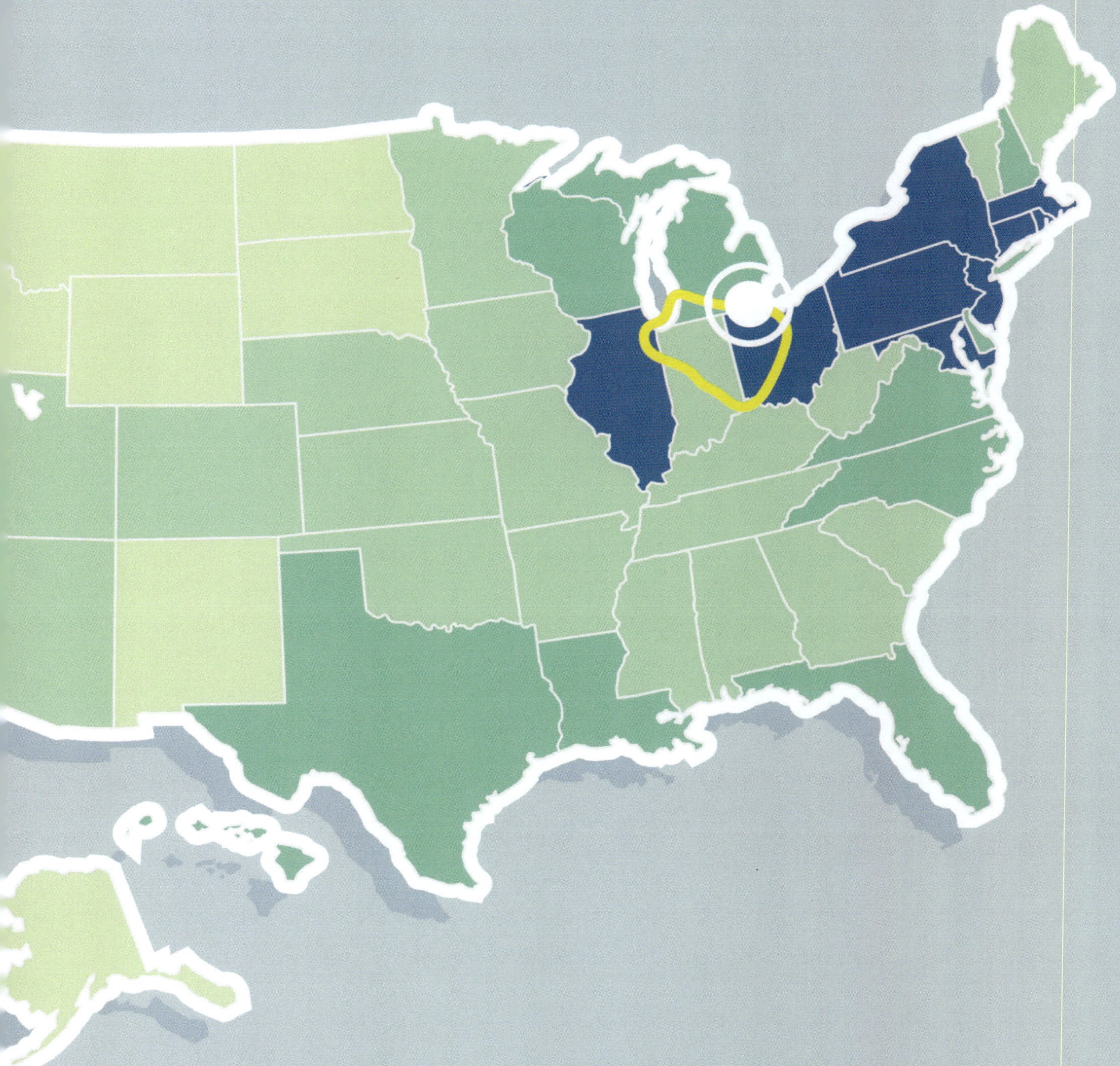

THE DETROIT HUB ROUTE 4

OFFBEAT AMERICA

In true Motor City style, follow the wheel-shaped route to the likes of Cincinnati, Indianapolis and Chicago before landing back at Detroit. From grandiose abandoned venues to towns you can traverse by white water raft, this trail is an urban explorer's dream. Take in the most opulent car park of all time, the grave of the original Psycho, see where the Empire State Building originated and of course no trip would be complete without visiting a giant egg.

1. GIANT COW HEAD
42.385, -82.96109
Near 13031 Mack Ave, Detroit, MI 48215
…for those who would want to visit a giant cow head.

2. VANITY BALLROOM
42.37224, -82.94642
1024 Newport St, Detroit, MI 48215
One of the last surviving intact (just) grand ballrooms of Detroit's dance hall era, the Vanity was built in 1929 and billed itself as 'Detroit's Most Beautiful Dance Rendezvous'. It closed in 1958,

Above: Vanity Ballroom

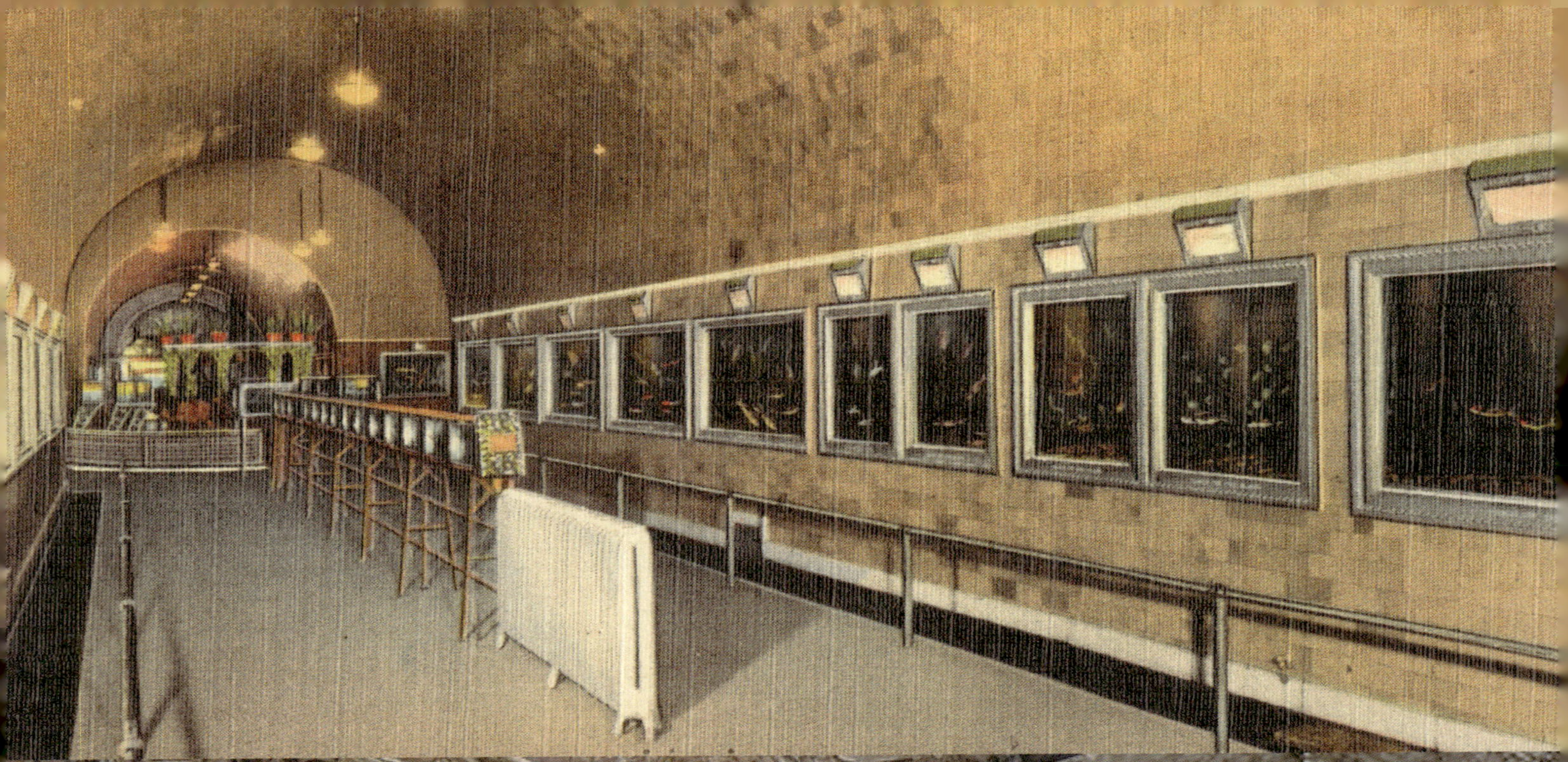
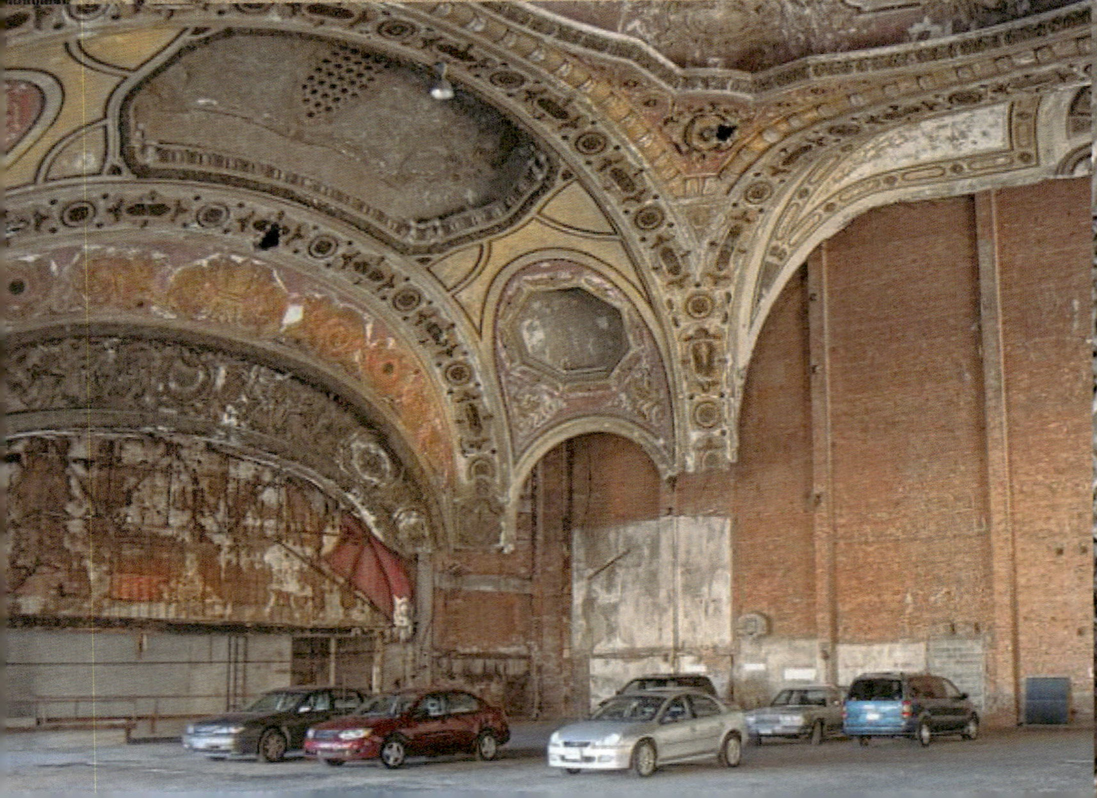
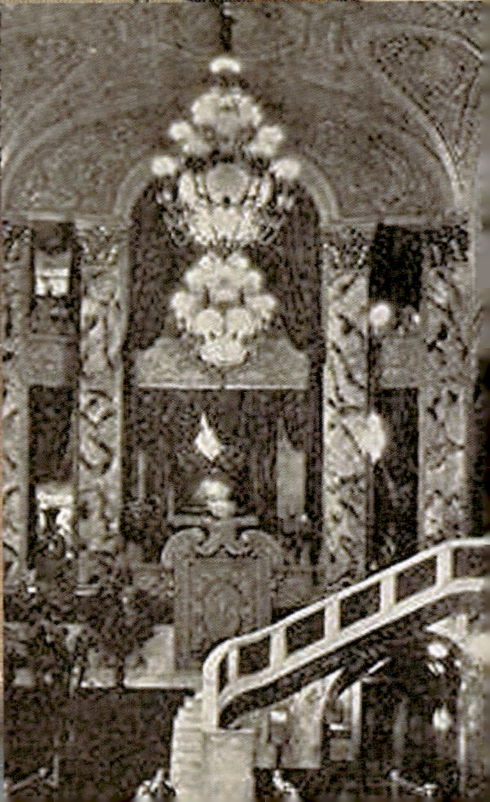

< Top: Belle Isle Zoo
< Bottom left, centre, right and overleaf: Michigan Theatre

before reopening for just one night a week for a couple of years. It has been abandoned ever since, apart from appearing as a backdrop to Eminem's 8 Mile movie in 2002. It is built in the Art Deco Aztec Revival style and was intended to fit 1000 couples on its 5600 sq.ft. dance floor in maple wood which incorporated an intentional bounce to add to the dancers' flare. There were three retail outlets inside, all built to reflect the Mayan/Aztec theme although some of this detail has since been lost.

3. BELLE ISLE ZOO
42.3406, -82.9813
Loiter Way, Detroit, MI 48207
The designer behind Manhattan's Central Park was also responsible for a more humble creation, the now abandoned Belle Isle Zoo of Detroit. Opened in 1895, it is heavily overgrown but still complete with deserted exhibits. It once had a bear den and an entire deer park, over 150 animals in all by 1909. Eclipsed by the newer Detroit Zoo which was created in 1928, Belle Isle was turned into a children's zoo in 1947 and it seems it was a lively place; baby elephant Kita famously swallowed a ball, a talking bird survived a kidnapping and lived to tell the tale and a kangaroo who staged a disappearance rocked up over 13 miles away hanging out on the other side of Detroit. It had an overhaul in the 1980s including smart raised wooden walkways above animal enclosures, but the Mayor of the time in 2002 saw a money saving opportunity and called for it to be closed to save some $700,000 dollars. Despite significant opposition, the now disgraced major (currently imprisoned) stuck to his guns and rather than maintaining Belle Isle, instead opened another zoo on the same island, the Nature Zoo that survives today (which at a guess may have cost over $700,000 to implement.)

4. MICHIGAN THEATRE
42.3345, -83.0531
220 Bagley Ave, Detroit, MI 48226
michigantheaterdetroit.com
With 4038 seats, the Michigan Theatre was a behemoth of performance arts, designed in French Renaissance style in 1925 and the jewel of Detroit in its day. It was built for over $3.5million dollars which today equates to about $42.4 million. Despite being located in Michigan, the theatre was slated to be named The Chicago, before some genius pointed out that the name The Michigan might be more fitting. Its Grande Lobby had 1000 square foot mirror panelling, a black and white chequered floor, Grecian columns, red velvet drapes, marble arches, giant crystal chandeliers and a wide sweeping staircase with carved balustrades and red carpet. Guests were entertained by a pianist each night whilst awaiting the movie. Works of art from the National Academy hung between every pair of columns (compare this to your local Odeon or Cineworld). The mezzanine was for black-tie wearing guests and was by invitation only. Grand cosmetics rooms for the ladies and retiring rooms for the men were included in the construction. There was also a Wurlitzer organ which could be raised to the stage and as films were silent until 1928, the Michigan Symphony Orchestra would play the soundtrack live. There were five showings daily, each consisting of a casual full scale concert by the symphony orchestra, singers, dancers, followed by the film. Prices ranged from 35 cents to 75 cents, time of day dependent. It was filled to capacity every day, with stars like the Marx Brothers, Sinatra, Louis Armstrong, Glenn Miller, Doris Day and Bette Davis all appearing on the stage. Memorably, Bob Hope once turned up thinking he was headlining, only to be billed after a performer called Joe Mendi; not best pleased, he was far less happy still when he discovered that Joe was a performing chimp. By the Forties, the style of cinemas changed and the focus was shifted to film rather than live performance; with that change came sound in theatres, rendering the orchestra and Wurlitzer redundant. Elements of the theatre, from the stage to the instrumentation began to sit unused and were slowly sold off. By the 1960s The Michigan became unprofitable and was sold for $1.5million in 1967, a fraction of its cost (only about $9.7million of today's money). It closed in 1967 with only a tenth of its capacity full at the final showing, a long shot from the four hours of queuing that people were prepared to undertake in its heyday. It was due to be demolished immediately

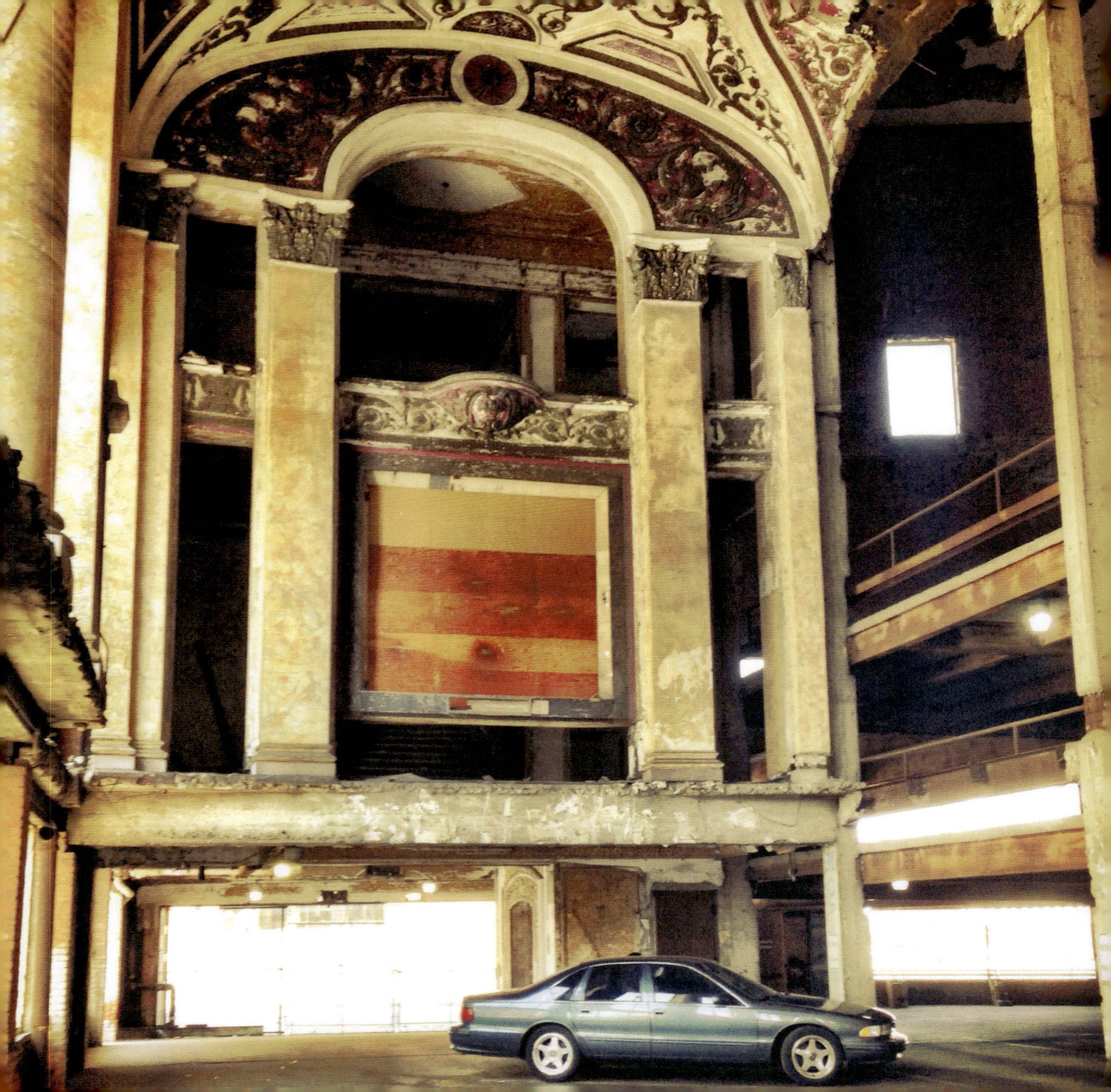

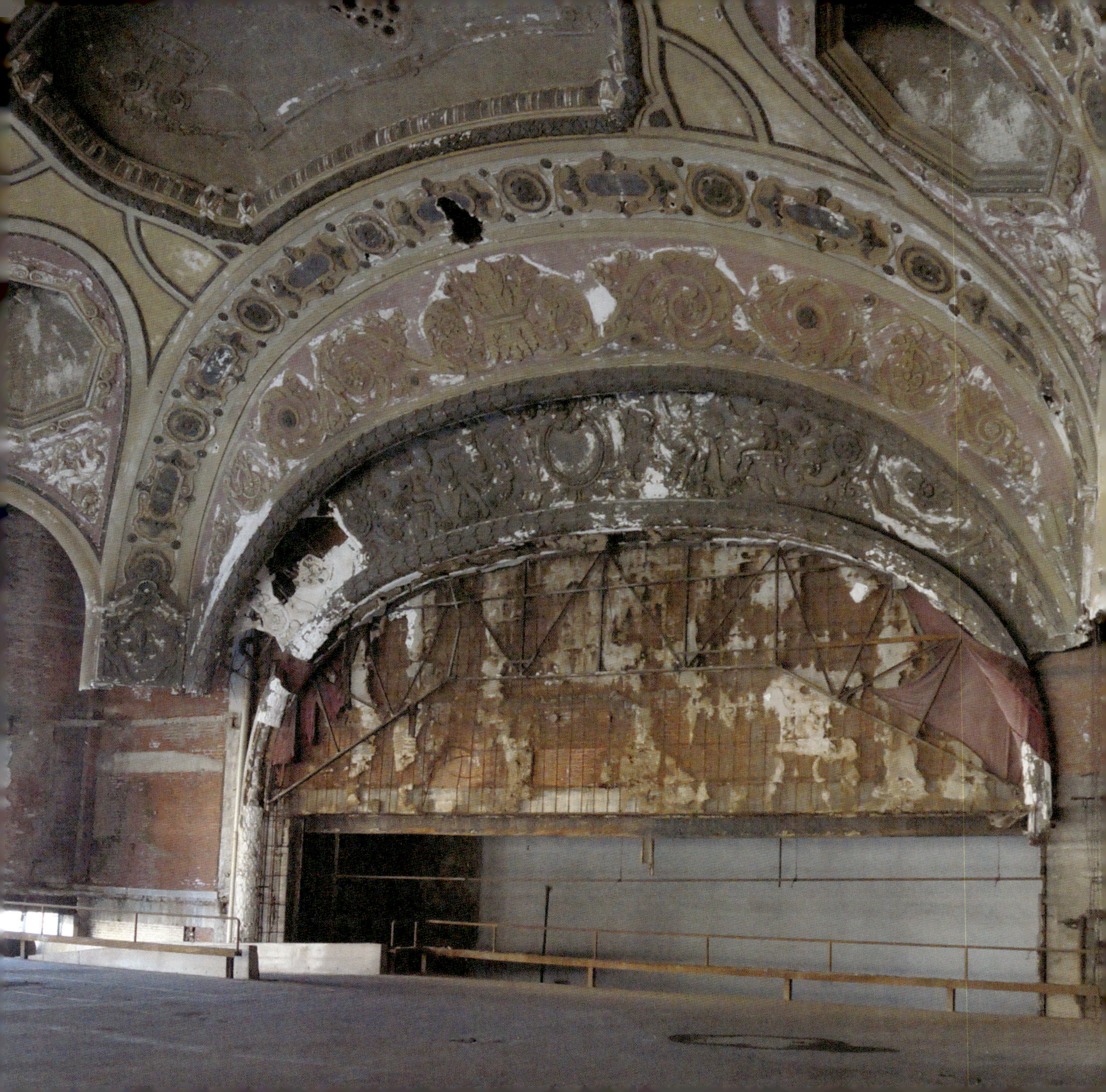

but was rescued by a showman who attempted to revive it. He too could not make the thing turn a profit and it closed again 3 years later. It briefly reopened as a theatre one final time but was shut for good in 1971. In 1972 a businessman opened it as a club, ripping out much of the interiors. In 1973 after failing as a club venue it was opened as a concert venue, featuring the likes of David Bowie, The Stooges and Aerosmith. Sadly the rock crowds took their toll on the building which suffered immeasurably and closed again in 1976. In a terrible twist of fate, it was opened as a secure parking location (!) - The parking plan had involved pulling the building down until it was decided that this would make the adjoining building unsound, so 3 levels and 160 spaces were simply built inside the theatre by ripping out the grand staircase, the mezzanine and the balcony. Today none the less, the ticket booth, four story lobby, part of the upper balcony and even the red velvet curtains can be seen. Why? Because the developers of the car park decided they wanted to quote unquote 'Leave some of the theatre's beauty intact'. Hooray for conservation. The location was in fact the site of the small garage where Henry Ford built his first car. The theatre planners tore it down and built upon it, but it seems the cars won out in the end. Go marvel at this unusual parking location for yourself.

5. SOUTHWESTERN HIGH SCHOOL
42.30337, -83.10881
6921 W Fort St, Detroit, MI 48209
This abandoned high school shut its doors in 2012, 97 years after its sister school John A. Nordstrum High School next door to which it was built as an extension first opened. The school's inaugural day was somewhat hampered as none of the desks had arrived; they were stuck in a mislaid railcar somewhere in Detroit's huge railyards. Southwestern was one of the first mandatory attendance schools of its day. Today it has been slated for a $32 million expansion into an engineering training centre and office space, but the developers are happily preserving the original gymnasium - to date development has yet to commence. Neurosurgeon Dr. Ben Carson, presidential candidate for 2016, is a Southwestern graduate along with 4 former MLB players and 3 former NBA players. An auction was held to sell off anything of value within the school buildings with prices as low as $1, but much went unclaimed leaving desks in situ.

6. KELLEYS ISLAND WINERY RUINS
41.6014, -82.7294
Maple Drive, Kelleys Island, OH 43438
Ohio was once at the forefront of USA wine production and this winery was very well considered before it later fell into ruin.

7. OHIO STATE REFORMATORY
40.78421, -82.50248
100 Reformatory Rd, Mansfield, OH 44905
This historic prison was built between 1886 and 1910, remaining in operation until 1990 when it was ordered closed by federal court. It was used in numerous films and TV shows, mostly while it was operating; the most famous was The Shawshank Redemption (1994) which was filmed in the building just after it closed. Today many of the grounds and support buildings have been torn down, as has the outer wall, but thankfully the rest has been turned into a museum by those who would save it in 1995, leaving one able to tour. The prison has seen some dark times: From 1935 to 1959 Mr Arthur Lewis Glattke was the Superintendent, residing in the family quarters on the property. He was well liked and had radio music piped into cell blocks to improve the inmates' lives. In 1950, his wife Helen was in an accident in which, whilst reaching into a jewellery box in her quarters, she accidentally discharged a handgun and died of pneumonia three days later. Arthur himself died in 1959 of a heart attack just 9 years later in his office on the premises. Over 200 others died at the facility, including two guards during escape attempts.

8. BIBLEWALK WAX MUSEUM
40.78599, -82.49577
500 Tingley Ave, Mansfield, OH 44905
livingbiblemuseum.org
As many biblical waxworks as anyone would care for.

9. CORNHENGE
40.085, -83.12351

> Top: Kelleys Island Winery Ruins
> Bottom: Ohio State Reformatory

OFFBEAT AMERICA

KELLEYS ISLAND,
OHIO. 33.

4995 Rings Rd, Dublin, OH 43017
Built to immortalise the inventor of a new species of corn, this…maize…of corn traps happy guests for hours.

10. THE NATIONAL BARBER MUSEUM AND HALL OF FAME
39.84282, -82.80566
135 Franklin St, Canal Winchester, OH 43110
www.nationalbarbermuseum.org
Hairdressers, get your own museum.

11. DEADMAN CROSSING
39.2725, -82.92806
Deadman Crossing, OH 45601
Strange location name, etymology unknown.

WHILE IN CINCINNATI: , WHY NOT CHECK OUT:

MUSHROOM HOUSE – p.140
OHIO'S LUCKY CAT MUSEUM – p.140
AMERICAN SIGN MUSEUM – p.140
VENT HAVEN MUSEUM – p.140
FLORENCE Y'ALL – p.144
CREATION MUSEUM – p.140
USS SACHEM RUINS – p.138

12. GRAVES OF THE RENO GANG
38.9676, -85.8906
200 E 9th Street, Seymour, IN 47274
This was the location in which America's first train robbers were strung up and buried.

13. EMPIRE QUARRY
38.9009, -86.5253
375-719 E Smithville Road, Bloomington, IN 47401
This most beautiful of holes in the ground was left behind after the stone was extracted from it to build the Empire State Building. The way in which the 18,630 tons of stone were removed leave behind an extremely deep and sharp sided pit which then fills with rain and ground water to give the water an unnaturally aquamarine colour. Be aware that quarry waters are unsafe to swim in due to the changes in depth and jagged areas. Admire from a photographic distance.

14. STATUE OF JOE PALOOKA
38.90079, -86.529
109 Main St, Oolitic, IN 47451
Joe Palooka is a now largely forgotten comic book hero, but was notable for being the first comic book character to be enlisted in the military when in 1940 he spent five years fighting the Nazis. When in 1948 at the dawn of the Cold War the Indiana Limestone Company, (the organisation responsible for Empire Quarry on p. X), wanted a statue to commemorate their 100th anniversary, they therefore chose Joe as a topical figure representative of someone ready to stand proudly and face any danger.

15. KNIGHTRIDGE SPACE OBSERVATORY

39.15005, -86.47038
4000-, 4400 E Lampkins Ridge Rd, Bloomington, IN 47401
Abandoned space observatory built in the Thirties deep in a forest… need we say more.

WHILE IN INDIANAPOLIS, WHY NOT CHECK OUT:

All entries from MOORESVILLE GRAVITY HILL to THE RUINS – pages 136 to 138

WHILE IN CHICAGO. WHY NOT CHECK OUT:

All entries from THE MURDER CASTLE SITE to SHOWMEN'S REST – pages 113 to 122

16. WORLD'S LARGEST BALL OF PAINT
40.25875, -85.70912
10696 N 200 W, Alexandria, IN 46001
Kudos to anyone who can make paint into a ball. A genuine spherical marvel.

17. ALBANY SHOE TREE
40.2924, -85.25239
Edgewater Road, Albany, IN 47320
A tree, full of shoes, in Albany.

18. MODOC'S MARKET
40.79662, -85.82198
205 S Miami St, Wabash, IN 46992
www.modocsmarket.com
Modoc is known as the Most Famous Elephant in America; when the Great American Circus put on a performance at the local High School in 1942, Modoc stormed out mid spectacle and marauded downtown. Where she smelt the freshly roasted peanuts at the Bradley Brothers Drug Store, she promptly smashed straight through the front door, consumed every peanut in sight, and thus fuelled, embarked on a 5 day trip across two counties hitting national headlines as she went. Bradley Brothers was renamed Modoc's in honour of this momentous occasion.

19. MENTONE EGG
41.1734, -86.0349

< Top: Cornhenge
Above left: World's Largest Ball of Paint
Above right: Mentone Egg

THE DETROIT HUB ROUTE 4

180

202 E Main St, Mentone, IN 46539
It's a large egg, found in Mentone.

20. BENDIX WOODS
41.67169, -86.48859
32132 Indiana 2, New Carlisle, IN 46552
Established by the Studebaker Corporation as a million dollar test facility for cars with a track featuring a variety of terrains and road conditions, the woodland that the track surrounded formed one of the largest living advertisements the World has ever seen when in 1938it was planted to read the word 'STUDEBAKER' spelled out in 8,000 pine trees.

21. EAST RACE WATERWAY
41.6769, -86.2446
East Race Waterway
South Bend, Indiana, 46617
A little light white water rafting straight through the midst of an Indiana city.

22. AMERICAN MUSEUM OF MAGIC
42.27228, -84.95835
107 E Michigan Ave, Marshall, MI 49068
www.americanmuseumofmagic.org
This private collection, situated not far from famed illusionist Harry Blackstone Snr's home, is extensive and housed in a pretty building in Marshall, Michigan. Among other treasures are many gimmicks belonging to Blackstone himself.

23. STEELCASE PYRAMID
42.7998, -85.6229
Steel Case, off 6262 E Paris Ave SE (Paul Henry Thornapple Trail), Grand Rapids, MI 49512
Steelcase, a furniture manufacturer, built this pyramid as its Corporate Development Center in the late 80s for over $100 million in a bid to outclass its office decor competitors so that it could test its furniture out fully, some might say excessively; the building allowed for furniture to be plunged into freezing temperatures and to be blasted with different acoustic levels. Shockingly this venture didn't prove profitable, leading Steelcase to abandon the building in 2011, putting it up for sale for $19.5 million. Today it sits abandoned amongst lush fields, a bizarrely futuristic eyesore on the land covering what are cavernous underground workspace bunkers. The pyramid is currently in the process of being sold to a Nevada tech firm who are planning to convert it into a giant data centre creating 1000 jobs with an investment level of $5 Bn., but as of today the pyramid still lies forlorn.

24. GRAVE OF ED GEIN
M 44.2167, -89.5204
Packer Dr NE, Belmont, MI 49306
The original Psycho and Leatherface, severely troubled Ed made entire outfits out of human skin which he wore around his house, which was itself decorated in turn with macabre

< Left: Bendix Woods
Right: East Race Waterway

< Left: Grave of Ed Gein (prior page)

furnishings such as skull bowls and skin lampshades. His grave has been vandalised many times but still remains.

25. BATH SCHOOL MASSACRE MEMORIAL
42.8187, -84.4486
13751 Main Street (Between Main St and Webster Rd, North of Clark Road)
Bath Township, Michigan, 48808

Andrew P Kehoe didn't process his defeat in the local election well, and suffering from significant financial stress, lost the plot and went on a murderous rampage in which he killed his wife, lit a bomb at a local elementary school which killed 38 children and 6 adults, injured 58 others and finally blew himself up in his truck in what is to this day the deadliest mass murder at a school in US history.

26. HELL
42.43472, -83.985
Hell, MI 48169

There a several theories as to the etymology of this township: 1. Hell was built around a grain mill which produced a large amount of moonshine - when wives were asked where their husbands had gone, they would reply 'He's gone to Hell' and the name stuck. 2. Two German travellers exited a stagecoach one sunny afternoon in the 1830s, one saying to the other 'So schön hell!' or 'So beautifully bright!', which overheard by locals, stuck. 3. Founder George Reeves was asked what he should call it and he replied 'I don't care, you can name it Hell for all I care', the name becoming official on October 13,1841. 4. The name came from the hell-like conditions encountered by early explorers including mosquitos, thick woodland and wet marshy land. The jury is still out.

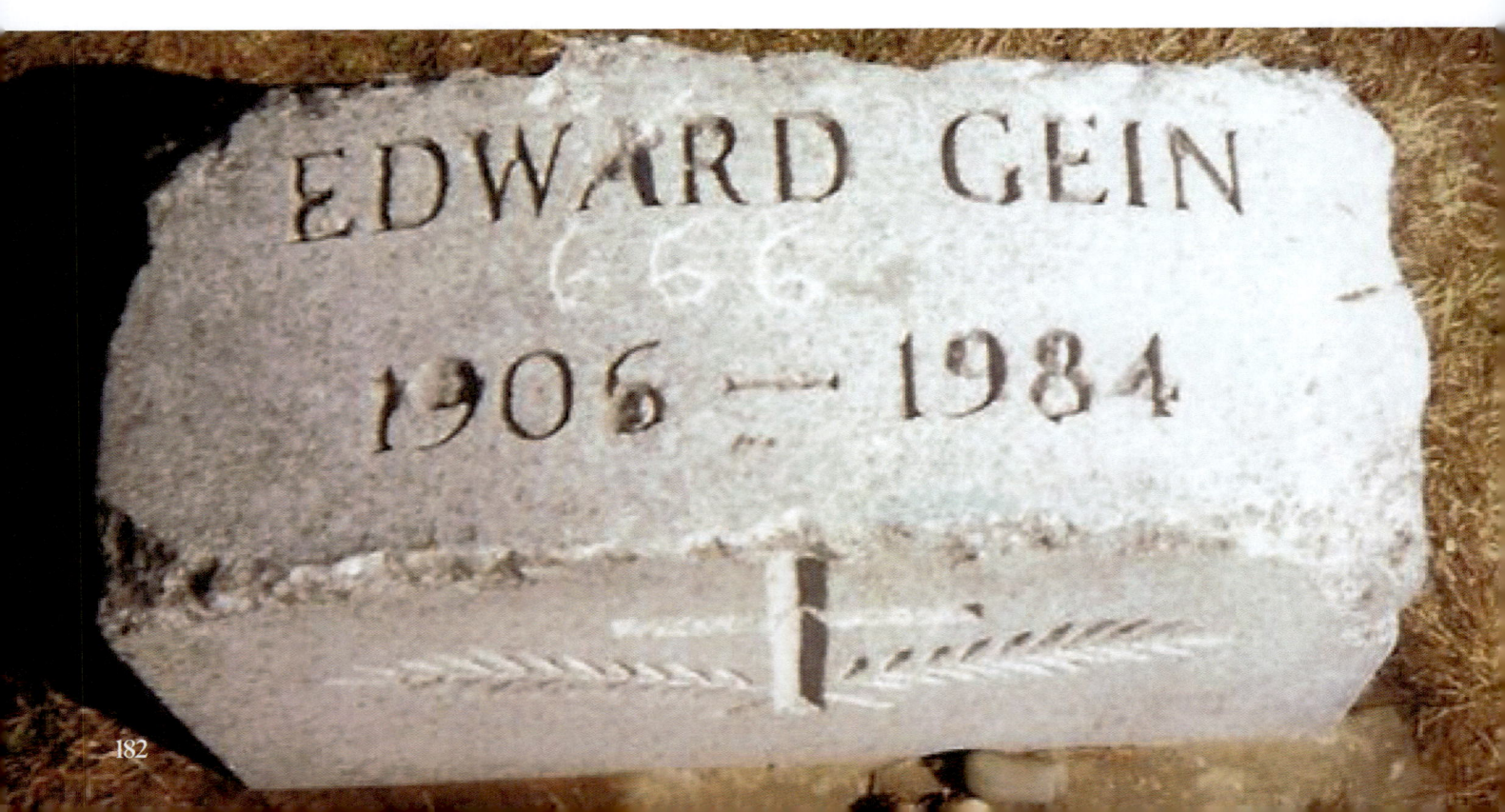

Top and bottom left: Bath School Massacre Memorial
Bottom right: Hell

THE DETROIT HUB ROUTE 4

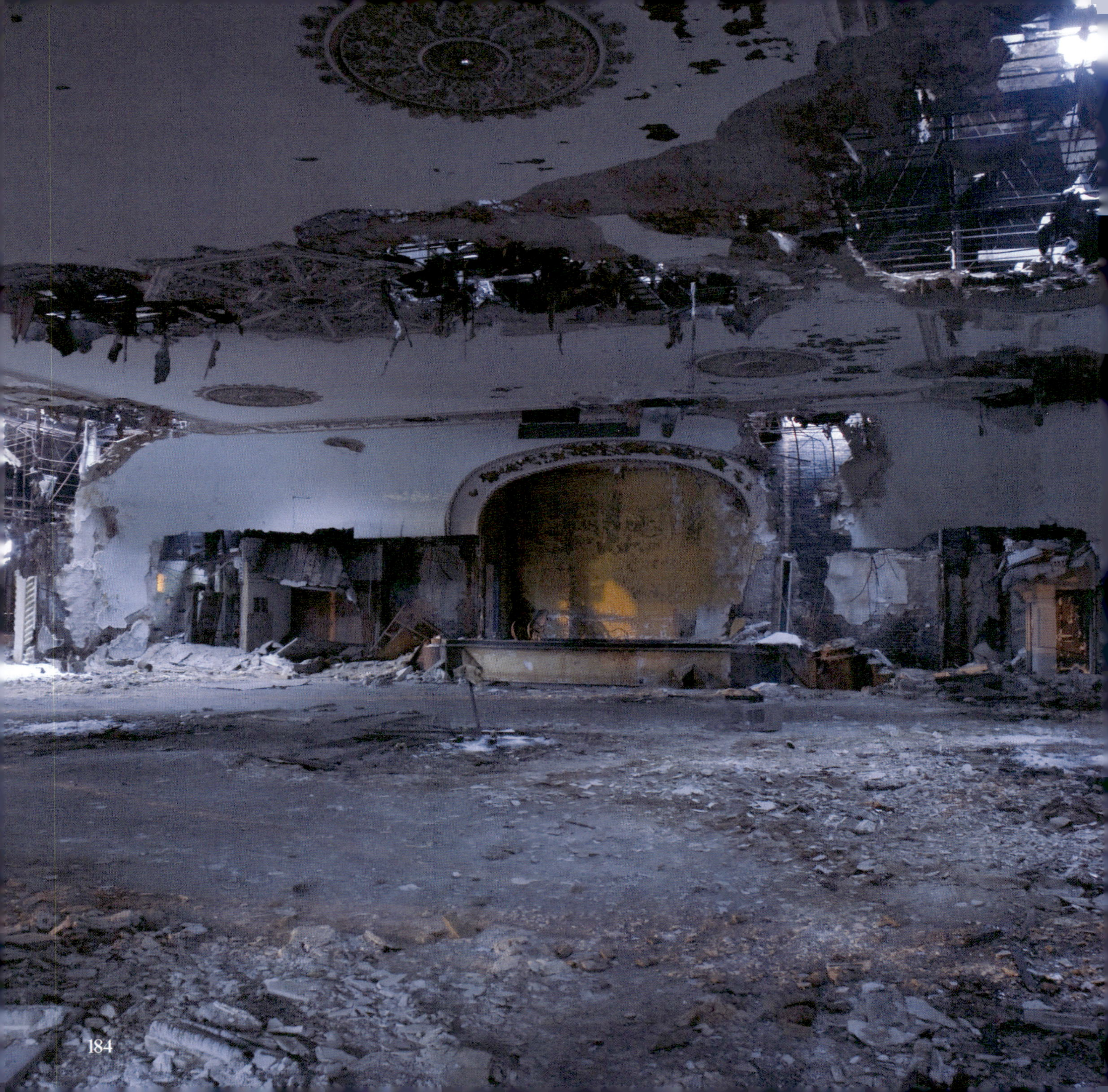

< Left: Grande Ballroom
Below: Bronner's Christmas Wonderland

27. BRONNER'S CHRISTMAS WONDERLAND
43.31402, -83.73708
25 Christmas Ln, Frankenmuth, MI 48734
www.bronners.com
At Bronner's CHRISTmas Wonderland where the Christ comes capitalised, you can revel in the magic of xmas all year round in a store 1.5 football fields in size filled with 50,000 plus decorations.

28. THE WORLD'S LARGEST STOVE
42.4393, -83.1176
Michigan State Fairgrounds
1120 W. State Fair Ave.
Detroit, Michigan, 48203
Here once stood, but no longer stands, the World's Largest Stove. This fact is included merely to note the irony that it is no longer present as it burnt to the ground.

29. ST AGNES CHURCH AND SCHOOL
42.36642, -83.09381
W Bethune Ave, Detroit, MI 48202
This ex-Catholic school is now a decrepit ruin.

30. ABUNDANT LIFE CHRISTIAN CENTER
42.36049, -83.1181
8240 Grand River Ave, Detroit, MI 48204
This somewhat ironically named church has fallen into glorious disrepair and is entirely lacking in any signs of life.

31. GRANDE BALLROOM
42.36484, -83.12833
8952 Grand River Ave, Detroit, MI 48204
This famed location is a stunning tribute to decay and has featured performances from the likes of Led Zeppelin, Janis Joplin, Pink Floyd, The Grateful Dead, Procol Harum and The Who. Designed in 1928 to incorporate ground floor retail and an upstairs dance hall, it became a major venue for music in 1966 and closed in 1972, rarely used since with no plans in the pipeline for redevelopment to date.

THE SOUTHBOUND TRAIL ROUTE 5

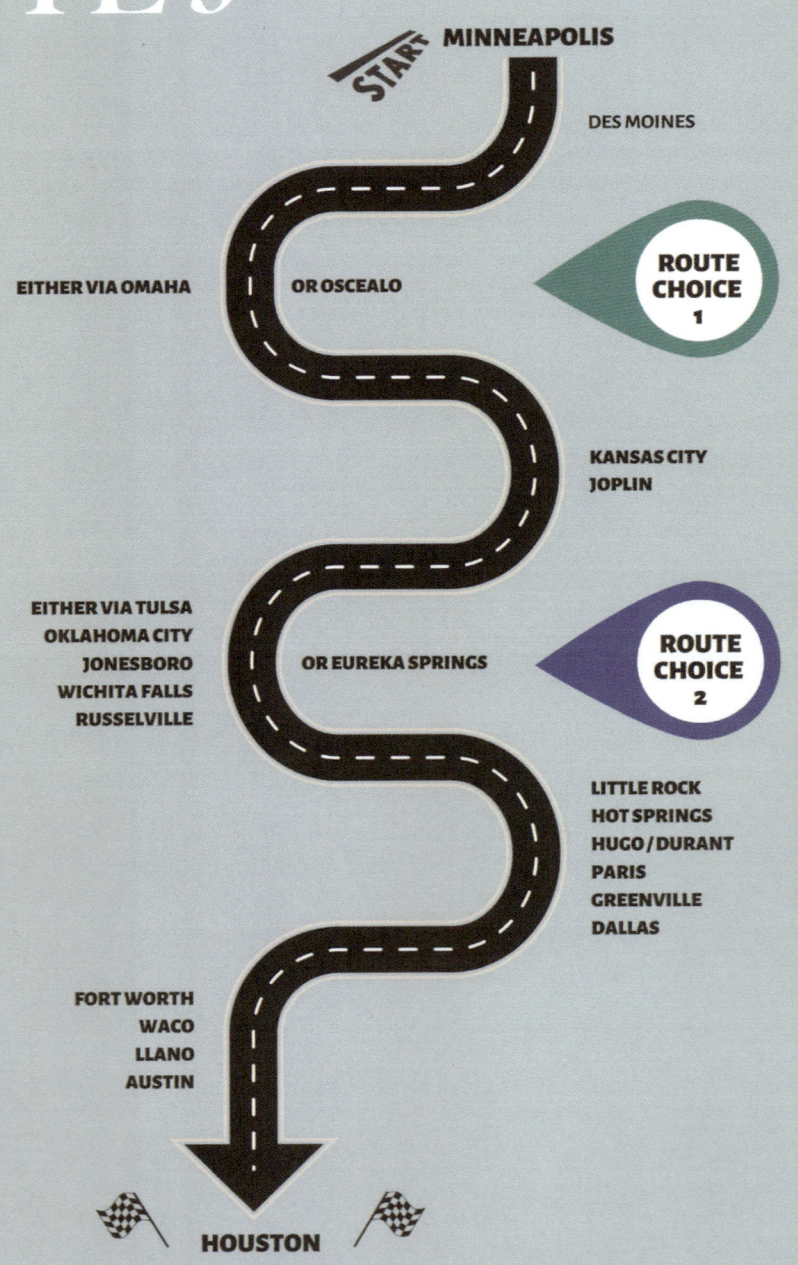

START — MINNEAPOLIS

DES MOINES

EITHER VIA OMAHA   OR OSCEALO

ROUTE CHOICE 1

KANSAS CITY
JOPLIN

EITHER VIA TULSA
OKLAHOMA CITY
JONESBORO
WICHITA FALLS
RUSSELVILLE

OR EUREKA SPRINGS

ROUTE CHOICE 2

LITTLE ROCK
HOT SPRINGS
HUGO / DURANT
PARIS
GREENVILLE
DALLAS

FORT WORTH
WACO
LLANO
AUSTIN

HOUSTON

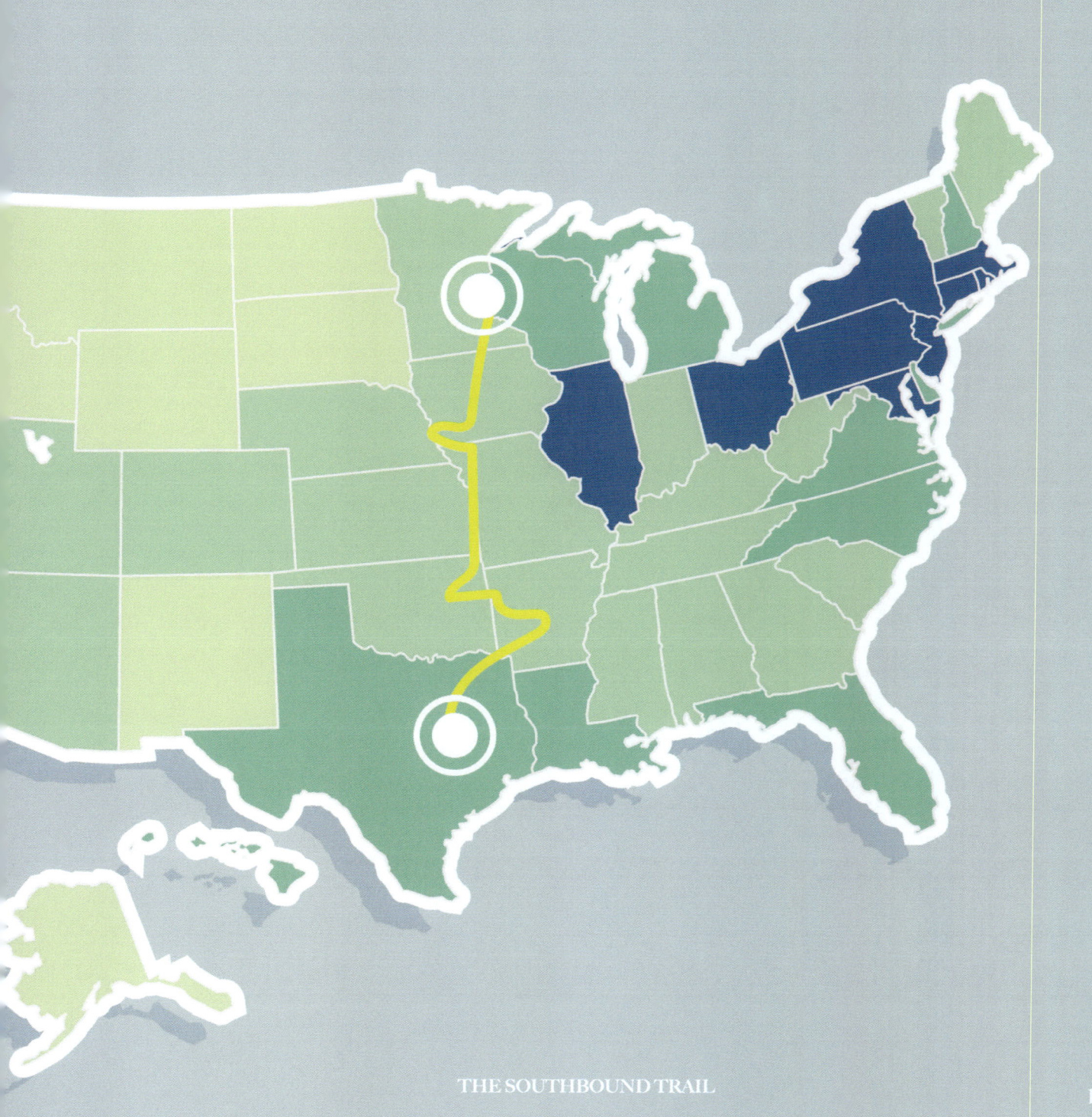

THE SOUTHBOUND TRAIL

THE SOUTH BOUND TRAIL ROUTE 5

Above: Hidden Beach

'Everything is Bigger in Texas' or so the saying goes, although if there is one thing you will learn from this book, it's that each State has its own share of stupidly large versions of everyday things. Travel down the Northern reaches of Minneapolis to the Gulf of Mexico via giant cutlery, a bigger Billy Bass collection than you will ever have felt the need to see and a giant bull - plus the world's smallest skyscraper by way of juxtaposition. Unleash your inner Cryptozoologist by hunting the frequently sighted Bigfoot in the wooded swamplands of atmospheric Uncertain where residents live in steam barges under the Spanish Moss and read the epitaphs of fire-eaters in the Showmen's cemetery.

1. HIDDEN BEACH
44.96107, -93.31807
2000 S Upton Ave, Minneapolis, MN 55405
www.minneapolisparks.org
Recently renamed 'Cedar Lake East Beach' as part of a renovation initiative, this somewhat notorious alternative lake side location in Minneapolis was once the only nudist beach in the Twin Cities

THE SOUTHBOUND TRAIL ROUTE 5

although few nudists are actually to be found there today. The name is appropriate; it is hidden down a very long trail through the woods which leads to the shore. A very mixed bag of high class to homeless people rub shoulders at the beach which is also frequented by the Rainbow Family of Living Light, a hippie group who refer to one another as Brother, Sister or simply Sibling by way of gender-neutrality. Proponents gather at camps known as Rainbowland whilst the outside world is referred to as Babylon. Barter is preferred over the use of cash. Another Hidden Beach attraction worth a visit is the mud pit on the eastern side of the area, complete with diving board. Speak to the Mud Man who famously greets visitors and advises them of the prevailing mud status that day. He also keeps a running tally of mud pit visitors. Try to also find 'Kevin' and ask him for a special free hand made tie dye t-shirt complete with lion crest and black star on the shoulder to wear on your visit to Hidden Beach - he has given away 12,000 of them to date. The area whilst friendly in the day is known to be dubious at night and somewhat notorious for police brutality claims and illegal stop and searches. Technically it is not legal to be in the water or mud pit (it is not entirely clear why) and tickets have occasionally been issued. One man was memorably maced for not having a fishing license. Extensive clearing of vegetation in the area to enable it to be observed by the authorities more clearly has taken its toll somewhat, so see this quirky spot before it goes the way others have gone before.

2. SPOONBRIDGE AND CHERRY
44.97023, -93.28905
Loring Greenway, Minneapolis, MN 55403
Located in one of the largest sculpture gardens in the country, this original piece has delighted visitors since the 80s.

3. HOUSE OF BALLS
44.96828, -93.25123
1504 S 7th St, Minneapolis, MN 55454
houseofballs.com
A local artist opened a public space 28 years ago which is still alive and well today; it remains unlocked 24 hours a day, filled with creations which demonstrate the artist's belief that objects acquire a tangible life force when they come into contact with living beings. The name comes from the presence of copious bowling balls in the venue as well as from the artist's motto that 'we all possess creative impulse and we owe ourselves the balls to express it.'

4. FREDERICK R WEISMAN ART MUSEUM
44.97318, -93.23702
333 E River Pkwy, Minneapolis, MN 55455
www.weisman.umn.edu
A beautiful collection of art which is totally upstaged by the simply extraordinary building in which it is housed, designed by renowned architect Frank Gehry in 1993. One side of the building blends with its surroundings, whilst the other side is a futuristic come steampunk joy of abstraction which represents a waterfall and a fish. Gehry has been labelled by Vanity Fair as 'the most important architect of our age; his portfolio includes the Guggenheim of Bilbao, the Walt Disney Concert Hall of LA, the Louis Vuitton Foundation Paris, the New World Center in Miami Beach and many others.

5. THE SOAP FACTORY
44.9831, -93.24971
514 2nd St SE, Minneapolis, MN 55414
www.soapfactory.org
The National Purity Soap Factory did a roaring trade in the Twenties at this cool old space, now reappropriated as an awesome non-profit independent art gallery. A maze of rooms in the decrepit building show off the structure as it once was whilst up to the moment art sets a great juxtaposition.

6. MINNEAPOLIS MANHOLE COVERS
44.9833, -93.2667
The character of this fine city is demonstrated by the fact that artists were commissioned between 1983 and 1990 to design its manhole covers individually. Once the most talked about piece of art in the town, they have now fallen into almost total obscurity

> Right: Spoonbridge and Cherry
Overleaf: Frederick R Weisman Art Museum

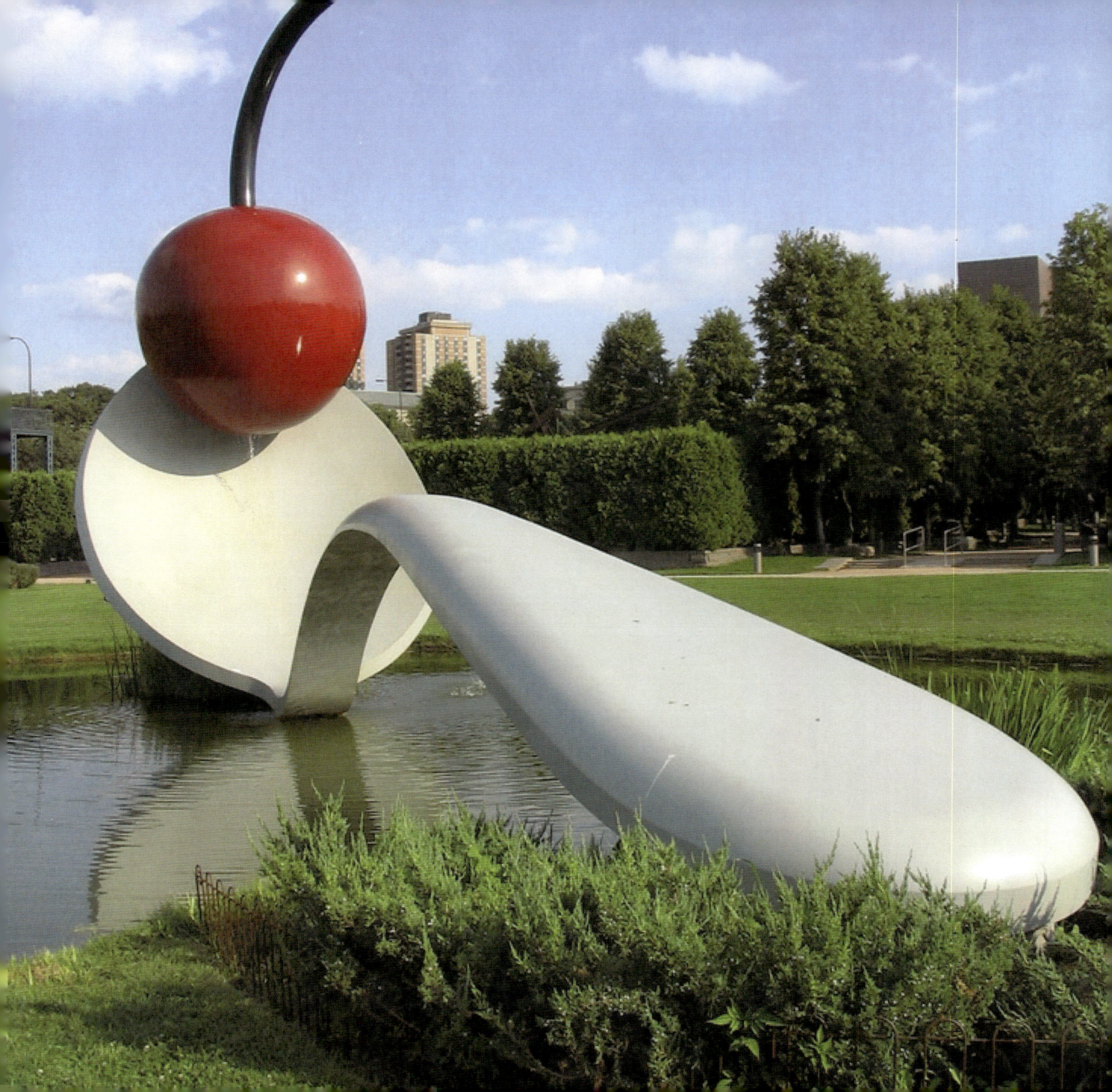

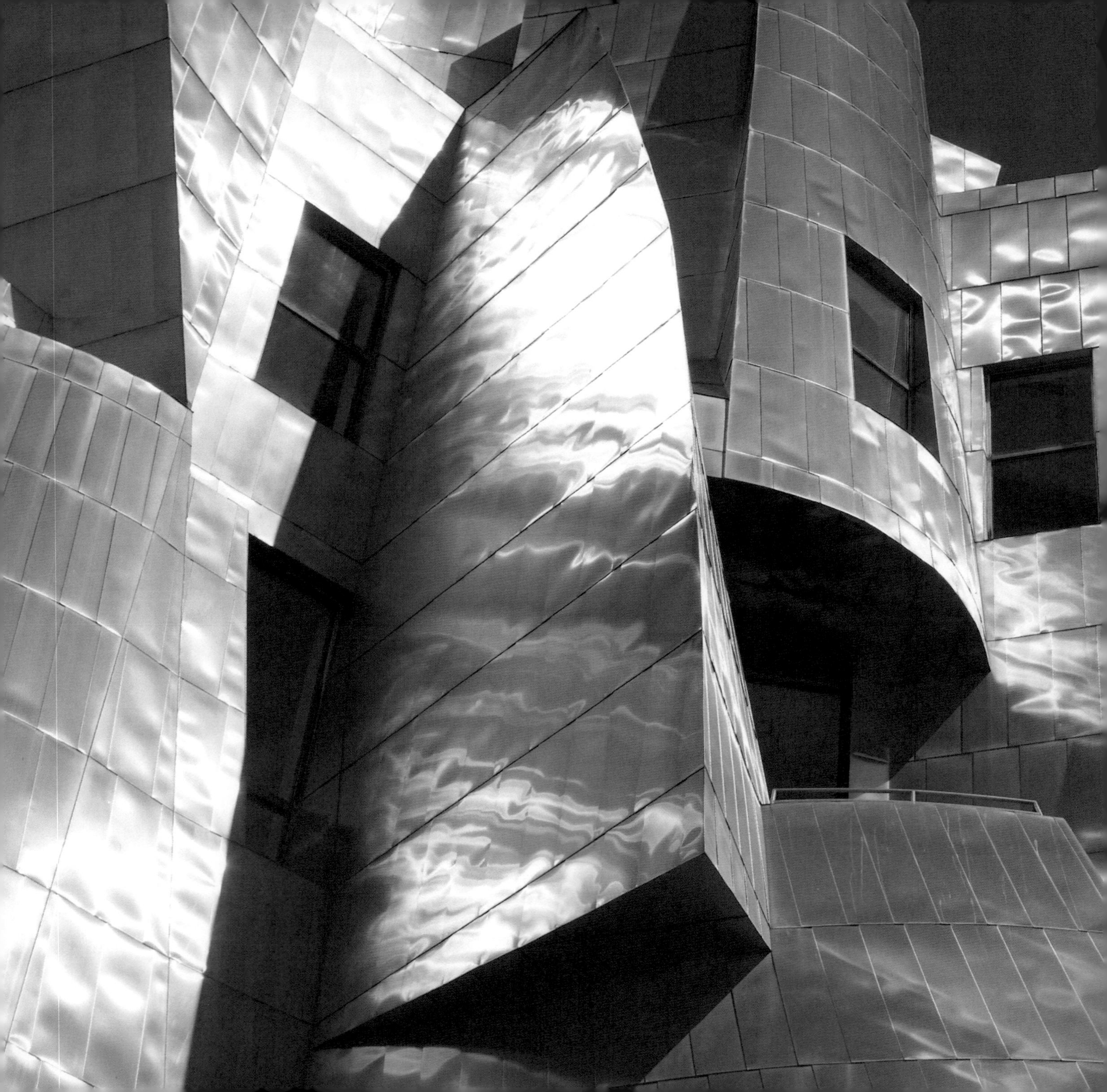

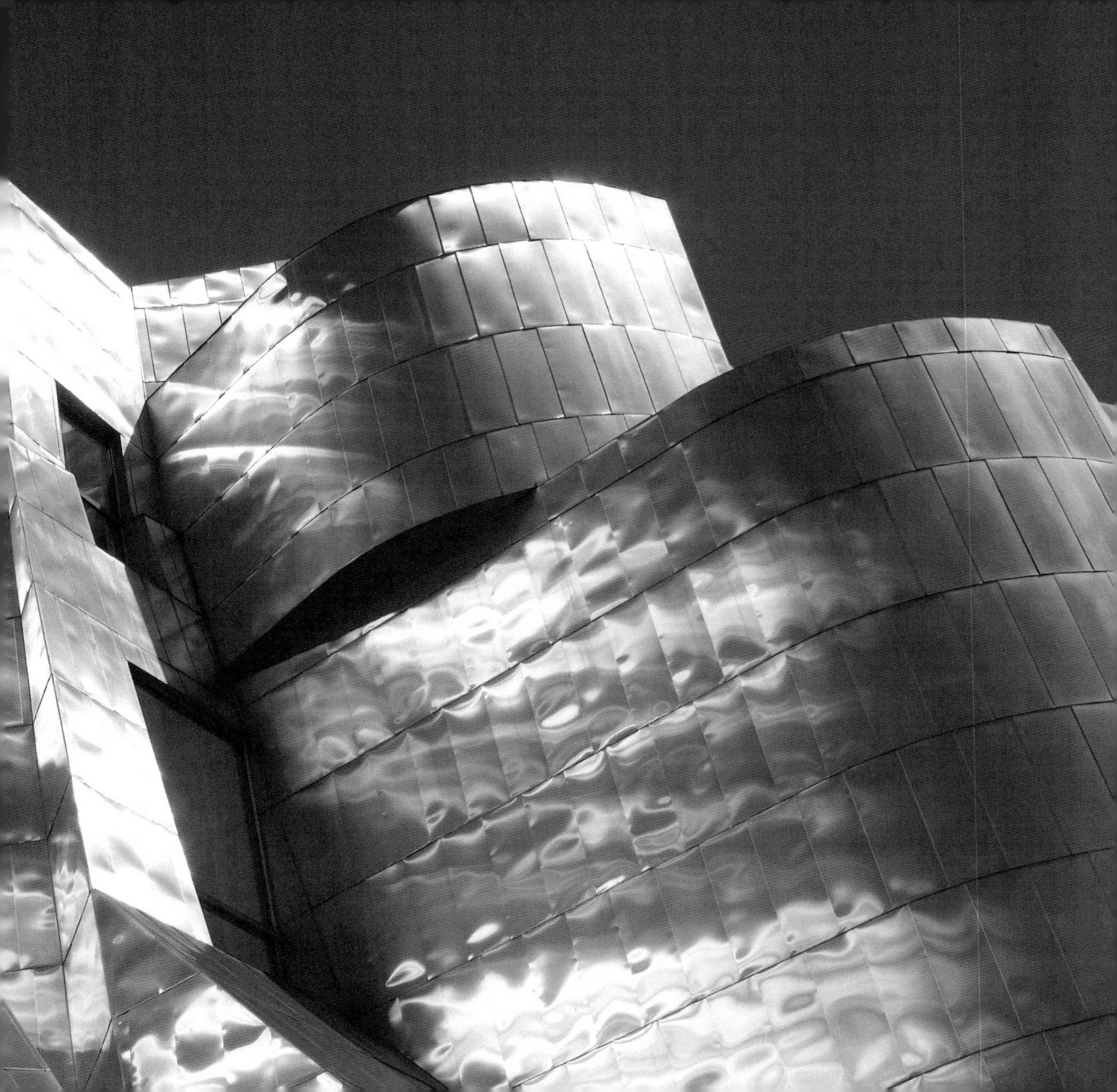

Hobo Signs & Symbols

(spiral)	A judge lives here
⊗	Good place for a hand-out
⊕ with dot	Doctor won't charge here
⊃	Owner is out
⌂ (hat)	Kind gentleman lives here
(cat)	Kind lady lives here
₪	Vicious dog here
(folded papers)	Owners will give to get rid of you
oxo ~~~	Fresh water safe campsite
∿∿	Barking

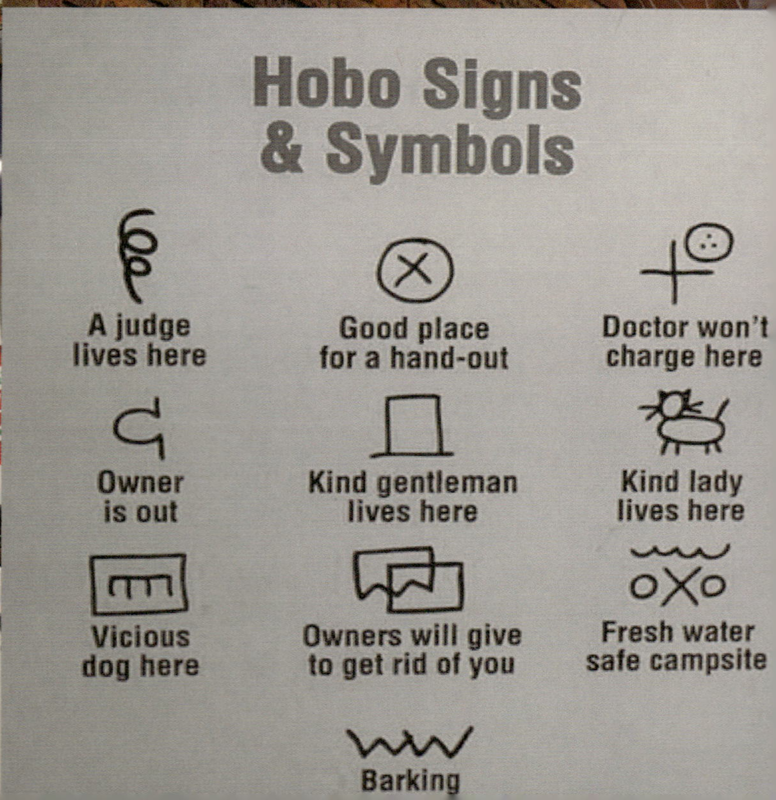

< Top left and top right: The Herbivorous Butcher
< Bottom left: Spam Museum
< Bottom right: National Hobo Convention

having become entirely part of the day to day. Visit http://www.minneapolismn.gov/wcm1/groups/public/@cped/documents/webcontent/wcms1p-087364.pdf for the only walking tour map we can find.

7. THE HERBIVOROUS BUTCHER
44.99041, -93.25398
507 1st Ave NE, Minneapolis, MN 55413
www.theherbivorousbutcher.com
The most disappointing butcher's shop for meat lovers in existence – vegans, form an orderly queue.

8. ZORAN'S SCULPTURE GARDEN
44.9996, -93.27179
Near 77 13th Ave NE, Minneapolis, MN 55413

This stone sculpture park is a quirky work in progress.

9. CITY SALVAGE
45.00855, -93.2815
2800 N Washington Ave, Minneapolis, MN 55413
www.citysalvage.com
The place to go in Minneapolis for all things kooky, reclaimed, salvaged and discarded.

10. SPAM MUSEUM
43.6666, -92.9746
101 3rd Ave NE, Austin, MN 55912
www.spam.com
Does exactly what it says on the tin.

11. NATIONAL HOBO CONVENTION
43.09645, -93.80144
51 Main Ave S, Britt, IA 50423
hobo.com
Hobos come together every year from all over the US to celebrate Hobo culture and have done since the 1900s.

12. FATHER DOBBERSTEIN'S GROTTO OF THE REDEMPTION
42.9639, -94.44559300 N Broadway Ave, West Bend, IA 50597
www.westbendgrotto.com
One man's journey into religion via gemstones, shells and quite possibly mental illness. Visit the Grotto Café while you're in town.

13. WORLD'S LARGEST POPCORN BALL
42.4223, -94.9927
401 N 13th St, Sac City, IA 50583
noblepopcorn.com
Resist the urge to nibble this baby in passing.

14. ELWOOD THE WORLD'S TALLEST CONCRETE GNOME
42.0114, -93.6381
1407 S University Blvd, Ames, IA 50011
Hate gnomes? This monster is a Guinness World Record Breaker. Does this make it any more appealing? …no.

Above: Zoran's Sculpture Garden
Right: World's Largest Popcorn Ball

THE SOUTHBOUND TRAIL ROUTE 5

> Top left: Woodland Palace
> Centre left: The Black Angel of Oakland Cemetery

15. IOWA'S LARGEST FRYING PAN
42.3146, -92.0076
800-850 Main St, Brandon, IA 52210
The World's Largest Frying Pan!? you say? No. Just…the largest in Iowa.

16. RAVEN'S GRIN INN
42.10207, -89.97987
411 N Carroll St, Mt Carroll, IL 61053
www.hauntedravensgrin.com
This creepy house is booby trapped and gimmicked by its owner to give tour guests a fright. Be ready for the unexpected!

17. WOODLAND PALACE
41.27874, -89.8597
N 900th, Kewanee, IL 61443
An inventor called Fred Francis built this home in 1889 or rather started building it as it did not reach 'completion' for another 37 years when he finally died in another story reminiscent of San Jose's Winchester House. The house contained innumerous futuristic creations such as air conditioning (an elaborate series of fans) and heating, automated doors and windows, hidden shutters and storm windows and clean running water, all without the use of electricity. He added elaborate columned roof detailing plus a glass solarium, designed to aid his wife's tuberculosis recovery. All the internal decor and furnishings are also works of his. Tours are available to the public.

18. THE BLACK ANGEL OF OAKLAND CEMETERY
41.66966, -91.52219
1000 Brown St, Iowa City, IA 52245
Urban legend has it that this statue was originally white, turning black with grief over time.

19. THE TOWN OF WHAT CHEER
41.40139, -92.35462
What Cheer, IA 50268
The town's name may come from the old English greeting 'What cheer with you' which was in use from the 15th century, or it may have been the exclamation of a Scottish miner who cried 'What cheer!' upon discovering coal nearby. Another line of thinking is that a Joseph Andrews chose the name due to recall one of the myths of his native town of Providence Rhode Island which holds that the founder of Providence, a Roger Williams, was greeted in 1636 by Native Americans with 'What cheer, Netop', 'Netop' meaning friend, and the 'what cheer' learned from English settlers.

20. ZOMBIE BURGER & DRINK LAB
41.56913, -93.80379
101 Jordan Creek Pkwy #12514, West Des Moines, IA 50266
www.zombieburgerdm.com
Brraaaiiinnnss. Or just dead good burgers.

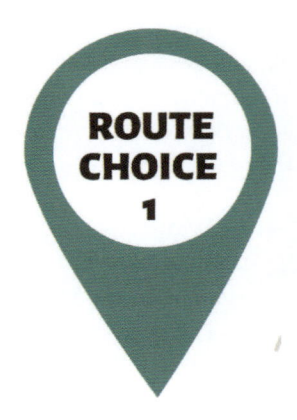

ROUTE CHOICE 1

ROUTE A VIA OMAHA

To instead follow Route B via Osceola, turn to p. 200

21. ALBERT THE BULL
41.71106, -94.92686
Audubon, IA 50025
A 30 ft. tall bull weighing 45 tonnes, mostly in solid concrete, with a steelwork frame made from abandoned Iowa windmills. Albert was named for a local businessman who came up with an annual beef 'drive' called Operation T-bone. The lesser known Operation Pork Chop failed to rope a giant windmill-framed Pig into its publicity and therefore fell into obscurity. Why not stay in the nearby Albert the Bull Campground?

22. WILLIAM THOMPSON SCALPED SCALP
41.2581, -95.93529

> Bottom left: The Town of What Cheer
> Right: World's Largest Frying Pan
> Overleaf: Albert The Bull

OFFBEAT AMERICA

EXIT 201
21
Belle Plaine
What Cheer

BRANDON, IOWA

ALBERT

AUDUBON I

E BULL
50025

< Bottom left: Villisca Axe Murder House
< Bottom right: World's Largest Ball of Stamps

215 S 15th St, Omaha, NE 68102
www.omahalibrary.org
Probably the only library to receive a donation of a scalp from the live, if somewhat foreshortened, previous owner himself.

23. WORLD'S LARGEST BALL OF STAMPS
41.26256, -96.12698
13628 Flanagan Blvd, Boys Town, NE 68010
www.boystown.org
Where better than the fantastically named Boys Town to construct a giant ball of stamps weighing 600 lbs and containing over 4.5 million pieces of legal tender – a true philatelist's dream. Licked by tongue or wetted using a sponge? We just don't know. We're not sure we want to either; perhaps this is also a contender for Guiness' World's Largest Ball of Saliver. Stop in at the Boys Town Gift Shop while you're there, or visit the Boys Town National Landmark at 13628 Flanagan Blvd, Boys Town, NE 68010 to take a picture of the town sign.

24. VILLISCA AXE MURDER HOUSE
40.9307, -94.97331
508 E 2nd Street, Villisca, IA 50864
6 members of the Moore family, 43 year old Josiah, 39 year old Sarah, Herman (11), Mary (10), Arthur (7) and Paul (5) and their two young guests (Ina (8) and Lena (12) were bludgeoned to death in their home, all of them with severe head wounds from an axe. The case remains unsolved and open to this day despite there being numerous credible suspects, several of whom had been convicted of axe murder sprees carried out in a very similar way.

JUMP TO WORLD'S LARGEST SHUTTLECOCKS p. 201 TO CONTINUE YOUR JOURNEY

ROUTE B VIA OSCEOLA

25. ADAM-ONDI-AHMAN
39.98392, -93.97622
Adam-ondi-Ahman, MO 64647
This historic site is, according to Mormon doctrine, where Adam and Eve lived after their ejection from Eden. The Mormon church had planned to build a temple on the site, which they believe holds significance

for the Second Coming of Christ, however during the 1838 Mormon War (yes, there was one) which was prompted by settlers' concerns that the Mormons would seize political control of the County, the church was evicted from Missouri laying such plans to rest and the area renamed Cravensville.

ROUTES A & B CONVERGE IN KANSAS CITY

26. FRITZ'S
39.08258, -94.58269
2450 Grand Blvd, Kansas City, MO 64108
www.fritzskc.com
This 1954 restaurant has dispensed with waiters in favour of a tiny rail road – simply use the telephone at your table to order your food, and wait for the overhead train to chug your food around to you.

27. WORLD'S LARGEST SHUTTLECOCKS
39.0451, -94.581
4525 Oak St, Kansas City, MO 64111
www.nelson-atkins.org
...Very large shuttlecocks.

28. WORLD'S LARGEST SMALL ELECTRIC APPLIANCE MUSEUM
36.9959, -94.3757
51 Highway 59, Diamond, Missouri, 64840
Very much what it says it is. Why? Who knows.

29. WORLD'S LARGEST FORK
37.14537, -93.32325
2215 W Chesterfield St, Springfield, MO 65807
It's a very big fork.

Top: Adam-Ondi-Ahman
Right: World's Largest Fork
Overleaf: World's Largest Shuttlecocks

THE SOUTHBOUND TRAIL ROUTE 5

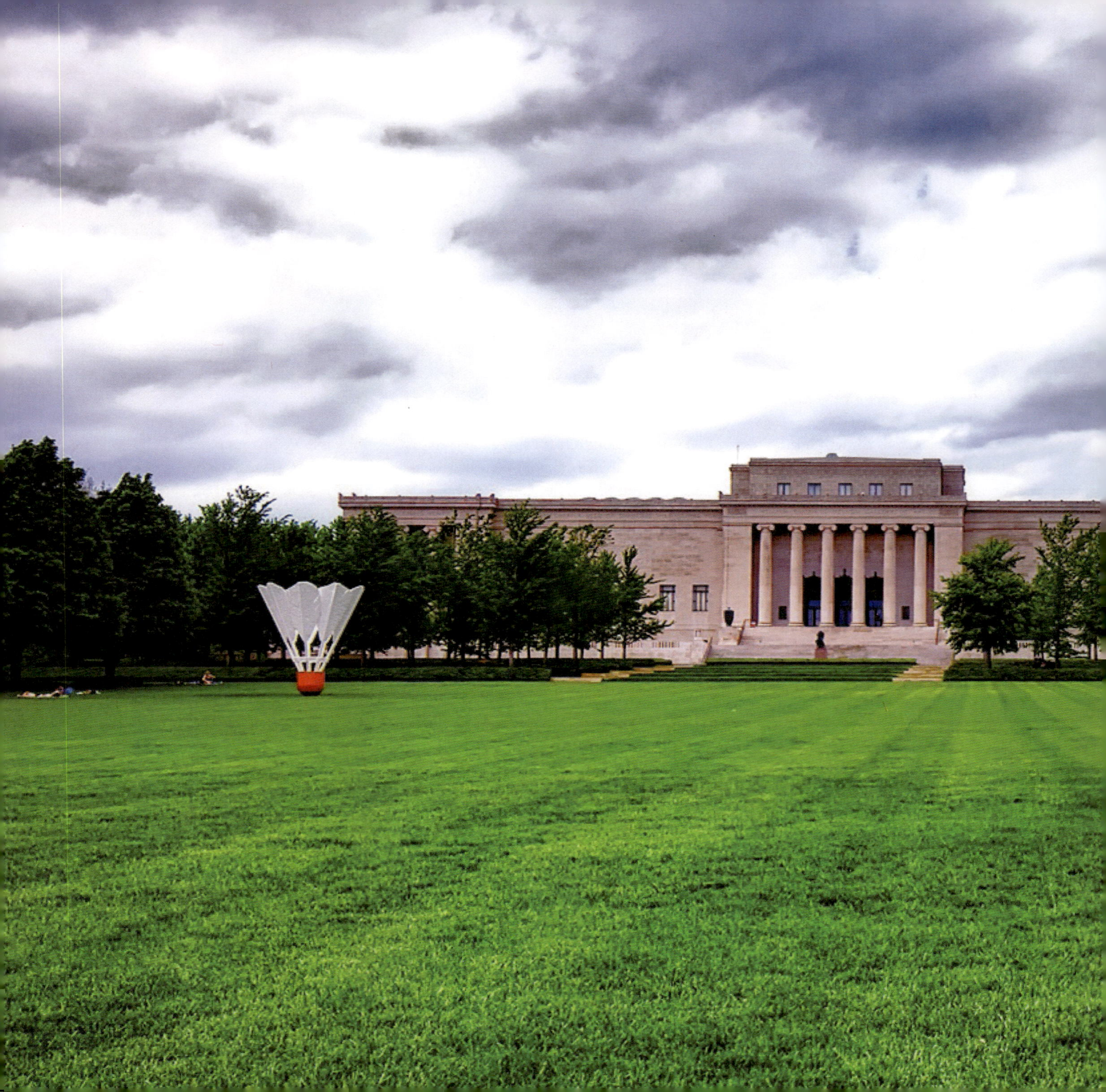

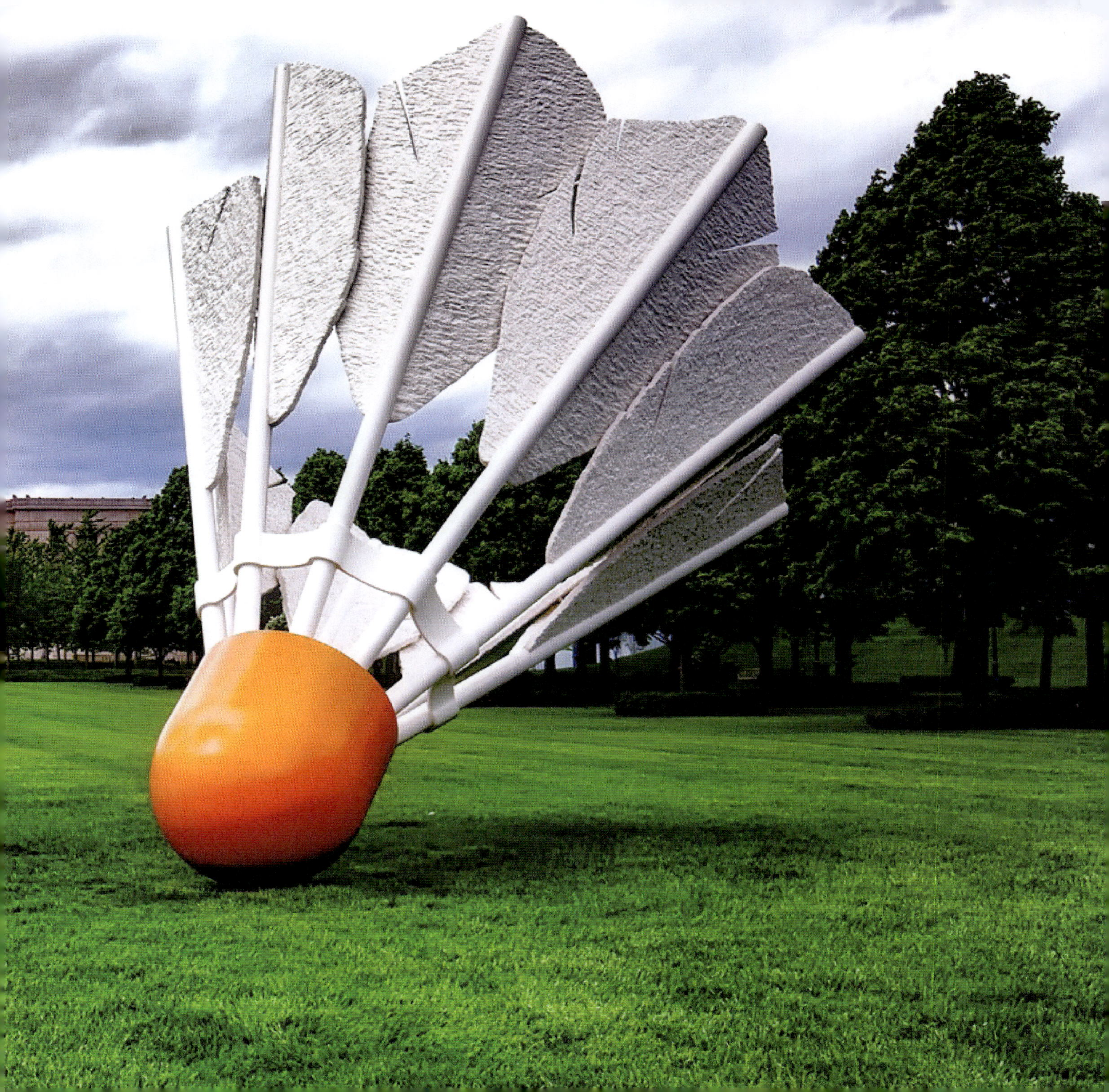

ROUTE CHOICE 2

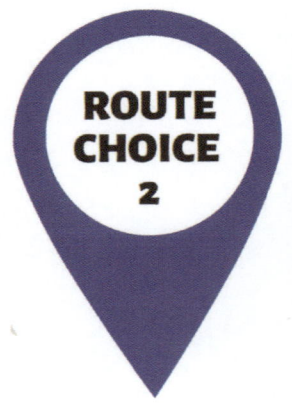

ROUTE A VIA TULSA

(or for Route B via Eureka Springs, turn to p. 209)

30. GRAVE OF THE EMBALMED BANDIT
35.8979, -97.4067

Guthrie Summit View Cemetery, 1808 N Pine St, Guthrie, OK 73044 (Boot Hill section)

Elmer McCurdy was an outlaw who was killed following a shootout with the police in 1911. His body was passed to a local funeral director, who waiting some time for someone to collect the body, decided to embalm it to keep it fresh until someone turned up. When no one did, the funeral director, decidedly out of pocket for his work, decided to hang onto it and use it as a tourist attraction to earn back the money that the funereal processes had cost him and which went unpaid. Eventually two men, claiming to be McCurdy's long lost brothers, contacted the local sheriff and gained permission to take the body back with them to San Francisco for proper burial. It later transpired that these gentlemen were in fact the Patterson brothers, owners of the Great Patterson Carnival Shows, who then displayed the corpse as 'The Outlaw who would Never Be Captured Alive' until 1922 when the carnival was sold. The new owner displayed the corpse in his travelling Museum of Crime amongst other waxworks, before it was sold onto another entrepreneur who displayed the body in theatres' lobbies to promote his film Narcotic! , claiming the now much shrunken body to be that of a 'dead dope fiend'. After the entrepreneur's death, the body sat in storage in LA for a while before being lent to a filmmaker who featured it in 1967's She Freak. In 1968 it was resold with other wax figures to the owner of the Hollywood Wax Museum, but it was somehow deemed both not lifelike enough and too gruesome to be exhibited. It was then sold to an amusement zone in Long

Above: Pops Soda Ranch on Route 66
> Top right and bottom right: The American Pigeon Museum
> Bottom left: Grave of the Embalmed Bandit

OFFBEAT AMERICA

Beach where, in 1976, it hung in the 'Laff in the Dark' funhouse exhibit. The same year, the production crew of The Six Million Dollar Man who were filming scenes in the funhouse realised that the waxwork was in fact a body and called police - an autopsy determined that the now entirely petrified body which through the years had been covered with layers of phosphorous paint, was in fact that of Elmer McCurdy.

31. SCOTTISH RITE TEMPLE
35.8781, -97.41337
900 E Oklahoma Ave, Guthrie, OK 73044
www.guthriescottishrite.org
Tour a grandiose masonic temple built with oil money in the Twenties.

32. OKLAHOMA TERRITORIAL MUSEUM
35.87835, -97.42094
406 E Oklahoma Ave, Guthrie, OK 73044
www.okterritorialmuseum.org
A wonderful museum for a general browse, but specifically the home of outlaw come arsenic painted mummy Elmer McCurdy.

33. GANDINI'S CIRCUS
35.6591, -97.4979
N Kelly Avenue between Swan Lake Road and Pruett Drive
Edmond, Oklahoma, 73003
An abandoned circus camp. Need we say more.

34. POPS SODA RANCH ON ROUTE 66
35.65827, -97.33547
660 OK-66, Arcadia, OK 73007
pops66.com
An American 'soda ranch' on historic Route 66, this extraordinary roadside store sells over 700 types of fizzy drink and has a giant soda bottle sculpture to mark the spot.

35. THE AMERICAN PIDGEON MUSEUM
35.53631, -97.47135
2300 NE 63rd St, Oklahoma City, OK 73111
www.theamericanpigeonmuseum.org
Someone had to capture the rich history of pigeons before it was lost forever.

36. RODEO ANIMAL CEMETERY
35.5352, -97.48309
1700 NE 63rd St, Oklahoma City, OK 73111
nationalcowboymuseum.org
Oklahoma City's National Cowboy and Western Heritage Museum incorporates a graveyard for trusty rodeo steeds, a bull and even the museum mascot.

37. AMERICAN BANJO MUSEUM
35.4668, -97.51149
9 E Sheridan Ave, Oklahoma City, OK 73104
www.americanbanjomuseum.com
The most Oklahoma-n museum imaginable.

38. THE TOWN OF SLAUGHTERVILLE
35.08729, -97.33502
Slaughterville, OK, 73051
The area is named for a Mr Slaughter but was nonetheless the focus of a PETA protest who asked the town to change its name to Veggieville in return for a donation of $20k of veggie burgers to the local school. As Slaughterville doesn't have a local school, the name change never occurred.

39. DEAD WOMEN CROSSING
35.56778, -98.65055
Dead Women Crossing, OK 73096
This small backwater town is named after a grisly crime in which a woman who was running away from her husband was murdered by her sister in law in retribution… although the name sounds more like a road safety warning. Keep your eyes peeled.

40. WICHITA MOUNTAINS BUFFALO HERD
34.73284, -98.71319
32 Refuge Headquarters Road, Indiahoma, OK 73552
wichitamountains.fws.gov
One of the few locations where American bison are allowed to roam freely, this herd was released from a conservation program in the Bronx Zoo via being transported all the way to the Wichitas by train and are now thriving.

41. THE HOLY CITY OF OKLAHOMA
34.74267, -98.5911
262 Holy City Rd, Cache, OK 73527
Much resembling how one might picture Israel in biblical eras gone by and the site of the longest running Passion play in the USA, this area is essentially a giant stage set,

Above: Rodeo Animal Cemetery

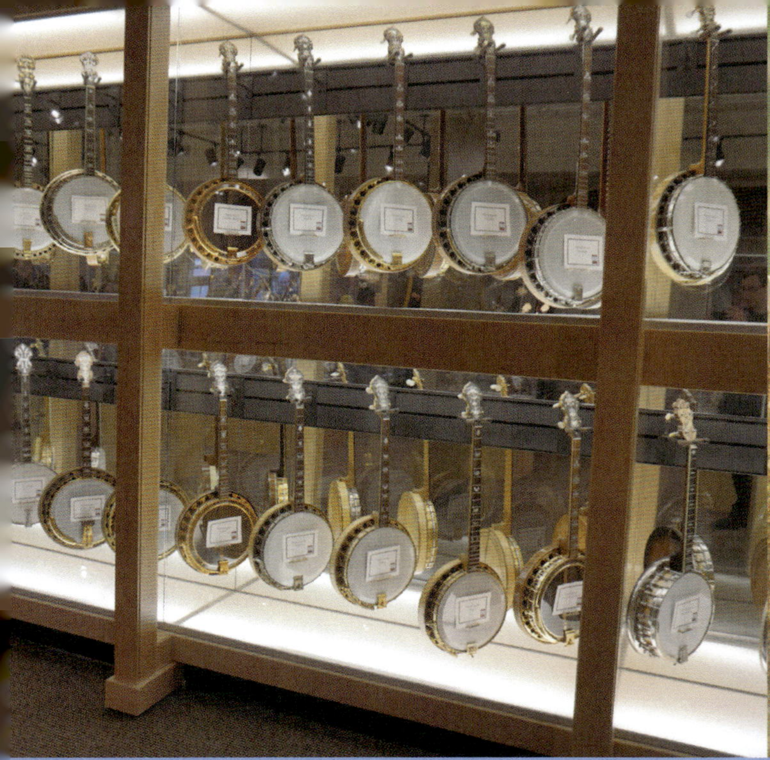
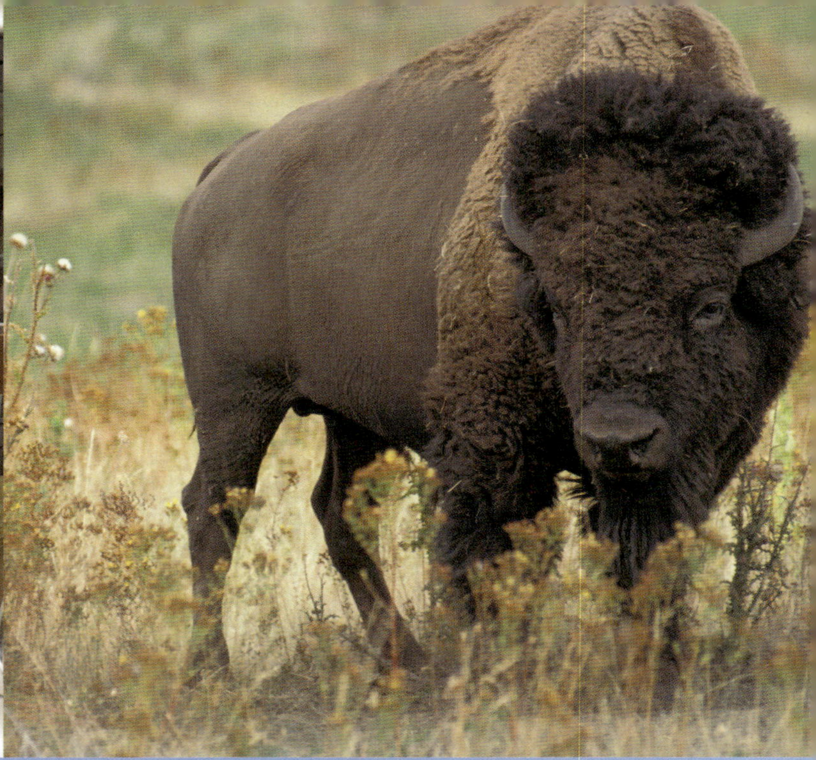
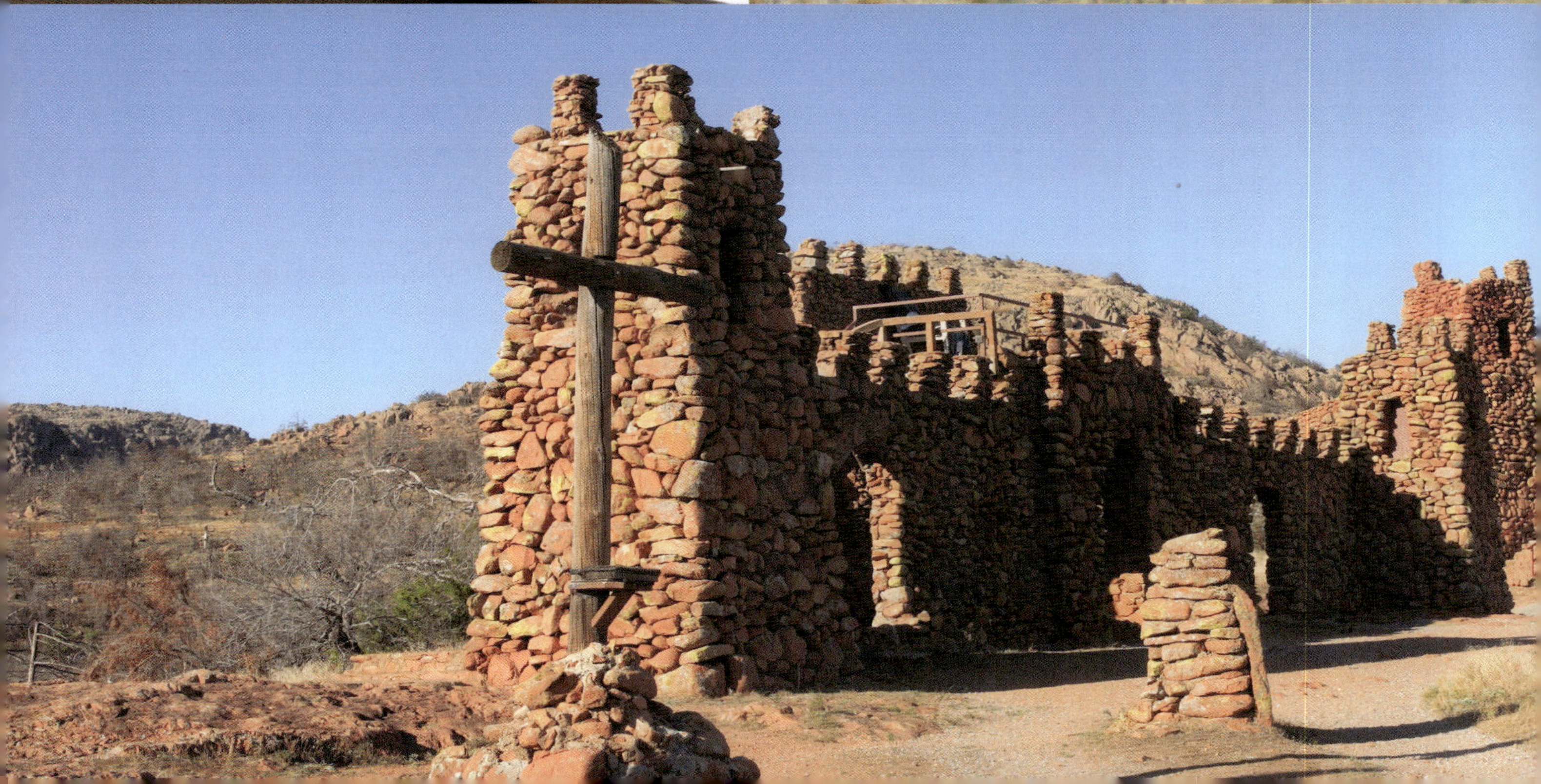

founded in 1926 in a location slightly to the east of its current situation by a Reverend to put on a traditional passion play which grew and grew, attracting first hundreds, then thousands, then hundreds of thousands of visitors a year. By the Thirties and with 100,000 plus attendees, US theatres showed footage of the event and in '37 the government filmed a feature length film of the production; another came about in 1949, with the Oklahoma accents much derided by the studios involved. The site you see today was built in 1934 as an up-scaled version of the original.

42. NEWBY-MCMAHON BUILDING
33.91444, -98.48975
World's littlest skyscraper, Wichita Falls, TX 76301

Also known as the World's littlest skyscraper, this charming building is the result of a fraudulent investment scheme by a con-man and represented a huge loss of face to the city of Wichita Falls when it was built in 1919. The scam held that McMahon would build a high-rise addition to the Newby building to provide the wealthy Wichita Falls with much needed office space and investors were quick to jump on board. He however never quite mentioned when speaking about the proposal how high the building would actually be, collecting $200,000 dollars which at the time would have had a value equivalent to $2.9m in today's money based on a blueprint plan which quite clearly labelled the building as being comprised of 4 floors and 480 inches high, all approved by investors who wholesale read the prints as 480ft high. This fact made a legal battle impossible to win for those defrauded. As an extra flourish, McMahon failed to build a stairway to access the floors as again, none was added into the blueprint and investors had simply made the assumption it would be featured, and instead magnanimously offered a ladder instead before making off with the cash. In the Twenties, the building featured in Ripley's Believe it or Not

Above and left: The 1886 Crescent Hotel and Spa
> Top: Newby-Mcmahon Building
> Bottom: Quigley's Castle

museum.

JUMP TO BILLY BASS ADOPTION CENTER p. 210 TO CONTINUE YOUR JOURNEY

ROUTE B VIA EUREKA SPRINGS

43. THE 1886 CRESCENT HOTEL AND SPA
36.4085, -93.7374
75 Prospect Ave, Eureka Springs, AR 72632
www.crescent-hotel.com

A historic hotel with a rep of being one of the most haunted in the USA. Built in 1886, it was first a resort for celebrities and the rich, before being converted into a variety of uses including a college, a summer hotel and a hospital run by a most dubious individual, a Mr Baker, who called himself a doctor, had absolutely no medical training, had been run out of Iowa for practicing without a licence, claimed to find a cure for cancer and derided conventional medicine for being profit-driven. Baker opened the Crescent as a cancer hospital, renaming it a 'health resort' for legal resources. His cure consisted of drinking natural spring water from the area. He spent four years in prison in 1940 leaving the Crescent empty until 1946 when it was bought for shared ownership by four individuals. In '97 the hotel was purchased and restored by Mr and Mrs Roenigk although tragically Mr Roenigk died in a car crash in 2009. Mrs Roenigk remains the current owner. Legend has it that the building is haunted by a woman who jumped or was pushed from the roof in the 20s, a nurse who worked in the former hospital, a stonemason who lost his footing during its construction, a cancer victim who died in Baker's 'care', a boy who died from complications from appendicitis and Mr Baker himself.

44. QUIGLEY'S CASTLE
36.3452, -93.7547
274 Quigley Castle Rd, Eureka Springs, AR 72632
www.quigleyscastle.com

Designed by Elisa Quigley, this house was built using all the rocks she had collected since her childhood and incorporated a two storey space for tropical plants. Today the house is open for tours.

45. DOGPATCH USA
36.1068, -93.1322
Marble Falls Township, Arkansas, 72648
This theme park opened in 1968, based on the comic strip Li'l Abner set in a fictional town called Dogpatch. An early hit, investors tried to build a sister park but this failed, leading to Dogpatch's financial collapse in '93. In 2014 it was bought by a pair of entrepreneurs and by Christmas it was open for business again. In 2016 the park was up for sale again, with one entrepreneur selling out and one staying in the venture. It remains closed for business awaiting an investor with $3M dollars to spare; ironically a similar amount was awarded to a youth who was nearly decapitated on the land in an ATV accident in 2005.

46. PEPPERSAUCE GHOST TOWN
36.1176, -92.1412
Rand Hill St
Calico Rock, Arkansas, 72519
This six block area east of Main Street is named for illegal spirits sold in what was a disreputable part of town. Now you can read placards about each building and although there is no trespassing on the private properties, the old city jail tempts urban explorers.

47. GRAVE OF A MAN AND HIS HORSE KILLED BY A TRAIN
36.0769, -90.94459
213 AR-34, Walnut Ridge, AR 72476
Self-explanatory, if unusual. Was John A. Rhea (38) killed, in 1893, committing suicide by horse/train or was it accidental? We may never know. Their grave is by a small tree in the middle of a field under a mound marked by an ornate headstone and is easily visible from the road.

48. THE TOWN OF TOAD SUCK
35.07564, -92.55988
Toad Suck, Union Township, AR 72016
Once the proud owner of the most votes for America's most unfortunate town name, the moniker originated from local church women referring to drunk men by saying that so and so was 'sucking on a bottle so much he's swollen up like a toad'. An alternative explanation holds that since the first Europeans to fully explore the area were French, the name could be an English corruption of a French word in the way that Aux Arcs became Ozarks – possibly eau d'sucre, chateau d'sucre or cote eau d'sucre.

ROUTES A & B CONVERGE HERE

49. BILLY BASS ADOPTION CENTER
34.7474, -92.2653
511 President Clinton Ave, Little Rock, AR 72201
flyingfishinthe.net
Ever wondered where Billy Basses go when they no longer adorn walls, approximately 2 days after purchase?

50. MAXWELL BLADE'S ODDITORIUM
34.51825, -93.05518
121 Central Ave, Hot Springs, AR 71901
www.maxwellblade.com
Arkansas illusionist Maxwell Blade shares his bizarre collection of odd with the world.

51. TREE SURGEON BURIED IN A TREE
34.08025, -92.48993
Hampton Springs Cemetery, Dallas 427, Carthage, Arkansas, 71725
In a tree by the entrance of a cemetery in

Above: Town of Toad Suck
> Right: Dogpatch USA
Overleaf: Billy Bass Adoption Centre

OFFBEAT AMERICA

2 MILES AHEAD

DOGPATCH USA

FREE ADMISSION

SHOWS

BRING US YOUR BILLY BASS FOR A FREE BASKET OF CATFISH!

THE WORLDS FIRST
*LY BASS ADOPTION CENTER

THE ONE THAT GOT AWAY

SIR DOUGLAS "DOUGIE" EDWARDS
2-19-07

BE NICE OR LEAVE!

Carthage, local legend has it that a tree surgeon is buried behind some large bricks sunken into the trunk.

52. THE GURDON GHOST LIGHT
33.95294, -93.16634
739 AR-53, Gurdon, Arkansas, 71743 (Exit I-30 at State Road 53, look for where old tracks cross I53 on map, turn right on dirt track here)
This light is said to be blue, green, white or orange and bobs around both in the day and the night in a wooded area of Arkansas. Legend tells that it is the light of a worker killed on the railroad that was mown down by a train, the head being cleaved from his body and never found thereafter. He searches for it by the light of a lantern. In reality it is thought the light is either passing cars on the highway in the distance creating an illusion, or perhaps the effect known as piezoelectricity, energy from the constant stress enacted on underground quartz crystals as the area in question sits above significant quantities of such crystals and on a fault line.

53. CRATER OF DIAMONDS STATE PARK
34.03272, -93.67542
209 State Park Rd, Murfreesboro, AR 71958
www.craterofdiamondsstatepark.com
Is it a 'pick your own' diamond mine, is it a field of mud? Try your luck and find out.

54. BONNIE AND CLYDE AMBUSH MUSEUM
32.54475, -93.05326
2419 Main St, Gibsland, LA 71028
bonnieandclydeambushmuseum.com
Run by L.J. 'Boots' Hinton, the son of a local sheriff, this low key museum in the town which is home to the last place that Bonnie and Clyde visited, Ma Canfield's Café, collects all the ephemera related to the duo who grabbed a couple of takeout sandwiches before being killed 8 miles down the street, Bonnie with sandwich in hand.

55. UNCERTAIN
32.71208, -94.12129
Uncertain, TX 75661
Incredibly creepy Lake Caddo-side location of swamp dwellings and Bigfoot sightings - photogenic beyond belief. Follow Lake Caddo signs and look out for hairy shapes amongst the trees. Check out the wonderful Uncertain documentary before you go. The city was named due to difficulty encountered by surveyors attempting to delineate the border between Texas and Louisiana who were uncertain as to which side of the line

they were on when they began surveying this area of Lake Caddo. Keep an eye out for the somewhat over active fauna in the area, especially those of the bloodthirsty variety in and around the water.

56. THE TOWN OF LOONEYVILLE
31.76323, -94.84438
Looneyville, Texas 75760
Named for John Looney in the 1870s who owned a store here.

57. APACHE DRIVE-IN THEATRE
32.35775, -95.1905
13180 TX-31, Tyler, TX 75705
Swing past while no movie is playing for a chance to see a proper US drive-in movie theatre. Stay if X rated adult movies are your thing!

58. GRAND SALINE SALT PALACE
32.6745, -95.7096
100 W Garland St, Grand Saline, TX 75140, USA
One museum that has missed the memo that you should cut back on salt. Literally… all things salt. And the building housing it is made…of salt. In a town called Grand Saline featuring a Grand Saline High School.

59. TEXAS EIFFEL TOWER
33.63987, -95.52387
s 75460, 2025 S Collegiate Dr, Paris, TX 75460
www.paristexas.com

< Bottom left: Crater of Diamonds State Park
< Bottom right: Texas Eiffel Tower
Right: Showmen's Rest
Overleaf: Uncertain

Why go to France when you have the same wonder in both Vegas AND Texas.

60. SHOWMEN'S REST
33.9987, -95.5012
Mt Olivet Cemetery, E Trice St & 8th St, Hugo, OK 74743
Hugo Oklahoma is a common winter retreat for travelling circus men, hence its nickname 'Circus Town, USA'. Nowadays the circuses of Carson & Barnes and Kelly Miller reside there - Kelly himself is buried along with other circus performers including animal trainers and wire walkers in a Showmen's Rest section (of which there are several across America), beneath a monument decorated with an elephant. There is also a grand life-size statue of a Ringmaster described as 'the man with more friends than Santa Claus'. One man, an elephant handler, died in a more common than you might think circus train wreck, whilst another elephant trainer might have had enough of the creatures as he was crushed to death by one, but nonetheless has been immortalised by a grave decorated with a large pachyderm. Graves of rodeo stars are also featured, often with spectacular names, some of whom died naturally, others of whom were gored to death. Kelly's brother and fellow circus master D.R. Miller purchased Kelly his plot upon his death, and has now joined the cemetery himself, his epitaph reading 'Dun Rovin'.

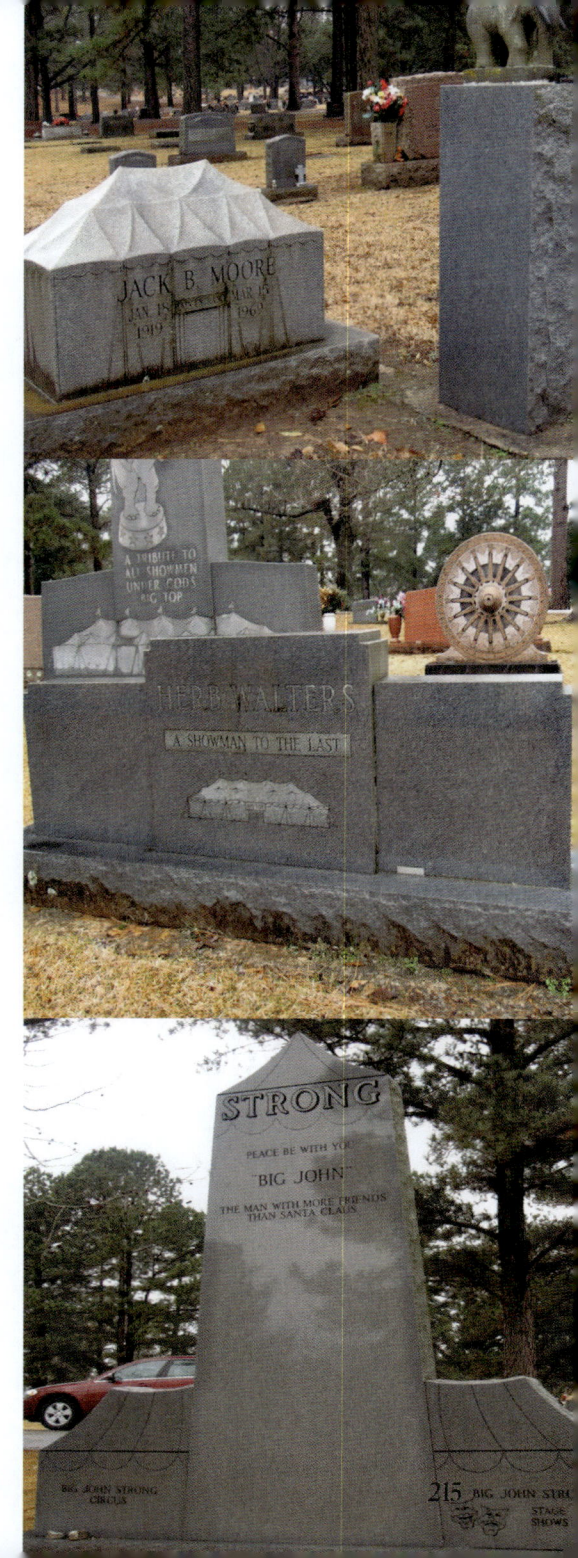

THE SOUTHBOUND TRAIL ROUTE 5

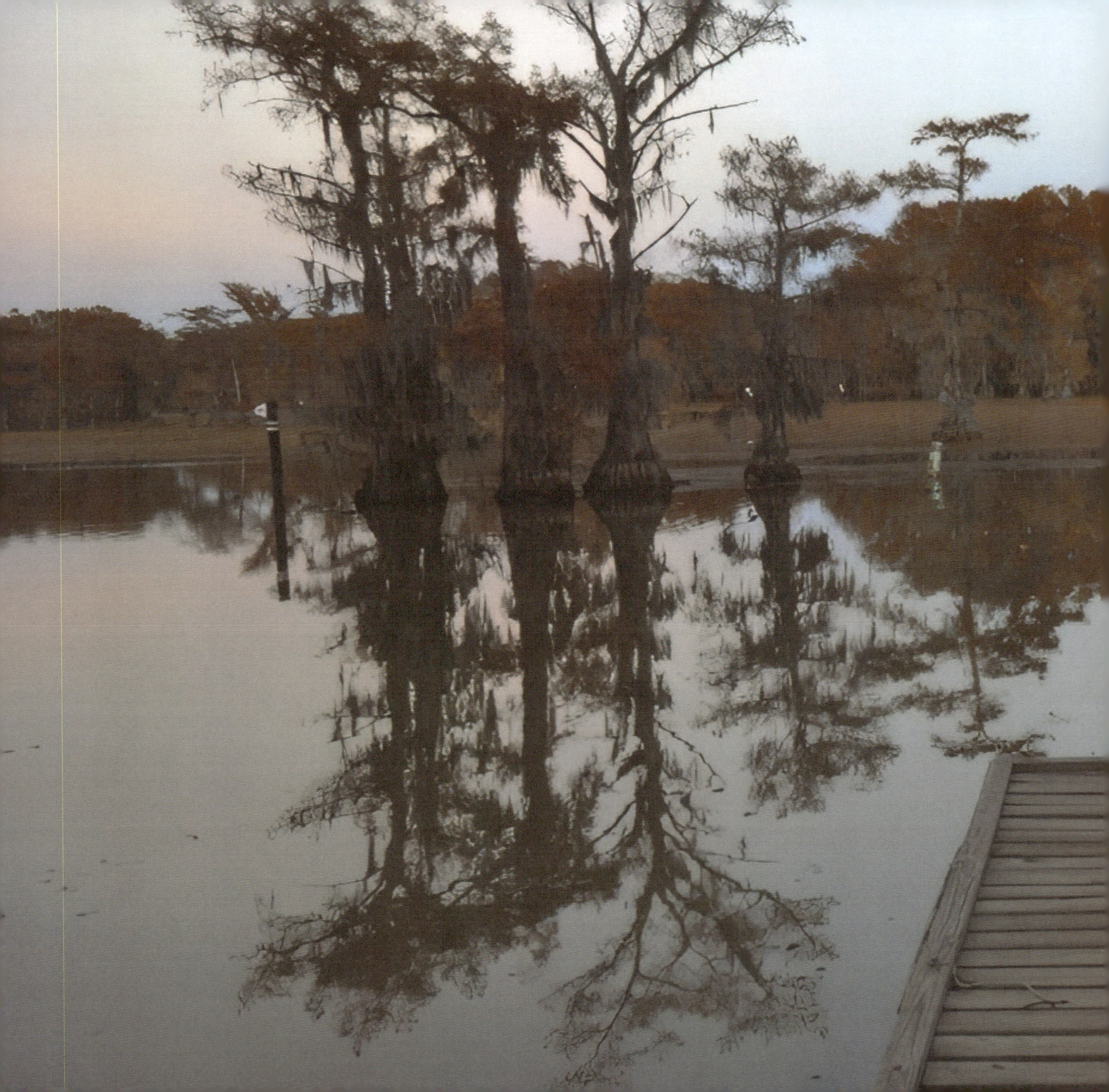

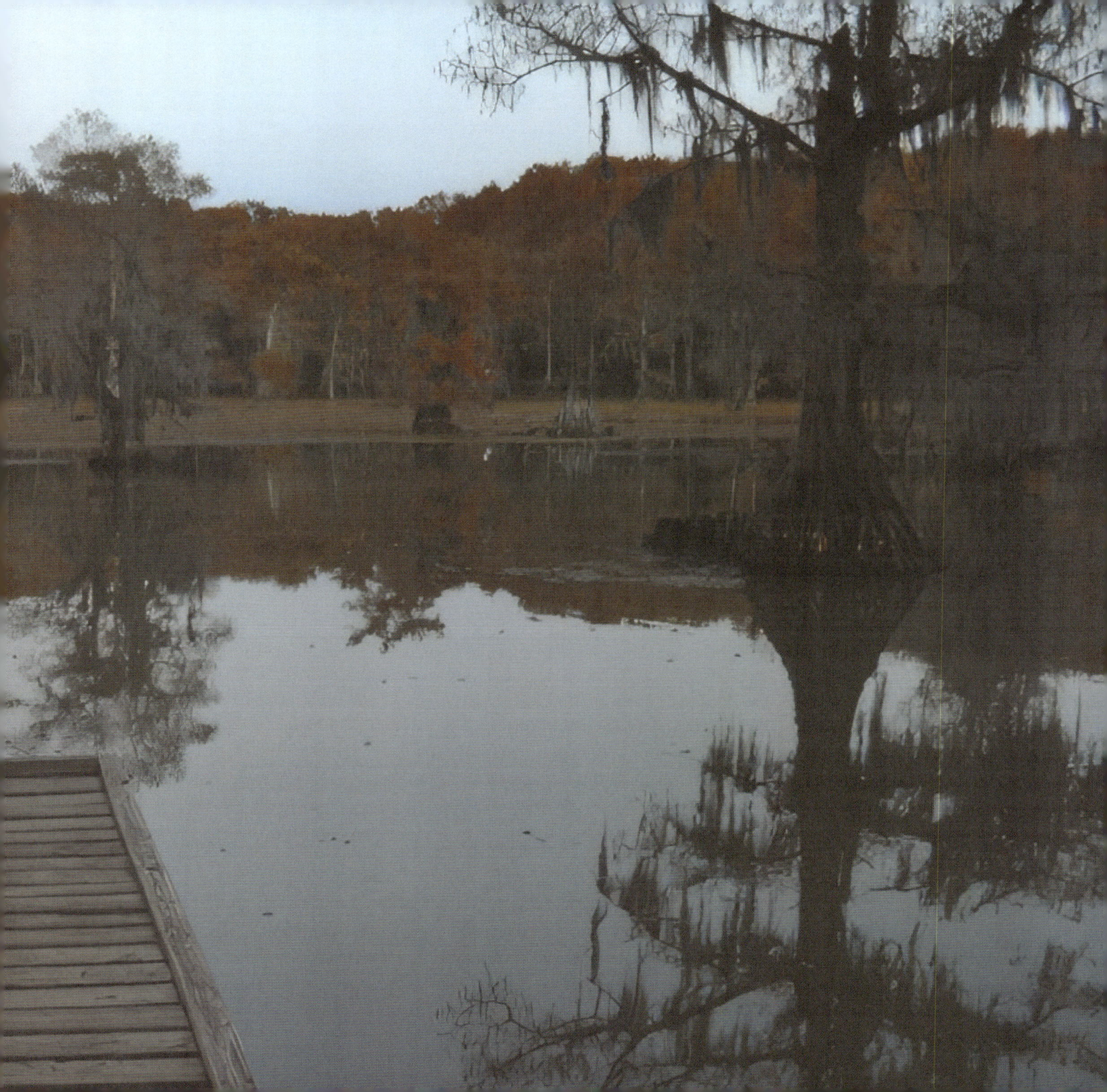

61. WORLD'S LARGEST PEANUT
33.9927, -96.3783

201 N 3rd Avenue, Durant Oklahoma, 74701(corner of Evergreen St. and N 3rd Ave)

Is this Durant peanut the largest, or does that title go to Ashburn Georgia or Pearsall Texas? Well apparently no one is in agreement on this so to be even handed let's just say this is one of three very large peanuts.

62. ROYSE CITY FUTURO HOUSE
32.89805, -96.30007

9573 TX-276, Royse City, TX 75189

www.thefuturohouse.com

Designed as an innovative and desirable portable ski chalet in 1968 by Matti Suuronen, this icon of the Sixties 'the Futuro House' has very few surviving examples and this is one of them (albeit abandoned). Fewer than 100 were built due to public negativity towards the look of them - they were thought too futuristic to be sympathetic to their environment.

63. AURORA ALIEN GRAVE
33.05336, -97.50002

Aurora Cemetery, Aurora, TX 76078

In 1897 a UFO is said to have crashed after hitting a windmill (clearly their technology isn't that advanced), resulting in the death of the alien pilot whose body is allegedly buried in an unmarked grave at the local graveyard.

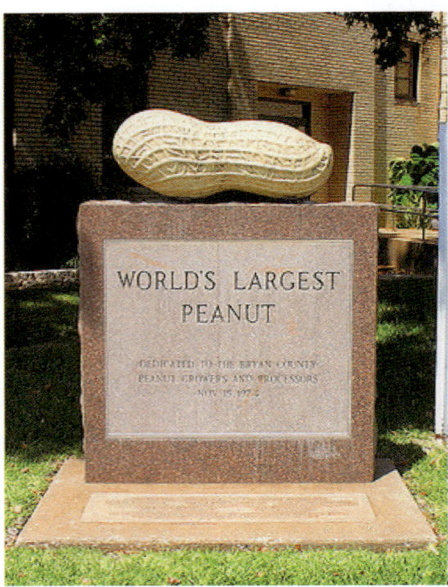

Top and overleaf: Royse City Futuro House
Bottom: World's Largest Peanut (prior page)

OFFBEAT AMERICA

Others have theorised that when the town was in decline after being beset by a number of disasters, one resident may have written the hoax article to bring notoriety and success to the failing town.

64. THE PALACE LIGHT BULB
32.78949, -97.34659
The Stockyards Museum, 131 E Exchange Ave # 113, Fort Worth, TX 76164
www.stockyardsmuseum.org
Almost as impressive as the longest ever burning light bulb, this is the... second... longest... ever burning light bulb. Someone get a solar panel.

65. THE CAFÉ AND CAR LOT
32.7231, -97.48217
3400 W Loop 820 S, Fort Worth, TX 76116
Grab an 'OMG Burger' whilst perusing vehicles at Frank Kent Honda in this Texas café which really does cater to all aspects of the American dream at once.

66. MAN WITH A BRIEFCASE
32.7505, -97.3337
Burnett Park, Fort Worth, TX 76102
A unique 2D sculpture.

67. FORT WORTH WATER GARDENS
32.7478, -97.3265
Fort Worth Water Gardens, W Lancaster Ave, Fort Worth, TX 76102
An arresting oasis in downtown Fort Worth that makes for great photos.

68. MUNSTER MANSION
32.4361, -96.8107
3636 FM 813, Waxahachie, TX 75165
www.munstermansion.com
This residence is one couple's faithful reproduction of the iconic home featuring identical externals and internals as well as many original props from the series and is open once a year for special tour events.

69. DINOSAUR VALLEY STATE PARK
32.43558, -96.81083
1629 Park Rd 59, Glen Rose, TX 76043
www.tpwd.state.tx.us

Bottom left: Man with a Briefcase
Bottom centre: Fort Worth Water Gardens
Bottom right: Munster Mansion

THE SOUTHBOUND TRAIL ROUTE 5

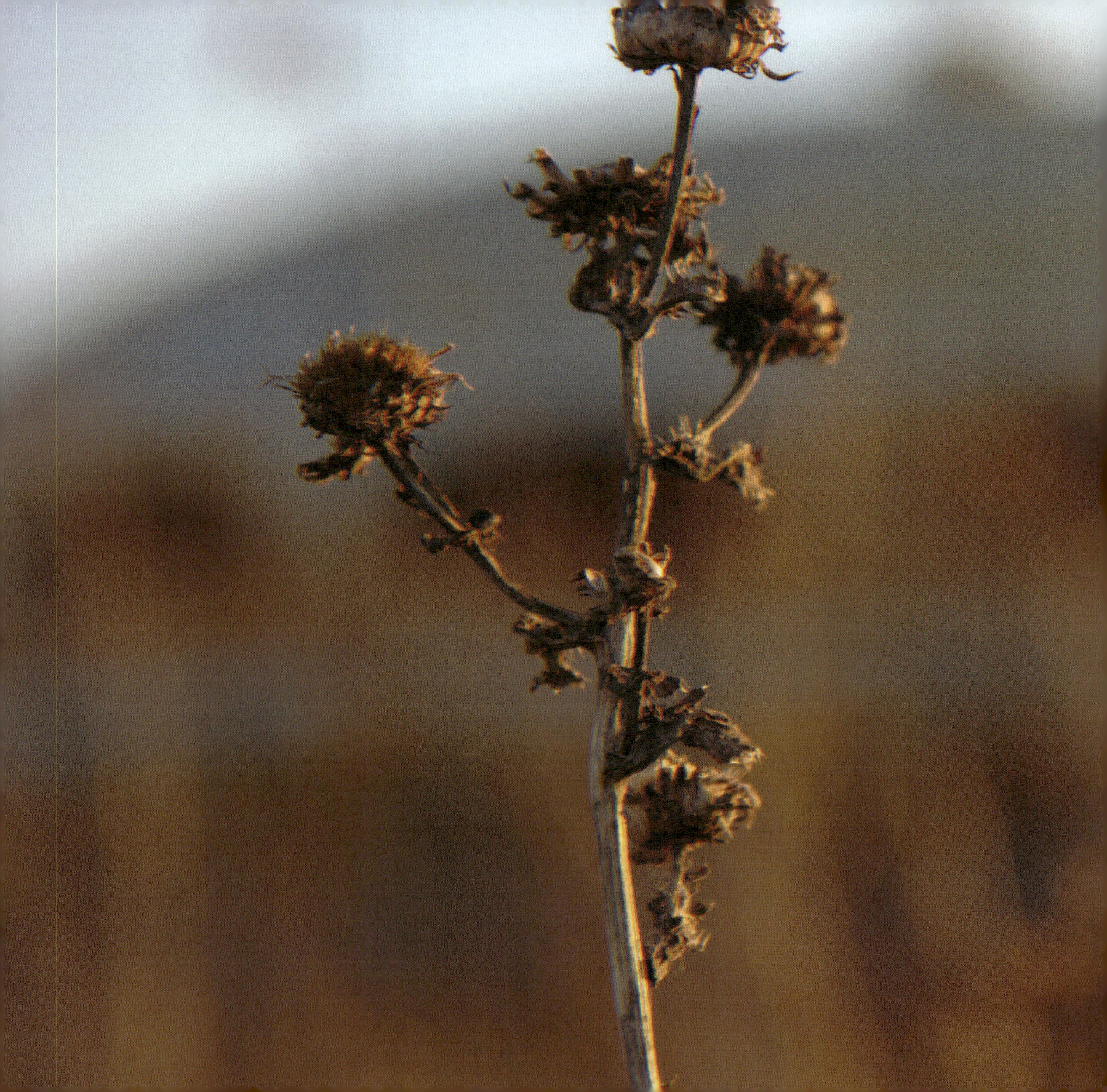

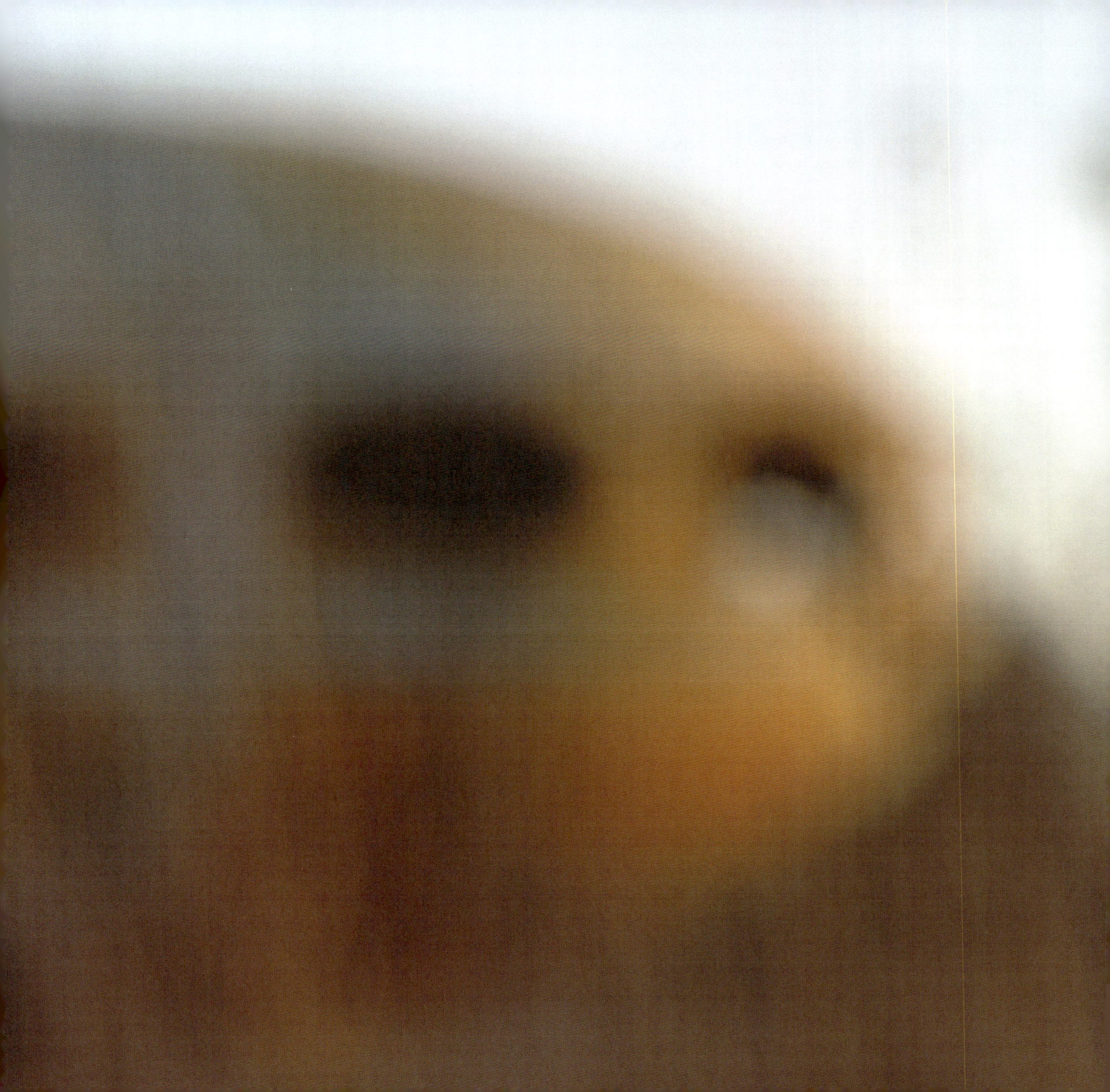

Bottom left: Grave of Rope Walker
Bottom centre: Dinosaur Valley
Bottom right: Beer Can House (next page)

This state park contains authentic dinosaur tracks in the riverbed - visit and walk in their footsteps.

70. STARSHIP PEGASUS
32.19609, -96.89844
100 Kinfolk Rd, Italy, TX 76651
A spaceship sitting in the geographically confusing Italy, Texas. Apparently it's up for sale, takers?

71. GRAVE OF ROPE WALKER
32.0851, -96.4905
2301-2399 W 2nd Ave, Corsicana, TX 75110
Legend has it this one-legged tightrope walker fell off his rope whilst attempting to cross it strung across Corsicana's Beaton Street. To make his life more of a challenge he was carrying a cast iron stove on his back, leading him to land beneath the stove with only the time to request a Jewish burial as he breathed his last without revealing his name. Much speculation and research has gone into filling in his story; his name is thought to be Daniel De Houne, a performer of some renown in Texas, California, Nevada and Louisiana, who also used the alias Joseph Berg and may have carried the title Professor. It is thought his death occurred on the 14th March and that he in fact survived for at least 3 days, having his only remaining leg amputated in that time.

72. CULT SWIMMING POOL AND MASSACRE SITE
31.596, -96.98789
1781 Double Ee Ranch Road, Waco, TX 76705
This is the site of the extraordinary standoff between Branch Davidian cult leader David Koresch and the FBI which resulted in the deaths of 76 so called Davidians, including Koresch himself, after the FBI began to (accurately) fear that the cult was stockpiling weapons and besieged its compound. The only remaining structure is a swimming pool used for relaxation by cult members and as a bunker during the deadly standoff.

73. BABY HEAD CEMETERY
30.88771, -98.6561
Llano, TX 78643
Various accounts are said to explain the name of Babyhead Mountain which is the area in which this cemetery finds itself - all seem

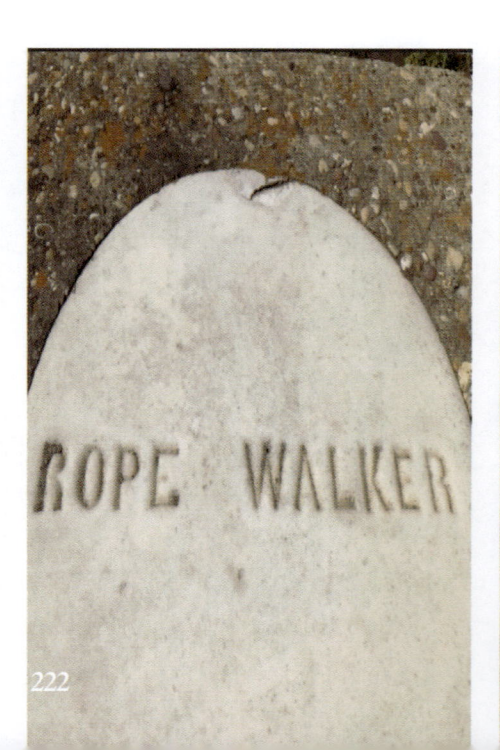

Below: Cult Swimming Pool & Massacre Site

to agree that it is due to a small child being found dead on the mountain, or possibly more than one. The most widely held belief is that a young child was killed by Indians and its remains left on the mountain.

74. TRAVIS STATE SCHOOL FARM COLONY
30.2732, -97.6400
509 Deaf Smith St, Austin, TX 78724 (Cemetery can be found on south side of the campus)

Founded in 1933 as a branch of Austin State School, this 241 acre site on the Colorado River provided a home for mentally underdeveloped boys who were deemed unable to benefit from wider schooling, providing them work in farming, dairying and tending to the grounds. At its peak, 1800 students lived here, transferring from other institutions to join the education program. Female students were admitted from 1973 but the general population declined in the seventies and eighties as such individuals were deemed better served by integration into the wider community. It was closed in 1995 due to law suits pending against the so called Texas Department of Mental Health and Mental Retardation. Incidentally for anyone observant who might be wondering as to the etymology of the Street the colony is found upon, 'Deaf Smith Street', it is named for an American frontiersman Erastus 'Deaf' Smith, a.k.a. El Sordo ('The Deaf') noted for his part in the Texas Revolution and the Army of the Republic of Texas who did indeed suffer hearing loss. His name inspires several locations and brand names in the US, although most are curiously pronounced 'Deef' rather than deaf. His gravestone in Richmond Texas Episcopal churchyard reads 'Deaf Smith, The Texas Spy.'

75. THE BOTTLE HOUSE
30.2438, -97.75779
2209 S 1st St, Austin, TX 78704 (Around the back of End of an Ear Records, check open days or make an appointment via the website https://www.facebook.com/thebottlehouseaustin)

Located in the wonderfully named Slackerville, this house is not decorated with bottles but rather made out of them. Not only that, it contains actual carved peanuts (yes, literally peanuts which have been

THE SOUTHBOUND TRAIL ROUTE 5

Bottom: National Museum of Funeral History (prior page)
Top and > Right: Art Car Museum (prior page)

carved), with pun related names such as the Sage of the Leguminati or The Wizard of Aus(tin).

76. NATIONAL MUSEUM OF FUNERAL HISTORY
29.9895, -95.4306
415 Barren Springs Dr, Houston, TX 77090
www.nmfh.org
All things dead and dying and the practices used to deal with them. Look out for the bus.

77. ART CAR MUSEUM
29.77203, -95.39686
140 Heights Blvd, Houston, TX 77007
www.artcarmuseum.com

This museum aims to recognise the talents of artists who have gone beneath the radar of other art institutions and specialises in art created using vehicles - Closed Monday and Tuesday.

78. BEER CAN HOUSE
29.7638, -95.4190
222 Malone St, Houston, TX 77007
www.beercanhouse.org
Taking a love of beer to a whole new level.

224 OFFBEAT AMERICA

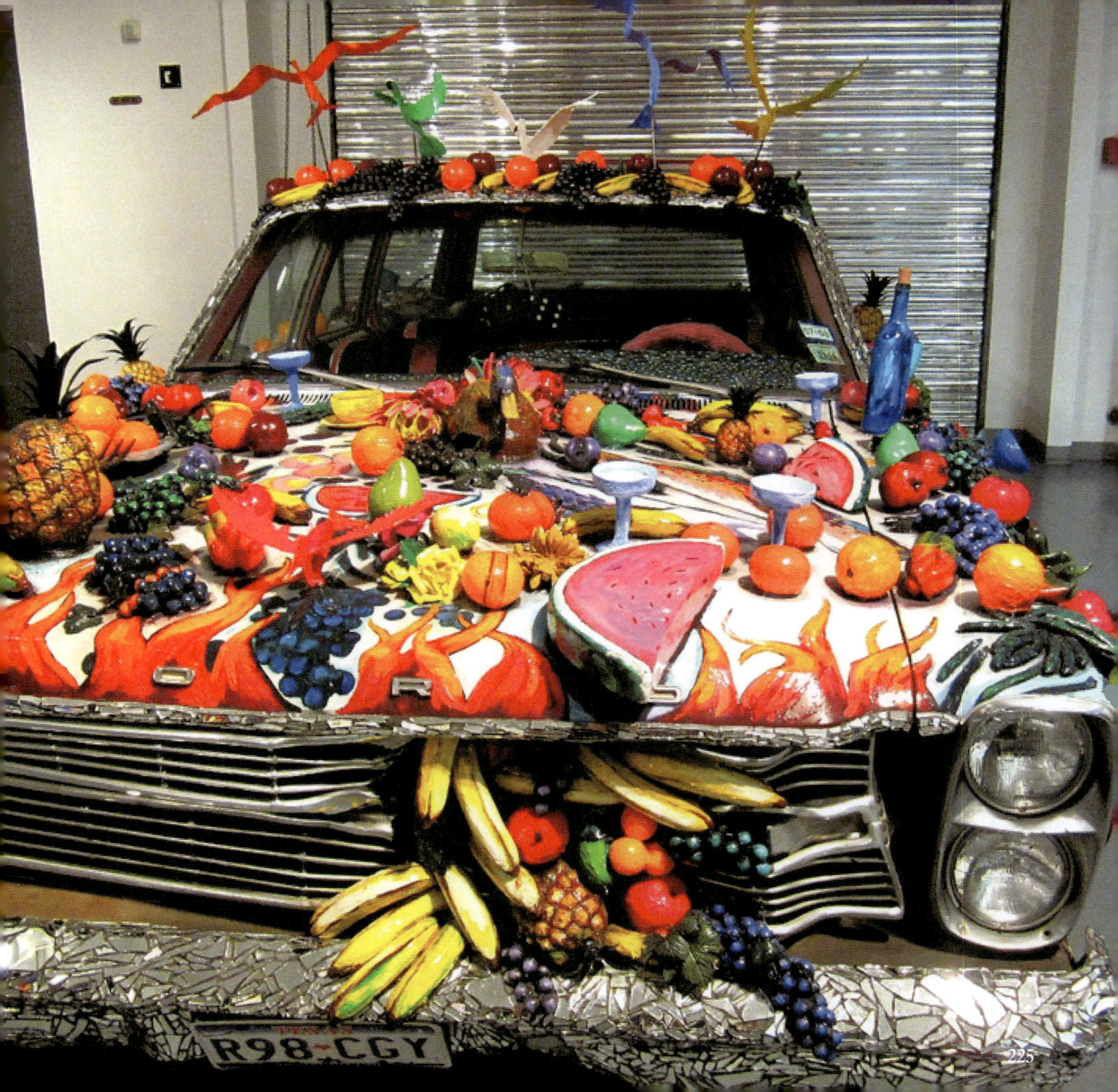
R98-CGY

THE SOUTHERN TRAIL ROUTE 6

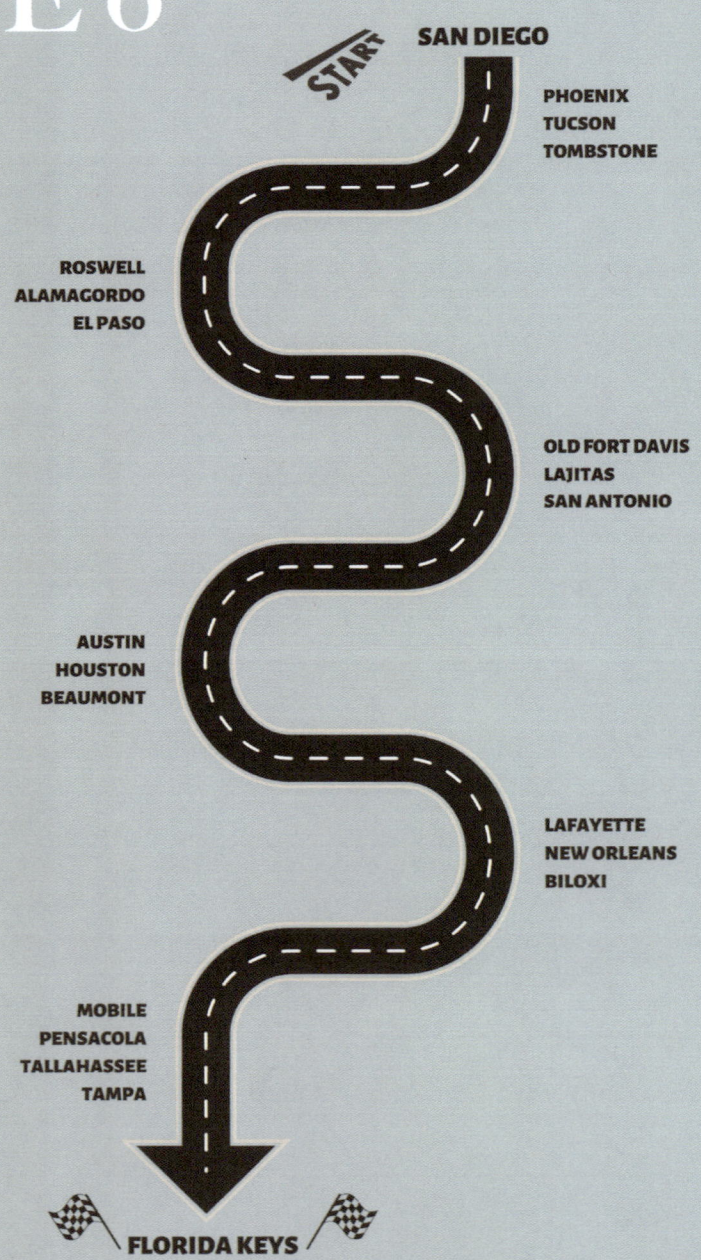

START — SAN DIEGO

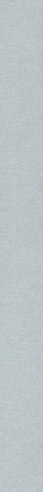

PHOENIX
TUCSON
TOMBSTONE

ROSWELL
ALAMAGORDO
EL PASO

OLD FORT DAVIS
LAJITAS
SAN ANTONIO

AUSTIN
HOUSTON
BEAUMONT

LAFAYETTE
NEW ORLEANS
BILOXI

MOBILE
PENSACOLA
TALLAHASSEE
TAMPA

FLORIDA KEYS

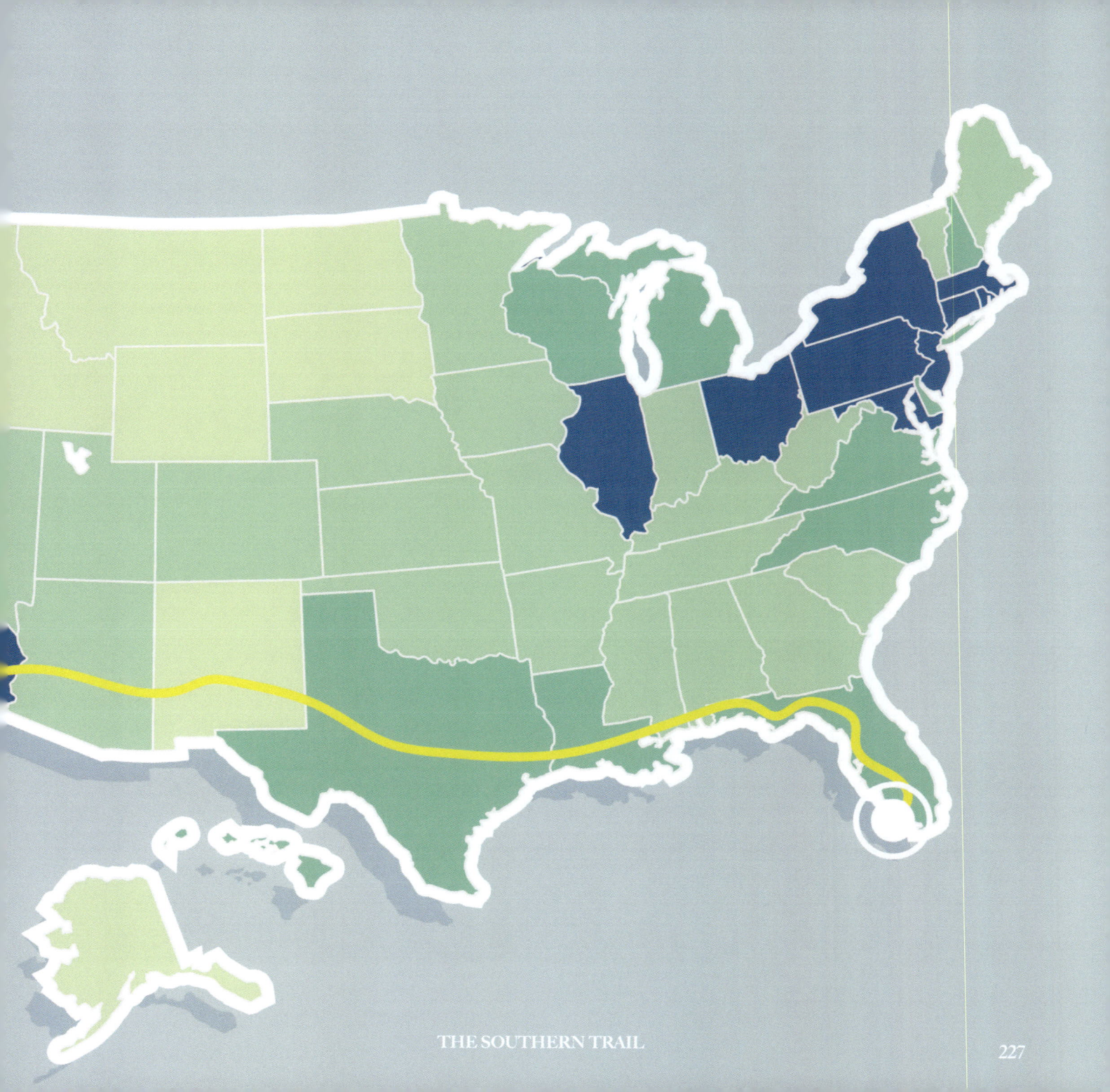

THE SOUTHERN TRAIL

THE SOUTHERN TRAIL ROUTE 6

Follow the Mexican borderlands all the way to the Keys on the Southern Trail, travelling through America's tropics. Here you will truly see the vast range of landscapes that the States has to offer, from the desolate deserts of the Wild West to UFO country, from cowboy ranches to the eerie mangrove swamps of Louisiana, from French colonial voodoo Nola to utopian Tampa. Travel across the Everglades stopping in at grandiosely named Everglade City, shoot past alligators across seemingly solid grasslands on an airboat and finally kick back with a Mojito in the charmingly ramshackle Florida Keys, America's answer to the Caribbean. Meet the mayor of a town (but don't be surprised if he is drunk or you find yourself butting heads with him) and if the timing's right, join an amphibian festival.

1. THE INDESTRUCTIBLE MUSHROOM HOUSE OF BLACK'S BEACH

- 32.872310, -117.252048
- 9036 La Jolla Shores Ln, La Jolla, CA 92037
- This unusual guest house was built for Sam Bell, a snack food

Above: The Indestructible Mushroom House of Black's Beach

"WEREN'T DINOSAURS TOO BIG TO GO ON THE ARK?"

entrepreneur, in 1968, to the brief that the house had to be futuristic and withstand any rock slide, earthquakes and waves (or teenagers, as he has since added) as well as be accessible via a nigh on vertical 300 ft funicular set into the cliff face (tracks still visible in the picture). One assumes he wasn't a fan of close guest proximity. Whilst now abandoned, the house still stands proud just south of Black's Beach and the exterior can be reached via a canyon hike.

2. LEMON GROVE MUMMIES AND LARGEST LEMON

32.73175, -117.15231
San Diego Museum of Man, Balboa Park, 1350 El Prado, San Diego, CA 92101
www.museumofman.org
32.7425, -117.0310
3365-3599 Main St, Lemon Grove, CA 91945

When life gives you lemons…go hunting for Mummies? A place famous for its giant lemon, and for two young boys who whimsically went Mummy hunting south of the Mexican border and managed to return with a real life mummy which they promptly hid in their garage. The Mummies themselves can now be found in a San Diego Museum within Balboa Park, whilst the giant lemon is a proud feature of Lemon Grove, a town which also features a Lemon Grove Ave, Lemon Grove Way, Lemon Ave, Lemonwood Lane, Citrus St, a Citronica building as well as a Berry St just to throw you off.

3. HARPER'S TOPIARY GARDEN

32.7412, -117.176
Harper's Topiary Garden, Union St, San Diego, CA 92103

A local artist has created a topiary front yard of Edward Scissorhands proportions.

4. MUSEUM OF CREATION AND EARTH HISTORY

32.8451, -116.9594
10946 N Woodside Ave, Santee, CA 92071
creationsd.org

The place to go to learn about how man and dinosaur lived hand in claw, the exact size of the ark and where the triceratops were stored on it, how God's hand is seen in all scientific discoveries and why religion can explain all the great mysteries of space.

5. CHRISTMAS CARD LANE

32.9664, -117.1310
9106 Ellingham St, San Diego, CA 92129

The most festive street in sunny San Diego – visit in the holiday season for twinkling festivities American style.

6. THE AIRMAIL LANE MAIL BOX

33.01107, -116.93125
17358 CA067 (Junction of Airmail Ln), Ramona, CA 92065

This mailbox on the corner of Airmail Ln is at perfect cruising altitude.

< Left: Museum of Creation and Earth History
Right: Lemon Grove Mummies & Largest Lemon

THE SOUTHERN TRAIL ROUTE 6

If you have time whilst in San Diego, why not view the outside of the Mormon Temple, a stunning structure - sadly no entry for non-Mormons permitted.
7474 Charmant Dr, San Diego, CA 92122

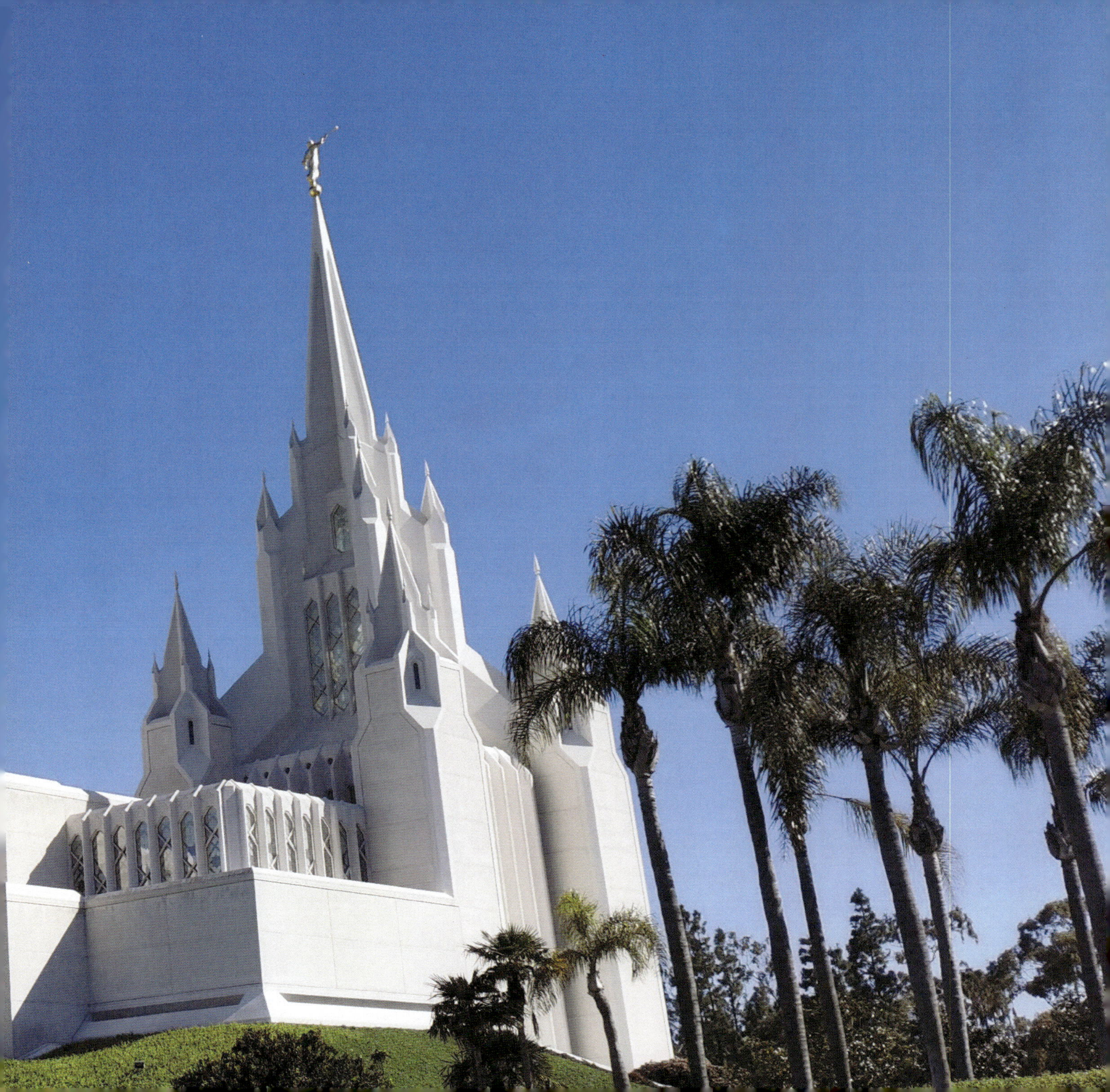

Left top: Christmas Card Lane (prior page)
Left centre: The Airmail Lane Mail Box
Bottom left and > right: Bombay Beach at the Salton Sea

7. GALLETA MEADOWS ESTATE
33.30503, -116.40529
Galleta Meadows, Borrego Springs, California 92004
Extraordinary metal sculpture park in the midst of the desert where arresting metal scorpians, camels and Chinese dragons by artist Ricardo Breceda rise out of the dust. Drive right up to them on the off road tracks to get spectacular photographs.

8. BOMBAY BEACH AT THE SALTON SEA
33.3479, -115.7298
Avenue E, Niland, CA 92257
The Salton Sea in the Coachella Valley (better known for its hip beyond belief festival) was envisioned as a utopian resort in the middle of the desert and briefly played host to tourists on shiny speedboats visiting from Palm Springs and LA as well as boasting Sonny Bono as the town mayor. The Sea, which fills the lowest elevation of the Salton Sink in the Colorado Desert, was historically in a constant state of flux between freshwater lake, saline lake and dry desert basin depending on the balance between the flow of the river into and out of the valley and the evaporative loss. In order to create greater water flow into the area for local farms, the California Development company in 1905 dug irrigation canals and a cut into the local river, which overflowed the engineered banks and filled the historic dry lake bed creating the Salton Sea of today which entirely submerged the town of Salton and the Torres-Martinez Native American Land. Due to the constant inflow and lack of outflow created by the artificial canals to nearby farms, the Salton Sea lost its natural balancing system; low water levels due to farm water use, ancient salt deposits in the lake bed combined with high salinity of inflow create an ever increasing salinity level, with a concentration currently increasing at around 3% per year and approximately 4 million short tonnes of salt deposited in the valley annually. This created a toxic environment of astronomic proportions; with water significantly saltier than seawater, the freshwater fish which once resided in the lake began to die off in their millions, leaving the area a natural disaster zone with scenes of mass dead fish littering the beaches. The remaining fish are highly toxic and the water rancid; the lake as a result now lies abandoned but for a few hangers oners who, having spent their funds on their ideal retirement home in the glamourous resort, are now unable or unwilling to move away. In what is one of the lonliest and most folorn places one could imagine living, some locals are said to still eat the fish from the lake due to a lack of alternative services in the area although the wise steer clear. A mecca for urban explorers and fans of decay photography and a stark warning about messing with the natural balance in favour of capitalism. The Grand Theft Auto V location Alamo Sea is based on the Salton Sea, whilst documentaries Plagues & Pleasures

Overleaf: Galleta Meadows

OFFBEAT AMERICA

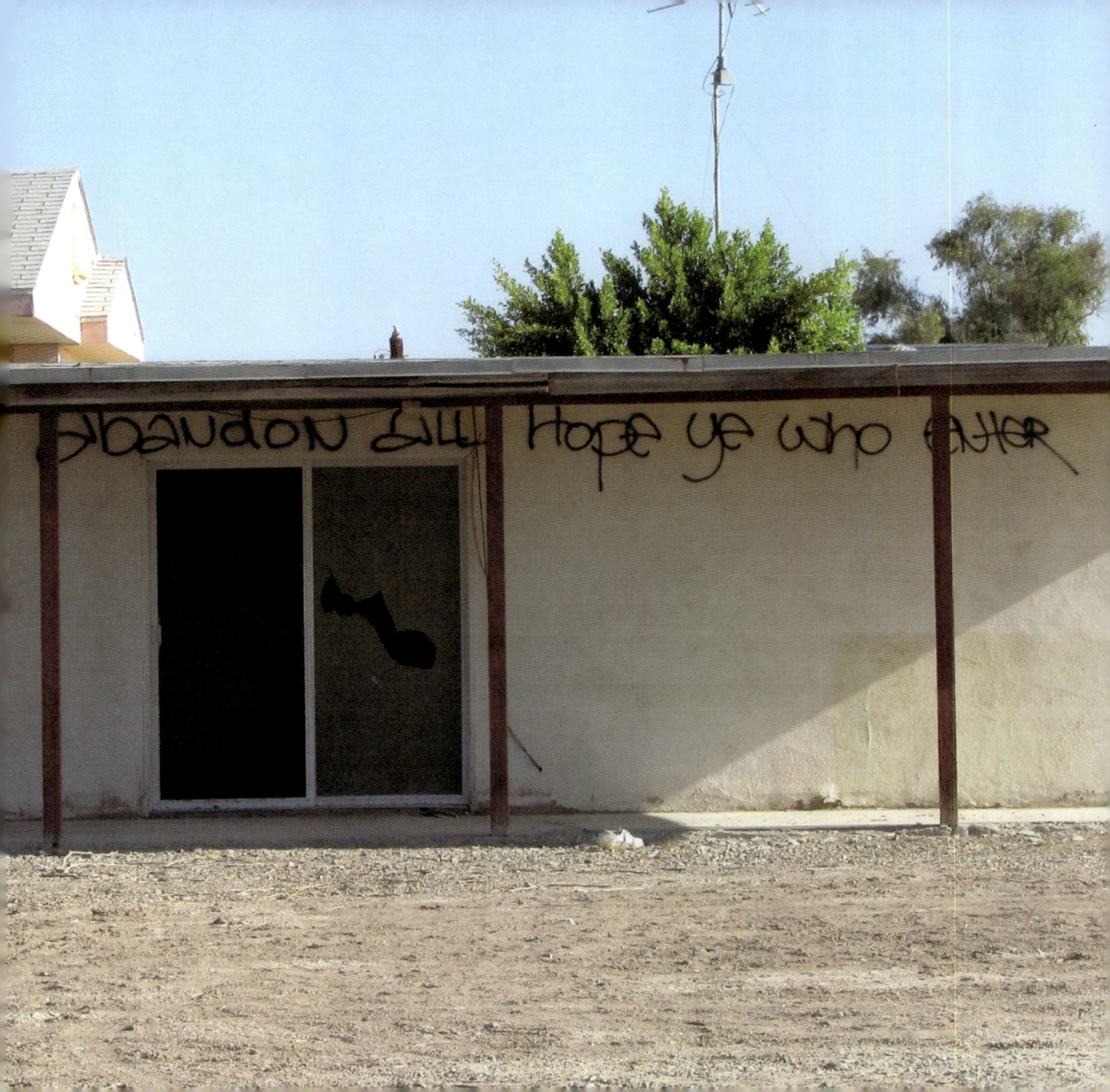
Abandon All Hope ye who enter

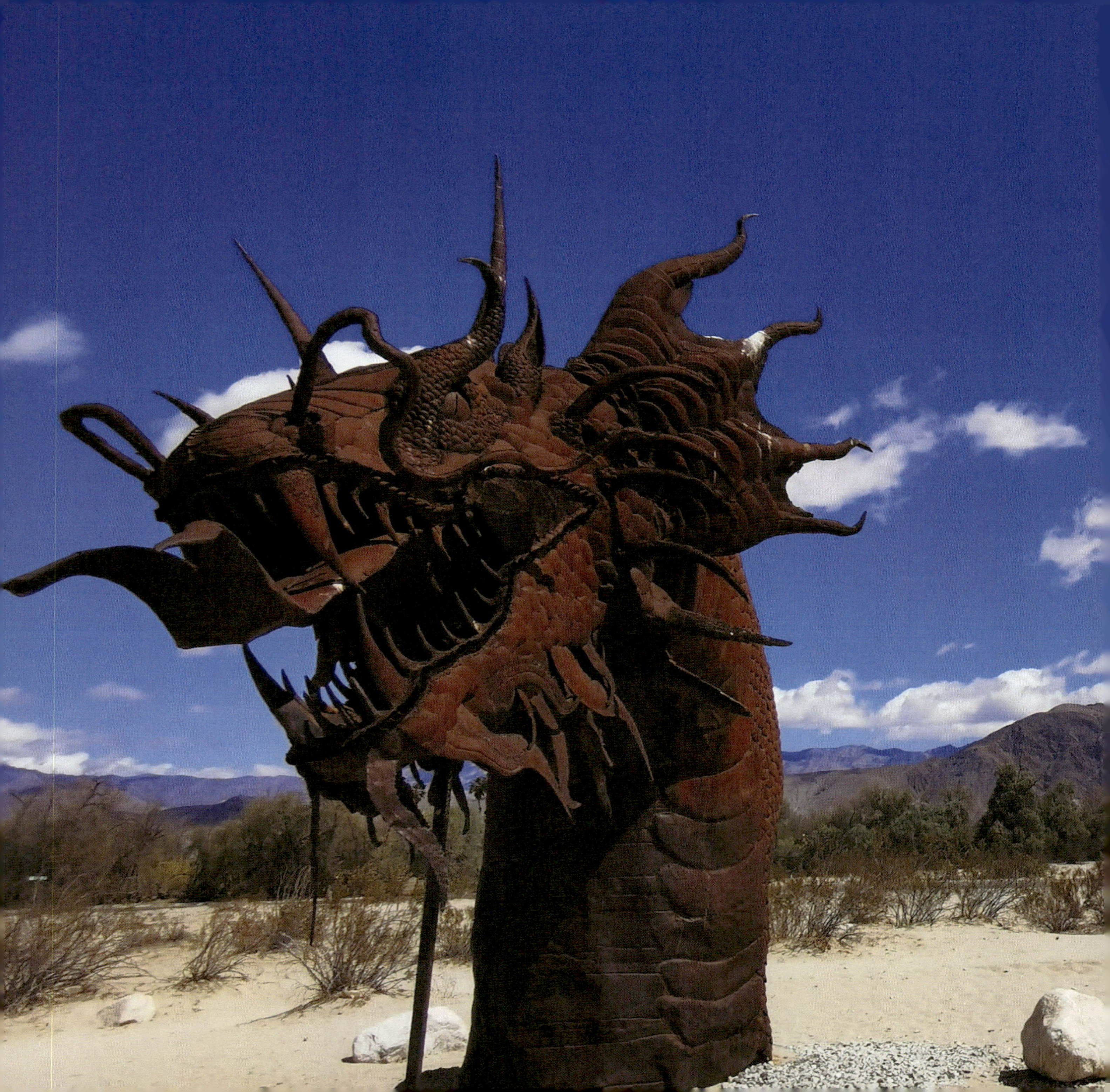

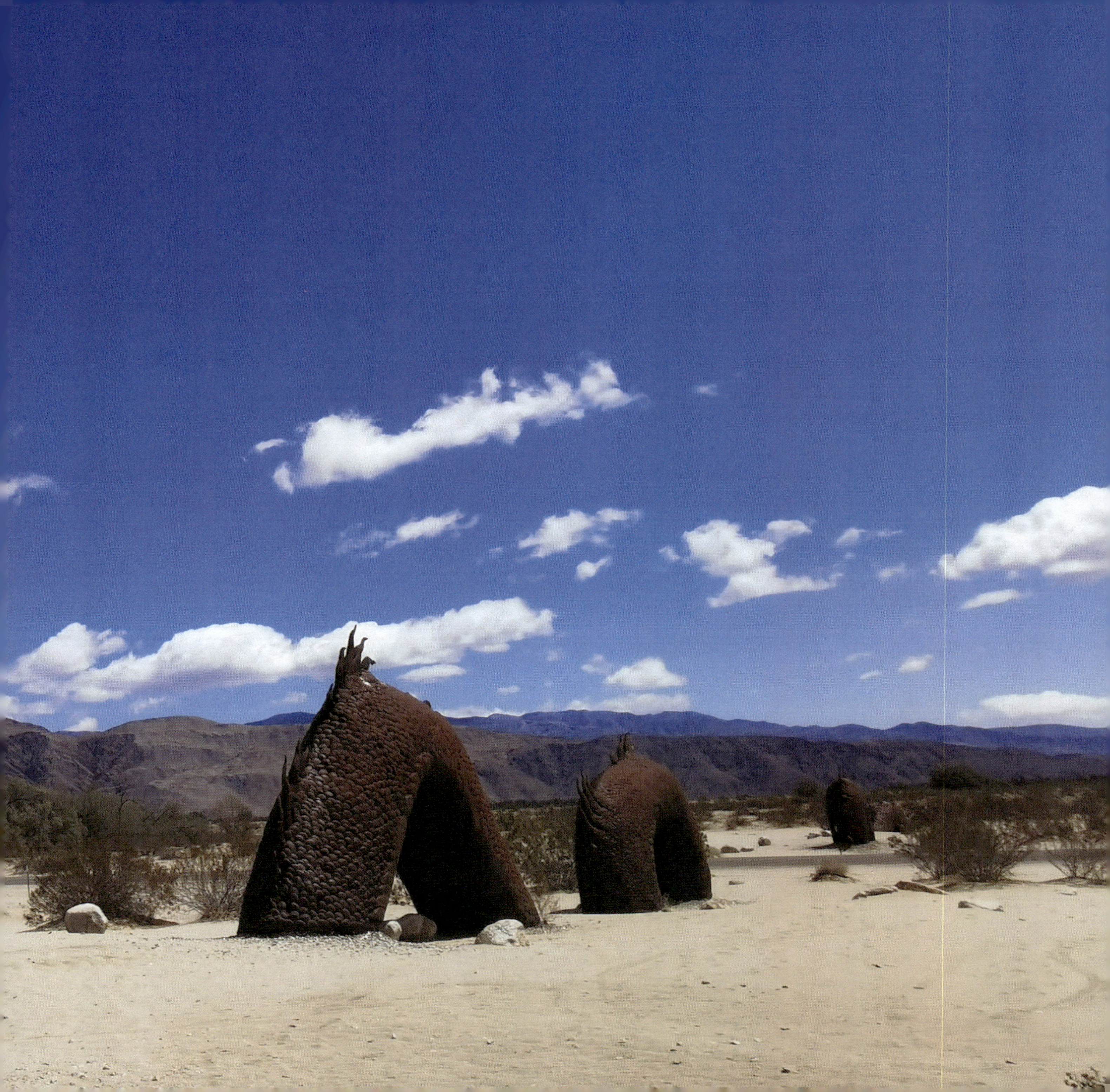

on the Salton Sea and Bombay Beach both provide strong accounts of the area.

9. SALVATION MOUNTAIN
33.25414, -115.47264
Beal Rd, Niland, CA 92257
www.salvationmountain.us

This Slab City (see below) stalwart collects paint from passers by to make his one man shrine to the Creator, visible from Google Earth. 'Got Paint?'

10. SLAB CITY INCLUDING EAST JESUS
33.25797, -115.46233
Slab City, CA 92233

In a scene straight out of Mad Max, this commune of artists and antiestablishmentarians congregate on an abandoned Air Force Base bang smack in the middle of the desert to live an alternative but by no means easy life far from capitalism, reality tv and school runs. Considerate it the Louvre of the homeless, with installations to rival the Tate Modern made largely from old shoes, abandoned tv sets and scrap metal all set in a bizarre Martian landscape. Pass the toll booth that marks the end of civilisation as you know it, hang your shoes in the shoe tree and remember to come bearing gifts of whiskey and construction/art materials – oh, and paint.

11. THE TOWN OF WHY
32.26867, -112.73875
Why, AZ 85321

Named for two major highways, state routes 85 and 86 which originally intersected here at a Y-intersection. Founders had wanted to call the town Y but Arizona law required all city names to have at least three letters, so it was named Why instead. The intersection has since been changed to a T-junction but as of yet no one appears to have made the rational suggestion that the town be renamed Tea.

12. THE TOWN OF SURPRISE
33.62923, -112.36792
Surprise, Phoenix, AZ

A town founded in 1938 by Flora Mae Statler who named it Surprise as she 'would be surprised if the town ever amounted to much'.

13. GOLDFIELD GHOST TOWN
33.45705, -111.49197
4650 N Mammoth Mine Rd, Apache Junction, AZ 85119
goldfieldghosttown.com

Why not evade the hordes by trying your hand at horseback riding at Superstition's O.K. Corral Stables in this otherwise undeniably touristy ghost town, entering the Superstition Mountains, one of the US's most iconic regions, for as much as a whole day.

14. TOMBSTONE
31.71286, -110.06757
Tombstone, AZ 85638

'The town too tough to die'. Tombstone, complete with its brilliantly named Mayor Dusty Escapule, was founded in 1879 and was the site of the Gunfight at the O.K. Corral in which Sheriff Virgil Earp and his temporary deputies and brothers Wyatt Earp and Morgan Earp chased down the Cowboys Gang for shooting dead two victims in a stagecoach during a holdup worth in the region of $639,000 in today's money. This culminated in the killing of gang members Tom McLaury, Frank McLaury and Billy Clanton. Three months later in 1881, Virgil was ambushed and wounded and by 1882 Morgan had been killed by a shot that passed through his spine whilst playing billiards. This would cause Wyatt to lead a posse and kill four of the men held responsible in what

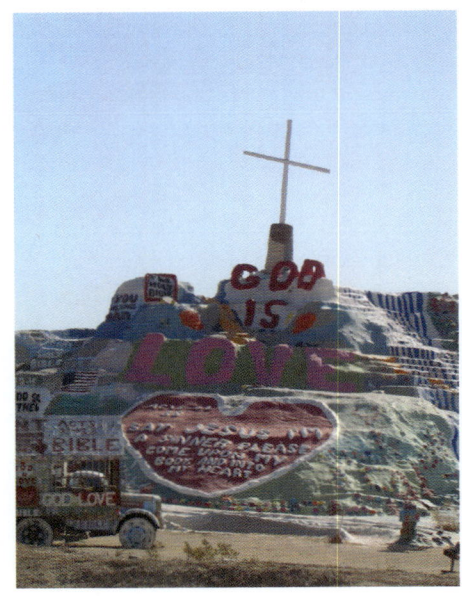

< Left and > right: Slab City including East Jesus
Top left: The Town of Why
Top centre: Goldfield Ghost Town
Top right: Tombstone

THE SOUTHERN TRAIL ROUTE 6

was later known as the Earp Vendetta Ride. Tombstone was one of the last wide open frontier boomtowns in the Old West. How did it get its morbid name? When the town's founder voiced his plans to colonise the area, a passerby recounted tales of the death of several previous visitors by Indians, stating 'The only rock you will find out there will be your own tombstone' or variously 'Better take your coffin with you; you will find your tombstone there and nothing else.'

15. PRADA MARFA
30.60346, -104.51848
US-90, Valentine, TX 79854
An entire replica of a Prada store complete with (cunning anti-theft versions of) wares in the middle of nowhere. Not only that, it is designed to biodegrade back into the desert as a comment on materialism. Although…it keeps being rebuilt to be more resilient due to vandalism and it is unclear where this has left the store regarding biodegradability - perhaps materialism has won out after all.

16. BALMORHEA STATE PARK POOL
30.94461, -103.78536
9207 TX-17, Toyahvale, TX 79786
www.tpwd.state.tx.us
Swim or scuba in this spring water pool built in the 1930s.

OFFBEAT AMERICA

17. CONTRABANDO
29.2796, -103.8412
Farm to Market 170
Redford, Texas, 79846
This old movie set/ghost town in the Contrabando Trail area of Texas stands a quick drive away from Big Bend National Park and remains reasonably intact on the evocative 'Farm to Market' road. The set was constructed for the 1985 Roy Clark film 'Uphill all the Way' as well as providing a backdrop for Lone Star in 1996. The area is known for its Candelilla plants (small stands of slender blue-gray stems clustering together in the desert with small pale pink blooms if you are keeping an eye out) from which it is possible to extract wax which during World War I was a valuable commodity in ammunition and canvas waterproofing. This plant helped give Contrabando its name, as large amounts of this Candelilla wax were shipped across the Mexican border into the US to avoid playing Mexican export duty. This wasn't the only smuggled good to have crossed Contrabando's environs; cattle rustling played a big part in securing the town's name between border ranches whilst Mexican liquor was transported by mule to the bootleggers during Prohibition. The Contrabando Trail's smuggling days died off with the advent of America's new found predilection for mass produced narcotics and super highways.

18. LAJITAS GHOST TOWN
29.26158, -103.77657
Lajitas, TX 79852
The only critical thing to note about this ghost town is that it has a goat (name of Clay Henry III) for its mayor. Specifically, a goat which is famed for drinking beer straight from the bottle. That is all.

19. TERLINGUA GHOST TOWN
29.32029, -103.61314
Terlingua Ghost Town, Terlingua, TX 79852
This mercury mining town had a population of 2000 in its heyday before the mining company heading production went bust at the beginning of WW2, leading to its current ghost town status.

20. THE TOWN OF UTOPIA
29.61522, -99.52699
Utopia, TX 78884
Originally called Waresville, citizens chose the name Utopia after finding that their preferred option 'Montana, Texas' was already taken, much to their disappointment. The cemetery still holds the name Waresville. The name was also tied to plans for a utopian community nearby, however these were cancelled when the La Reunion Utopian Socialist community of 1855 in Dallas (which planned to allow participants to share in profits for labour performed) collapsed after only 18 months due to financial insolvency, a lack of skilled participants, poor weather, lack of capability in farming and

< Top: Balmorhea State Park Pool
< Bottom: Terlingua Ghost Town
Right: Lajitas Ghost Town
Overleaf: Prada Marfa

THE SOUTHERN TRAIL ROUTE 6

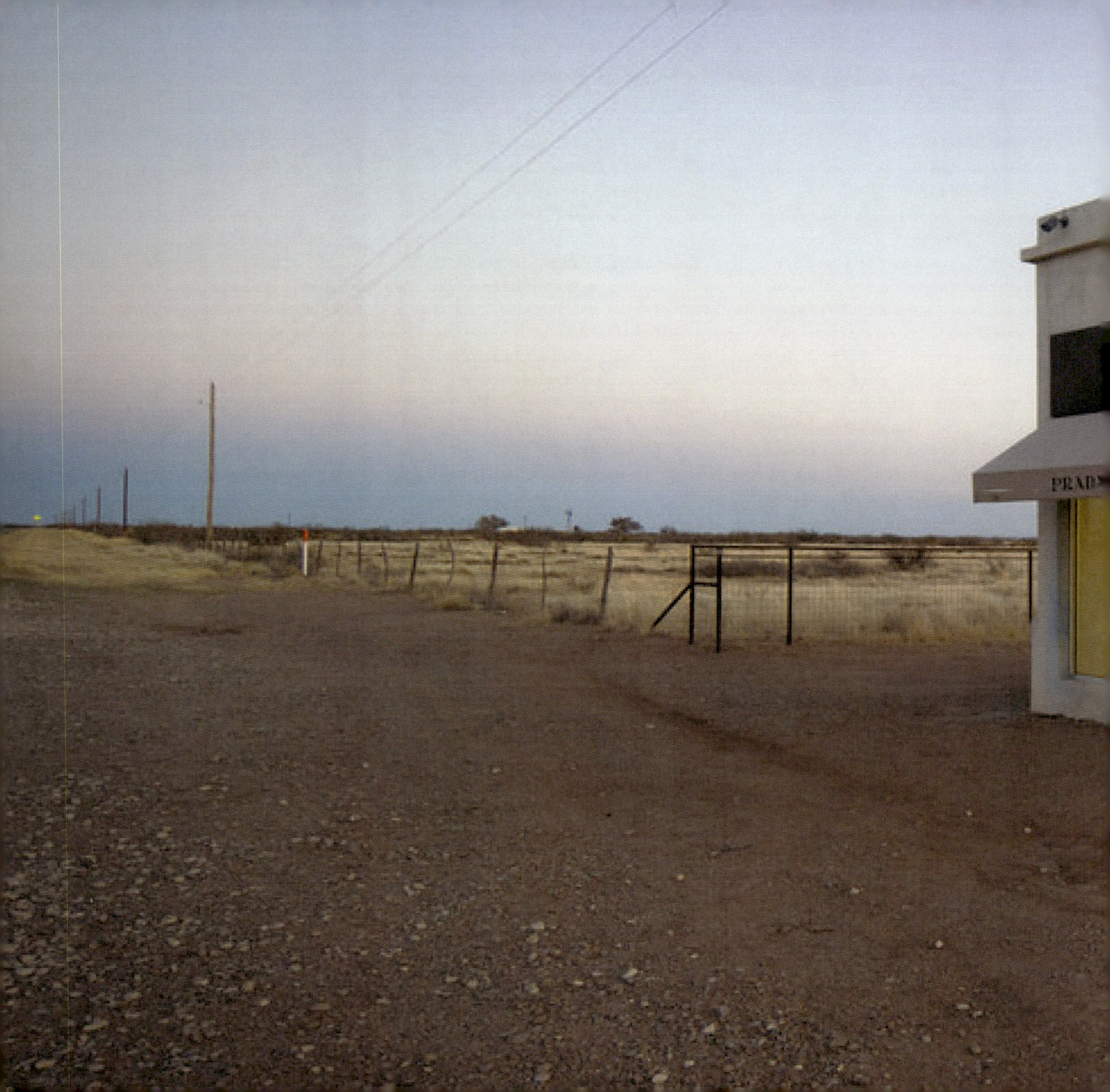

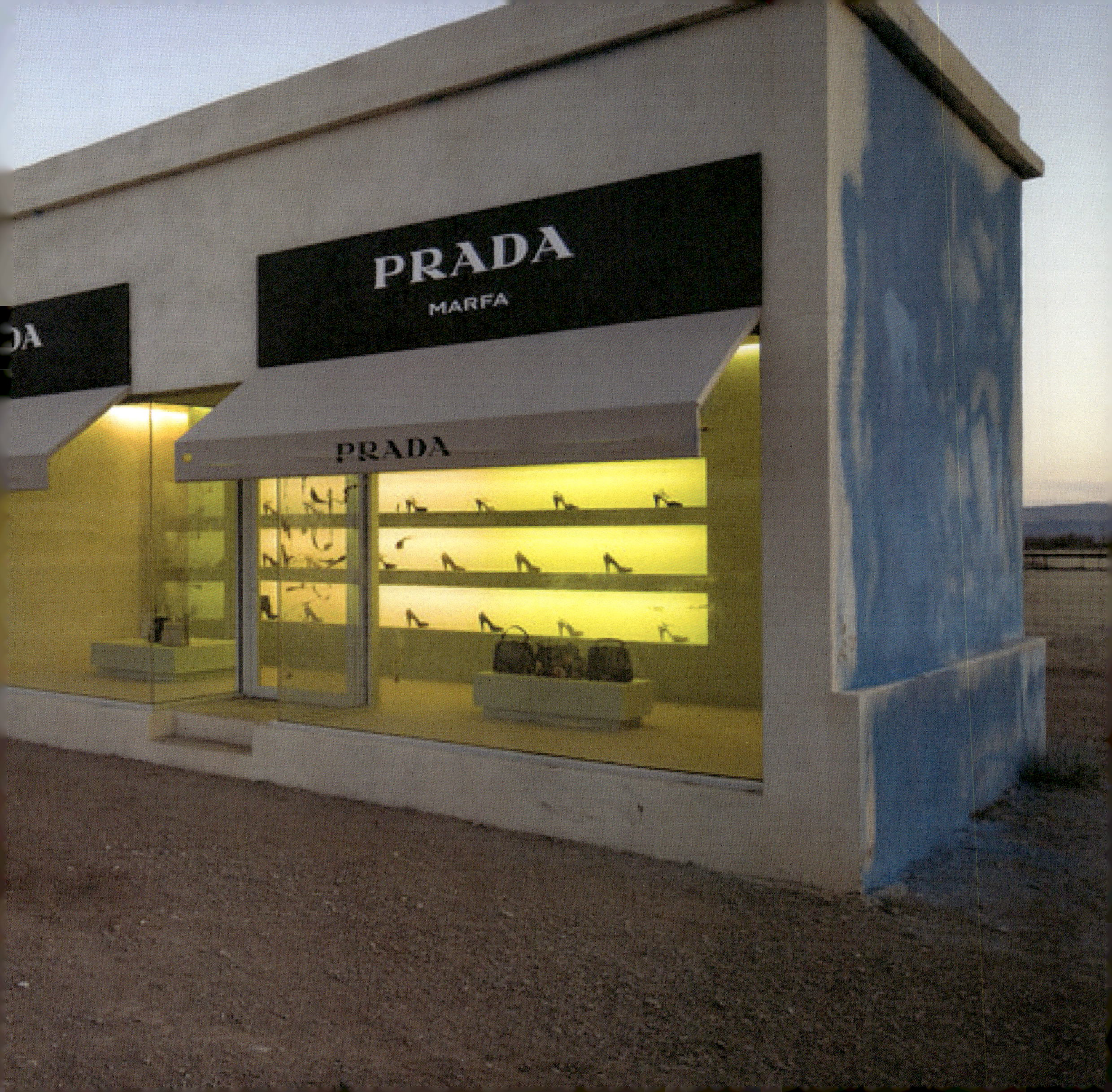
PRADA
MARFA
PRADA

high costs. It was unlikely to work out, all things considered.

21. BOOT HILL CEMETERY
28.4616, -98.5480
Main St, Tilden, TX 78072 (On the corner of Live Oak St and Main St, between Wheelers Mercantile & Shell Gas Station and McMullden County Sheriff's Office.)
This graveyard is so named because the majority of its interred died, so say, 'with their boots on', i.e. of violent, unnatural, accidental or sudden deaths, taking them before their time. The term was first used to describe cemeteries for gun fighters who died with their boots on - graveyards with this name are common across the US West, the most famous being Boot Hill in Tombstone Arizona, linked to the aforementioned OK Corral.

22. HOT WELLS HOTEL AND SPA
29.36584, -98.47076
Koehler Ct, San Antonio, TX 78223
Once a hangout for Valentino, Roosevelt and Chaplin, this spa resort was first built in 1893 before burning down the following year and being rebuilt in grander style. This one lasted 30 years and had three large swimming pools to take advantage of the local sulphurous healing spring waters as well as luxurious rooms which included marble bath tubs and individual phones in the rooms. An ostrich farm was even established on the premises to ensure a ready supply of fashionable feathers to the visiting ladies.

23. BARNEY SMITH'S TOILET SEAT ART MUSEUM
29.48174, -98.46978
239 Abiso Ave, San Antonio, TX 78209
An art museum composed entirely of toilet seats - keep the lid down.

NOW WHY NOT CHECK OUT:

BOTTLE HOUSE - p.223

< Bottom: The Town of Ding Dong
Top right: Boot Hill Cemetery
Bottom: Barney Smith's Toilet Seat Art Museum

TRAVIS STATE FARM COLONY AUSTIN - p.223
BABY HEAD CEMETERY - p.222

24. THE TOWN OF DING DONG
30.97463, -97.77729
Ding Dong, TX, 76542
This tiny town was founded in the thirties by two settlers, Bert and Zulis Bell. They were the proprietors of a hardware shop and hired a painter by the name of C.C. Hoover to paint their store sign. This gentleman was in turn encouraged, by a man named Fred Foster of Florence (just revelling in the names in this entry), to paint two bells on the sign and label them Bert and Zulis, underneath which he

should write Ding Dong. Hoover did as he was told, and ever since the community was known as Ding Dong, with the game Ding Dong Ditch running rampant and causing an immense problem for local dwellers. The town features in Ripley's Believe It or Not and is unincorporated, with a mere 15 residents. One resident recently claimed via Facebook 'Ding Dong is thriving! We have a new café and two new houses are being built! It's a boom town!'. If anyone has any sense, they have installed door knockers.

NOW WHY NOT CHECK OUT:

All entries from *MUSEUM OF FUNERAL HISTORY* to *BEER CAN HOUSE* – p.224

25. RAYNE FROG FESTIVAL
30.24953, -92.27619
Rayne, LA 70578
Meet a frog wearing tiny clothes (and then become emotional as people around you eat frog's legs) during May. Year round frog adoration also present, as is a road called Frog Festival Drive (see coordinates).

WHILE IN BATON ROUGE, WHY NOT CHECK OUT:

All entries from *ANGOLA PRISON RODEO & ARTS* to *THE MYRTLES PLANTATION* - p.162 - 163

WHILE IN NEW ORLEANS, WHY NOT CHECK OUT:

All entries from *CUT OFF* to *SIX FLAGS AMUSEMENT PARK* – p. 163

26. WORLD'S LARGEST ROCKING CHAIR
30.45441, -89.13746
11451 Canal Rd, Gulfport, MS 39503
Is it the largest or the second largest? There is much debate. Once standing on giant functional rockers in order to classify as a rocking chair, this was eventually securely welded to prevent onlooker squashage.

WHILE IN TALLAHASSEE, WHY NOT CHECK OUT:

All entries from *AIRPORT CEMETERY* to *RUINS OF THE HAMPTON SPRINGS HOTEL* - p.57

WHILE IN TAMPA, WHY NOT CHECK OUT:

All entries from *WHIMZEYLAND* to *DOME HOMES* – pages 62 - 67
ED LEEDSKALNIN'S CORAL CASTLE - p.70

WHILE IN THE FLORIDA KEYS, WHY NOT CHECK OUT:

UNDERWATER HOTEL - p.70
BETSY THE LOBSTER - p.70

> Right: Rayne Frog Festival

LOUISIANA FROG COMPANY
"ONE OF THE LARGEST SHIPPERS OF FROGS IN THE WORLD"

Pho. 96

RAYNE, LA.

THE NORTHERN ROUTE
ROUTE 7

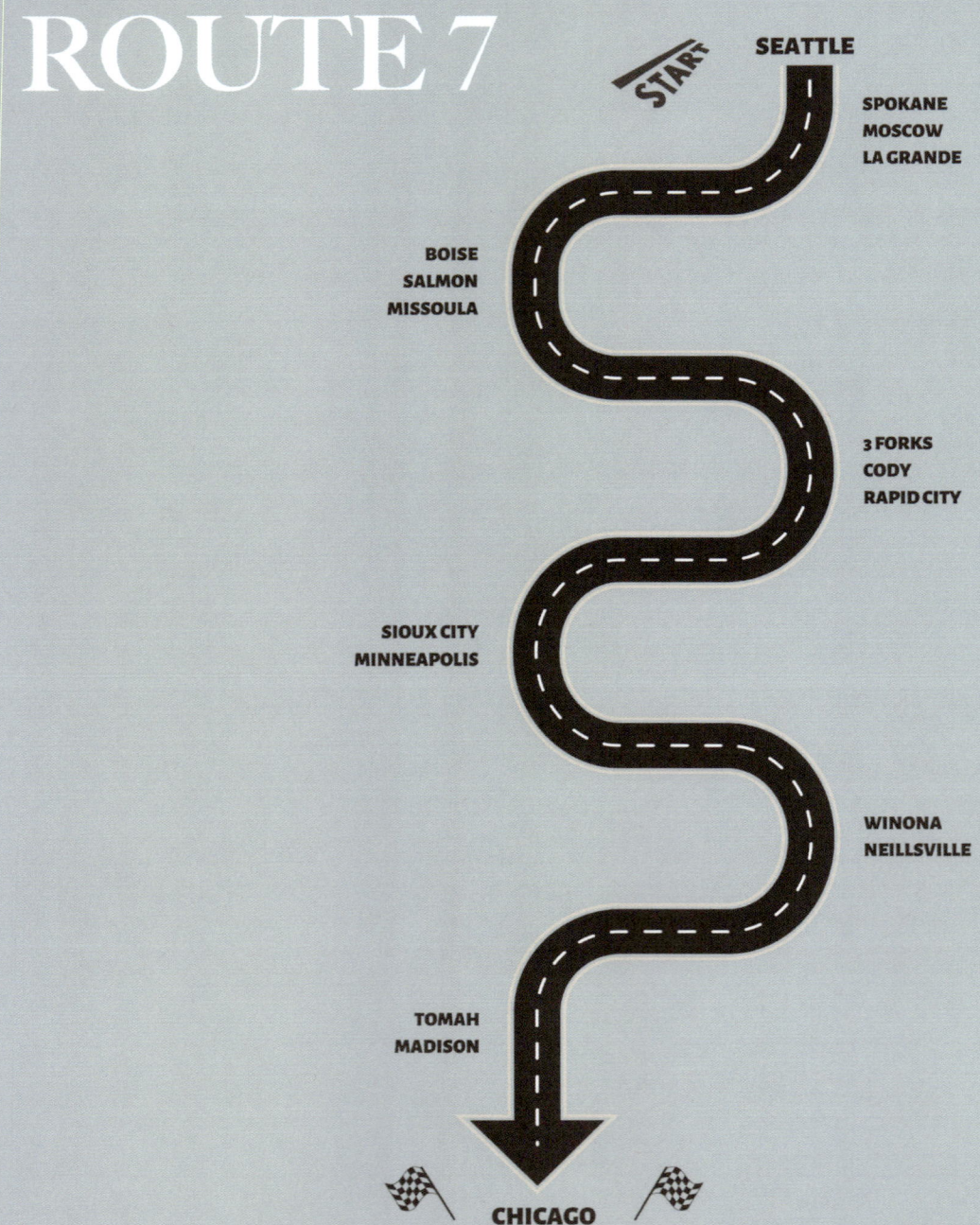

START

SEATTLE

SPOKANE
MOSCOW
LA GRANDE

BOISE
SALMON
MISSOULA

3 FORKS
CODY
RAPID CITY

SIOUX CITY
MINNEAPOLIS

WINONA
NEILLSVILLE

TOMAH
MADISON

CHICAGO

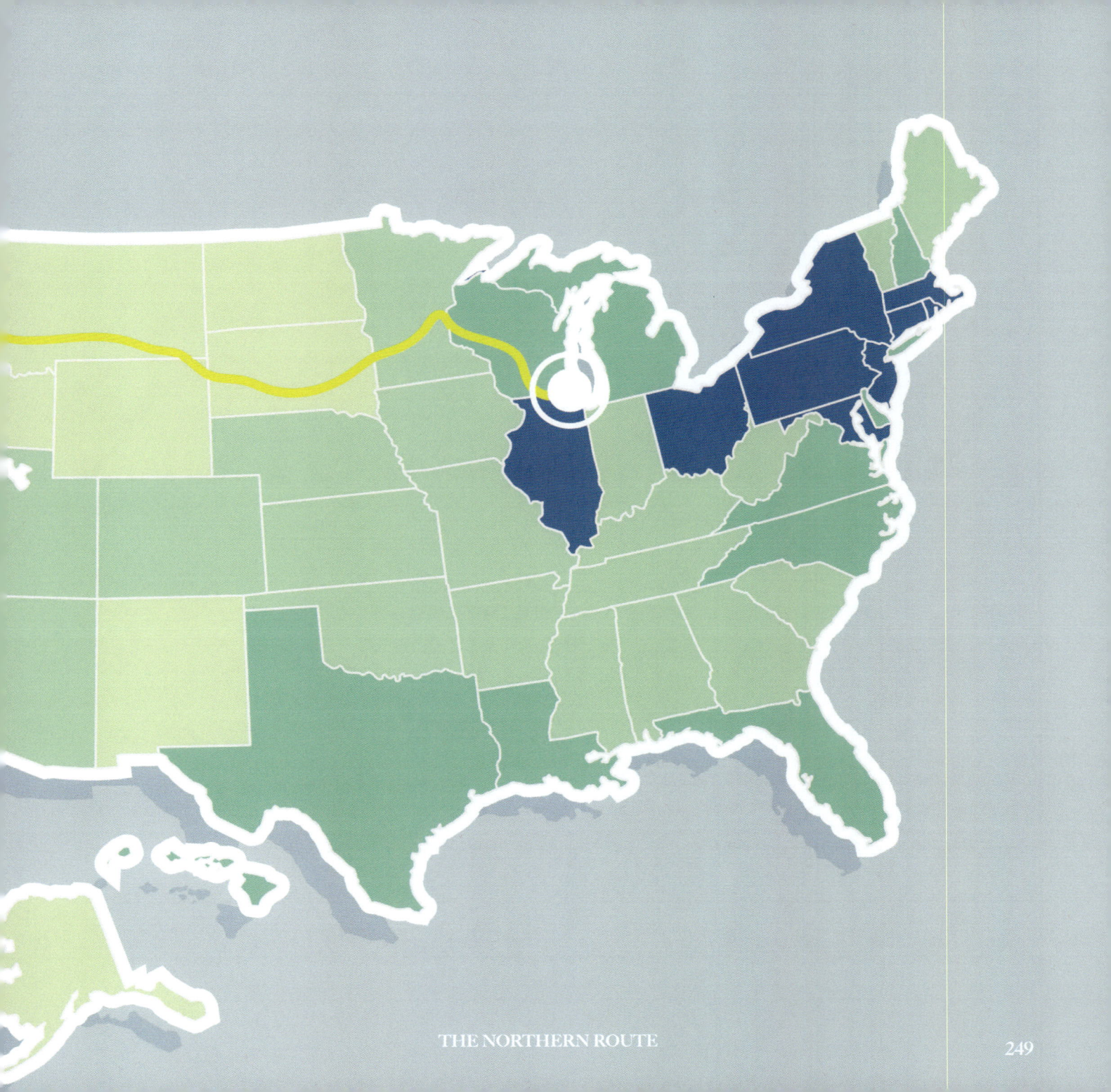

THE NORTHERN ROUTE

THE NORTHERN ROUTE - ROUTE 7

You may want to pack your anorak for this one; travel from famously wet and wuthering Seattle where you can huddle with your Original Starbucks coffee (surprisingly enjoyable) before heading out into cult 80s TV show territory in Big Bend. Drawn by the bright lights of attractions such as the Idaho Potato Museum, view stunning natural wonders such as the Prismatic Spring, not to mention the somewhat more unnatural giant talking cow of Wisconsin.

1. THE BIKE TREE
47.42299, -122.46008
99th Ave SW, Vashon, WA 98070
See a bike being devoured by the tree it was casually leaned against. Town sheriff Don Puz claims the bike was his and he left it there in 1954.

2. NEVERTOLD CASKET COMPANY
47.60641, -122.31549
509 13th Ave, Seattle, WA 98122
nevertoldcasket.com

Above: The Bike Tree

Why sell products when you can sell haunted products.

3. STEVE'S WEIRD HOUSE
47.6031, -122.3301

A beautiful example of the phobia Horror Vacui (or a fear of empty spaces) at work, Steve really has filled his house with quite a lot of weirdness. This is a private residence and is not open to touring but tour it virtually online here: Http://www.bohonus.com/special-projects/virtual-tour-steves-weird-house/

OFFBEAT AMERICA

< Top left: Freemont Troll
< Bottom left: Ye Olde Curiosity Shop
Bottom left: Seattle Underground
Bottom right: Mike's Chilli Parlor

4. YE OLDE CURIOSITY SHOP
47.6042, -122.3390
1001 Alaskan Way, Seattle, WA 98104
yeoldecuriosityshop.com
Purveyor of the macabre.

5. WORLD FAMOUS GIANT SHOE MUSUEM
47.6084, -122.3414
1501 Pike Place, # 424, Seattle, Washington, 98101
This sideshow-esque wonder in the Old Seattle Paperworks store in Pike Place may be small but boy it contains some big shoes. The collection belongs to a Danny Eskenazi who became obsessed with giant shoes when he discovered that his grandfather once owned one belonging to Robert Wadlow, the world's tallest man. With big shoes to fill (sorry), Danny offered $1000 to anyone able to track down his huge heirloom but sadly it has never been found - in the meantime however he has accumulated quite a few more sizeable footwear specimens. He is still looking for that long lost shoe (emphasis on the long) but in the meantime, catch his collection made all the more enjoyable by its coin operated slot viewing mechanic.

6. FREMONT TROLL
47.6509, -122.3472
Troll Ave N, Seattle, WA 98103
This area became a dumping destination, leading to a design competition to revitalise the area. The winner? A troll made entirely in that most versatile of substances, good ol' concrete.

7. SEATTLE UNDERGROUND
47.6015, -122.3343
614 1st Avenue, Pioneer Place Park, Pioneer Square, Seattle, WA, 98104 (between Cherry and James Street)
Visit the subterranean remains of this fire-hit area of Seattle and walk the original tunnels beneath the downtown streets that link local businesses, shops and bars.

8. MIKE'S CHILI PARLOR
47.66283, -122.37576
1447 NW Ballard Way, Seattle, WA 98107
This dive eatery has served chilli in Seattle since 1922 and has been featured on the Food Network.

9. THE SEATTLE METAPHYSICAL LIBRARY
47.6691, -122.38581
2220 NW Market St, Seattle, WA 98107
www.seattlemetaphysicallibrary.org
Est. 1961 this library of the metaphysical holds more than 14,000 books and much more regarding all things esoteric, spiritual and eye opening.

> Top left: Salish Lodge
> Top right/bottom: Ronette's Bridge - Twin Peaks

10. SEATTLE'S OFFICIAL BAD ART MUSEUM OF ART
47.67148, -122.31716
5828 Roosevelt Way NE, Seattle, WA 98105
www.officialbadartmuseumofart.com
Open 7am to 2am, this Seattle cafe doubles as the curator of some of the worst art you will lay your eyes on.

11. TWEDE'S CAFÉ
47.49516, -121.78685
137 W North Bend Way, North Bend, WA 98045
www.twedescafe.com
Fire may have walked with it but this diner has stood the test of time, restored to bring the Double R Diner of Twin Peaks back to reality.

12. SALISH LODGE
47.54208, -121.83664
6501 Railroad Ave, Snoqualmie, WA 98065
www.salishlodge.com
This lodge overlooking Snoqualmie Falls will be familiar to fans of Twin Peaks but is also just a stunning place with its cascading waterfall and tranquil location.

13. RONETTE'S BRIDGE - TWIN PEAKS
47.52987, -121.80684
40412–40430 SE Reinig Road, Snoqualmie, WA 98065
Fans of Twin Peaks can not only picture this disused trestle bridge as a scene from the movie and find innumerous quotes and references etched into it, but also imagine the old railroad which used to run through here until shortly post-filming; the bridge used to cross the road and carry tracks although now is the domain of joggers and cyclists.

14. WELLINGTON AVALANCHE SITE
47.7471, -121.1274
Iron Goat Trail, Leavenworth, WA 98826
The worst avalanche in the history of the US in terms of lives lost, this disaster plunged the little town of Wellington under meters of snow, hurling a passenger train into a river costing 93 people their lives. The community of Wellington has since been renamed Tye (hence the Tye River and Tye Scenic Road) in an effort to distance itself from the death toll, but the name change could not prevent the town from collapsing into obscurity. Hike the Iron Goat Trail to find debris that the avalanche left behind.

15. UMATILLA CHEMICAL DEPOT
45.8082, -119.4001
Hermiston, OR 97838
A storage unit for bonafide chemical weapons situated off Gun Club Road, operated from 1962 to 1994, the facility also destroys such weapons at the Umatilla Chemical Agent Disposal Facility which was built in 2001.

16. THE JUNK CASTLE
46.7313, -117.1796
Armstrong Road, Pullman, WA 99163

Top: Twede's Cafe
Bottom: Wellington Avalanche Site

255

Think you can't build a house for $500? Think again.

17. HOT LAKE SPRINGS
45.24338, -117.95853
66172 OR-203, La Grande, OR 97850
www.hotlakesprings.com

The first commercial building in the world to use geothermal energy from its hot spring as its main source of heat, this hotel boasted 105 rooms, a 60 bed surgical ward (diversification at its best but quite common in a time when serious mental and physical sickness was often treated with 'taking the waters' (although the fact that the owner and manager Dr. Phy died of pneumonia perhaps speaks to its efficacy), a ballroom, a barber shop, a sweet shop, flight school (!), drug store, 'show barn', news stand, laboratories and more, garnering the name The Town Under One Roof. It was largely self-sufficient producing its own vegetables, dairy products, meats and eggs. Given its self-heated claim to fame, it is rather ironic that half of the hotel burned down in 1934, the remaining half used as an asylum and nurse's training school among other things until its eventual abandonment in 1991. It sat empty for a long time due to its rumoured hauntings by a gardener who committed suicide and residents of the insane asylum. A piano on the third floor was said to play by itself for hours on end. Reports of screaming and crying from the surgery room abounded, as did rocking chairs rocking and the like. By 2003 it was falling apart but was purchased by an entrepreneur, who took to restoring it despite it missing 368 windows and most of its roof. In 2005 he opened it for tours, but in 2008 the entire west wing collapsed. Since 2010 it has operated as a bed and breakfast, museum and spa, making it accessible.

18. MITCHELL SHOE TREE
44.5529, -119.8032
Mitchell, OR, 97750
A tree, with shoes, in Mitchell.

19. OLD IDAHO STATE PENITENTIARY
43.60279, -116.16197
2445 Old Penitentiary Rd, Boise, ID 83712
This prison has operated for 101 years,

Left: Old Idaho State Penitentiary
Right: Hot Lake Springs

processing over 13,000 inmates over the years; around 600 at any given time. 215 of the prisoners were female, one of whom was an infamous murderess called Lady Bluebeard who killed her husbands to secure their insurance pay-outs.

20. IDAHO CITY
43.8285, -115.83455
Idaho City, ID 83631
Once the largest city in the Pacific Northwest during the gold rush, this western town remains much as it always was, full of history, original features such as fine wooden sidewalks and excellent antiques stores to boot. The times when you could buy your wares in return for gold powder may be gone but much remains to be enjoyed.

21. MUSEUM OF CLEAN
42.8596, -112.4417
711 S 2nd Ave, Pocatello, ID 83201
museumofclean.com.s158603.gridserver.com
Presumably set up by rival museum entrepreneurs ready to take on the stiff competition set by the Idaho Potato Museum, this collection honours all things spotless. An OCD dream.

22. IDAHO POTATO MUSEUM
43.18955, -112.34365
130 NW Main St, Blackfoot, ID 83221
idahopotatomuseum.com
Idaho is so proud of their spuds that they've dedicated an entire museum to them.

23. GARNET
46.8253, -113.3381
Garnet, Drummond, MT 59832
Located in the marvellously named First Chance Gulch, the town of Garnet sits in a beautiful mountain location and was founded in 1895 under the name Mitchell. Built on a gold mine on the Garnet Lode, it had just 10 buildings when it began but just two years later when the boom hit 1000 people were living there. The excitement only lasted 20 years until the gold ran out and a fire wiped out much of the rest of Garnet in 1912. None the less, as ghost towns go this one is still very well preserved with the original Wells Hotels, Kelly Saloon and Davey's Store. Back in the day, Garnet had not only 13 saloons but the three hotels charged customers between 1 and

Above: Garnet
Overleaf: Idaho City

Copenhagen
ROUTE
US
66
ROOT BEER
RAIL ROAD
CROSSING
call for

BLATZ
Heidelberg
DAD'S
IDAHO CITY
1862
MILK
Coca-Cola
Coca-Cola
KEEP
GATE CLOSED
NO
PARKING
ANY
TIME

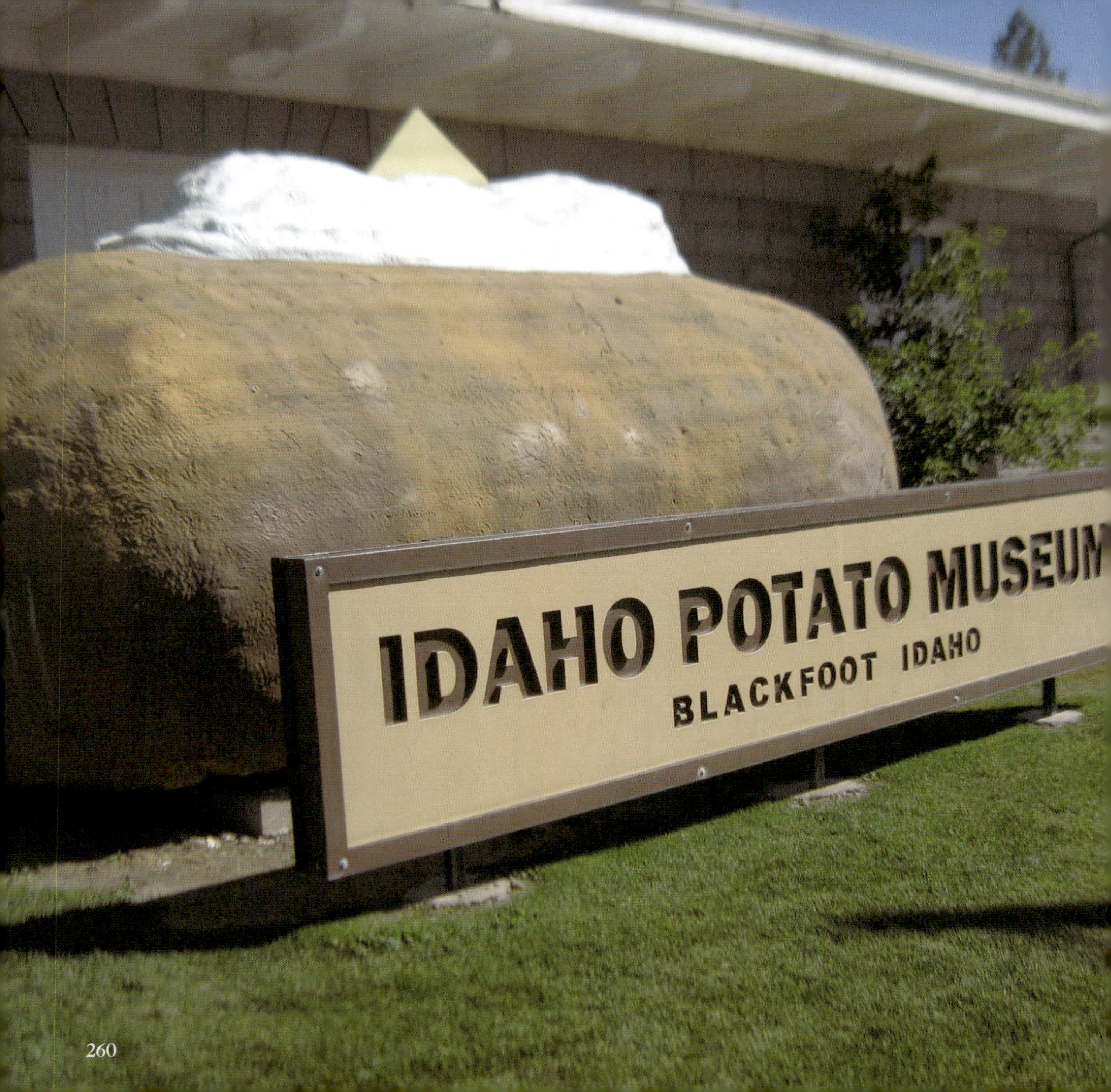
IDAHO POTATO MUSEUM
BLACKFOOT IDAHO

< Left: Idaho Potato Museum
Right: Castle Town
Overleaf: Bleu Horses, / Wyoming Grand Prismatic Spring

3 dollars a night, whilst miners unable to pay this steep price could sleep in the windowless loft for a quarter.

24. BLEU HORSES
45.9788, -111.5962
10493 US-287, Three Forks, MT 59752
Haunting equine sculptures against a striking backdrop.

25. CASTLE TOWN
46.44133, -110.67186
Castle Town, MT 59053
Calamity Jane was resident in Castle Town, arriving to open a restaurant and lead a life on the right side of the tracks. This plan did not of course last long. Castle City was founded in the 1870s and Jane lived with a good 1999 other townspeople, despite it having absolutely no transportation by way of railroad, meaning all the silver and lead mined there had to be dragged out manually. In 1893 silver was demonetised and the town disbanded, leaving a few lead mining hangersoners. When lead crashed the rest left, bar two who managed to hang in there until their deaths in 1938. Little remains but what does is certainly worth a visit.

26. WYOMING GRAND PRISMATIC SPRING
44.52508, -110.83812
Grand Loop Rd, Yellowstone National Park, WY 82190

The largest hot spring in the USA, this psychedelic pool is composed of red, orange, yellow, green and blue colourations hence its name, due to microbial beetles that reside around the edges of the water. Due to its extreme heat, the centre of the pool is sterile and is so vivid a blue due to blue light being scattered by particles suspended in the water. This colour is particularly visible in mid spring when the beetles are fewer and farther between.

27. THE OLD FAITHFUL INN
44.4597, -110.83029
1 Grand Loop Rd, Yellowstone National Park, WY 82190
The Old Faithful Inn is a Yellowstone hotel with a great view of the Old Faithful Geyser. Built in what is known architecturally as the Golden Age Rustic Resort style or National Park Service Rustic Style, it is one of the few log hotels still present in the US and was the first of its kind in the American West in 1903. It is the largest log hotel in the world and may be the largest log building in the World too. The Crow's Nest is a platform above the second level of a double level balcony which provides an excellent view of the Geyser and was originally built for entertainers to play to guests.

28. THE E C WATERS WRECK
44.51506, -110.38643
Stevenson Island, Yellowstone Lake, Yellowstone National Park, WY 82190

E C Waters was well renowned in Yellowstone business circles in the very early 1900s as the most obnoxious man one could possibly run into. His successful boating company already ran one large steamer and built another, the eponymously named E C Waters, capable of carrying 500 passengers, and launched it onto Yellowstone Lake. Sick of complaints regarding Mr Waters' approach to customer service, park officials decided they had to force E C Waters out of business by launching a competing passenger service. With the boat already in the water, Waters asked for another passenger permit for the new steamer and the Park

THE NORTHERN ROUTE - ROUTE 7

261

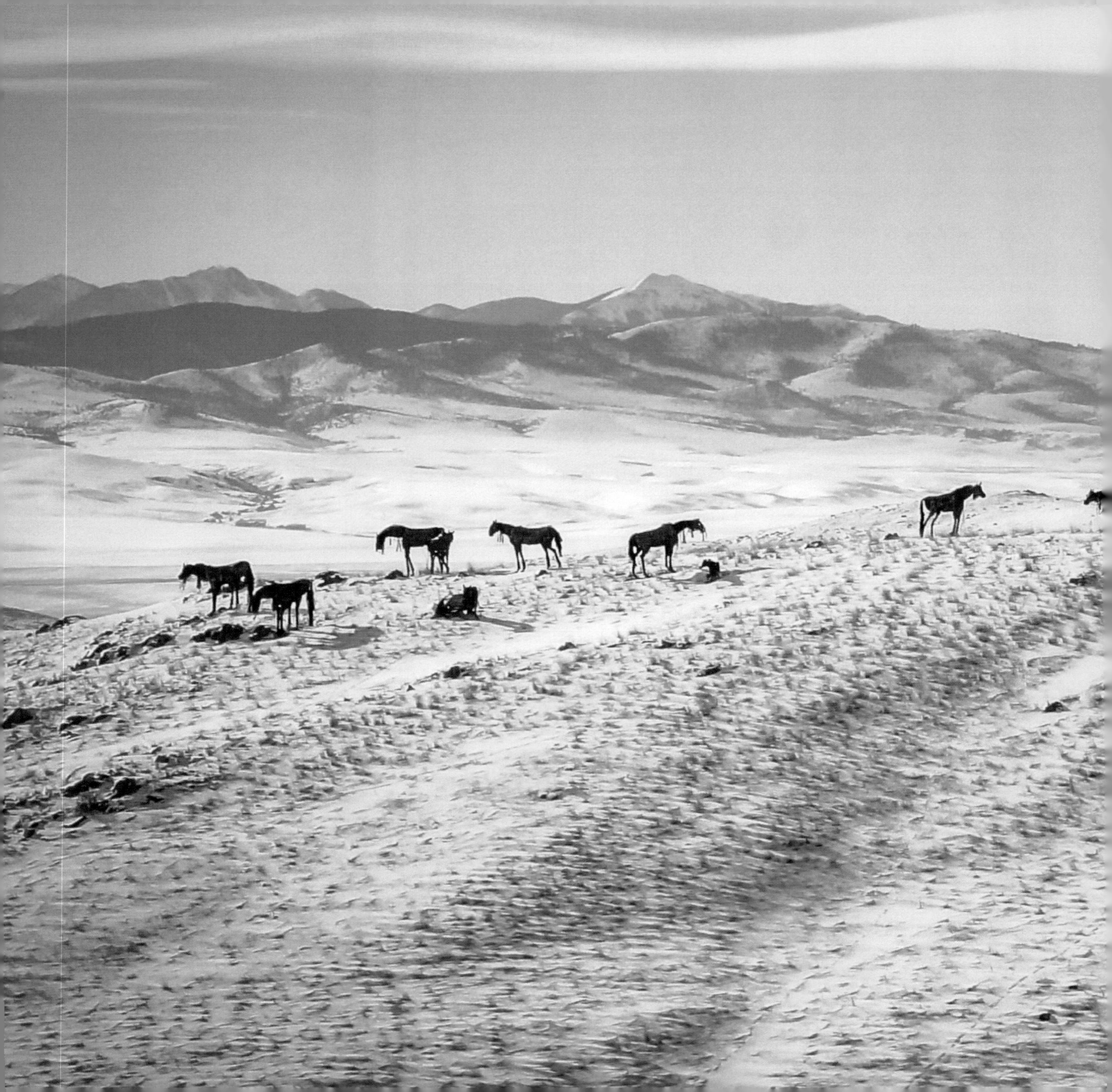

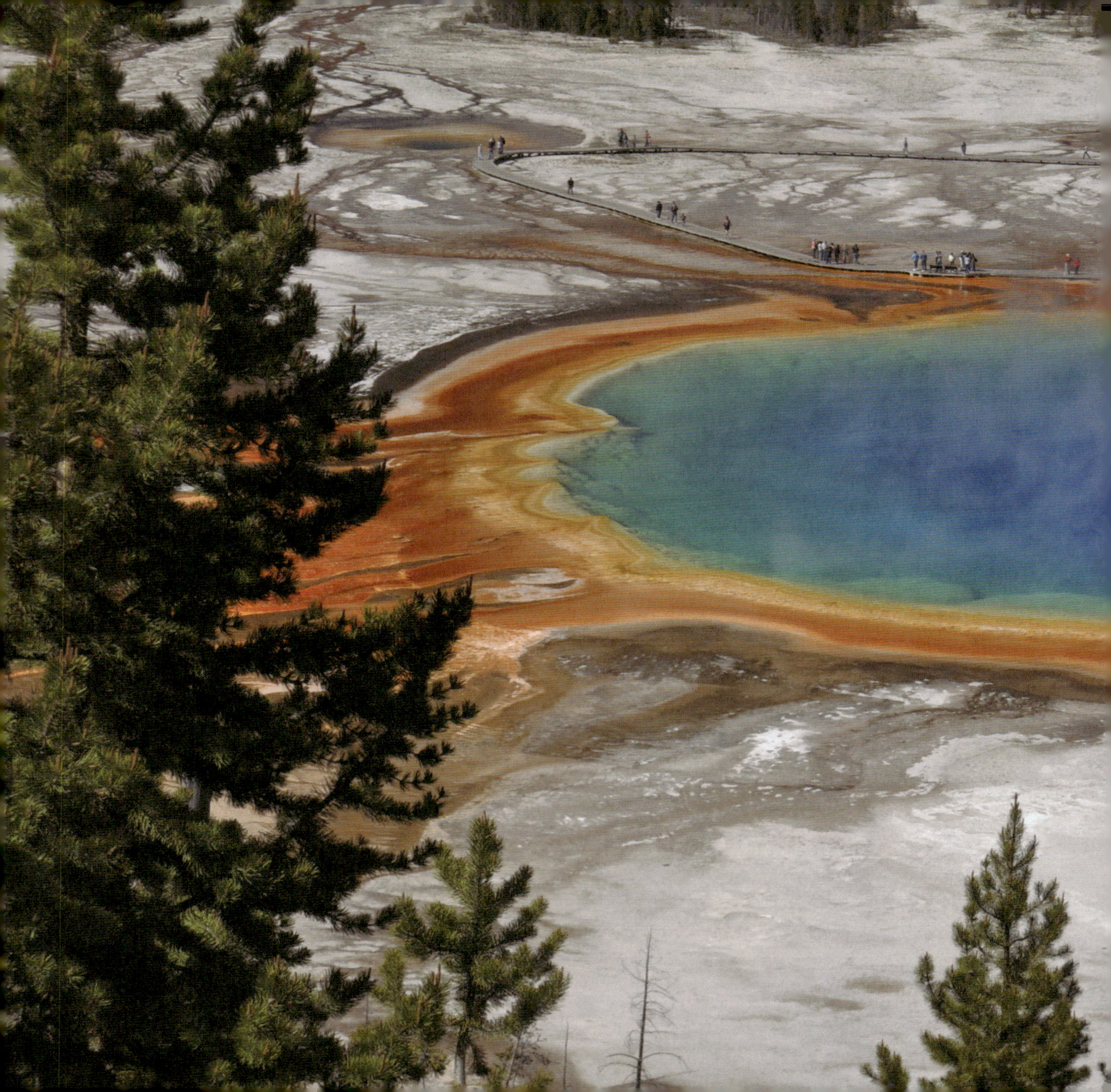

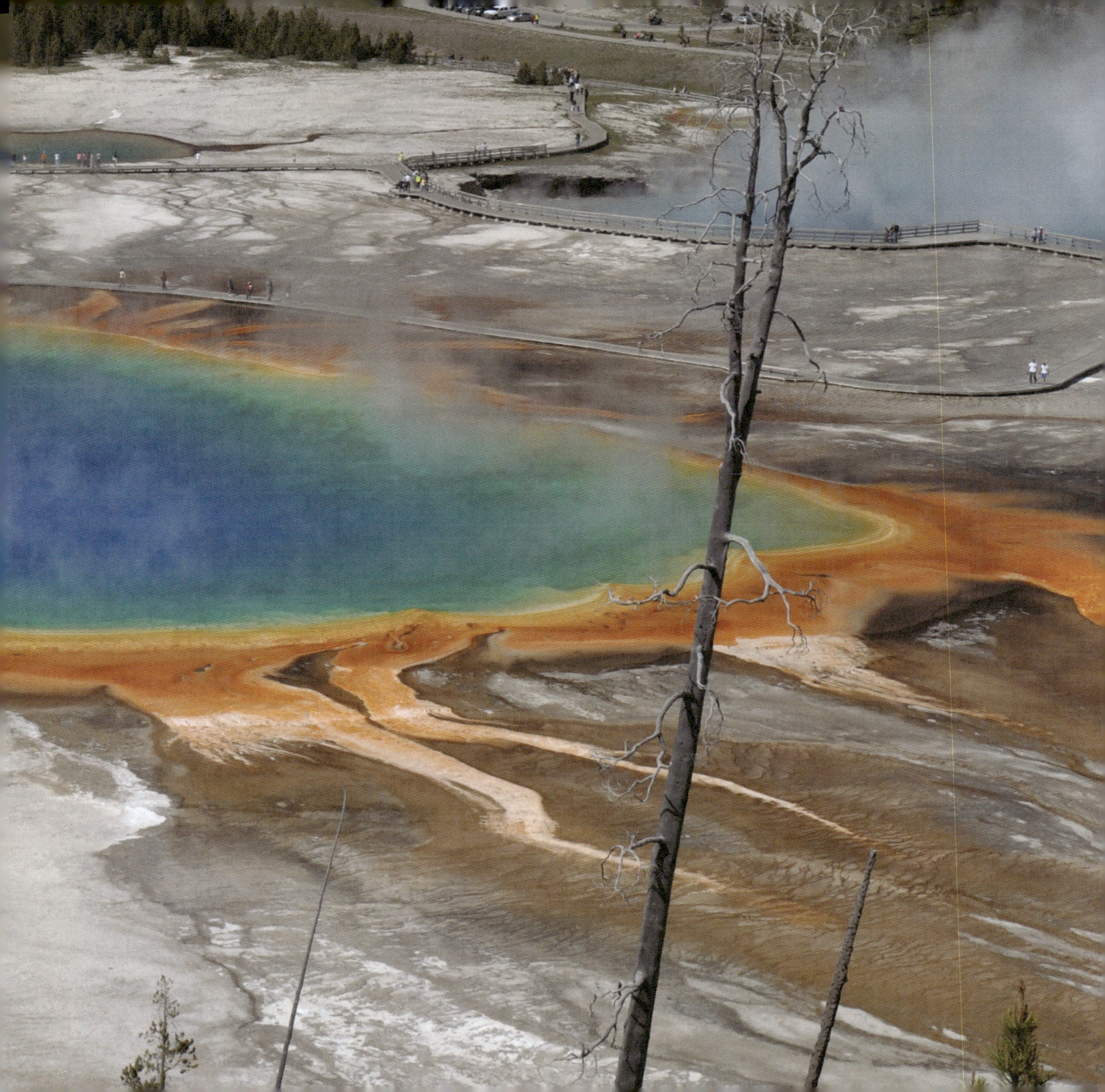

> Right: The Old Faithful Inn
Below: Wyoming Grand Prismatic Spring

Service duly refused on mere principal. In 1906 some three years later, Waters hired a man to care for the ship through the winter, but he died of a heart attack attempting to row to the boat. The replacement guard fared no better when he was locked up for 3 months for being drunk and disorderly, and without anyone caring for the steamer, park officials promptly instructed Waters to take his boat and leave. They didn't mince their words either, writing that 'E.C. Waters, having rendered himself obnoxious during the season of 1907, is debarred from the park'. Waters wasn't going to give up that easily, and had to be forcibly removed in 1909. As such, he left the boat by way of protest right where it sat, and for years there it decayed. The boat proved fairly useful - Its steam engine was removed by the local hotel where it was used for the next half a decade as a kind of boiler to heat its rooms and skiers crossing the frozen lake would huddle within the ship for refuge. Finally some resourceful rangers took it upon themselves to clean it up their own way, by chucking kerosene all over it in 1930. Their superiors were not best pleased and one man was sent to the East Coast for the rest of his working life as penance. The boat didn't so much get cleaned up as thoroughly blackened and sits there still, rotting and skeletal but refusing to budge as a testament to obnoxiousness winning out over entrepreneurialism. Waters died in 1926. In order to view the wreck you must first gain access via water to Stevenson Island.

29. THE SMITH MANSION
44.46102, -109.49429
2891-, 2903 N Fork Hwy, Cody, WY 82414
The house that appeared to a man in a vision? A lookout tower guarding an

267

OFFBEAT AMERICA

< Left: The Smith Mansion
Below: Bighorn Medicine Wheel

underground volcano in Yellowstone Park? Simply the work of a madman? All of these are commonly held legends regarding this bizarre structure although none are in fact accurate as Sunny Larsen, daughter of the builder in question, confirms - she grew up there with her brother Buckles. Mr Smith their father was an engineer and singlehandedly built the extraordinary design over 12 years in a folly somewhat reminiscent of The Winchester House, San Jose. In 1992, he tragically fell to his death from one of the house's balconies in one of a series of falls he suffered whilst working on the roof in the Wyoming winds. Her brother tragically drowned in a river near the property. The backstory was that Mr Smith was divorced by his wife mid-way into building her and their children a home, and when she up and took the kids, he could only throw himself into the construction. However, the strange plan cannot be attributed entirely to their troubles - Mr Smith in fact never had a plan for the house and built on whim around the clock, contributing to their divorce, and not a single one of the many rooms is built with the purpose of being a bedroom - instead some rooms were Hot rooms, others Cold rooms, some had sleeping bags, others hammocks. Still not sound like madness? The remaining family are insistent that he was an entirely sane man and simply an artist, and are now desperate to restore the house which is slowly falling apart - Sunny wants her children to see what a marvel it is and through it share with them her Father's legacy. Hopefully one day with enough funding it will open as a museum.

30. BIGHORN MEDICINE WHEEL
44.82615, -107.92159
Lovell, WY 82431

This construction of stones to form a giant wheel with spokes, aligned to the constellations, was built by Plains Indians as much as 800 years ago. The site has been used for centuries by one tribe in particular, Crow Nation youth for fasting and so called Vision Quests. The Medicine name is due to the location being used for prayers asking for healing as well as atonement made for wrongs against others. The Crow Nation

> Top: Crazy Horse Memorial
> Bottom left: Giant Prairie Dog
> Bottom right: Jolly Green Giant Statue

in this area are divided into four groups: Mountain Crow (in Native speak the spectacular Awaxaawaxammilaxpaake), River Crow, Kicked in the Bellies and Beaver Dries its Fur. Today there are 12,000 enrolled members in the tribe, speaking Crow, English and Plains Sign Talk and following the religions of Crow Way, Tobacco Society and Christianity.

31. HOLE-IN-THE-WALL GANG HIDEOUT
43.54635, -106.81116
Hole-In-The-Wall, Wyoming 82639
A remote mountain pass and the meeting place of the Hole in the Wall Gang and Butch Cassidy's Wild Bunch gang. The location was chosen as the outlaws could see the law coming from a long way off.

32. LOST SPRINGS
42.7656, -104.92647
Main St, Lost Springs, WY 82227
A coal mining town which crashed when the mine shut like so many others in 1930, by the sixties only a handful of people were based in the town. Currently 3 people are officially residents. Check out the Lost Bar while you visit.

33. HUDSON-MENG BISON BONEBED
42.82847, -103.60154
Meng Drive, Harrison, NE 69346
A bison kill (or potentially natural death) site, linked to the Alberta Culture, featuring the skeletons of over 600 bison from over 10,000 years ago, of a species that was an evolutionary step between the now-extinct Bison Antiquus species and those alive today#.

34. CRAZY HORSE MEMORIAL
43.8368, -103.6244
12151 Ave of the Chiefs, Crazy Horse, SD 57730
www.crazyhorsememorial.org
This is the biggest sculpture hewn into rock anywhere in the world and came about in retaliation by the Native Americans who objected to the carving of Mount Rushmore into their land.

35. COSMOS MYSTERY AREA
43.9232, -103.4204
24040 Cosmos Rd, Rapid City, SD 57702
www.cosmosmysteryarea.com
A place where nothing is quite as it seems and your eyes just may deceive you.

36. SPOKANE GHOST TOWN
43.8418, -103.3809
Spokane Ghost Town, Hermosa, SD, 57744
This all but forgotten 1890s lead, zinc and gold mining town still contains its original mill as well as remnants of other buildings including a schoolhouse, water tower and miners' cabins.

37. GIANT PRAIRIE DOG
43.8211, -101.9001
21290 SD-240, Philip, SD 57567
Marking the spot of an actual prairie dog colony.

38. DEVIL'S GULCH
43.72219, -96.50004
Devils Gulch, Garretson, SD 57030
See the famed 20ft foot ravine that Jesse James was said to leap on his trusty steed to evade capture by a raging horde.

39. JOLLY GREEN GIANT STATUE
43.6510, -94.0957
Green Giant Statue Park, Green Giant Ln, Blue Earth, MN 56013
At over 55ft in height, this statue exists due to a radio DJ who hosted a show in 1979 in which he would interview travellers passing through the town, giving them the local delicacy of Green Giant canned veg as a take

Bottom: Lost Springs

271

272

away gift at the end of each show. When he learnt that a new road system would divert travellers away from the town and his show, he decided (as you do) that constructing one of the largest statues in America of the Jolly Green Giant might induce them to return to him. Green Giant, who one assumes were over the moon, none the less gave only their approval but not a cent to the operation. Notably, sculptors struggled with his giant rear, which had never been shown in Green Giant advertising, but which is now immortalised forever.

NOW WHY NOT CHECK OUT:

SPAM MUSEUM - P 195

WHILE IN MINNEAPOLIS, WHY NOT CHECK OUT:

All entries from *HIDDEN BEACH* to *CITY SALVAGE* – pages 189 to 195

40. LARK TOYS
44.30209, -92.00404
63604 170th Ave, Kellogg, MN 55945
www.larktoys.com
This huge toy store has a hand carved ride-able carousel as well as a plethora of beautifully fashioned wooden toys and games. It also naturally offers miniature llamas and an 18 hole mini golf course.

41. THE ROCK IN THE HOUSE
44.13556, -91.72433
440 N Shore Dr, Fountain City, WI 54629
This is very much what it says it is.

42. WORLD'S LARGEST SIX PACK
43.80284, -91.25326
3rd St S, La Crosse, WI 54601
When a keg just won't do.

43. FAST FIBERGLASS MOULD GRAVEYARD
43.9691, -90.7823
14177 Co Hwy Q, Sparta, WI 54656
www.fastkorp.com
These abandoned moulds make for fantastic urban decay photography, a must see.

44. CHATTY BELLE
44.5527, -90.5804
1031 E Division St, Neillsville WI 54456
Sitting in the vicinity of the World's largest 'replica' cheese, this giant cow has a sporadically functioning coin-operated voice box making it if not the largest cow, at least the world's largest TALKING cow. Chatty Belle pleasingly is marked with a serial number '109', suggesting that a further 108 giant talking cows were produced. In the words of Midwest Marvels, "Thanks for stopping at the WCCN Radio headquarters, which is housed in that building right over there" Chatty says to kids who already want their twenty-five cents back. Once upon a time Chatty had a small companion heifer, Bullet, but as he cost 600 dollars of

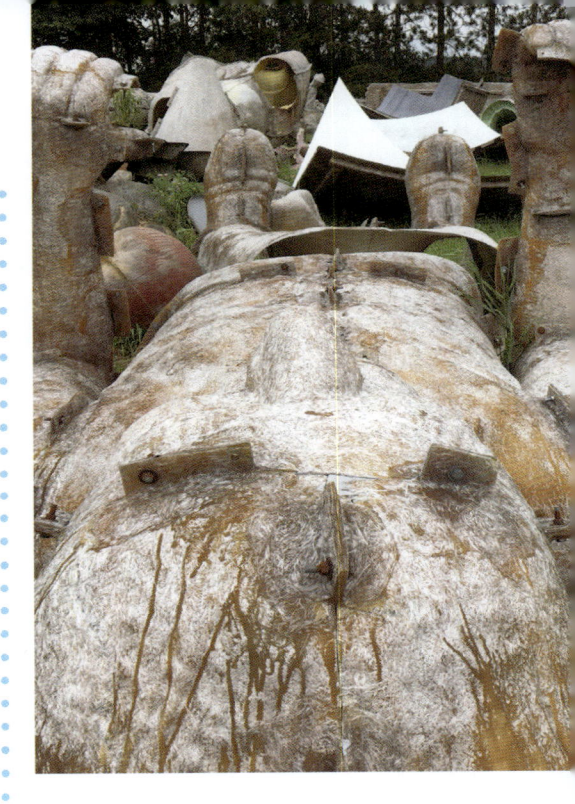

< Top left: Lark Toys
< Top right: World's Largest Six Pack
< Bottom left / > right: Fiberglass Mould Graveyard
< Bottom right: Chatty Belle

THE NORTHERN ROUTE - ROUTE 7

fibreglass to fix when visitors regularly poked his eyes out, he was unceremoniously dumped in the trash. Bizarrely, Chatty is situated next to a small yet elaborate Pavilion which featured in the 1964 New York World's Fair, currently home to both Wisconsin radio station WCCN AND (naturally) the Pavilion Cheese and Gift Store, complete with signs advising 'Central Wisconsin Broadcasting – closed to the public after 1pm.' Presumably cheese aficionados need to time their purchasing carefully. The Pavilion also contains a private collection of World's Fair memorabilia. In the words of a Neilsville resident 'It's just a weird-looking building from some old fair'. Had you have visited Chatty back pre-2005, you could have enjoyed another Wisconsin Historical Society favourite; Further along the highway stood the Cheesemobile, a refridgerated truck once used to haul the Largest Cheese in the History of Mankind, made with the milk of sixteen thousand cows to the New York World's Fair along with Chatty and Bullet (who have travelled more than some Neillsville residents may have.) Obviously the Cheesemobile was glass sided to show off the cheese to its fullest whilst en route. After showing the self-same cheese for the second consecutive year in row, the Wisconsin Dairymen and Cheesemakers Association got together in 1965 and ate all seventeen and one quarter tonnes of the cheddar. In place of the real cheese, the Cheesemobile for many years contained a giant plywood yellow cube, known better as the marketable World's Largest Replica Cheese. Sadly in '05, the truck was no more and with it died the giant cheese dream of Neillsville.

45. CIRCUS WORLD MUSEUM
43.4838, -89.7583
550 Water St, Baraboo, WI 53913
circusworldbaraboo.org
A museum dedicated to the renowned Ringling Bros as well as circus culture in general. Live performances take place in Summer months.

46. MAN MOUND
43.48853, -89.67148

Man Mound Park, Man Mound Road, Baraboo, WI 53913

An enigmatic giant figure of a man with an unknown history can be seen in outback Baraboo.

47. PARDEEVILLE
43.53776, -89.30011
Pardeeville, WI 53954

It's an Amish town to top it all. The name derives from founder John Pardee in the 1800s.

48. THE TOWN OF EMBARRASS
44.66553, -88.70732
Main St, Embarrass, WI 54933

The name caught on from French Canadian lumberjacks (then the majority of the early lumberjack population in the town) who found it almost impossible to send logs down the river because of the many snags and debris, leading them to call it the Riviere Embarrase, embarrase meaning to impede, snag or obstruct.

49. MUSTARD MUSEUM
43.0954, -89.5114
7477 Hubbard Ave, Middleton, WI 53562
www.mustardmuseum.com

It cuts…the..

50. EPIC SYSTEMS CAMPUS
42.99623, -89.56923
1979 Milky Way, Verona, WI 53593
www.epic.com

Founded in 1979, Epic, an IT systems company, employs 9000 plus people on the new campus it moved to in 2005 which is something like a mini universe of joyful work where the employee comes first. Referred to as their Intergalactic Headquarters where their employees 'superpowers' can be released, the phenomenal work environment is world class, every employee has their own office or shares with one other, it has super casual dress code, offers Ultimate Frisbee, basketball, Jiu Jitsu, board gaming, volunteering and another 65 plus clubs, has its own Epicycles brigade who cycle trails together - it even has a sledding hill and skating pond for God's sake. Not only that but the food is award winning, vacation time is lengthy, sabbaticals are encouraged and you can get your car seen to while you work or leave your dirty whites at 'The New York Sock Exchange'. Heading to your cubicle on Monday just got more depressing.

51. THE LOST CITY OF MADISON
43.04492, -89.42064
University of Wisconsin-Madison Arboretum, 1207 Seminole Hwy, Madison, WI 53711 (follow trails labelled 'L')
arboretum.wisc.edu

Planned as a huge suburban utopia by developers in the early 1900s, this 800 acre area was due to be a new era of residential living with trams, playgrounds and schools all set to rival Madison. The town was going

< Left: Circus World Museum
Top right: Mustard Museum
Bottom right: Epic Systems Campus

THE NORTHERN ROUTE - ROUTE 7

275

Bottom left: Mary Nohl House
Bottom right: The Safe House

to be a beautiful mix of natural and urban, 7000 houses each of which would be situated on or near a lake or picturesque woodland. Roads were laid and foundations duly poured, but unfortunately at this point it became abundantly clear that Lake Forest was rather too much Lake and rather too little Forest, and the entire area began to sink - fast. There had been cunning plans for 7000 ft. worth of canal to lessen the marshy quality of the land but when greed hastened the project and the best laid plans were put on hold in favour of building for a quick buck, things began to unravel. Very little remains to be seen of the only 6 houses that were built before building was halted indefinitely but a keen eye can find a few remaining items of that bygone age from the construction crews of the day and perhaps even a step or sidewalk here and there. Most have forgotten Lake Forest or as it is better known the Lost City of Madison.

52. MARY NOHL HOUSE
43.1503, -87.8921
7328 N Beach Dr, Fox Point, WI 53217
A weird house belonging to 'The Witch of Fox Point' which local residents have not been able to get rid of.

53. THE SAFE HOUSE
43.04055, -87.91032
779 N Front St, Milwaukee, WI 53202
www.safe-house.com
Dine like a spy on dishes such as the Agent Provocateur Steak Sandwich or the Cuban Missile Crisis in this restaurant which requires a password to get in. Don't have it? Try waddling like a penguin for 30 seconds and they may unlock the door…

54. T H STEMPER CO
42.9977, -87.89429
1125 E Potter Ave, Milwaukee, WI 53207
www.stempers.com
Where the holy go to buy their wares.

55. AMERICAN SCIENCE AND SURPLUS
42.9877, -87.9990
6901 W Oklahoma Ave, Milwaukee, WI 53219
www.sciplus.com
If The Big Bang Theory had a store, this would be it.

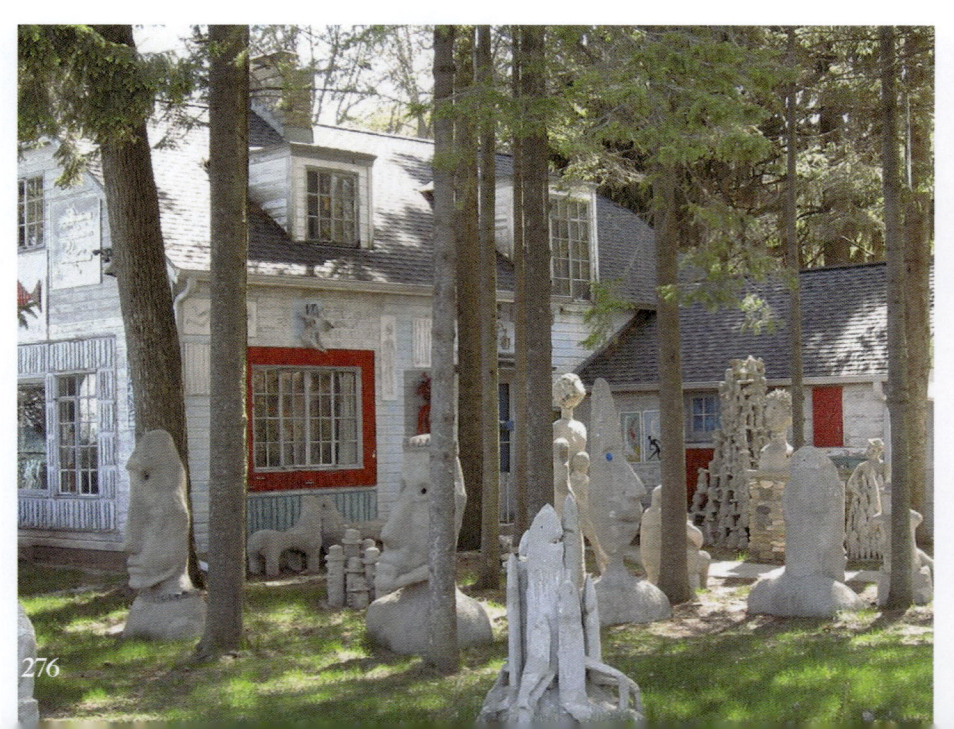

56. ORGAN PIPER PIZZA PALACE
42.9652, -88.0483
4353 S 108th St, Greenfield, WI 53228
www.organpiperpizza.com

This Milwaukee landmark has been running for 40 some years, entertaining pizza munching hoards with the dulcet tones of a fabulous Mighty Wurlizer theatre pipe organ dating from the 1920's. The skilled organists take requests and can play a wide variety of music from the classical to rock, to…dare we say it…Let It Go.

57. ONAN'S GOLD PYRAMID HOUSE
42.4135, -87.9449
37921 N Dilleys Rd, Wadsworth, IL 60083
goldpyramid.com

As homes go, this one is elaborate and was built specifically to support its owners' belief in 'pyramid power', a cult theory that emerged in the early 70s. This folk belief holds that the pyramid shape itself can confer a variety of benefits, including for example the ability to preserve food, to sharpen or maintain the sharpness of razor blades, to improve health, to stimulate thought, to trigger sexual urges and many more. Such beliefs are collectively termed Pyramidology. Naturally, there is no scientific basis for any such beliefs whatsoever. The idea was developed by Antoine Bovis, a French ironmonger in the Thirties, who came up with the food preservation concept based on allegedly having visited the King's Chamber of the Great Pyramid of Egypt and noticing that a trash can filled with dead animals who had entered the structure had not decayed, drawing the conclusion that it

Top: American Science & Surplus
Right: Organ Piper Pizza Palace

THE NORTHERN ROUTE - ROUTE 7

277

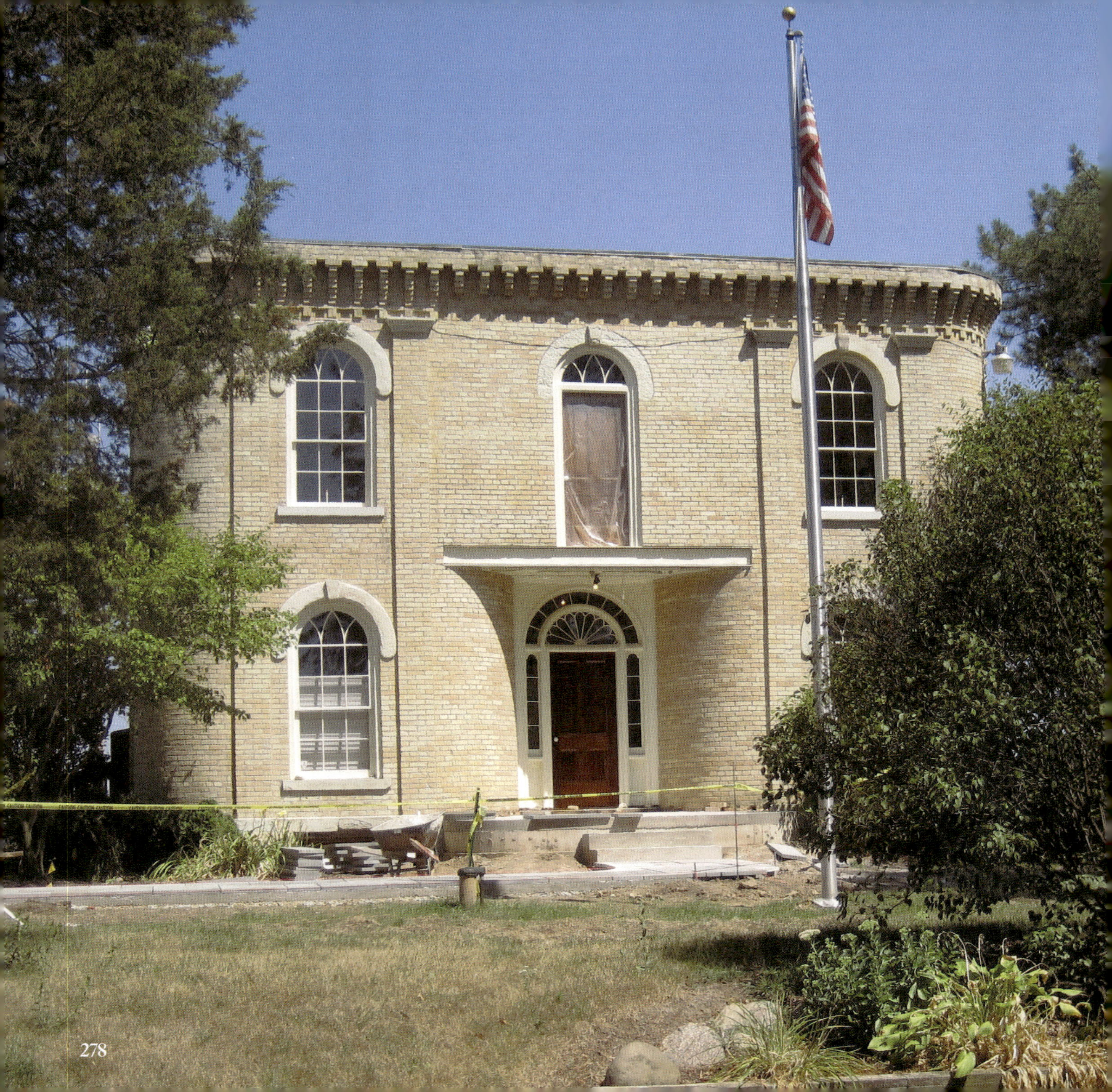

must have been the pyramid which preserved them. His book describes the depth of research solidly backing up his claims: 'I have supposed that Egyptians were already very good dowsers and had oriented their pyramid by means of rod and pendulum. Being unable to go there to experiment and verify the radiations of the Keops Pyramid, I have built with cardboard some pyramids that you can see now, and I was astonished when, having built a regular pyramid and oriented it, I found the positive at the East, the negative at the West, and at the North and the South, dual-positive and dual-negative...A new supposition: since with the help of our positive 2000° magnetic plates we can mummify small animals, could the pyramid have the same property? I tried, and as you can observe with the small fish and the little piece of meat still hanging, I succeeded totally.' A Czech man by the name of Drbal patented a 'Pharoah's shaving device' in 1949 which he claimed maintained razor blades at their sharpest by orientating them to magnetic fields. Such theories clearly inspired the Onan Family who were hotel and condo developers to build this structure in 1977 - It is entirely gold plated but luckily is a bit too large to be nicked. A Winery in British Columbia has followed suit, building a four storey replica of the Great Pyramid which is said to improve the quality of wine aged within it. Terry Pratchett's Pyramids novel explores the theory via the development of an industry based on the pyramid's ability to halt time. Should you dare open a New Age magazine, you may be lucky enough to spot an ad for open metal pole pyramids under which one can meditate. See also the Summum Pyramid (Chapter 11, entry 12.)

58. GEORGE STICKNEY HOUSE
42.3007, -88.3522
1904 Cherry Valley Road, Woodstock, IL 60098
The house which today is the Bull Valley Police Headquarters is of bizarre design based largely upon George and Sylvia Stickney's beliefs in spiritualism and is said to be haunted by 200 plus ghosts. Both of the Stickney's were 'accomplished' mediums and hosted parties and séances for their friends, hence the choice of an isolated location for the house. They entered Spiritualism to commune with their deceased children, of which they had had ten with only three surviving to adulthood. The police officers confirm that they have experienced sightings personally whilst working in the house.

NOW WHY NOT CHECK OUT:

CHICAGO, all entries from T*HE MURDER CASTLE SITE* to *SHOWMEN'S REST* - pages 113 to 122

< Left: George Stickney House
Top right: Onan's Gold Pyramid House

THE NORTHERN ROUTE - ROUTE 7

THE CANADIAN BORDERLANDS
ROUTE 8

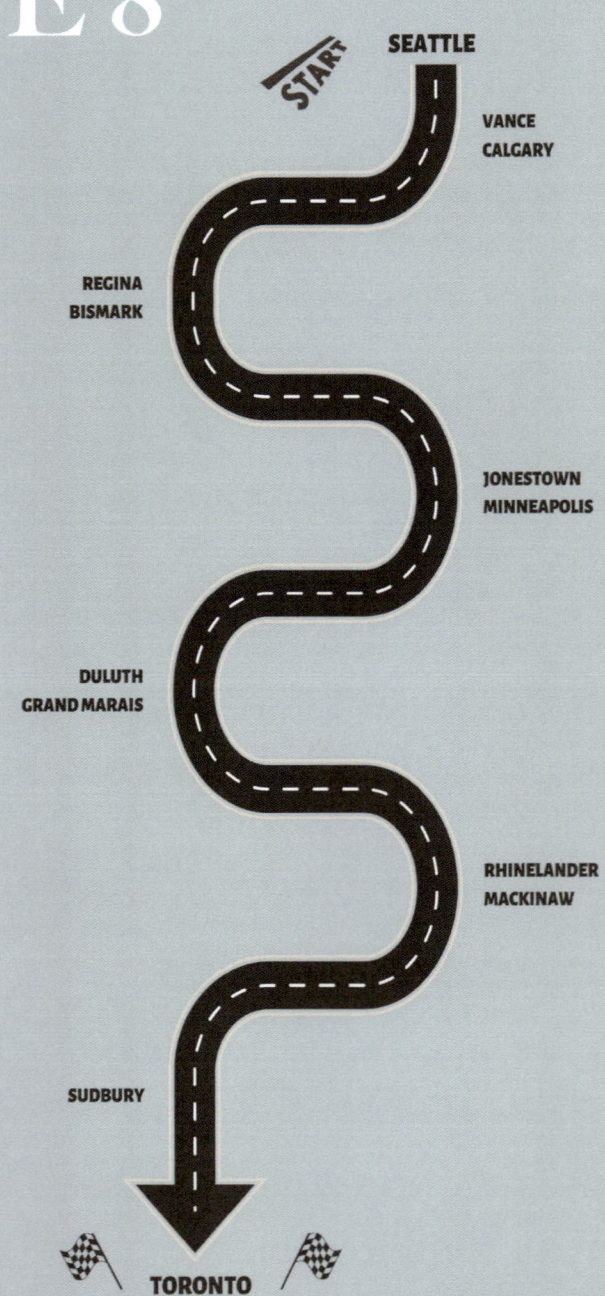

START — SEATTLE
VANCE
CALGARY
REGINA
BISMARK
JONESTOWN
MINNEAPOLIS
DULUTH
GRAND MARAIS
RHINELANDER
MACKINAW
SUDBURY
TORONTO

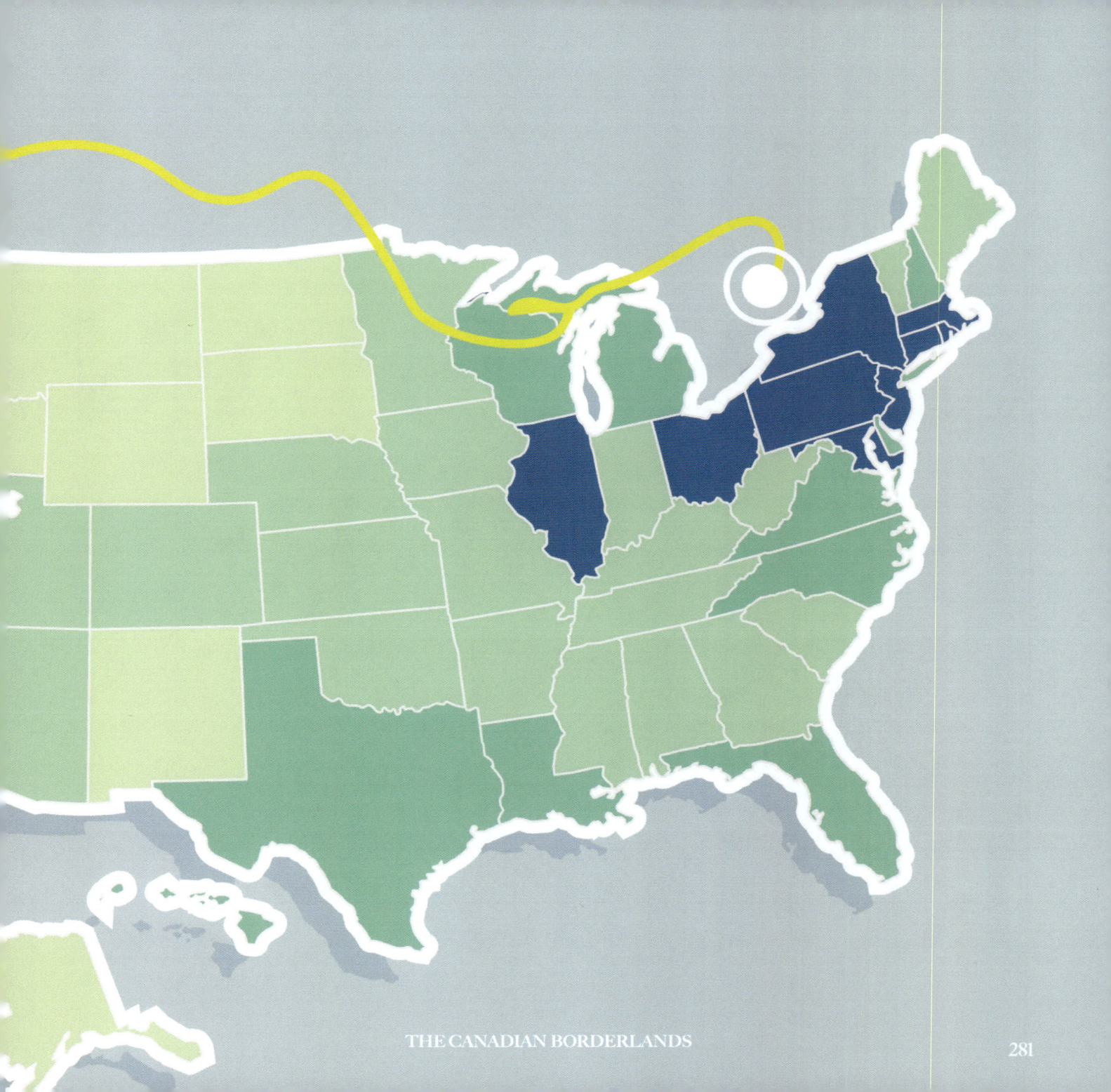

THE CANADIAN BORDERLANDS

281

THE CANADIAN BORDERLANDS ROUTE 8

Above: Mcmillan Mausoleum

Taking a slight detour from Seattle, zig-zag your way up to America's neighbours in the North and back again, putting on your winter warmers and tracking down a bowl of Poutine, or as it's better known, chips covered in gravy and cheese curd. Prepare yourself for stunning natural beauty, peppered with the remains of plane crashes, a giant pixellated Killer Whale, a climable T-Rex and the most Canadian museum of all time.

WHILE IN SEATTLE, WHY NOT CHECK OUT:

All entries from *VASHON BICYCLE TREE* to *RONETTE'S BRIDGE*, pages 251 to 254

1. MCMILLIN MAUSOLEUM
48.61594, -123.149
664 Afterglow Dr, Friday Harbor, WA 98250
This symbology-filled tomb structure in Roche Harbour incorporates three flights of stairs, the first flight of which has three steps, representing the three ages of man. The second has five, to symbolise the

five orders of classic architecture and the five senses and the final flight has seven, representing the seven liberal arts and sciences as well as the number of days in a week. There is a classic broken column which is used to represent death cutting a life short in an untimely manner, and a large table in the centre which represents the McMillin family sitting for dinner together, each with a named chair containing their ashes. The family's personal secretary is interred with them.

2. ABANDONED PLANE CRASH SITE

49.138, -122.2885

7494 Mary St, Mission, BC V2V6Y9, Canada

(Take trail closest to St Mary's School and keep walking around until you find it!) Wedged between two branches of a tree in Heritage Park are the remains of a crashed single seater plane. Few are aware of its existence and it takes some hunting to find. No one appears to know anything about the crash, or whether for some reason the crashed parts were moved from elsewhere and wedged in the tree, although it has been there a while - graffiti on the wing piece dates back to 1971.

3. THE SPOTTED LAKE

49.0780, -119.5675

Spotted Lake, Okanagan-Similkameen A, BC V0H, Canada

A beautiful polka-dotted lake caused by mineral and salt deposits considered sacred by First Nations, surrounded by what are thought to be ancient graves.

4. RIVERVIEW HOSPITAL

49.24585, -122.80485

2601 Lougheed Hwy, Coquitlam, BC V3C 4J2, Canada

This mental hospital operated from 1913 until 2012 and was originally designed to house 480 patients although by the end of its first year in operation it already held 919. In a move that was either excellent rehabilitation or a clever use of cheap labour, the Colony Farm adjacent that kept patients busy was within that 1 year producing more than 700 tons of crops and 20,000 gallons of milk every year. By 1955, the hospital had a Tuberculosis unit, a Veteran's Unit known as Crease Clinic, a Female Chronic Unit, an Acute Psychopathic Unit, an arboretum and a plant nursery. By 1956 it had 4,306 patients but by the Sixties numbers were declining

Above: The Spotted Lake
> Top left: Plane Wreck of Heritage Park
Top right and bottom: Riverview Hospital

OFFBEAT AMERICA

285

and continued to do so until 2004 when there were just 800 beds owing to the introduction of anti-psychotic medications, psychiatric units being introduced into acute care hospitals and an increasing emphasis on outpatient care. Buildings were closed one by one until the facility was completely closed in 2012. It was slated to reopen in 2019 complete with new facilities.

5. THE MCBARGE
49.2922, -122.9809
Adrian St, Burnaby, BC V5C 1L7, Canada
This water bound McDonald's, officially named The Friendship 500, has seen better McDays.

6. LEG-IN-BOOT SQUARE
49.26726, -123.1193
Leg in Boot Square, Vancouver, BC V5Z, Canada
A square nostalgically named after a severed leg washed up on the shore nearby. No one ever claimed the leg, so the police gave it to a stray dog. Apparently that's how it's done in Canada.

7. DIGITAL ORCA
49.28977, -123.11676
Vancouver Convention Centre West Building, 1055 Canada Pl, Vancouver, BC V6C 0C3, Canada
Have a pixelated whale of a time at this cool sculpture in Vancouver.

8. CAPILANO SUSPENSION BRIDGE
49.34295, -123.11494
Capilano Suspension Bridge, West Vancouver, BC V7S 1J5, Canada
This bridge was built in 1889 out of just rope and a few planks as one man's challenge to his buddies to cross the span and be duly declared courageous - thankfully for the rest of us, it was fully rebuilt in 1956 and whilst requiring no less courage to cross, at least now promises full life preservation into the bargain.

9. INTERNATIONAL YARN BOMBING DAY
49.6935, -122.8418
Lethbridge, T1J 4C9
Also known variously as yarn storming, guerilla knitting, urban knitting, graffiti knitting

Top left: Digital Orca
Bottom left: Capilano Suspension Bridge
Top: The Mcbarge

OFFBEAT AMERICA

or the frankly excellent KNIFFITI, this is the (sport?) of creating street art using crocheted or knitted wool. This festival began in 2011 in Alberta when revellers get their knit on across town. Why not join in or just watch and wonder why.

10. THE EMPRESS HOTEL
48.42166, -123.36784
721 Government St, Victoria, BC V8W 1W5, Canada
www.fairmont.com

Renowned for its stunning crystal ballroom, this beautiful Vancouver Island landmark hotel on the Victoria harbour was designed by Brit Francis Rattenbury and built in 1904 over a four year period in grand Imperial style, servicing film stars and royalty. By the Twenties Rattenbury was married with children but on a night out at the Empress he fell in love with a 27 year old stunner called Alma Packenham, had an affair and leaving his family behind, took a boat for England with her to sunny Bournemouth. Sadly karma won out when he was brutally beaten to death by a large croquet mallet in his Bournemouth drawing room, with the lovely Alma confessing to the horrific murder. Shortly later however she passed the blame to her 17 year old driver, who it transpired she was also having an affair with. She was acquitted as both she and the boy were as high as kites on cocaine, but stabbed herself multiple times in the heart before throwing herself into a river for good measure a few days later. The driver served seven years for Rattenbury's murder.

11. WORLD'S LARGEST HOCKEY STICK AND PUCK
48.7829, -123.70249
Side of Cowichan Aquatic Centre, 2653 James St, Duncan, BC V9L 2X5, Canada

...Because someone else had the World's Largest Hockey Stick without the puck.

12. OLD COUNTRY MARKET
49.3055, -124.423
2326 Alberni Hwy, Coombs, BC V0R 1M0, Canada
oldcountrymarket.com

A market store of Norwegian ownership with goats casually hanging out on its roof.

13. THE TREE ON THE LAKE
48.5894, -124.3498

Top: International Yarn Bombing Day
Bottom: The Tree on the Lake

121B-141B Aspen Drive, Sparwood, BC V0B 2G0, Canada
1st the worst, 2nd the best.

15. FRANK
49.5999, -114.3943
Frank Slide Interpretive Centre, Hwy 3 Crowsnest Pass, Blairmore, AB T0K 0E0, Canada

In 1903, over 90M tons of stone hurtled down the innocuously named Turtle Mountain towards the town of Frank, wiping out, within just 1 minute 40 seconds, a portion of the town and around 90 of its residents, most of whom are buried under the rubble to this day. By 1906 the town's population had actually doubled although by 1917 with the closure of the town's mine, most left. Currently Frank has a population of around 200 and the disaster site is almost totally untouched. The deadliest landslide in Canadian history, it is thought that the death toll may be considerably higher as around 50 passers-through were camped at the foot of the mountain at the time and it is not clear whether they had passed on or not prior to the accident. Worse, 17 miners were underground when the slide blocked their tunnels - one miner knew of a way to tunnel out and his team dug for hours whilst the air ran out steadily; only 3 had the strength to continue and finally broke into the open air, all 17 surviving after a 13 hour ordeal when the rest were pulled to safety. Tragically, it was only after surveying the scene around them that they discovered that some of their families had been killed. A horse called Charlie was found after a month having survived in the mine underground on ground water and wood bark, but died soonafter when his rescuers overfed him oats and brandy. Not all the news was tragic however, 128 men were due to arrive to work in the area and were delayed by the trains, thus avoiding the slide. One man, Sid Choquette, ran through falling debris and a thick dust cloud for 1.2 miles to flag down an oncoming passenger train, the Spokane Flyer, warning it that the track was covered with rocks. He was commended a hero and given a $25 cheque for his trouble. Only 12 bodies could be recovered from the disaster at the time although in 1924 six more were found by labourers working on a road in the area. A legend persisted for a long time that a bank containing half a million dollars was buried under the rubble - it was in fact untouched by the slide on the other side of town. The legend arose after the bank's subsequent demolition - road crews building in the area did so under police guard in case they unearthed the bank and fell prey to the greedy.

16. HEAD-SMASHED-IN-BUFFALO JUMP
49.70533, -113.65341
Fort MacLeod, AB T0L 0Z0, Canada
headsmashedin.org

Buffalo jumps were used by Native people as

Fairy Lake, Pacific Marine Road, Port Renfrew, BC V0S, Canada
It's a rock. With a tree on it. In a lake. A pretty good tree.

14. FORMERLY THE WORLD'S BIGGEST TRUCK
49.7316, -114.88409

Top: Formerly The World's Biggest Truck
Centre: Head-Smashed-In Buffalo Jump
> Right: Frank

OFFBEAT AMERICA

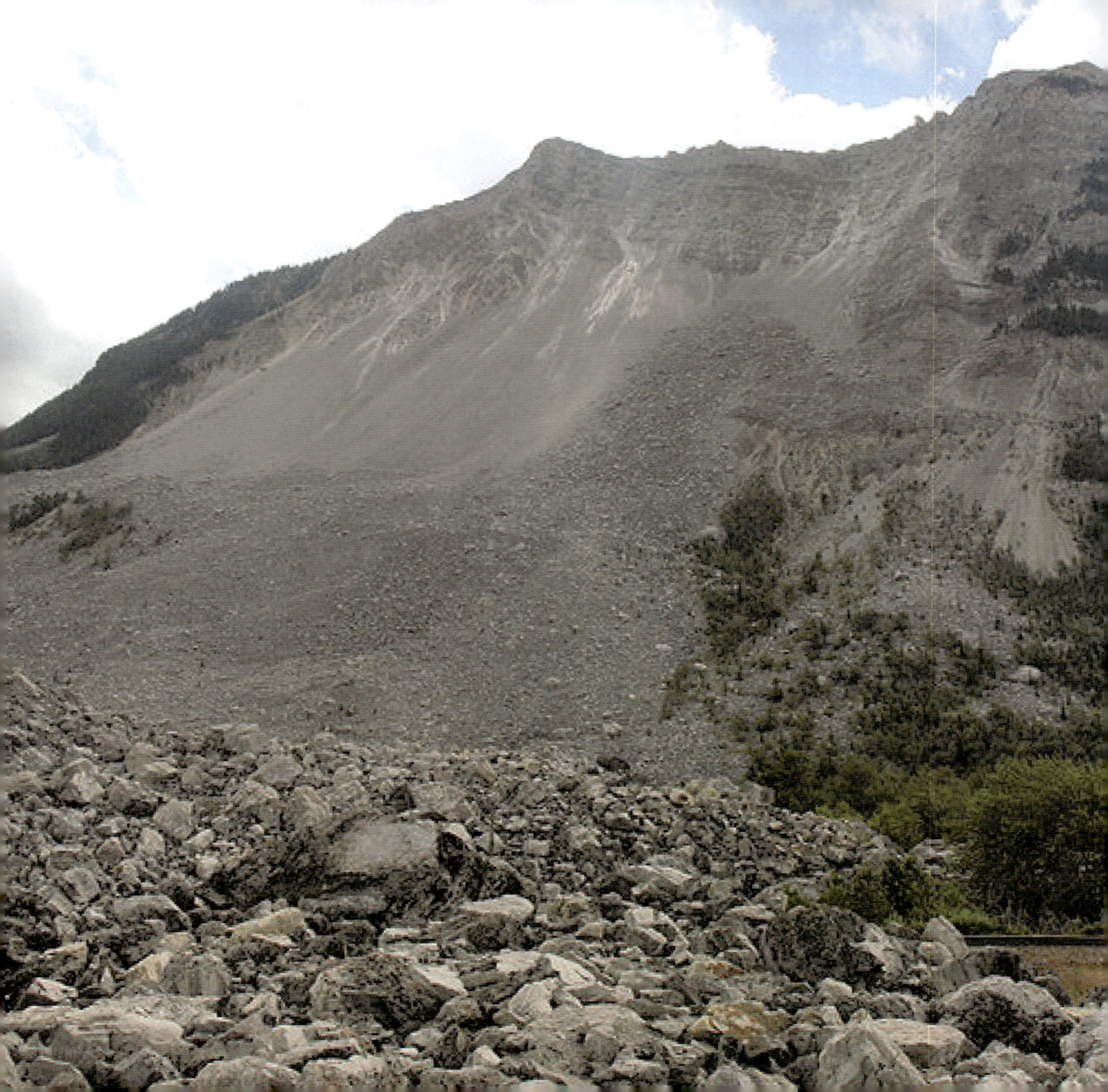

a hunting method, making use of their excellent knowledge of both geography and bison behaviour, for over 6000 years - this jump is a UNESCO World Heritage Site.

17. THE WORLD'S LARGEST DINOSAUR
51.46726, -112.7088
60 1 Ave W, Drumheller, AB T0J 0Y0, Canada
www.worldslargestdinosaur.com
Built from fibreglass and steel, this 26.3 metre high attraction is much larger than the world's biggest specimens of the actual dinosaur it represents (which were approximately half this height, although commonly they would have been about 4 times smaller). It weighs 65 tonnes and has 106 stairs leading to its mouth/viewing area.

18. GALAXYLAND
53.52351, -113.62198
8882 170 Street #2784, Edmonton, AB T5T 4J2, Canada

The Edmonton Mall is not only absolutely gigantic, it contains its own indoor amusement park with 24 full scale rides and the world's largest indoor triple loop roller coaster. Ride at your peril however - in 1986 disaster struck when missing bolts caused a car to separate from its track at the back of the ride and start to swerve wildly, releasing the safety bars keeping the riders in their seats, throwing them off the ride before the ride stalled, slid backwards and crashed into a concrete pillar, killing three and crushing one man's legs. After the crash, the train which derailed was scrapped; the cars came in three colours, yellow, red and blue and as it was a yellow car which crashed, the other yellow cars were repainted red and blue as passengers were scared of yellow roller coasters featuring in the media images of the crash. In more recent years, the yellow colour has bizarrely returned. In 2000 in an unrelated incident, a man was found drowned at the bottom of a pool in the mall near the replica of the Santa Maria ship, once shown at the World's Fair.

19. THE WORLD'S LARGEST SAUSAGE
53.5952, -112.3366
5321 Sawchuk St, Mundare, AB T0B 3H0, Canada
Not the brat-worst thing you'll see on your trip. Sometimes listed more apologetically as 'The World's Largest Garlic Sausage', leading one to believe that larger sausages may be out there.

< Bottom left: Mac the Moose
< The World's Largest Dinosaur
Bottom: The Weyburn Mental Hospital
Overleaf: The Vegreville Pysanka

20. THE VEGREVILLE PYSANKA
53.4926, -112.03744
45 St, Vegreville, AB T9C, Canada
www.vegreville.com
The Easter bunny must have had his work cut out with this one - a pysanka is an Ukranian Easter egg and this is a biggun at 31ft tall. Ukrainian due to Vegreville's huge Ukrainian population, the egg was made using incredibly complex mathematical calculations to piece together 2732 individual metal pieces.

21. GIANT PYROGY
54.2484, -111.15449
5029 Pyrogy Drive North, (Pyrogy Park), Glendon, AB T0A 1P0, Canada
What happens when Polish ravioli take on epic proportions? This does.

22. MAC THE MOOSE
50.4131, -105.5101
450 Diefenbaker Dr, Moose Jaw, SK S6J 1N2, Canada
The World's Largest Moose.

23. THE WEYBURN MENTAL HOSPITAL
49.67403, -103.86103
Saskatchewan Dr, Weyburn, SK S4H 2Z9, Canada
Now demolished, spare a thought as you pass for the alcoholics who were fed LSD by their doctors in early LSD experiments here, at the hospital where the term 'psychedelic' was coined.

24. PAPERCLIP COTTAGE CAFÉ
50.10209, -102.63095
503 Main St, Kipling, SK S0G 2S0, Canada
The phenomenal outcome of one man's now famous quest to barter his way up from a paperclip to a home, the home in question has since be bartered again this time to a restaurant owner who has opened it as a café - drop in and take note of the nearby marker memorialising the world record for the most trades and find the town's giant paperclip commemorating the event forever.

25. ENCHANTED HIGHWAY
46.4217, -102.5557
607 Main St, Regent, ND 58650
enchantedcastlend.com
One man's dream to put his home town of Regent North Dakota on the map rather than see it fall into obscurity; single handedly and with no prior experience at all, Gary Greff built the most stunning giant sculptures along the roadside which make

THE CANADIAN BORDERLANDS ROUTE 8

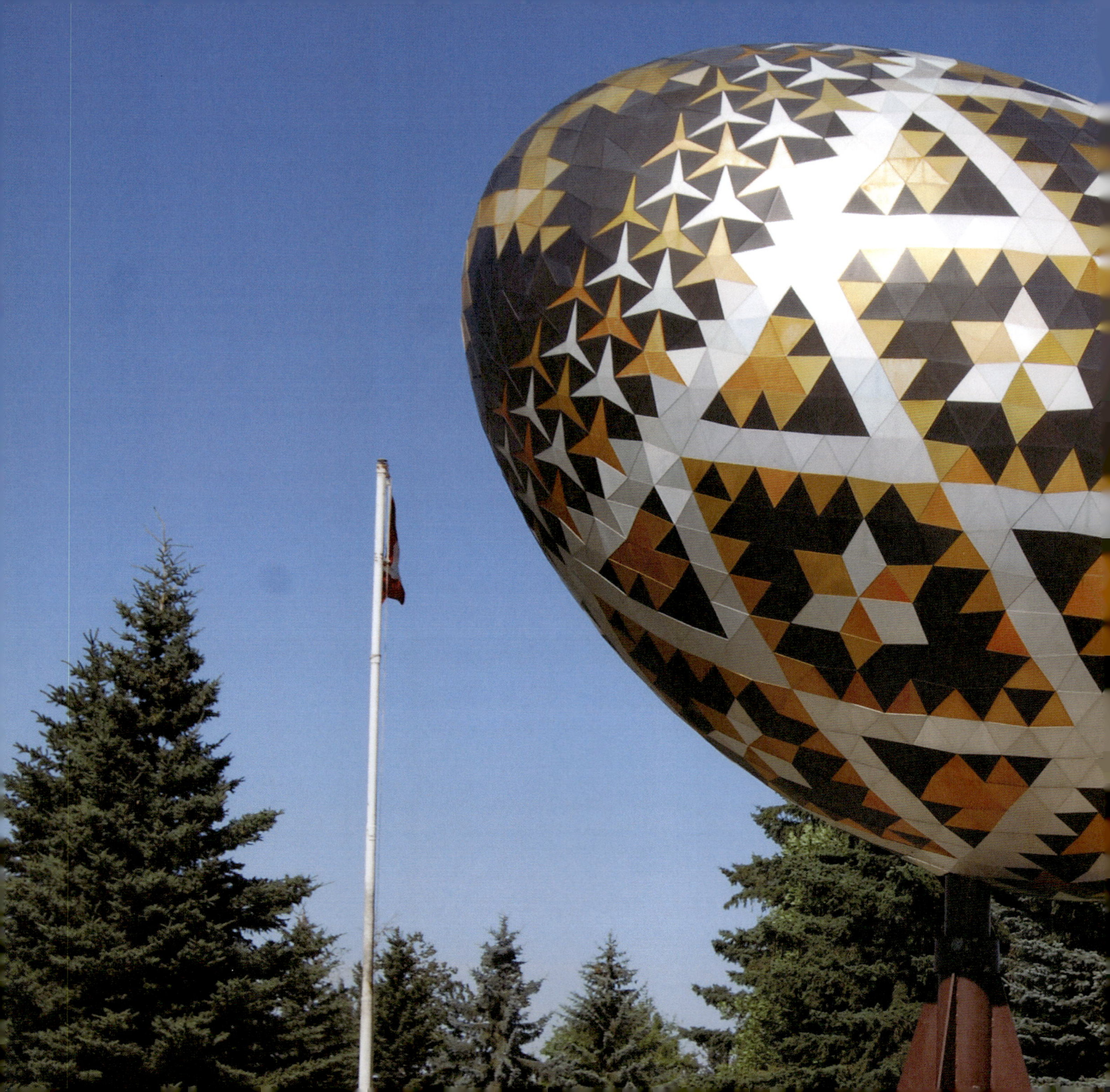

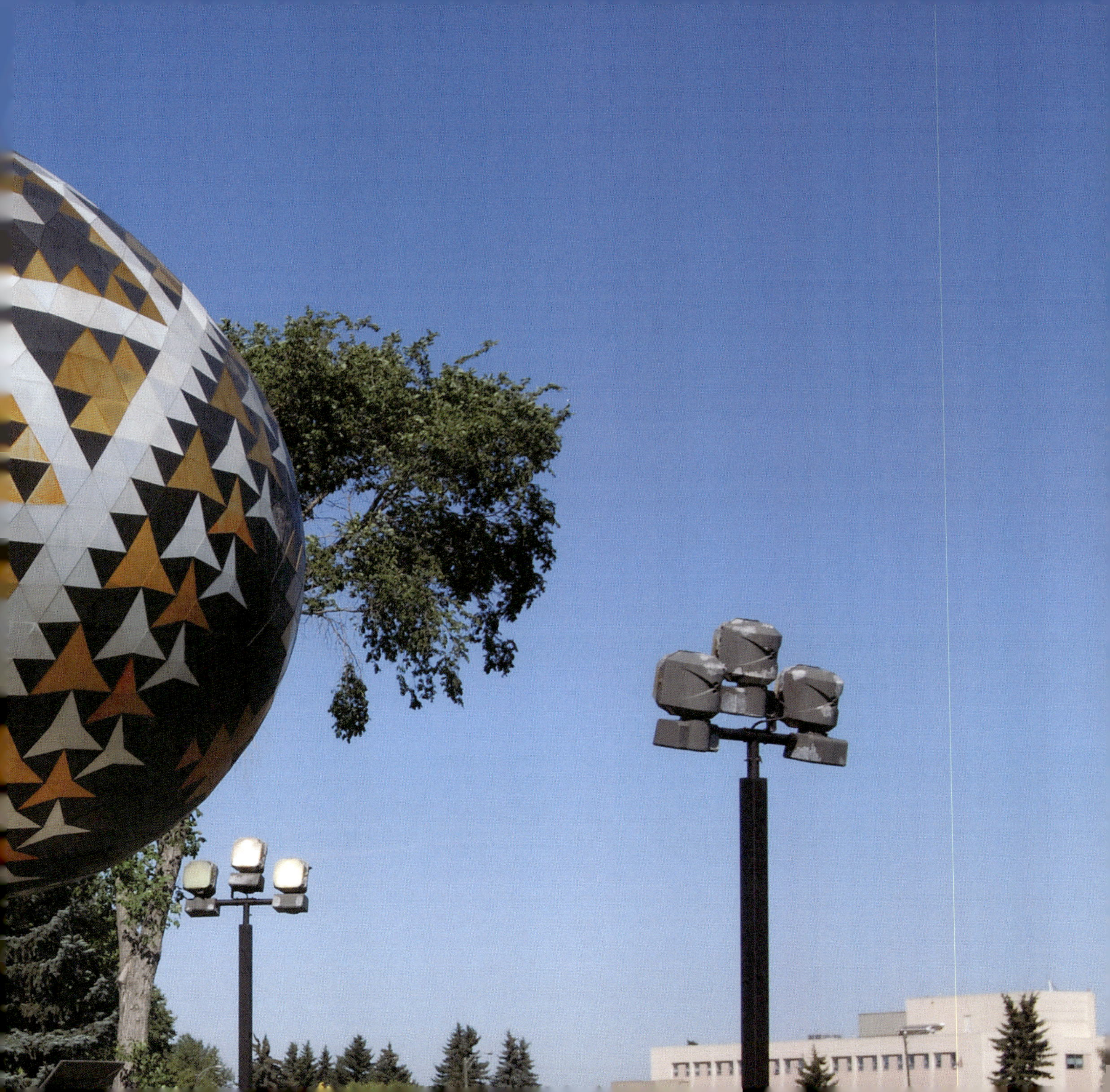

for phenomenal Americana photography - his creations continue to be built out of donations alone so be sure to show your appreciation

26. MCFARTHEST SPOT
45.4595, -101.9135 (Off road)
Sick of McDonalds' bid for world domination? Then this spot is for you, placing you further away from a McDonalds than any other location in America.

27. THE ALBINO BUFFALO OF NORTH DAKOTA
46.8905, -98.7388
Interstate 94, Jamestown, North Dakota, 58401 (view from the road)
White buffalo are held extremely sacred to Native Americans and Jamestown has not one but 3 roaming about for all to see. The Native Americans pass down variations of the same story regarding White Buffalo from generation to generation and deem it highly significant; the legend is that Man had lost his ability to talk to the Great Spirit, who therefore sent the White Buffalo Calf Woman to aid him. She taught Man how to pray with the sacred bundle, a Pipe, giving him also seven sacred ceremonies to follow to ensure future harmony, peace and balance. The seven ceremonies, still performed today, are the Sweat Lodge

Top: Enchanted Highway (prior page)
Left: World's Largest Buffalo

for purification, the Naming Ceremony for child naming, the Healing Ceremony for health, the Adoption Ceremony for the making of relatives, the Marriage Ceremony for uniting people, the Vision Quest for communing with the Creator and the Sundance Ceremony to pray for wellbeing for all. When White Buffalo Calf Woman had imparted her wisdom, she told them she had within her four Ages, and that she would leave them and return again, looking back upon them in each of the four Ages and returning again in the Fourth Age to restore peace to a troubled land. She walked away a short distance, sat, and arose as a black buffalo. A little further away she again sat, before arising as a yellow buffalo. The third time, she arose as a red buffalo and the fourth, as a white buffalo calf, signalling the fulfilment of the prophecy. The colours referred to the four colours of man as they were then deemed to be as well as the four directions of North, East, South and West. One man still holds the sacred Pipe - his name is Arvol Looking Horse and he lives on the Cheyenne River Indian reservation in South Dakota. Today White Buffalo still signify prayers being heard, that the sacred Pipe is being honoured and prophetic promises fulfilled, as well as a time of abundance and plenty.

28. WORLD'S LARGEST BUFFALO
46.8892, -98.6984
17th St SE, Jamestown, ND 58401, USA

It's an exceptionally large buffalo. Check out the National Buffalo Museum while you're nearby (500 17th St SE, Jamestown, ND 58401, buffalomuseum.com , +1 701-252-8648).

29. BUTTZVILLE
46.50802, -97.62981
Buttzville, ND 58054
Etymology unknown.

30. AMERICA'S LARGEST VIKING
45.89106, -95.37729
Central Lakes Trail, Alexandria, MN 56308
Was Alexandria visited by Vikings? The jury is out on this claim to fame, but assuredly not by ones as big as 'Big Ole'.

31. WORLD'S LARGEST CROW
45.453, -95.0045
Belgrade Centennial Memorial Park, Highway 71, Belgrade, Minnesota
What better way to celebrate a city's anniversary than building… the Largest Crow in the World?

32. WORLD'S LARGEST BALL OF TWINE ROLLED BY ONE MAN
45.0963, -94.4101
World's Largest Twine Ball, Darwin, MN 55324
As opposed to The Largest Ball of Twine NOT rolled by one man. That one man is sadly no longer with us but his whimsy lives on to put a smile of the faces of countless visitors.

Right: World's Largest Ball of Twine Rolled by One Man

Bottom left: Museum of Quackery & Medical Frauds
Bottom Right: Naniboujou Lodge

NOW WHY NOT CHECK OUT:

MINNEAPOLIS, All entries from *HIDDEN BEACH* to *CITY SALVAGE* – pages 189 to 195

33. MUSEUM OF QUACKERY AND MEDICAL FRAUDS
44.9435, -93.0957
Science Museum of Minnesota, 120 W Kellogg Blvd, St Paul, MN 55102
Charlatans abound in this temple to all things fraudulent and misleading.

34. WORLD'S LARGEST HOCKEY STICK
47.4612, -92.5401
412 Monroe St, Eveleth, MN 55734
Another 'The World's Largest Hockey Stick', this time sans puck.

35. EMBARRASS
47.65908, -92.19794
Embarrass, MN 55732
French fur traders found the river here very shallow and narrow and thereby difficult to navigate leading them to apply the term 'embarras' to it, or 'obstruct/block'.

36. NANIBOUJOU LODGE
47.81706, -90.04941
20 Naniboujou Trail, Grand Marais, MN 55604
www.naniboujou.com
This Native American and Art Deco-influenced private VIP resort was built in the Jazz Age by an entrepreneur from that bastion of Fargo pop culture, Duluth. Babe Ruth was a member of the club which was planned to include a golf course, pool, tennis courts, marina, clubhouse and hunting lodge. The Great Depression dampened plans however and only a reduced scale version of the clubhouse was built, although in the most phenomenal grand Native American influenced style with arresting hand painted interiors in colourful themes which have remained untouched since its opening in the Twenties. It foreclosed in 1935 and was sold off in 1939. Much of the land was repurposed as a state park but the property went to a private owner and has since existed variously as a hotel chain, a family resort and of course a

OFFBEAT AMERICA

Bottom left: Pickle Barrel House
Centre: Mackinac Island
Right: The Canadian Canoe Museum
Overleaf: Big Nickel

ubiquitous religious outfit.

37. WORLD'S LARGEST SOUP KETTLE

45.5636, -88.6740

US-8, Laona, WI 54541 (just south of Mill on your left half way down the side of the park on your left as you travel south)

What is a soup kettle? Why is this one so large? Can an entire event be held purely to laude soup? Find out in Laona.

38. PICKLE BARREL HOUSE

46.67092, -85.98468

Lake Ave & Randolph Street, Grand Marais, MI 49839

If you are going to live on a lake, you might as well do so in a house that looks like a pickle barrel, or so the logic goes. What is a pickle barrel I hear you say? Well in the true American tradition of saying what you see… it is a barrel made to contain pickles.

39. MACKINAC ISLAND

45.86831, -84.62756

Mackinac Island, MI 49757

When Mackinac (pronunciation: Mak-in-aw) Island banned cars (or 'horseless carriages') in 1898, it really meant it. The ban has remained to this day. Want to see the entire population of an entire island attempt to rely on horses, bikes and foot for transport? This is your place. Before you think you can avoid the ban yourself, scooters, golf carts and the like are all banned, although they have magnanimously made allowances for motorised wheelchairs and emergency vehicles. Visit the M-185, the only highway in the US where cars are outlawed.

40. BIG NICKEL

46.47916, -81.03045

Dynamic Earth, 122 Big Nickel Mine Dr, Sudbury, ON P3C 5T7, Canada

A 9 metre high Canadian Nickel, built wholly against the wishes of the local council to commemorate the Canadian Centennial by one man with a giant Nickel-shaped dream that he refused to let die. He purchased the land it sits on for $1M using a $25 down payment and despite multiple planning rejections for both the Nickel and road access, he eventually acquired enough property to be able to build the nickel, with access, just outside of city limits and therefore without the need for a permit

41. THE CANADIAN CANOE MUSEUM

44.28795, -78.33034

910 Monaghan Rd, Peterborough, ON K9J 5K4, Canada

www.canoemuseum.ca

Arguably the most Nationalistic museum in the history of Nationalistic museums.

THE CANADIAN BORDERLANDS ROUTE 8

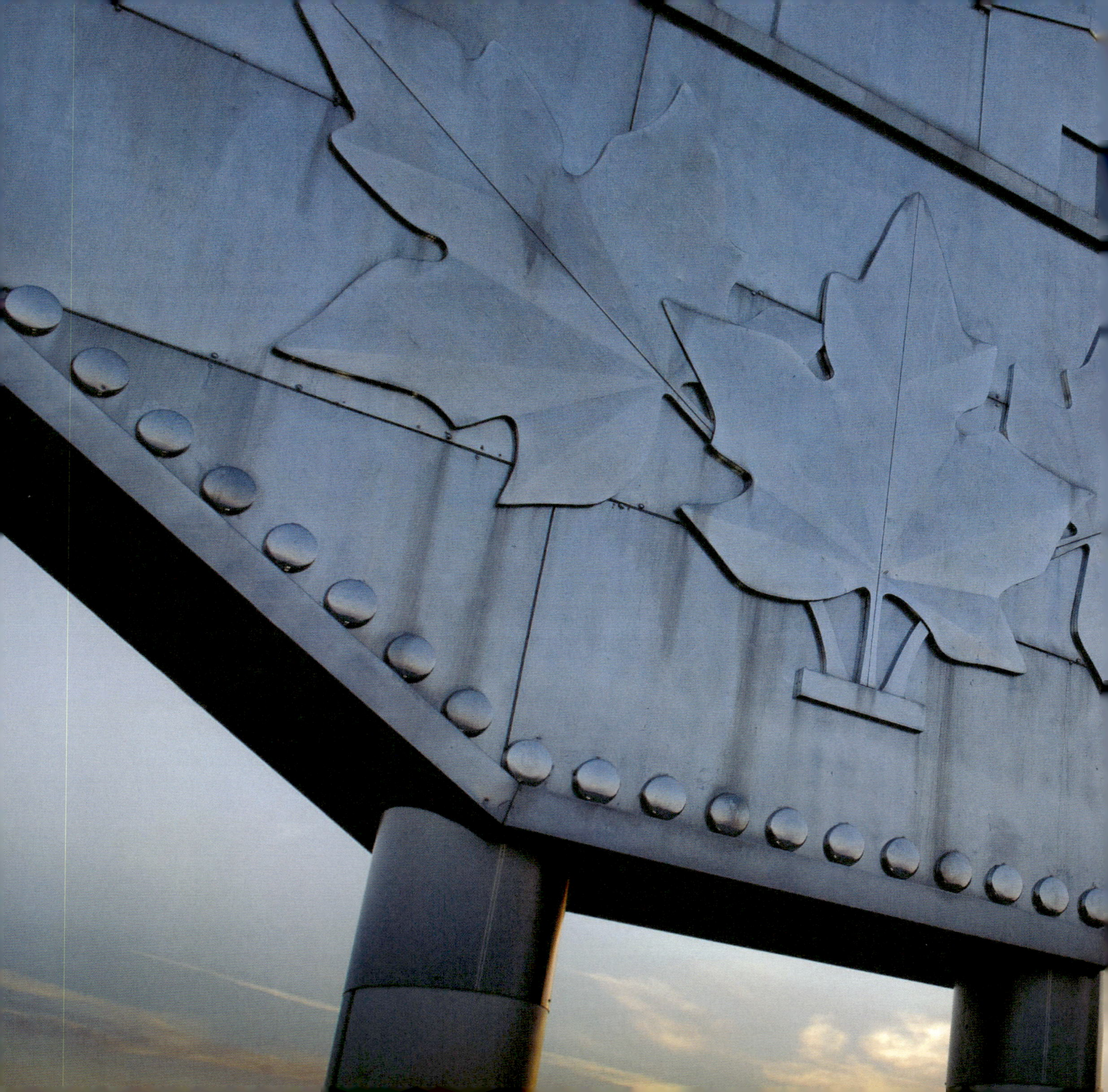

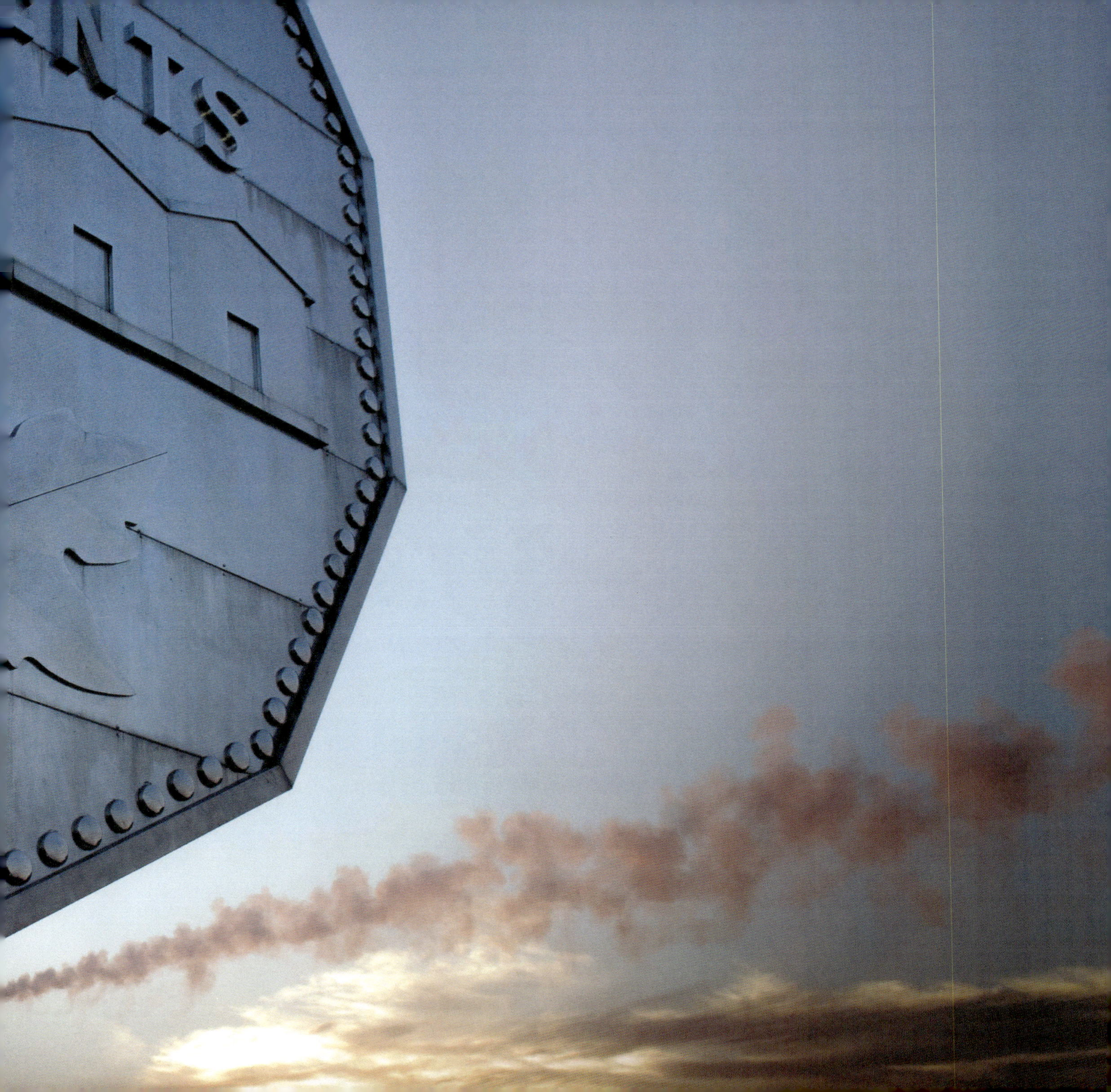

THE PACIFIC TRAIL ROUTE 9

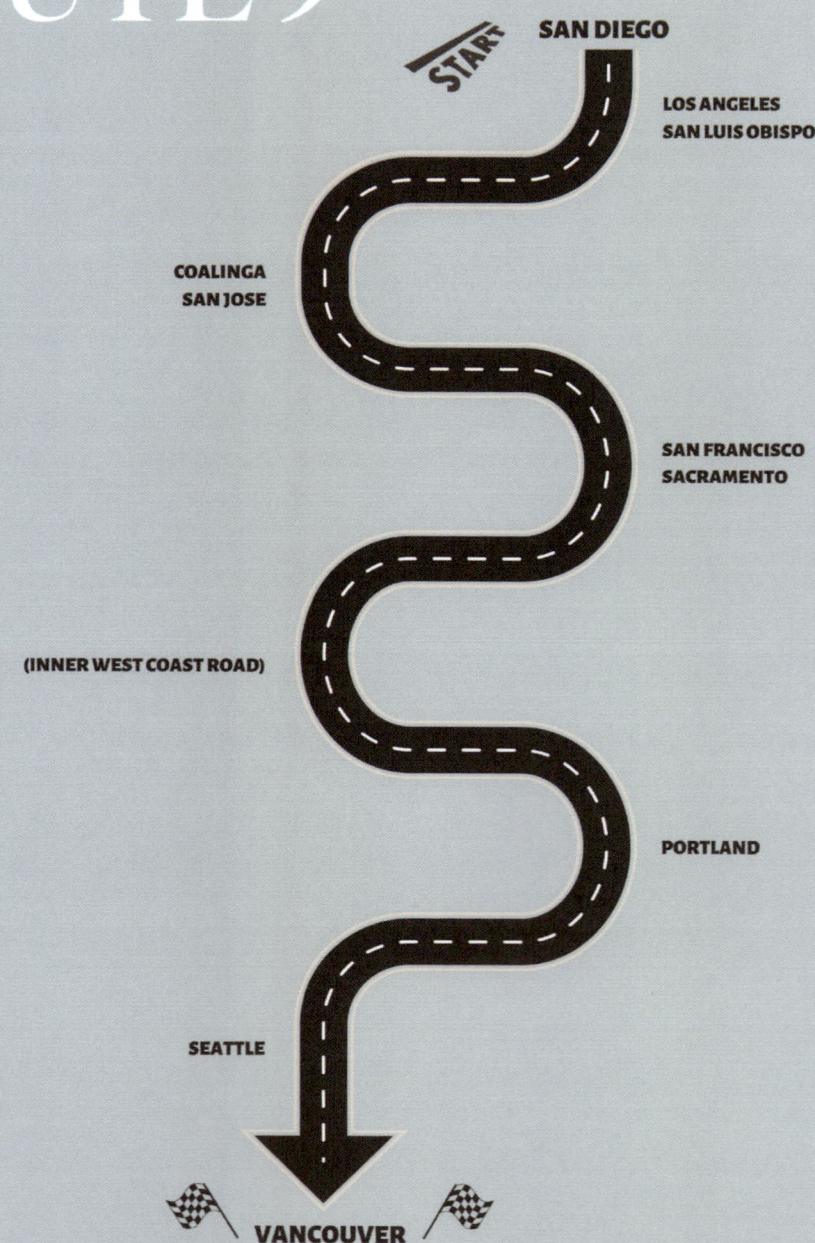

START

SAN DIEGO

LOS ANGELES
SAN LUIS OBISPO

COALINGA
SAN JOSE

SAN FRANCISCO
SACRAMENTO

(INNER WEST COAST ROAD)

PORTLAND

SEATTLE

VANCOUVER

300

THE PACIFIC TRAIL

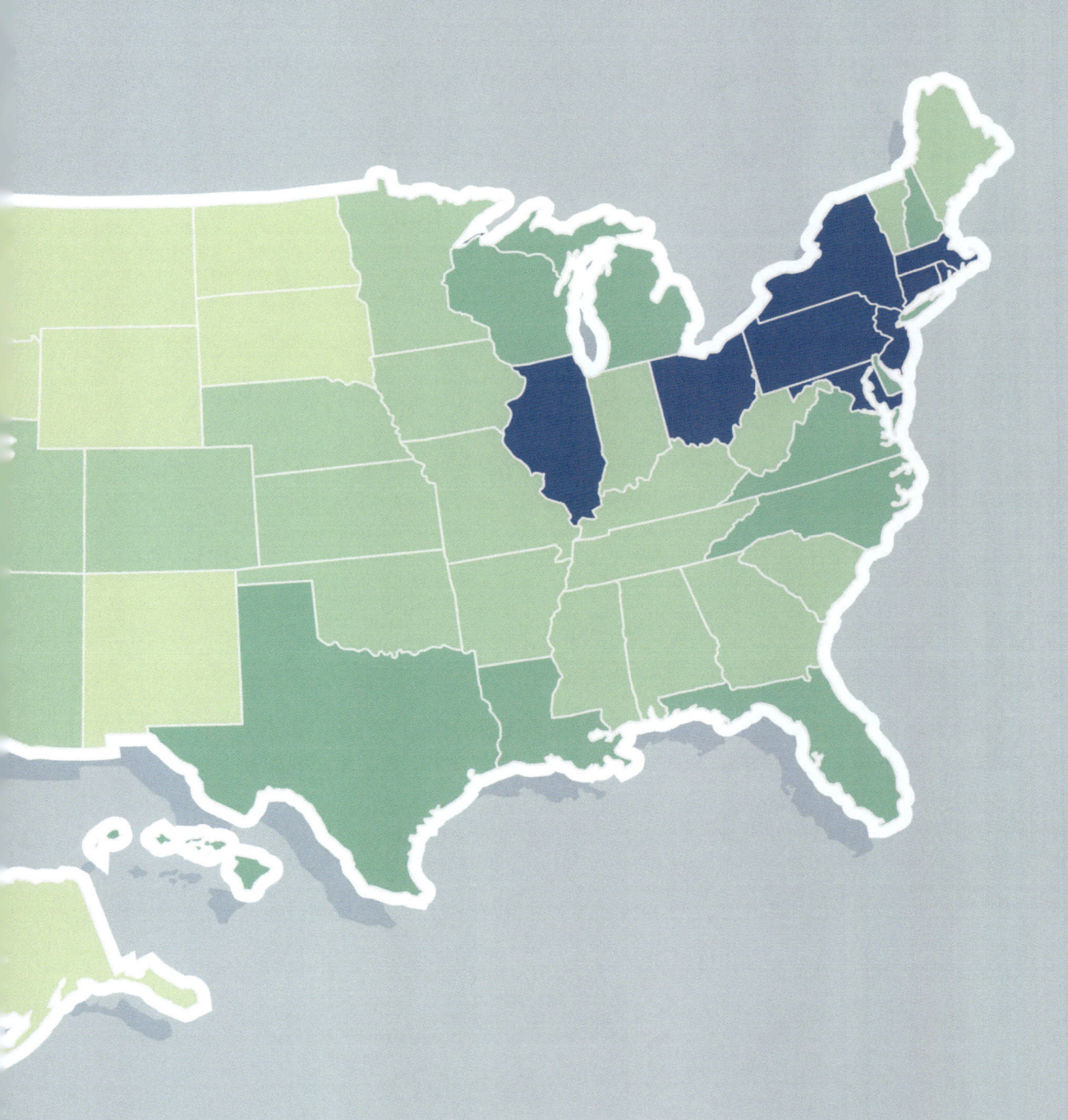

THE PACIFIC TRAIL ROUTE 9

Now is the time to hire yourself a convertible Mustang - go! Done? Ok now you're ready to embark on the iconic Pacific Trail - but not as you know it. Are you going to drive up Big Sur? Not much! Are you going to see a house with an obelisk made of bricks, used to interfere with submarine activity? Yes! From beaches made entirely of glowing coloured glass beads to a house whose passageways to nowhere and doors to fatal drops was under construction 24/7 for a lifetime to avoid torment by evil spirits, this route will take you from out there Southern California to more sensible Washington, ensuring you track down all the weird and wonderful things that the North has to offer.

Above: Moon Amtrak

SAN DIEGO:
Why not check out:
LEMON GROVE - p.231
HARPERS TOPIARY GARDEN - p.231

1. MOON AMTRAK
33.5654, -117.6737

THE PACIFIC TRAIL ROUTE 9

27324 Camino Capistrano #101, Laguna Niguel, CA 92677

Since the happy day that one man in 1970 told his mates he would buy a drink for anyone willing to moon a passing train, thousands gather on the second Saturday of July every single year to moon the poor trains en masse outside the equally blighted Mugs Away Saloon. It goes without saying that there is an official website.

2. THE FLOWER FIELDS

33.12309, -117.31787
5704 Paseo Del Norte, Carlsbad, CA 92008
www.theflowerfields.com

50 acres of colour and beauty open March through mid May.

3. SPADRA CEMETERY

34.05144, -117.80091
Behind 2882 Pomona Blvd, Pomona, CA 91766

The cemetery of a ghost town originally founded by a double murderer and renowned in its day for its own incredibly high incidences of murder, suicide and unexplained deaths. The town, once an important coach stop, became forgotten after a neighbouring town boomed and a mental hospital was built, driving people away (presumably given the circumstances, the hospital was in high demand) and causing the collapse of the town. The last burial at the cemetery was in 1971.

4. SAYDEL INC

33.9894, -118.228
2475 Slauson Ave, Huntington Park, CA 90255
www.saydel.com

Where mystical meets wholesale. This long running institution has been serving the needs of those dealing in the occult, spiritual, odd, religious, quirky or hucksterish for 25 years and claims to be the biggest such supplier in the world. Be greeted by a voodoo deity on entry and educate yourself on the beliefs that underlie LA whilst picking up a spell or two (they come in all shapes and sizes, although seemingly with something of an underlying theme towards avoiding police detection and/or wooing unrequited loves).

5. LINDA VISTA HOSPITAL
34.0382, -118.2172
Approx 610 S St Louis St, Los Angeles, CA 90023

Originally opened in 1904 as one of America's Railroad Hospitals purely to service railroad employees (a concept which really highlights how critical the railroads once were to the country), the hospital had its own Jersey cows, chickens and a garden which provided patients with fresh goods. Razed and rebuilt in 1924, the hospital suffered as the area around it in the 70s became less and less affluent and hospital funding was cut, particularly as railroad employees started to have medical insurance policies held by standard non-railroad companies. During this period, the hospital dealt with high numbers of gunshot wounds and stabbings from the surrounding areas, hitting its mortality statistics and reflecting poorly upon it. By 1991 it had shut. Since that time, it has been the subject of multiple major paranormal investigations and is now converted into apartment blocks in this somewhat dubious area of LA (be careful where you drive). Linda Vista has featured in over fifty tv series and films including as the location of the Bay Harbour Butcher's base in Dexter as well as in ER, Buffy the Vampire Slayer, Charmed, True Blood, Criminal Minds, NCIS Los Angeles, Children of the Corn: Isaac's Return, Pearl Harbour, Day of the Dead 2, Insidious: Chapter 3 and, obviously, in Zombie Strippers as well as in over 25 music videos (Duran Duran's 'Falling Down', Garbage's 'Bleed Like Me', Foo Fighters 'Best of You', Nine Inch Nails 'Closer', Fall Out Boy's 'Just One

< Left: Linda Vista Hospital
Above: The Flower Fields

THE PACIFIC TRAIL ROUTE 9

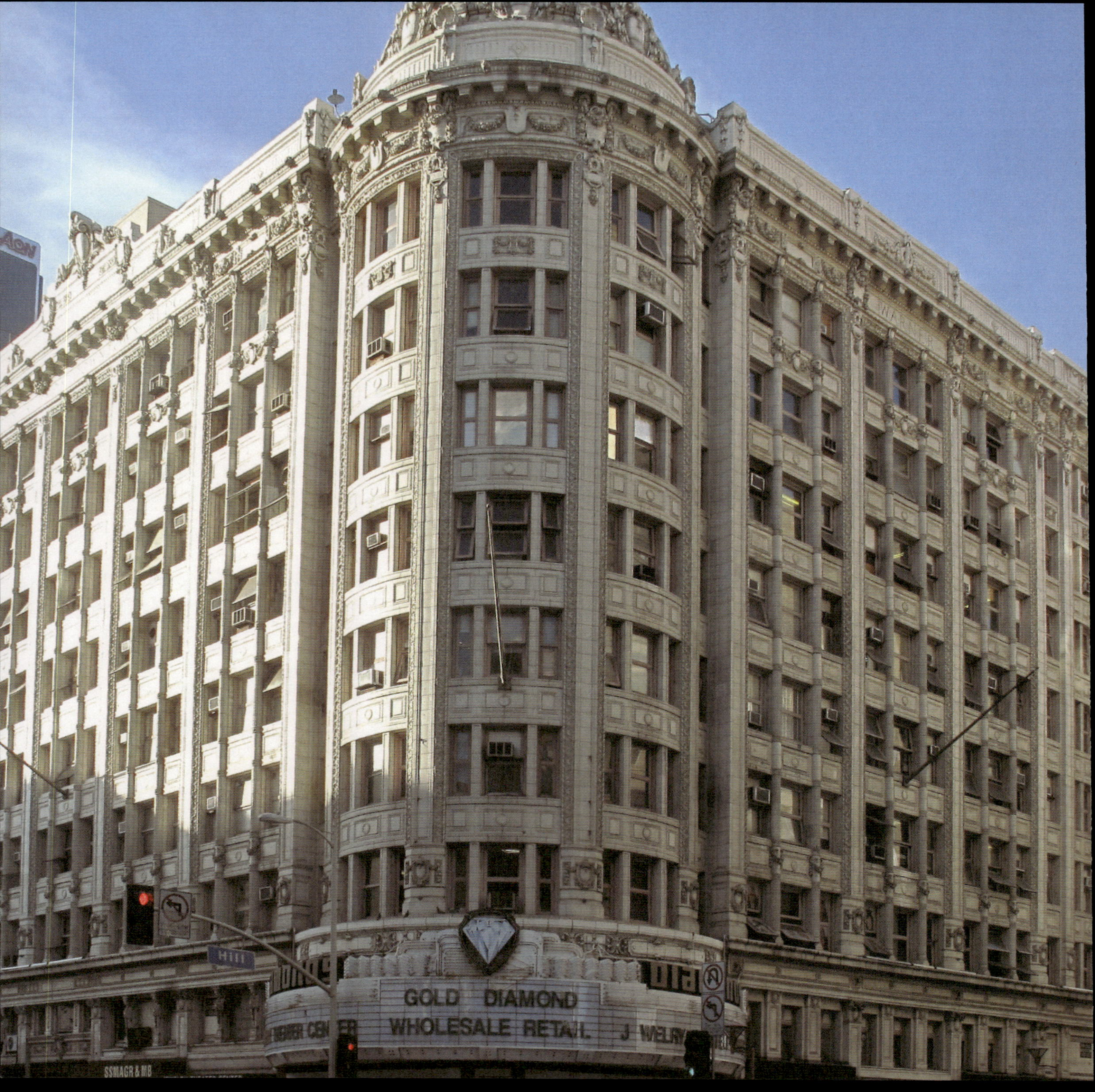
GOLD DIAMOND
WHOLESALE RETAIL

Yesterday', 'Alone' and 'Where Did The Party Go' and Alice Cooper's 'Vengeance is Mine', 'Feminine Side' and 'Killed By Love'.).

6. BOTANICA REINA DE MEXICO
34.03704, -118.19383
3425 E 1st St, Los Angeles, CA 90063

On the second storey of El Mercado de Los Angeles you will find a stall packed with Santeria spells, the like of which can aid you to evade capture by the police, prevent snitches from snitching or snare the object of your affections. Be aware that these are taken seriously by vendors and locals! Santeria is practiced by around 22,000 practitioners in the US alone, although the number is thought to be significantly higher than that disclosed to nationwide censuses. The religion is mainly found in the Spanish speaking Americas including predominantly Cuba, Puerto Rico, Dominican Republic, Panama, Colombia, Venezuela and Mexico and amongst migrants from those countries to the USA. The religion has a murky history regarding animal sacrifice and numerous major court cases have been heard regarding religious freedoms vs. the protection of animal rights; in each case to date, religious freedom has won out and been protected, including by the US Court of Appeals for the Fifth Circuit and the US Supreme Court. Numerous articles have documented the quantity and brutality of such practices and these are far from a backwater hidden practice – major Los Angeles Santeria Churches complete with websites will openly discuss their animal sacrifice practices, usually accompanied by a mention of the Supreme Court ruling which allows them to do so. FYI these stores have a habit of closing down, but a quick google will find plenty more, there is even a hypermarket version!

7. ABANDONED WARNER BROS THEATRE INSIDE JEWELRY STORE
34.0460, -118.2545
405 7TH St, Los Angeles, CA 90014

The Downtown Jewellery Exchange's logo over the door may seem reminiscent of the Warner Bros Shield - that is because the building was the 1920s Pantages Warner Bros Theatre, LA's second ever theatre, in a

< Left and above: Old Warner Bros Theatre Inside Jewelry Store
Right: Botanica Reina De Mexico

previous life. It closed in 1975, was used as a church and then converted to retail space in the 1980s. The parapet continues to read 'Warner Bros. Downtown Building'. Much of the interior's baroque ornamentation and theatre look remains, including the elaborate auditorium ceiling, albeit with a modern chandelier obscuring the once grand sunburst mural beneath. The original Corinthian columns also flank the stage.

8. STAY ON MAIN HOTEL
34.0442, -118.2508
640 S Main St, Los Angeles, CA 90014
This now swanked up hotel is trying hard to forget its past as the Hotel Cecil, a refuge for serial killers and a crime scene for suicides

OFFBEAT AMERICA

and murders, including one particularly infamous case involving scary and bizarre CCTV footage from one of the lifts and a water tank. Someone really should tell them that despite the re-brand, the giant ghost sign reading HOTEL CECIL covering the entirety of the building's side is giving the game away somewhat.

9. MILLENNIUM BILTMORE HOTEL
34.04981, -118.25392
506 S Grand Ave, Los Angeles, CA 90071
millenniumhotels.com

This hotel has been used as a movie location for Spiderman, Ghostbusters, Beverly Hills Cop, True Lies, Independence Day, Ocean's 11, The Nutty Professor, Wedding Crashers, The Italian Job, Daredevil, National Treasure, Cruel Intentions, Fight Club, Charlie's Angels, Entourage, ER, NYPD Blue, The West Wing, CSI: NY, Nip/Tuck, Mad Men, Glee, Scandal and 24 among many others and features luscious interiors including frescoed ceilings hand painted in 1922 by Italian artist Giovanni Smeraldi, known for his work in the Vatican and the White House. The hotel additionally featured in music videos for Janet Jackson's 'Son of a Gun', Britney Spears' 'Overprotected' and Ed Sheeran's 'Thinking Out Loud'. In 1952, a well-known yogi and author Paramahansa Yogananda dropped dead of a heart attack whilst giving a speech at the hotel – the site is now revered by many who view it as the location of his 'mahasamadhi', or conscious leave of the body. John F. Kennedy and Lyndon B. Johnson each had their respective campaign headquarters in the Music Room (now Lobby) and Emerald Room, their press conferences held in the Crystal Ballroom heavily documented. The Beatles stayed in the hotel's Presidential Suite whilst conducting their first US tour in 1964, and were so mobbed that they had to access their room by landing on the roof of the hotel in a helicopter.

10. UNDERGROUND TUNNELS OF LOS ANGELES
34.0558, -118.24469
Los Angeles County Hall of Records, Nr N Hill St, Los Angeles, CA 90012

LA is networked with extensive underground tunnels which have been used for years to conduct secret business far from prying eyes - from transporting mobsters and serial killers to court in the 50s, to carrying $1Bn payments in cash from the city's Hall of Records to the Hall of Administration, to Charles Manson's Family plotting to use the tunnels to bust him out of his trial. An elevator in a corner of Grand Park marked 222 N.Hill St still enters the tunnels to this day with directions available online to the unscrupulous, although sadly the tunnels are now considered officially closed.

11. SKELETONS IN THE CLOSET
34.0485, -118.2088
1104 N Mission Rd, Los Angeles, CA 90033
lacoroner.com

This has to be the best located shop imaginable for those with a love of the macabre - it is found in the LA Coroner's office. This store has a short life expectancy as higher ups are beginning to consider it a bit of a social faux-pas (what???!!!) so catch this while you still can and grab yourself some body toe tags, a body bag or two or some official coroner's reporting stationary – call prior to visiting to ensure its current status as it has been under threat for some time. Never fear, you can still buy your tasteless merchandise elsewhere if LA kills off this treasure in favour of political correctness; Las Vegas can always be relied upon to be the purveyor of all things ill-conceived and Clark County Coroner's office provides a similar store, as do plenty of other US coroner's offices.

12. THE TIME TRAVEL MART
34.0773, -118.2589
1714 Sunset Blvd, Los Angeles, CA 90026
www.timetravelmart.com

The trippiest shop in LA, emblazoned with the motto 'Whenever you are, we're already then'. Purveyor of everything one could want then or soon, this is arguably the only store in town where you can simultaneously purchase a centurion helmet, a robot replacement arm, candles dedicated to the Patron Saints of time travel, Einstein and Hawking, canned Mammoth chunks, time travel sickness pills and Condensed Primordial Soup.

< Top: The Time Travel Mart
< Bottom left: Stay on Main Hotel
< Bottom right: Millenium Biltmore Hotel

13. ANGELUS TEMPLE
34.0761, -118.2613

1100 Glendale Blvd, Los Angeles, CA 90026
www.angelustemple.org
This megachurch can seat 10,000 and is worth a visit to comprehend this style of US church culture. Why not join a Men specific ministry where Men can learn to 'lead in the Church, in the home or in the workplace' or a Women specific ministry where Women can learn to help others. Perhaps we could all use some time spent at the Angelus 'Financial Breakthrough Conference', which 'combines solid Biblical principals with creative ideas to help you maximise your earning potential…for the glory of God.' If you have attended the conference and now earn a sufficient amount, you probably want to know more how to be an Angelus Faith Builder, or high income earning individual who gives a large amount of money to the Church; do follow this link which lays out the process in detail: http://www.angelustemple.org/ministries/faith-builders/ This Church is one of many which practice tithing (the concept that God commanded everyone to give at least 10% of their gross income to the church – apparently the Bible specifies gross rather than net) but churches of this type also encourage 'love gifts', or donations beyond the 10% level. Most can take your donations by app, online pay portal, credit card, debit card, over the phone or of course in cash. The selfless belief generally holds that the more you give, the more you are blessed by God in return.

14. GALCO'S SODA POP STOP
34.1186, -118.1935

5702 York Blvd, Los Angeles, CA 90042
www.galcos.com
Want to shop for more quirky flavours of soda than you possibly ever wished to see in one place? Galco's is for you.

15. THE BUBBLE HOUSE
34.1268, -118.14159

407-499 Wallis St, Pasadena CA 91106
One man's intriguing answer to a housing shortage. Designed by famed architect to the stars Wallace Neff, they were conceptualised as a quick and cheap way to ease the crisis, by inflating a giant balloon then covering it in wire mesh and gunite prior to its deflation, leaving behind a perfect open plan spherical home in what Neff believed would be a phenomenon but which in fact failed to catch on. 3000 such homes were built, but this is now the sole example remaining in the USA.

16. FORK IN THE ROAD
34.13135, -118.15482

S St John Ave, Pasadena, CA 91105
A pun and roadside marvel, all in one. Located, naturally, in Fork Plaza.

17. A'FLOAT SUSHI
34.14593, -118.14861

87 E Colorado Blvd, Pasadena, CA 91105
Marvel as tiny boats piled with sushi float past your table.

18. FOREST LAWN MEMORIAL PARK
34.12524, -118.24371

1712 S Glendale Ave, Glendale, CA 91205
forestlawn.com
LA's cemetery of the rich and famous including Walt Disney, Clark Gable, Jimmy Stewart, Michael Jackson, Elizabeth Taylor, Humphrey Bogart among others.

19. MUSEUM OF NEON ART
34.1438, -118.2547

216 S Brand Blvd, Glendale, CA 91204
www.neonmona.org
This collection celebrates America's rich history of neon in captivating Technicolor.

20. OLD ZOO PICNIC AREA
34.1340, -118.2881

Fire Road, Los Angeles, CA 90027
The City of Los Angeles Zoo, situated in Griffith Park, was open from 1912 to 1965 before the current Los Angeles Zoo was opened at a different location. See the original cages where bears, lions, monkeys, parrots, elephants and more once enchanted visitors.

21. HOLLYWOOD SIGN
34.1347, -118.3209

Mt Lee Drive, Los Angeles, CA 90068
www.hollywoodsign.org
Iconic, surprisingly hard to spot, unaweinspiringly small in photos taken at a distance and really tricky to get close to.

> Top Right: Angelus Temple
> Bottom right: Old Zoo Picnic Area

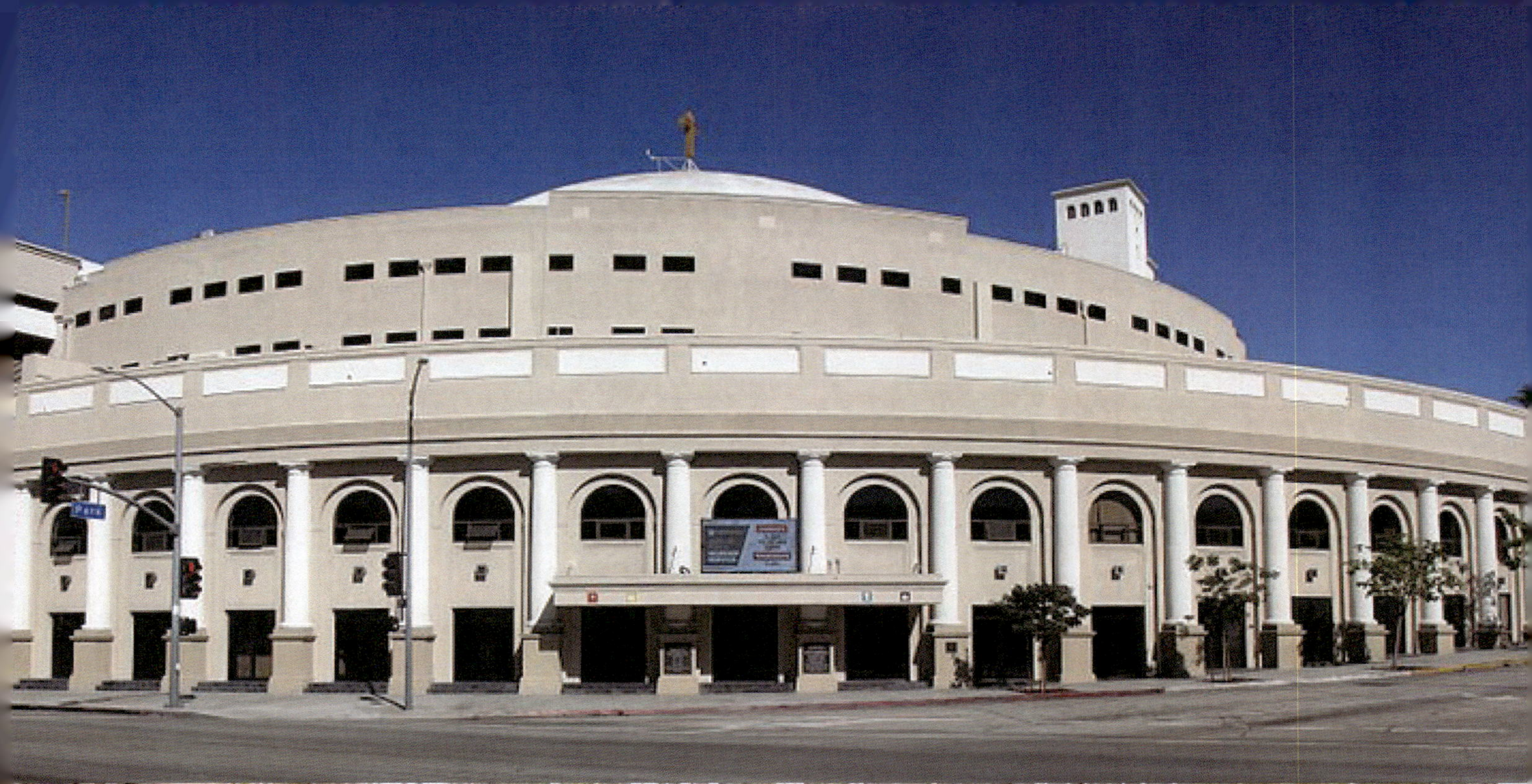

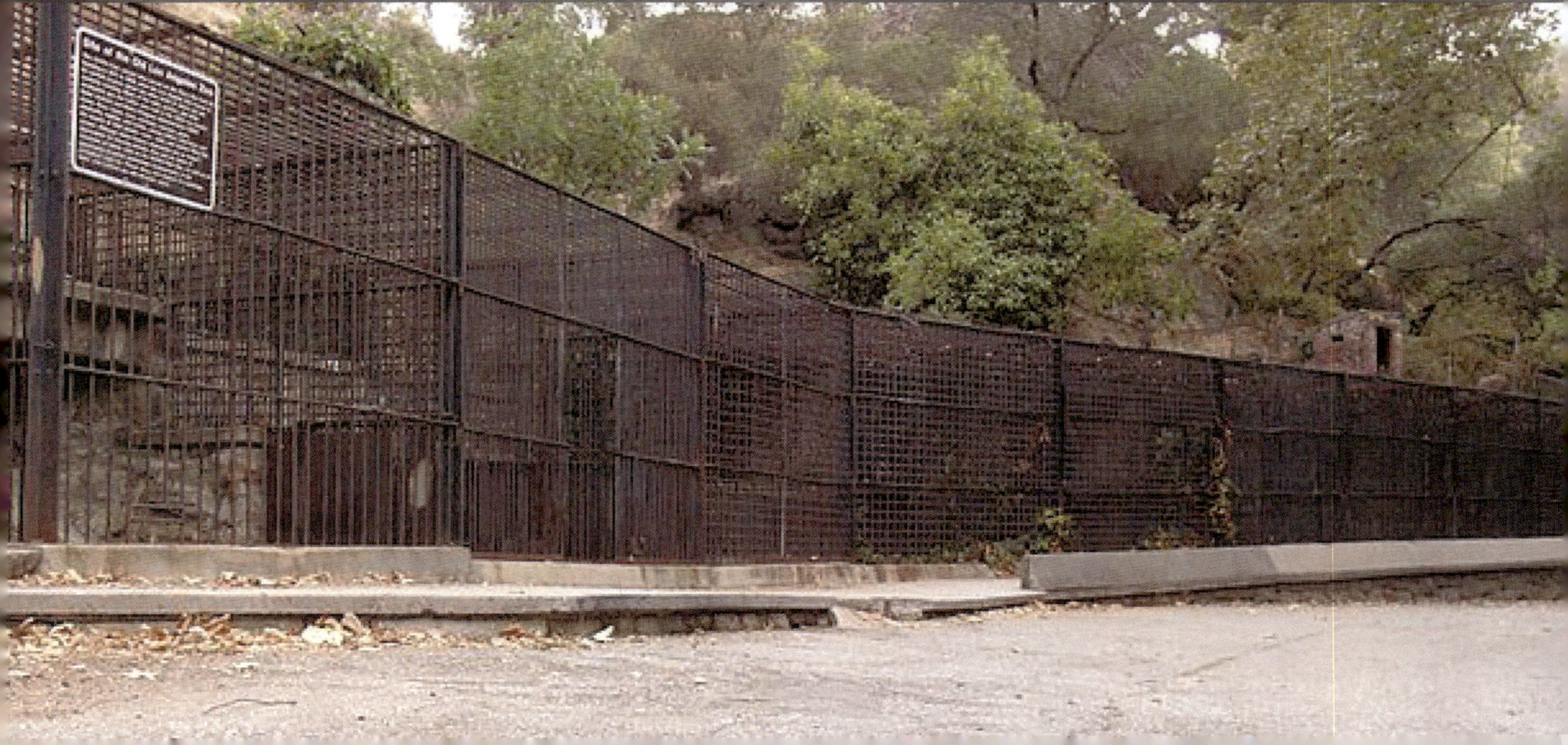

22. CALIFORNIA INSTITUTE OF ABNORMALARTS (CIA)
34.17198, -118.37742
11334 Burbank Blvd, Los Angeles, CA 91601
This nightclub come freak show come carnival museum which includes a mummified clown is the best place to hang out of an evening if you like bizarre acts coupled with mirror mazes.

23. BRONSON CAVE
34.12133, -118.31433
3200 Canyon Dr, Los Angeles, CA 90068
This area of Griffith Park in LA is frequently used by movies looking to shoot scenes of woodland loneliness without leaving the confines of the City of Angels. Movies and series shot here include Invasion of the Body Snatchers, The Lone Ranger, Cabin Fever, The A-Team, Batman, The Dukes of Hazzard, Mission: Impossible, Star Treks Deep Space Nine, Enterprise, The Next Generation, The Original Series and Voyager, Twin Peaks and most vitally Mega Python vs. Gatoroid and Mega Shark vs. Crocosaurus.

24. LOS FELIZ MURDER MANSION
34.1157, -118.2934
2475 Glendower Place, Los Angeles, CA 90027
This house still remains untouched since a double murder-suicide occurred within its walls; it is said that the decor remains as it was in the 60s and there is even a fully decorated Christmas tree in one of the rooms.

25. PHILOSOPHICAL RESEARCH SOCIETY
34.1136, -118.2774
3910 Los Feliz Blvd, Los Angeles, CA 90027
A curious collection of some very esoteric books on subjects such as Satanism and demons.

26. HOLLYWOOD TOWER APARTMENTS
34.10486, -118.32419
6200 Franklin Ave, Los Angeles, CA 90028
www.thehollywoodtower.com
Opened in 1929 as La Belle Tour, this Golden Age tower was a residence for entertainment industry employees such as Humphrey Bogart and provided Disney with the inspiration for the Twilight Zone Tower of Terror attraction in Disney's Orlando, California, Tokyo and Paris. It also featured in 1984 thriller Body Double.

27. THE MUSEUM OF DEATH
34.1017, -118.3212
6031 Hollywood Blvd, Hollywood, CA 90028
museumofdeath.net
Not for the faint of heart, this museum contains all things macabre, including John Wayne Gacy's Clown shoes. Prepare to feel queasy upon exit.

Left: Hollywood Tower Apartments

OFFBEAT AMERICA

28. THE MAGIC CASTLE
34.10459, -118.34192

7001 Franklin Ave, Los Angeles, CA 90028

www.magiccastle.com

Rub shoulders with LA's Magic elite at this Magicians' members club – you can't get in without a guest pass and even then without a paying member accompanying you, you will be slapped with a hefty entrance fee but emailing a sympathetic magician performing on the night has oft been known to elicit guest list passes, or why not purchase a reasonably priced annual associate membership – no magical capabilities required.

29. PSYCHIATRY: AN INDUSTRY OF DEATH MUSEUM
34.0980, -118.3339

6616 Sunset Blvd, Los Angeles, CA 90028

Don't tell these people your name, come prepared with a fake moniker and email address and marvel at this somewhat biased view of the atrocities of modern medicine.

30. THE THOMPSON HOME FOR OLD LADIES
42.3547, -83.0655

4756 Cass Avenue, Detroit, MI 48201

This one time home for wealthy widows now lies empty, since the charitable institution established in 1884 fell into decline in the Seventies before closing in '77; the following tenants, Wayne State Uni and a Social Work school moved away too, leaving the building abandoned to its fate.

31. 'HALLOWEEN' MURDER HOUSE
34.0993, -118.36079

1537/1530 N Orange Grove Avenue, Los Angeles, CA 90046

Horror movie fans will remember this from their nightmares – the idyllic street Orange Grove Avenue was used as the set for the little Midwestern town of Haddonfield, Illinois in this creepy John Carpenter classic. Two of the house locations in the movie were shot here – many of the scenes featured the Doyle residence where Jamie was baby-sitting Tommy (1530 N. Orange Grove Avenue) whilst her best friend Annie was attacked while baby-sitting in the Wallace residence with the pumpkin lantern on the porch nearby at 1547 N. Orange Grove Avenue. These are private homes so please admire

Top left: The Museum of Death
Top centre: The Magic Castle
Top right: Psychiatry Museum

THE PACIFIC TRAIL ROUTE 9

314

< Top: Greystone Mansion
< Centre left: The Silent Movie Theater
< Centre right: Pink's Hot Dogs

from a distance.

32. GREYSTONE MANSION
34.09228, -118.40123
905 Loma Vista Dr, Beverly Hills, CA 90210
www.beverlyhills.org

This Tudor revival mansion with a dark past has beautiful grounds which are open as a park and offer free public entry. Originally gifted by oil tycoon Edward Doheny to his son Ned Doheny before the city purchased the estate to save it from demolition, the property is regularly used for filming and the house's staircase is one of the most famous sets in Hollywood. At the time of construction it was the most expensive home built in California. Four months after Ned, his wife and their five kids moved in, Ned was found dead in one of the guest bedrooms in a murder-suicide, killed by his secretary Hugh Plunket, apparently due to anger over lack of a raise, although the cynical have pointed out that Ned's gun was found to be the murder weapon and he was not buried in the Catholic cemetery with the rest of his family, suggesting suicide. Both men are now buried close to each other in Forest Lawn Memorial Park, Glendale. His wife remarried and remained in the house for some years. Movies shot here include Batman and Robin, The Big Lebowski, The Bodyguard, Dark Shadows 1991, Death Becomes Her, Entourage, Eraserhead, Garfield 2, Indecent Proposal, The Mentalist, The Muppets, NCIS, Rush Hour, Spider Man 1 2 and 3, The Social Network, There will be Blood and X Men amongst countless others.

33. THE SILENT MOVIE THEATER
34.0820, -118.36156
611 N Fairfax Avenue, Los Angeles, CA 90036

The last silent movie theatre in the US, this was opened by a couple who wanted to keep the dream of the silent theatre alive. They eventually sold out to a family friend, who was gunned down in the lobby in 1997 by a hitman working on behalf of his business partner who was less than keen to share the takings. Since then it has changed hands again and is still being lovingly curated, offering periodic silent movie screenings complete of course with organ accompaniment. A cherished piece of Americana.

34. PINK'S HOT DOGS
34.08384, -118.3443
709 N La Brea Ave, Los Angeles, CA 90038
www.pinkshollywood.com

Famed roadside dogs with a wide range of toppings, an LA must-eat.

35. TEMPLO SANTA MUERTE
34.08338, -118.30713
4902 Melrose Ave, Los Angeles, CA 90029
templosantamuerte.com

This authentic LA temple dedicated to the Angel of Death in which proponents describe themselves as 'believing in God, adoring Jesus but [acting as] the voice of Santa Muerte' contains spectacular full scale Santa Muerte figures; ask to be let in via the tiny shop. Keep an eye out for the unusual skull behind the door to the right. This religion which has been around for generations in Mexico has had dubious associations in the past – in 2012, eight members of the same family were charged with murder after they killed two ten year old boys and a 55 year old woman as an offering to Santa Muerte. Describing itself as 'the fastest growing popular faith in the Americas', links have been made to drug lords and gangs, but devotees in LA claim that what happens in Mexico is a different mode of practice to that in LA. In the words of the Professor who leads worship in this temple has no issue with detractors terming the gathering a cult: 'They say we are a cult. Yes, and what's a service or mass in the Catholic Church? A cult'. Despite the desire to distance itself from negative associations, the religion has certain rituals built into it (as listed in the La Santa Muerte Biografia y Culto which contains 26 such rituals) which bely its past, including the Ritual para socorrer a quienes estan presos or Ritual to comfort those in prison.

36. ROSENHEIM MANSION
34.04999, -118.3174
1120 Westchester Pl, Los Angeles, CA 90019

This property which featured in Season 1 of American Horror Story and Buffy, was listed for $4.5M in 2011, then for a whoppingly optimistic $17 Mil after AHS finished shooting, before being reduced to $7.8M shortly

< Bottom left: Templo Santa Muerte
< Bottom right: Rosenheim Mansion

thereafter due to lack of interest. It finally sold last year for just $3.2M. Perhaps the series was a little too realistic.

37. GIANT SCISSORS
34.182, -118.59109
6109 De Soto Ave, Woodland Hills, CA 91367
There is no way of missing this hairdressers.

38. VALLEY RELICS MUSEUM
34.24727, -118.60117
21630 Marilla St, Chatsworth, CA 91311
www.valleyrelicsmuseum.org
If it's unusual, Americana-orientated and cool, this man has collected it.

39. ANTELOPE VALLEY POPPY RESERVE
34.7349, -118.396
15101 Lancaster Rd, Lancaster, CA 93536
A stunning panorama of California's state flower - visit in Spring for the best views.

40. HONDA'S MUSICAL ROAD
34.7259, -118.2019
W Ave G, Lancaster, CA 93536
www.musicalroad.net
West Avenue G in Lancaster, north of LA, is a very special road courtesy of Honda's advertising department, which uses a concept based on the humble rumble strip. The team created a musical stretch of road which, when driven over at certain speeds, plays the theme from the Lone Ranger, the William Tell Overture. It was first built close to town where it was used for the filming of a Honda advert, creating traffic jams and chaos with tourists flocking to try it, before it was later moved a little further out by the council. Some have argued that whilst the rhythm is correct, the melody is vague, and it is thought that the designers may have made

a systematic miscalculation when designing the groove spacings. Musical roads today exist in Denmark, Japan, South Korea, the USA, China, San Marino (strangely), Taiwan and the Ukraine. The first musical road is generally held to be the Asphaltophone and was created in October 1995 in Gylling Denmark by two Danish artists, although the musical airport runway created by Disney into Orlando which played Wish Upon a Star (see page X) was dreamt up far earlier in 1971 and undoubtedly inspired all such projects. As of 2016, in Japan over 30 'melody roads' as they are known in the area exist, some of which are polyphonic so that both a melody and harmony can be heard beneath the left and right tires of a car and most of which play Japanese folk songs. The primary aim of the roads in both Denmark and Japan was to attract tourists. In South Korea, the 'Singing Road' in Anyang (one of two in the country) was designed to keep drivers awake as 68% of road accidents are due to sleeping or inattentive drivers. The song it plays is 'Mary Had a Little Lamb' (which one could argue is quite soporific). In Tijeras Nex Mexico, a musical road plays America the Beautiful if you lower your speed to 45 mph and was installed as an innovative safety measure.

41. CALIFORNIA CITY
35.1768, -117.7880
California City, CA 93505
Founded in 1958 by a developer, this suburb was going to be the next big metropolis, due to rival LA in both size and economy. Now home to just 14,000 people who are congregating to the Southwest of the empty grids leaving the rest all but a ghost town, this area idyllically situated between a Honda test track, a prison and the largest open-pit mine in California, boasts a network of named boulevards and culs-de-sac but nothing much else has materialised. The fate that befell California City is like that of Salton Sea and many other utopian projects across America which have fallen foul to some natural disaster, demographic issue or simply a lack of demand compared to commercial expectations, in which developers bought land assuming that people would flock, yet they never did. In the case of California City, the clearing of the land led to massive dust storms rendering the land rather inhospitable.

42. LAKE SHORE INN
35.1317, -117.94259
21330 Lake Shore Dr, California City, CA 93505
This abandoned lakeside hotel and golf course set in the desolate remnants of California City has been standing in this state for 20 odd years and still remains relatively intact.

43. RANDSBURG
35.3686, -117.65809
35 Butte Ave, Randsburg, CA 93554
www.randsburg.com
Randsburg is Old West at its best; gold was discovered here in 1895 and a mining camp was quickly constructed, named Rand Camp. Today you can visit the general store come ice cream parlour and check out their 1904 soda fountain - the store even sells antiques local to the area. More antiques stores, galleries, gift shops, a mining museum and an original jail are open to the public. Please bear in mind that the General Store shuts on Tuesdays and Wednesdays. As of 2010, the population of the town was set at 69 and the locale was used to film Calvin Harris' platinum track 'Feel So Close'.

44. THE ASYLUM'S DAIRY
34.177, -119.0294
Federal Youth Division Road off Old Dairy Road, Camarillo, CA 93012
An asylum's farm, now an abandoned ruin.

45. PENNY BAR
35.3003, -119.6245
23273 Highway 33, McKittrick, California, 93251
We've all wondered what to do with those pennies. Few of us however have taken the thought and run with it as much as this property owner.

46. BUBBLEGUM ALLEY
35.2790, -120.6638
733.5 Higuera St, San Luis Obispo, CA 93401
An art installation or a disgusting and somewhat saliva-orientated eyesore?

< Left: Bubblegum Alley
Overleaf: Antelope Valley Poppy Reserve

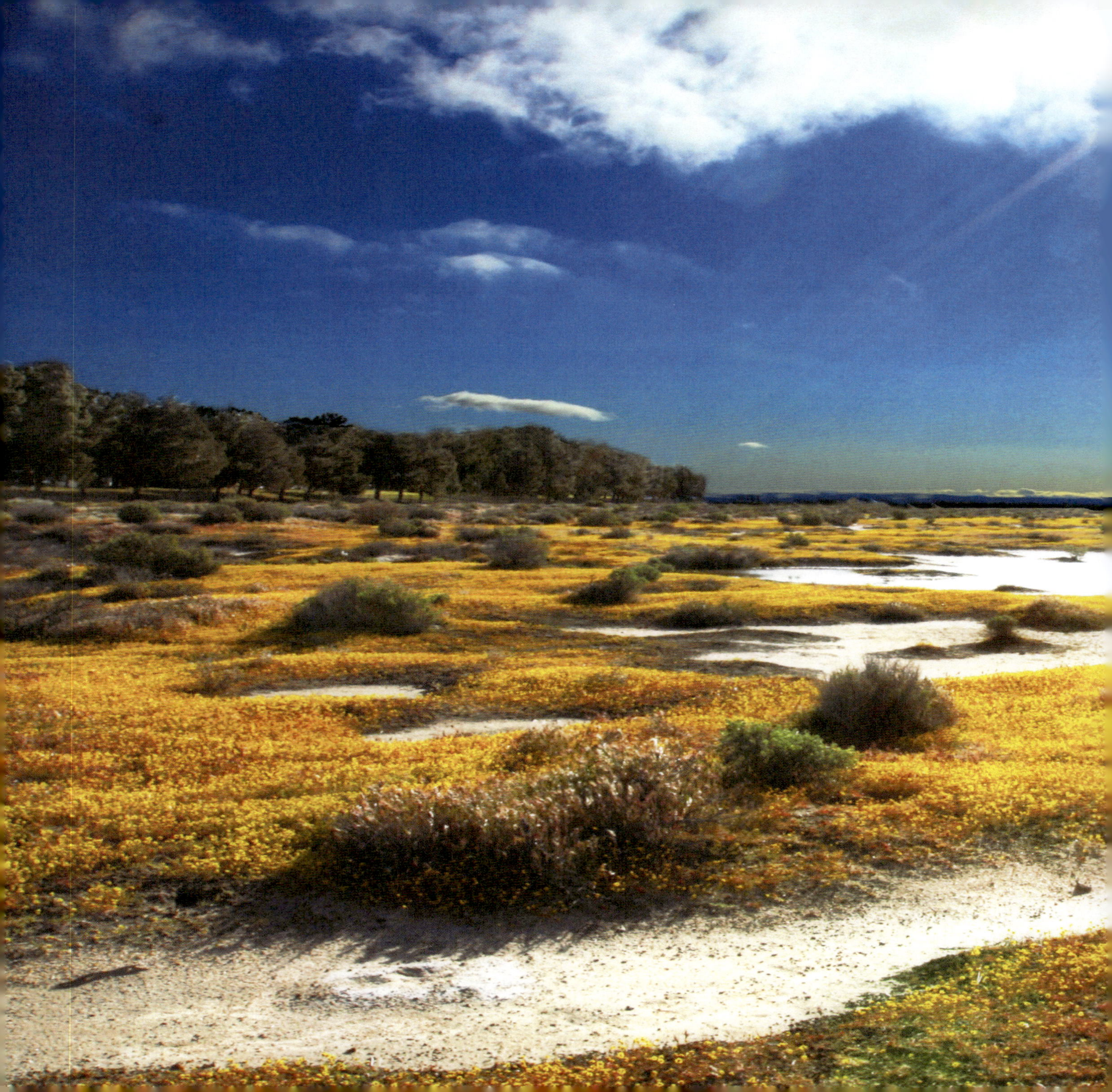

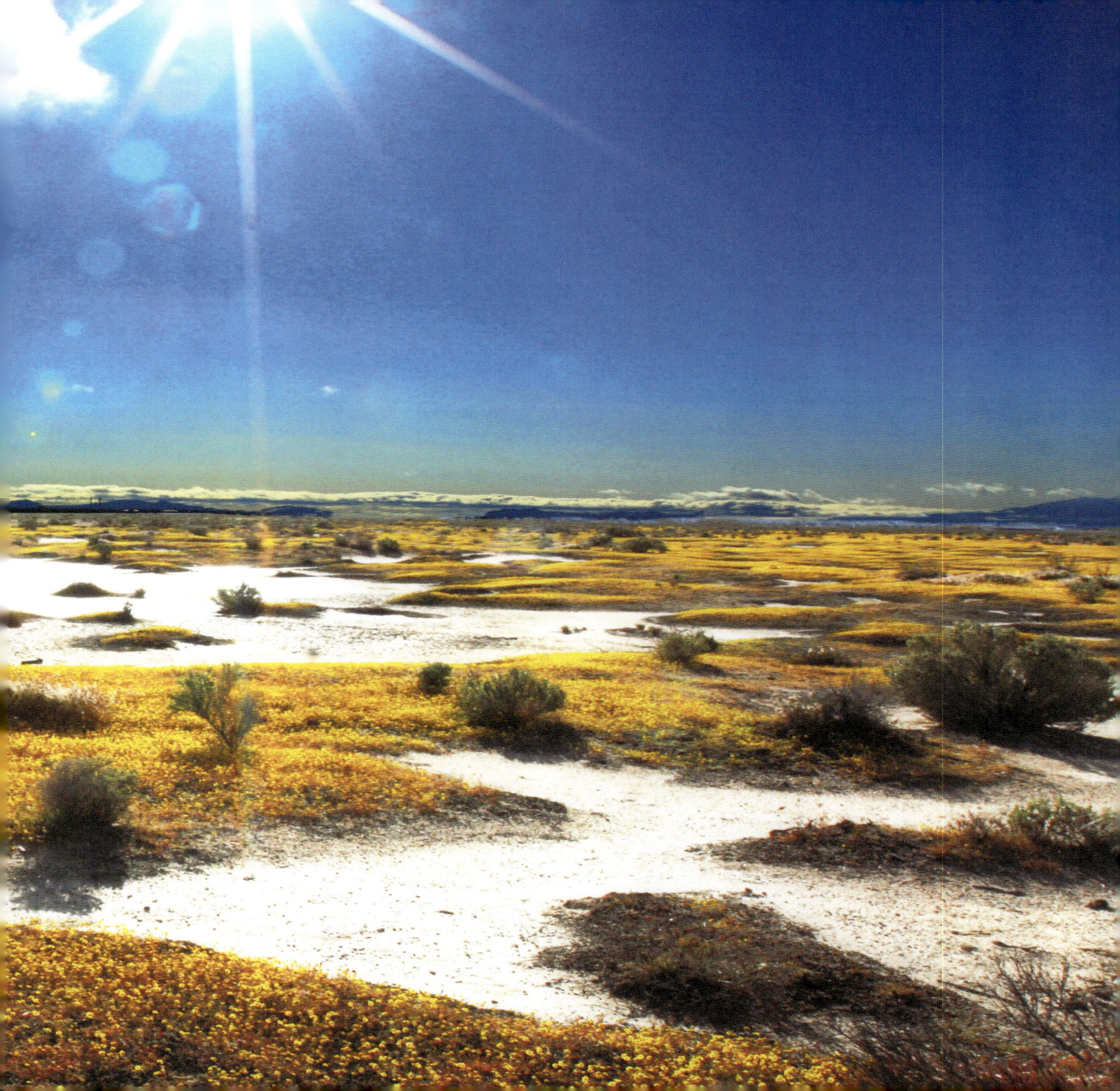

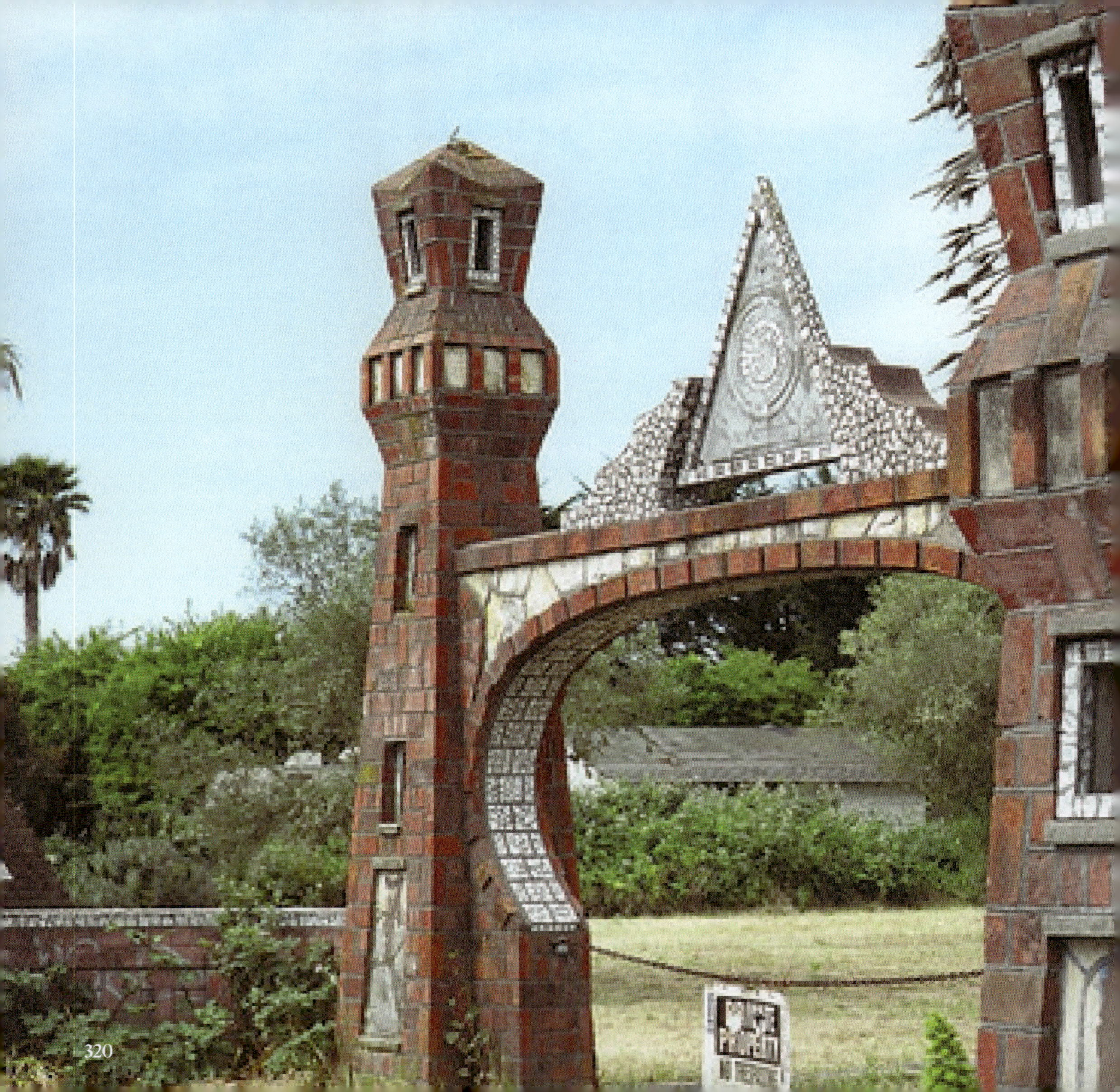

47. IRON ZOO
36.23898, -120.31461
33241-, 33287 Fresno Coalinga Rd, Coalinga, CA 93210
Oil and animals mix at this bizarre roadside sculpture area.

48. WORLD'S LARGEST TREE
36.5817, -118.75144
Sequoia National Park, Generals Hwy, Sequoia National Park, CA 93262
The World's Largest Tree (currently living, historically others have been even larger). Known as General Sherman, it is actually neither the tallest, nor the widest, nor the oldest tree on Earth, but is thought to be the largest by volume and remains one of the tallest, widest and longest living of all trees on our planet.

49. THE UNDERGROUND GARDENS
36.8078, -119.8822
5021 W Shaw Ave, Fresno, CA 93722
www.undergroundgardens.com
This unusual location is a hand-built network of underground rooms and passages in which long-standing fruit trees, shrubs and vines are grown, built as a private home.

50. THE RED PALACE
36.95498, -122.04507
515 Fair Ave, Santa Cruz, CA 95060
Santa Cruz prides itself on its weirdness and early proponents of this badge of pride were the follies-a-deux-esque Kitchen Brothers. One, Kenneth, a bricklayer with a penchant for submarine interference, one, Raymond, a stonemason who built fireplaces for a living, in 1946 they embarked on building their oeuvre and homage to their Spiritual beliefs, a mystical temple known variously as the Court of Mysteries, Watts Towers and the Red Palace, working under the cover of darkness by the light of the moon, due in part to their mystical beliefs, in part due to their lack of building permits (this may have been the greater of the two parts). The architecture of the building is certainly unusual; its Gate of Prophecies was built to feature a form of clock in inlaid shells with the crescent moon at 12 and the sun at 6 which Kenneth appears to have believed could move at will despite being made entirely of inanimate objects without a mechanism, and which when aligned would signal the apocalypse. It is said that he and his brother built the temple to win the heart of a woman that Kenneth was in love with. A lovely quirk of the property is that two tall stone pillar obelisks topped by pyramids are found in the grounds, both of which were built by Kenneth as 'submarine stopping devices' - a spoked wheel made of railroad ties was laid on the center of the property with these two pillars acting as a sender and receiver of radio signals to submarines, jamming the signals of enemy craft. Kenneth had an eighth-grade education. To render these EVEN more effective than they already undoubtedly were, Kenneth was said to hose down the mattress he slept on every night so as to remain alert for radio signals. He would lie on it for days at a time listening, his brother Raymond bringing him food from the outside world. It is alleged but unconfirmed that the devices functioned and that the Navy moved Kenneth to Florida to remove his influence from the area, whilst another rumour alleges that the government broke into the temple to steal the plans for his obelisks. He returned however and resumed his construction, before disappearing from Santa Cruz without a trace in 1953. For a long time there was no known death certificate for him (although there is for his brother) and no clues as to his final location. His death certificate was later unearthed but

< Left: The Red Palace
Above: The World's Largest Tree

inconsistencies regarding his age and date of birth have led many to suspect it was forged in a cover up. Today the temple, which was transformed into a Greek Church during which time it was known as the Unorthodox Chapel, has now been purchased (for $1.1M in 2016 after going on the market at $2.2M just 2 years previously with no interested takers) by a couple, a tech firm consultant and artist, who plan to restore it sympathetically and may run tours.

51. SANTA CRUZ MYSTERY SPOT
37.0173, -122.0038
465 Mystery Spot Rd, Santa Cruz, CA 95065
www.mysteryspot.com

This mystery spot, one of the classic US 'illusion phenomenon' locations, may be a little more touristy than some but is worth a visit if in the area. The illusion experienced by visitors is due to the oddly tilted environment combined with standing on a tilted floor. Heights and orientation misperceptions occur and make for fun photos.

52. BIGFOOT DISCOVERY MUSEUM
37.0415, -122.0726
5497 Hwy 9, Felton, CA 95018
bigfootdiscoveryproject.com

Are you likely to discover a Bigfoot here? Probably not.

53. THE KINGDOM OF BOOMERIA
37.0897, -122.1440
112 Molina Drive, Bonny Doon, CA 95060

Preston Q. Boomer has been a physics and chemistry teacher in San Lorenzo Valley High in the Santa Cruz area for over five decades and has been known to cut off local police communications via a Tesla coil by accident. He is the all round ideal mad scientist figure that every child hopes will feature in their life, teaching them how to create green flames out of thin air. Boomer had the idea for Boomeria the day he took a defensive stance against students egging his home, firing at them with water pistols. He built a wooden castle complete with dungeon, battle turrets, water cannons, a pneumatic pipe organ and an underground series of tunnels which interconnect to join the various areas of the kingdom together. It also has a Main Aqueous Ammunition Bunker (swimming pool to you and me) as well as a chapel. Nor was this array casually thrown together; students dug the tunnels over a three year time period in the Sixties. The Kingdom also boasts a fully functional and full size guillotine (for slicing watermelons) and a reconstructed skeleton of some animal bones found on the property, as yet unidentified. Warning communication sirens and bells feature throughout including a Navy foghorn which can be heard for miles around. Students frequently attempt to conquer Boomeria but have yet to be successful, largely due to the giant water cannons which are controlled by the main engine room. Telegraph systems and steam engines power other areas of the Kingdom and a laboratory is on hand in case any experiments need to be urgently undertaken. The Boom (for so he is known) greets visiting students with a 'Who goes there?!'. If you desire a similar welcome and are not lucky enough to be a student at the school, you can attend the annual Boomeria Extravaganza, a charitable fundraiser which costs $50 per ticket but allows you to tour. Christmas carol singing events are also scheduled and failing that...well contact The Boom and be nice.

54. MONOPOLY IN THE PARK
37.32824, -121.89319
330 W San Carlos St, San Jose, CA 95110
www.monopolyinthepark.com

Do not pass go.

55. THE WINCHESTER MYSTERY HOUSE
37.3189, -121.9506
525 S Winchester Blvd, San Jose, CA 95128
www.winchestermysteryhouse.com

This (albeit now touristy) extraordinary building is officially the strangest in the world and has inspired many a horror movie including Stephen King's Rose Red mini-series. Mrs Sarah Winchester of the Winchester gun dynasty was told by a psychic that the thousands of deaths wrought by her family's guns had made the spirits angry and that the only way of keeping them at bay was to keep construction workers building her property day and night, without any break whatsoever or any master plan, for as long as she lived (funded by her inheritance from her

Right: The Winchester Mystery House
Overleaf: Monopoly in the Park

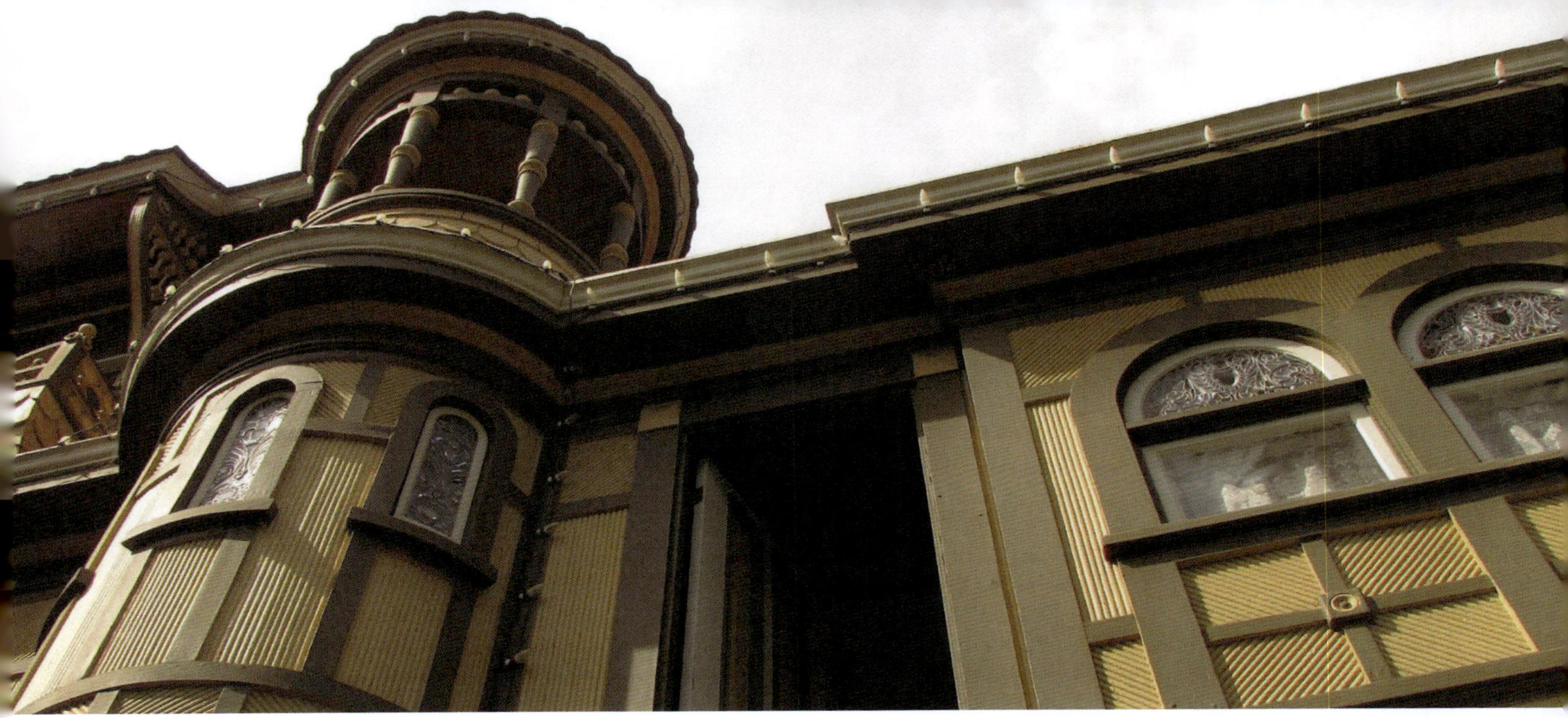

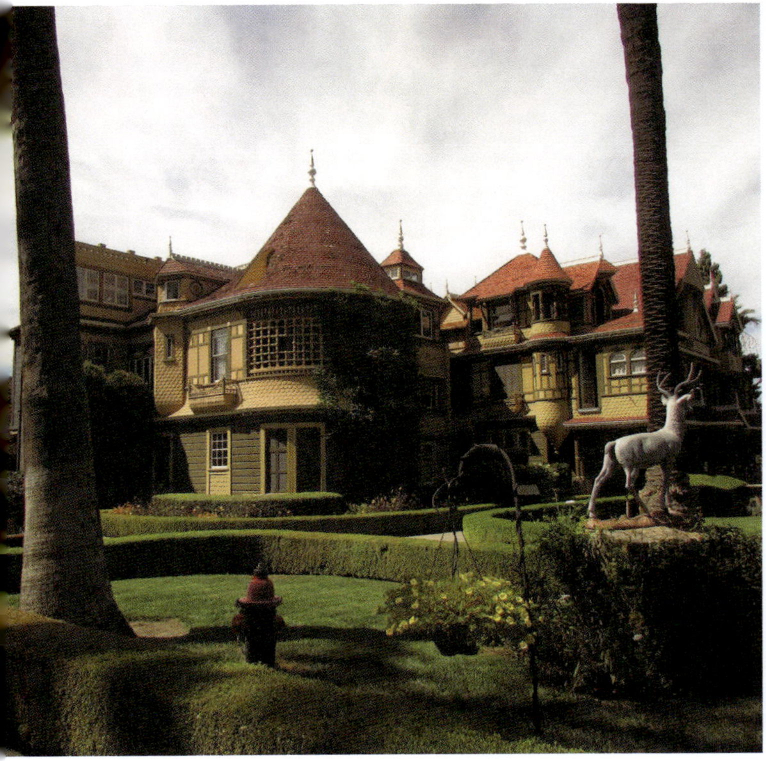

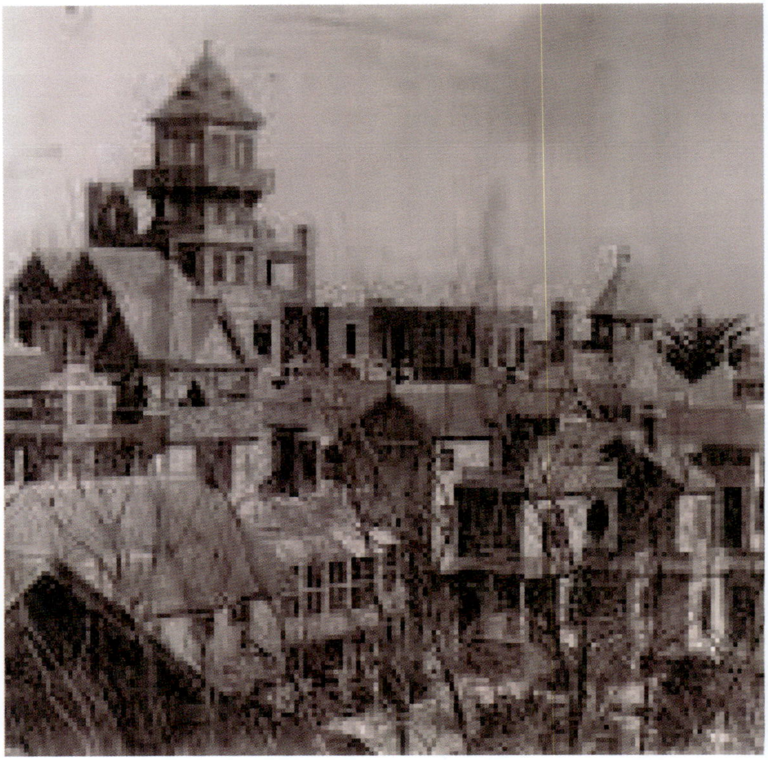

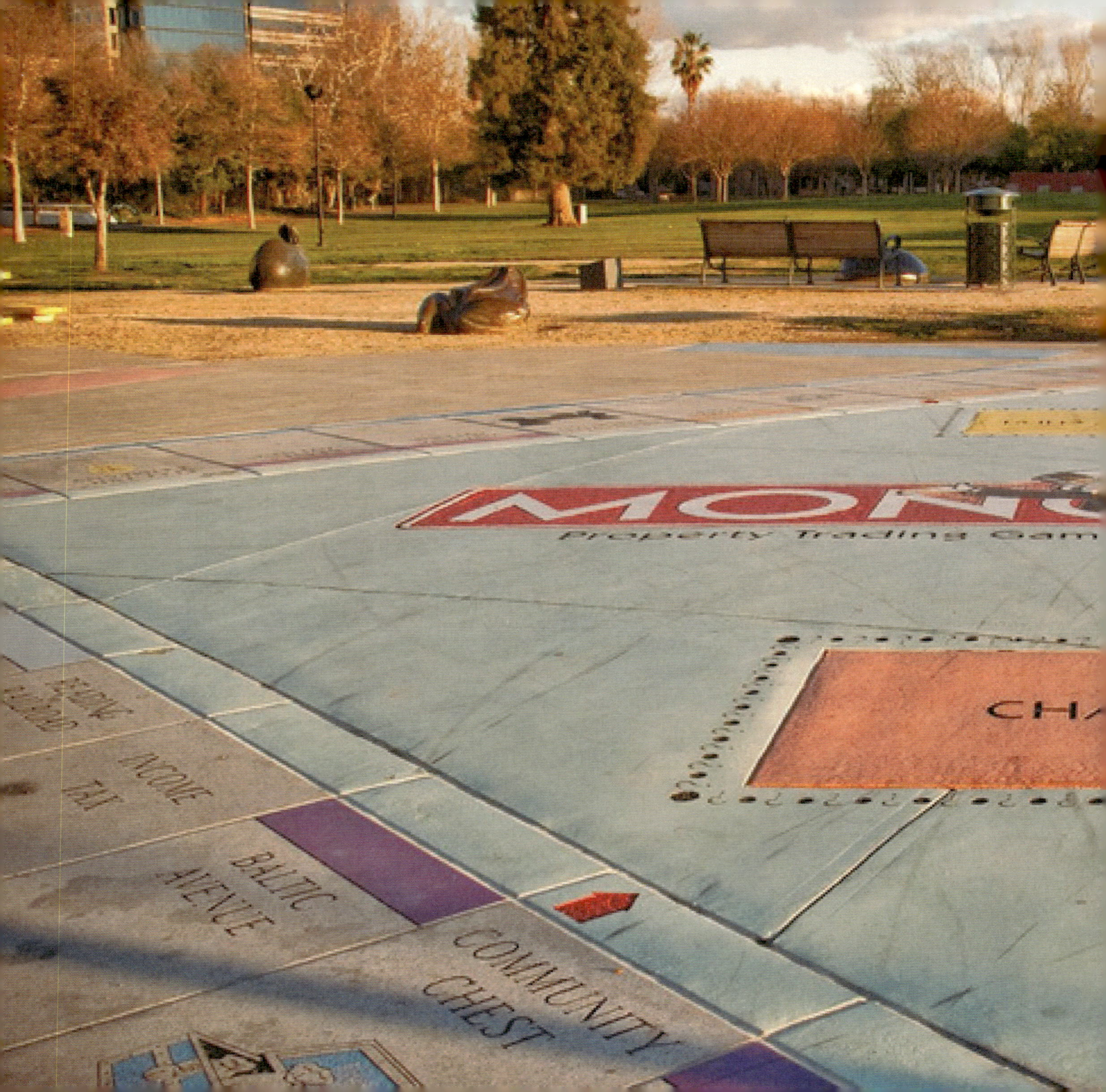
INCOME TAX
BALTIC AVENUE
COMMUNITY CHEST

POLY

from Parker Brothers

LUXURY
TAX

PARK
PLACE

late husband of $20.5 million as well as an income from the Winchester Repeating Arms Company of what in today's money would be around $23,000 dollars per day.) And so she did. Work was carried out around the clock for thirty eight years until the moment of her death in 1922, resulting in the most bizarre seven story haphazard creation which is not only absurdly huge but also contains doors to nowhere, decorations aimed at thwarting malevolent spirits and a car park where your car will get broken into if you leave any valuables on display (you have been warned). Today only four stories remain after a major earthquake in 1906, during which only the house's 'floating foundation', aka the fact that it is not fully attached to its base and can freely flex, prevented it from total collapse. The house has around 161 rooms, including 40 bedrooms and 2 ballrooms (one unfinished). The house contained 13 bathrooms (13 is a common number theme throughout the house which includes a chandelier altered to hold 13 candles, clothes hooks in multiples of 13, 13 panels of stained glass in windows, drain covers on sinks containing 13 holes and the like) only one of which functioned to confuse the spirits as decoys; Mrs Winchester slept in a different room every night for the same reason. There is a storage room on the property with a contents value of $25,000 at the time, now equivalent to $357,704 as of 2016, containing items designed by people such as Tiffany himself as well as one window designed by Sarah featuring the 13 theme and spider web designs, again to put off spirits. Upon her death, her niece took any items she wanted then sold the rest at a private auction with six trucks allegedly taking six weeks worth of 8 hour days to remove all the furniture from the home. Her will failed to mention the mansion, which was deemed worthless after the earthquake and due to its bizarre construction and was sold at auction for just $135,000 to a local investor. It was opened to the public by the lease holders for the first time in 1923, and Harry Houdini toured the house. It took until 2016 for one room to even be found, an attic space containing a pump organ, couch, dress form, sewing machine and paintings. A 2018 film, Winchester, was filmed on the property starring Helen Mirren.

56. LIBBY'S WATER TOWER
37.38112, -122.03496
490 W California Ave, Sunnyvale, CA 94086

Once the world's largest cannery, now just a water tower in the form of a very large can of fruit cocktail where it once stood after its demise in 1985. The tower was painted like this in its heyday but when the Libby factory was torn down it was painted out, leading furious residents to protest and have it repainted in its 1900s style.

57. DRAWBRIDGE
37.4625, -121.9735
Drawbridge, Fremont, CA 94538

Previously known as Saline City, this ghost town complete with a deserted station is located on Station Island in the San Fran Bay. When it was built in 1876 it had one cabin in which resided the operator of the railroad's two drawbridges crossing the wonderfully evocative Mud Creek Slough and Coyote Creek Slough. In its heyday in the 1880s, ten trains a day stopped there bringing around 1000 visitors to the town every weekend. By the '20s it had 90 some buildings divided into two separate areas, one for the Catholics and one for the

Above: Libby's Water Tower

Protestants. It was once reported, just after the drawbridges were removed, that the town was a ghost town with valuables left behind by the departed, leading to locals having their houses looted and vandalised. The last resident actually left in 1979. The drawbridges are long gone, the only remaining route now the Union Pacific Railroad track - take a glimpse as you pass from Altamont Commuter Express, Capitol Corridor or Coast Starlight trains.

58. MUSEUM OF PEZ
37.5791, -122.3441
214 California Dr, Burlingame, CA 94010
www.burlingamepezmuseum.com
We aren't sure how to pronounce Burlingame nor why anyone would have this many Pez.

59. MCCLOSKEY CASTLE
37.6348, -122.4884
900 Mirador Terrace, Pacifica, CA 94044
This residence was built as a refuge from an earthquake in 1906 and since then has been an illegal abortion clinic, a prohibition speakeasy and a communications centre during WWII for defence against the Japanese. It was finally bought by a theatre painter at 20th Century Fox who built a museum to theatre decor and props within it, and it is still run by his estate.

60. NIKE MISSILE SITE SF-51
37.63973, -122.47894
Milagra Creek Overlook Trail, Pacifica, CA 94044
Abandoned Cold War missile defence complex with plenty of intact buildings and tons of stunning graffiti.

61. WYATT EARP'S GRAVE
37.67506, -122.45546
Hills of Eternity Memorial Park, 1301 El Camino Real, Colma, CA 94014
Memorial of the archetypal Old West sheriff, famed for the shootout at the O.K. Corral in Tombstone, Arizona.

62. FLEISHHACKER POOL RUINS
(Car Park, San Francisco Zoo)
37.7335, -122.5063
1 Zoo Road, San Francisco, CA 94132

Top right: Fleishhacker Pool Ruins
Bottom right: Wyatt Earp's Grave
Overleaf: Museum Of Pez

THE PACIFIC TRAIL ROUTE 9

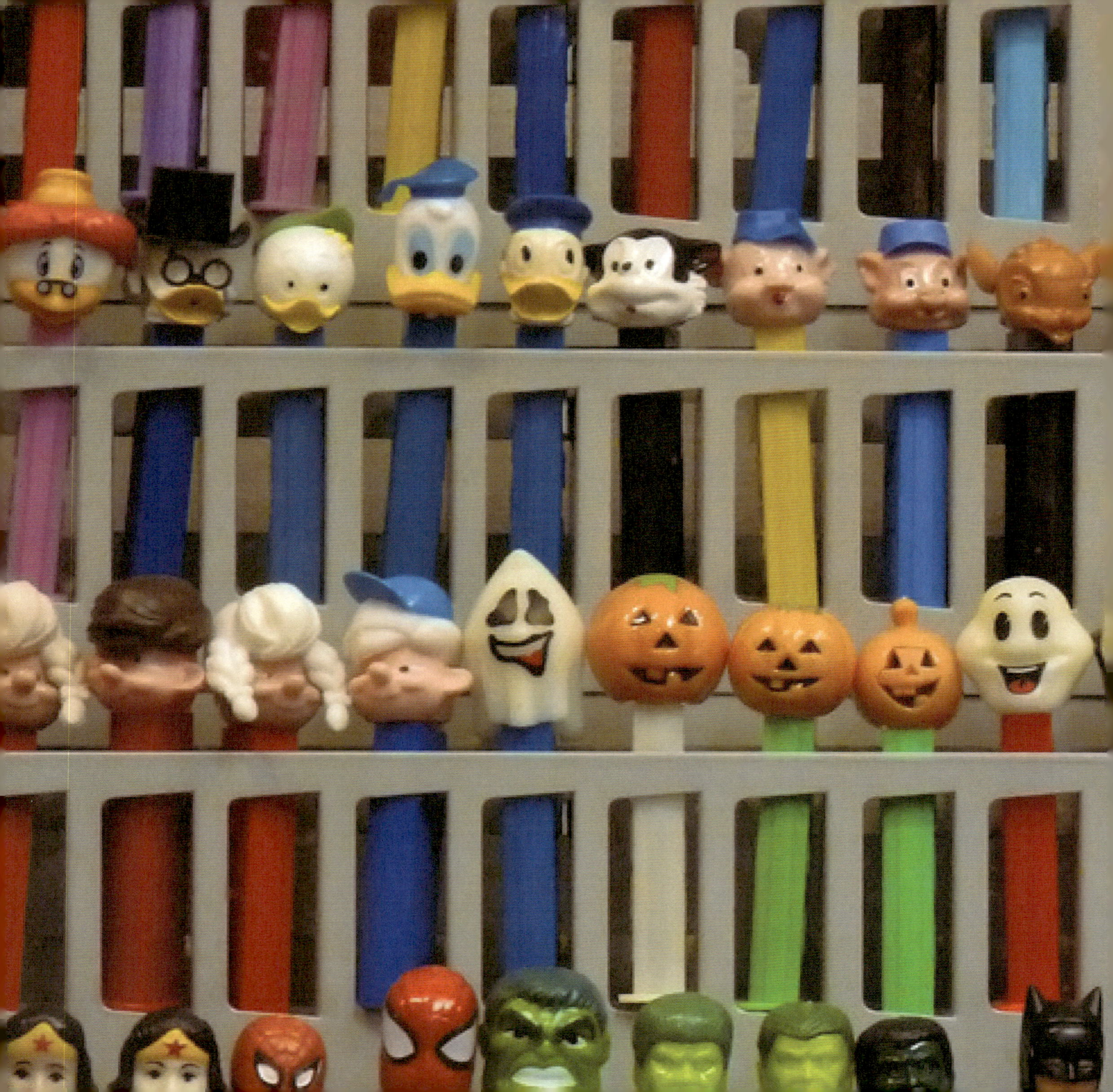

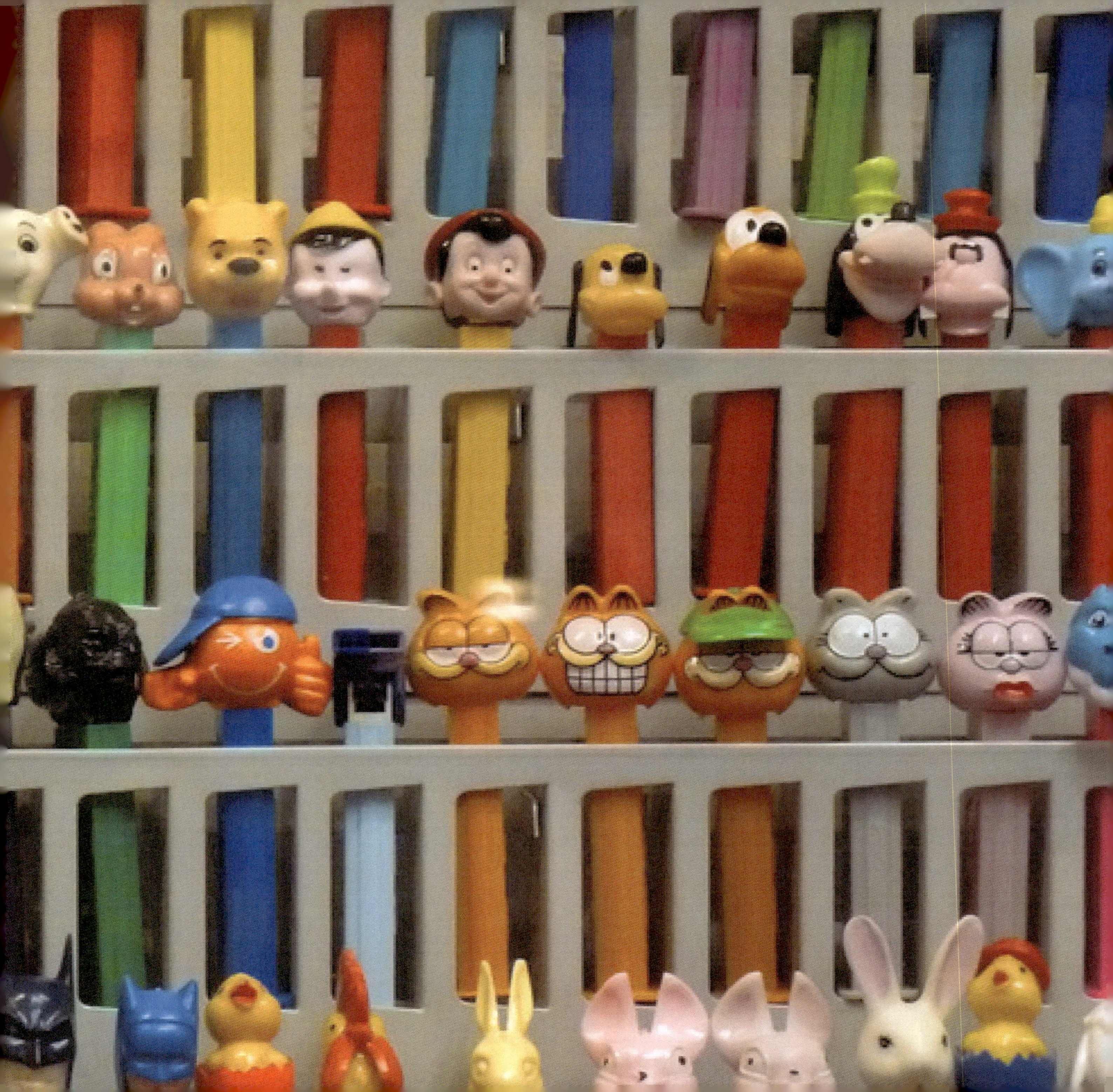

Top left: Bacon Bacon
Top right: Ruins of the Sutro Baths
Bottom left: Bourn Mansion
Bottom right: San Francisco's Pet Cemetery

Popular saltwater San Fran public pool next to the San Francisco zoo completed in 1925 and in its day the largest heated outdoor swimming pool in the world. It was demolished but you can still see three of the beautiful original main entrances freestanding as a memory to what once was.

63. CIRCUS CENTER
37.7658, -122.4571
755 Frederick St, San Francisco, CA 94117
www.circuscenter.org
Learn to clown around like a pro.

64. LOVED TO DEATH
37.76941, -122.45021
1681 & 1685 Haight St, San Francisco, CA 94117
www.lovedtodeath.com
Wonderful shop full of the bizarre, the old, the beautiful.

65. BACON BACON
37.76706, -122.44666
205 Frederick St, San Francisco, CA 94117
www.baconbaconsf.com
The wording of their website's contact page reads 'Need to talk bacon? Contact Bacon Bacon. We'd love to talk about bacon with you.' This is really all you need to know about this restaurant which is the proud purveyor of, in its words, 'bacon goodness', as well as throwing a mechanical pig in for good measure. Try 'The Almost Veggie Sandwich'. Spoiler alert: It contains bacon. It is also the proud owner of the quite possibly the most unbeatable side dish to ever have graced a menu, 'The Bacon Bouquet', described as 'Bacon, Bacon, Bacon, Bacon, Bacon.'

66. BRAINWASH
37.7763, -122.4087
1122 Folsom St, San Francisco, CA 94103
www.brainwash.com
Eat, drink AND get your laundry done all at once at this Laundromat come eatery.

67. ALBION CASTLE
37.7315, -122.3756
881 Innes Ave, San Francisco, CA 94124
This property owner built a castle in 1870 in

order to brew the perfect English beer from imported Scottish hops using a local spring and extensive tunnels beneath the property for storage; the brewing continued until his widow died in 1919.

68. BOURN MANSION
37.7941, -122.4332
2550 Webster St, San Francisco, CA 94115
Built by one of the richest men in San Francisco, this grandiose town house is a historical landmark that has fallen into disrepair.

69. RUINS OF THE SUTRO BATHS
37.7799, -122.5137
Point Lobos Ave, San Francisco, CA 94121
Once a grand public saltwater swimming pool complex in Lands' End, Richmond District complete with its own rail line which over looked the Golden Gate, this 1896 bath house was once the world's largest indoor swimming pool establishment, with a natural flow of water from the ocean which recycled the water in the pools at high tide. Sadly it burned down in 1966 and has remained in ruins ever since. The building was built by ex-mayor of San Francisco Adolph Sutro and it struggled financially since its conception owing to exorbitant running costs. As soon as it was closed and slated to be demolished, it burnt down, the developers promptly claimed the insurance money and left the San Francisco Bay area. You can still see the concrete walls, blocked off stairs and passageways from the original construction. It originally boasted six saltwater and one freshwater pool with 7 slides, 30 swinging rings and a diving board, 517 private dressing rooms, an ice skating rink, a 2700 seater amphitheatre, club rooms for 1100 and a museum of taxidermy.

70. SAN FRANCISCO'S PET CEMETERY
37.8026, -122.4674
McDowell Ave, San Francisco, CA 94129
Picturesque pet cemetery, featuring a lot of pets owned by military families who have been given military style burials; monuments feature the rank of the owner as well as comments such as 'A GI pet. He did his time.' It is thought that the origins of the cemetery may be a burial ground for horses of the cavalry from the 19th century or perhaps WWII dogs, as cemeteries such as this on military ground are fairly unusual.

71. OCTAGON HOUSE
37.79779, -122.42744
2645 Gough St, San Francisco, CA 94123
This quirky house in San Francisco is one of only three octagonal houses in the city hailing from a time when a brief craze to build your house in the shape of an octagon rather than a square hit in the 1860s; it was claimed that the design was healthier with more light and ventilation and more economical because the shape approached that of a sphere therefore maximising volume of interior space with a more compact floor plan. Most were built with a dome over a central stairway.

72. AQUATIC PARK TOMBSTONES
37.80705, -122.42615
3260 Van Ness Ave, San Francisco, CA 94109
A storm in 2012 revealed the ruins of gravestones and tombs which were used decades ago to shore up a seawall. The bodies were moved to local cemeteries whilst there was room, before many more were dumped in landfill

73. ALCATRAZ
37.82697, -122.42295
Alcatraz Island, San Francisco, CA 94133

Top right: Aquatic Park Tombstones

Left: The Alameda Spite House
Right: Alcatraz

A San Fran must-see, The Rock is packed with history; be sure to read Inside Alcatraz: My time on the Rock by Jim Quillen prior to visiting to fully appreciate the context.

74. HOTEL VERTIGO
37.78858, -122.41599
940 Sutter St, San Francisco, CA 94109
hotelvertigosf.com
Ever wanted to step into a Hitchcock movie? This is for you. When this hotel featured in the movie it was called the Empire and the film still plays on loop in the lobby as the venue fully embraces its heritage.

75. ALAMEDA SPITE HOUSE
37.76189, -122.24009
1343 Broadway, Alameda, CA 94501

A spite house is a genre of building designed deliberately to irritate neighbours by blocking out light, access or generally to be obnoxious. The Alameda house is situated on the only remaining strip of land left to an Alameda resident who had planned to build his palatial dream house on his large plot before the city took a large chunk of it in order to build a side street. To spite the city and particularly a neighbour who had been unsupportive and unsympathetic, Mr Froling built a house of absurd proportions immediately adjacent to the neighbour's property.

76. DUNSMUIR-HELLMAN HISTORIC ESTATE
37.74423, -122.14386
2960 Peralta Oaks Ct, Oakland, CA 94605
www.dunsmuir-hellman.com
Beautiful neo-classic revival home built in 1899 by the son of a wealthy coal magnate as a wedding gift for his wife - sadly he was taken ill and died on his honeymoon in New York, leaving her to return to live in the home alone. She herself died soon after in 1901. It has changed hands several times since but the beautiful house can today be toured and has been used for a number of films and TV series including Phantasm, A View to a Kill, So I Married an Axe Murderer and True Crime.

77. CHILDREN'S FAIRYLAND
37.8087, -122.26036
699 Bellevue Ave, Oakland, CA 94610
www.fairyland.org
This early young children's theme park,

launched as part of a Lake Meritt Park improvement project, opened its doors some 65 years ago and has since served as both a muse for what was to become Disneyland as well acting as a proving ground for puppeteer talents such as Frank Oz of Miss Piggy fame.

78. FISH HOUSE
37.85629, -122.28589
2747 Mathews St, Berkeley, CA 94702
The most photographed house in Berkley in an otherwise unremarkable street, this house is in fact not in the shape of a fish at all, but a microscopic marine creature.

79. ADVENTURE PLAYGROUND
37.86317, -122.31447
160 University Ave, Berkeley, CA 94710

Top left: Dunsmuir-Hellman Historic Estate
Top right: Adventure Playground
Bottom Right: The Fish House

This bizarre take on childhood freedom is enough to terrorise your average parent - this adventure playground was built by kids, for kids. Literally, in return for helping to pick up litter, they are handed hammers, nails, saws and chunks of wood and are told to crack on.

80. THORNBURG VILLAGE
37.8771, -122.2656
1781-1851 Spruce St, Berkeley, CA 94709
Pretty, rural-European style buildings which stick out from their surroundings.

81. MARK OLIVER'S YARD ART
37.8863, -122.2785
1118 Colusa Ave, Berkeley, CA 94707
One man combats the dumping of trash by creating art in his front yard.

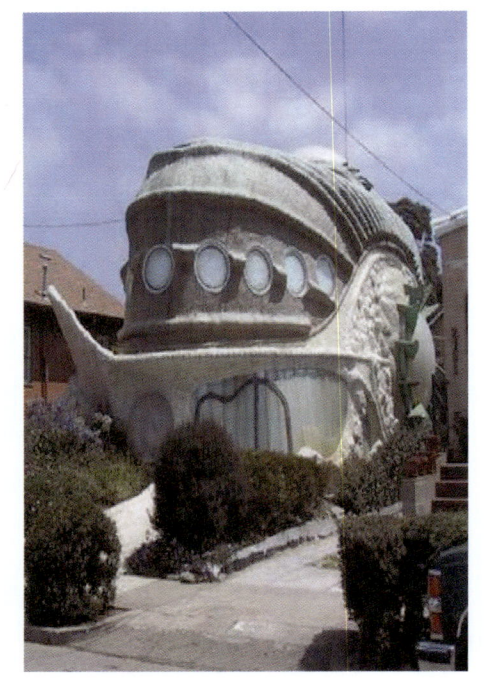

THE PACIFIC TRAIL ROUTE 9

82. FAIRY POST OFFICE
37.8992, -122.2525
Off Brook Road (Curran Trail), Berkeley, CA 94708

A tiny post office hidden in a tree which is actually functional. Leave a letter or package for another whimsical itinerant hiker - but it needs to be miniature.

83. PLAYLAND NOT AT THE BEACH
37.91686, -122.31287
10979 San Pablo Ave, El Cerrito, CA 94530
www.playland-not-at-the-beach.org

Playland amusement park opened in San Francisco in 1928, a 10 acre site complete with the staples of the time like borderline racist rides, terrifying dummy automatons and a curiosity display. One little boy lived just down the road from the park and could see the terrifying laughing dummy head of Laughing Sal, of which 287 were made back in the day; he could hear her laughing all day long every day of his childhood. Rather than put him off for life, Marvin Gold became obsessed and when the amusement park closed in 1972, he was not only there to watch the wrecking ball move in in horror but his desire was cemented to collect amusement paraphernalia and put them on public display. Playland not at the Beach is his collection of all things arcade and amusement park and operates on weekends. Playland's carousel still operates today at Yerba Buena Gardens in San Francisco.

84. CENTENNIAL BULB
37.6822, -121.7411
Fire Station #6, 4550 East Avenue, Livermore, CA 94550
www.centennialbulb.org

Longest continually lit bulb in existence. Eco friendly? No.

85. BYRON HOT SPRINGS HOTEL
37.84825, -121.63325
Old Byron Hot Springs Hotel, Byron, CA 94514

This abandoned 1900s hotel was once a major film star haunt. Its first incarnation, built in 1889 out of wood was destroyed by fire, leading to a rebuild in 1901 in stucco. This too burnt down in 1912, leading to the construction of the final hotel in 1913, the ruins of which remain today. Since its closure in 1938, it was repurposed by the military in 1941 and used as an interrogation camp housing German and Japanese POWs.

The building was sold in 1947 to the Greek Orthodox Church for $105,000 whereupon it served as a monastery and then via various owners as a resort, club and private home. It is due to be redeveloped.

86. THE PRESTON SCHOOL OF INDUSTRY
38.35963, -120.93466
201 Waterman Road, Ione, CA 95640
www.prestoncastle.com

This building was formerly one of the oldest and best known reform schools in the USA; it opened in 1894 when 7 wards, minors who were guardians of the state and/or juvenile offenders, were moved there from San Quentin Prison. Known by locals as simply The Castle, it was left empty in 1960 when other buildings replaced it. In 1999, its name was changed to Preston Youth Correctional Facility although that too closed in 2010. Now abandoned, it has often been used in film and is open for public tours. Events are also held throughout the year including decorations at Christmas and a haunted house for Halloween. Some of the original wards of Preston were: Neal Cassady who prominently featured in the first draft of Kerouac's On the Road (as himself) as well as in his later works as Cody Pomeray - he was in Preston for possession of stolen goods. Rory Calhoun, an actor and producer, appeared in Sergio Leone's The Colossus of Rhodes and alongside Marilyn Monroe in both How to Marry a Millionaire and River of No Return (he had been incarcerated for stealing a revolver and once escaped Preston's adjustment centre- a jail within the main prison). Eddie Anderson was a comedian and actor who started out in vaudeville (his father was a minstrel, his mother a tight rope walker until she fell from a rope) and was the first African American to have a regular role on a nationwide TV program. Don Jordan, a boxer and World Welterweight Champion, died later in his life after being robbed and seriously assaulted in an LA parking lot in 1995. Signer songwriter Merle Haggard was in Preston due to a troubled childhood after the death of his father. He went on to receive a Grammy Lifetime Achievement Award in 2010, a BMI Icon award in 2006 and was entered into the Nashville, Oklahoma and Country Music Halls of Fame. Eddie Machen dropped out of high school to become an amateur boxer but was arrested and convicted of armed robbery after just 3 bouts. Upon his release he had a 64 bout career leading him to be highly rated, fighting most big names of his era and winning 50 games, 29 by KO; he is considered by some to have been the perfect fighting machine. Pancho Golzales was given a $0.51 tennis racquet by his mother when he was 12. This lead him to lose all interest in school and become a troubled teen, always truant from school and being picked up by truancy officers which in turn ostracised him from the sport as a youth. He was arrested for burglary at age 15. Upon his release from Preston he joined the Navy and went on to become the World Tennis No. 1 player for an all time record eight years

< Left: Playland Not At The Beach
< Right: Centennial Bulb
Right: Byron Hot Springs Hotel

THE PACIFIC TRAIL ROUTE 9 335

from 1952 to 1960, winning 17 Major singles titles including 15 Pro Slams and 2 Grand Slams and twice winning the United States Championships. He is still widely considered one of the greatest tennis players in history and Sports Illustrated said of him 'If earth were on the line in a tennis match, the man you want serving to save humankind would be Ricardo Alonso Golzalez'. Tony Cornero aka The Admiral and Tony the Hat was a bootlegging gambling entrepreneur born in Piedmont, Italy. He ended up running gambling ships, a major mobster occupation of the era before building the iconic Stardust Resort & Casino (the original neon sign of which takes pride of place in the Vegas neon boneyard (see page X). After surviving a shooting from point blank range of four bullets to the stomach when he answered the door to a contract killer, he eventually died on the casino floor in dubious circumstances when the day after informing investors he would need an extra $800,000 to pay for liquor in the venue, he suddenly dropped dead with a drink in his hand. His body was immediately removed from the casino floor prior to the calling of the police, his glass washed by staff and therefore never examined – his death was ruled a heart attack although many contend he was poisoned. Caryl Chessman was sent to Preston for stealing a car and stole another a month after his release - he went on to be the first modern American executed for a non-lethal kidnapping in 1960. Joseph Paul Cretzer started in crime early and went on to be a prisoner at Alcatraz, slain in the bloody battle there in 1946 after a failed escape plan. He was the backbone of the Cretzer-Kyle Gang, big-time bank robbers and was number 4 on the FBI's most wanted list. Eddie Bunker is a crime fiction writer and actor who wrote the book Animal Factory, acting also as a screenwriter on the film. He had alcoholic parents and ended up in foster care at 5 when they divorced and ran away, committing shoplifting and leading him to be kept in Preston. Here he met hardened young criminals who encouraged him to go on to engage in bank robbing, drug dealing, extortion, armed robbery and forgery, for which he was eventually convicted. He played one of two criminals killed during a heist in Reservoir Dogs.

87. GOTHIC ROSE ANTIQUES & CURIOSITIES
38.72951, -120.7998

Above: The Preston School of Industry, Eddie Anderson, Joseph Paul Cretzer, Pancho Gonzales
> Right: Mormon Island
Overleaf: Glass Beach

484 Main St, Placerville, CA 95667
www.gothicroseantiques.com
Shop the weird and bizarre.

88. MORMON ISLAND
38.7021, -121.115
Folsom Lake State Recreation Area, El Dorado Hills, CA 95762, USA
You might think that Mormon settlers weren't in the business of seeking gold during the Rush - you would be wrong. When two such men hit gold whilst hunting in 1848, about 150 others flocked to the site in what was the first major gold strike in California. The community at Mormon Island, Folsom Lake died a post-gold-rush death and the vast majority was razed, the only remnant now a recreation area and at a separate location, a relocation cemetery on the dry side of the Dam which also contains remains exhumed during the deliberate flooding of Folsom Lake and some found during the construction of a road near Prairie City. The relocation cemetery can be found at 2547 Shadowfax Lane, El Dorado Hills, El Dorado County, CA 95762.

89. COOL PATCH PUMPKINS CORN MAZE
38.48459, -121.82007
6585 Milk Farm Rd, Dixon, CA 95620
www.coolpatchpumpkins.com
The world's largest temporary corn maze.

90. LEARN BOONTLING IN BOONVILLE
39.00897, -123.36715
Boonville, CA 95415
Visit the small town with its very own language spoken by only 12 surviving people, 140 years after its inception. First spoken in the 1870s, the language is an amalgamation of English, Scottish Gaelic, Pomoan Indian and Spanish and is said to have originated to help the town gossip about a visiting pregnant

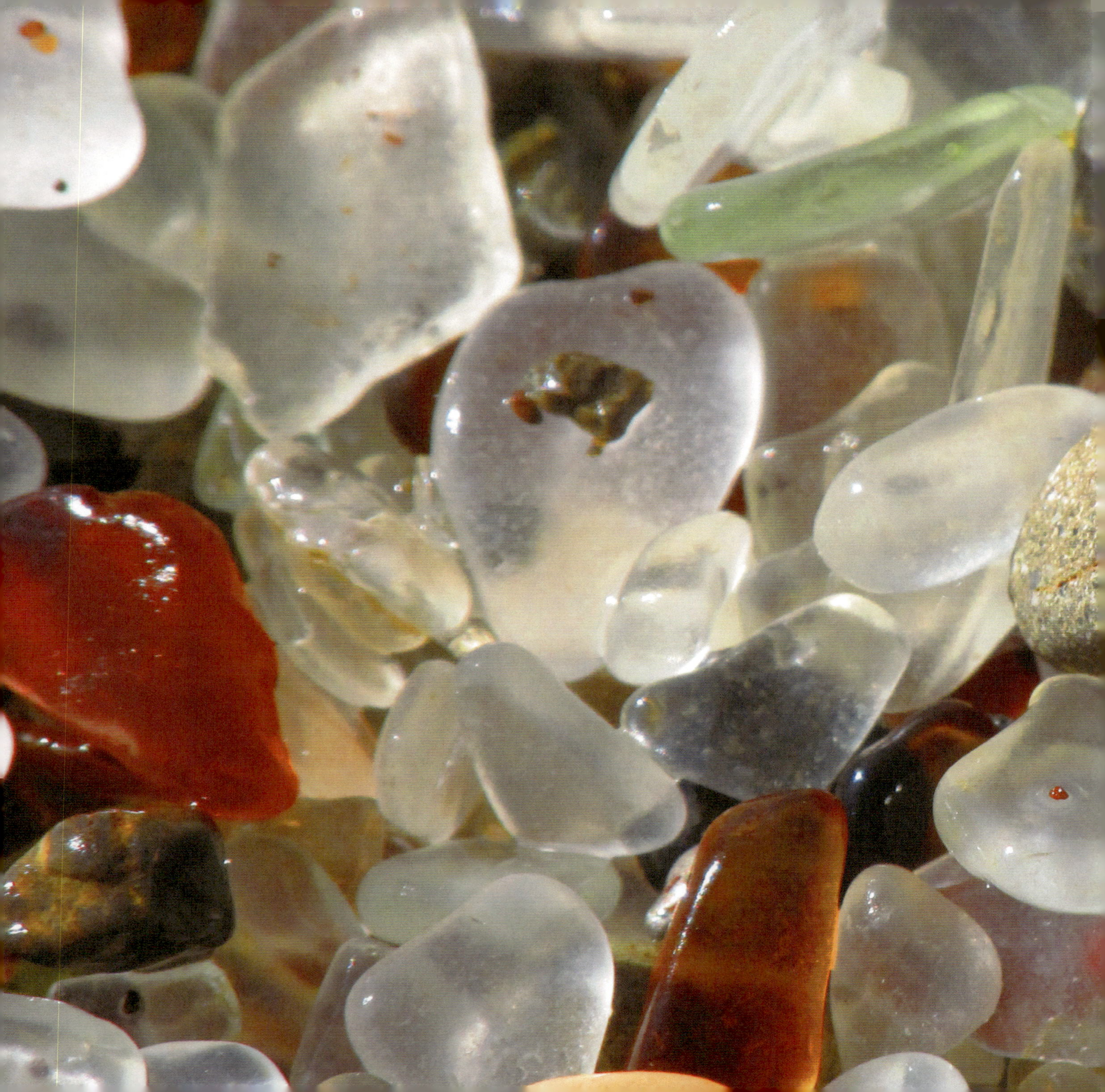

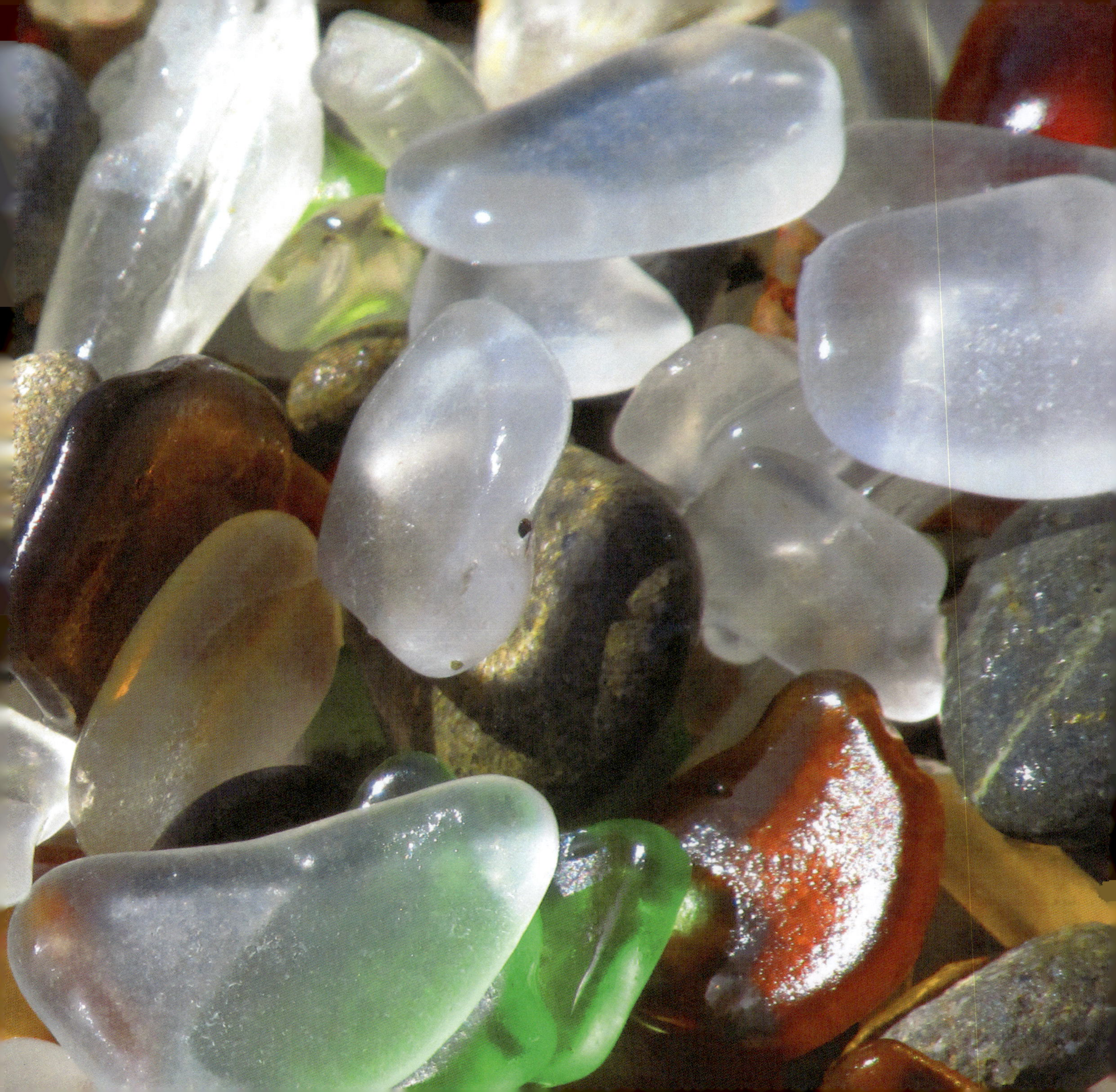

woman who they disapproved of due to her out-of-wedlock status, without her understanding. The language is composed of 1600 words and anyone, including visitors, can make up a new word as long as it is vetted by the other speakers. The language's name comes from 'Boont' for Boonville and 'ling' for lingo.

91. GLASS BEACH
39.45259, -123.81349
Glass Beach, Fort Bragg, CA 95437
This stunning beach is composed entirely of smooth coloured glass pebbles, the remnants of what was known as Site 3, the Union Lumber Company's third rubbish dumping site. The beach remained an active dump site until 1967. Often these smooth coloured pieces of glass are of jewellery quality. There are two further such beaches in the Fort Bragg area (sites one and two.)

92. SALTAIR
Current location (Saltair III)
40.7457, -122.1901
12408 West Saltair Drive, Magna, UT 84044
thesaltair.com
Original location (Saltair I, II, now defunct)
40.7763, -112.1702
N Temple Frontage, Salt Lake City, UT 84116
The first incarnation of this spectacular pavilion was in 1893, a resort serving Salt Lake hoisted upon 2000 posts many of which are still standing 110 years later. Its aim was to provide a healthy family atmosphere in-line with Mormon teachings and under the supervision of church leaders, to combat the spiritually devoid resorts it competed with. It was also intended to rival Coney Island to the East, and was one of the first US amusement parks. Controversially, the Saltair did sell coffee, tea and alcohol and opened on Sunday despite this being against Mormon dogma. The old rail tracks that brought hordes of clean-cut revellers to dance the night away can still be seen at the original location. Variations of the pavilion have come and gone due to natural disaster and fire, and in something of a moral turnaround, Kesha recently held her Get Sleazy tour at the most recent version of the venue which sits just down interstate 80 from the original.

93. WYNTOON
41.19154, -122.06444
McCloud, CA 96057
William Randolph Hearst's lesser known estate after Hearst Castle, built from the remnants of grand estates throughout Europe.

94. THE JUNIPER LODGE MOTEL
41.7584, -122.0632
Volcanic Legacy Scenic Byway (97 – between Mud Lake Road and Jerome Road cross streets), Macdoel, CA 96058
An intact 70s abandoned motel - pleasingly Bates-esque.

95. OLD FORT ROAD GRAVITY HILL
42.2517, -121.74259
Old Fort Road, Klamath Falls, OR 97603
A classic US gravity location where poured water flows uphill and cars roll the wrong way. All a cunning illusion but particularly effective at night, it is a classic location of urban legend.

96. OREGON STATE HOSPITAL MUSEUM OF MENTAL HEALTH
44.93869, -123.00303
2600 Center St NE, Salem, OR 97301
Notably the filming location for One Flew Over the Cuckoo's Nest, this fascinating museum and hospital provides a great insight into mental health through the ages. Keep an eye open for the purple glass tiles in the floors, which exist to let in light to the underground tunnels which were a feature of many hospitals which needed to transport quarantined patients from building to building without them coming into contact with others.

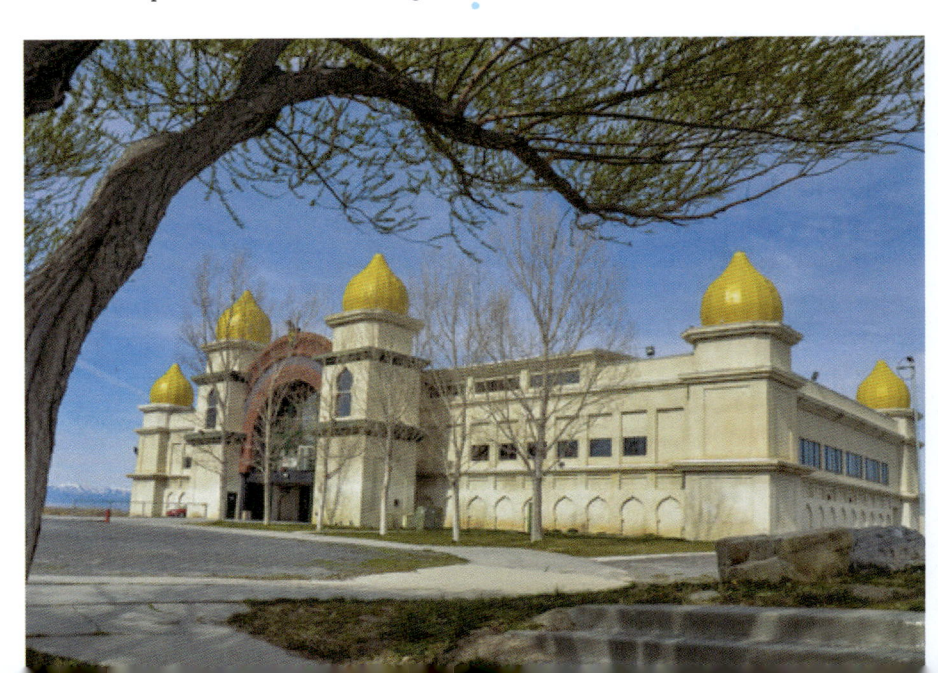

97. MOUNT ANGEL ABBEY MUSEUM
45.05728, -122.77567
1 Abbey Dr, St Benedict, OR 97373
www.mountangelabbey.org
In a beautifully bizarre combination, this museum is both curated by Benedictine monks, and is the home of a giant hairball from a large pig. That's not the only weird artefact on display - revel in an 8-legged calf and a Siamese cow and question the monks' thinking.

98. WANKERS CORNER STORE
45.30252, -122.76437
8499 SW Main St, Wilsonville, OR 97070
www.wankerscorner.com
Named for the Wanker family who still own the property, pronounced (understandably) after the German, 'Wonker'.

99. TREE CLIMBING PLANET
45.31205, -122.6303
20451 S Central Point Rd, Oregon City, OR 97045
Free your inner 8 year old and learn tree climbing techniques with access to the canopy above.

100. TIMBERLINE LODGE
45.33096, -121.71128
Mt Hood National Forest, Government Camp, OR 97028
Better known as the Overlook, this hotel was featured in aerial shots as part of the opening scene of Kubrick's The Shining and provided

Overleaf & right, Saltair
< Top right: Oregon State Hospital Museum of Mental Health
< Bottom Right: The Juniper Lodge Motel

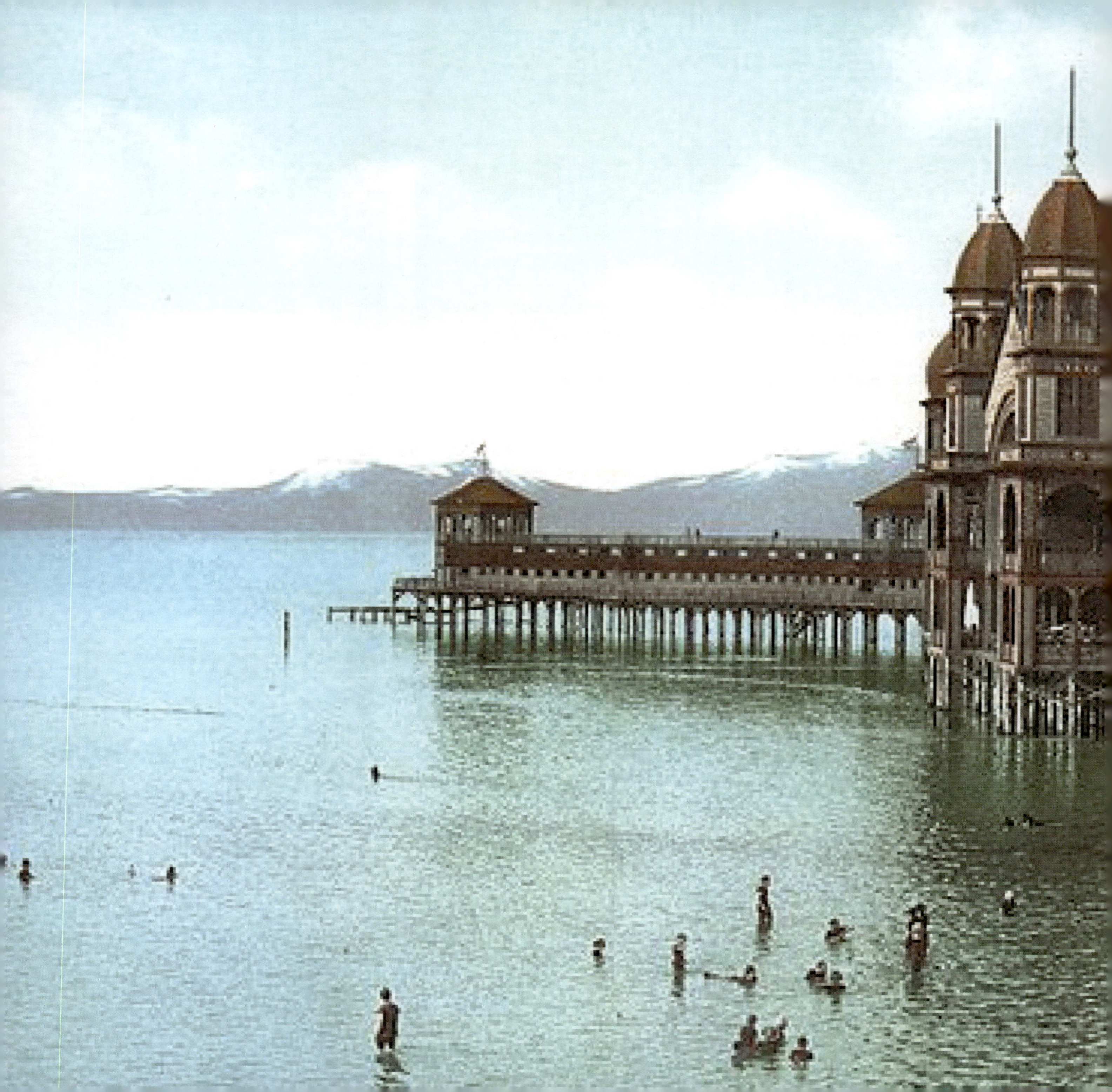

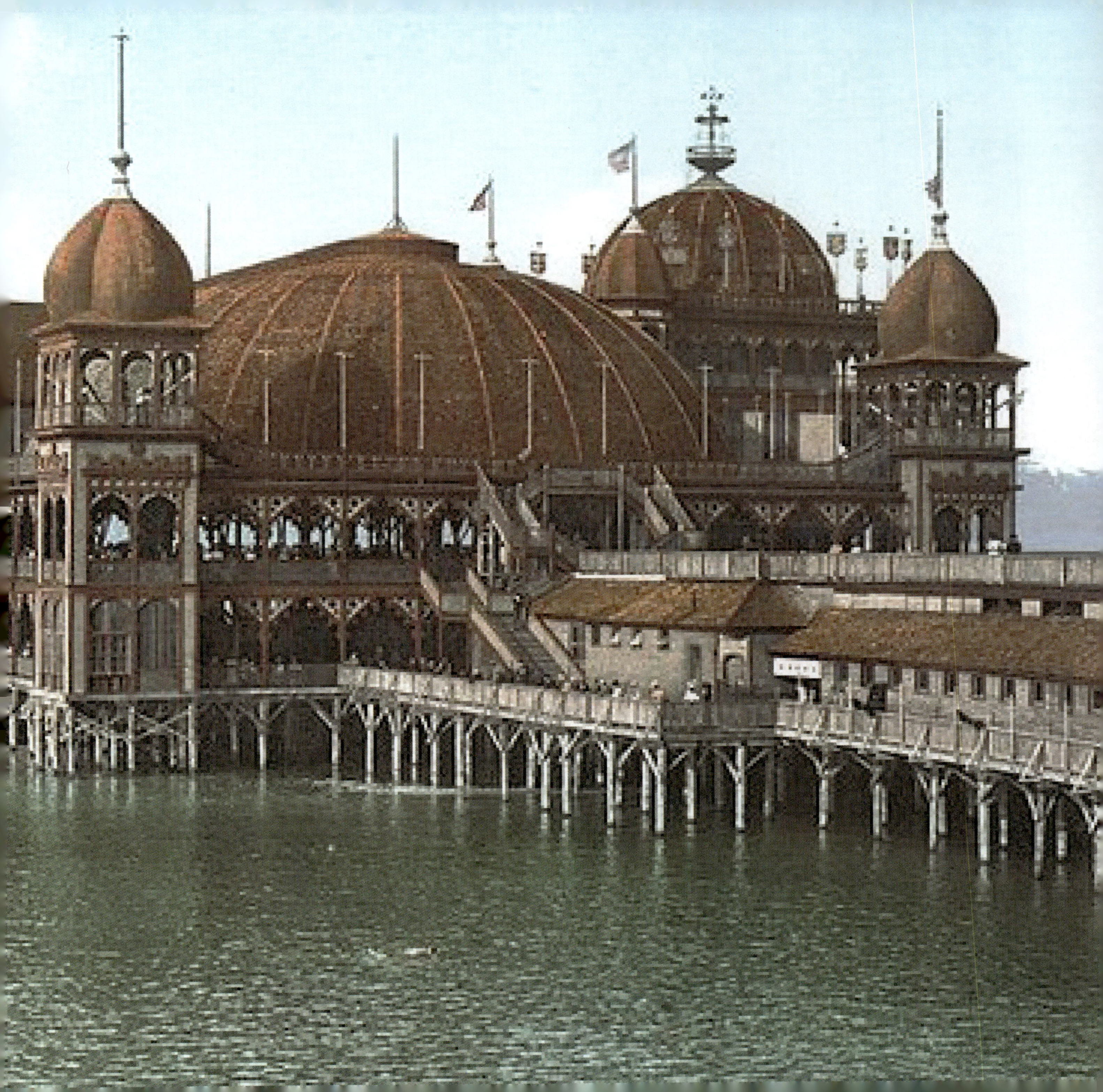

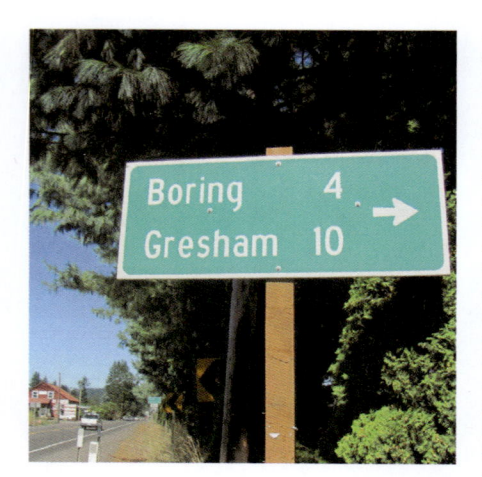

the exterior footage. The rest of the film, including the maze scene, were shot at British studios. Kubrick was requested not to show room 217 as featured in Stephen King's novel lest guests refuse to stay there again thereafter. Instead, a non-existent room 237 was included. In typical fashion, room 217 is the most requested in the hotel, and the manager is now undoubtedly kicking himself.

101. ZIGZAG
45.344, -121.94313
Zigzag, Mt Hood Village, OR 97067
Named for the Zigzag River in Zigzag Canyon. Crossing the canyon was described by one pioneer in 1845 as this: 'The manner of descending is to turn directly to the right, go zigzag for about one hundred yards, then turn short round, and go zigzag until you come under the place where you started from; then to the right, and so on, until you reach the base', explaining the origins of the Zigzag moniker.

102. THE TOWN OF BORING
45.43136, -122.37346
Boring, OR, 97009
Named for William Harrison Boring, a former Union soldier and farmer who settled in the area in 1874. While you're in town, why not grab a bite at The Not So Boring Bar and Grill, 28014 SE Wally Road, Boring, OR 97009.

103. AIRPLANE HOME IN THE WOODS
45.408, -123.0079
15270 SW Holly Hill Rd, Hillsboro, OR 97123
www.airplanehome.com
Why live in a caravan when you can live in a Boeing 727.

104. IDIOTVILLE
45.61944, -123.41805
Idiot Creek Camp, Idiot Creek Loop, Tillamook, OR 97141
So named as logging camp 'Ryan's Camp' which was the main industry in the community was so remote that locals claimed only an idiot would live and work there. The surrounding area thus garnered the name Idiotville, whilst the local stream became Idiot Creek.

105. THE WITCH'S CASTLE
45.52857, -122.72446
Lower Macleay Trail, Portland, OR 97210
The current crumbling building was built as a ranger station in the '50s on what was thought to be the site of a witch's house from the 16th century and which later became an estate owned by a Danford Balch. The old Balch family cabin was nearby, scene of a bloody argument between Balch himself and itinerant worker named the rather Pratchett-esque Mortimer Stump, with whom Balch had been clearing the land. Stump had fallen in love with Balch's fifteen year old daughter and was threatening marriage, to which Balch replied that he would kill Stump if the pair eloped. After they did so and were married in 1858, they returned to the estate for supplies, upon which Balch promptly shot Stump with a shotgun in the cabin – he was hanged for the crime, and a plaque now commemorates

Top: The Town of Boring (and Dull)
> Right: The Timberline Lodge (prior page)

344   OFFBEAT AMERICA

345

Left: Voodoo Doughnut and Wedding Chapel
Right: Slappy Cakes (prior page
> The Wreck of the Peter Iredale

the event. In more recent years, a witch coven used one of the rooms which still contains satanic etchings on the walls.

106. THE FREAKYBUTTRUE PECULIARIUM

45.53542, -122.69758

2234 NW Thurman St, Portland, OR 97210

www.peculiarium.com

This store-come-exhibit is ideal for any fan of the weird, macabre and just plain gross. The place to go for alien autopsy selfies.

107. VOODOO DOUGHNUT AND WEDDING CHAPEL

45.52261, -122.6731

22 SW 3rd Ave, Portland, OR 97204

voodoodoughnut.com

Want to get married and eat doughnuts at the same time? Of course you do. Live the dream at Voodoo.

108. THE HAT MUSEUM

45.50935, -122.64989

1928 SE Ladd Ave, Portland, OR 97214

www.thehatmuseum.com

Like Hats? Like Museums? This is for you.

109. SLAPPY CAKES

45.5164, -122.6184

4246 SE Belmont St, Portland, OR 97215

www.slappycakes.com

Make your own pancakes DIY style at this happy go lucky eatery – 'batter up' and add all the 'fixins' you can think of before flipping your globular beauty onto your plate.

110. SLOTH CAPTIVE HUSBANDRY CENTRE

46.089, -122.9359

74320 Larson Road, Rainier, Oregon, 97048

More sloths than you could possibly shake a stick at, or would want to.

111. THE PETER IREDALE WRECKAGE

46.1784, -123.981

Peter Iredale Rd, Hammond, OR 97121

Visit Warrenton at low tide and you will be able to walk right up to a 1906 shipwreck.

112. WINLOCK EGG

46.49332, -122.93788

Fir St, Winlock, WA 98596

Reminiscent of the Mentone egg, this egg is also of a size, but this time located in Winlock. Grab a bite at the Winlock Eggspress in celebration of all things eggtastic.

113. SUCHER & SONS STAR WARS SHOP AND KURT COBAIN MEMORABILIA & INFO CENTER

46.97613, -123.81376

413 E Wishkah St, Aberdeen, WA 98520

sucherandsonsstarwarsshop.com

The ultimate Star Wars fan shop. Also.. the ultimate Kurt Cobain fan shop. Diversification at its best in this wonderful corner of kitsch joy.

WHY NOT CHECK OUT:

SEATTLE, all entries from *VASHON BICYCLE TREE* to *RONETTE'S BRIDGE*, pages 251 to 254

VANCOUVER, all entries from Leg in Booth Square to Capilano Suspension Bridge,e, p286

THEN, WHY NOT CHECK OUT

All entries from *PLANE WRECK OF HERITAGE PARK* to *THE TREE ON THE LAKE*, pages 290 - 298

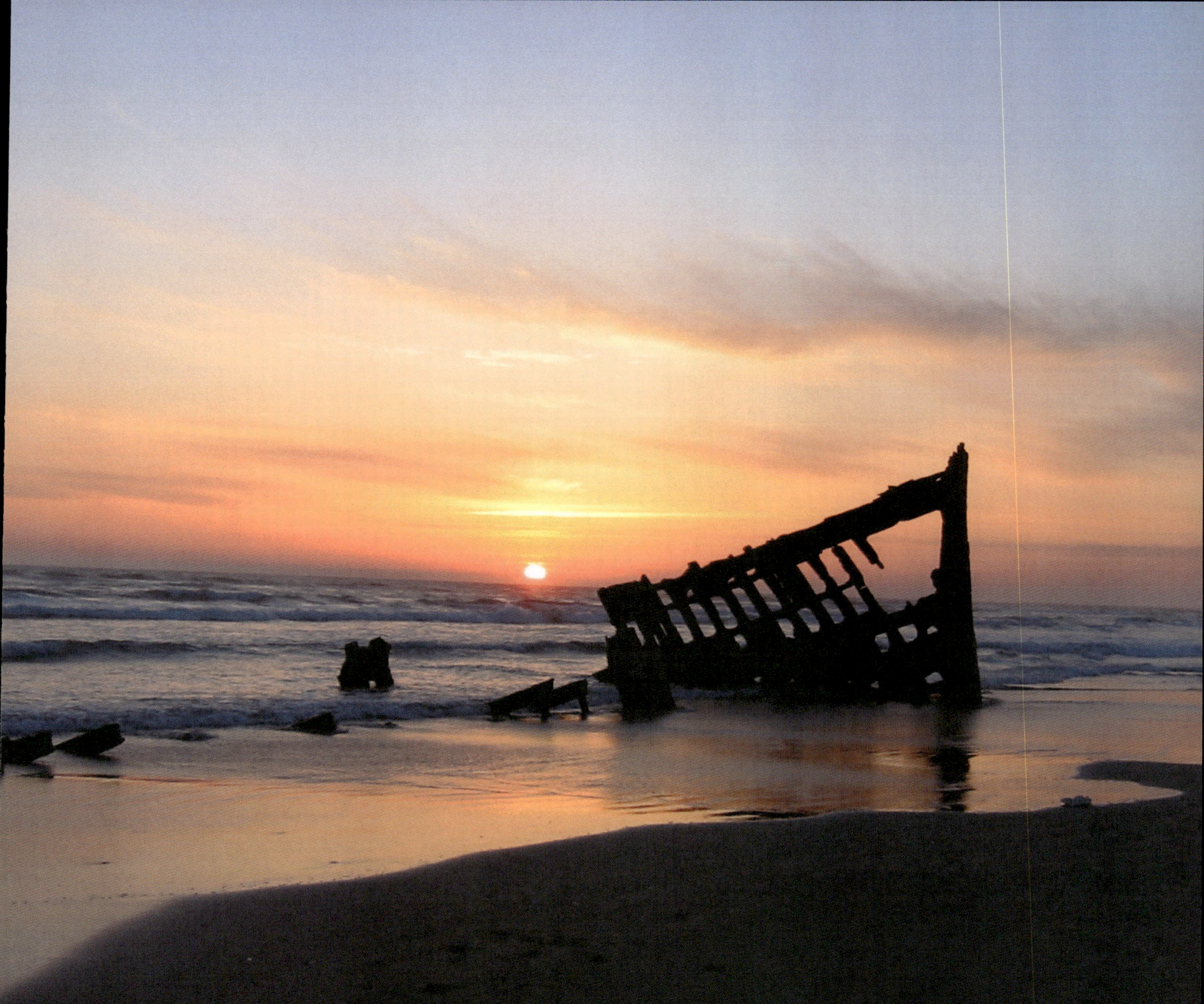

THE INNER NEVADA TRAIL ROUTE 10

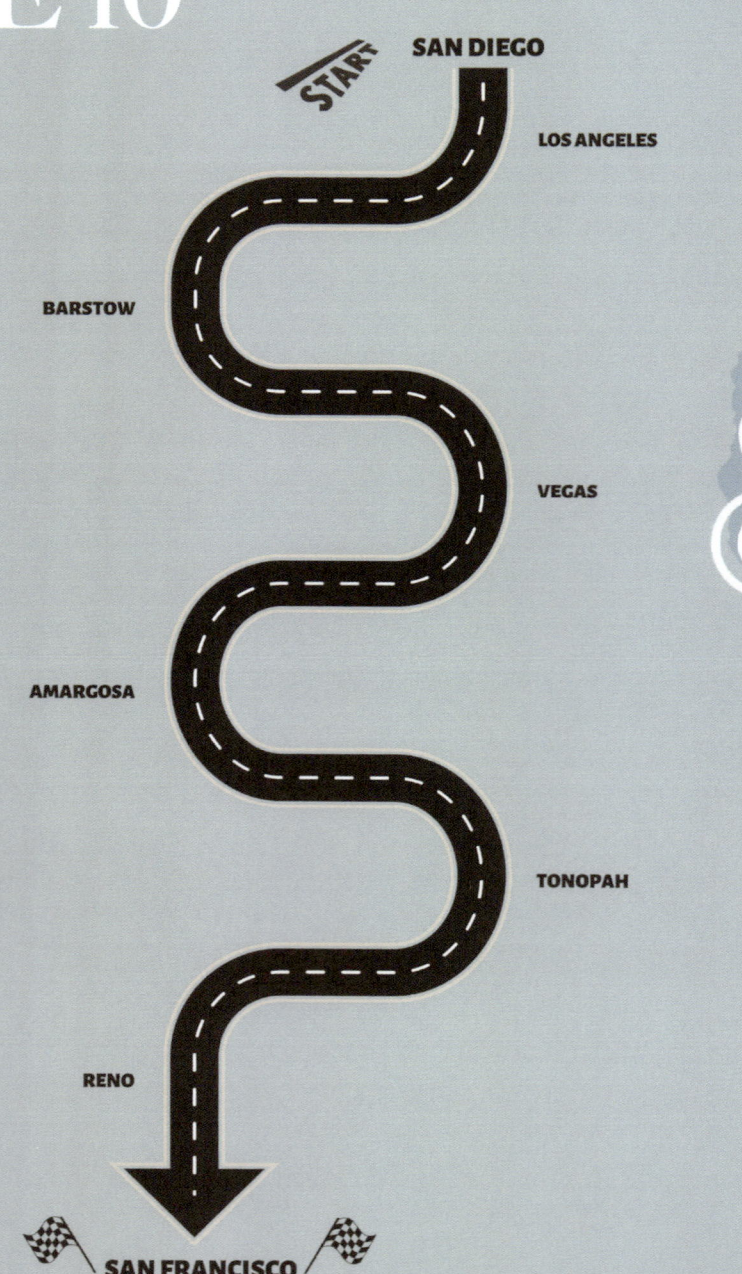

START — SAN DIEGO
LOS ANGELES
BARSTOW
VEGAS
AMARGOSA
TONOPAH
RENO
SAN FRANCISCO

THE INNER NEVADA TRAIL

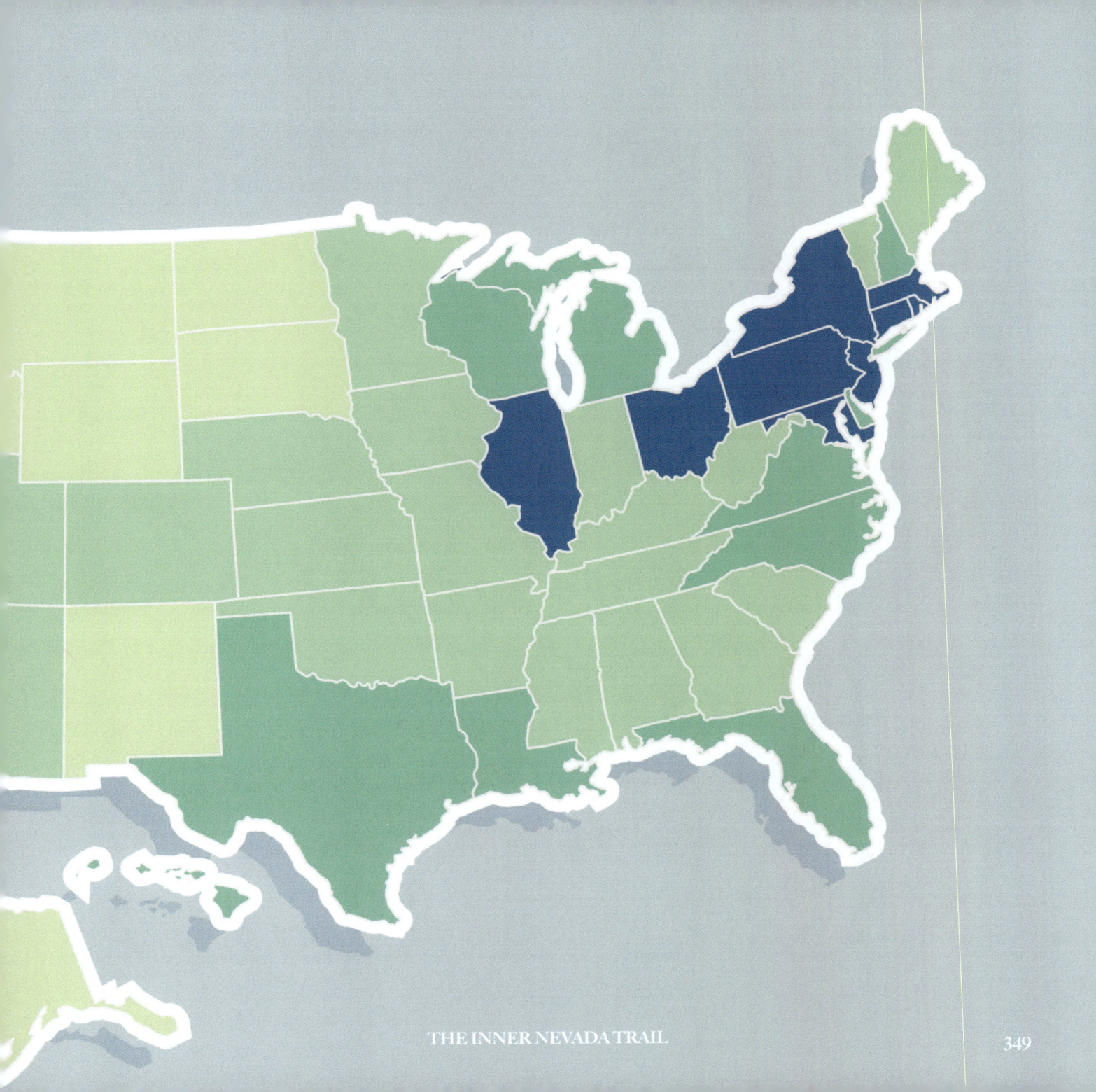

THE INNER NEVADA TRAIL ROUTE 10

Pack your sunscreen as you head towards some of the hottest places in the USA. Contrast the wastelands of Route 66 in which motels lie abandoned, keys still hanging in Reception awaiting guests that will never come, with the brash lights of the Strip which never sleeps. Forego the roulette table in favour of exploring the fascinating history behind Las Vegas, in which gangsters and con artists thrived and entrepreneurs thought bigger and better than ever before. Watch closely to see the brides in wedding dresses gamble away their ATM balances or talk to a minister who conducts upwards of 80 weddings a day. Learn to spot the original downtown casinos within the now pedestrianised and covered mall-like gambling areas and track down a million dollar photo opportunity. See unbelievably untouched ghost towns like Bodie to appreciate what life would have been like for those pre-Cirque de Soleil.

WHILE IN SAN DIEGO, WHY NOT CHECK OUT:
LEMON GROVE - p.231
HARPERS TOPIARY GARDEN - p.231

Above: Mojave Phone Booth

THE INNER NEVADA TRAIL ROUTE 10

352

< Top: Calico Ghost Town
< Left: The Bottle Tree Ranch
< Centre: Rock-a-Hoola Water Park
< Zzyzx Mineral Springs (Curtis Howe Springer)

WHILE IN CENTRAL L.A., WHY NOT CHECK OUT:

All entries from *MOON AMTRAK* to *GIANT SCISSORS*, pages 303 to 315

1. SANTA'S VILLAGE
34.23307, -117.17137
28950 CA-18, Skyforest, CA 92385
www.skyparksantasvillage.com

A (currently shut but due to reopen) entire amusement park dedicated to all things festive and gaudy, Santa's Village opened one month ahead of Disney Land (which clearly afforded it no competitive advantage whatsoever). Revenue drops (perhaps caused by an unforeseeable seasonality issue) caused it to close in 1998 but in a testament to tenacity, it reopened back in December 2016. Go see it as a ghost town or to feel festive depending on how this development pans out.

2. MOZUMDAR TEMPLE
34.26566, -117.3225
865 Mozumdar Dr, Crestline, CA 92325
www.unification.net

A miniature Taj Mahal of sorts in the middle of the Cali woods built by A.K.Mozumdar, a preacher who dreamt of a place of unity where all could worship as one. He died before it could be completed leading it to be sold first to the YMCA and then, naturally, to the Moonies (in a move which presumably would not have sat well with Mozumbdar's dreams of oneness among men). Now it sits in ruins in the middle of a dark forest and is often explored by passers-by. It is private property and is now guarded but its gold dome and walls are visible from the gate.

3. GEORGE AIR FORCE BASE
34.58905, -117.37139
George AFB, Victorville, CA 92394

A defunct US Army Air Corps base opened in the early Forties, closed at the end of World War II and officially decommissioned in 1992. A three-prison strong Federal Correctional Complex is located on some of the former land and some of the remaining abandoned buildings are used as urban warfare training areas for the Army and Marines - so beware wandering about. It was used as a location for The War of the Worlds (1953), Face Off, Jarhead, Six Million Dollar Man.

4. THE BOTTLE TREE RANCH
34.69018, -117.3395
National Trails Hwy, Oro Grande, CA 92368

One man's glass forest creation creates a cool photo stop on Route 66. Chat to Elmer Long the creator to learn more.

5. AMBOY GHOST TOWN
34.5586, -115.74366
County Rte 66, Amboy, CA 92304
www.rt66roys.com

With a classic Motel sign to die for, Amboy is an abandoned motel where the room keys are still hanging in Reception and the rooms are largely intact, albeit complete with some bizarre Blair Witch-esque additions from itinerant visitors.

6. CALICO GHOST TOWN
34.94848, -116.8649
36600 Ghost Town Rd, Yermo, CA 92398
www.calicoattractions.com

This former mining town in the Calico Mountains of the Mojave Desert was founded in 1881 to mine silver, restored in the '50s and has the dubious distinction of having been proclaimed California's Official Silver Rush Ghost Town by then Governor Schwarzenegger.

7. ROCK-A-HOOLA WATERPARK
34.94886, -116.68591
Cherokee Road/Hacienda Road, Newberry Springs, CA 92365

A cautionary tale of entrepreneurship; do people want to be around water when they are in the desert? Yes. Is that because it is wholly unavailable? Yes. Is it therefore advisable to attempt to build a water park? One man clearly thought the answer was a resounding affirmative.

8. ZZYZX MINERAL SPRINGS AND HEALING CENTER
35.1431, -116.1042
ZZyzx Road, Baker, CA 92309

Curtis Howe Springer, named 'King

Overleaf: Amboy Ghost Town

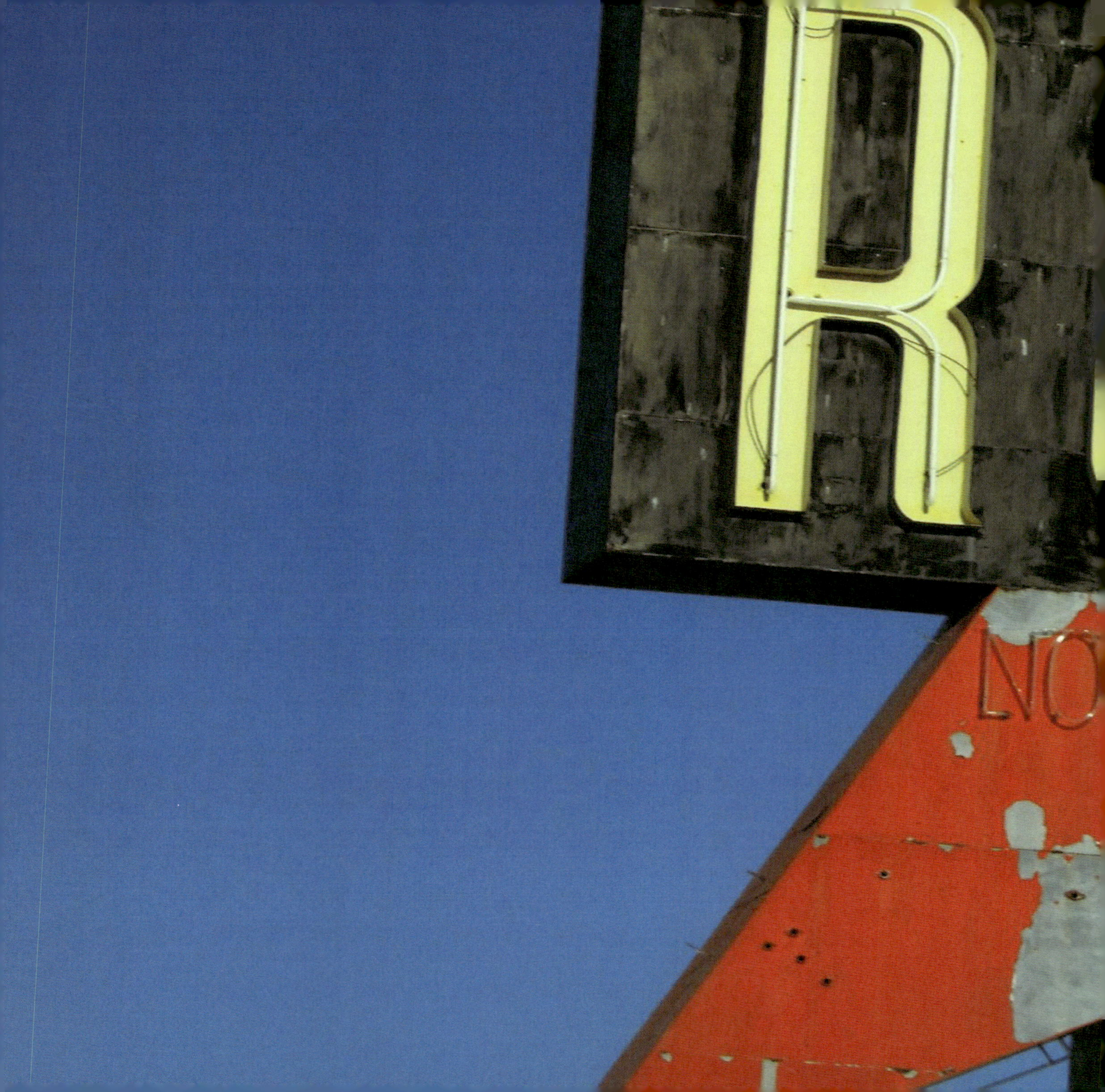

OY'S

VACANCY

MOTEL

of the Quacks' by the American Medical Association in 1969, is undoubtedly one of America's greatest hucksters. A serial liar and self-promoter a la L. Ron Hubbard, the most concrete thing one can state of the man is that he was born in Alabama in 1896, after which the details become somewhat more fuzzy. Beyond his regular role as a radio evangelist, he claimed to be (all with little to no evidence) a WWI boxing instructor, a preacher in the fight against 'demon rum', a Florida teacher, an attendee of a college in Chicago as well as holder of an M.D., D.O., Ph.D. and/or an N.D., none from real institutions. He claimed variously to represent 'The National Academy', 'Westlake West Virginia College', The American College of Doctors and Surgeons' and the eponymous 'The Springer School of Humanism' among others, again none of which had any basis in reality. As one journalist, Dan Nosowitz noted in 2015, 'Let's take a moment and reflect on the cojones to not only give yourself a false honorific but also to insist it was issued by a school that doesn't exist that you have named after yourself'. The American Medical Association published many a damning report calling Springer out for his falsification ('a most thorough search fails to show that Springer was ever graduated by any reputable college or university, medical or otherwise') although this does not appear to have impeded his entrepreneurialism – this included the creation of healing beverages under a variety of names, liquid miracle cure-alls which he hawked over the radio. In 1931 he upgraded, building himself his very own health spa called the somewhat funereal 'Haven of Rest' in Fort Hill, Pennsylvania, from which to better flog his products. Six years later, it was shut due to tax non-payment. Other resorts included Wilkes-Barre, Johnstown (see page X) as well as locations in Pennsylvania, Maryland and Iowa. In 1944 he found a murky oasis in the Mojave Desert and rather than acquiring the land, merely filed a mining claim to it (without any intention of mining) and then effectively squatted on the site. Using the homeless from L.A's Skid Row as free labour in return for room and board to build a cut price hotel, he named the spa ZZYZX Springs, or what he termed the 'last word in health' (alphabetically in the English language). This is very roughly pronounced a little like 'isaacs', but with a Z in front of it 'z-eye-saks' or to give it its less unwieldy former name, Soda Springs/Camp Soda. He also attributed the name to his desire to own the last word in the English language overall. There weren't actually any hot springs in the area, but not a man to be deterred by such trifles, Springer installed imitations in secret using a boiler to heat pools; no one knew the difference. In time the complex came to contain a 60 room hotel, church, health spa/mineral baths, radio studio (so as to sell more products), a private landing strip known as Zyport, a park called the 'Boulevard of Dreams' and a small castle. His radio show, carried at its peak by 221 stations in the US and 102 abroad, requested that listeners send in donations to obtain his cures which could solve everything from a headache to hitherto-terminal cancer. One of the many products Springer had on sale, just to set the tone, was 'Mo-Hair' (a mixture of salt and mud to be rubbed on the head whilst holding one's breath, with facial redness listed as an indicator that the product was working). Visitors were also fed goat milk, two sermons a day over loud speaker plus further requests for cash, a haemorrhoid cure and life-prolonging tea largely made from parsley juice. Springer was eventually evicted in '74 and convicted of false advertising, for which he served jail time before moving to Las Vegas (of course) where he died in 1985. The name Zzyzx was featured in a book called Beyond Language in 1977, having been spotted on an old San Bernardino map, leading further atlases to relabel the area as 'Zzyzx' without the 'Springs'. The names were subsequently approved as a place name by the US Board on Geographic Names in 1984 and remains the USBGN's lexicographically greatest (alphabetically last in Latin order) place name. It featured as a site in which bodies were buried in Michael Connelly novel 'The Narrows': 'I knew the road. Or more accurately, I knew the sign. Anybody from L.A. who made the road trip to and from Las Vegas as often as I had in the last year would have known it. At just about the halfway point on 15 Freeway was the Zzyzx Road exit, recognizable by its unique name

> Top: Amboy Ghost Town
> Bottom: Zzyzx Mineral Springs

THE INNER NEVADA TRAIL ROUTE 10

if nothing else. It was in the Mojave and it appeared to be a road to nowhere. No gas station, no rest stop. At the end of the alphabet and at the end of the world.' A prehistoric quarry site (which leads the area to yield arrow heads and rock art to this day), the remains of a wagon stop and railroad artefacts can also be seen lying around.

9. THE MOJAVE DESERT MAILBOX
35.1854, -115.6928

Old Government Road, Nipton, CA 92364
Don't expect the postal service to be quick from this mail box, the most deserted in the USA, but do open it and sign the guestbook.

10. MOJAVE PHONE BOOTH
35.28567 -115.68443
Nipton, CA 92364 (defunct)
deuceofclubs.com
A phone booth installed in the Sixties six miles from the nearest asphalt road, 15 from the nearest highway and many more from anywhere meaningful may since have died a death, but its legacy lives on in the digital space. The number is (760) 733 9969. It was built for local miners, first as a hand-cranked device and then as a payphone. Visitors have been known to await calls at the location, recording the conversations they have. In '99 an LA Times Writer reported on a man at the booth who claimed that the Holy Spirit had directed him to answer a call, leading him to spend 32 days there answering over 500 of them including several from one man called 'Sergeant Zeno from the Pentagon'. The phone booth has recently been removed but its number has been reinstated using Voice Over IP; calling it connects to a conference line allowing one to connect to strangers in a similar manner as before. SMSs with the words SUBSCRIBE ALIAS to 760-733-9969 will join group chat.

11. PIONEER SALOON
35.83253 -115.43191
310 NV-161, Goodsprings, NV 89019
www.pioneersaloon.info
Clark Gable drank in this saloon after receiving word of the death of his wife. It has been featured in endless movies and shoots and is a great place to visit to get a feel for the real old Wild West.

12. SEVEN MAGIC MOUNTAINS
35.8384, -115.27091
S Las Vegas Blvd, Las Vegas, NV 89054
sevenmagicmountains.com
Colourful 2 year public art installation by Swiss artist Ugo Rondinone, featuring seven 35 ft. high day-glow totems; makes for great desert photography.

13. NELSON
35.7096, -114.8037
Nelson Cutoff Rd, Searchlight, NV 89046
Notorious Techatticup Mine, scene of killings so regular as to be an ordinary daily occurrence due to management disagreements. Named for Charles Nelson, a camp leader

murdered in his home with four others in 1897 by the renegade Indian, Avote, the town was previously called Eldorado and has a population of 37.

14. THE SIMPSONS' HOUSE
36.0773 , -115.0154
712 Red Bark Ln, Henderson, NV 89011
Visit one of the most iconic family homes in the USA, built as a competition prize.

15. LONNIE HAMMARGRENS HOUSE
36.1114, -115.0921
4318 Ridgecrest Drive, Las Vegas, NV 89121
This American politician and retired NASA flight neurosurgeon has spent his life collecting curious Vegas antiques such as old Nevada casino signs and an Apollo space capsule as well as casually purchasing the High Roller roller coaster from the Stratosphere, as we all would if we were better off than we are. He also notably held what he termed an 'Awake Wake' for himself, in which he held a funeral service in full New Orleans Jazz Funeral style, and buried himself in a sarcophagus in the Egyptian tomb in his garage, emerging an hour later, in a scene which Gob of Arrested Development would have appreciated.

16. PINBALL HALL OF FAME
36.10131, -115.13051
1610 E Tropicana Ave, Las Vegas, NV 89119
www.pinballmuseum.org
Now twice the size of its previous incarnation, the sparkling new Pinball Hall of Fame or 'PHoF' as it is better known is now closer to the Strip and replete with even more pinball. 10,000 foot of pinball to be exact.

17. HEART ATTACK GRILL
36.16945, -115.14075
450 Fremont St #130, Las Vegas, NV 89101
www.heartattackgrill.com
This hospital themed restaurant aggressively and proudly promotes an unhealthy diet of incredibly large hamburgers, and who are we to disagree with that. Customers are referred to as 'patients', orders are 'prescriptions', waitresses are nurses and special treatment is given to those weighing over 350 pounds – they are provided unlimited free food provided they weigh themselves

< Top: The Simpsons' House
Top: Heart Attack Grill
Overleaf: Seven Magic Mountains

THE INNER NEVADA TRAIL ROUTE 10

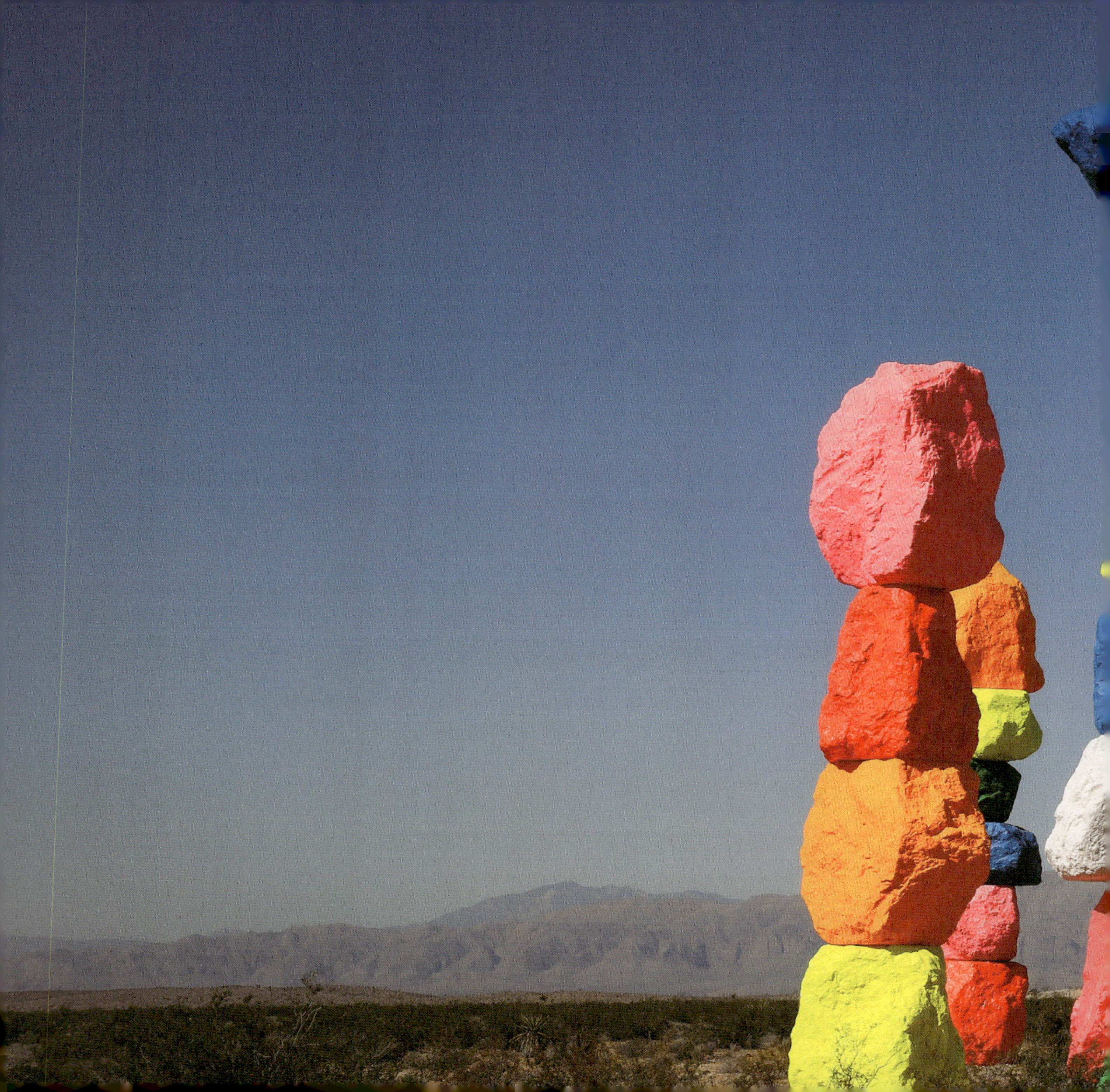

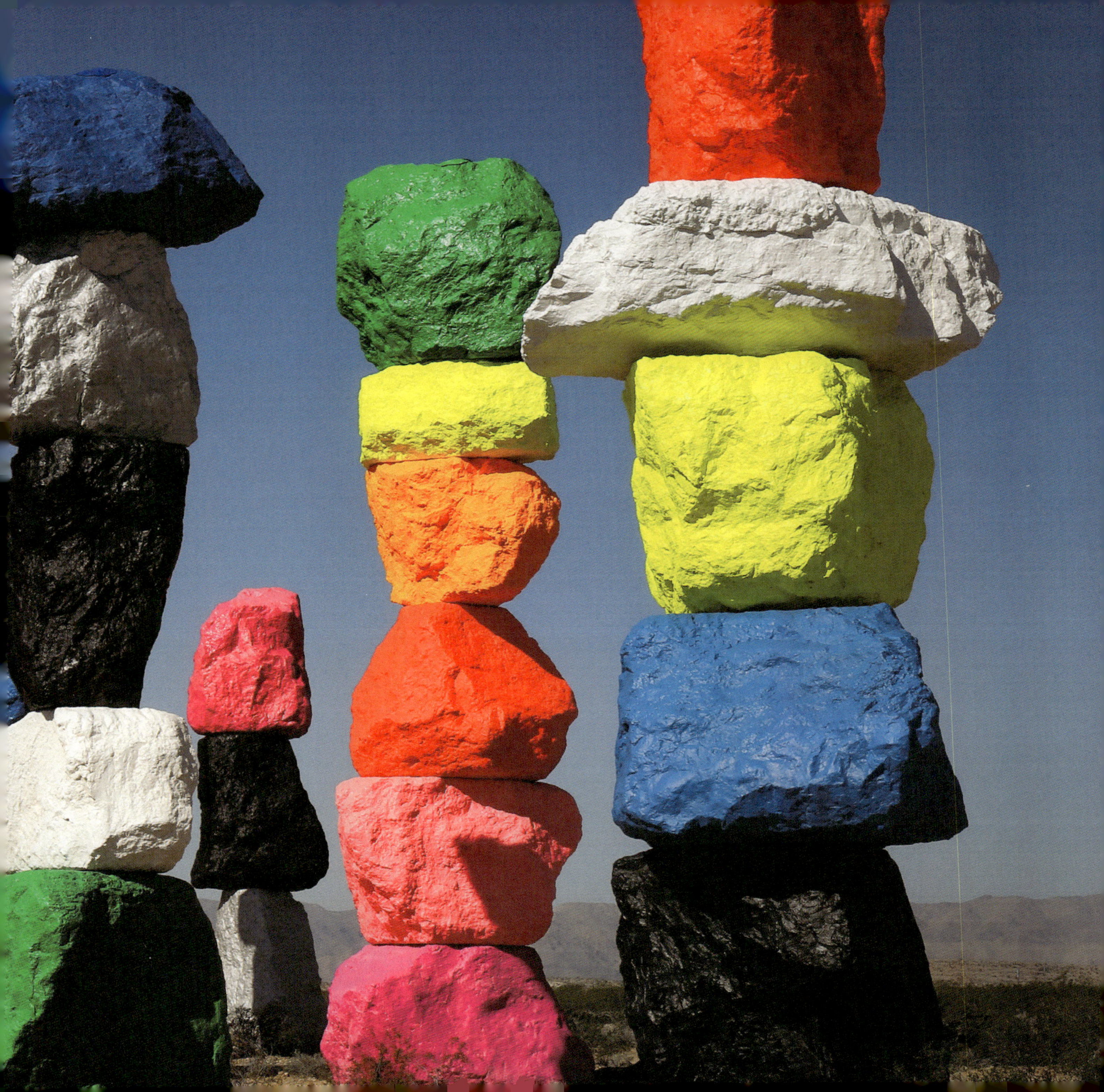

OFFBEAT AMERICA

on an electronics cattle scale in front of cheering hoards. Choose from the Single Bypass Burger®, Double Bypass Burger®, Triple Bypass Burger®, Quadruple Bypass Burger®, Quintuple Bypass Burger™, Sextuple Bypass Burger™, Septuple Bypass Burger™, and the Octuple Bypass Burger™, the latter reaching four pounds of beef, or why not try the Flatliner Fries® cooked in pure lard, the Coronary Dog™, or Lucky Strike no filter cigarettes all washed down with a ton of alcohol, or perhaps for the kids, the Butterfat Milkshakes™, full fat coke or candy cigarettes. Should you be enough of a failure at life to neglect to empty your plate, guests are the recipients of hardcore spankings by the staff. The folks at Guiness have awarded the Quadruple Bypass Burger®, the World's Most Calorific Burger at a whopping 9,983 calories, although they have yet to consider the Quintuple through to the Octuple, perhaps out of fear for their health. Free wheelchair service is provided to anyone finishing their Quadruple Bypass Burger®, and the owner of the joint, Dr. Jon (a non-AMA recognised doctor of course), divides his time between flipping patties in a lab coat and being hounded by the press and government; in 2006 he staved off a public threat of closure from the Attorney General's Office. Rarely far from the press, the Heart Attack Grill in 2010 was the globally number one most searched term on Google when its 570 pound spokesman died at 29, whilst in 2012 it again hit the limelight when two customers actually suffered heart attacks whilst dining in the establishment – Dr. Jon's response? That such occurences were inevitable when dealing with a clientele at the quote unquote 'avant-guarde of nutritional risk takers'. The following year the restaurant's second spokesman died, this time of a heart attack while leaving the premises having never missed a single day's attendance in the restaurant – his ashes are displayed above the bar.

18. GOLDEN NUGGET
36.17057, -115.14546
129 Fremont Street Experience, Las Vegas, NV 89101
www.goldennugget.com
Few appear to actually be aware that deep inside the renowned casino The Golden Nugget lies an actual large golden nugget for which it was named back at its inception.

19. ST THOMAS
36.46631, -114.37066
Old Saint Thomas Road, St Thomas, NV 89040
A Nevada ghost town on the Colorado River, abandoned when nearby Lake Mead flooded the entire town; it was founded by Mormon settlers led by Thomas Smith himself in 1865 and had over 500 inhabitants. The Mormons left due to a fabulous quirk in 1871 - the state line was shifted one degree longitude to the east in a land survey, meaning that the Mormons had failed to settle in the Promised Land of Utah by one degree - they had in fact settled in Nevada. Nevada then excitedly welcomed them by landing them with a tax bill, conveniently payable only in gold, for all their unpaid previous years of occupancy, whereupon they went on the lam without paying.

20. AVIATION NAVIGATION ARROW
37.06483, -113.59541
St George, UT 84790
In the 1920s, when the first regularly scheduled overland passenger flights were being made in the USA, 50 foot concrete arrows such as this (one of four in the St. George area) were placed at 10 mile intervals to aid the navigation of mail and passenger planes, alongside steel towers which held coal oil lamps which illuminated the arrows after dark. In the absence of radar or radio guidance, when visual guidance was the only method available to pilots, some 1500 such beacons and arrows were built from New York to San Francisco to help pilots fly by night in what was the world's first such system. A white beacon light similar to a light house would flash regularly, whilst red and green lights beneath would flash a Morse Code letter to identify the beacon. Many still exist across the USA.

21. THE NARROWS
37.305, -112.94911
The Narrows Bottom Up, Hurricane, UT 84737
Situated next to the alluringly named 'Mountain of Mystery', this stunning river

< Left: Golden Nugget
< Right: Aviation Navigation Arrow

THE INNER NEVADA TRAIL ROUTE 10

Bottom: Atomic Survival Town
> Right: The Narrows
Overleaf: Neon Boneyard

canyon is not to be missed. Research of the area will provide you with numerous natural beauty spots to visit here.

22. NEON BONEYARD
36.1776, -115.1342
770 N Las Vegas Blvd, Las Vegas, NV 89101
www.neonmuseum.org
A stunning tribute to old Vegas, this collection of giant original Casino signs and the stories behind them will give you real insight into the history underlying the Strip and the wacky entrepreneurs that established it.

23. LITTLE A'LE'INN
37.64681, -115.74588
1 Old Mill Rd, Alamo, NV 89001
www.littlealeinn.com
You know you are in outback Nevada when the first thing an inn's website says is 'there is no gas available in town, please fill your tank in Alamo from the east or Tonopah from the west'. This charming inn, run by Pat for over 25 years, says of its UFO-centric name: 'Some believe the name to sound like an inn that serves ale (ale inn), while others believe it to mean alien. We leave this up to you to decide. We like the sounds of both.' They also advise 'Look up as the truth lies there. Always keep your eyes to the skies whenever you can. You just never know when that special event will happen. At those times there may be no answers, leaving you only to wonder what just happened or what you saw, and having to ask more questions... getting no answers. Life is a mystery, enjoy the ride. The events and unidentified flying objects we see and only hear at times in this area often leave us shaking our heads. The unknown is what we live for. The times when logic escapes us and the knowledge of things to come are before us. We welcome it all'. Nuff said.

24. ATOMIC SURVIVAL TOWN
37.0688, -116.04419
Tours required from National Atomic Testing Museum, see belowhttp://nationalatomictestingmuseum.org/
Once the site of 1955 Pleasantville style houses filled with lifelike human dummy families who were nuked so that the effects upon them could be viewed. The location inspired Call of Duty's Nuketown and today remains open for public tours which depart from the National Atomic Testing Museum (755 E Flamingo Rd, Las Vegas, NV, 89119). Google Earth reveals giant blast sites.

25. DEVIL'S HOLE
36.42523, -116.29087
Devils Hole, Nevada 89060
This hole is a tiny body of water in an otherwise arid area of Death Valley and contains its very own species which exist only in this one location on Earth - the pupfish. In 1965, kids David Rose and Paul Giantontieri and one other jumped the fence and entered the area – one turned tail and returned home but David and Paul never made it back out. Divers dived to 315 foot deep to try to locate them, a record diving depth at

OFFBEAT AMERICA

THE INNER NEVADA TRAIL ROUTE 10

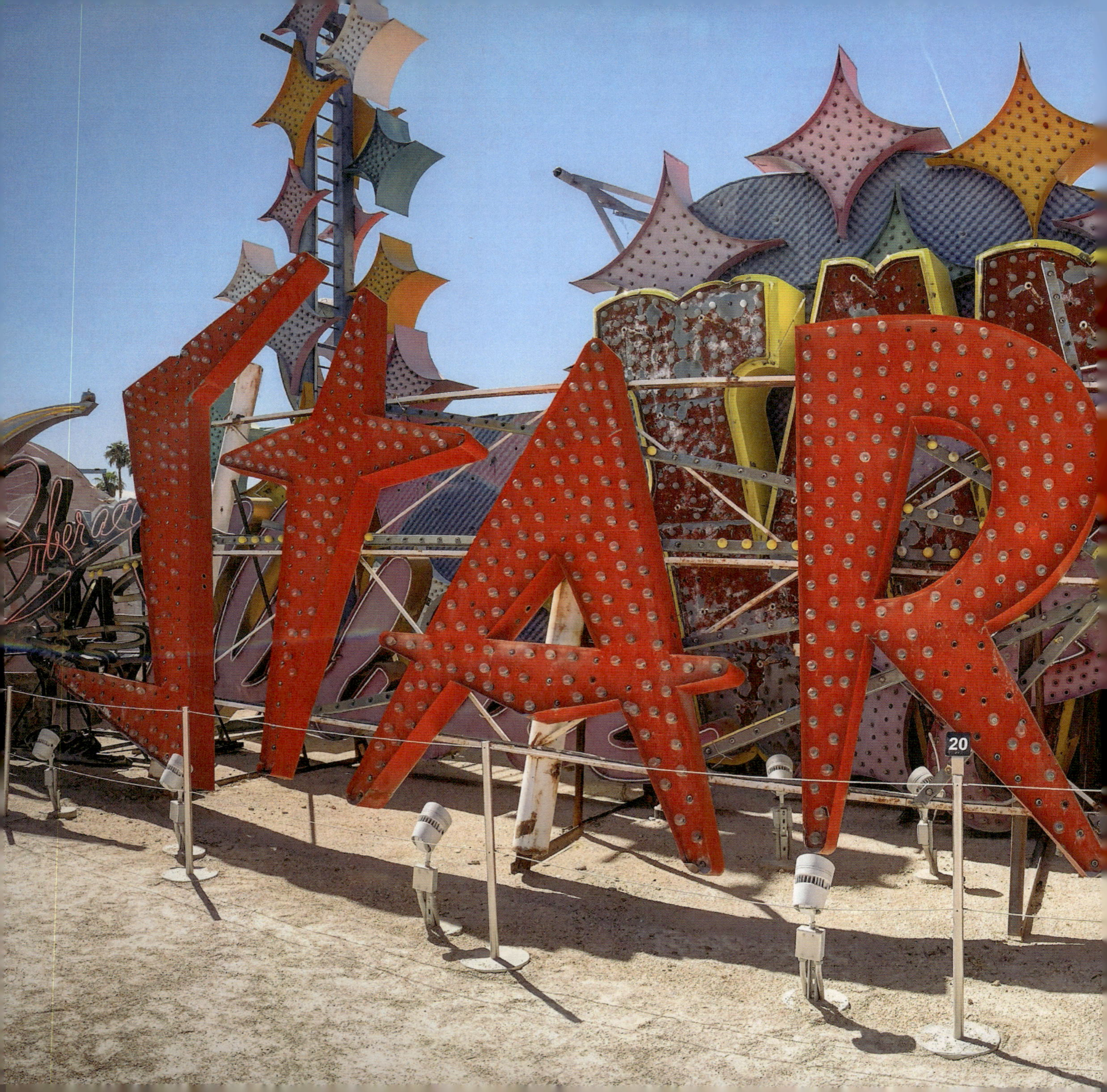
STAR
20

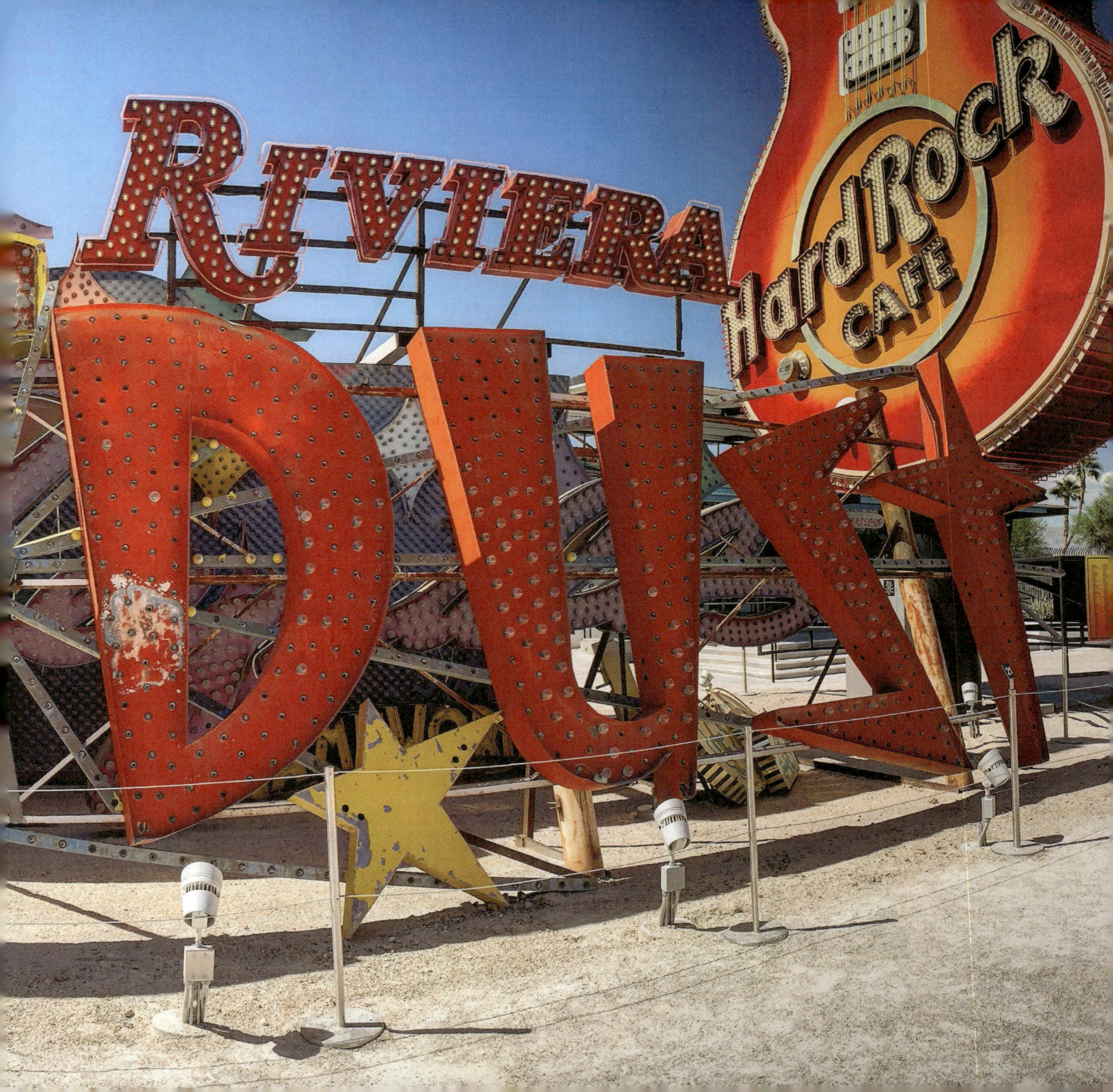
RIVIERA
Hard Rock
CAFE

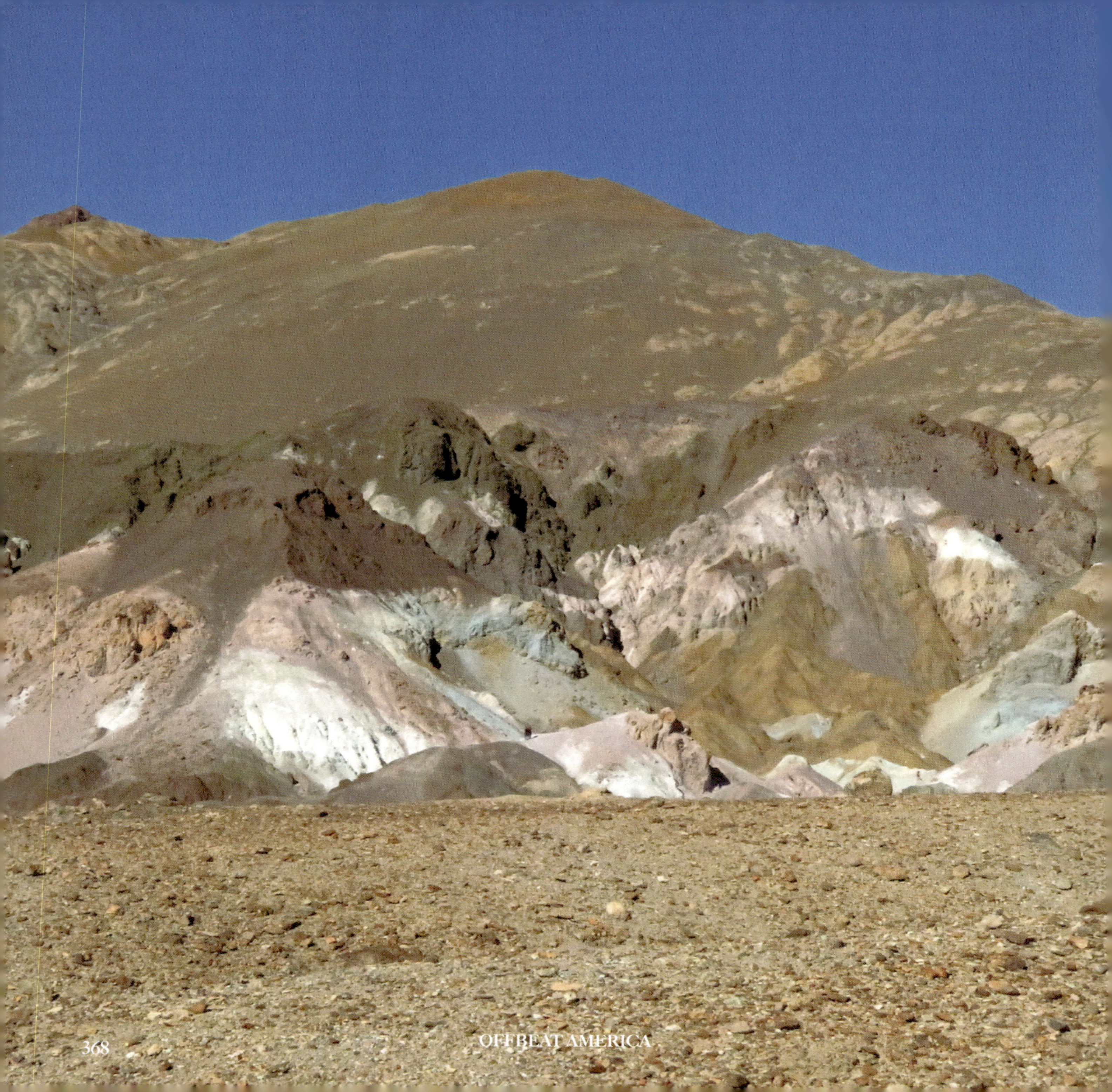

< Left: Artist's Drive
Below: Badwater Basin

the time but found no bodies, only their dive chart and a failing flashlight. It was thought that air pockets exist in the incredibly deep dark water-filled cavern hole, but no one knew where and they were so deep that they were unreachable. Experts trying to recover the boys went to extraordinary lengths (and depths), struggling in the darkness to retain their sense of bearings to find the boys, but despite locating a mask, snorkel and one fin, they said that at such a depth one begins to get 'nitrogen narcosis', a drunken state of confusion and light headedness and were only able to establish that the depths go down to over 900 foot.

26. ARTIST'S DRIVE
36.37042, -116.82419
Artists Dr, Furnace Creek, CA 92328
Naturally occurring colours make this Death Valley drive ultra photogenic.

27. THE SAILING STONES OF DEATH VALLEY
36.6816, -177.5633
Death Valley National Park, Racetrack Playa, California
These famed moving stones leave trails in their wake but are never seen to move to the naked eye.

28. BADWATER BASIN
36.24608, -116.8185
Badwater Basin, California
These much photographed salt flats are a wonder to behold and a death valley must see.

29. BALLARAT GHOST TOWN
36.04757, -117.22416
Ballarat Rd, Trona, CA 93592
Ballarat, an 1897 town named by an itinerant Australian, has one full time resident, most recently Rocky Novak who lives in the town with his dogs Potlicker and Brownie; in its heyday the town claimed some 500 residents including renowned Death Valley prospector Seldom Seen Slim. Each summer, a lady called June and her son arrive in town and stay in the former morgue (perhaps it's cool?). Charles Manson was also a fan of the area; he

and his Family lived in Barker Ranch to the south of the town, and left graffiti in some Ballarat buildings as well as what was rumoured to be one of his abandoned desert trucks, a 1942 Dodge power wagon driven by Charlie and Tex Watson which can be found on the left of the main intersection in the town. Tex Watson fled in this vehicle from the police when they raided Barker Ranch (located in a remote area of the mountains above Ballarat). Closer inspection of the interior roof will reveal pentagram graffiti left by Manson and his followers including Bobby Beausoleil who confirmed from prison that this is indeed the power wagon he left at Spahn's Ranch in LA before he got arrested for the initial Manson family murder in July 1969 (www.beausoleil.net/wizard/index.html). Tex Watson is also on record stating that he drove one of the power wagons through the area and got stuck in the flats before hitch hiking to Trona and never came back.

30. RHYOLITE GHOST TOWN
36.90115, -116.82891
Beatty, NV 89003

A ghost town originally established in 1905, which due to the onset of the gold rush boasted electric lights, water mains, telephones, newspapers, a hospital, a school, an opera house and its very own stock exchange just two years later. It had a peak population of around 5,000 in 1908. A combination of the crash and the San Francisco 1906 quake hit the town badly leading the mine to close in 1911, marking the end of the mining town like so many others of the era. By 1920, almost no one was resident in the town. Today the ruins of the Famous Players Lasky Corporation which owned Paramount Pictures, the Cook Bank building and others are still standing and can be visited. Slightly south of Rhyolite visitors can find the Rhyolite-Bullfrog Cemetery featuring many original wooden grave markers which have survived due to the dry conditions of the area. The area of Bullfrog in which the town sits is so named for its big green and yellow spotted rocks, whilst Rhyolite is a type of rock found in the area. The Amargosa River is named for the Spanish amargo or bitter, due its saline taste.

31. RHYOLITE'S DISTRICT OF SHADOWS
36.895, -116.83029
Beatty, NV, 89003

An important location relating to the Kcymaerxthaere project (a parallel universe that intersects with our own) - see a marker relating to it here and explore this world for yourself. If you are not familiar with the concept, Google it to discover this worldwide viral phenomenon invented by a Geographer called Eames Demtrios.

32. TOM KELLY'S BEER BOTTLE HOUSE
36.89739, -116.82909
Beatty, NV, 89003

This Rhyolite home was built during the gold rush in 1905 using 51,000 beer bottles and mud, standing as a testament to a man who presumably drank a lot and explained his folly by stating 'it's very difficult to build a house with lumber from a Joshua tree'. A fair point and a great example of the common practice of the era of building your castle out of whatever is lying around. Paramount Pictures restored the building for a movie in 1925.

33. INTERNATIONAL CAR FOREST OF THE LAST CHURCH
37.69819, -117.22857
Off Reed St, Goldfield, NV 89013

If there is one thing Nevada is good at, it's combining religion and scrap. Go for the name alone.

34. GOLDFIELD HOTEL
37.70805, -117.23568
69-79 Columbia Ave, Goldfield, NV 89013

At its opening in 1908, this hotel was the most spectacular in Nevada (which goes some way to reveal Nevada of the time). At its launch, champagne apparently flowed down its front steps. It stood unoccupied after WWII for many years until in 2003 it was bought by the evocatively-named Red Roberts, a rancher who hoped to refurbish it. As of yet this is incomplete.

35. CLOWN MOTEL
38.07215, -117.23777

> Top: Clown Motel
> Bottom left: Rhyolite's District of Shadows
> Bottom right: Goldfield Hotrel

CLOWN
MOTEL
SINGLE $3950 TAX
CLEAN RO OM 5
PETS OK DISH TV
CLOWN MOTEL
Single 3950
2 Persons 4250
3 Persons 4550
FREE INTERNET
TRUCKERS
GOOD RATES
PETS O.K.

GOLDFIELD HOTEL

OFFBEAT AMERICA

521 N Main St, Tonopah, NV 89049

It is probably unnecessary to describe this further, other than to confirm that all the rooms are fully clown decorated and to add that it is located next to a graveyard. Coulrophobic's beware. A recent Kickstarter campaign funded an author to live in the Motel for a month and document his experiences, which included discovering fake blood on the curtains and staving off the many resident feral black cats. A favourite with truckers, a box on the check-in desks sells clown noses for $1 just to ensure that all guests are rendered as disturbing as the décor. Look out for the cleaner who works dressed as a clown and if the clown portrait above your bed is disturbing you, just let the management know and they will cover it.

36. OLD TONOPAH CEMETERY

38.07213, -117.2388

917-923 N Main St, Tonopah, NV 89049 (next to the Clown Motel)

Because every clown motel needs a creepy cemetery and every creepy cemetery needs a clown motel.

37. COALDALE

38.02711, -117.89009

Off US 6, Nevada

What happens if a town bases all its income on one diner and one gas station? In short, it had better hope they don't go out of business. Sadly the gas station did as it was leaking gas into the ground (not looked upon favourably) which in turn killed the diner traffic, and took the town with it. At last check, the diner was complete with cooking utensils sitting on the hob, abandoned like the Marie Celeste.

38. ERICK SCHATS BAKKERY (sic)

37.36784, -118.3957

763 N Main St, Bishop, CA 93514

www.erickschatsbakery.com

This delicious bakery bakes ten loaves of bread for every resident in its town, every single day.

39. DEVIL'S POSTPILE NATIONAL MONUMENT

37.62509, -119.0849

Devils Postpile Access Road, Mammoth Lakes, CA 93546

A stunning natural occurrence that makes for wonderful landscape photography.

40. THE AHWAHNEE HOTEL

37.74615, -119.57433

1 Ahwahnee Drive, Yosemite National Park, CA 95389

www.travelyosemite.com

This Yosemite hotel provided the interiors for Kubrick's The Shining.

41. SQUABBLETOWN

38.01464, -120.3863

Squabbletown, CA 95370

It is thought that this town was literally named for an argument, either over a girl or over a gold mining claim, although which we may never know. The town sign is repeatedly stolen, particularly since Squabbletown made the Top 10 Most Embarrassing Or Unfortunate Town Names list.

42. MERCER CAVERNS

38.1453, -120.4497

1665 Sheep Ranch Rd, Murphys, CA 95247

www.mercercaverns.com

Show caverns first discovered by Walter Mercer in 1885 which were originally an ancient burial ground for a prehistoric Indian Tribe called the Yokuts. The tribe treated it as a mortuary cave, rolling bodies

< Left: International Car Forest (prior page)
Right: The Ahwahnee Hotel

down inside from the opening as the area was sacred and entry was forbidden. It was originally named New Calaveras Cave (New Skull Cave) for the skeletons Mercer found inside but as it was being used as a show cave, to avoid claims of indecency the name was changed.

43. BODIE STATE HISTORICAL PARK
38.21176, -119.01148

Hwy 270, Bridgeport, CA 93517

This slice of the American gold rush remains almost perfectly immortalised in the breathtaking hills of Yosemite National Park, featuring buildings such as hotels, saloons and a school where the writing is still clearly on the blackboard. A stunning visit worth every bit of the drive.

44. GRIMES POINT PREHITORIC ROCK ART & HIDDEN CAVE
39.40672, -118.62692

Off Lincoln Hwy, Fallon, NV 89406

This petroglyph-filled cave was first visited by Native Americans some 8000 years ago and was still filled with their ancient treasures when it was discovered.

45. THE SHOE TREE, MIDDLEGATE
39.2943, 117.9867

The Shoe Tree, 41763 Lincoln Hwy, Fallon, NV 89406

A shoe tree on the Loneliest Road in America, allegedly commemorating the day when a newlywed pair had an argument beneath a tree where they were camping; when she threatened to leave, her husband threw her shoes into the tree to ruin her plan, before marching off to the nearby Middlegate Station Bar for a drink. Add your shoes and try the Station Bar burger challenge while there to win a t-shirt.

WHILE IN SACRAMENTO, WHY NOT CHECK OUT:

All entries from *COOL PATCH PUMPKINS* to *PRESTON SCHOOL OF INDUSTRY*, pages 337 to 335 (it is more convenient to follow the entries in reverse order from Cool Patch to Preston)

WHILE IN SAN FRANCISCO, WHY NOT CHECK OUT:

All entries from *BURLINGAME MUSEUM OF PEZ* to *PLAYLAND NOT AT THE BEACH*, pages 327 to 334

Above and right: Bodie State Historical Park

THE INNER NEVADA TRAIL ROUTE 10

SAN FRAN TO THE MIDWEST ROUTE 11

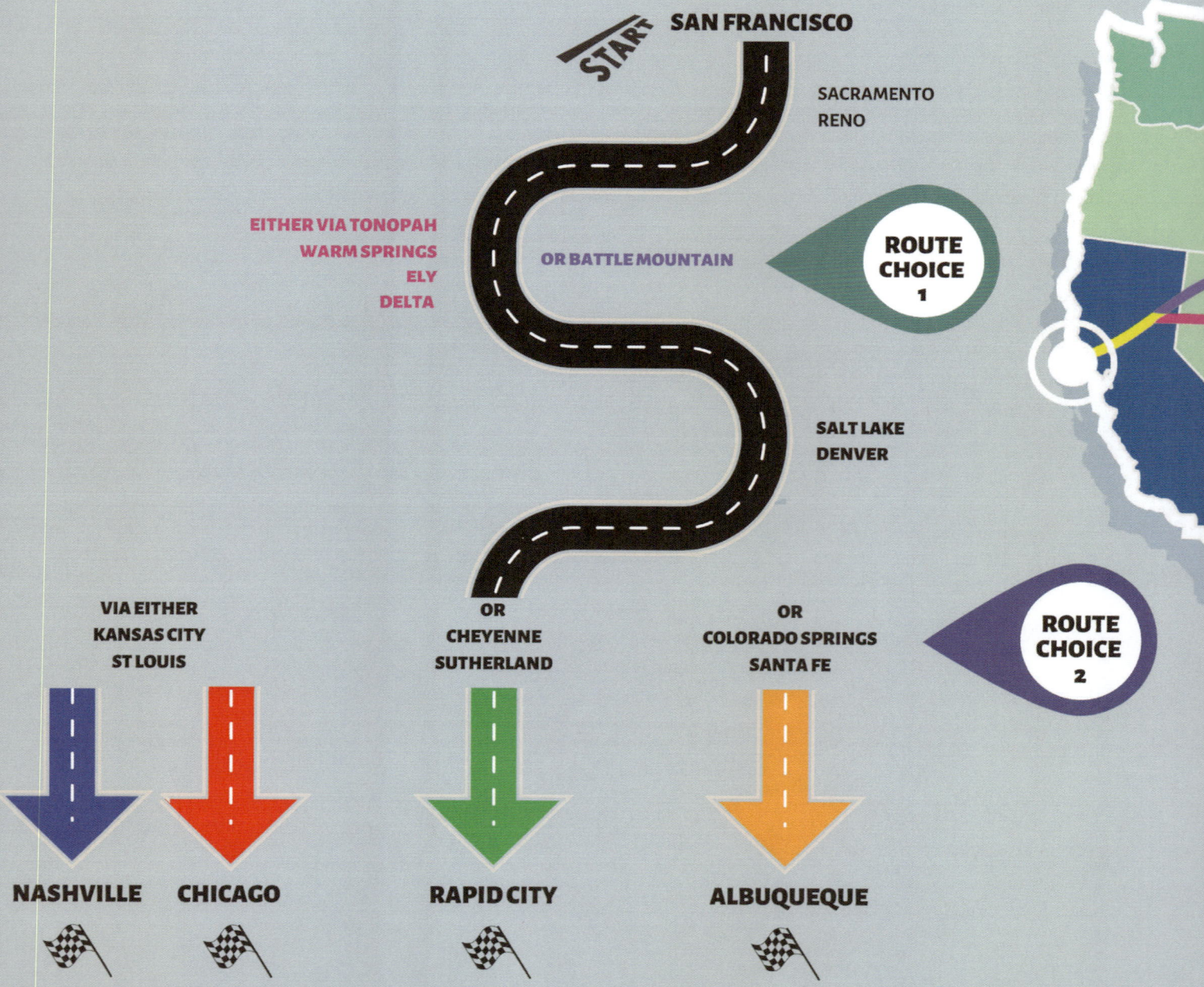

START — SAN FRANCISCO

SACRAMENTO
RENO

EITHER VIA TONOPAH
WARM SPRINGS
ELY
DELTA

OR BATTLE MOUNTAIN

ROUTE CHOICE 1

SALT LAKE
DENVER

ROUTE CHOICE 2

VIA EITHER
KANSAS CITY
ST LOUIS

OR
CHEYENNE
SUTHERLAND

OR
COLORADO SPRINGS
SANTA FE

NASHVILLE   **CHICAGO**   **RAPID CITY**   **ALBUQUEQUE**

SAN FRAN TO THE MIDWEST

377

SAN FRAN TO THE MIDWEST ROUTE 11

Begin your journey at hippy-chic San Fran, home of Silicon Valley and The Rock, filling up on top price coffee and fortune cookies in China Town in preparation for your journey to the Mormon's Promised Land. Visit Utah's answer to Holi festival, broaden your comparative religion horizons by glimpsing the Summum Pyramid, before promptly narrowing your cultural view again with a drive past the 'Up' house. See stunning petroglyphs along Nine Mile Canyon, bring yourself back to earth with a selfie infront of a giant Goose before eating at the most wonderfully gaudy Mexican restaurant ever created.

WHILE IN SAN FRANCISCO, WHY NOT CHECK OUT:

All entries from *BURLINGAME MUSEUM OF PEZ* to *PLAYLAND NOT AT THE BEACH*, pages 327 to 334

WHILE IN SACRAMENTO, WHY NOT CHECK OUT:

All entries from *COOL PATCH PUMPKINS* to *PRESTON SCHOOL OF INDUSTRY*, pages 337 to 335 it is more convenient to follow the entries in reverse order from Cool Patch to Preston)

Above: Summam Pyramid (later in chapter)

SAN FRAN TO THE MIDWEST ROUTE II

379

AT RENO, NOW CHOOSE:

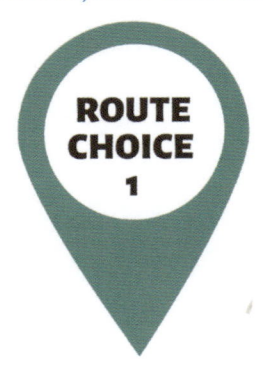

ROUTE CHOICE 1

PINK ROUTE

Or skip to page 381 to follow **PURPLE ROUTE** to Battle Mountain
WHY NOT CHECK OUT:
HIDDEN CAVE AT GRIMES POINT – SEE P 374

1. LEHMAN CAVES
39.00558, -114.21989
5500 NV-488, Baker, NV 89311
Cave full of intricate and rare formations.

2. U-DIG FOSSILS
39.3474, -112.56759
U-Dig Fossils, 350 East 300 South Delta, Utah, 84624
Where the prehistoric is up for grabs – the average visitor finds ten to twenty trilobites in a four-hour period.

3. THISTLE GHOST TOWN
39.9919, -111.4946
Thistle, UT 84629
A landslide killed this town and it lies much as it was left in the intervening days after the disaster.

4 SRI SRI RADHA KRISHNA TEMPLE
40.0757, -111.66211
8628 S State Rd, Spanish Fork, UT 84660
Try to time this one to coincide with their phenomenal festival of colour, akin to Holi festival in India.

5. SATAN'S LAND
40 -111.6199
Between Sierra Vista Way and Mountain Vista Pkwy, Provo, UT 84606
In the midst of Mormon country sits this area of undeveloped land, previously an old iron factory and now a refuge for misspent youth, leading to its local and somewhat judgemental moniker of 'Satan's Land'.

JUMP TO THE UP HOUSE p. 385 TO CONTINUE YOUR JOURNEY

PURPLE ROUTE TO BATTLE MOUNTAIN

6. BIG RIG JIG
3 -115.1 40
1028 Fremont St, Las Vegas, NV 89101
This phenomenal installation of two giant upended artic trucks has to be seen to be believed - it is soon to be installed permanently in Vegas, after recently travelling to the UK to be a part of Banksy's Dismaland exhibit.

WHILE IN THE VEGAS AREA, WHY NOT CHECK OUT ROUTE 10,

ENTRIES 12-22, p. 358 to 363

7. FLY GEYSER
4 -119.3319
County Rd 34, Gerlach, NV 89412
This awe-inspiring conical geyser displaying naturally occurring fantastic colours was the result of human drilling for geothermal water leaving behind an abandoned geyser, which then accumulated deposits around the drill site over time, building to its present conical form.

8. ARMPIT OF AMERICA
40.6365, -116.94299
Broad St., Battle Mountain, NV 89820
Situated on a road variously described as running through 'a desert, but lacking in any desert-type beauty', 'nondescript scrub that resembles acre upon acre of toilet brushes buried to the hilt' and 'flatter than any cliché – even pancakes have a certain doughy topology', it was proclaimed as the Armpit of America by a Washington Post Sunday Magazine writer in 2001 and has since taken on the moniker as a certain point of pride (perhaps by default, devoid of any other). Upon his return some time later, in a piece pitched at revealing the beauty of the location and redeeming his view of it, the Post journalist added that to appreciate Battle Mountain, you would need to 'take a small town, remove any trace of history, character, or charm. Allow nothing with any redeeming qualities within city limits – this includes food, motel beds, service personnel. Then place this pathetic assemblage of ghastly buildings and nasty people on a freeway in the midst of a harsh,

< Right: Sri Sri Radha Krishna Temple
< Left: U-Dig Fossils Trilobite Cemetery
Above: Fly Geyser
Overleaf: Big Rig Jig

SAN FRAN TO THE MIDWEST ROUTE 11

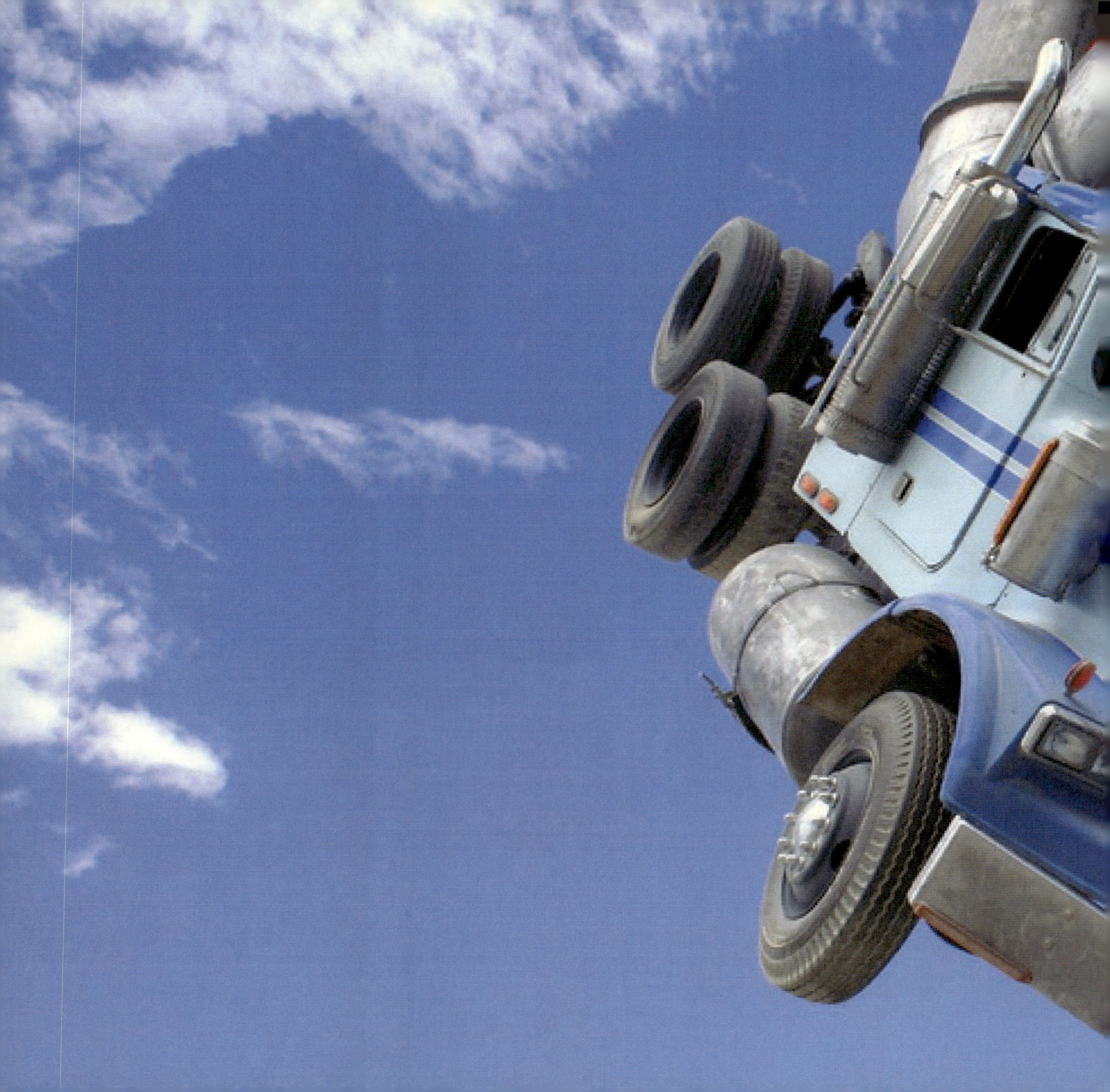

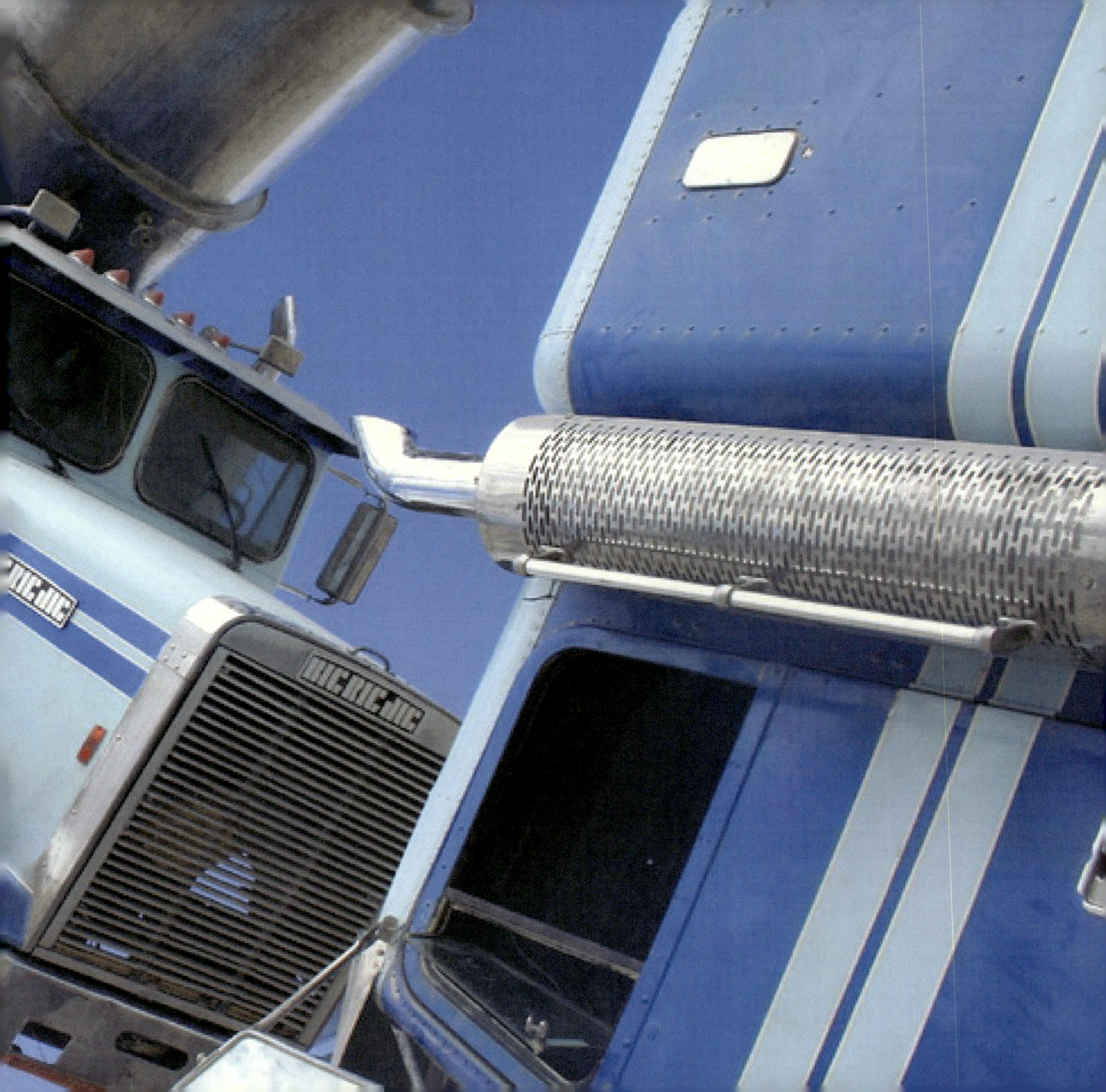

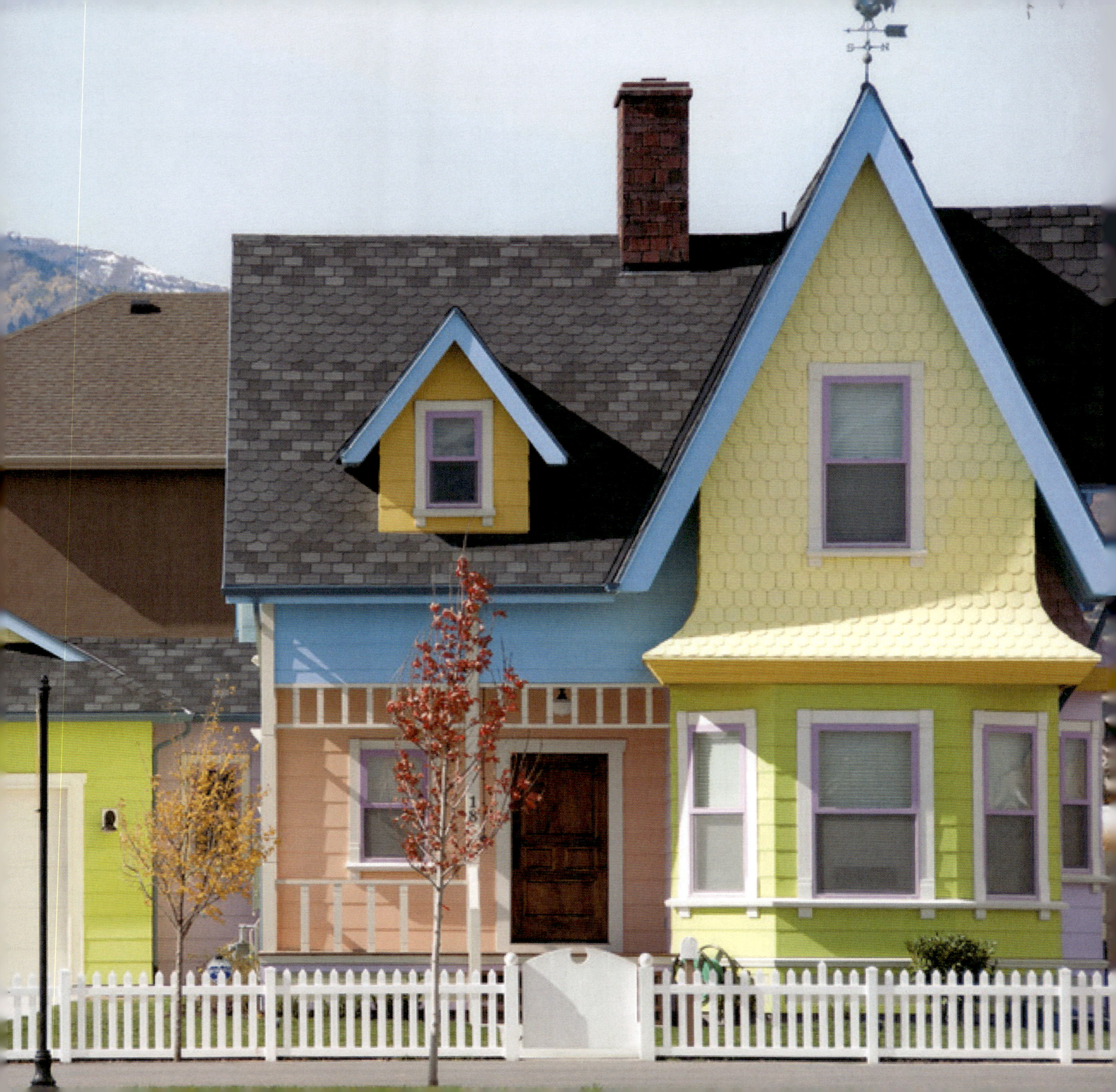

uninviting wilderness, far enough from the nearest city to be inconvenient but not so far for it to develop character of its own. You have now created Battle Mountain, Nevada'. The town has two famous ex-residents, the first a General James H. Ledlie described by President Ulysses S. Grant as 'the greatest coward of the Civil War' and journalist W. J. Forbes, who having attempted to launch an intelligent newspaper for thinkers in the town which promptly failed, spiralled into depression and drink. Upon his death it was said that he was 'One of the brightest geniuses the coast had ever seen, but he lived in communities where his mental brightness was more envied than appreciated', leading the Washington Post to add that the town is 'where genius comes to die'. Battle Mountain's true name came from an attack by Shoshones on a group of white people back in 1857, (it generally appears to be the rule that a location is deemed a 'battle' if the whites won, or a 'massacre' if the Indian's came out on top.)

9. WORLD'S LARGEST STUFFED POLAR BEAR

40.8314, -115.764
Commercial Casino, 345 4th St, Elko, NV 89801
http://www.rollingstone.com/culture/features/fear-and-loathing-in-elko-19920123

The world's largest stuffed polar bear, immortalised in print by Hunter S. Thompson in his article for Rolling Stone 'Fear and Loathing in Elko' written in 1992.

NOW PINK AND PURPLE ROUTES CONVERGE IN SALT LAKE

10. THE UP HOUSE

40.51205, -112.01932
13218 Herriman Rose Blvd, Herriman, UT 84096
www.therealuphouse.com

Cute as a button, for animation fans.

11. GRAVESITE OF UTAH'S FIRST JEDI PRIEST

40.6816, -111.9946
4335 W 4100 S, West Valley City, UT 84120

...Presumably the Force was weak in this one.

12. THE SUMMUM PYRAMID

40.7506, -111.9116
707 Genesee Ave, Salt Lake City, UT 84104
www.summum.us

A rather culty group with a penchant for mummification. What's not to like. The religion formed in 1975 after Mr Corky Nowell encountered beings called 'Summa Individuals' who introduced him to the nature of creation and he decided to share these gifts with others. In 1980, he changed his name to the catchy Summum Bonum Amon Ra, or Corky Ra for short. The word 'summum' is Latin meaning 'highest' and in the context of this philosophy means 'the sum total of all creation'. The religion also differentiates between Summum (the name of the

< Left: The Up House
Right: White King

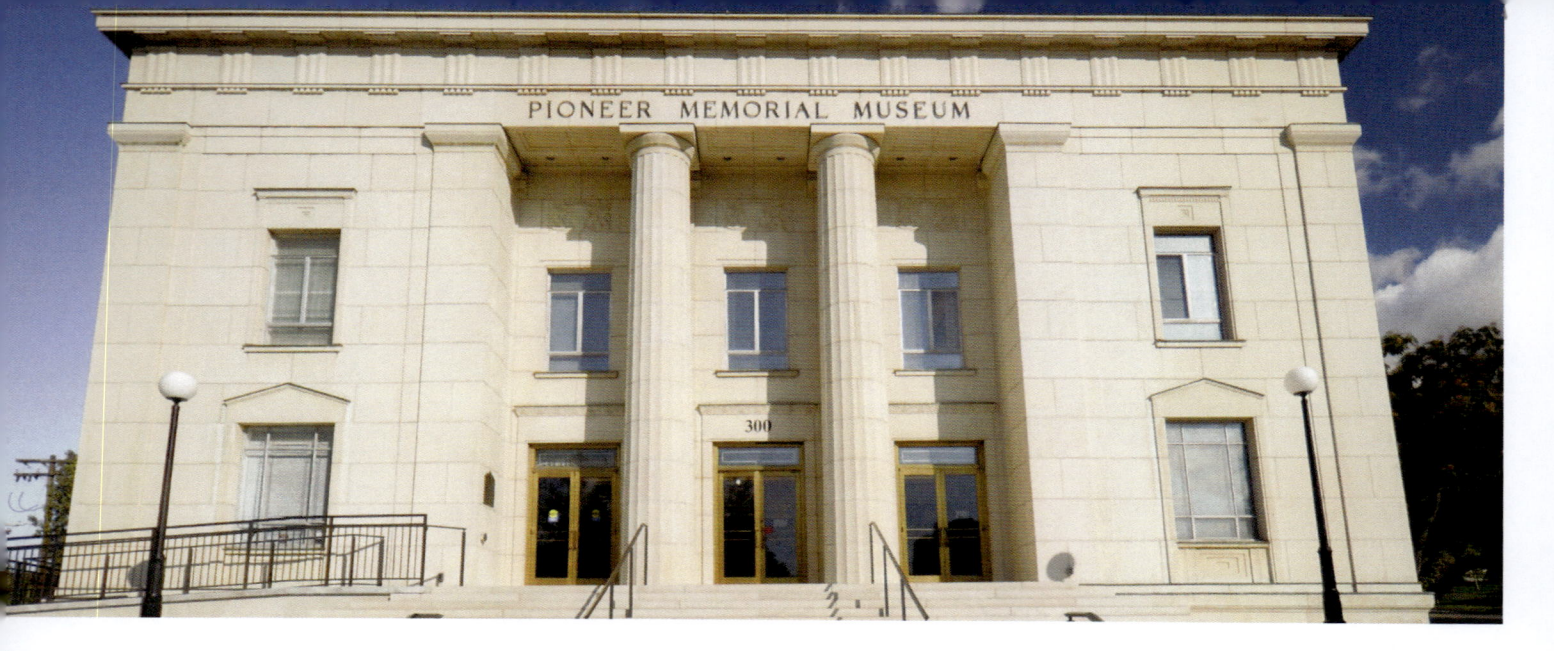

organisation) and SUMMUM (the totality of existence). Defining the religion's beliefs is somewhat convoluted but there is seemingly no recognised deity per se, rather that people are all part of the mind of the universe and that one must study and meditate upon that fact. It is said, rather logically, that our mental state dictates our feeling of wellbeing and harmony and that the resulting experiences we engender become part of our memories which then hold us captive. The religion also produces its own 'nectars' inside the pyramid, which are wines used in the practice of meditation. The government consider these nectars as wines and Summum therefore had to obtain a winery license to make them, rendering them Utah's first federally bonded winery. The group practices what it refers to as 'Modern Mummification', for which it was granted a religious exemption from the IRS for its mummification service. Both humans and pets may be mummified, with Nowell himself the first to undergo the process upon his death in 2008. His body is now held within a gold mummiform casket standing inside the pyramid. Read more about Pyramidology in Route 7 (page X).

13. THE PIONEER MEMORIAL MUSEUM
40.77661, -111.89114
300 North Main Street, Salt Lake City, UT 84103
www.dupinternational.org
The Mormons followed Joseph Smith to the promised land a.k.a. Utah and this museum documents their travels via related relics.

14. THE ANDERSON TOWER
40.776431, -111.883797
309 A St E, Salt Lake City, Utah
A misguided tourist attraction, this viewing tower was built on a hill to provide paying customers with a great view of the valley - unfortunately it suffered from the fact that non-paying customers already had a great view of the valley from the hill it was built on, rendering it entirely surplus to requirements.

15. THE SOLITUDE YURT
40.61985, -111.59188
12000 Big Cottonwood Canyon Rd, Solitude, UT 84121
www.skisolitude.com
If you are visiting in the winter, why not trek half a mile on snowshoes through a forest lit only by lanterns to reach a secluded yurt where gourmet chefs prepare a four course meal for you and your group.

16. VICTIM OF THE BEAST GRAVESTONE
40.7773, -111.8541

200 N St., Plot X- Block 1- Lot 169- Grave- 4 –East, Salt Lake City, Utah, 84116

Why was Lilly E. Gray deemed a 'Victim of The Beast 666' upon her death in 1958? Many theories abound including that she was a follower of Aleister Crowley (as he is known as The Beast 666) or that she was killed in a car crash on Highway 666 near her home. However, mental illness suffered by her incarcerated husband Elmer Gray is more likely to be the culprit: it is thought (based on rather outlandish writings in a Criminal Pardon's Application Gray sent to Utah State from prison) that not only did he believe himself 'kidnapped' by the government on account of allegedly being imprisoned without attending court (although this is unlikely to have been the case) but that he further attributed her death to similar 'kidnapping' and mistreatment by law enforcement, chosing this marker wording to reflect his feelings towards The Man. Her death certificate records that she died of 'natural causes'. In the application, he also ascribed his parents' deaths to grief at Lilly's 'kidnapping'. Unusually, Lilly married Elmer at the age of 72, (records indicate that her name was spelt Lily with one L rather than two, and her birth year as 1880 rather than 1881). Typos also pepper the Pardon application so this could have been in error. Elmer is buried in the same cemetery, although strangely some distance from Lilly. Their tombstones also hold clues: Lilly's is decorated with an evening primrose, symbolising hope, memory, sadness and eternal love, whilst Elmer's carries Narcissus, carrying connotations of narcissim, ego and vanity.

17. THE IS THE PLACE MONUMENT
40.75221, -111.81667
2601 Sunnyside Ave S, Salt Lake City, UT 84108
www.thisistheplace.org
A memorial to the place where Brigham Young brought his Mormon follows and declared the journey to the Promised Land complete.

18. THE SPIRAL JETTY
41.43769, -112.66885

< Top: The Pioneer Memorial Museum
Top left: Victim of the Beast Gravestone
Top right: This is the Place Monument

SAN FRAN TO THE MIDWEST ROUTE 11

387

Great Salt Lake, UT
www.spiraljetty.org
Making for a beautiful landscape shot if you time it right, this 1970 earth sculpture only appears above the water level at times of drought. The artist sadly died in a plane crash just 3 years after its creation.

NOW WHY NOT CHECK OUT:

SATAN'S LAND (p.380)
SRI SRI RADHA KRISHNA TEMPLE (p.380)
THISTLE GHOST TOWN (p.380)

19. NINE MILE CANYON
39.7762, -110.4964
9 Mile Canyon Road, Helper, UT 84526
An extraordinary stretch of open road adorned with 9 miles of ancient pictographs and petroglyphs by an ancient Native American people, many over 1,000 years old in origin.

20. SEGO
39.04145, -109.7115
Sego, UT 84540
This coal mining town was made rich by the railroad but died a death when the trains converted to diesel and two fires hit the wooden structures. Today a few structures, foundations and trails of smoke from the coal mines burning below ground remain of the town that once had 150 employees operating the mine.

21. DINOSAUR
40.24357, -109.01456
Dinosaur, CO 81610
The town of Dinosaur was originally named Artesia, but was renamed in 1966 to capitalise on the town's proximity to Dinosaur National Monument. Look out for dinosaur-oriented place naming like Tyrannosaurus Trail, Antrodemus Alley and Cletisaurus Circle.

22. HANGING LAKE
39.60139, -107.19172
70 County Road 125, Glenwood Springs, CO 81601
One of the clearest lakes you are ever likely to see and a natural marvel.

Top left: The Spiral Jetty
Bottom left: Nine Mile Canyon
Top right and > top left: Dinosaur
> Bottom: Hanging Lake

OFFBEAT AMERICA

23. HUNTER S THOMPSON SHRINE
39.1868, -106.8186
Snowmass
Aspen, Colorado, 81611 (near Gunner's View run)
Popular US author and journalist Thompson, perhaps most famous for Fear and Loathing in Las Vegas, killed himself in his Aspen home in 2005. Following his own wishes, his ashes were fired from a cannon on top of a self-built 153 ft. tall tower in the shape of a fist holding a peyote button to the sound of 'Mr Tambourine Man' accompanied by fireworks, in proceedings financed by Thompson's close friend and collaborator Johnny Depp. The shrine is cared for by 5 cult followers of Thompson's who go by the names Rusty Hematoma, Mister Z, R.W. Featherstone, Phlegm Thrower and Mr. Quick.

24. GILMAN CONTAMINATED MINING TOWN
39.53271, -106.39389
Off Highway 24 at 39.5370, -106.3914. The town can be seen from the higher areas of the road as Hwy 24 sharply bends whilst crossing Rock Creek.
A disaster area that can still be glimpsed from a distance although is not accessible (nor would close proximity be advisable). The boomtown of Gilman went from strength to strength after its founding in 1879. Despite the many highs and lows of the industry, Gilman managed to continue to operate and prosper until the seventies when an inspection of the town found that it, along with its surrounding 250 acres of land, were highly contaminated with multiple harmful substances including arsenic and lead which had infiltrated the water supply, leading to an immediate and full evacuation. By '84 the town was entirely closed down and today is in the process of being environmentally cleansed but its buildings including its school and bowling alley are still standing.

25. LEADVILLE'S ABANDONED SILVERMINE
39.2477, -106.2608
Co Rte 1, Leadville, CO 80461
This silver mine lies in ruins, with some of its original workings and ruins still visible.

26. CONEY ISLAND HOTDOG STAND
39.40828, -105.49356
Coney Island Hot Dog Stand, Bailey, CO 80421
This 1950s diner is a long way from home.

389

- shaped like a giant hot dog, it has been named the best piece of architecture in the state.

27. FROZEN DEAD GUY DAYS
39.9617, 105.5109
Nederland, Colorado, CO 80466

One man's extreme efforts to cryogenically preserve his grandfather (as well as a random hopeful stranger) are lauded at this festival which, originally a one-off theme suggestion for a Spring event, is now an annual occurrence. The process occurred in his own DIY 'cryoshed' at unfeasibly warm temperatures relative to cryogenics, after which the individual in question was unfortunately deported from the country. The shed was left in the care of a paid 'cryocarer' and today a portion of proceeds from the event go back to the grandson himself for the continued dubious preservation of his grandfather. Dress in chilly morbid costume to fit right in.

28. CAROUSEL OF HAPPINESS
39.9601, -105.51006
20 Lakeview Dr, Nederland, CO 80466
www.carouselofhappiness.org

This beautiful carousel has an extraordinary history - Charles I.D. Looff, one of the great carousel builders of the 19th century, came to the USA from Denmark at the age of 18 and 6 years later had hand carved Coney Island's first carousel. During his life he carved carousels for all over America, including one with 4 rows of horses for the stunning Mormon Saltair resort on Salt Lake, Utah in 1910 (see p. X). This survived multiple fires and natural disasters including being crushed by a rollercoaster during high winds, yet 2 of the 4 rows of horses were still able to be salvaged. Upon the resort's eventual bankruptcy in 1959, the carousel was gifted to a Utah state school for the disabled where it remained for 27 years until it was sold in 1986 by the school to a buyer who sadly only wanted to retain the animals. A Colorado resident, an ex-Marine who during Vietnam had kept his mind distracted from the trauma of war by listening to a tiny music box which reminded him of a carousel, bought the rest of the frame on a whim and spent the next 26 years hand carving animals for it without any prior experience, determined to return it to its former glory. Now, complete with its 50 animals, it can be visited in Colorado.

29. DENVER'S DINOSAUR HOTEL
39.65444, -105.07952
3440 S Vance St, Lakewood, CO 80227
www.bestwestern.com

A Best Western - with dinosaurs. A must for kids big and small.

30. CASA BONITA
39.741, -105.0709
6715 W Colfax Ave, Lakewood, CO 80214
www.casabonitadenver.com

There is little to no point trying to describe Casa Bonita other than to tell you that it is self-dubbed 'The Most Exciting Restaurant in the World.' Just... expect the unexpectedly kitsch (think the whole of Vegas distilled into one Mexican themed restaurant), watch South Park for reference and bemoan the closure of the other Casa Bonitas in what was once a glorious chain.

31. LINGER EATUARY
39.75952 -105.01144
2030 W 30th Ave, Denver, CO 80211
lingerdenver.com

Death-centric yet tasty, who can resist a restaurant which was a morgue in a previous life? The sign for Olinger Mortuaries has been slightly amended to read Linger Eatuaries and many of the original features from the morgue which held Buffalo Bill's body for six months remain such as the metal body conveyor belts for tables - see how many such details you can spot when you visit.

32. CHEESMAN PARK
39.73351, -104.96517
Cheesman Park, Denver, CO 80218

A great location for lovers of the historically macabre, the entirety of the land now called Cheesman park and about 240 acres besides was, in 1858, set aside for a beautiful garden cemetery to be named Mount Prospect. The rich and those of ill repute were to be buried in distinct areas, however when the cemetery rapidly filled with those of ill repute who

> Top left: Coney Island Hotdog Stand
> Top right: Frozen Dead Guy Days
> Bottom left: Carousel of Happiness
> Bottom right: Linger Eatuary

391

had a tendency to die from frequently, it garnered the moniker Old Boneyard and the rich went elsewhere. Over the next decade or so, the cemetery fell into greater and greater disrepair as the families of the poor and criminal were unable to pay to maintain the lots. In the 1890s the city of Denver decided to take back control and repurpose the land, taking up a cheap contract with a company to remove the 5000 some human remains. Due to the cut-price and somewhat unscrupulous nature of the contractor, the agreement held that they would use 3.5ft long containers to transport the bodies, thus the public lined the area to watch as the bodies were unceremoniously hacked into pieces and slung into their new crates. Ghost stories were quick to follow and were so severe in quantity and content that City Hall officially stopped the operation to investigate the ghoulish goings on that were being reported. Some 3000 odd bodies remain buried, forgotten and now covered by the park.

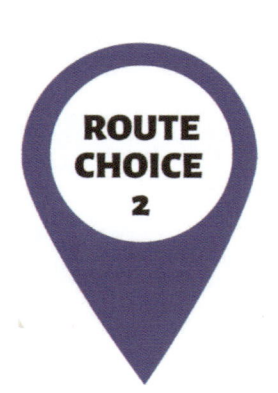

ROUTE CHOICE 2

Now choose to travel on one of the following 3 routes:

1. BLUE / RED ROUTES TOWARDS NASHVILLE / CHICAGO (you will choose your final destination for these routes further ahead on p. 399) or choose to travel the

2. GREEN ROUTE ENDING IN RAPID CITY - turn to p. 403, or the

3. ORANGE ROUTE ENDING IN ALBUQUEQUE - turn to p.408

1. BLUE / RED ROUTES TOWARDS NASHVILLE / CHICAGO

33. CLUTTER FAMILY HOME
37.9852, -100.99959
Off unmarked road where Oak Avenue and S West St, Holcomb, meet.
This house was the inspiration for Truman Capote's In Cold Blood: A True Account of a Multiple Murder and Its Consequences, after a family of four were tied up and shot to death in 1959 by two men out on parole who had heard a rumour that the family had money and kept it in the home. Both were hanged, after finding only $50. It has been up for sale several times by auction but has been taken off the market due to insufficient bids.

34. THE TOWN OF HOOKER
36.86002, -101.21349
Hooker, OK 73945
Named for ranch foreman John 'Hooker' Threlkeld, this town's motto is 'It's a location, not a vocation'.

35. KANSAS BARBED WIRE MUSEUM
38.52461, -99.31158
120 1st St, La Crosse, KS 67548
www.rushcounty.org
Finally, someone documents the history, life and times of our favourite type of wire.

36. ABANDONED LUTHERAN SCHOOLHOUSE
38.745950, -98.617046
198TH St, Dorrance, KS 97634
One for the photographers, a beautiful timber abandoned Lutheran church and schoolhouse in the midst of unadulterated nothingness

37. WORLD'S LARGEST CZECH EGG
38.82415, -98.47267
2520 Ave D, Wilson, KS 67490 (where Ave D and 27th St/Old U.S.40 intersect)
At 22 feet long, this egg has delighted viewers since 2012 when it arrived in white form, before its paint job was finished in 2015 and it was finally situated as an egg should be in a protective gazebo as of 2016. Located in the Czech capital of Kansas, its aim was to single-eggedly bring tourism to the town, and it's working. Allegedly there is a bigger egg in Canada but Wilsonites will be quick to retort that it's not painted. Grab a Czech 'kolache' pastry while you're in town.

38. WORLD'S LARGEST COLLETION OF THE SMALLEST VERSIONS OF LARGEST THINGS
39.0571, -98.5353
226 Kansas Ave, Lucas, KS 67648
www.worldslargestthings.com
Given the collective popularity and tourist pull of America's 'largest things' roadside attractions, entrepreneurism might dictate that one should build a collection of slightly larger versions of them and cash in. Some genius however had a much smarter and more financially viable idea, to create miniscule versions of the largest things...and lots of them... then come up with this fabulous title. Hats off to the legend behind this one.

39. THE GARDEN OF EDEN
39.0580, -98.5350
305 E 2nd St, Lucas, KS 67648
www.garden-of-eden-lucas-kansas.com
Bizarre sculpture garden in concrete creates striking silhouettes

40. WORLD'S LARGEST BALL OF TWINE
39.50921, -98.4337
Wisconsin St, Cawker City, KS 67430
www.kansastravel.org
It took 29 years but Francis A. Johnson kept rolling his twine ball single-handedly (actually he probably used both) for four hours straight a day, every day, until he was the proud owner of this beauty. This labour of love stands as testament to the man, now deceased, whose dedication to silliness still brings delight to all who visit.

41. TRUCKHENGE
39.07923, -95.60177
4124 NE Brier Rd, Topeka, KS 66616
www.lessmanfarm.com
Trucks rise up out of the earth in this uber cool art park.

NOW WHY NOT CHECK OUT:

WORLD'S LARGEST SHUTTLECOCKS, KANSAS CITY - p.183

< Left: Cheesman Park
< Right: Kansas Barbed Wire Museum
Right: World's Largest Ball of Twine
Overleaf: Abandoned Lutheran Schoolhouse

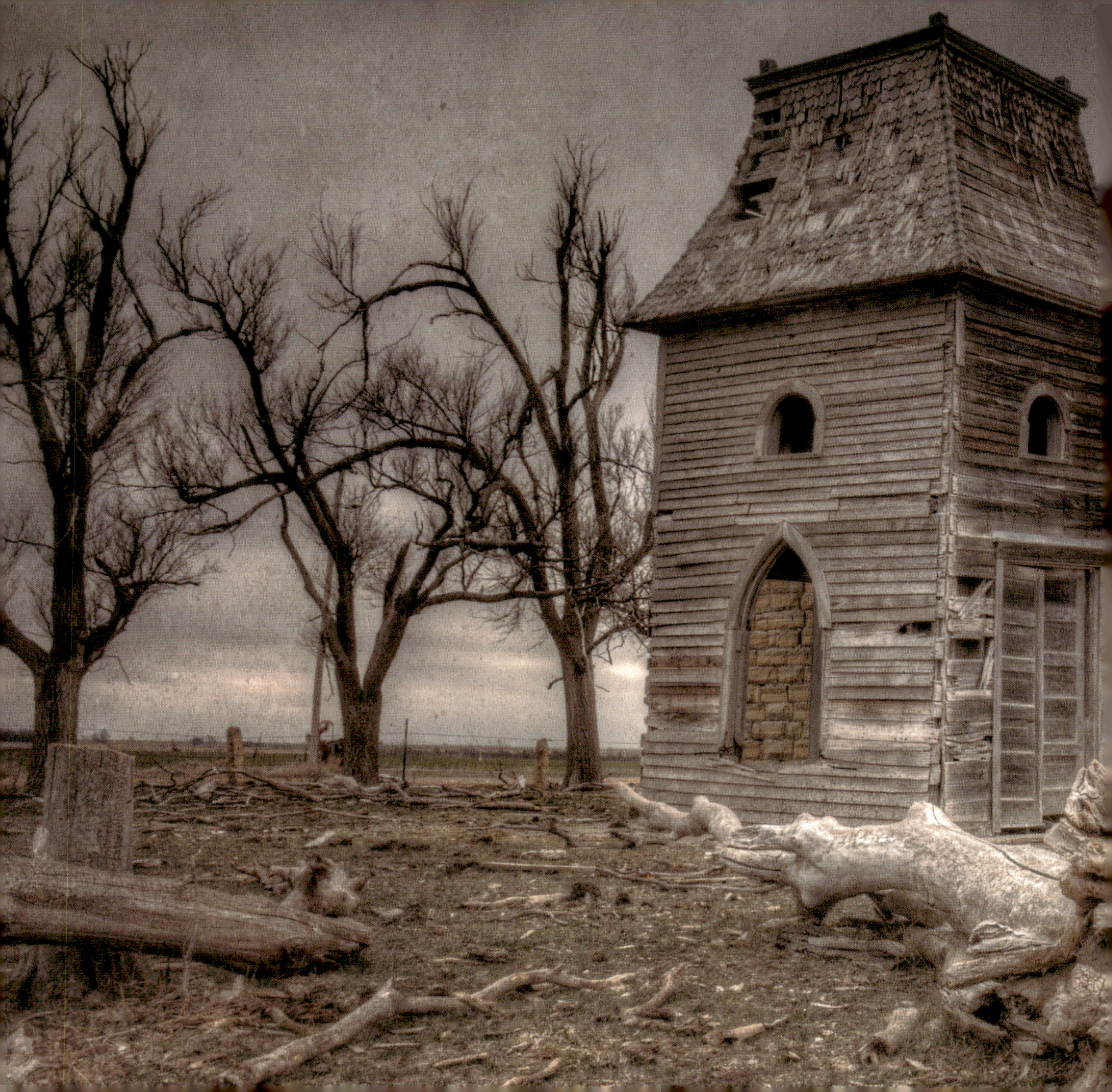

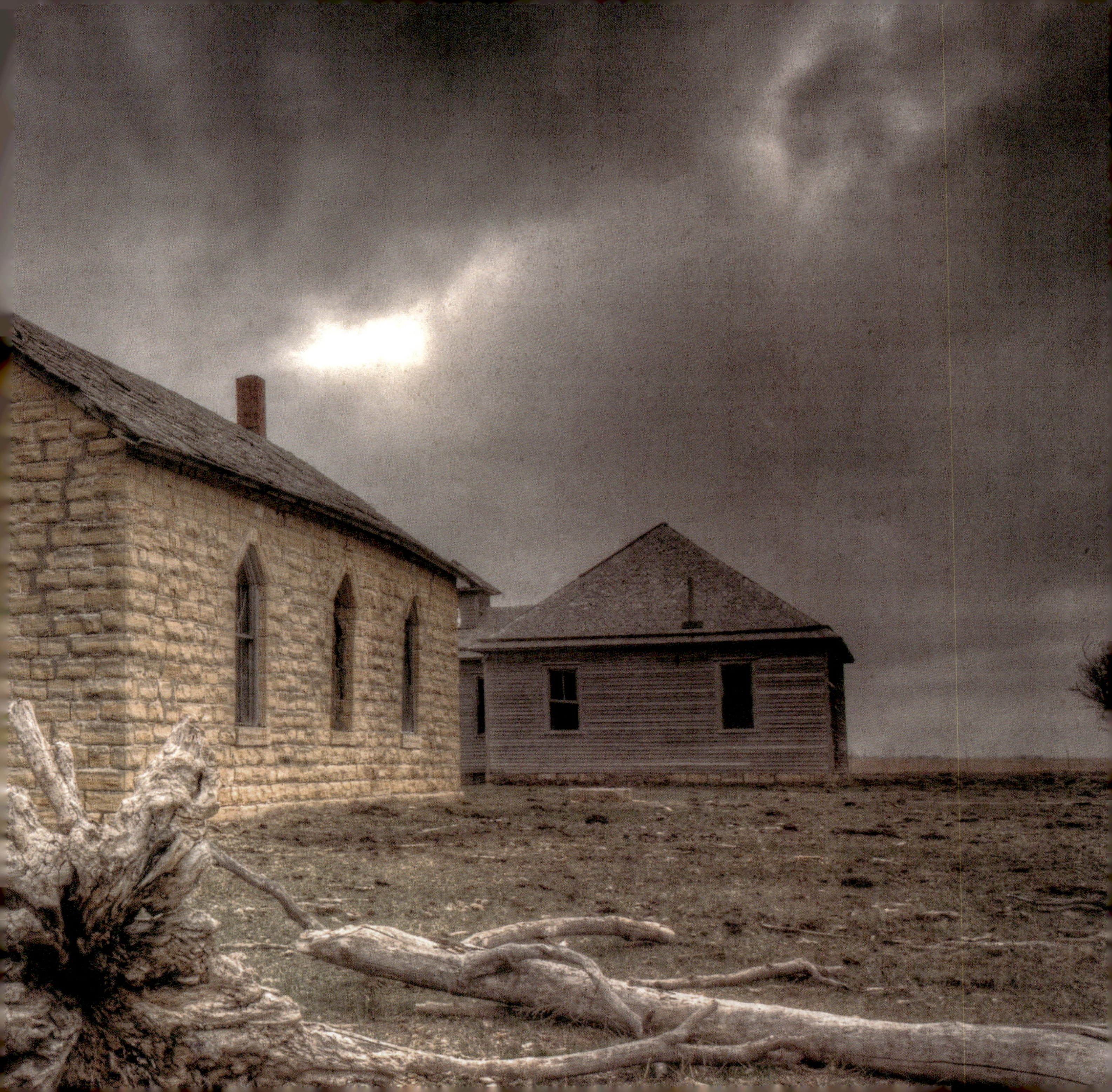

42. JIM THE WONDER DOG MEMORIAL GARDEN
39.12168, -93.19735

101-113 N Lafayette Ave, Marshall, MO 65340

www.jimthewonderdog.org

An entire memorial garden dedicated to an allegedly psychic dog who successfully predicted the winner of the Kentucky Derby 7 years on the trot, predicted the Yankee victory in the 1936 World Series and who was said to be able to deduce the sex of unborn babies and answer to orders in multiple languages unknown to his owner. He confounded several psychologists and the director of the Missouri School of Veterinary Medicine, who concluded that Jim 'possessed an occult power that might never come again to a dog in many generations'.

43. WORLD'S LARGEST PECAN
39.42342, -93.13069

119 W Broadway St, Brunswick, MO 65236

It's a very large pecan.

44. MAXIE THE WORLD'S LARGEST GOOSE
39.6534, -93.24599

Park Drive, off 1st St (139), Sumner, MO 64681

What else would you build in the self-proclaimed Wild Goose Capital of the World, particularly when several visitors to the area have pointed out a total lack of visible wild geese in the area. This goose may be made of fibreglass and at 40 ft. tall weigh a whopping 5,500 lbs., but it has actually flown; it was helicoptered into position in time for the annual Goose Festival and naturally was dedicated by the Miss Goose Pageant Queen. Locals like to point out that the World's Largest Pecan significantly outweighs Maxie.

45. KIRKSVILLE DEVILS CHAIR
40.19080, -92.55690

504 Jamison St, Kirksville, MO 63501

The urban legend term 'devil's chair' is often used to refer to funereal seat sculptures, common in the 19th century in the USA; it used to be standard practice to gather sociably

OFFBEAT AMERICA

at graveyards to spend time with extended family without the deceased being left out (many people assume the old taps you often see near tombs are modern for the use of caretakers – they were actually there to provide drinking water for visitors during their sometimes lengthy stays), thus many memorials featured chairs or benches for the comfort of visitors. They are referred to more correctly as 'mourning chairs' or in today's inimitable parlance, 'monu-benches' (not all progress is good progress). The 'devil's chair' moniker is attributed to a legend that the devil will appear to anyone brave enough to sit upon it and has made such monuments the subject of so called 'legend tripping', or the making of pilgrimages, often at night, by young people to test out urban legends. This particular chair carries the legend that a zombified hand will reach up from beyond the grave and drag whoever sits upon it into the depths of hell. This one should be quite easy to verify once and for all folks.

46. ADAM-ONDI-AHMAN
39.9839, -93.9763
22374 Koala Rd, Jameson, MO 64647 (church site)
39.971838, -93.985397
225th St., Jameson, MO 64647 (historic site)
Following 225th St, and keeping heading straight on the main road will take you to an area where the road becomes unnamed and starts to loop and bend in woodland – this is the Adam Ondi Ahman historic site. This historic site is, according to Mormon doctrine, where Adam and Eve lived after their ejection from Eden (which, according to the ever well-informed Joseph Smith was itself located near Independence, Missouri). The name is variously translated as 'Valley of God, where Adam dwelt', 'Adam's grave', 'Adam with God', or 'the Valley of God where Adam blessed his children'. Lyman Wight, an early leader in the LDS movement, built a home on the site and during a visit in 1838, Joseph Smith proclaimed that Adam had built either two or three altars in the area, one of which was by Wight's house, the other a mile to the north on top of Spring Hill. A couple of months later, Smith went further, claiming that the location was in fact where Adam and Eve went after being exiled from Eden, leading to the establishment of Adam-ondi-Ahman as an official Latter Day Saint settlement. A few months later it had a population of 1500, but concerns by non-Mormons that the group would attempt to take political control of Daviess County lead to fighting. When locals tried to prevent the Mormons from voting, things turned ugly; Mormon homes were burnt by vigilantes with LDS followers fleeing to Adam-ondi-Ahman for protection. The Mormons then gathered their own forces from Caldwell County in response, leading the then Govenor of Missouri to threaten to

< Top: Jim the Wonder Dog Memorial Garden
< Centre: World's Largest Pecan
< Bottom: Maxie the World's Largest Goose
Right: Adam-Ondi-Ahman

'exterminate' the Mormon community. Smith, Brigham Young and their followers dedicated the temple square on the highest point of the bluff, before ultimately surrendering in November 1838 on charges of murder, arson, theft, rebellion and treason, with Smith and Wight imprisoned almost immediately. No non-Mormons were brought to trial despite 17 Mormons dying in the Haun Hill massacre alone. That same tumultuous month, the LDS were told they had just ten days to leave the settlement and forfeit their property and were marched out by 2,500 state troups, relocating to Far West, Missouri. The following year, after being granted a change of prison, Smith was allowed to escape by his guards and successfully settled in Illinois after convincing the state that they were refugees, victims of religious oppression. During these wranglings however, the Mormons lost their rights to their land which was later bought by a John Cravens who selflessly renamed the town 'Cravensville'. Today the LDS Church has reacquired it and the 3000 acres of Adam-ondi-Ahman are now protected as a historic landmark.

47. TIGHTWAD BANK
38.30956, -93.54366
1160 SE Hwy 7, Clinton, MO 64735
The best named bank in America.

48. HA HA TONKA CASTLE RUINS
37.9763, -92.7696
Ha Ha Tonka State Park, Natural Bridge Rd, Camdenton, MO 65020
This castle and surrounding 5000 acre plot in the Ozarks was built in the 1900s by wealthy Kansas entrepreneur Robert Synder as his personal retirement home; he envisioned it as a European-inspired castle with a grand carriage house, saying of the property 'I will fish and loaf and explore the caves of these hills with no fear of intrusion'. Unfortunately just as this plan began to unfold, he died in 1906 in one of the state's first car crashes, leaving his sons to painstakingly complete the work. Financial struggles led the family to lease the property as a hotel for a few years, during which time a spark from a fireplace led it to be gutted in 1942 by fire. In 1976, the water tower too was burned down by arsonists, laying to rest any hopes that Synder had held of distancing himself from intrusion. Since then the roof has been repaired and the walls stabilised to preserve the artistry of the masons who were brought over from Scotland

to complete the work. Today one can tour the ruins, the boardwalks and trails as well as Snyder's much loved caverns and tunnels, springs and sinkholes. The area was named 'Ha ha tonka' by early settler Robert G. Scott to reflect the area's beauty and Native American heritage as home of the Osage and Cherokee tribes; it is said to mean 'laughing spirit' or 'smiling waters' in reference to the springs on the property.

49. THE WORLD'S SECOND LARGEST ROCKING CHAIR
38.03743, -91.46921
5957 State Hwy ZZ, Cuba, MO 65453
Is it the largest or the second largest? The scintillating debate continues.

50. WELCH SPRING HOSPITAL RUINS
37.39388, -91.57436
401-409 Watercress Rd, Van Buren, Missouri, 63965 (between Cedargrove and Akers on the Upper Current, best reached by canoe but by car head north past Akers Group Camp, park next to the river at the end of the road and walk a trail north along the river for half a mile. You will see the hospital on the opposite side of the spring.)
Welch Spring was purchased in 1913 by a doctor C. H. Diehl for $800, in order to capitalise on what he believed were its healing properties . He thought that beyond the effects of the water itself, cool air from the nearby cave could help those with asthma, tuberculosis and other consumptive illnesses.

< Bottom left: Tightwad Bank
< Centre: Ha Ha Tonka Castle Ruins
< Right: The World's Second Largest Rocking Chair

To make the most of these natural resources, he built a hospital over the cave mouth, damming off the water so as to close off the entrance and force more air out through the cave opening into the hospital. Little further medical treatment was offered, and the doctor also had the foresight to open an adjacent camp ground to capitalise on tourism and supplement his medical income. Unfortunately he had failed to recognise what an obstacle the Ozarks' poor road system would prove to be, as tourists were unwilling to make the trip - when he died in 1940, his family had little interest in maintaining the property leading to its decline and eventual collapse. Dr. Diehl (1879-1940) is buried in Oakridge Cemetery, Effingham, Illinois with his wife Jennie. Beware of wading into the spring as metal debris from the hospital period may cause injury.

ST LOUIS:

NOW WHY NOT CHECK OUT:

All entries from WORLD'S TALLEST MAN STATUE TO WORLD'S LARGEST CATSUP BOTTLE, pages 128 to 132

NOW CHOOSE EITHER NASHVILLE OR CHICAGO AS YOUR EAST ROUTE FINAL DESTINATION: BLUE ROUTE ENDING IN NASHVILLE

(skip to p.403 to follow red route ending in Chicago)

51. BALD KNOB CROSS OF PEACE
37.55131, -89.34648
3630 Bald Knob Rd, Alto Pass, IL 62905
www.baldknobcross.com
A giant white cross with a name liable to detract from its eminence.

52. MONUMENT TO BOOMER THE THREE LEGGED HERO DOG
37.617667, -89.209722
594 Makanda Road, Makanda, Illinois
A monument to a special 3 legged mutt who could outrun trains (they were slower back then), which reads "In memory of Boomer the hound dog. Tradition says he dashed his life out against the iron abutment of the railroad bridge 300 feet south of this point on September 2, 1859, while running along on three legs trying to put out the flame in a hotbox on the speeding train of his beloved fireman-master." The history of this special mutt goes that he was owned by a fireman working on the Illinois Central Railroad, whose bosses would not let dogs ride on the train leading Boomer to run alongside it every time it passed through town carrying his master. This lead to the Illinois Central train becoming the object of ridicule, when the public pointed out that it couldn't go faster than a dog, let alone one on three legs. To regain face, the heads of the railroad brought

SAN FRAN TO THE MIDWEST ROUTE II

the fastest train in their stock to Makanda, heaped it with as much fuel as possible and the firemen were told to take it to full speed. The boiler pressure rose so high that the firebox door started to glow red and the rivets looked ready to burst. Locals lined the streets to see if Boomer could keep up. And keep up he did, although meanwhile the wheels of the train started to overheat and the grease on the bearings caught light. Flames started to spew out of the side of the vehicle and it is said that seeing his master in peril, Boomer ran to the flames and peed on them, extinguishing them entirely (if you are wondering, it is unclear how he may have achieved this at speed). Tragically however, Boomer failed to notice an upcoming bridge which was obscured by the steam clouds from the train, ran into it and was killed on the spot. Due to the lives saved by this faithful dog, he was afforded a hero's funeral. Is it really possible that Boomer saved lives by single-pawedly extinguishing a burning train? If not, you have to ask yourself why the impressive full scale memorial would exist…

53. MERMET SPRINGS
37.2845, -88.85802

6724 US-45, Belknap, IL 62908
www.mermetsprings.com

Described as America's 3rd best underwater attraction, this scuba location offers an underwater petting zoo and….a sunken 727 Boeing airplane. That's right. Hire the gear or bring your own and first timers are welcome too. Did we mentioned the underwater Railroad Coal Car, subacqueous Cherokee 150 Aircraft, water-logged Cessna, submerged Ambulance, Firetruck and an overly damp motorbike? You may have gathered by now that this is not the most unlucky crash site in the world, these vehicles have been

400

placed here for lucky people like you to visit - but that makes them, and the underwater photography on offer, absolutely NO less cool.

54. MONKEY'S EYEBROW
37.18671, -88.98784
Monkey Eyebrow Road, Monkeys Eyebrow, Kentucky 42056

A town's whose favourite local pastime is to direct people to the city of Paducah by saying, quite accurately, 'it's halfway between Monkeys Eyebrow and Possum Trot (one can assume there isn't much by way of entertainment on offer). Monkey's Eyebrow is also next to Bandana, and near towns like Klondike, Mound City, Champion, Friendship and Perks but apparently these names are not unusual enough to register with locals. Theories behind the moniker are that when looking at a map of Ballard County, it looks much like a monkey's head, with Monkey's Eyebrow naturally in the location where the eyebrow would be found. As one would therefore logically expect, there were actually two Monkey's Eyebrows, known locally as Old Monkey and New Monkey, one at the top of a small hill and one at the bottom.

55. ABANDONED TOWN OF CAIRO
37.00532, -89.17646
Cairo, IL 62914

1920s shipping town which once had a population of 15,000, now revised down to 2. Today largely reclaimed by ivy, the remaining crumbling structures still give a great impression of the town's heyday.

56. LAMBERT'S CAFÉ
36.8878, -89.5464
2305 E Malone Ave, Miner, MO 63801
www.throwedrolls.com

You would be forgiven for not understanding what 'Throwed Rolls' are until you have visited Lambert's, a restaurant started by Earl and Agnes Lambert in 1942 with 14 cents between them and a loan of $1500 from a friend. Initially business was tough as World War II's severe rationing made the operation of restaurants extremely challenging, but over time and with the help of their young son Norman, the restaurant thrived. One day young Norman was struggling to pass the bread to a customer seated in a far corner who then shouted 'throw the #$@#$@ing thing'; since that time Norman developed the habit of throwing bread rolls at anyone who asked him for bread, estimating that back in the day he probably threw around 200 dozen homemade rolls a day during the week and 300 dozen a day

< Mermet Springs
Above: Abandoned Town of Cairo

on weekends. Today the restaurant advises patrons that 'dozens of hot rolls are flying through the air every few minutes, so be alert.' Norman also told people in wheelchairs that 'if you bring your own chair, you eat free' and stuck to this policy for his entire time at Lambert's. Norman may no longer be with us, but his spirit and kindness live on at this family establishment where famous customers have included Elvis Presley, Jay Leno, Clint Eastwood, Morgan Freeman, Ray Stevens and John Goodman, among many others.

57. THE STRANGE PROCESSION WHICH NEVER MOVES

36.75125, -88.63499

Maplewood Cemetery, N 6th St, Mayfield, KY 42066

Maplewood Cemetery houses The Wooldridge Memorial, built for Col. Henry G Wooldridge to remember his family and other loved individuals in his life. The Procession's construction commenced in 1892 when he lost the last of his sisters, leaving him with no immediate family and continued until he died in 1899. Represented are his mother (Keziah Nichols), his brothers (Alfred, Josiah and John), his sisters (Narcissa, Minerva and Susan stand at the rear of the lot and were completed by one sculptor), his great nieces Maud and Minnie, his favourite dogs Tow-Head and Bob, a fox and a deer as well as two statues of Henry himself, one at a lectern (this carved in Italy and shipped to the USA), one riding his favourite horse Fop (he raised and raced horses in the Mayfield area). Notably missing from the statuary is Henry's father. There are 18 monuments in total although these are statues rather than tomb markers; rather poignantly perhaps, Wooldridge is in fact buried alone at the site, but is surrounded by those that loved him. The estimated cost of the statues would have been around $160,000 of today's money. It is said that when the large statue of Henry astride his horse was shipped on a special flat train car by the Illinois Central Railway to the Mayfield cemetery, the town drunk climbed up behind the figure of Henry and rode all the way along the journey on the horse.

58. CAVE-IN-ROCK

37.46921, -88.1653

Cave-In-Rock, IL 62919

Outlaw stronghold and Wild West town which attracted the likes of serial killers and bandits such as the bloodthirsty Harpe Brothers ('Big' and 'Little' Harpe who killed between 39 and 50 victims), as well as famed counterfeiters, highwaymen and gangs. The town, which had a population of 318, was named for a large riverside cave used extensively by outlaws, notably including counterfeiters Philip Alston and John Duff for whom the cave was a key meeting point. The Harpe Brothers pushed a large number of couples as well as a man tied to his horse off the top of the cliff overhanging the cave to their deaths. Big Harpe met his comeuppance when he was decapitated by a vigilante posse with ties to his victims who displayed the head on a spike as was common for outlaws at the time when it was considered, probably rightly, as a decent deterrent to further criminal acts. The legendary Potts Inn, thought to be a human death trap for travellers caught unawares, was also built near this location. The Inn was run as a pirate operation by innkeeper Billy Potts and American civic leader and secret River pirate Jim Ford, a wealthy land owner, entrepreneur and illustrious military man whose hidden dealings including owning a large number of slaves and associating with John Hart Crenshaw to kidnap, enslave and illegally sell freed slaves to Southern plantations. Ford was well known for his cruel treatment of slaves, including an incident in which he bound an offending individual and dragged him to his death behind a mule through a field of tree stumps. Known as Satan's Ferryman, Ford also operated a ferry near the inn and was head of what came to be known as Ford's Ferry Gang; he would size up travellers and send word to Billy Potts of their imminent arrival at the inn. Billy would then welcome the traveller to his abode, direct them to a cold water spring at the back of the property, whereupon when they bent down to drink, Billy would murder them and take all their valuables. The deal went that anyone escaping the Harpe brothers were fair game for Ford and Potts. Billy Potts had a son who moved away from the area in his teens. Upon his return some years later completed with an aged face and beard, Ford sent word to Potts that a worthy client was due to arrive and Potts entirely failed to recognise him. The son decided to surprise his father at the last minute but unfortunately he timed this poorly and was promptly dispatched and buried in a shallow grave – Billy only realised his mistake when a visiting friend of his son's asked after him and Potts exhumed the body, identifying him belatedly by a birthmark. If you look at a map of Cave-in-Rock you will see E. Fords Ferry Road and Old Ford Ferry Road named for Ford and his dubious Ferry service. The site of the Potts Inn is thought to be at 37.580691, -88.189643 where an abandoned house still sits upon the original cellar and the original spring can still be found in woods behind the property. The property would have been situated on a busy intersection at the time, scars of previous roads can still be made out in the area. Please note that this is private land.

WHILE IN CENTRAL NASHVILLE, WHY NOT CHECK OUT:

CONCRETE PARTHENON & HERMITAGE HOTEL - p.158

RED ROUTE ENDING IN CHICAGO

Why not check out:

All entries from *SHOWMEN'S REST* TO *THE MURDER CASTLE SITE*, pages 122 to 113, following the entries in reverse order from Showmen's Rest to The Murder Castle Site.

- END OF RED ROUTE AND END OF SAN FRAN TO THE MIDWEST ROUTE 11 –

GREEN ROUTE ENDING IN RAPID CITY

59. OLE'S BIG GAME STEAKHOUSE AND LOUNGE
41.12376, -101.35603
123 N Oak St, Paxton, NE 69155
www.olesbiggame.com
Dating back to the '30s, this taxidermy stuffed steakhouse packs a meaty punch.

60. PANORAMA POINT
41.007463, -104.031270
Off the Co Rd 5, Pine Bluffs, NE 82082
The highest point in the State provides beautiful sweeping views of wild bison.

61. BUFORD WYOMING POP. 1 BUFORD
41.12368, -105.30229

Left/Overleaf: The Strange Procession Which Never Moves
Right:: Lambert's Cafe

SAN FRAN TO THE MIDWEST ROUTE 11

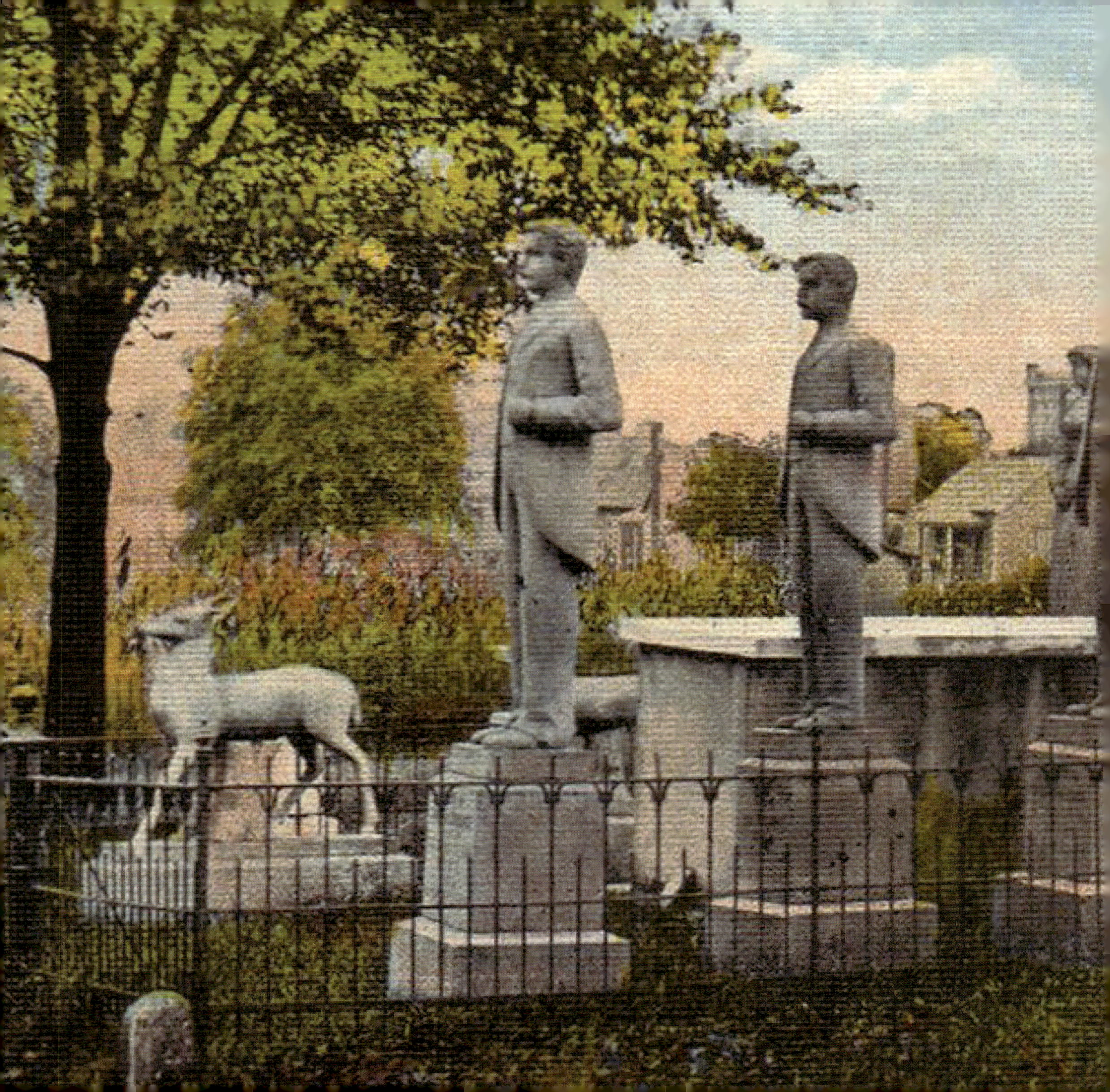

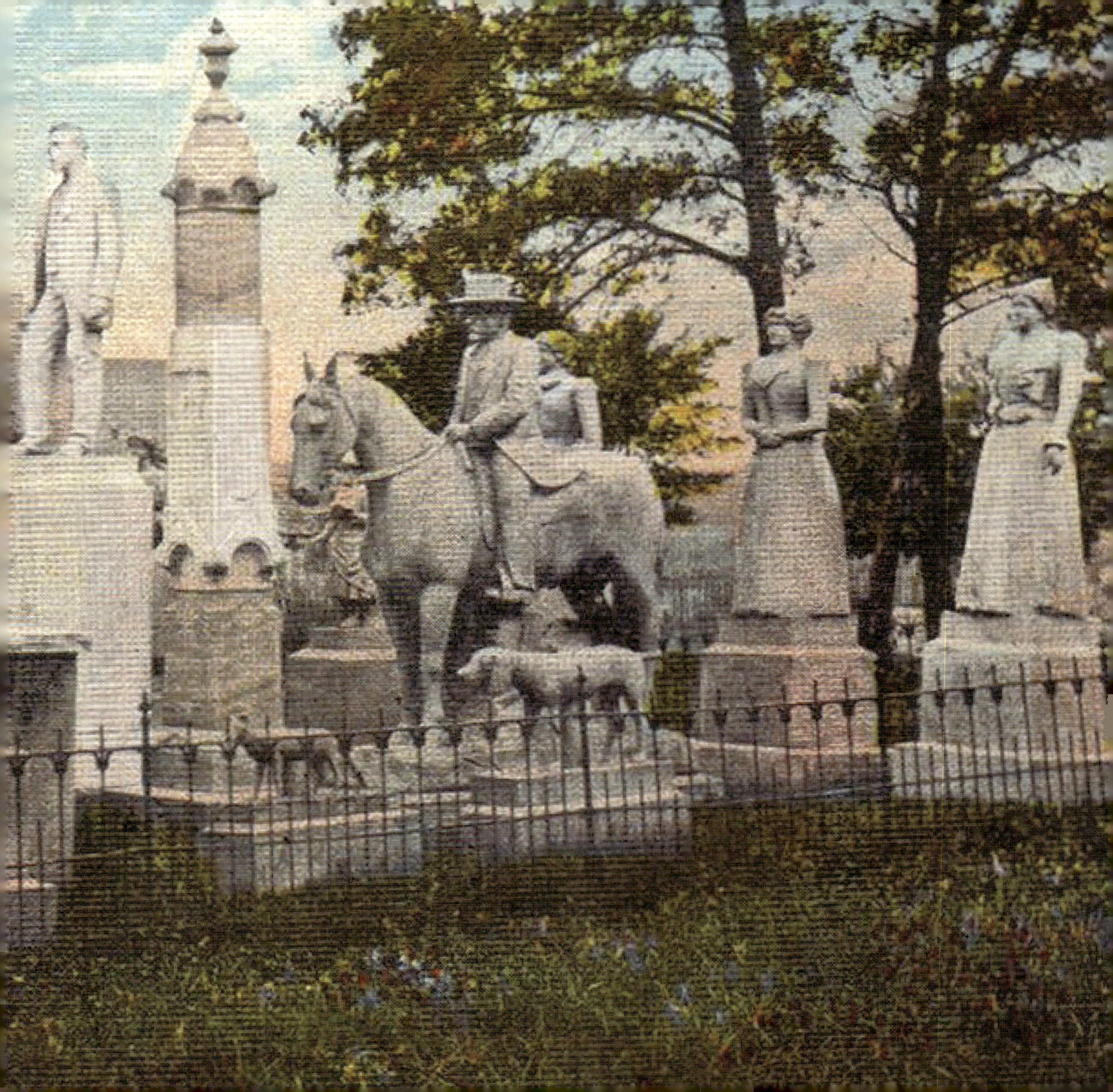

> Right: Fossil Cabin

2 Sammons Ln, Buford, WY 82052
www.bufordtradingpost.com
The one resident in question was until 2013 Don Sammons who moved to Buford in 1980 with his family, before purchasing the town in 1992. His wife died in '95 and his son moved elsewhere in 2007, leaving him Buford's only resident. Don eventually decided to relocate closer to his son, and so the town was put up for auction in 2012 and purchased for $900,000 by a Vietnamese duo, who sadly rebranded it 'PhinDeli Town Buford' as a promotional campaign intended to sell more PhinDeli brand coffee from the convenience store; the postal address however remains Buford.

62. FOSSIL CABIN
41.8650 , -106.0735
US Highway 30/287, Medicine Bow, Wyoming, 82329
This building stands as excellent testimony to the concept common in outback America back in the day that if you need to build a house in the middle of nowhere, build it out of whatever comes to hand - even if that happens to be ancient and valuable dinosaur skeletons. The home was discovered by a bemused palaeontologist in 1897 who couldn't quite believe his eyes when he came across it, but realised his suspicions were accurate when he stumbled across a quarry filled with dinosaur remains directly behind the house. Since that time it has been a part of Ripley's Believe it or Not collection and a public museum but has now reverted to a private home, although the 'Believe it or Not' faded sign outside recalls a previous life.

63. WYOMING FRONTIER PRISON
41.79263, -107.24259
500 W Walnut St, Rawlins, WY 82301
wyomingfrontierprison.org
Wyoming was outlaw hangout number 1 in the USA due to its myriad labyrinthine canyons which made for perfect dugouts in times of need. In 1901 Wyoming decided to put an end to this dubious claim to fame by building a large prison devoid of running water or electricity and soon home to notorious crooks, daring escapes, executions and stand offs. Reopened in 1988 after its closure in '81, you can still visit today but beware the prison closes when there is bad weather due to the poor road system used to reach it.

64. LOST SPRINGS
42.73633, -104.91291
401-439 Lost Springs Road, Manville, WY 82227
A coal mining town which once boasted a population of around 150 residents enjoying a lumber yard, post office, saloon, drugstore, mercantile, hotel, bank, restaurant, newspaper (The Lost Springs Times) and a shooting gallery but which subsequently crashed when the mine shut in 1930, like so many others of its kind. By the sixties only a

Top left: Ole's Big Game Steakhouse
Centre: Buford Wyoming Pop.1
Bottom: Wyoming Frontier Prison

OFFBEAT AMERICA

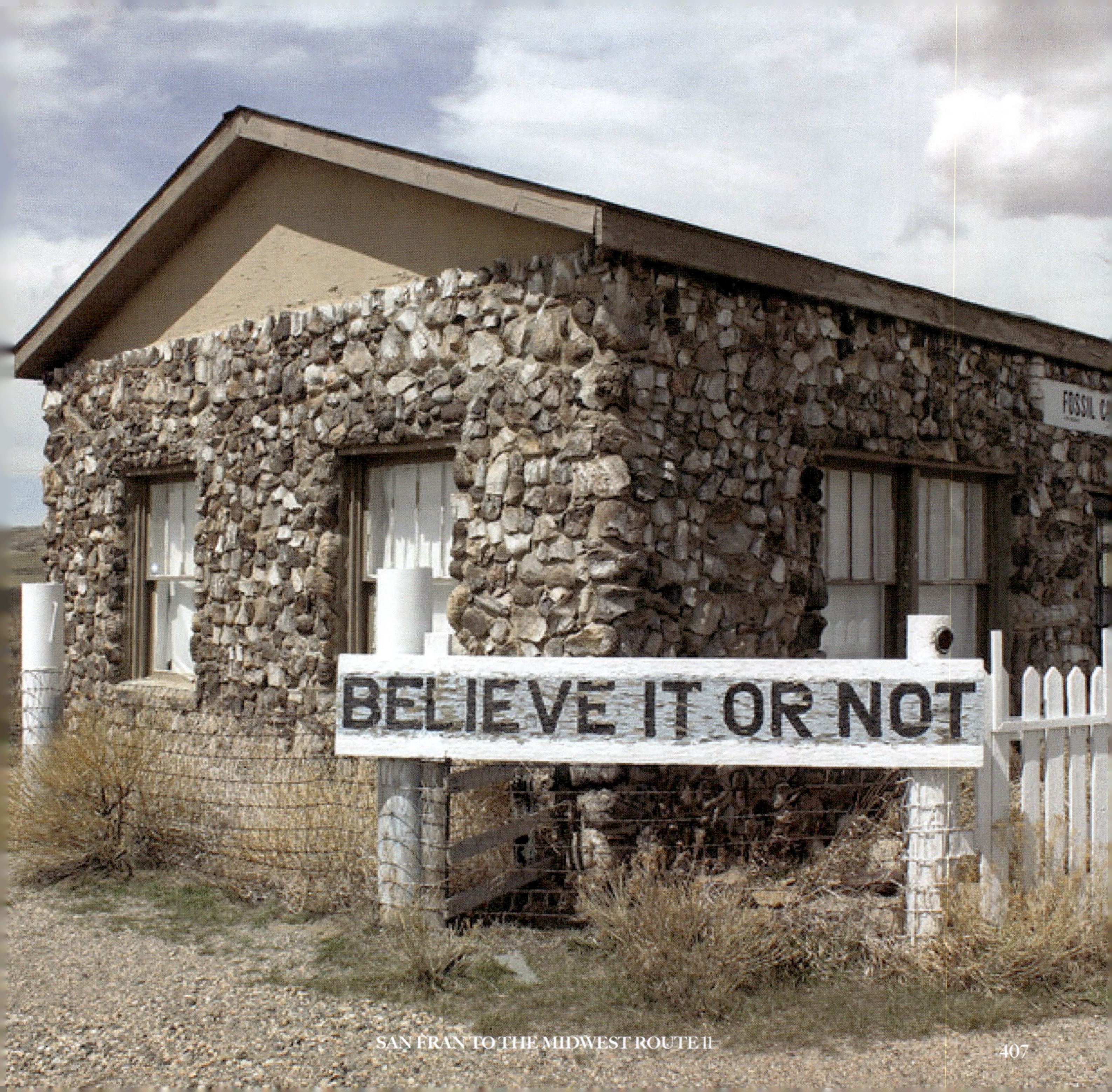
FOSSIL
BELIEVE IT OR NOT

handful of people were based in the town and today 3 people are officially residents.

NOW WHY NOT CHECK OUT:

All entries from FOR HUDSON-MENG & GIANT PRAIRIE DOG, see p. 270

65. SPOKANE GHOST TOWN
43.8187, -103.22019
Spokane Ghost Town, Hermosa, South Dakota, 57744 (unsigned, just to the North of Wolf Camp, or to the east of the 16A/Iron Mountain Road between N Playhouse Rd and S Playhouse Road)
This all but forgotten 1890s lead, zinc and gold mining town still contains its original mill as well as remnants of other buildings including a schoolhouse, water tower and miners' cabins.

- END GREEN ROUTE ENDING IN RAPID CITY AND END OF SAN FRAN TO THE MIDWEST ROUTE 11 -

ORANGE ROUTE ENDING IN ALBUQUEQUE

66. PAINT MINES INTERPRETIVE PARK
39.02033, -104.27157
Paint Mine Open Space, Paint Mine Rd, Calhan, CO 80808
A natural beauty spot spread over 750 acres containing evidence of human life as far back as 9,000 years ago. The area, which has long been linked to Native American culture when they were used as body paints, features Technicolour clay and sand deposits which can be viewed on a three mile hike trail complete with interpretive plaques.

67. THE AIRPLANE RESTAURANT
38.80628, -104.72666
1665 Newport Rd, Colorado Springs, CO 80916

408   OFFBEAT AMERICA

www.solosrestaurant.com

Make yourself feel even worse about the legroom and food options on your next flight by stopping in at this converted 1953 Boeing U.S. Air Force tanker and fueling up on Runway Crunchy Chicken, Air Tower Nachos or Wings Wings.

68. AMERICA'S HIGHEST DEEP FAT FRYER
38.839921, -105.043980
PSICC, Crystal Hills, CO 80829

At this mountain peak, air is so thin that the boiling point of water is dramatically altered. This makes the frying of donuts particularly challenging - fortunately, Pikes Peak has it down and remains the only place you can eat these donut one offs which are made using a receipe which literally only functions at altitudes over 14,000 feet due to high-altitude adjustments made to the recipe: 'Even if you take it down a couple thousand feet, the recipe will not work' in the words of the staff. Local rules state that these sugary beauties must be eaten at elevation rather than carted down the mountain for fear of flavour loss.

69. THE VINDICATOR TRAIL AT CRIPPLE CREEK
38.725071, -105.123500
Vindicator Valley Trailhead, Cripple Creek, CO 80813

How many gold mines can feature on one trail in a place as strikingly named as Cripple Creek? Well this one has 500. Yes, one trail, covered in 500 abandoned yet remarkably intact mines from the 1800s. Word to the wise - the gold mines are built on huge tracts of interconnecting tunnels, any one of which can cave in at any moment; this makes the area extremely high risk so stick to the designated paths!

70. BISHOP'S CASTLE
38.0610, -105.0942
12705 CO-165, Rye, CO 81069
www.bishopcastle.org

This bizarre self-built construction was developed by Jim Bishop as his personal residence, via a series of wranglings and disputes with local government who were seeking to charge him for the use of the stone he gathered from the surrounding land. When he and his wife were both diagnosed with cancer, he made his friend David Merrill a trustee of the castle, however Merrill promptly converted the property into Castle Church for the Redemption, leading the Bishop's to then spend $20,000 trying to clear the title and remove Merrill's name.

71. UFO WATCHTOWER
37.78587, -105.88901
201-249 CO-17, Center, CO 81125
www.ufowatchtower.com

A must for those keen to get under the skin of good old weird America, this campground and observation platform replete with UFO gimmicks galore has been established by a very devoted owner who is a firm believer in our other worldly visitors. Meet her and others like her, as well as enough esoterica to keep you happy along the way.

72. MOVIE MANOR
37.58669, -106.19864
2830 US-160, Monte Vista, CO 81144
www.bestwestern.com

A beautiful piece of pure Americana nostalgia, the entrepreneurial owner of the Star Drive-In theatre decided in the mid-sixties to add a motel built in an arc around the screen behind the cars with a perfect view of the movie, complete with sound piped into the rooms. Renamed Movie Manor, the concept was a resounding success, and despite having been sold by the original owner to Best Western, the motel continues to operate almost exactly as it did in its heyday, with screenings between May and September.

73. LUDLOW MASSACRE SITE
37.3392, -104.58389
Intersection of 44 and County Rd 61.5, Trinidad, CO 81082

During a major strike, the Colorado National Guard and guards from the Colorado Fuel and Iron Company attacked 1,200 coal miners and their families, leaving some 24 people dead, including wives and children. The miners fought back and over the next week and a half as many as 200 lives were cut short, rendering the episode the strike with the most fatalities in the history of the USA

< Top left: Lost Springs
< Top right: The Airplane Restaurant

74. SCIENTOLOGY'S TREMENTINA BASE
35.52733, -104.55492
County Rd C56A, Trementina, NM 88439
A secret base with the purpose of guiding L Ron Hubbard back to earth as and when he should choose to re-join us, where he will be welcomed back into his choice of office (one of which is kept ready and waiting for him in each Scientology base around the world). From the sky, giant symbols can be seen gouged into the earth (Google Earth it).

75. DARK BIRD PALACE
35.76939, -105.94569
2-16 Flea Market Road, Santa Fe, NM 87506
A shed come shrine belonging to folk artist Kelly Moore within Pueblo of Tesuque Flea Market, Aisle J. A strange creation in a bizarre location.

76. CANO'S CASTLE
37.0809, -106.0059
State St & E 10th Ave, Antonito, CO 81120
Ever thought of building yourself a life-size castle out of all those empty cans of beer mounting up around the living room?

77. THE CAVES OF RA PAULETTE
36.3031, -106.04669
Lamadera, NM 87539
An artist has spent 25 years hand carving these stunning edifices in various locations in the desert before moving on to another location, leaving many of the locations to be explored and enjoyed by those that come after him. http://originnewmexico.com/sandstone-art-caves-origin-new-mexico/ offer tours.

78. TWA FLIGHT 260 CRASH SITE
35.194686, -106.442695
Simms Park Road, Albuquerque, NM 87111
This Albuquerque to Santa Fe flight crashed just ten minutes after take-off due to navigational failure in 1955. The remains of the 16 dead including three crew were removed but the rest of the crash site remains largely in place. You will need to complete a reasonably hard-going hike through the forest for 3.5 miles with decent navigational equipment/map to find it as markings are scarce. The hike may be approximately 2-4 hours each way. https://www.hikingproject.com/trail/7006997/domingo-baca-trail-twa-flight-260-crash-site https://ondafringe.wordpress.com/2015/03/26/day-hike-domingo-baca-trail-to-twa-canyon-sandia-mountains-albuquerque-new-mexico-usa/ These websites may prove helpful in locating the site.

- END ORANGE ROUTE ENDING IN ALBUQUERQUE AND END OF SAN FRAN TO THE MIDWEST ROUTE 11 –

> Top left: Scientology's Trementina Base
> Top right: Cano's Castle
> Bottom left: Ra Paulette's Hand Carved Caves
> Bottom right: TWA Flight 260 Crash Site

411

SAN DIEGO TO TENNESSEE ROUTE 12

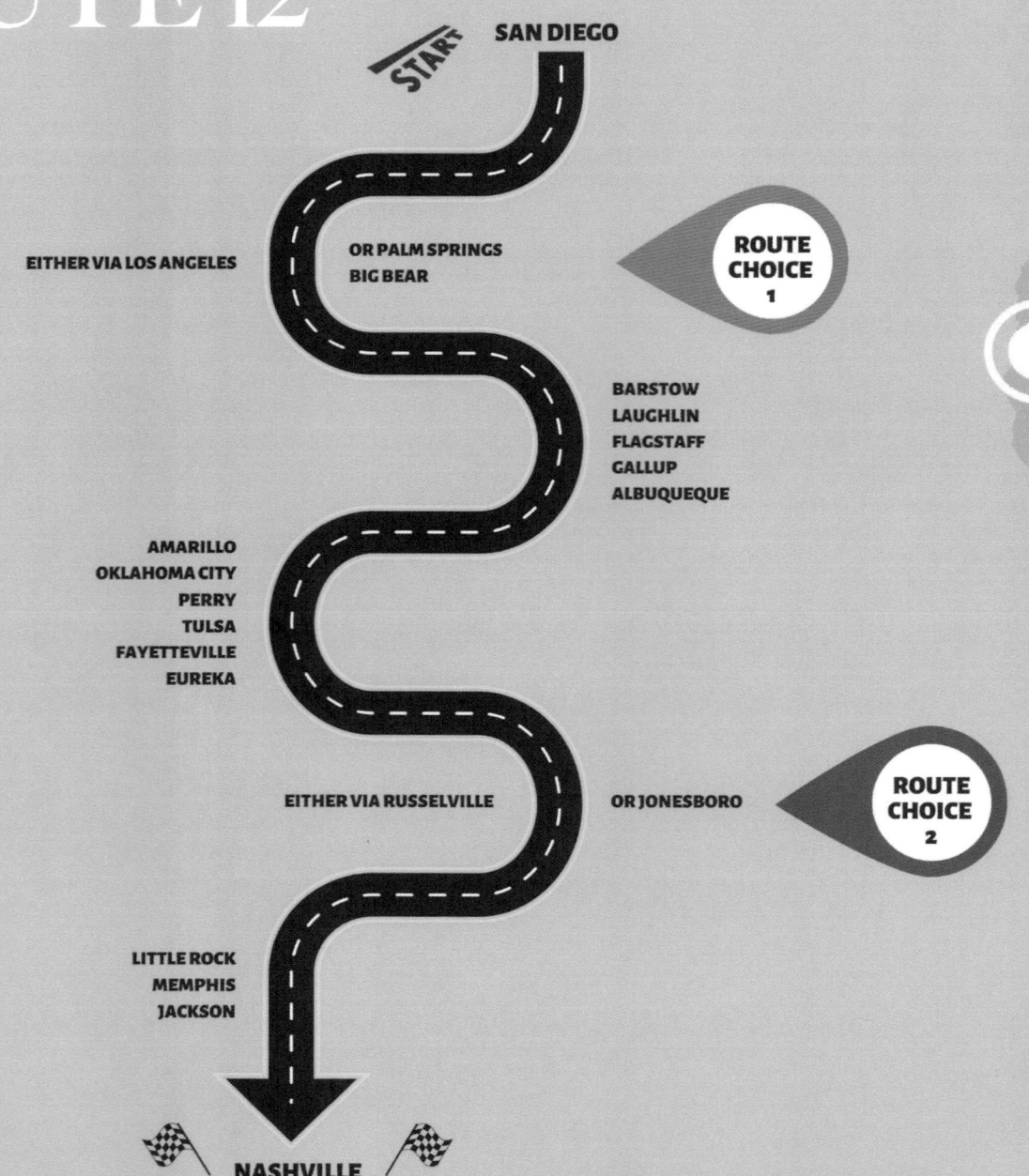

SAN DIEGO — START

EITHER VIA LOS ANGELES

OR PALM SPRINGS
BIG BEAR

ROUTE CHOICE 1

BARSTOW
LAUGHLIN
FLAGSTAFF
GALLUP
ALBUQUEQUE

AMARILLO
OKLAHOMA CITY
PERRY
TULSA
FAYETTEVILLE
EUREKA

EITHER VIA RUSSELVILLE

OR JONESBORO

ROUTE CHOICE 2

LITTLE ROCK
MEMPHIS
JACKSON

NASHVILLE

412

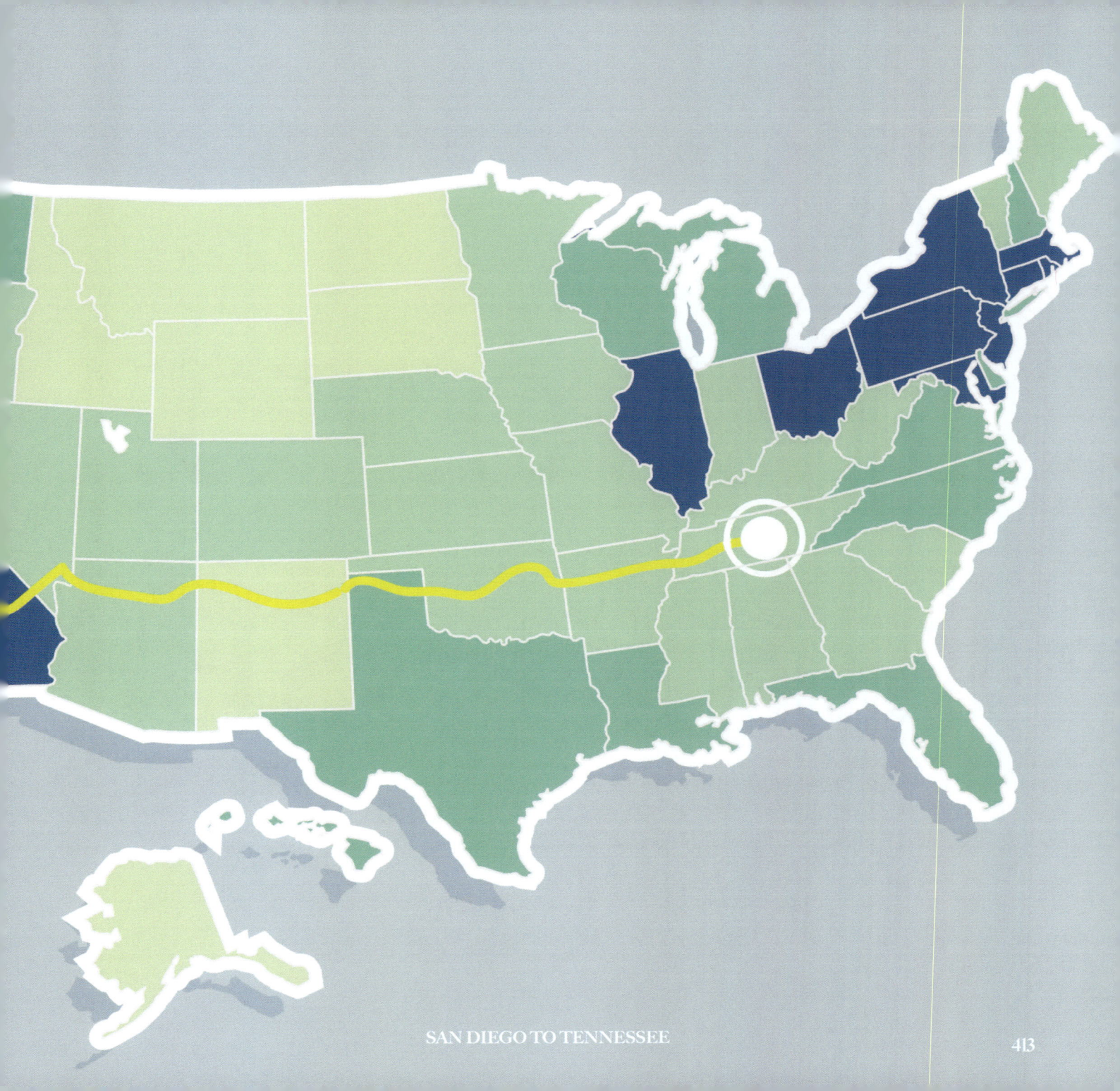

SAN DIEGO TO TENNESSEE

SAN DIEGO TO TENNESSEE ROUTE 12

From sunny San Diego with its giant Lemon, head east to Music City via the glamour of LA to experience Square Dancing and more live music than you could shake a stick at. Prepare to encounter sculptures that bring to mind Mad Max, ghost towns, the largest Pinball arcade anywhere in the world and the grave of a man and his horse killed by a train.

WHILE IN **SAN DIEGO:**, WHY NOT CHECK OUT:

LEMON GROVE – p. 230
HARPERS TOPIARY GARDEN - p.230

Above: World's Biggest Dinosaurs

SAN DIEGO TO TENNESSEE ROUTE 12

NOW CHOOSE:

ROUTE CHOICE 1

ROUTE 1 - VIA L.A.
or see Route 2 via Palm Springs on this page

Why not check out:
CHRISTMAS CARD LANE, p.230
All entries from *MOON AMTRAK* to *GIANT SCISSORS*, pages 303 to 315

JUMP TO CALICO GHOST TOWN p.353 TO CONTINUE YOUR JOURNEY

ROUTE 2. - VIA PALM SPRINGS

Why not check out:

All entries from *GALLETA MEADOWS* to *SLAB CITY INCLUDING EAST JESUS*, pages 234 to 238

1. ROBO LIGHTS
33.83168, -116.5354
1077 E Granvia Valmonte, Palm Springs, CA 92262
www.robochristmas.com
Once a one off event, artist Kenny Irwin Jr.'s creation Robolights, a melange of the robotic and the festive, now graces the streets as a landscape of sculptural art all year round involving robotic reindeer and microwave-carrying wise men.

2. LEE R BAXANDALL BRIDGE - BRIDGE OF THIGHS
33.8442, -116.54559
1568 N Indian Canyon Dr, Palm Springs, California, 92262
Better known as the 'Bridge of Thighs', this

OFFBEAT AMERICA

416

Palm Springs overpass allows nudists to cross the road in safety, presumably preventing major car crashes on a daily basis.

3. WORLD'S BIGGEST DINOSAURS
33.9229, -116.7743
50770 Seminole Dr, Cabazon, CA 92230
www.cabazondinosaurs.com
What to do with a giant hollow dinosaur other than build a creationism museum in it?

4. MUSEUM OF PINBALL
33.9203, -116.8588
700 S Hathaway St, Banning, CA 92220
www.museumofpinball.org
The biggest pinball arcade in the world.

5. HICKSVILLE TRAILER PALACE & ARTIST RETREAT
Nr 34.1347, -116.3131
Joshua Tree, CA 92252
http://www.hicksville.com/joshuatree/motel
This is a fantastic place to stay whilst in California, a motel with a difference opened by the wonderfully named LA writer and director Morgan Higby Night who started collecting vintage trailers and restoring them with a view to creating a quiet private space where he could retreat to work. When he eventually decided to open his creation to the public, he retained the private feel; you can't access the motel prior to signing paperwork, only guests are allowed inside and the gates are locked at all times. No GPS locators are permitted and the location is revealed to paid up guests only. As well as offering fire pits, Fort Dog (a doggie area), a 'corn hole' (we're not sure) and a roof deck with hot tub, this arty venue has taken all the most iconic ways one could possibly reside by the road in the USA and put them all in one place, each loving restored and cared for. Stay in a tipi, a pioneer cabin, a 60's caravan, a covered wagon, an airstream and more. People have been known to stay again and again with the aim of trying out each themed room.

6. WORLD FAMOUS CROCHET MUSUEM
34.13432, -116.31396
61855 CA-62, Joshua Tree, CA 92252
A homage to the humble hook.

< Top left: Museum of Pinball
< Top right: Hicksbille Trailer Palace & Artist Retreat
Above: World Famous Crochet Museum

OFFBEAT AMERICA

<Left: Pioneertown
Below: Oatman Ghost Town

7. PIONEERTOWN
34.15644, -116.49864
Pioneertown, CA 92268
Pioneertown, population 350, was built as a Wild West movie set in the Forties with Roy Rogers acting as an original investor in the project. It featured a bowling alley in which school age children were hired as 'pinsetters', laying out the bowling pins before each shot, as the automatic pinsetter was not invented until the 1950s. This bowling alley is one of the oldest in constant use in California. The town had a close call in a 2006 wild fire but fire-fighters managed to save all the beautiful historic wooden buildings which remain intact and in good condition. The local music club was saved and played host to Paul McCartney in 2016 in a secret concert played to 300 guests. Today the town, whose principal road is adorably called Mane Street, makes for a great visit, complete with realistic dummies in rocking chairs outside houses, fake crows tied to railings and carts of prop dynamite lying around. A quirky location where the real and fake blend.

ROUTES CONVERGE HERE

Why not check out:

CALICO GHOST TOWN – p.353
ROCK-A-HOOLA - p.353
AMBOY - p. 353

8. CARTY'S CAMP, NEEDLES
34.8332, -114.5959
207 E Broadway St, Needles, CA 92363
These residences from the twenties have fallen into disrepair since the advent of a newer motel directly next door.

9. OATMAN GHOST TOWN
35.0264, -114.3836
Oatman, AZ 86433
Once the largest producer of gold in Arizona, this ghost town still has 100 inhabitants down from its heyday 10,000, but is photogenic due to its proliferation of wild burros wandering the streets. The town is named for Olive Oatman, kidnapped by Apaches, sold to Mojave Indians and released five years later in

SAN DIEGO TO TENNESSEE ROUTE 12

1855 near the town.

10. SANTA CLAUS
35.33421, -114.21773
Santa Claus, AZ 86413

One quirky deserted Arizona desert town. The town only came into being in 1937, and was established by a woman in real estate who cunningly plotted to use the ubiquitous Santa concept to draw in buyers to her otherwise dusty land. The woman advertised herself as the 'biggest real estate agent in California', but weighing over 300lbs, it is unclear in which sense this was intended. Within 5 years tourists had begun to congregate at the quirkily named location but it never had enough pull to become a real estate mecca, leading the owner to sell out in 1949. Others have tried to cash in including a re-mailing service offering to postmark letters from the location but ultimately it fell into decline in the '70s and despite efforts to sell the land first for $95,000 then for $52,200, it never sold; compared to its heyday in which it featured a North Pole (obviously), a workshop and a perennial live Santa Claus as well as food such as Chicken a' la North Pole, it is now almost erased from the map but for a wishing well, a few ruined structures and a children's derailed train.

11. CHLORIDE GHOST TOWN
35.41395, -114.19859
Chloride, AZ 86431

A largely abandoned town where the remaining residents display bizarre trash art and murals adorn the surrounding cliffs.

12. THE TOWN OF NOTHING
34.48001, -113.33592
Nothing, AZ 85360

Small abandoned town which at its peak

Left: Santa Claus
Right: The Town of Nothing
Right: Chloride Ghost Town

SAN DIEGO TO TENNESSEE ROUTE 12

The Journey
images from an inward search for self

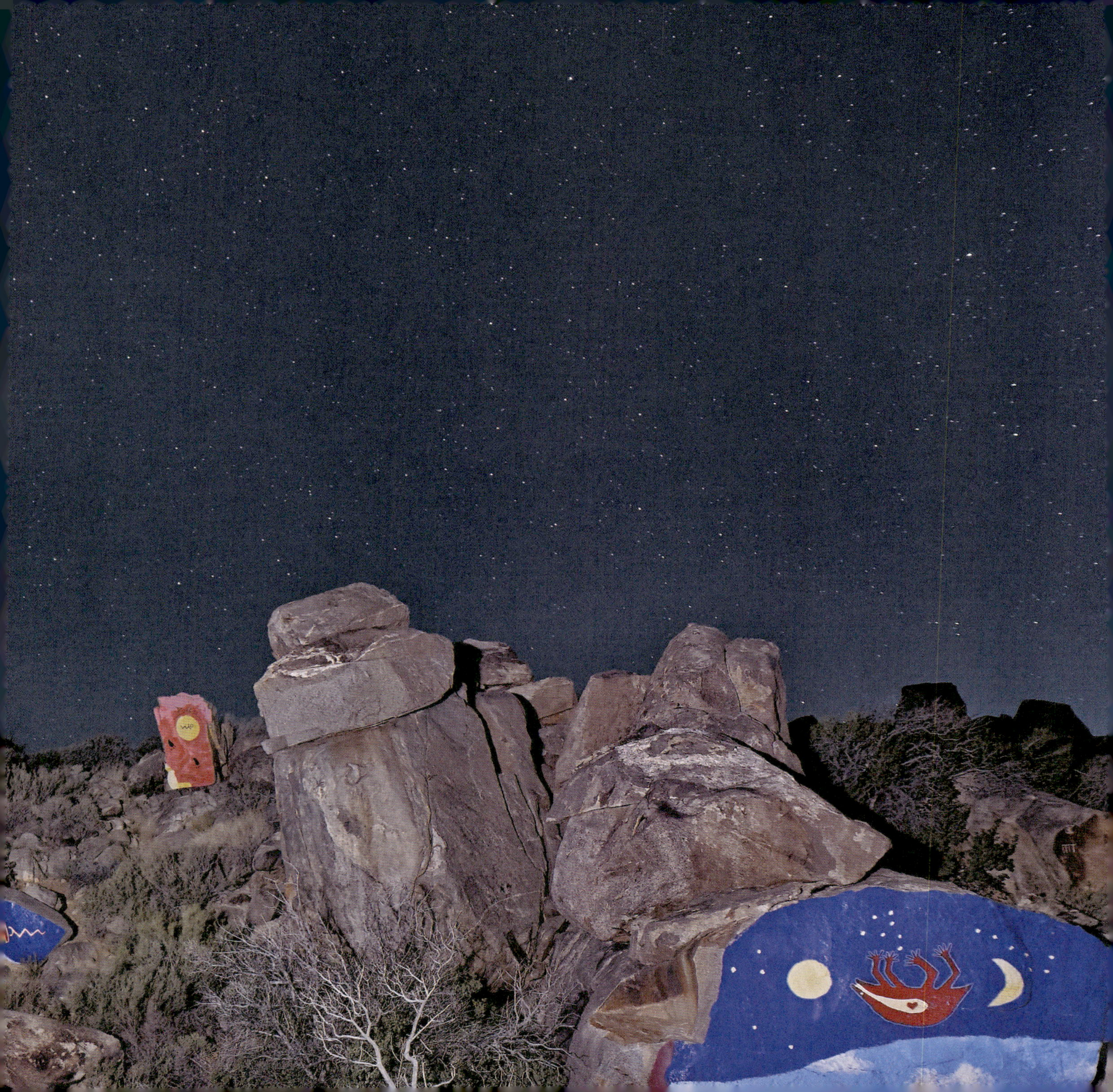

UNITED STATES POST OFFICE
TRUTH OR CONSEQUENCES NEW MEXICO
87901

North Entrance—TRUTH OR CONSEQUENCES, NEW MEXICO

PALACE MOTEL

boasted 4 residents. The common answer from locals as to the etymology of its name is 'it got named by a bunch of drunks'. The town sign once read 'Town of Nothing Arizona. Founded 1977. Elevation 3269ft. The staunch citizens of Nothing are full of Hope, Faith and Believe in the work ethic. Thru-the-years-these dedicated people had faith in Nothing, hoped for Nothing, worked at Nothing, for Nothing.' Century21 Estate Agents ran a campaign in 2016 entitled 'Give Dad Nothing for Father's Day', in which for 24 hours only people could purchase a tiny plot of land in Nothing complete with downloadable certificate.

NOW WHY NOT CHECK OUT:

SURPRISE - See p.238

13. THE TOWN OF PIE
34.29838, -108.13478
Halsell Road, Pie Town, NM 87827
An unincorporated community founded by the wonderfully named Leander Blankenship, a resident 'who really liked pie, regardless of kind'. Stop in at…ready… Pieoneer Pies while you're in town (US-60, Pie Town, NM 87827, www.pieoneer.com) The store is just off Mud Pie Lane. Seriously. Meanwhile nearby, the Pie Town Fire Department are presumably staving off oven fires and trying to be taken seriously, hotel The Toaster House is feeling as if it screwed up its branding and the Mormon Church established an outpost here because… well… literally everyone loves pies.

14. THE TOWN OF TRUTH OR CONSEQUENCES
33.1284, -107.2528
Truth or Consequences, NM 87901
Originally named Hot Springs, this town was renamed after the eponymous popular NBC Radio program when the host of the Truth or Consequences quiz announced that he would broadcast its 10th anniversary edition from the first town that renamed itself after the show. The host, Ralph Edwards, went on to broadcast from the town but also to visit it on

< Left and above left: The Town of Truth or Consequences
Right: Roswell Mcdonalds

SAN DIEGO TO TENNESSEE ROUTE 12

the first weekend of May for the next 50 years for the local 'Fiesta' event, which still occurs each year on the self-same weekend. A park is named Ralph Edwards Park in the host's honour.

15. ROSWELL MCDONALDS
33.400433, -104.522856
720 N Main St, Roswell, NM 88201
This McDonalds is truly out of this world.

16. THE CITY OF EARTH
34.23313, -102.41074
Earth, TX 79031
This city was originally named Fairlawn by William E. Halsell its founder, but was renamed Earth as the result of a competition submission by Ora Hume Reeves when it was discovered that there was already a Fairlawn in Texas.

17. OZYMANDIAS ON THE PLAIN SCULPTURE
35.10179, -101.90909
4743 W Sundown Ln, Amarillo, TX 79119
Visit a bizarre sculptor's view of Shelley's famed poem.

18. COMBINE CITY AND CADILLAC RANCH
35.0918, -101.76656
Combine City: 6001 East Farm to Market Road 1151, Amarillo, TX 79118
Cadillac Ranch: I-40, Amarillo, TX, west of the Amarillo city line, exit 60.
Combine harvesters, growing up out of the mud. Check out the nearby Cadillac Ranch while you are in the mood for vertical vehicles. This art installation was built by an art collective called The Ant Farm, backed by Amarillo billionaire Stanley Marsh III. The latter commissioned the piece, which pays tribute to the Cadillac tail fin's evolving design in 1974. Graffiti artists welcome, spray away.

19. VW SLUG BUG RANCH
35.21553, -101.38383
I-40 Frontage Rd, Panhandle, TX 79068
Where VWs go to rust and die.

Why not check out:

All entries from **GANDINI'S CIRCUS** *to* **DEAD WOMAN'S CROSSING**, *pages 205-206*

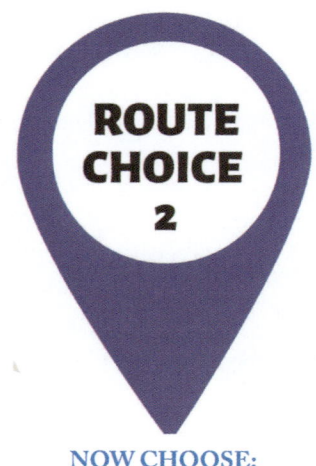

ROUTE CHOICE 2

NOW CHOOSE:

> Right: Ozymandias on the Plain Sculpture
Left: VW Slug Bug Ranch
Overleaf: Combine City and Cadillac Ranch

OFFBEAT AMERICA

426

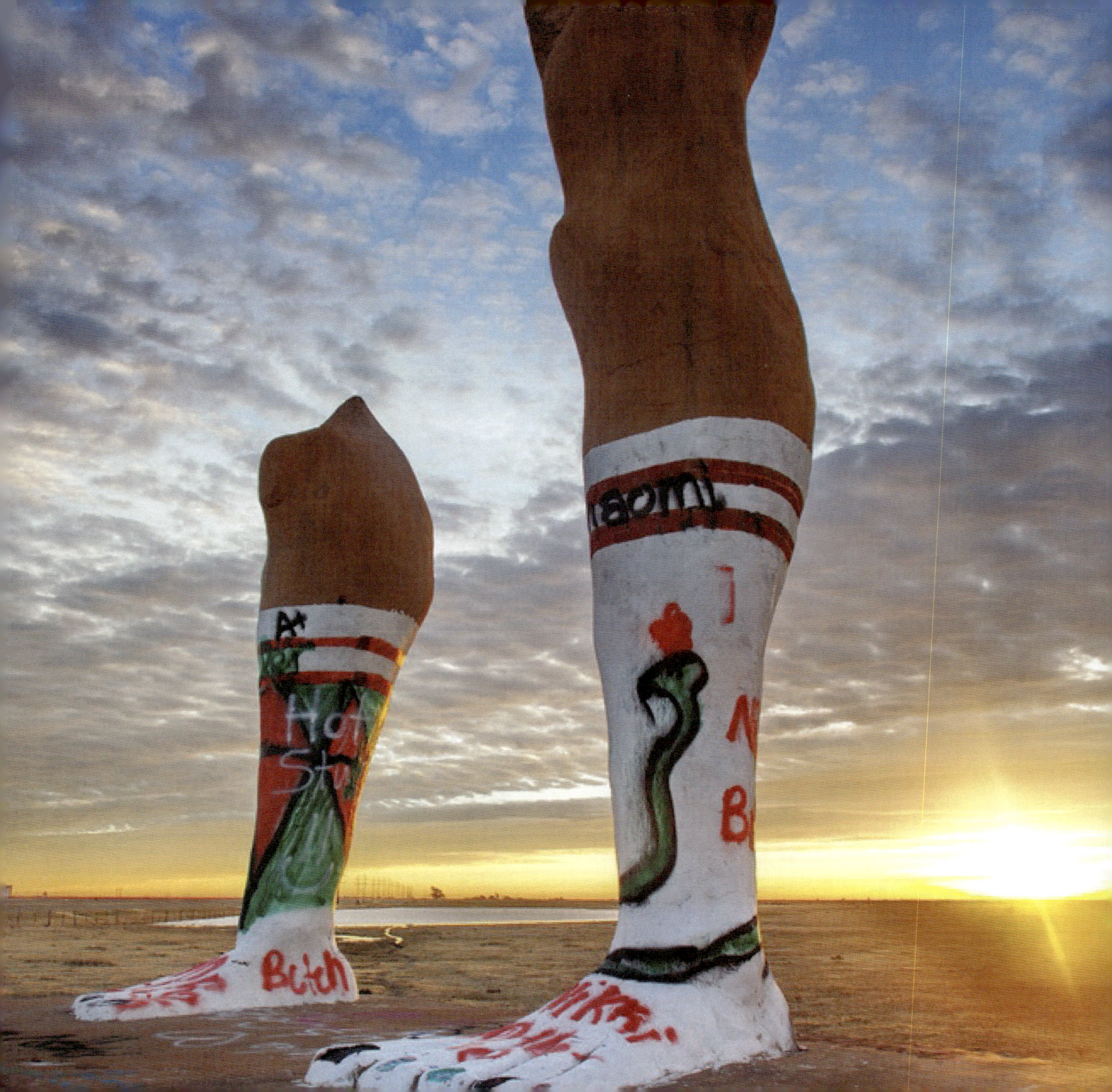

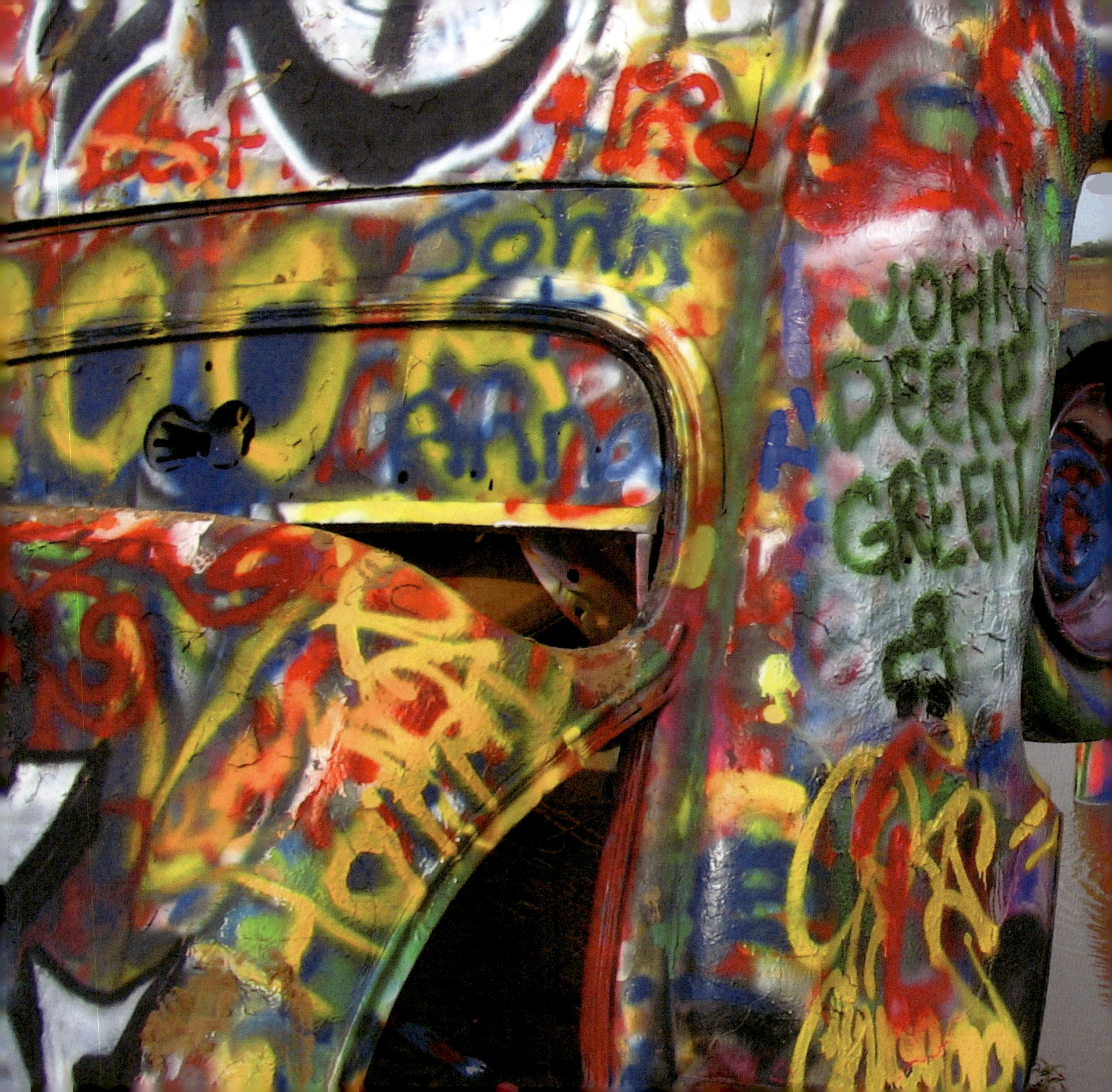
JOHN
DEERE
GREEN

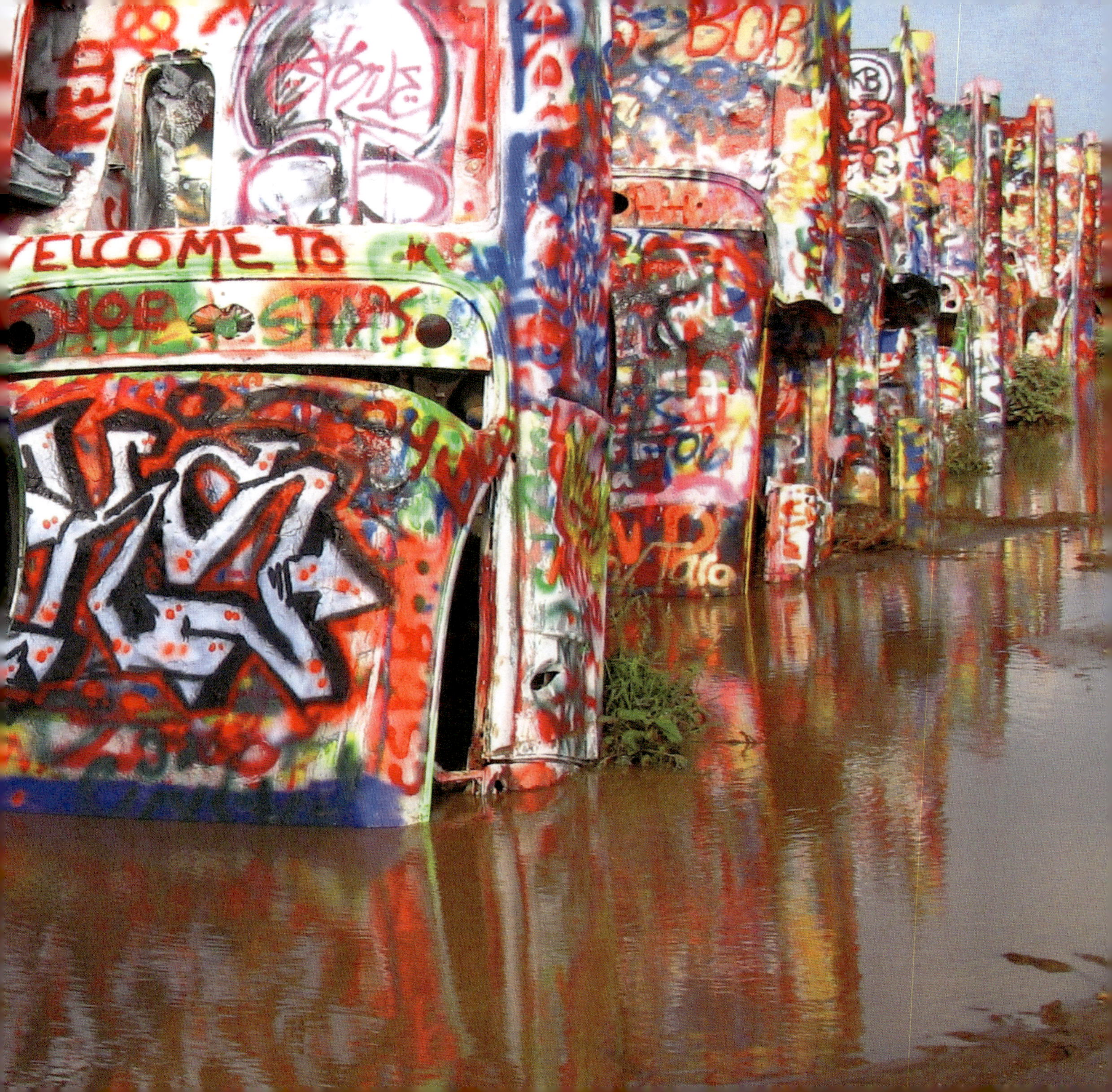
BOB
WELCOME TO

AID
LOST PROFIT
NOTES
MINDFIELD AMBRE JOE

ROUTE A via RUSSELVILLE

or jump to p. 431 to take Route B via Jonesboro

Why not check out:
TOAD SUCK, p. 208

NOW CONTINUE YOUR JOURNEY FROM THE ROUTE A & B CONVERGING POINT BELOW

ROUTE B via JONESBORO

Why not check out:

All entries from *THE 1886 CRESCENT HOTEL & SPA* to *GRAVE OF A MAN & HIS HORSE*, pages 209 to 210

ROUTES A & B CONVERGE IN LITTLE ROCK

WHILE IN LITTLE ROCK, WHY NOT CHECK OUT:

BILLY BASS ADOPTION CENTER, p. 210

20. THE CRYSTAL SHRINE GROTTO
35.10893, -89.87423
Memorial Park Funeral Home and Cemetery, 5668 Poplar Ave, Memphis, TN 38119
Built in the Thirties, this cave contains rock quartz crystal and semiprecious stones, subtlety illustrating Jesus' journey on Earth. The sculptor not only sculpted the attractive faux concrete tree stump the cave is situated in, but also created the fake wood stone mill featured in the opening of Gone With the Wind, as well as the tasteful concrete tree stump rubbish bins around the cemetery which houses the crystal cave.

21. BILLY TRIPP'S MINDFIELD
35.5920, 89.2699
1 Mindfield Alley/S Monroe Avenue, Brownsville, Tennessee, 38012
One man's voyage into his own psyche in giant mad metal form.

WHILE IN NASHVILLE, WHY NOT CHECK OUT:

THE CONCRETE PARTHENON & THE HERMITAGE HOTEL, p. 158

< Left: Billy Tripp's Mindfield
Right: The Crystal Shrine Grotto
Overleaf: Combine City and Cadillac Ranch

SAN DIEGO TO TENNESSEE ROUTE 12

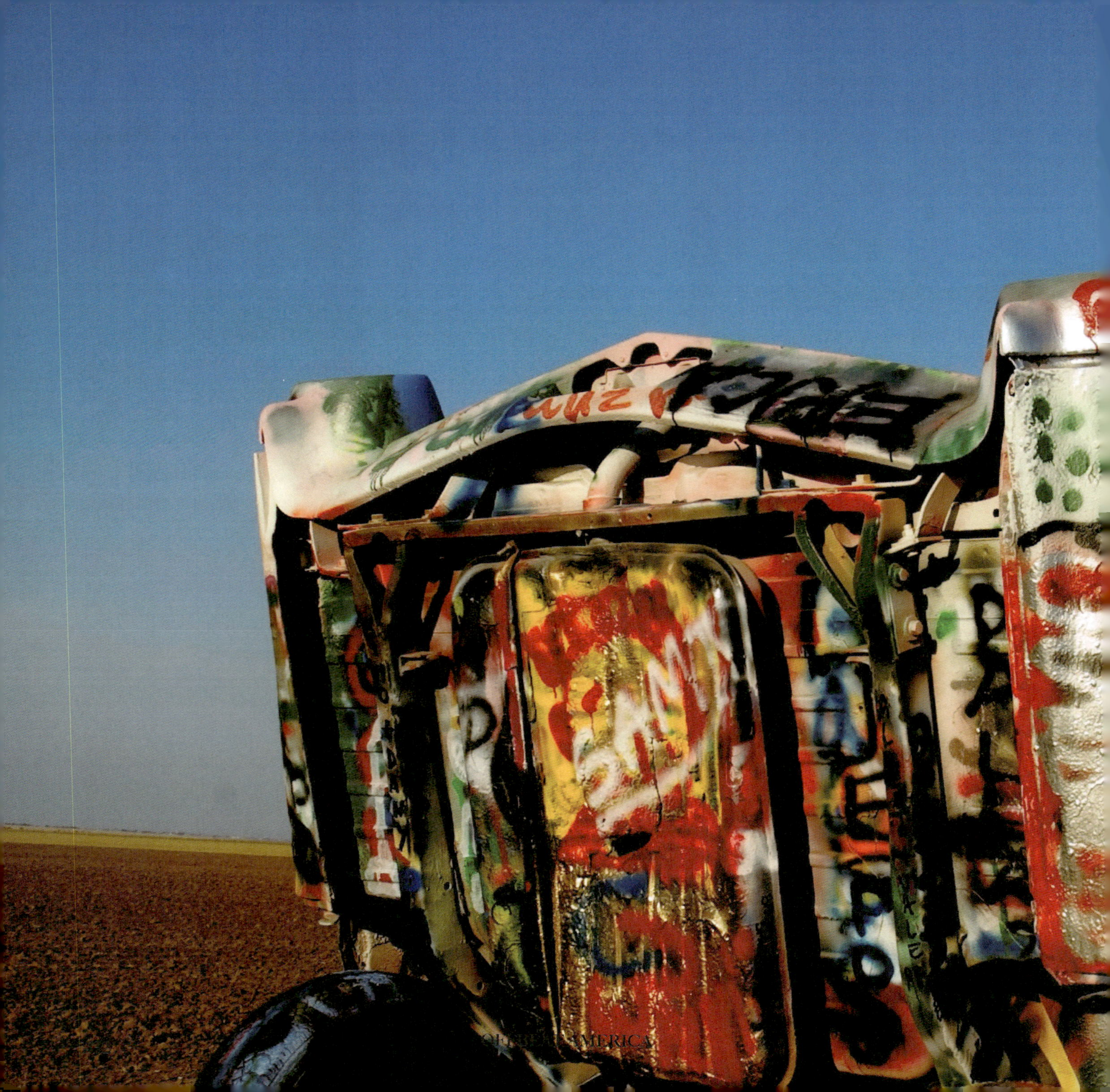

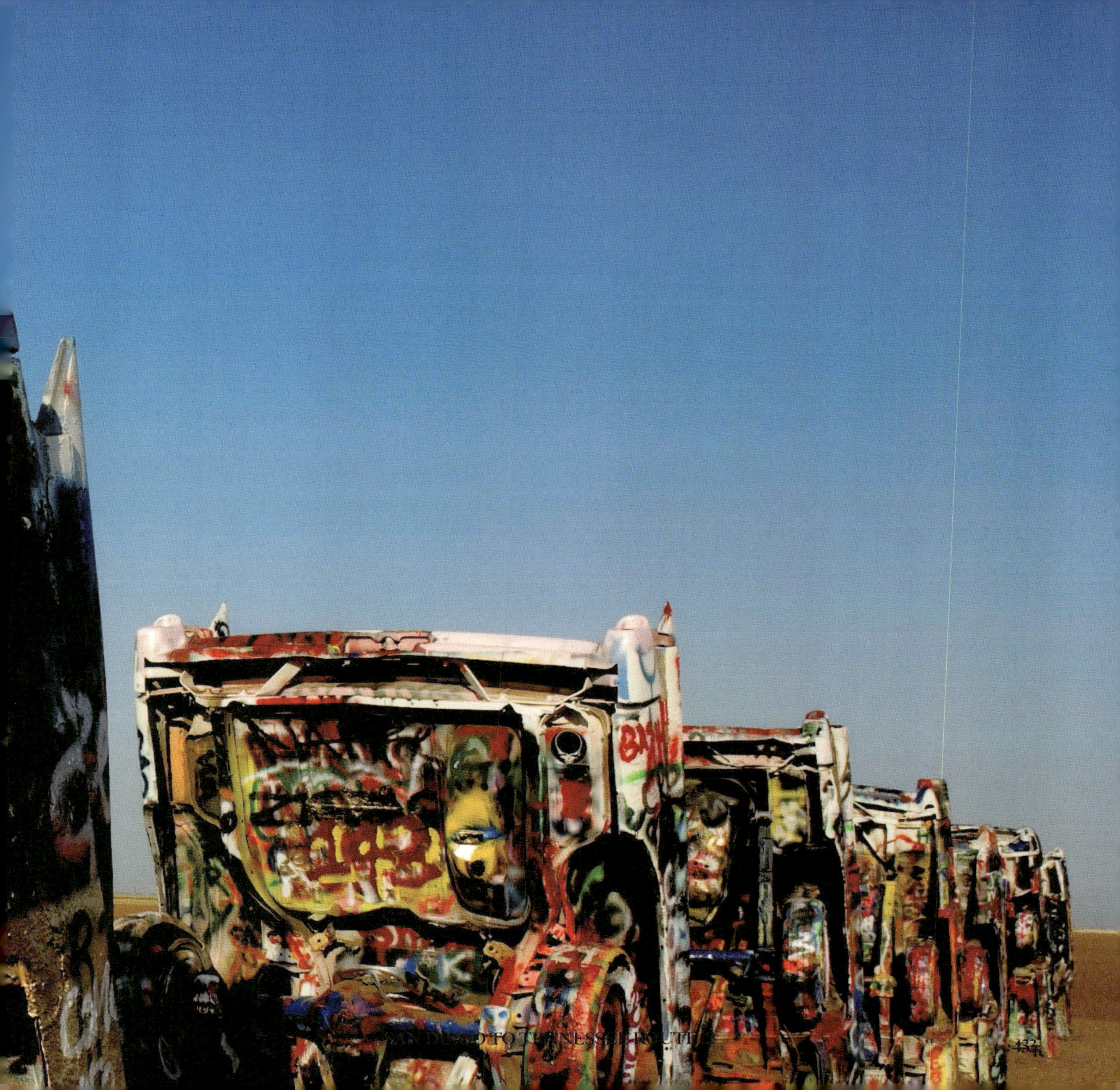

MANKIND·WHICH·ARE·DELIVERED·DOWN·FROM·GENERATIO

< Left: Largest Tiffany Glass Dome (p. 114)
End of book: Mount Moriah Cemetery (p. 26)

INDEX

112 OCEAN AVE 11

A

ABANDONED HENRY RIVER MILL VILLAGE 40

ABANDONED LUTHERAN SCHOLHOUSE 393
ABANDONED RIVER COUNTRY PARK 60
ABANDONED TOWN OF CAIRO 401
ABUNDANT LIFE CHRISTIAN CENTER 185
ACCIDENT 79
ADAM-ONDI-AHMAN 200, 397
ADVENTURE PLAYGROUND 333
A'FLOAT SUSHI 310
AHLGRIM FAMILY FUNERAL SERVICES 122
AIRPLANE HOME IN THE WOODS 344
AIRSTREAMS OF SEFFNER 62
AIRTIGHT BRIDGE 136
ALAMEDA SPITE HOUSE 332
ALBANY SHOE TREE 179
ALBINO SQUIRRELS OF OLNEY 133
ALBION CASTLE 330
ALCATRAZ 331
ALEISTER CROWLEY'S MAGICKAL RETIREMENT 106
ALEX RASKIN ANTIQUES 59
AMBOY GHOST TOWN 353
AMERICAN BANJO MUSEUM 206
AMERICAN CELEBRATION ON PARADE 35
AMERICAN MUSEUM OF MAGIC 181
AMERICAN NUMISMATIC SOCIETY 14
AMERICAN SCIENCE AND SURPLUS 276
AMERICAN SIGN MUSEUM 140
AMERICA'S HIGHEST DEEP FAT FRYER 409
AMERICA'S LARGEST VIKING 295
ANGELUS TEMPLE 310
ANGOLA PRISON RODEO 162
ANTELOPE VALLEY POPPY RESERVE 316
APACHE DRIVE-IN THEATRE 215
AQUARIUM RESTAURANT 158

AQUATIC PARK TOMBSTONES 331
ARK ENCOUNTER 144
ARMPIT OF AMERICA 381
ART CAR MUSEUM 224
ARTIST'S DRIVE 369
ASSAWOMAN 27
Atlanta 46
ATLANTA PRISON FARM 49
ATLANTA WHITE HOUSE 46
ATOMIC SURVIVAL TOWN 364
AURORA ALIEN GRAVE 218
AVIATION NAVIGATION ARROW 363

B

BABY HEAD CEMETERY 222
BACON BACON 330
BADWATER BASIN 369
BAHA I HOUSE OF WORSHIP 119
BALD KNOB CROSS OF PEACE 399
BALLARAT GHOST TOWN 369
BALMORHEA STATE PARK POOL 240
BARBECUE 37
BARBOURSVILLE RUINS 35
BARNEY SMITH'S TOILET SEAT ART MUSEUM 244
BARTLETT YARNS MILL 100
BATH SCHOOL MASSACRE MEMORIAL 182
BEARTHA 94
BEAVERLICK 144
BEER CAN HOUSE 224
BELCHERTOWN 85
BELLE ISLE ZOO 173
BELLEVUE HOSPITAL 18
BEN AND JERRYS FLAVOUR GRAVEYARD 109
BENDIX WOODS 181
BENSONS PARK 93
BETSY THE LOBSTER 70
BETTY AND BARNEY HILL 106
BETTY AND BARNEY HILL ARCHIVE 94
BIBLEWALK WAX MUSEUM 176

BIG BEND POWER PLANT MANATEE VIEWING AREA 62
BIG BUTT MOUNTAIN SIGN 40
BIG CHICKEN 46
BIGFOOT DISCOVERY MUSEUM 322
BIGHORN MEDICINE WHEEL 269
BIG NICKEL 297
BIG RIG JIG 381
BILLY BASS ADOPTION CENTER 210
BILLY TRIPP'S MINDFIELD 431
BIRTHPLACE OF H H HOLMES 94
BISHOP'S CASTLE 409
BITTER END 40
BLACK DAHLIA MEMORIAL 87
BLEU HORSES 261
BLUE FLASH BACKYARD ROLLER COASTER 151
BLUE GHOST FIREFLIES 40
BODIE STATE HISTORICAL PARK 374
BOK TOWER GARDENS & SINGING TOWER 61
BOMBAY BEACH AT THE SALTON SEA 234
BONNIE AND CLYDE AMBUSH MUSEUM 214
BOOT HILL CEMETERY 244
BOTANICA REINA DE MEXICO 307
BOURN MANSION 331
BRAINWASH 330
BRONNER'S CHRISTMAS WONDERLAND 185
BRONSON CAVE 312
BROOKLYN SUPERHERO SUPPLY STORE 13
BUSTED PLUG PLAZA 43
BUSY BEAVER BUTTON CO 118
BUTTZVILLE 295
BYRON HOT SPRINGS HOTEL 334

C

CAGLE CASTLE 46
CAHOKIA MOUNDS 130
CALICO GHOST TOWN 353
CALIFORNIA CITY 317
CALIFORNIA INSTITUTE OF ABNORMALARTS (CIA) 312
CANO'S CASTLE 410
CAPE ROMANO DOME HOUSES 67
CAPILANO SUSPENSION BRIDGE 286
CAROUSEL OF HAPPINESS 390
CARTY'S CAMP 419
CASA BONITA 390

CASTLE TOWN 261
CAVE HILL CEMETERY 148
CAVE-IN-ROCK 402
CDC MUSEUM ATLANTA 48
CEMENTLAND 129
CENTENNIAL BULB 334
CHATTY BELLE 273
CHEDDAR 43
CHEESMAN PARK 390
Chicago 113
CHICAGO MUNICIPAL TUBERCULOSIS SANITARIUM 118
CHICAGO SWEATLODGE 118
CHICAGO'S WOODEN ALLIES 118
CHILDREN'S FAIRYLAND 332
CHLORIDE GHOST TOWN 420
CHRISTMAS CARD LANE 231
CHUTTERS CANDY STORE 106
CIRCUS CENTER 330
CIRCUS TRAIN WRECK VICTIMS MEMORIAL 52
CIRCUS WORLD MUSEUM 274
CITY HALL STATION 14
CITY SALVAGE 195
CLOWN MOTEL 370
CLUTTER FAMILY HOME 392
COALDALE 373
COLEBROOK MURDER VICTIMS MEMORIAL 100
COLONEL BUCK AND THE WITCH'S CURSE 97
COLONEL SANDERS GRAVE 148
COMBINE CITY AND CADILLAC RANCH 426
CONCRETE PARTHENON 158
CONEY ISLAND HOTDOG STAND 389
CONFLICT KITCHEN 79
CONTRABANDO 240
COOL PATCH PUMPKINS CORN MAZE 337
CORINNE ELLIOT LAWTON'S GRAVE 59
CORNHENGE 176
CORPSEWOOD MANOR 158
COSMOS MYSTERY AREA 270
COTTAGE PLANTATION 162
CRATER OF DIAMONDS STATE PARK 214
CRAZY HORSE MEMORIAL 270
CROWN FOUNTAIN 114
CULT SWIMMING POOL AND MASSACRE SITE 222
CUT OFF 163

D

DANVERS HOSPITAL FOR THE CRIMINALLY INSANE 90
DARK BIRD PALACE 410
DARTH VADER GROTESQUE AT THE WASHINGTON NATIONAL CATHEDRAL 30
DEAD CHILDRENS PLAYGROUND 158
DEADMAN CROSSING 178
DEAD WOMEN CROSSING 206
DEMOULIN MUSEUM 132
DENVERS DINOSAUR HOTEL 390
DEVIL'S GULCH 270
DEVIL'S HOLE 364
DEVIL'S POSTPILE NATIONAL MONUMENT 373
DIGITAL ORCA 286
DINE WITH AN ASTRONAUT 60
DINOSAUR VALLEY STATE PARK 219
DINOSAUR WORLD 155
DOG MOUNTAIN 100
DOGPATCH USA 210
DOTSON RUNWAY GRAVES 59
DRAWBRIDGE 326
DUNSMUIR-HELLMAN HISTORIC ESTATE 332

E

EAST CORINTH 107
EASTERN CEMETERY 148
EAST RACE WATERWAY 181
EBENEZER FLOPPEN SLOPPERS 122
ECKLEY MINERS VILLAGE MUSEUM 80
EDISTO ISLAND TREE 58
ED LEEDSKALNIN'S CORAL CASTLE 70
ELBERTON GRANITE MUSEUM 43
ELLAVILLE GHOST TOWN 57
ELWOOD THE WORLD'S TALLEST CONCRETE GNOME 195
EMBARRASS 296
EMILY'S BRIDGE 109
EMPIRE QUARRY 178
EPIC SYSTEMS CAMPUS 275
ERECT 37
ERICK SCHATS BAKKERY 373
E T WICKHAM SCULPTURE TRAIL 158
EXCHANGE BAR & GRILL 19

F

FAIR PLAY 43
FAIRY POST OFFICE 334
FAST FIBERGLASS MOULD GRAVEYARD 273
FATHER DOBBERSTEIN'S GROTTO OF THE REDEMPTION 195
FLEISHACKER POOL RUINS 327
FLOATING BRIDGE OF BROOKFIELD 107
FLORENCE Y'ALL WATER TOWER 144
FLORIDA CITRUS TOWER 60
FLOYD COLLINS MUSEUM 151
FLY GEYSER 381
FOAMHENGE 37
FORD TRUCK GRAVEYARD 56
FOREST HAVEN ASYLUM 30
FOREST LAWN MEMORIAL PAR 310
FOREST PARK 122
FORK IN THE ROAD 310
FORMERLY THE WORLD'S BIGGEST TRUCK 288
FORT KNOX 97
FORT WORTH WATER GARDENS 219
FOSSIL CABIN 406
FRANK 288
FREDERICK R WEISMAN ART MUSEUM 190
FREMONT TROLL 253
FRITZ'S 201
FROZEN DEAD GUY DAYS 390
FUNSPOT 106

G

GAFFNEY PEACHOID 40
GALAXYLAND 290
GALCO'S SODA POP STOP 310
GALLETA MEADOWS ESTATE 231
GALLOPING GHOST ARCADE 122
GANDINI'S CIRCUS 205
GARNET 257
GEMINI GIANT MUFFLER MAN 122
GEORGE AIR FORCE BASE 353
GEORGE FIRESTONE PRISON 57
GEORGE STICKNEY HOUSE 279
GHOSTBUSTERS FIREHOUSE 14

GIANT COW HEAD 171
GIANT PRAIRIE DOG 270
GIANT PYROGY 291
GIANT SCISSORS 316
GIBSONTON 62
GILMAN CONTAMINATED TOWN 389
GLASS BEACH 340
GLEN ECHO AMUSEMENT PARK 35
'GNOME CHOMSKY' 80
GOLDEN NUGGET 363
GOLDFIELD GHOST TOWN 239
GOLDFIELD HOTEL 370
GOOD INTENT 27
GOTHIC ROSE ANTIQUES & CURIOSITIES 336
GRANDE BALLROOM 185
GRAND SALINE SALT PALACE 215
GRAVE OF A MAN AND HIS HORSE KILLED BY A TRAIN 210
GRAVE OF ED GEIN 181
GRAVE OF ROPE WALKER 222
GRAVE OF SARAH WARE 97
GRAVE OF THE EMBALMED BANDIT 204
GRAVESITE OF UTAH'S FIRST JEDI PRIEST 385
GRAVES OF THE RENO GANG 178
GRAVES OF THE SMUTTYNOSE MURDER VICTIMS 94
GRAVITY RESEARCH FOUNDATION MONUMENT 48
GREENBANK'S HOLLOW 109
GREYSTONE MANSION 315
GRIMES POINT PREHI TORIC ROCK ART & HIDDEN CAVE 374

H

HA HA TONKA CASTLE RUINS 398
HAMPTON SPRINGS HOTEL 57
HANGING LAKE 388
HARPER'S TOPIARY GARDEN 231
HARRY HOUDINI GRAVE 13
HARRY JENNINGS RAT PIT OF THE FIVE POINTS 13
HEAD-SMASHED-IN-BUFFALO JUMP 288
HEART ATTACK GRILL 359
HELL 182
HELL HOUSE ALTAR 30
HENRYS RABBIT RANCH 129
HERMITAGE HOTEL 158
HESS' TRIANGLE 18
HICKSVILLE TRAILER PALACE & ARTIST RETREAT 417
HIDDEN BEACH 189

HOLE-IN-THE-WALL GANG HIDEOUT 270
HOLLIDAY PARK 138
HOLLYWOOD CEMETERY 35
HOLLYWOOD SIGN 310
HOLLYWOOD TOWER APARTMENTS 312
HONDA'S MUSICAL ROAD 316
HOTEL VERTIGO 332
HOT LAKE SPRINGS 256
HOT WELLS HOTEL AND SPA 244
HOUDINI MUSEUM 21
HOUSE OF BALLS 190
HOWE CAVERNS 84
HUDSON-MENG HARRISON 270
HUNTER S THOMPSON SHRINE 389

I

IDAHO CITY 257
IDAHO POTATO MUSEUM 257
IDIOTVILLE 344
INTERCOURSE 77
INTERNATIONAL CRYPTOZOOLOGY MUSEUM 94
INTERNATIONAL YARN BOMBING DAY 286
IOWA'S LARGEST FRYING PAN 196
IRON ZOO 321

J

JAMES RIVER PARK PIPELINE WALKWAY 36
JEKYLL ISLAND CLUB 59
JIM THE WONDER DOG MEMORIAL GARDEN 396
JOHN DILLINGERS GRAVE 138
JOLLY GREEN GIANT STATUE 270
JOSIE LANGMAID MONUMENT 94
JULES UNDERSEA LODGE 70
JUNKMANS DAUGHTER 48

K

KAATSKILL KALEIDOSCOPE 80
KANSAS BARBED WIRE MUSEUM 393
KELLEYS ISLAND WINERY RUINS 176
Kentucky 145

KEY UNDERWOOD COON DOG CEMETERY 162
KILLER PILLAR 57
KIRKSVILLE DEVILS CHAIR 396
KNIGHTRIDGE SPACE OBSERVATORY 178

L

LAJITAS GHOST TOWN 241
LAKE SHORE INN 317
LAMBERT'S CAFÉ 401
LARGEST PANCAKE GRIDDLE IN THE WORLD 80
LARGEST TIFFANY GLASS DOME 114
LARK TOYS 273
LAUREL HILL CEMETERY 22
LAWYERS WINTERBROOK FARM 27
LAZARETTO QUARANTINE STATION 27
LEADVILLE'S ABANDONED SILVERMINE 389
LEARN BOONTLING IN BOONVILLE 337
LEE R BAXANDALL BRIDGE - BRIDGE OF THIGHS 416
LEG-IN-BOOT SQUARE 286
LEHMAN CAVES 380
LEMON GROVE MUMMIES AND LARGEST LEMON 231
LEMP MANSION 131
LIBBYS WATER TOWER 326
LICK FORK 22, 158
LINDA VISTA HOSPITAL 305
LINGER EATUARY 390
LITTLE A'LE'INN 364
LITTLE HEAVEN 27
LIZARD LICK 36
LONNIE HAMMARGRENS HOUSE 359
LOS FELIZ MURDER MANSION 312
LOST COVE 40
LOST SPRINGS 270, 406
LOVE 37
LOVED TO DEATH 330
LOVELADIES 27
LUCKY CAT MUSEUM 140
LUCY THE ELEPHANT 27
LUDLOW MASSACRE SITE 409
LUNA CAFÉ 130

M

MACKINAC ISLAND 297
MAC THE MOOSE 291

MAMMOTH CAVE 151
MAN-EATING RUGS 113
MAN MOUND 274
MAN WITH A BRIEFCASE 219
MARGARET'S GROCERY AND MARKET 162
MARK OLIVER'S YARD ART 333
MARY NOHL HOUSE 276
MAXIE THE WORLD'S LARGEST GOOSE 396
MAXWELL BLADE'S ODDITORIUM 210
MCCLOSKEY CASTLE 327
MCFARTHEST SPOT 294
MCMILLIN MAUSOLEUM 283
MENTONE EGG 179
MERCER CAVERNS 373
MERMET SPRINGS 400
Miami 67
MIAMI MARINE STADIUM 67
MICHIGAN THEATRE 173
MICKEY MOUSE TELEGRAPH POLE 61
MIDDLEGATE 374
MIKE'S CHILI PARLOR 253
MILLENNIUM BILTMORE HOTEL 309
MINNEAPOLIS MANHOLE COVERS 190
MITCHELL SHOE TREE 256
MODOC'S MARKET 179
MOJAVE PHONE BOOTH 358
MONKEY'S EYEBROW 401
MONOPOLY IN THE PARK 322
MONUMENT TO BOOMER THE THREE LEGGED HERO DOG 399
MONUMENT TO THE WORLD'S TALLEST MAN 129
MOON AMTRAK 303
MOORESVILLE'S GRAVITY HILL 136
MORMON ISLAND 337
MOUNT ANGEL ABBEY MUSEUM 341
MOUNT MORIAH CEMETERY 22
MOVIE MANOR 409
MOZUMDAR TEMPLE 353
MUNSTER MANSION 219
MURDER IN SMALL TOWN X STATUE 97
MUSEUM OF CLEAN 257
MUSEUM OF CREATION AND EARTH HISTORY 231
MUSEUM OF NEON ART 310
MUSEUM OF PEZ 327
MUSEUM OF PINBALL 417
MUSEUM OF QUACKERY AND MEDICAL FRAUDS 296
MUSTARD MUSEUM 275

N

NANIBOUJOU LODGE 296
Nashville 158
NATIONAL CORVETTE MUSEUM SINKHOLE 155
NATIONAL FIREARMS MUSEUM 35
NATIONAL HOBO CONVENTION 195
NATIONAL MUSEUM OF FUNERAL HISTORY 224
NATIONAL PARK SEMINARY 30
NEEDLES 419
NELSON 358
NEON BONEYARD 364
NEPTUNE MEMORIAL REEF 67
New 163
NEW 11
NEWBY-MCMAHON BUILDING 208
NEW SALEM AIRPORT CEMETERY 56
NEW YORK FEDERAL GOLD VAULT 13
NIKE MISSILE SITE SF-51 327
NINE MILE CANYON 388
NINJA 14

O

OATMAN GHOST TOWN 419
OCTAGON HOUSE 331
ODD FELLOWS REST 163
OHIO STATE REFORMATORY 176
OKLAHOMA TERRITORIAL MUSEUM 205
OLD COUNTRY MARKET 287
OLD FORT ROAD GRAVITY HILL 341
OLD IDAHO STATE PENITENTIARY 256
OLD TONOPAH CEMETERY 373
OLD WARNER BROS THEATRE INSIDE JEWELRY THEATER CENTER 307
OLD ZOO PICNIC AREA 310
OLE'S BIG GAME STEAKHOUSE AND LOUNGE 403
ONAN'S GOLD PYRAMID HOUSE 277
OREGON STATE HOSPITAL MUSEUM OF MENTAL HEALTH 341
ORGAN PIPER PIZZA PALACE 277
Orlando 60
ORLEANS SIX FLAGS AMUSEMENT PARK 163
OZYMANDIAS ON THE PLAIN SCULPTURE 426

P

PAINT MINES INTERPRETIVE PARK 408
PANORAMA POINT 403
PAPERCLIP COTTAGE CAFÉ 291
PAPER HOUSE 90
PARDEEVILLE 275
PASAQUAN 52
PAUL BUNYAN STATUE 97
PEANUT-TASTIC DOTHAN 56
PENNY BAR 317
PEORIA STATE HOSPITAL 122
PEPPERSAUCE GHOST TOWN 210
PET SEMETARY FILMING SITES 97
Philadelphia 22
PHILOSOPHICAL RESEARCH SOCIETY 312
PHONE BOOTH ON A ROOF 128
PICKLE BARREL HOUSE 297
PINBALL HALL OF FAME 359
PINECRAFT 63
PINKS HOT DOGS 315
PIONEER SALOON 358
PIONEERTOWN 419
PLANE WRECK OF HERITAGE PARK 284
PLAYLAND NOT AT THE BEACH 334
POPE LICK TRESTLE BRIDGE 145
POPS SODA RANCH ON ROUTE 66 205
PRADA MARFA 240
PRISONERS' RESTAURANT 87
PRUITT-IGOE RUINS 131
PSYCHIATRY: AN INDUSTRY OF DEATH MUSEUM 313
PUNXSUTAWNEY 79

Q

QUIGLEY'S CASTLE 209

R

RACCOON MOUNTAIN CAVERNS 158
RANDSBURG 317
RA PAULETTES HAND CARVED CAVES 410
RATTLESNAKE SALOON 162

RAVEN'S GRIN INN 196
RAYNE FROG FESTIVAL 246
RHYOLITE GHOST TOWN 370
RHYOLITE'S DISTRICT OF SHADOWS 370
RIVERVIEW HOSPITAL 284
ROACHTOWN 132
ROBO LIGHTS 416
ROB ZOMBIE SIGN 93
ROCK-A-HOOLA WATERPARK 353
ROCK 'N' ROLL MCDONALDS AND MUSEUM 114
RODEO ANIMAL CEMETERY 206
RONETTE'S BRIDGE - TWIN PEAKS 254
ROSE ISLAND AMUSEMENT PARK 144
ROSENHEIM MANSION 315
ROSICRUCIAN PYRAMIDS OF BUCKS COUNTY 77
ROSWELL MCDONALDS 426
ROTARY JAIL MUSEUM 136
ROWAN OAK 162
ROYSE CITY FUTURO HOUSE 218
RUINS OF THE SUTRO BATHS 331

S

SALEM VILLAGE WITCHCRAFT VICTIMS MEMORIAL 90
SALISH LODGE 254
SALTAIR 340
SALVATION MOUNTAIN 238
SAN FRANCISCO'S PET CEMETERY 331
SAN LUIS OBISPO'S BUBBLEGUM ALLEY 317
SANTA CLAUS 151, 420
SANTA CRUZ MYSTERY SPOT 322
SANTA'S VILLAGE 353
SATANS KINGDOM 85
SATAN'S LAND 380
Savannah 59
SAYDEL INC 304
SCIENTOLOGYS TREMENTINA BASE 410
SCOTTISH RITE TEMPLE 205
SEATTLE'S OFFICIAL BAD ART 254
SEATTLE'S OFFICIAL BAD ART MUSEUM OF ART 254
SEATTLE UNDERGROUND 253
SEGO 388
SEVEN MAGIC MOUNTAINS 358
SHIT FOUNTAIN 118
SHOPSINS 18
SHOWMEN'S 215

SHOWMEN'S REST 122
SINGING RUNWAY 61
SKELETONS IN THE CLOSET 309
SKULL CLIFF 87
SLAB CITY INCLUDING EAST JESUS 238
SLAPPY CAKES 346
SLOTH CAPTIVE HUSBANDRY CENTRE 346
SOLOMON'S CASTLE 63
SOUTH UNION SHAKER VILLAGE 155
SOUTHWESTERN HIGH SCHOOL 176
SPACESHIP HOUSE 158
SPADRA CEMETERY 304
SPAM MUSEUM 195
SPECTRE SET RUINS 52
SPOKANE GHOST TOWN 270, 408
SPOOK HILL ANTI-GRAVITY ZONE 61
SPOONBRIDGE AND CHERRY 190
SQUABBLETOWN 373
SRI SRI RADHA KRISHNA TEMPLE 380
ST AGNES CHURCH AND SCHOOL 185
STARSHIP PEGASUS 222
STATUE OF JOE PALOOKA 178
STAY ON MAIN HOTEL 308
STEELCASE PYRAMID 181
STEPHEN KING'S HOUSE 97
STEVES AUTHENTIC KEY LIME PIES 13
STEVE'S WEIRD HOUSE 252
STILTSVILLE 70
ST THOMAS 363
SUCHER & SONS STAR WARS SHOP AND KURT COBAIN
    MEMORABILIA & INFO CENTER 346
SUMMUM PYRAMID 385

T

TANNEN'S MAGIC STORE 21
TEMPLO SANTA MUERTE 315
TERLINGUA GHOST TOWN 241
TEXAS EIFFEL TOWER 215
THE 1886 CRESCENT HOTEL AND SPA 209
THE ADAMS MEMORIAL 30
THE AHWAHNEE HOTEL 373
THE AIRMAIL LANE MAIL BOX 231
THE AIRPLANE RESTAURANT 408
THE ALABAMA BOLL WEEVIL MONUMENT 52
THE ALBINO BUFFALO OF NORTH DAKOTA 294

THE AMERICAN PIDGEON MUSEUM 205
THE AMERICAN TOBY JUGMUSEUM 119
THE ANDERSON TOWER 386
THE ASYLUM'S DAIRY 317
THE AWAKING MUSE 122
THE BAPTIST MURDER HEADSTONE 93
THE BELL WITCH CAVE 158
THE BIG BIRDCAGE 136
THE BIG COIN 135
THE BIG PENCIL 135
THE BIG YARDSTICK 136
THE BIKE TREE 251
THE BLACK ANGEL OF OAKLAND CEMETERY 196
THE BLUE FUGATES OF TROUBLESOME CREEK 41
THE BODY FARM 43
THE BOTTLE HOUSE 223
THE BOTTLE TREE RANCH 353
THE BUBBLE HOUSE 310
THE CAFÉ AND CAR LOT 219
THE CANADIAN CANOE MUSEUM 297
THE CARNEGIE RUINS 59
THE CINCINNATI MUSHROOM HOUSE 140
THE CITY OF EARTH 426
THE COMMUNITY OF RAPTURE 151
THE CREATION MUSEUM 138
THE CRYSTAL SHRINE GROTTO 431
THE CUP HOUSE 37
THE DOGTOWN GHOST TOWN & BOULDERS 87
THE E C WATERS WRECK 261
THE EMPRESS HOTEL 287
THE ENCHANTED HIGHWAY 291
THE EVIL DEAD CABIN 41
THE FISH HOUSE 333
THE FLOWER FIELDS 304
THE FREAKYBUTTRUE PECULIARIUM 346
THE FUGITIVE TRAIN WRECK 43
THE GARDEN OF EDEN 393
THE GHOST TOWN OF LAUSANNE 80
THE GRAND KUGEL 35
THE GRAVE OF HARRY L COLLINS 148
THE GRAVE OF THE BOSTON STRANGLER 87
THE GRAVE OF WILLIAM G BRUCE 94
THE GURDON LIGHT GURDON 214
THE 'HALLOWEEN' MURDER SCENE HOUSES 313
THE HAT MUSEUM 346
THE HERBIVOROUS BUTCHER 195
THE HEX HOUSE 79

THE HOLY CITY OF OKLAHOMA 206
THE HOLY LAND EXPERIENCE 60
THE HOME ALONE HOUSE 122
THE INDESTRUCTIBLE MUSHROOM HOUSE OF BLACK'S BEACH 229
THE IS THE PLACE MONUMENT 387
THE JOHN & MABLE RINGLING MUSEUM OF ART 62
THE JUNIPER LODGE MOTEL 341
THE JUNK CASTLE 254
THE KAZOOBIE KAZOO FACTORY & MUSEUM 58
THE KINGDOM OF BOOMERIA 322
THE LEANING TOWER OF NILES 122
THE LEGEND OF ETERNAL SILENCE 118
THE LOST CITY OF MADISON 275
THE MAGIC CASTLE 313
THE MANHATTAN WELL MURDER 14
THE MARKEL BUILDING 35
THE MARKET STREET CATACOMBS 137
THE MCBARGE 286
THE MEATPACKING PLANT 131
THE MISSISSIPPI RIVER BASIN MODEL 162
THE MISTAKE HOUSE 129
THE MOJAVE DESERT MAILBOX 358
THE MONROE INSTITUTE 37
THE MURDER CASTLE SITE 113
THE MUSEUM OF DEATH 312
THE MUSEUM OF EVERYDAY LIFE 100
THE MYRTLES PLANTATION 162
THE NARROWS 363
THE NATIONAL BARBER MUSEUM AND HALL OF FAME 178
THE NEVERTOLD CASKET COMPANY 251
THE NEW YORK NEW CHURCH 21
THE OLD BATHHOUSE 118
THE OLD FAITHFUL INN 261
THE OLD SLAVE MART MUSEUM 57
THE PALACE LIGHT BULB 219
THE PENN HILLS RESORT 80
THE PEST HOUSE MEDICAL MUSEUM 37
THE PIONEER MEMORIAL MUSEUM 386
THE PRESTON SCHOOL OF INDUSTRY 335
THE RAILSPLITTER COVERED 129
THE REBECCA NURSE HOMESTEAD 90
THE RED PALACE 321
THE ROCK IN THE HOUSE 273
THE RUINS 138
THE RUINS OF SWEETWATER CREEK 49

THE SAD TINY DINER 18
THE SAFE HOUSE 276
THE SAILING STONES OF RACETRACK PLAYA 369
THE SEATTLE METAPHYSICAL LIBRARY 253
THE SHOE TREE 374
THE SILENT MOVIE THEATER 315
THE SIMPSONS HOUSE 359
THE SINGING OAK 163
THE SMITH MANSION 266
THE SOAP FACTORY 190
THE SOLITUDE YURT 386
THE SPIRAL JETTY 387
THE SPOTTED LAKE 284
THE STRANGE PROCESSION WHICH NEVER MOVES 402
THE THOMPSON HOME FOR OLD LADIES 313
THE TIME TRAVEL MART 309
THE TINY MUSEUM 85
THE TOWN OF BACON 151
THE TOWN OF BORING 344
THE TOWN OF DESIRE 79
THE TOWN OF DING DONG 245
THE TOWN OF EMBARRASS 275
THE TOWN OF HAPPYLAND 84
THE TOWN OF HOOKER 393
THE TOWN OF LOONEYVILLE 215
THE TOWN OF MOONSHINE 133
THE TOWN OF NORMAL 122
THE TOWN OF NOTHING 420
THE TOWN OF PIE 425
THE TOWN OF SLAUGHTERVILLE 206
THE TOWN OF SURPRISE 238
THE TOWN OF TOAD SUCK 210
THE TOWN OF TRUTH OR CONSEQUENCES 425
THE TOWN OF UTOPIA 241
THE TOWN OF WHAT CHEER 196
THE TOWN OF WHY 238
THE TREE ON THE LAKE 287
THE TREE THAT OWNS ITSELF 46
THE UNDERGROUND GARDENS 321
THE UP HOUSE 385
THE VARSITY 49
THE VEGREVILLE PYSANKA 291
THE VERDURA PLANTATION 57
THE VINDICATOR TRAIL AT CRIPPLE CREEK 409
THE WEARY CLUB OF NORWAY 100
THE WEYBURN MENTAL HOSPITAL 291
THE WILLARD ASYLUM SUITCASES 79

THE WINCHESTER MYSTERY HOUSE 322
THE WITCH HOUSE OF SALEM 87
THE WITCH'S CASTLE 344
THE WORLD'S LARGEST DINOSAUR 290
THE WORLD'S LARGEST SAUSAGE 290
THE WORLD'S LARGEST STOVE 185
THE WORLDS LARGEST TELEPHONE 100
THE WORLD'S LARGEST TREE 321
THE WORLD'S SECOND LARGE T ROCKING CHAIR 399
THE WORLD'S SMALLEST POLICE STATION 56
THE WRECK OF THE PETER IREDALE 346
THISTLE GHOST TOWN 380
THORNBURG VILLAGE 333
T H STEMPER CO 276
TIGHTWAD BANK 398
TIMBERLINE LODGE 341
TINY DOORS ATL 48
TOMBSTONE 239
TOM KELLY'S BEER BOTTLE HOUSE 370
TRAVELLER'S RESTAURANT 84
TRAVIS STATE SCHOOL FARM COLONY 223
TREE CLIMBING PLANET 341
TREE SURGEON BURIED IN A TREE 210
TRUCKHENGE 393
TUNNELVISION 43
TWA FLIGHT 260 CRASH SITE 410
TWEDES CAFÉ 254
TWO STORY OUTHOUSE 133

U

U-DIG FOSSILS TRILOBITE CEMETERY 380
UFO WATCHTOWER 409
UFO WELCOME CENTER 57
UMATILLA CHEMICAL DEPOT 254
UMBRELLA COVER MUSEUM 94
UNCERTAIN 214
UNDERGROUND TUNNELS OF LOS ANGELES 309
US NATIONAL TICK COLLECTION 58
USS INAUGURAL SUNKEN MINESWEEPER 131
USS SACHEM RUINS 138
UTOPIAN FALLSCHASE 57

V

VALLEY RELICS MUSEUM 316
VANITY BALLROOM 171

INDEX

VAN SANDT CRYBABY BRIDGE 22
VENETIAN POOL 67
VENT HAVEN MUSEUM 140
VERMONTASAURUS 107
VICTIM OF THE BEAST GRAVESTONE 386
VILLISCA AXE MURDER HOUSE 200
VIZCAYA MUSEUM AND GARDENS 67
VOODOO DOUGHNUT AND WEDDING CHAPEL 346
VW SLUG BUG RANCH 426

W

WANKERS CORNER STORE 341
WARM MINERAL SPRINGS 63
WARP DRIVE STREET SIGN 35
Washington 30
WASHINGTON DC MORMOM TEMPLE 30
WAVERLY HILLS SANITORIUM 148
WELCH SPRING HOSPITAL RUINS 399
WELCOME 43
WELLINGTON AVALANCHE SITE 254
WEST BADEN SPRINGS HOTEL 150
WEST SIDE COW TUNNELS 21
WHIMZEYLAND 61
WHITE KING 385
WICHITA MOUNTAINS BUFFALO HERD 206
WICKER PARK SECRET AGENT SUPPLY CO 118
WIGWAM VILLAGE 2 154
WILD BLUEBERRY LAND 97
WILKES-BARRE ABANDONED TRAIN STATION 80
WILLIAM THOMPSON SCALPED SCALP 196
WINLOCK EGG 346
WOODLAND PALACE 196
WOOLLY MAMMOTH ANTIQUES AND ODDITIES 118
WORLD FAMOUS CROCHET MUSUEM 417
WORLD FAMOUS GIANT SHOE MUSUEM 253
WORLD'S BIGGEST DINOSAURS 417
WORLD'S FIRST CHOCOLATE BROWNIE 114
WORLDS LARGEST AXE 100
WORLD'S LARGEST BALL OF PAINT 179
WORLD'S LARGEST BALL OF STAMPS 200
WORLD'S LARGEST BALL OF TWINE 393
WORLD'S LARGEST BALL OF TWINE ROLLED BY ONE MAN 295
WORLD'S LARGEST BUFFALO 295
WORLD'S LARGEST CATSUP BOTTLE 132
WORLD'S LARGEST COLLETION OF THE SMALLEST VERSIONS OF LARGEST THINGS 393
WORLD'S LARGEST CROCHET HOOK & KNITTING NEEDLES 135
WORLDS LARGEST CROSS 133
WORLD'S LARGEST CROW 295
WORLD'S LARGEST CZECH EGG 393
WORLD'S LARGEST FORK 201
WORLD'S LARGEST GOLF TEE 134
WORLDS LARGEST HAMMOCK 36
WORLD'S LARGEST HOCKEY STICK 296
WORLD'S LARGEST HOCKEY STICK AND PUCK 287
WORLD'S LARGEST MAILBOX 135
WORLD'S LARGEST PEANUT 218
WORLD'S LARGEST PEANUT MONUMENT 49
WORLD'S LARGEST PECAN 396
WORLD'S LARGEST PITCHFORK 134
WORLD'S LARGEST POPCORN BALL 195
WORLD'S LARGEST ROCKING CHAIR 246
WORLDS LARGEST ROCKING CHAIR 133
WORLD'S LARGEST SHUTTLECOCKS 201
WORLD'S LARGEST SIX PACK 273
WORLD'S LARGEST SMALL ELECTRIC APPLIANCE MUSEUM 201
WORLD'S LARGEST SOUP KETTLE 297
WORLD'S LARGEST WIND CHIME 134
WORLD'S LARGEST WOODEN SHOES 135
WORLDS TALLEST FILING CABINET 109
WORLD TRAVELER SIGNPOST 100
WYATT EARP'S GRAVE 327
WYNTOON 341
WYOMING FRONTIER PRISON 406
WYOMING GRAND PRISMATIC SPRING 261

Y

YE OLDE CURIOSITY SHOP 253
YORK WITCH GRAVE 94

Z

ZIGZAG 344
ZOMBIE BURGER & DRINK LAB 196

ZORAN'S SCULPTURE PARK 195
ZZYZX MINERAL SPRINGS AND HEALING CENTER 353

WITH THANKS

This book would not have been possible without the adventurers who generously share their photographic spoils with others on an Attribution basis. Any images which do not contain Attributions are either the Author's own or are rights free.

Intro

UFO Watchtower -

Panorama Point -

Route 1

1. 112 Ocean Avenue - Doug Kerr
2. Houdini Grave - Anthony22
3. Brooklyn Superhero Supply - Jeffrey O Gustafson
5. Conflict Kitchen - Ragesoss
5. Federal Gold Value - ?
7. City Hall - Salim Virji
8. Ninja - Dion Hinchcliffe
8. Willard Briefcases - Peter Caroll
9. Ghostbusters Firehouse - Phillip Ritz
14. Hess' Triangle - Jasoneppink
15. Bellevue - Teri Tynes
21. Crybaby Bridge - Scotty Emerle
22. Laurel Hill Cemetery - Ron Cogswell
24. Mount Moriah - Cortland V. D. Hubbard
24. Mount Moriah - Thomas
24. Mount Moriah Cemetery - Mourningarts
25. Lazaretto Quarantine - Smallbones
28. Lucy the Elephant - Harriet Duncan
29. Little Heaven - Jeffrey A. Brown

30. Assawoman Bay - Smoorenburg
31. Lawyers Farm - Maryland Govpics
32. Hell House Altar - Forsaken Fotos
32a. John Eckart
32b. Elijah Jefferson
33. Forest Haven - Will Fisher
34. National Park Seminary - Eli Pousson
35. Mormon Temple - Jerry
35. Mormon Temple - Joe Ravi
35. Mormon Temple - Mamageek
36. The Adams Memorial - Mike Maguire
36. The Adams Memorial - ncindc
37. Darth Vader Grotesque - ted
38. Glen Echo Amusement Park - EnLorax. G Edward Johnson
39. Warp Drive - Famartin
40. NRA - m01229
43. The Markel Building - Eli Pousson
44. Kugel Fountain - Ewen Roberts
45. Hollywood Cemetery - KH Wilt
45. WW Pool Grave - RVA Allday
46. James River Park Walkway - Jim
48. Windchimes - John Manard
54. Foamhenge - Ben Schumin
58. Lost Cove - Whweller
59. Gaffney Peachoid - Ken Lund
60. Blue Ghost Fireflies - Mike Lewinski

61. Big Butt - Thomson200
64. Bodyfarm - Tyrone - Anil 1956
69. Busted Plug Plaza - Jason Eppink
70. Tunnelvision - Questermark
71. Elberton Granite Association - Egaonline.com
72. Tree that Owns Itself - Boston Public Library
74. Big Chicken - Idawriter
75. Atlanta White House - Wendy Harman
76. CDC Museum - Anokarina
77. Gravity Research Monument - Elizabeth
78. Junkman's Daughter - Joaquin Uy
79. Tiny Doors ATL - Eddie Krebs
81. Atlanta Prison Farm - RJ
82. Sweetwater Creek - John Murphy
83. World's Largest Peanut - Ajrhobby
84. Pasaquan - Rives Langley
86. Spectre - Jason Biro
87. Boll Weevil Monument - Michael Rivera
87. Boll Weevil Monument - Tampags
87. Boll Weevil Monument - Martin Lewison
88. World's Smallest Block - An Errant Knight
89. World's Smallest Police Station - Ebyabe
90. Harveys Ford Truck Collection - Rachel Kramer
95. Ellaville - Ebyabe
96. Hampton Springs - Michael Rivera
98. UFO Welcome Center - Mongollon _1

Attribution 2.0 Generic (CC BY 2.0) - https://creativecommons.org/licenses/by/2.0/legalcode

Attribution-ShareAlike 4.0 International (CC BY-SA 4.0) - https://creativecommons.org/licenses/by-sa/4.0/legalcode

OFFBEAT AMERICA

99. The Old Slave Mart - Brian Stansberry
101. The Kazoo Museum - bobisrtravelling
104. Alex Raskin - Danielle Grace
104. Alex Raskin - Lauren Mitchell
104. Alex Raskin - Marthinus Duckitt
105. Corinne monument - Ann Gav
106. Jekyll Island Club - Ebyabe
109. The Holy Land Experience - David Joyce
110. Citrus Tower - Ebayabe
111. River Country - Coreyjune12
113. Mickey Pylon - dough4872
114. Bok Tower - Rain0975
117. Airstream Ranch - soupstance
119. Manatee - Public
120. Ringling - Roger Wollstadt
121. Pinecraft - Richard Elzey
121. Pinecraft Amish Church - Witherpshins
122. Solomons Caste - Sam Howzit
123. Warm Mineral Springs - Ebyabe
124. Dome Houses - Andy Morffew
125. Venetian Pool - Ines Hegedus-Garcia
126. Vizcaya - Ines Hegedus-Garcia
127. Miami Marine Stadium - Ines Hegedus-Garcia
127. Miami Marine Stadium - Craig Oneill
127. Miami Marine Stadium - Golden Dusk Photography
128. Neptune Memorial Reef - Todd Murray
129. Stiltsville - Justdweezil
129. Stiltsville - Ebyabe
131. Jules Hotel - Eric Falconi
132. Betsy The Lobster - Matt Kleffer

Route 2

2. Intercourse, Derek Ramsey 2006
5. Conflict Kitchen, Ragesoss

6. Punxsutawney - Doug Kerr
8. Willard Suitcases - Peter Caroll
11. Eckley Miners Village - Jerrye and Roy Klotz MD
13. Penn Hills - R'iyeh Imaging
13. Penn Hills - Foresaken Fotos
13. Penn Hills - Jonathan Haeber
15. Kaleidoscope - Jason Eppink
16. Howe Caverns - Leah
19. Belchertown - Matthew Bennet
25. Salem - Witch2
25. Sales Witch House - Paul Rocheleau
29. Rebecca Nurse Hous - Willijay
30. Salem Memorial - Dana Huff
31. Danvers - John Phelan
34. Cutter Grave - J. W. Ocker
42. Umbrella Cover Museum - PIGUY101
43. Eartha - Paul Vanderwerf
47. Paul Bunyon Statue - Dennis Jarvis
48. Stephen King's House - Cliff
50. Wild Blueberry Land - Larry Miller
52. World's Largest Axe - Nackawic NB Hohum
56. Maine Sign - 90494
59. Dog Chapel - Bazusa, Ann Dabney, Alans1948, Carol M. Highsmith
60. Chutters - J Cardinal 18
63. Aleister Crowley - Magus
64. Vermontasaurus - Steph Flanders
66. Brookfield Floating Bridge - Summerlovin6411
67. Greenbank Hollow - Corey Ann
68. Emily's Bridge - Mfwills
69. Ben and Jerry's Flavour Graveyard - Doug Kerr

Route 3

4. Crown Fountain - Serge Melki

5. Tiffany Dome - Jax House
5. Tiffany Dome (rear of book) - wsilver
6. Rock & Roll McDonalds - Antonio Vernon
8. Shit Fountain - Brandie Heinel
13. Eternal Silence - Leyla. A
17. Baha I Temple - Jelloneck
17. Bahi I Temple - Purpy Pupple
18. Home Alone House - Famartin
19. Niles - Ken Lund
24. Showmen's Rest - 6th Happiness
25. Gemini Giant -
26. Normal -
27. Peoria State - Willijay
31. Tallest Man - Ulstein Bild
31. Robert Wadlow - Ethajek
33. Cementland - PASA47
37. Pruitt-Igoe Ruins -
38. USS Inaugural - Paul Sableman
39. Lemp Mansion - Paul Sableman
39. Lemp Mansion - Matt Huck
41. Largest Catsup - Andrew Keith
43. Effingham Cross - Daniel Schwen
44. Two Story Outhouse - Senoranderson
45. Albino Squirrel - Patrick Boyle
47. Largest Rocking Chair - Abe Ezekowitz
48. Largest Wind Chimes - John Manard
49. Largest Golf Tee - Drew Tarvin
60. Rotary Jail - dok1
62. Dillinger - Wildhartlivie
63. The Ruins - Karl Bitter
65. Creation Museum - David Berkowitz
65. Creation Museum - John Scalzi
66. American Sign Museum - David Berkowitz
66. American Sign Museum - Geoffrey Galloway
67. Lucky Cat Museum - ?

WITH THANKS

68. Mushroom House - Dave Menninger
69. Vent Haven - Schw5r7z
70. Florence Water Tower - Allen Burt
70. Florence Water Tower - Madaise
72. Ark Encounter - Scott1346
73. Rose Island - Bedford
74. Pope Lick - Marcus O. Bst
75. Cave Hill - Garden State Hiker
77. Colonel Sanders Grave - Bedford
79. Waverly - Aaron Vowels
80. West Baden Springs Hotel - Sarah Ewart
80. West Baden Springs Hotel - Sarah Wilkerson Poole
81. Blue Flash - Colin
84. Santa Claus - Udalumni
88. Dinosaur World - MCDLTTX
89. National Corvette Museum - Zombieite
91. Bell Witch - Brad06
93. Aquarium Restaurant - Cliff
94. Hermitage Hotel - Nashpual
95. Concrete Parthenon - Michael Brown/Kaldari
96. Spaceship House - Heavybluesman
102. Key Underwood Coon Dog Cemetery - Terri
108. Myrtles Plantation - Bogdan Oporowski
110. Odd Fellows Rest - ?
112. Six Flags - Keoni Kabral

Route 4

2. Vanity Ballroom - Albert Duce
4. Michigan theater - Jedimentat44
4. Michigan theater - Rex Brown
4. Michigan theater - TNS Sofres
4. Michigan theater - Lisa Picard
5. Southwestern - notorious4life
7. Ohio State - rain0975

9. Cornhenge - Miguelcastaneda
9. Cornhenge - Web2jordan
13. Quarry - eli duke
16. Ball of Paint - Steven Pierson
19. Mentone Egg - Nyttend
21. East Raceway - Michael J Lane
22. American Magic Museum - Battlecreekcvb
23. Steelcase - drtel
24. Ed Gein grave - bryanwake
25. Bath School Memorial - jtmichcock
26. Hell - sswonk
26. Hell - Ashleigh Bennett
26. Hell - Danielle Walquist Lynch
27. Bronners - Ken Lund
31. Grande Ballroom - Albert Duce

Route 5

1. Hidden Beach - Oneconscious
1. Hidden Beach - Tony, Oneconscious
2. Spoonbridge - Rob Marquardt
4. Weisman - Carol M. Highsmith
7. Herbivorous Butcher - Tony Webster
7. Herbivorous Butcher - Paul Vanderwerf
10. Spam Museum - Darb02
11. Hobo Symbols - Ryan Somma
12. Father Dobberstein - Alejandro Pulido
13. Popcorn - Videovik
15. Iowa Frying Pan - Neil Conway
17. Woodland Palace - Kepper66
18. Black Angel - Bill Whittaker
19. What Cheer - Quinn Anya
19. What Cheer - Tony Webster
20. Zombie Burger - Alan Light
21. Albert the Bull - Neepster

23. World's Largest Ball of Stamps - Andrew Seaman
24. Villasca - Jennifer Kirkland
25. Adam - Ondi - Ahman - Americasroof
27. Shuttlecock - JD Redding
27. Shuttlecocks - Pexels
29. World's Largest fork - Fishepat000
30. Elmer McCurdy - WG Boag
31. Scottish Rite - Allison Meier
34. Pops - Carol M. Highsmith
35. Pigeon - Sheila Scarborough
36. Rodeo Cemetery - Joseph Novak
37. American Banjo Museum - Michael Barera
40. Bison - Jack Dykinga & Agricultural Research Service
41. Holy City - Doug Miller
42. Newby Building - Chuck Coker
43. Cresent Hotel - Brad Holt
44. Quigley's Castle - Brandon Rush
45. Dogpatch USA - Whiterabbit@undergroundozarks.com
48. Toad Suck - Spider Dog
49. Billy Bass - Kevin Burkett
53. Diamonds - Doug Wertman
54. Bonnie & Clyde - Billy Hathorn
59. Texas Eiffel - Nancy I'm gonna snap!
60. Showmen's Rest - Joseph Novak
61. World's Largest Peanut - Chuck Coker
62. Futuro - Steve Rainwater
66. Man with a Briefcase - Sashafatcat
67. Fort Worth Water Garden - Paul Joseph
68. Munster House - prayitno
69. Dinosaur Valley - Diane Turner
70. Starship Pegasus - lfwlfw
71. Rope Walker - @Maggiel_42, seh256
72. Branch Davidian - Daniel Tobias
76. Funeral History - A Yee
77. Art Car - Cali4beach

77. Art Car - Alex Brogan

78. Beer Can House - Andrew Wiseman

Route 6

1. Mushroom House - R Gourley

4. Famous Air Mail Box - Robert DuHamel

7. Galleta Meadows - Author's Own

11. Why - Michael Fiegle

13. Goldfield - Marine 69-71

14. Tombstone - Grombo

14. Boothill - Ken Lund

15. Balmorhea - Chris Mcinnis

15. Prada Marfa - Nan Palmero

16. Balmorhea - Larry D. Moore

18. Lajitas - 12fh

19. Terlingua - Jerrye & Roy Klotz MD

23. Toilet Seat - Julie Gomoll

24. Ding Dong - oyoyoy

25. Rayne - ny1938

Route 7

4. Ye Old Curiosity Shop - Joe Mabel

5. Giant Shoes - Christine592

6. Fremont Troll - Roshan Vyas

7. Seattle Underground - JVL

8. Mike's Chilli Parlor - Visitor7

14. Hot Lake Springs - Visitor7

19. Idaho State - Dieseldemon

20. Idaho City - Brian Teutsch

21. Museum of Clean - Ethan Prater

22. Idaho Potato Museum - Rayb777

23. Garnet - Mypubliclands

24. Bleu Horses - W&J

25. Castle Town - Sshreeves

26. Grand Prismatic - James St. John

26. Grand Prismatic - Yellowstonenps

27. Crows Nest - Jinx McCombs

27. Old Faithful - Jim Peaco

29. Smith Mansion - Paul Hermans

30. Medicine Wheel - Djonsons

31. Hole in the Wall - Sam Beebe / Bureau of Land Man.

32. Lost Springs - idunno00923

34. Crazy Horse memorial - Stockypics

35. Cosmos - Shelby Bell

37. Giant Prairie Dog - Scott Robinson

38. Devils Gulch - Punkerstin

39. Jolly Green Giant - Doug Kerr

40. Lark Toys - Minnemom

42. Largest Six Pack - Tony Webster

43. Fibreglass - Shannon McGee

44. Chatty Belle - La Vaca Vegetariana

45. Circus World - bdunnette

48. Embarass - Corey Taratuta

49. Mustard Museum - Minnemom

49. Mustard Museum - Jonathunder

50. Epic - Allison Meyer

50. Epic - YLEM

52. Mary Nohl House - Freekee

53. Safe House - Richie Diesterheft

55. American Science - yossarian22

56. Organ Piper - purple slog 2

57. Onan - Chuck Falzone

58. Stickney Mansion - Teemu008

Route 8

1. McMillan Mausoleum - Joe Goldberg

2. Plane Wreck - Brock Anderson

3. Spotted Lake - Andrew Enns

4. Riverview - Justus Hayes

5. McBarge - Taz

7. Digital Orca - Faruk Ates

8. Capilano - David Davies

9. Kniffiti - Founzy

9. Kniffiti - Rebmobnray

9. Kniffiti - Michellecornelison

10. The Empress - miladiaferrari

11. Hockey Stick - Smileygrl

13. Tree on the Lake - Shawn McCready

14. Truck - Hojusaram

15. Frank - Marek Slusarczyk

16. Head Smashed - lazarus000

17. Dinosaur - prakahsubbarao

18. Galaxyland - iqremix

20. Vegreville Pysanka - Myke2020

22. Mac - Matt Boulton

22. Mac - Lisa

23. Weyburn - Briyyz

25. Enchanted Highway - Mineemom

27. Albino Buffalo - Mongo

28. Buffalo - Jennifer Kirkland

30. Big Ole - Amy Meredith

32. Ball of Twine - Alecpie

33. Quackery - Andrew Kuchling

34. Hockey Stick - Mykl Roventine

36. Naniboujou - Kablammo

37. Soup Kettle - Lanyap

38. Pickle Barrel - Kristina_5

38. Pickle Barrel Historic - Wystan

39. Mackinac - notorious4life

40. Big Nickel - deashoot

41. Canadian Canoe Museum - p199

WITH THANKS

449

Route 9

1. Moon Amtrak - Chuck Coker
2. Poppies - Vision
3. Carlsbad - Fastily
5. Linda Vista - downtowngal
6. Santeria - amy nicholson
7. Jewelery Theater - downtowngall
9. Biltmore - P G Roy Photography
13. Angelus Temple - Bruce Boehner
18. Grave of Buster Keaton - Alan Light
19. Neon Art - DavidPLP
20. Old LA Zoo - Junkyardsparkle
21. Hollywood Sign - Thomas Wolf
23. Inside Bronson Cave - Sam Howzit
26. Hollywood Tower - Loren Javier
26. Hollywood Tower - bdesham
27. John Wayne Gacy - The Orchid Club
28. Magic Castle - Minnaert
29. Industry of Death - Gruntooki
31. Halloween House - Bryanwake
33. Silent Movie - Charlesconstantine
24. Pinks - Minnaert
36. Rosenheim Mansion - Michael J Locke
39. Antelope Valley- doncram
43. Randsburg - CC Pierce
43. Randsburg - Don Graham
43. Randsburg - Pretzelpaws
44. Scary Dairy - Magic Madzik
46. Bubblegum - penubag
47. Iron Zoo - Jay Galvin
48. General Sherman - Jim Bahn
49. Forestiere - Scott Harrison
50. Court of Nocklebeast
51. Illustion spot - Lawrence Lansing
51. Santa Cruz - Ted Drake
52. Bigfoot Museum - Bod Doran
53. Boomeria - Greymalkn
54. Monopoly - Harshlight
56. Libby's - lps.1
57 Drawbridge - Andre Engels
58. Museum of Pez - Ingrid Taylar
60. Nike Missile - Travis Wise
61. Wyatt - broken sphere
65. Bacon Bacon - www.baconbaconsf.com
68. Bourn Mansion - djinn415
69. Sutro Baths - Jonathan Dinh
70. Pet Cemetery - Dave Parker
72. Headstone - Cirruspop
75. Alameda Spite House - ELF
76. Dunsmuir - David Brossard
77. Fairyland - Ted Eytan
78. Fish House - John Weber
79. Adventure Playground - charlievinz
83. Playland - Sonny Abesamis
84. Centennial Bulb - John Fink
85. Bryon Hot Springs - Captdelta
86. Preston Castle - A mad scientist
91. Glass Beach - Moximox
92. Saltair today - r.nial. bradshaw
92. Saltair - Ken Lund
94. Juniper Motel - Tom Hilton
96. Oregan State - Wistungsten
102. Boring - Robert Ashworth
102. Dull & Boring - Peter Mercator
107. Voodoo Doughnut - Oh Captain my Captain
109. Slappy Cakes - Jason Lander
109. Slappy Cakes - Pouregon
111. Peter Iredale - Robert Bradshaw
112. Winlock Egg - Robert Ashworth
113. Sucher - Heyrocker

Route 10

6. Calico - Justin Ennis
6. Calico - tech109
8. Zzyzx - Ken Lund
10. Mojave Phone Booth - Mwf95
12. Seven Magic Mountains - Kimberly Reinharft
14. The Simpsons' House - Scott Jones
17. Heart Attack - Bcgrote
17. Heart Attack - Daryll Mitchell
17. Heart Attack - Einar Jorgen Haraldseid
17. Heart Attack - Mary Sue
18. Golden Nugget - Ken Lund
20. Concrete Arrow - Dppowell43. Fibreglass - Shannon McGee
21. Narrows - N4rwhals
22. Neon Boneyard - Evan Wohrman
24. Atomic Survival - Unknown
25. Devils Hole - Ken Lund
30. Rhyolite - Bim Nevada
33. International Car Forest - Kimberly Reinhardt
34. Goldfield - Vivaverdi
35. Clown Motel - Famartin
40. Ahwahnee Hotel - Ben Churchill
Extraterrestrial highway - Ken Lund

Route 11

2. Trilobite - James St John
4. Krishna Temple - pastelitodepapa
4. Holi - steven gerner
6. Big Rig - H Dragon
7. Fly Geyer - Jeremy C Munns

9. White King - famartin
10. Up - Brett Neilson
12. Cat & Pyramid summum
13. Pioneer Museum - Tracie Hall
17. This is the Place - Cory Maylett
18. Spiral - NL Bradbury
19. Nine Mile - Bureau of Land Man.
20. Sego - Thomas
21. Dinosaur - James St. John
22. Hanging Lake - Don Becker
22. Hanging Lake - Wasif Malik
26. Coney - David Adams
27. Frozen Dead Guys - Jon Fischer
28. Carousel - Shammim Mohamed
29. Denver Dinosaur Hotel - Jimmy Thomas
30. Casa Bonita - Seren Wild
31. Linger - Catherine Shyu
33. Clutter - Spacini
34. Hooker - Dennis Yang
35. Kansas Barbed Wire Museum - Leeanne Adams
36. Abandoned Church - Lane Pearman
39. Garden of Eden - Kim Newell
40. Kansas Ball of Twice - David Heckman
31. Truckhenge - Thomas And Ron Lessman
42. Jim the Wonder Dog - Amercasroof
43. World's Largest Pecan - Lezlie K King
44. Maxie - Sector001
45. Baird chair - David Oaks
46. Adam-Ondi-Ahman - Americasroof
47. Tightwad - Bhall87
48. Ha Ha Tonka - Jason Runyon
49. Largest Rocking Chair - Abeezekowitz, Cuba Missouri
53. Mermet - Paddlefish
55. Cairo - Hickory Hardscrabble
55. Cairo - Litherland

56. Lamberts - Infrongmation
58. Cave in Rock - Daniel Schwen
59. Ole's - Nick Taylor
60. Panorama Point
61. Buford - travelingotter
62. Fossil House - Jeffrey Beall
63. Lost Springs - Idunno00923
67. Airplane - Dave Dugdale
70. Bishops Castle - husvedt
71. UFO Watchtower - Plazak
73. Ludlow - Beverly
76. Cano's Castle - Michael Rael
77. Ra Paulette - Max Shred
78. TWA - Adventurejay.com

Route 12

3. Cabazon Dinosaurs - Jllm06
4. Pinball - Michael Moore
5. Hicksville ?
6. Crochet Museum - Amanderson2
7. Pioneertown - catchpenny
9. Oatman - Roger Howard
10. Santa Claus - Todd Huffman
11. Chloride - John Fowler
11. Chloride - Beth Woodrum
12. Nothing - Alex
12. Nothing - Skarori
13. Pie - teofilo
14. Truth or Consequences - Laura Hertzfeld
14. Truth or Consequences - CGP Grey
15. Flying Saucer - Allens
16. Earth Sign - Leaflet
17. Ozymandias - Dave Weber
18. Cadillac - CGP Grey

19. Cadillac - Mtsrs
19. VWs - Jennifer Kirkland
19. VW2 - Iwishmynamewasmarsha
20. Crystal Shrine - Thomas R Machnitzki
21. Billy Tripps - Lindsey Turner

WITH THANKS

451

RIQUET
GOU
1857 DAVI
1867 SARA
1888 FLORE
CHARLES L.
1894
SARAH C.
JENNIE MANN

© Daisy Laramy-Binks 2023

Printed in Great Britain
by Amazon